Ottoman-Turkish
Conversation-Grammar

A practical method of learning the
Ottoman-Turkish language

V. H. Hagopian

Alpha Editions

This edition published in 2020

ISBN : 9789354034602

Design and Setting By
Alpha Editions
email - alphaedis@gmail.com

METHOD GASPEY-OTTO-SAUER.

OTTOMAN-TURKISH
CONVERSATION-GRAMMAR

A PRACTICAL METHOD OF LEARNING
THE OTTOMAN-TURKISH LANGUAGE.

BY

V. H. HAGOPIAN, M. A.

PROFESSOR OF THE TURKISH, ARABIC AND PERSIAN LANGUAGES
IN ANATOLIA COLLEGE, MERZIFOUN, TURKEY;
AUTHOR OF ENGLISH - ARMENIAN DICTIONARY etc.

LONDON.
DAVID NUTT, 57—59 Long Acre.   DULAU & CO., 37 Soho Square.
SAMPSON LOW, MARSTON & CO., 100 Southwark Street.
NEW YORK: BRENTANO'S, 5—9 Union Square.
DYRSEN & PFEIFFER (F. W. Christern) 16 West 33rd Street. G. E. STECHERT
& Co., 129—133 West 20th Street. E. STEIGER & CO., 25 Park Place.
BOSTON: C. A. KŒHLER & CO., 149a, Tremont Street.

HEIDELBERG.
JULIUS GROOS.
1907.

مُقَدَّمِس

Preface.

The Turkish language is of Tartar origin, as the Turks came from Central Asia, and is consequently quite distinct from Arabic and Persian, although it is true that in modern times the Arabic characters have been adopted for all three languages, and that the Turkish language is now half filled with Arabic and Persian words. Yet these words have been incorporated without affecting the nature or framework of the Turkish, which is as different from Arabic and Persian as Anglo-Saxon dialects are from Hebrew or Hungarian. In fact pure Turkish is Turanian, while Arabic is Semitic and Persian Aryan, and the resulting modern Ottoman-Turkish is compounded not only of three languages but of representatives of the three great families of languages. The original Turkish tongue, which is called Chaghata (Jagatai), was somewhat barbarous, but extremely forcible and concise when spoken. The adoption of Arabic and Persian words is arbitrary. To master the language it is necessary to have at least an elementary knowledge of the Arabic and Persian languages.

It is an extraordinary and lamentable fact that the language of the Turks has hitherto received little or no attention in England, although it is spoken by millions of people belonging to a vast empire with which we are closely connected by mutual vital interests, and is more or less used, in official circles, from Tunis in Africa to the walls of China. It is the court language of Persia, and in many provinces of that country, of South Russia and Afghanistan is spoken as much

as Persian. It is difficult to account for the absolute neglect of the study of such an important language, considering that it is used by a people who once influenced half the world, who overturned and established empires, who have possessed the thrones of Persia, Greece, Egypt and Arabia; whose power was once dreaded by Italy, Germany and France, and to whom our proud Queen Elizabeth applied for aid against the Spanish Armada. The Turkish has always been of the greatest consequence to us, owing to the importance of our political and commercial relations with the Ottoman Empire, and the complete ignorance of it on the part of our countrymen has greatly impeded proper communication and intercourse between the two nations and given rise to most serious misunderstandings and difficulties both in the diplomatic and commercial world. [*Dr. Ch. Wells.*]

Besides, not a small body of earnest men from the great Anglo-Saxon republic of the Trans-Atlantic continent have long been established in Constantinople and in the provinces of Turkey, labouring to unfold the treasures of modern science, temporal and spiritual, to the people of Turkey; losing no opportunity to place themselves in friendly communication both with the governing Ottoman element and with the numerous races and religious denominations subject to the Imperial sway.

To meet the need of the representatives of these two great nationalities in Turkey, there arose the necessity for conversation-books, grammars and lexicons. There have appeared a number of Turkish grammars and other books in the English language, but they seem little fitted to acquaint the learner fully with Turkish, chiefly because they are not sufficiently practical in the strict sense of the word, or they are composed only of rules. The appearance of a new Ottoman-Turkish Gram-

mar which combines in itself the theoretical and the practical elements of the language, it is expected will be cheerfully welcomed.

The so-called Conversation-method, originated by Drs. Gaspey and Otto, is now applied for the first time by the writer of this present book to the Ottoman-Turkish language also. It is his mother tongue and besides for more than 20 years he has practised this method in teaching the language in an important American institution to the natives of Turkey and to English-speaking foreigners. Therefore his own experience enables him to speak with some little authority on this subject. He thinks he has introduced a new element too in the Gaspey-Otto conversation-method, by inserting the word exercises which appear on pp. 121—125, 215, 256 etc.

The First Part of this work is devoted to conversational language and in it all the peculiarities of the language are given in a very easy and comprehensive way. The study of the First Part being finished it will soon be seen that Turkish is a very regular language, and that it is far more easy than is generally thought.

In the Second Part the elements of the Persian and Arabic languages are treated of as they are used in Ottoman-Turkish, and all the difficulties of both languages are explained, in a concise way. This is the Literary and Official language. There are then added some very valuable matters and a vocabulary.

As to the Exercises and Reading Lessons for translation, most of them are on subjects referring to Turkey and Turkish literature. Many characteristic specimens of poetry and prose illustrative of the literature and of the country, especially in modern phraseology, are given, so that the learner will feel himself in Turkey, and will have a glimpse into the geography, the history and the manners and customs of the country.

I recommend as a help to the student the excellent Turkish-English Dictionary of Sir J. Redhouse and the valuable Turkish Dictionary of Samy Béy, which latter is the most reliable guide to the student after finishing the First Part of this Grammar. And as a purely Turkish Grammar I recommend that of Mihran Efféndi Apigian (Mihri), to which I am much indebted.

I am much indebted also to Rev. Dr. W. St Clair-Tisdall, the C. M. S. missionary at Ispahan, Persia, who has carefully revised the MS. and has made valuable suggestions. Himself being a ripe scholar in the language, these have been of great service to me.

I must also express my sincere thanks to Dr. J. Wright, of Oxford, for the kindness and care with which he has looked over the proofs of this work.

V. H. Hagopian.

Anatolia College, Merzifoun (Marsovan), Turkey.

A List of Books indispensable to the Student of the Turkish Language.

Redhouse's Turkish-English Lexicon . . . . 25/—
     W. W. Peet: Bible House, Constantinople.
Samy Béy's Turkish Dictionary (*Qamousou Túrki*) .   . . 8/—
Mihri's Larger Turkish Grammar (*Moutavvél Sarf*) . . . . 1/—
Turkish Reader: 1, 2, 3 parts (*Talimi Qra"at*) . . . . . . 2/—
Turkish Reader: With Nésikh and Riqa (*Réhbéri Qra"at*) . —/8
Turkish Reader: With 6 different characters (*Qra"at Hojasi*) — 8
Penmanship Master (*Yazî Hojasî*) . . . . —/4
Blanks for Penmanship (*Réhbéri Sûbian*, by Mihri) 1, 2, 3 parts —/2
     Library Téféyyûz, 36 Grand Rue de la Sublime Porte, Constantinople.

فهرست

Contents.

VIII   Contents فهرست Fihrist.   ح

ط Contents فهرست *Fihrist.* IX

Page

Appendices.

The Official Part.

————›X‹————

مدخل

Introduction.

A. Letters of the Alphabet.

§ 1. The following table shows the shape of the Ottoman-Turkish letters, when they are connected with a preceding or a following letter, or with both, and when isolated:

Names	Isolated	Final	Medial	Initial	Proper sounds	Numerical values	Remarks
élif	ا	ﺎ	ﺎ	ا	—	1	See § 29.
bé	ب	ﺐ	ﺒ	ﺑ	b	2	
√pé	پ	ﭗ	ﭙ	ﭙ	p	2	Tur., Pers.
té	ت	ﺖ	ﺘ	ﺗ	t	40	
sé	ث	ﺚ	ﺜ	ﺛ	s	500	Arabic.
jim	ج	ﺞ	ﺠ	ﺟ	j	3	
chim	چ	ﭻ	ﭽ	ﭼ	ch	3	Tur., Pers.
ha	ح	ﺢ	ﺤ	ﺣ	ḥ	8	Arabic.
khî	خ	ﺦ	ﺨ	ﺧ	kh	600	
dal	د	ﺪ	ﺪ	د	d	4	
zal	ذ	ﺬ	ﺬ	ذ	z	700	Arabic.
ré	ر	ﺮ	ﺮ	ر	r	200	
zé	ز	ﺰ	ﺰ	ز	z	7	
√zhé	ژ	ﮋ	ﮋ	ژ	zh	7	Persian.

Names	Isolated	Final	Medial	Initial	Proper sounds	Numerical values	Remarks
sin	س	س	ـسـ	سـ	s	60	
shin	ش	ش	ـشـ	شـ	sh	300	
sad	ص	ص	ـصـ	صـ	ṡ	90	
dad	ض	ض	ـضـ	ضـ	d, z	800	Arabic.
tî	ط	ط	ـطـ	طـ	t, d	9	
zî	ظ	ظ	ـظـ	ظـ	z	900	Arabic.
ayn	ع	ع	ـعـ	عـ	ʿ	70	» § 35.
ghayn	غ	غ	ـغـ	غـ	gh	1000	
fé	ف	ـف	ـفـ	فـ	f	80	
qaf	ق	ـق	ـقـ	قـ	q	100	
kéf	ك	ـك	ـكـ	كـ	k	20	
géf	گ	ـگ	ـگـ	گـ	g	20	Tur., Pers.
lam	ل	ـل	ـلـ	لـ	l	30	
mim	م	م	ـمـ	مـ	m	40	
noun	ن	ن	ـنـ	نـ	n	50	
vav	و	و	و	و	v	6	
hé	ه	ـه	ـهـ	هـ	h	5	
yé	ى	ى	ـيـ	يـ	y	10	

§ 2. The letters of the Ottoman-Turkish Alphabet are 32 in number, and consist of 28 Arabic letters, together with some which the Persians have added (پ چ ژ گ). The Turks, as most other Oriental nations, read and write from right to left, instead of from left

to right as we do; and a book consequently begins where it would end in English. Capital letters are unknown, and the punctuation marks have been adopted recently. They are the same as in English.

§ 3. There are four kinds of writing:

I. *Riqá*, which is the ordinary current handwriting used in letters and in all kinds of civil and official documents.

II. *Nésikh*, is the common print of books, newspapers etc.

III. *Divanee*, is a style of large handwriting used in the Imperial Chancery for engrossing letters-patent.

IV. *Taliq*, is the Persian model of Arabic characters, it is used by Persians, and also in documents of the Ottoman Canonical court. Examples of these and other forms of rarer occurence are given at the end of this work.

§ 4. There is always more or less difficulty in representing the sounds of one language by those of another. This is true also in the case of the Ottoman-Turkish language. It belongs to a family or group of tongues different from the English, possessing sounds entirely foreign to English ears. To express these sounds, we have made some modifications of some of the English vowels and consonants. It is necessary to master these sounds before going on. They must be pronounced fully; all having only one regular sound. For instance: *a* has only *one* sound, and not five or more as in English: *e* has only one, as in *pet*, though the name itself will cause some blunder. *i*, *o*, *u* also have only one sound each.

There are eight vowel sounds in Turkish.

§ 5. The vast population of Turkey, especially the Christians, do not all use the Ottoman characters in their writing. The Armenians and the Greeks have adapted them to their characters. There are books and papers in Turkish, in Armenian and Greek characters, published in Constantinople. Most of the Englishmen and Americans, resident in Turkey, find it easier to begin Turkish with English or Armenian characters, and after mastering the pronunciation and the elements of the language, they turn to begin it with the Arabic

characters, which they find very easy then. The method adapted by us in this work, will remove all these difficulties.

Single and Double Vowels.

§ 6. In reading the names in the above Table and in pronouncing the proper sounds, written in the English characters, the learner must always remember:

1. Not to pronounce *a*, as in *fate, mortal* or *all;* but as in *far, art* or *father*.

2. *é* is always as *e* in *met* or *send*. Take care not to pronounce it as in *mere, verb* or *cane*.

3. *i* is always *i*, as in *pin* or *ship;* never as I, or as in *tire*.

4. *î* must be pronounced as *o* in *seldom* and *e* in *heaven*.

5. *o* must not be pronounced long as in *oat, prose;* but very short as in *no*.

6. *ou* pronounce always as in *youth, bouquet, foot;* and not as in *pour, couple, about*.

7. *û* is not as that of *pure, turn, rule;* it has no equivalent in English, but is the French *tu, sur*.

8. *eô* has no equivalent in English, it is in French *feu, coeur;* or German *ö* in *Zöllner, völlig*.

Compound Consonants.

§ 7. Turkish orthography does not employ combinations of two or three consonants and vowels to represent a single sound; we are under the necessity, however, of making use in this work of some combinations to represent Turkish sounds, for which there is no equivalent in English. These combinations are made by the addition of some vowels and consonants to *h* or *y*.

kh has the sound of *ch*, as in the Scotch *loch*.

gh, as the Greek γ, Armenian ղ.

zh must be pronounced as *z* in *azure*.

§ 8. The combinations *tch* and *dj*, so often to be seen in the transliteration of Turkish words, are but French notations of the English *ch* and *j* in *church* and *joy*.

§ 9. *y* must always be considered a consonant, and never allowed to degrade the sound of any vowel that may precede it; particular care must be taken by

Englishmen in this matter. It is always as in *yell*, *yoke*, *buy*.

§ 10. *y* is combined with other vowels to form a diphthong as will be seen in the next Table.

ay	Ex.: *qaymaq;*	as in		lime, high, I.
éy	»	*déymék;*	» »	fate, prey, hey.
iy	»	*chiy;*	» »	here, clear.
îy	»	*qîyma;*	» »	— —
oy	»	*doymaq;*	» »	boy, toy, going.
ouy	»	*douymaq;*	» »	cooing, doing.
ûy	»	*gûya;*	» »	Fr. essuyer, Guyot.
êôy	»	*êôylén;*	» »	Fr. deuil.

§ 11. In the transliteration of Ottoman words, *h* must be emphasized at the beginning, middle and end of words; at the end of the syllables it is generally accented; as: *Al-lah', qah'vé, hékim*. This is a most particular rule and requires a good deal of attention and practice in Englishmen; as a pernicious mode of orthography prevails among Englishmen, of introducing *h* mute very frequently at the beginning or end of words; as in *honest, Jehovah* etc. (§ 49 V.)

R is used as in English; except that it must never be allowed to be uttered obscurely; it must be pronounced fully and strongly; it is generally accented at the end of syllables. (§ 17.) Take care not to vitiate the pure sound of any vowel that may precede it.

G is always hard; as in *give, got, get*.

Numerals and Numeration by Letters.

§ 12. The numerical figures, ten in number, have been adapted by the Ottomans from the Arabs. They are the same that we make use of, calling them Arabic, because we took them from the Arabs. Their forms, however, differ considerably from thoses, which our digits have assumed, as the following table shows:

١ ٢ ٣ ٤ ٥ ٦ ٧ ٨ ٩ : ١٠ ٢٠ ٣٠ : ١٠٠

1   2   3   4   5   6   7   8   9;   10,   20,   30;   100

They are compounded in exactly the same way as our numerals. ١٩٠٢ = 1902.

§ 13. The apparent strangeness of the fact that those numbers seem to be written and read not from

right to left, but from left to right is due to the circumstance that, in Arabic, the smaller numbers are *read* as well as *written* first. Thus an Arab would read ١٩٠٢ 'two and nine hundred and a thousand'. This, however, a Turk does not do. (§ 691.)

§ 14. If the Arabic alphabet is arranged according to numerical values, there appeares the ancient order, which is still used for notation and numeration. In this order, that of the old Phoenician, Hebrew, Syriac, Greek and Latin alphabets: the first nine letters represent the units; the second nine the tens; the third nine the hundreds and the last one غ, one thousand; compare

the Table of the Alphabet. ابجد ؛ هوز ؛ حطى ؛ كلمن ؛ سعفص ؛ قرشت ؛ ثخذ ؛ ضظغ *Ebjéd, hév'véz, hout'ti, kélémén, safés, qaréshét, sakhéz, dazíghi.* Therefore the numeration by letters, is called *Ebjéd hisabî.*

§ 15. The method of numeration by the letters of the alphabet was a great task; it is fast going, if not entirely gone, out of practice, as puerile; but formerly great significance was attached to any combination of letters that expresses in one or more words an event or date. Thus خراب *kharab* is 600 + 200 + 1 + 2 = 803, the Hejira date when Timurleng laid Damascus in 'ruins'; and بلدة طيبه *béldéyi tay'yibé* is 2 + 30 + 4 + 400 + 9 + 10 + 2 + 400 = 857, date of the year when the 'Beautiful City', Constantinople, was taken by the Ottomans.

Exercise a.

Write and give the names of the following letters; they are arranged according to their numeral value:

ا ب پ ج چ د ؛ ه ه و ز ژ ؛ ح ط ى ؛ ك گ ل م ن ؛

س ع ف ص ؛ ق ر ش ت ؛ ث خ ذ ؛ ض ظ غ ٠

Division of the Letters.

§ 16. The Ottoman alphabet is divided into four classes: vowels; hard, soft, and neuter letters.

Vowel letters: ا و ه ی, which are vowels generally, when they are the second letter of the syllable.

Hard letters: ح خ ص ض ط ظ ع غ ق.

Soft letters: ت س ك گ ه.

Neuter letters: ب پ ث ج چ د ذ ر ز ژ ش ز ف ل م ن and ا و ی, when at the beginning of the syllables; as is the case with *y* and *w* in the English language.

B¹. Pronunciation of Letters.

§ 17. All the Ottoman letters in the Alphabetical Table are considered to be consonants, except ا و ه ی, which are often used as vowels, and call for further elucidation. (§ 29 ff.)

We now proceed to the phonetic value of the consonants:

ب *bê* has the value of English *b*, as: بد *béd* bad, برادر *biradér* brother. But when ending a syllable or word, it sometimes, anomalously, takes the value of *p*, as: شراب *sharap* wine, ابتدا *iptida* beginning. Especially is this the case with the Gerunds in ـوب, as: گیدوب *gidip*, آلوب *alip*. (§ 435.)

پ *pê* is the English *p*, as: پدر *pédér* father.

ت *tê* is the German *t*, as: تاتار *tatar* a Tartar; courier. It is sometimes changed into *d* in derivation when it is originally final; as: گیت *git* go, گیدر *gidér* he goes. Also (دمیر) تیمور *démir* iron, (دپه) تپه *dépé* a hill.

ث *sê* is found in Arabic words only, and is pronounced as *s*; as: ثابت *sabit* firm, امثال *émsal* proverbs.

ج *jim* is pronounced as *j*, as: جان *jan* soul.

چ **chim** has the value of the English **ch**, in *church*; as: چام *cham* the pine, چالی *chali* bush. (§ 8.)

ح **ha** has the harshly aspirated sound of English **h**, in *horse*. It is chiefly used in Arabic words; as: حاجی *haji* pilgrim.

خ **khî** has no equivalent in English. It is the counterpart of the Scotch *ch* in *loch* and German *Rache*. It is generally transliterated **kh**. But there are a good many words in which it is commonly pronounced as **h**, as: خواجه *hoja* teacher; خانه *hané* house.

د **dal** is German **d**, as: درد *dérd*.

ذ **zal** is found in Arabic words alone; its value is **z**, as: ذره *zér'ré* atom.

ر **ré** is in all positions a distinctly articulated lingual **r** as in *rain*. There are two important remarks, however, which is necessary for the English student to bear in mind with respect to this, *to him*, peculiar letter. Firstly, it must always be pronounced and accented (never dropped or slurred over, as in the pronunciation of *part, pa't*); and secondly, the value of the vowel before it in the same syllable must never be corrupted (as when it is pronounced *pot* pat; *for* far; *cur* car), but always kept pure, as with any other consonant; thus قور *qor'*, قیر *qîr'*, زار *zar'*; not *qo'*, *qî'*, *za'*. (§ 49 V.)

ز **zé** is English **z**, as: گز *géz*.

ژ **zhé** is only found in Persian and French words; it is of the value of the English **s** in *treasure*, and is transliterated **zh**; as: مژده *mûzhdé* tidings, آژدر *azh'dér* dragon, ژورنال *zhour'nal* journal. It is often pronounced

j, as: زنكار *jéngér* verdigris, ژیوه *jiva* quicksilver, ژاندارمه *jandarma* a county policeman.

س *sin* is a soft *s*, always followed by a soft vowel in all Ottoman words, as: سوز *seoz* word.

ش *shin* is English *sh*, as: ایش *ish* work.

ص *sad* is a hard *s*, it designates a hard vowel, as: صاغ *sagh* right, صول *sol* left.

ض *dad* is used in Arabic words only. It is generally pronounced as a hard *z*, but sometimes as a hard *d*; thus: راضی *razee* content, ضبطیه *zaptiyé* a gendarme, قاضی *qadi* judge, خضر الیاس *khidir élyas* St. Elias.

ط *tî* is pronounced as *t*, thus: طوپ *top* ball. But sometimes in Turkish words it is pronounced as *d*. طاغ (داغ) *dagh* mountain, اوطه (اودا) *oda* room.

ظ *zî* is used in Arabic words only, as a very hard *z*, thus: ظالم *zalîm* cruel.

ع *ayn*, غ *ghayn*, ق *qaf*, ك *kéf*. See §§ 33—36.

ف *fé* is the English *f*, in all cases, فنا *féna*.

ل *lam* is the English *l*, in all cases.

م *mim* is the English *m*, as: مال *mal*.

ن *noun* is like the English *n*, as: نان *nan* bread. But before *bé* ب it is pronounced as *m*. Thus پنبه *pémbé* light rose colour, استانبول *istambul* Constantinople (Stambul).

§ 18. *Note.* The reason why so many *s* and *z* sounds occur in Ottoman is that Arabic words intro-

duced into the language have to be written as in Arabic. In the latter tongue the sounds of ث ، س ، ص and again those of ظ ، ض ، ز ، ذ are quite distinct from one another, as are those of ح and ه, of ا and ع. But these distinctions are not observed by the Ottoman.

C¹. The Orthographic Signs.

§ 19. There are five kinds of orthographic signs used in Ottoman-Turkish. The vowel signs, Jezma, Medda, Shedda and Nunation. These are put under or over the letters.

The Vowel Signs.

§ 20. There are three kinds of vowel signs: *ûstûn*, *ésré*, *eôtré*. These are named *haréké* 'movements'; but by the Europeans they are commonly called *vowel points*.

§ 21. These three vowel signs have two values each.

I. With a soft or neuter consonant, *ûstûn* has the value of *é*; and with a hard consonant *a*.

II. With a soft or neuter consonant, *ésré* has the value of *i*; and with a hard consonant *î*.

III. With a soft or neuter consonant, *eôtré* has the value of *û*, *eô*; and with a hard one *o*, *ou*.

a) Hard Vowels.

§ 22. Hard vowels are used with hard letters.

I. *Ûstûn* is a diagonal stroke drawn from right to left, placed above the letter thus ـَ; it indicates that the hard letter over which it is placed, is to be followed in pronunciation by *a*, as in English *bar, star*.

قَ غَ عَ ظَ طَ ضَ صَ خَ حَ

Key. Ha ûstûn *ha*, khî ûstûn *kha*, ayn ûstûn *á*, etc.

II. This sign ـِ is called *és-ré*, under hard letters it is pronounced *î*, as *e* in *heaven*.

قِ غِ عِ ظِ طِ ضِ صِ خِ حِ

Key. Ha és-ré *hî*, khî és-ré *khî*, sad és-ré *sî*, etc.

III. This sign ٝ is *eôtré*, over the hard letters it is pronounced **o** or **ou**, as in *cold, could.*

$$ قُ عُ غُ ظُ طُ ضُ صُ خُ حُ $$

Key. Ha eôtré *ho, hou,* khî eôtré *kho, khou,* dad eôtré *do, dou,* etc.

b) Soft Vowels.

§ 23. Soft vowels are pronounced with soft or neuter letters.

I. *Ûstûn* when put over a soft or neuter letter, is pronounced like *é,* as in *met.*

$$ نَ دَ شَ بَ هَ گَ كَ سَ $$

Key. Sin ûstûn *sé,* kéf ûstûn *ké,* géf ûstûn *gé,* etc.

II. *Esré* when put under a soft or neuter letter, is pronounced *i,* as in *pit, him.*

$$ ژِ ثِ تِ جِ زِ فِ لِ مِ $$

Key. Mim ésré *mi,* lam ésré *li,* zé ésré *zi,* etc.

III. *Eôtré* when put over a soft or neuter letter, is pronounced *û, eô,* which have no equivalent in English. (§ 6, 7, 8.)

$$ چُ نُ ذُ رُ سُ كُ شُ پُ دُ $$

Key. Dal eôtré *dû, deô,* pé eôtré *pû, peô,* shin eôtré *shû, sheô,* etc.

Exercise b.

$$ قُ قِ قَ سُ سِ سَ صُ صِ صَ هُ هِ هَ حُ حِ حَ $$

$$ زُ زِ زَ مُ مِ مَ دُ دِ دَ طُ طِ طَ تُ تِ تَ كُ كِ كَ $$

$$ ژُ رِ رَ ذُ خَ جُ جِ شَ شُ شِ شَ بُ بِ بَ ظُ ظِ ظَ $$

$$ ئى وَ غِ فَ عُ $$

The Connection of the Letters.

§ 24. The letters of the Ottoman alphabet are divided into two other divisions: *connected* and *unconnected* letters.

I. The *unconnected letters* are ‍‍ا د ذ ر ز ژ و, which are never joined to the following letter, and when they occur the word is broken; that is, the pen is taken up, and the second part of the word is resumed unconnected. They may be joined only to the letter preceding them, as thus exhibited اداره *idaré* (administration) ‘ براقدم *braqdim* (I left).

II. The *connected* or *joinable letters* are those which may be joined to the letters which follow or precede them; the remaining letters are connected letters; as:

منفصل *múnfasil* (unconnected).

Exercise c.

‍	‍	‍	‍	‍	‍	‍	‍
ژَف	وَج	وَر	زَل	زَن	رَس	ذَم	دَك
ژِف	وِج	وِر	زِل	زِن	رِس	ذِم	دِك
ژُف	وُج	وُر	زُل	زُن	رُس	ذُم	دُك

Key. Dal kéf ûstûn *dék*, dal kéf ésré *dik*, dal kéf eôtré *dúk, deôk*.

§ 25. In dealing with the letters of the Ottoman alphabet on the preceding pages, we have shown only the shapes they take when standing alone; when they are combined with other letters, they are sometimes slightly modified, according as they stand at the beginning, in the middle, or at the end of the word. These various changes will be seen from the Table of the Alphabet (P. 1 and 2).

§ 26. There is also a compound character in use, which is always to be found inserted in alphabets, and which, for that reason, cannot be passed over in silence. It is the character ﻻ, called *lam élif*, being, in fact, nothing more than ل *lam* joined calligraphically to a following ا *élif*, in a similar manner to that whereby the English printers continue to join the *f* and *l* in fl, or *f* and *i* in fi, etc. When this double character is

connected with a preceding letter, it has the shape of لا, as: بلا *béla* (evil).

Exercise d.

ي نط لخ نتخ نيتلبثينيا نجخنلا ج س ص پش ين بف بغ بق يث

بج بنجبا ذ ء ف غ ق لك ك بهّا حجا حہا يحا

Key. *yé* initial; *noun* initial, *tí* final; *té* initial, *khí* medial; *noun* initial, *té khí* medial; *noun* initial, *yé*, *té*, *lam*, *bé*, *sé*, *yé*, *noun*, *pé* medial, *élif* final.

Exercise (Connected Monosyllables) e.

(بَ ش) بَش ؛ (پَ ر) پَر ؛ (تُ ل) تُل ؛ (ثَ م) ثَم ؛ (جَ م) جِم ؛

(چُ ك) چُك ؛ (شَ ش) شَش ؛ (سَ س) سَس ؛ (كُ م) كُم ؛ (قِ ل) قِل ؛

(فَ س) فَس ؛ (حَ ج) حَج

Key. Bé shin ûstûn *bésh*; pé ré ûstûn *pér*; té lam eôtré *túl*, etc.

Vowel Letters.

§ 27. Besides the vowel signs, sometimes the vowel letters ا و ه ى are used, to indicate vowel sounds.

I. **Elif** indicates the *hard vowel ûstûn*, provided that it is the second letter of the syllable. Instead of حَ طَ ظَ is written حا طا ظا; here *élif* is substituted for *ûstûn*.

II. **Yé**, sometimes when it is the second letter of the syllable, indicates the vowel ésré. Instead of جِ لِ دِ is written جى لى دى; here *yé* is substituted for *ésré*.

III. **Vav**, generally when it is the second letter of the syllable, indicates the eôtré. Instead of مُ قُ صُ is written مو قو صو; here *vav* is substituted for *eôtré*.

IV. **Hé**, when it is the second letter of the syllable, generally indicates the ûstûn, either hard or soft. Instead of دَ رَ پَ is written ده ره په; here *hé* is substituted for ûstûn (*pé*, *ré*, *dé*).

§ 28. *Note.* The Arabic and Persian long vowels are represented by the Letters of Prolongation ا و ى. These letters correspond respectively with the vowel points: ustûn, esré, êôtré (§§ 29—31). But there are no letters of prolongation in purely Turkish words; the use of these letters is limited only to indicating the vowel signs, as has been said above. Therefore they are called in Turkish *orthographic letters* also, as they serve only for the correction of the orthography.

Exercise f.

Read and write the following exercises:

I. با به بی بو ؛ ما مه ﻰ مو ؛ نا نه نی نو ؛ سا سه سی سو ؛ دا

ده دی دو ؛ فا فه فی فو ؛ غا غه غی غو ؛ لا له لی لو

Key. Bé élif ûstûn *ba*, bé hé ûstûn *bé*, bé yé ésré *bi*, bé vav êôtré *bou*, *bo* etc.

II. قَل = قال ، قِل = قيل ، قُل = قول ؛ قِش = قاش ،

قِش = قيش ، قُش = قوش ؛ لاف ، ايف ، لوف ؛ بال ، بيل ،

بول ؛ خام ، خيم ، خوم ؛ چام ، چيم ، چوم

Key. Qaf lam ûstûn *qal*, which is equivalent to qaf élif lam ûstûn *qal*; qaf lam ésré *qîl*, or with a vowel letter qaf yé lam ésré *qîl* etc.

III. Short sentences. صول قول ؛ چور چوپ ؛ بول مال ؛

يول وار ؛ قوپ كيت ؛ موم صات ؛ دار يول ؛ چوق طوز

Key. Sad vav lam êôtré *sol*, qaf vav lam êôtré *qol*, *sol qol* etc.

IV. چاقی ، باقی ، پاشا ، ياشا ، يالی ، ياتاق ، بوداق ، قوراق ،

قوناق ، خالی ، صاری ، چوبان ، باتاق ، صولاق ، صوغان ، يازی ،

دولاب ، چوراب ، اوغلان

Key. Chim élif ûstûn *cha*, qaf yé ésré *qî*, *cha-qî* etc.

V. توتون ؛ اوقو ؛ قوقو ؛ اوطور ؛ اوموز ؛ اوتوز ؛ اوجوز ؛ قوردو ؛

دودوك ؛ چوروك ؛ بوغو ؛ چولاق ؛ سولوك ؛ كوتوك

Key. Té vav êôtré *tû*, té vav noun êôtré *tûn,* *tû-tûn* etc.

B². Pronunciation of Letters (continued).

§ 29. ا *Élif.* There are four kinds of *élif* in Ottoman:

a) The *initial* or *hémzé élif*, which is a consonant, not a vowel. Like any of the initial consonants, it takes the three vowel points and letters; as: اَت *ét* meat, ایت *it* dog, اوت *ot* grass (§ 38).

Note. Initial *élif* is not generally indicated in transcription, it being understood that whenever an Ottoman word begins with a vowel, in the original it begins with *élif*.

b) *Orthographic* or *vowel élif*, which stands to show only the hard *ûstûn* vowel: it is used exclusively for Turkish and foreign words; as: بال *bal* honey, پاریس *paris* Paris, آوروپا *avropa* Europe.

c) *Shortened élif*, which is written generally in the shape of ی *yé*, but pronounced short; it is used only in Arabic words; as: مولا or مولی *mévla* God, عیسا or عیسی *ee-sa* Jesus.

d) *Elongated élif*, which is found only in Arabic and Persian words; it lengthens the hard *ûstûn* vowel; as: p. پاشا *pasha,* a. آمین *ā meen*, p. آباد *ā bad.*

§ 30. و *Vav.* There are four kinds of *vav* in Ottoman:

a) *Consonantal vav*, it has the phonetic value of *v*; as: اَو *év* house, وقت *vaqit* time, آلو *alév* flame.

b) *Orthographic* or *vowel vav*, which stands for the vowel êôtré; it is used only in Turkish and foreign words; as: یول *yol* way, لوندره *londra* London.

c) *Elongated vav*, which lenghtens the vowel êôtré,

and is found only in Arabic and Persian words; as:
p. دوست do̅st friend, a. ممنون mémnoon glad.

d) *Silent vav*, which is found only in some Persian
words, between the letters خ *khi* and ا *élif*, and is not
pronounced; as: خواجه *khajé* teacher, خواننده *khanéndé*
singer.

§ 31. ى **Yé** has three sounds:

a) *Consonantal yé*, which has the value of the consonant **y**, whether it be initial, medial or final, simple
or reduplicated; as: يل *yél* wind, سير *séyr* looking, مى
méy wine.

b) *Orthographic* or *vowel yé*, which stands to show
only the vowel *ésré*, it is used only in Turkish and
foreign words; as: قيش *qísh* winter, ديلين *Dublin*.

c) *Elongated yé*, which is used only in Arabic and
Persian words and lengthens the ésré; as: p. پير *peer*
old man, a. والى *valee* governor.

§ 32. ه **Hé** has three sounds:

a) *Consonantal hé*, which is a guttural and aspirated
as the **h** in *horse*; as: p. هنر *hünér* skill, قهوه *qahvé* coffee.

b) *Orthographic* or *vowel hé*, which stands for
ûstûn; as: آصمه *asma* vine, p. بنده *béndé* slave.

The vowel hé, when in the middle or at the end
of words, is never joined to the next letter in writing;
as: كله‌جكم *géléjéyim*, آصمه‌يه *asmaya*.

c) *Substitutive hé*, which is changed from ت *té*, and
is found only at the end of Arabic words; as: حكايه
hikyaiyé for حكاية *hikyaiyét* story.

§ 33. ق **qaf**, ك **kéf.** The Ottoman alphabet
distinguishes sharply between the hard letter *qaf* and

the soft letter *kéf*. The transliteration of this present work in accordance with the judgment of the ripest scholars, represents the ق by *q* and ك with *k*. The common people pronounce the *qaf* as *ghayn* at the beginning and the middle of words, and as *khi* at the end. The *kéf* also at the end of words is pronounced *kh* by the common people. Ex.: قوچاق *qochaq* com. *ghochakh* (brave), قان *qan* com. *ghan* (blood), قايش *qayish* com. *ghayish* (thong), كيدهجك *gidéjék* com. *gédéjékh* (he will go).

§ 34. ك *kéf* is appropriate only to soft syllables or words; it is so pronounced as to represent in Turkish four different sounds; to distinguish these four sounds the letter may be slightly modified in form. But in general, in Ottoman, the ك alone is used to express all four sounds, and the student can learn how to pronounce it only by practice.

I. The first of these four forms is called *kéf* or *kâif* (*kéfi Arabi*, Arabic kéf, by the grammarians); it is pronounced as *k*. Ex.: كور *kéôr* blind, كتاب *kitab* book, كول *kúl* ashes.

II. The second is called *géf* or *gîaf* (*kéfi Farisi*, Persian kéf, by the grammarians), and it is pronounced as hard *g*; it is sometimes distinguished by a modification in shape, thus گ. Ex.: گور *géôr* see, گول *géôl* lake, گل *gél* come.

Note. When ك represents the sound either of *k* or of *g* hard, and is followed by an *élif*, it takes before the vowel a short and incipient sound of *i*, which we have united thus *îa*. Ex.: كاغد *kîaghîd* paper, كامل *kîamil* perfect, آكاه *a-gîah* aware: not *ka-ghîd*, *ka-mil*, *a-gah*; because ك being a soft letter cannot go with a hard vowel *a* (§§ 22, 37).

III. The third is called *saghîr kéf*, or *néf* (surd kéf), and is pronounced as *ng* in the words *ring, sing* etc.; it is a nasal *n*, and is represented by *ñ*. It is sometimes written ݣ ك with three dots over it. It is never to be found elsewhere than at the middle of Turkish words; and consequently never can be initial. Ex.: دكز *déñiz* sea, يالڭز *yaliñiz* alone, سنڭ *séniñ* your.

IV. The fourth is called *yaf*, and is pronounced like the English *y* consonant; it is found only in Turkish words. Ex.: دكل *déyil* it is not, اكرى *éyri* crooked, بك *béy* prince.

Exercise g.

قاو ، كاو ، آقمَقْ ، اكمَك ¹⁴ ، اكيمَك ¹ ، آكْمَقْ ³ ، قول ، كُوْل ² ؛ قار ، كَار ، اكَ ¹ ، اآكَ ³ ، قيو قَيونِك ³ ؛ بنده بَنْدَه كِنز ³ ؛ يازدق يازديكِنز ³ ؛ كُول ¹ قول ؛ كَاتِب ؛ اوكود ⁴ ؛ اوكوز ⁴ ؛ دَكِرمَن ¹ ؛ بَكْمَز ⁴ ؛ دَكْنَك ⁴ᐟ¹ ؛ ايكَه ⁴ ؛ اِيكيت ⁴ ؛ كُونْش ² ؛ طوكوز ² ؛ طُقوز ³ ؛ كُوكَرْتَه ²ᐟ⁴ ؛ كُوكَرْچين ²ᐟ⁴ ؛ صوكُرَه ³ .

Key. Qaf élif vav ûstûn *qav*, géf élif vav ûstûn *gîav*; *aqmaq, ékmék, éymék, añmaq; qol, géôl; qar, kîar* etc.

§ 35. ع *'ayn.* The *ayn* has no equivalent in European languages; it characterizes only Arabic words. Its phonetic value in Arabic and in the mouth of an Arab, is a harsh guttural catch or hiatus. As pronounced by a Turkish scholar the letter is either entirely silent or only the slightest hiatus is perceptible. The common people pronounce it like an *élif*, and there is no harm in pronouncing so. In this work sometimes, when necessary, the vowel sound is accompanied by the sign ع, and it is generally marked by an apostrophe.

معلوم *ma'-lûm* or *ma-ɛa-lûm*, علم *'a'-lém* or *a-ɛa-lém*.

§ 36. غ *ghayn* is represented by *gh*; as اغا *a-gha*

or com. *a-a'* sir, باغ *bagh* vineyard, اوغلان *ogh'lan* com. *o'lan*, *ou-lan* boy. After a vowel *vav* و, with the sounds **o, ou**, غ has very much the sound of *w*; like the *gh* of *throughout*. Thus اوغلاق *ov-laq* or *ogh-laq* kid; قوغه *qova* not *qogha* (a pail); صغوق *sovouq* not *soghouq* cold; قوغمق *qovmaq* to expel; اوغهلامق *ovalamaq* to rub.

§ 37. *Note.* In the transliteration of the foreign proper names or nouns, the hard **g**, when followed by a hard vowel, is represented by غ and not by ك. Ex.: Hugo هوغو *hou-gho*, Gladstone غلادیستون *ghladiston*, guardian غاردیان *ghardiyan*, gazetta غزته *ghazéta* newspaper, gas غاز *ghaz*.

§ 38. ء *Hémzé*. The *élif* at the beginning of words is a consonant (§ 29), which is called *hémzé* or *hémzé élif*, because naturally there is a sign of *hémzé* over the *élif*, which is not generally written. اول *ol* is originally أول, اثر *é-sér* is أثر, ال is أل, ایت is أیت.

§ 39. The combination of *hémzé élif* with a vowel *élif* (ا أ) is expressed by *médda*, which is the vowel élif put over the consonant *hémzé élif* (§§ 29 d, 47) ا = آ; as: آلمق = أألمق *almaq*, ات *ét*, آت = أت or آت.

§ 40. But when *hémzé* is found in the middle of words, if it ends the syllable, it is like an accent or a hiatus. Ex.: تأثیر *té-é'-sir* influence, مأمور *mé-é'-mour* officer.

§ 41. At the beginning of syllables it is pronounced as **y** consonant; as: قائل *qayil*, دائر *dayir*.

Note. The pronunciation of *hémzé* and the changes

2٠

it undergoes, are in accordance with the rules of Arabic Grammar.

C². Other Orthographic Signs.

a) Jezma جزم

§ 42. The letters in a syllable are either vowelled or quiescent; the first letter of any syllable is naturally vowelled, the others quiescent. The *vowelled* letters are accompanied by a vowel sign, but those which are *quiescent*, are marked with the sign (ْ), called Jézma. Ex.:

بَشْلِك *bᵉsh-lⁱk*: the letters ب *b* and لِ *l* are vowelled, as they are the first letters of the two syllables; شْ *sh* and كْ *k* are quiescent; therefore marked with Jezma.

بَرْبَر *bᵉr-bᵉr* (barber): the two ب *bés* are vowelled and both of the ر *rés* quiescent and therefore marked. مَكْتَبْ *mᵉk-tᵉb* (school) م *mim* and ت *té* are vowelled, كْ *kéf* and بْ *bé* quiescent.

§ 43. The vowel letters cannot have the mark of quiescence, as they are substituted for the vowel signs, and indicate their kind; as بالِق *bᵃlⁱq* (fish), where *élif* stands for *ûstûn*, and does not need the sign.

Exercise h.

Read and write the following exercises:

I. ساعَتْ ' لايِقْ ' طاوُقْ ' چوجوق ' چوُجقْ ' صاحِبْ '
قاوِشْ ' چالِشْ ' راحَتْ ' چِيچَكْ ' چِيلَكْ ' دِيلَكْ ' وِشْنه ' گَلْدى '
گِيتْدى ' گِتْدى ' تَخْته ' بَشْقه ' كِتاب

Key. Sin élif ûstûn *sa*, ayn té ûstûn *at*, *sa-at*; Lam élif ûstûn *la*, yé qaf ésré *yiq*, *la-yiq*; Tî élif ûstûn *ta*, vav qaf ôtré *vouq*, *ta-vouq*: *yé* and *vav* are consonants, because they begins the syllable.

II. آخْشام ' اِسْلام ' اِقْرار ' اِقْبال ' اِثْبات ' اِسْراف ' اِنْسان '

تَبْدِيل ، تَشْرِيف ، تَعْرِيف ، تَسْلِيم ، تَقْسِيم ، مَخْصُوص ، مَظْلُوم ،

مَشْهُور ، مَكْتُوب ، مَحْبُوس

Key. Elif khî ûstûn *akh*, shin élif mim ûstûn *sham* ^akh-*sh*^am; ^is-*l*^am, ^iq-*r*^ar, ^iq-*b*^al, ^is-*b*^at, ^is-*r*^af, ^in-*s*^an; *t*^{b}-*d*^il, *t*^ésh-*r*^if etc.

III. كِتَاب ، كِتَابِى ، كِتَابه ؛ قَپُو ، قَپُوِنى ، قَپُوِيه ؛ يالى ، يالِىِى ،

يالِىِيه ؛ پاره ، پارهِنى ، پارهِيه ؛ يَاره ، يارهِنى ، يارهِيه ؛ بَابا ، بَابَالِى ، بَابَايَه ؛

آنَا ، آنَانِى ، آنَايَه ؛ قَنَاد ، قَنَادِى ، قَنَاده

Key. Kéf ésré *ki*; té élif bé ûstûn *tab*, *ki-tab*; kéf ésré *ki*, té élif ûstûn *ta*, *ki-ta*, bé yé ésré *bî*, *ki-ta-bî*; *kitaba* etc.

IV. شَرْبَتْجِى ، كِتَابِينِكْ ، كِتَابْجِيده ، كَبَابْجِى ، حَلْوَاجِى ،

مَجْلِسِده ، مَكْتَبْده ، سَرمَايه ، خَبَرْدَار ، دَوْلَتْلِى ، هَوَسْلِى ، مُطْلَقَا ،

بَاغْچَه ده ، يِكِيجَه ده

Key. Shin ré ûstûn *shér*, bé té ûstûn *bét*, *shér-bét*, jim yé ésré *ji*, *shér-bét-ji*; *ki-ta-bî-niñ*, *ki-tab-ji-da* etc.

§ 44. In most cases, indeed, the vowel points are not inserted, except in quotations from the Qoran, or in writing a foreign word or name, and in some poetical works. This at first causes a little embarrassment to the learner; he must accustom himself to pronounce the word as if such vowels did not exist, until he can supply them by a knowledge of the word. The difficulty will vanish by dint of a little practice.

b) Shedda تَشْدِيد

§ 45. A consonant which is to be doubled without the interposition of a vowel, is written only once, but marked with the sign ـّـ, which is called *shéd'da* or *tésh-deed* (strengthening). This reduplication is not a mere matter of orthography as it is in the English language; when a letter is doubled in writing, it must be doubled in pronunciation, as is done in English with the letters *d, l, n* in the words *mid-day, mad dog, full lips, thin nose.*

§ 46. The sign shedda belongs only to Arabic (700), in Turkish words the letter is simply written twice, as: صالامق *sal'-la-maq* not as صالّامق. Ex.: حدّت is changed into the form حدّت *hid'dét* (anger), ملّت = ملّت *mil-lét* nation.

Exercise i.

Write and read the following exercise:

سَقَا ، بَقَال ، مَدَاح ، بِلاد ، صَرَاف ، قَزَاز ، حَمَال ، جَرَاح ،

مُكَرَّم ، مُحَرِّك ، حَنَّا ، جَنَّت ، هِمَّت ، دَلَّاك ، شَمَّاس ،

Key. Jim ré ûstûn *jér*, ré élif ha ûstûn *rah'*, *jér'-rah'* etc.

c) Medda مدّ

§ 47. This sign is called *méd'da* ـٓ, which means long; it is put over *élif* to show that it must be pronounced with hard ûstûn *a*, and not as *e, i, o*. In Arabic and Persian words it serves to lengthen the *élif* (§§ 39, 603, 701 d); as: t. اَز *éz* (crush), but آز *az* is *few*; اَت *ét* (meat), آت *at* (horse). a. اَمين *émeen* (faithful), a. آمين *a̅ meen* (amen).

Read and write the following exercises:

اَه *éh* well!	اَل *él* hand	اَش *ésh* companion
آه *ah* alas	آل *al* take	آش *ash* food
اَو *év* house	اَی *éy* hallo!	اَك *ek* sow
آو *av* hunting	آی *ay* mouth	آق *aq* white

p. آتش ! a. آلَت ! a. آدم ! p. آباد ! a. آلدم ! آغّه

Key. Elif hé ûstûn *éh*, élif hé medda ûstûn *ah* etc.

d) Nunation تنوین

§ 48. The marks of vowels when doubled, are pronounced with the addition of the sound *n*, ـً *én*,

ـــِ *in*, ـــٌ *ûn*. This is called *tén-veen* i. e. 'giving the sound of *noun*'; it occurs only at the end of an Arabic word. The vowels thus doubled are spoken of as *iki ûstûn, iki ésré, iki êôtré* respectively (§§ 670, 681). Ex.:

تَ té ûstûn *té*: تً or تٌ or ةً té iki ûstûn *tén*.

دَ dal ûstûn *dé*: دٍ dal iki ûstûn *dén*.

فَ fé êôtré *fû*: فٌ fé iki êôtré *fûn*.

نِظَاماً ، قَرْضاً ، مُضَافٌ ، حَقّاً ، حَدّ ، اُطْفاً ، يَوْماً ، ثَانِياً

Key. Noun ésré *ni*, zî élif ûstûn *za*, *ni-za*, mim élif iki ûstûn *mén*, *ni-za-mén* etc.

D. Accent.

§ 49. It is difficult and wearisome to give absolute rules and their exceptions in regard to the accent in Ottoman Turkish, as it varies much. Some general rules are given in the following lines, while in all cases which cannot be included under these rules, the accent will be indicated.

I. Usually every Turkish word is accented on the last syllable; as: او *év'* house, كوپك *keô-pék'*, آغلامق *agh-la-maq'*.

II. Words with double consonants have the accent on the first consonant; as: صاللامق *sal'-la-maq* to shake, a. صرّاف *sar'-raf* banker, ايسّيز *is'-siz* lonely, تقدّم *té-qad'-dúm* progress.

Note. The shedda in Arabic words serves as an accent (§ 45).

III. In Persian and Arabic, the vowel letters or the Letters of Prolongation are pronounced long and are accented (§ 28); a. جاهل *jā-hil* ignorant, a. كريم *ké-reem'* merciful, p. آتش *ā-tésh* fire, a. خصوص *khou-soos'* a point, respect.

IV. In case of emphasis among words the accent is on that word which receives prominence. Ex.: 1. *Sén dûn' mû géldiñ?* Was it *yesterday* that you came? 2. *Dûn sén' mi géldiñ?* Was it *you* that came yesterday? 3. *Sén dûn géldiñ' mi?* Did you *come* yesterday? (§ 66).

V. The letters *h*, *r*, when they are in the middle and at the end of words, are accented; as آلیر *a-lir'*, الله *al'lah'*, قهوه *qah've* coffee (pp. 5, 8).

E. Euphony or Harmony of the Vowels.

§ 50. A very remarkable peculiarity of Ottoman is the attention paid to euphony in pronunciation, and the changes of the sounds of vowels and consonants which take place in consequence. Thus the collision of hard and soft letters in the same word is always avoided. And when one declines a word or adds a particle or letter to it, whatever be the leading letter the others must be pronounced so as to agree with it (§ 87).

§ 51. There are two simple rules of euphony in the language for the words of purely Turkish origin:

a) If the first syllable of the word contains a hard vowel, all the vowels in that word should be hard. اولدی *ol-dou* it became, آلتی *al-tî* six, آله‌جغمزی *a-la-ja-ghî-mî-zî* our credit; not *ol-di*, *al-ti*, *a-lé-jé-ghi-mi-zi* etc.

b) If the first vowel be soft, then the others should be soft also. سوزی *séo-zú* the word, کوردی *géor-dú* he saw, اللر *él-lér* hands, کوسته‌ره‌جکمز *géos-té-ré-jé-yi-miz*; not *so-zi*, *el-lar* etc.

§ 52. *Remark:* 1. On the above principles, when one declines a word or adds a particle to it, the vowel of the syllable added is generally so pronounced that:

î comes after *a*: طام ' طامی ' طامه *dam*, *damî*, *dama*;

i   »   »   *é*: ال ' الی ' اله *él*, *éli*, *e-lé*;

ou   »   »   *o*: قول ' قولی ' قوله *qol*, *qolou*, *qola*;

û comes after   *êô*: كورور ، كولى   *gêôlû, gêôrûr*;

a   »   » *o, ou*: قوله ، چوله   *choula, qola*;

é   »   » *u, êô*: كولش ، كورن   *gûléñ, gêôrén*.

2. On the same requirements of euphony, in words of Turkish origin which end in ت, ق, ك these letters are changed into *y, gh, d* (§§ 88, 89).

§ 53. When a word ending in a vowel receives a grammatical ending beginning with a vowel, a hiatus results, which is practically a difficulty in pronunciation. This is very common in Ottoman. To avoid this difficulty it is necessary to insert a consonant ى *y* (see §§ 91, 284, 287, 528, 543 etc.):

آنا *ana*: آنايه *anaya*, p. آرا *ara*: آرايش *arayish*.

§ 54ᵃ. As a list of words supposed to be exceptions by some grammarians, we note الما *élma*, which was originally *alma* 'apple', and is still so pronounced in many places; while قهوه *qah'-vé* coffee, پيلاو *pi-lav*, كيميون *kim-yon*, ليمون *li-mon* (lemon) are not Turkish.

§ 54ᵇ. As real exceptions to these rules are the ending of the Present tense ‑يور, which is always pronounced —*yor*, and the pronominal particle كى —*ki*, which is never changed (§§ 140, 319).

F. Orthography.

§ 55. As the orthography of every Arabic and Persian Ottoman word is fixed and unchangeable, it is only in pure Turkish and foreign Ottoman words that the orthography varies. The Vowel or Orthographic letters (ى , ه , و , ا) as they are called in Ottoman without any inflexible rule are added or left out arbitrarily; as: قيلندى ، قيليندى *qilindi*, are بتون and بوتون *bútún*; all admissible.

§ 56. The true rule is: 1. Never introduce a vowel letter into a Turkish or foreign Ottoman word without removing a possible doubt as to pronunciation; 2. Never leave out a vowel in such a word, if by omission a doubt is created as to the pronunciation.

§ 57. The following two points must be regarded as exceptions to this rule:

a) In any syllable which is composed of two consonants, if the vowel is soft *ústún*, none of the orthographic (vowel) letters is added; but, if it is composed of one letter ه *hé* is added to indicate the vowel; as: كلدی *gél-di*, بش *bésh*, ايستهمك *is-t⁶-mék*.

b) None of the grammatical affixes take the orthographic or vowel letters; as كلدم *gél-dim*, باشلر *bash-lar*, اوچلك *uch-lûk*, آلمق *al-maq*.

Note. The use of the orthographic or vowel letters is fully discussed and shown on pages 13—16.

§ 58. There are some words in Ottoman, the orthography of which is the same, but the pronunciation and meanings are different; as:

اون *on* ten; *oun* flour; *ún* fame.

شكر *shékér* sugar; a. *shúkúr* thanks.

كوز *geôz* eye; *gúz* autumn; *keôz* an ember.

چول *choul* sackcloth; *cheôl* desert, wilderness.

قول *qoul* servant; *qol* arm; a. *qavl* word.

كورك *gévrék* biscuit; *kúrk* fur; *kúrék* shovel; *keôrûk* bellows.

كل *gél* come; *kél* scald-head; p. *gúl* rose; a. *kúll* all.

اولو *eôlú* dead; *oulou* big.

First Part.
Turkish Grammar.

درس ١   Lesson 1.

The Definite and Indefinite Articles.

§ 59. There is no Definite Article in Turkish; all nouns, when used alone in a sentence, are usually considered as definite. Ex.: بابا *baba* the father, آنا *ana* the mother, قرداش *qardash* the brother.

§ 60. The Indefinite Article is بر *bir* a, an. Ex.: بر آت *bir at* a horse, بر كوپك *bir keôpék* a dog, بر قیز *bir qîz* a girl, بر آدم *bir adém* a man.

§ 61. The Adjective always precedes the noun. Ex.: كوزل *gûzél* beautiful, ایی ' ایو *éyi* good, كوتو *keôtû* bad, *gûzél qîz* the beautiful girl, *é-yi adém* the good man, *bir keôtû chojouq* a bad boy.

§ 62. As in English, there is no unnatural distinction of Gender in Turkish, that is to say: the names of males are masculine; those of females feminine, and those of inanimate objects, neuter. Thus: *baba* is masculine, *ana* feminine, قیز *qîz* feminine, اوغلان *ogh-lan* 'the boy' masculine. دكز *dé-ñiz* the sea, p. شهر *shé-hir* the city, كوی *keôy* 'the village', are neuter.

§ 63. The *Personal Pronouns* are: بن *bén* I, سن *sén* thou, او *o* he, she, it. بز *biz* we, سز *siz* you, اونلر *onlar* they.

§ 64. The *Demonstrative Pronouns* are: بو *bou* this, شو *shou* that (near by), او *o* that (distant).

§ 65. The Present Tense of the Turkish Substantive Verb is the following:

Affirmative Present

بن ايم *bén' im* I am   بز ايز *biz' iz* we are

سن سين *sén' sin* thou art   سز سكز *siz' siñiz* you are

او در *o' dour* he is.   اونلر درلر *onlar' dirlar* they are.

Interrogative Affirmative Present.

بن مى ميم ؟ or بن ميم ؟ *bén' mi yim?* (§ 53).

سن مى سين ؟ » سن ميسين ؟ *sén' mi sin?*

او مى در؟ » او ميدر ؟ *o' mou dour?*

بز مى ايز ؟ » بز ميز ؟ *biz' mi yiz?*

سز مى سكز ؟ » سز ميسكز ؟ *siz' mi siñiz?*

اونلر مى درلر ؟ » اونلر ميدرلر ؟ *onlar' mi dirlar?*

Am I? art thou? is he? etc.

§ 66. As will be seen, the question is expressed by adding مى *mi, mou* after the word emphasized by the question (§ 49 IV). Ex.:

بن ميم ؟ *bén' **mi** yim?* Am I? (§ 53).

كل بياض ميدر؟ *gûl béyaz' **mî** dîr?* Is the rose white?

بو بر كل ميدر؟ *bou bir gûl' **mû** dûr?* Is this a rose?

كل بو ميدر؟ *gûl bou' **mou** dour?* Is this the rose?

§ 67. The third person در is the Copula; its pronunciation, like that of *mi* مى, is governed by the preceding vowel, and is: *dir, dîr, dour, dûr*, as the case may be (§ 52).

لغتلر *Loughétlér,* Words.

وَ *vé* and

اوت *év'-rét* yes

اَو *év* the house

اوكوز *ô-kûz* the ox

قوش *qoush* the bird   آق *aq* white

a. قلم *qalém* the pen   قره *qara* black

a. هوا *hava* air, weather   قرمزی *qirmîzi* red

قیز قرداش *qiz qardash* a sister   a. فقیر *faqir* poor

بویوك *beô-yûk* great   زنكین *zéngin* rich

كوچوك *kû-chûk* little   گنج *génj* young

طاغ (داغ) *dagh* mountain   صیجاق *sîjaq* warm. hot

اوزاق *ouzaq* far   صغوق *so-rouq* cold (§ 36)

یاقین *yaqin* near   p. دره *déré* valley.

Note 1. These words, as well as those contained in the preceding rules, must be thoroughly committed to memory, before doing the exercise and translation.

Note 2. Those words without any mark are Turkish in origin, those with an *a* Arabic, those with a *p* Persian, and those with an *f* foreign in origin.

تعلیم ۱ *Taleem,* Exercise 1.

۱ بر چوجوق • چوجوق • ۲ بر قوش • قوش • ۳ او كوز • بر او كوز •
٤ شو دره • بر دره • ۵ بر یاقین كوی • یاقین بر كوی • ٦ یوكسك
برطاغ • بر یوكسك طاغ • ۷ اوزاق شهر • شهر اوزاقدر • او شهر اوزاق
میدر ؟ ۸ بو بویوك طاغ • بو طاغ بویوك میدر ؟ طاغ بویوك میدر ؟ بر
بویوك طاغ • ۹ ایكی چوجوق • چوجوق ایودر • او ایو چوجوق • او چوجوق
ایو بر چوجوقدر • ۱۰ بو آت • بر آت • ایی آت • بو بر آت در •
بر ایی آت • آت ایی در • ۱۱ اوزاق بر شهر • بر یاقین شهر • شهر یاقین
میدر ؟ شهر اوزاقدر • ۱۲ هوا ایی در • هوا صیجاق میدر ؟ هوا
صغوقدر • ۱۳ قرداش وَ قیز قرداش زنكین درلر • قرداش ، قیز
قرداش ، بابا وَ آنا ایو درلر • ۱٤ سن بویوك میسین كوچوك میسین ؟
۱۵ قره قوش (eagle) • قره طاغ (Montenegro)[1] • قره دكز (Black
Sea) • آق دكز (Mediterranean) • آق بابا (vulture) • آق طاغ •

---

[1] Observe that a parenthesis (. . .) encloses a word *to be*

ترجمه ۲ *Térjémé*, Translation 2.

1. The horse. A horse. A good horse. The good horse. A horse and **an ox**. 2. A house. A large house. The large house. The house is large. 3. A man. The man. A white man. The white man. 4. The Black Sea. The Black Mountain. The White Sea. The White Mountain. 5. A white rose. The white rose. The red rose. 6. A bad boy. This is a bad boy. This is the bad boy. 7. The house is near. The city is far. 8. A horse, a bird and an ox. The good horse and the big ox. 9. This bird is white. Is this bird white? It is black. 10. The brother is young. He is a good man. 11. The eagle is a large bird. That bird is a beautiful eagle. 12. The Mediterranean is a great sea.

Correct the following sentences.

۱ بن ايم كوچوك ۰ ۲ سين سن گنج ۰ ۳ اونلار درلر زنكين ۰

٤ بابا درلر ايو ۰ ٥ آت دركوتو ۰ ٦ او شهر در اوزاق ۰ ۷ شهر اوزاق

در؟ ۸ در هوا صيجاق؟ ۹ اوت او در ۰ ۱۰ قوش بويوك در ؟

مكالمه *Mûkialémé*, Conversation.

سؤال *Sival*, Question	جواب *Jévab*, Answer
Sén zéngin'mi sin?	Ev'vét, zéngin'im.
Qardash faqir'mi dir?	Ev'vét, faqir'dir.
Ogh'-lan é-yi'mi dir?	Ev'vét, oghlan é-yi'dir.
Sén é-yi'mi sin, kêotû'mû sûn?	Bén é-yi'yim (§ 53).
Qiz qardash é-yi'mi?	Ev'vét, qîz qardash éyi'bir qîz dir.
Bou dagh yûksék'mi?	Ev'vét, yûksék'dir.
Onlar génj'mi dir?	Ev'vét, génj'dirlér.
Siz faqir'mi siñiz?	Biz zéngin'iz.
Aq-Déñiz bêoyûk'mû?	Qara-Déñiz' kûchûk dûr.
Aq baba bêoyûk bir qoush'mou dour?	Ev'vét, bêoyûk bir qoush'dour.

---

translated, or an annotation, whereas brackets [. . .] signify "leave out".

[1] In such answers the predicate cannot be omitted. It must be *evvét, sijaq dir.*

درس ٢   Lesson 2.

The Substantive Verb.

§ 68. The Turkish Plural is formed by adding the affix لر to the singular. This affix is pronounced *lar*, after hard vowels, and *lér* after soft ones. Ex.:

دكنك *déynék* stick: دكنكلر *déyneklér* sticks.

كدى *kédi* cat: كديلر *kédilér* cats.

كوپرى *kéôprû* bridge: كوپريلر *kéôprûlér* bridges.

قپو *qapou* door: قپولر *qapoular* doors.

خصم *khî-sîm* relative: خصملر *khî-sîmlar* relatives.

§ 69. Titles of respect are given to persons according to their dignity, office and occupation. افندى *éffen'di* Sir, Mr., is peculiar to clergymen and educated people. اغا *a-gha* or vulg. *a-a'*, to tradesmen, labourers and old men; it means Mr., Esq. بك *béy*, prince, is given to civil functionaries and popularly to any person of supposed distinction. Each of these titles is put after the name of the person himself, not after his family name, as in English (§ 495). Ex.: احمد افندى, احمد بك , احمد اغا *Ah'méd éffendi, Ah'méd agha, Ah'méd béy.*

§ 70. When the subject is a pronoun it is often omitted (§ 120). Ex.: بن ايو ايم *bén éyi'yim* or ايوايم *éyi'yim* I am well; سز تنبل سكز *siz ténbél' siñiz* or تنبل سكز *ténbél' siñiz* you are idle.

§ 71. In Turkish, as in English, the adjective precedes the noun, and never varies, being the same whether it qualifies a singular or a plural substantive, a masculine or a feminine noun. Ex.: كوزل چيچك *gûzél chichék* beautiful flower: كوزل چيچكلر *gûzél chichéklér*

beautiful flowers; بویوك آغاج *beŏyúk a-ghaj* a big tree: بویوك

آغاجلر *beŏyúk aghajlar* big trees.

§ 72. The Negative of the Present Tense of the Substantive verb is as follows:

Negative Present.

دكل ايم or دكايم *déyil'im,* دكل ايز or دككز *déyil'iz.*

دكل سين » دك سكز *déyil'sin,* دكاسين » دكسين *déyil'siñiz.*

دكل در, » دك درلر *déyil'dir,* دكالر » دكل در *déyillér'.*

I am not, thou art not, he is not, etc.

Interrogative Negative Present.

دكل می ايم ؟ or دكايم ؟ *déyil'mi yim?*

دك می سين ؟ » دكاميسين ؟ *déyil'mi siñ?*

دكل می در ؟ » دكاميدر؟ *déyil'mi dir?*

دكل می ايز ؟ » دكلميز ؟ *déyil'mi yiz?*

دكل می سكز؟ » دكامیسكز؟ *déyil'mi siñiz?*

دكل می درلر؟ » دكاميدرلر؟ *déyil'mi dirlér?*

Am I not? art thou not? is he not? etc.

Note. It is very useful for the learner to conjugate the adjective with the verb and to write the latter in both its forms, the full and the abbreviated ones; as:

یورغون در or یورغونسین or یورغون سین، یورغونم، یورغون ایم or

یورغون دكلم، یورغونميسين، یورغونميم ؟ or یورغون می ايم ؟ ؛ یورغوندر

یورغون دكلدر etc.

لغتلر Words.

خیر افندم ! *khayr' éffendim!* No, Sir!	خیر ! خایر ! *khayr'* no!
اوّت افندم ! *év'vét éffendim!* Yes, Sir!	اوّت ! *év'vét* yes! t.
یاپراق *yapraq'* leaf	قونكشو *qon-shou'* neighbour
باغچه *bah'-jé*[1] garden p.	دشمن *dúshmén'* enemy p.
آطه *a-da* island	دوست *dost* friend p.

---

[1] This is the common pronunciation, the correct pronunciation is: *khas'-ta, ikh'-ti-yar, khosh'-noud, bagh'-ché* (p. 8).

a. عسكر *askér* soldier

قهوه *qah'vé* coffee

ویر *vér'* give

آرتین *Artin* Pascal

تپه ، دپه *tépé, dépé* hill

صو *sou* water

a. حاضر *hazîr'* ready, present

یشیل *yéshil'* green

پك *pék* very

یورغون *yorghoun'* tired

جومرد *jéômérd'* generous

a. p. طمعكار *tama'kiar* avaricious

p. تازه *tazé* fresh

چالیشقان *chalishqan* diligent

اختیار *ih'-ti-yar*[1] old (age)

p. خشنود *hosh'-noud*[1] content, happy

p. خسته *hasta'*[1] sick

پك ایو *pék éyi* very well!

تعلیم ٣ Exercise 3.

۱ فقیرمیسین ؟ زنكین میسین ؟ — بن فقیردكلم ؛ اختیار آدم فقیردر. ۲ كوزل دپهلر ، یوكسك طاغلر ، بوك آطهلر وَ یشیل یاپراقلر. ۳ زنكین قوكشولر ، فقیر دوستلر وَ بر اختیار عسكر. ٤ بر تازه صو وَ قهوه ویر ! — صو تازه در ، قهوه تازه دكلدر. ٥ یاپراق یشیل می در ، قیرمیزی میدر ؟ — افندم ! یاپراق یشیل در ، قیرمیزی دكلدر. ٦ چوجوقلر تنبل می در ؟ — خیر افندم ! چوجوقلر تنبل دكلدرلر ، چالیشقان درلر. ۷ عسكر اختیار می كنج می ؟ — افندم ! عسكر پك اختیار وَ خسته در. ۸ او جومرد دوست پك خسته در. ۹ بز تنبل دكاز ، چالیشقان ایز. ۱۰ سن پك تنبل سین. — بن تنبل دكلم ، تنبل سن سین. ۱۱ خیر افندم ! ۱۲ احمد افندی دوست وَ خصم در ، دشمن دكلدر. ۱۳ آرتین (Artin) بك قوﻧشو و دوست در. ۱٤ قهوه حاضر میدر ، دكلمیدر ؟ — اوت افندیلر ! قهوه وَ صو حاضر در. ۱٥ جورجی بك خسته میدر ؟ — خیر افندم ! خسته دكل یورغوندر.

---

[1] See the Note page 32.

ترجمه ٤   Translation 4.

1. Little hills. Red flowers. The green leaves and the beautiful gardens. 2. Is not the house large? — Yes, Sir, it is large. 3. The islands are small. That island is not small. 4. The coffee is very good. It is not ₃(a) ₁very ₂good ₄coffee. 5. The gardens and the trees are very nice. 6. Is the coffee ready? — No, Sir! 7. Are you ready? — Yes, gentlemen! I am ready. 8. Who is Mr. Charles? — He is a good neighbour. 9. Is the water fresh? — No, Sir, it is not fresh. — Give (a) fresh water. 10. Is the garden very far? — No, Sir, it is not very far, it is near. 11. Ahmed Bey is a good soldier. 12. He is a generous man. 13. That gentleman is not avaricious. 14. Master Georgie is very young.

To be corrected.

١ دكلميدر احمد افندى پك جومرد؟ — خير! احمد افندى در طمعكار پك۰ ٢ اغا آرتين پك كوزل بر آدم در دكل۰ ٣ اونلر كوزلر آدملر درلر۰ ٤ يشيللر ياپراقلر ٬ بيوكلر باغچهلر۰ ٥ سين مى سن حاضر؟ ٦ دكلم بن حاضر؟ ٧ درلر مى دكل چوجوقلر چالیشقان؟

مكالمه   Conversation.

جواب Jévab Answer	سؤال Sival Question
اوت افندم ٬ پك جومردم۰	افندى! جومرد ميسكز؟
خير افندم ٬ خسته دكلدر۰	عسكر خسته ميدر؟
ایی در افندم۰	چوجوق خسته مى ايو مى؟
خير افندم ٬ يوكسك دكلدر۰	او طاغ پك يوكسك مى؟
خير! دپه كوچوك بر طاغ در۰	دپه بيوك بر طاغ ميدر؟
اوت! طاغ بر دپه ميدر۰	طاغ بيوك بر دپه ميدر ٬ دكلميدر؟
خير افندم! ايو قهوه حاضر دكل ٬ صو حاضر۰	ايو قهوه حاضر ميدر؟
اوت افندم! پك خسته در۰	جومرد دوست خسته مى؟

او کوزل اَولر قیرمیزی می؟   خیر افندم! ایاض در.

او اوغلانلر کوزل میدرلر؟   اوت! کوزل وَ چالیشقان درلر.

دلرس ٣   Lesson 3.

The Substantive Verb. (Continued.)

§ 73. The Preterite or Past Tense of the Substantive Verb is as follows:

بن ایدم *bén′ idim* I was	بز ایدك *biz′ idik* we were
سن ایدك *sén′ idiñ* thou wast	سز ایدیكز *siz′ idiñiz* you were
او ایدی *o′ idi* he was	اونلر ایدیلر *onlar′ idiler* they were.

The Negative Past Tense.

بن دكل ایدم *bén déyil′ idim*	بز دكل ایدك *biz déyil′ idik*
سن دكل ایدك *sén déyil′ idiñ*	سز دكل ایدیكز *siz déyil′ idiñiz*
او دكل ایدی *o déyil′ idi*	اونلر دكل ایدیلر *onlar déyil′ idilér.*

I was not, thou wast not, he was not, etc.

The Interrogative Forms of the Same.

Bén′ mi idim? sén′ mi idiñ? o′ mou idi?
Biz′ mi idik? siz′ mi idiñiz? onlar′ mi idilér?
Was it I? was it thou? etc.

Bén déyil′ mi idim? sén déyil′ mi idiñ? o déyil′ mi idi?
Biz déyil′ mi idik? siz déyil′ mi idiñiz? onlar déyil′ mi idilér? or déyil′ler miyidi?
Was it not I? was it not thou? etc.

§ 74. The Numerals are used just like all other adjectives. Like them, they precede the noun. The noun qualified by cardinals always remains in the singular (§ 71). Ex.: ایکی چوجوق بر آدم *bir adém* a man, *iki chojouq* two boys.

ایکی *iki* two		آلتی *altî* six	
اوچ *ûch* three		یدی *yédi* seven	
درت *déôrt* four		سكز *sékiz* eight	
بش *bésh* five		طقوز *doqouz* nine	

اون on ten   اون بر *on bir* eleven

اون ايكى *on iki* twelve, etc.

§ 75. The English word "half" is expressed in two ways, by يارم *yarîm* and by بوچوق *bouchouq* (§ 207). **Yarîm** is used before a noun like an adjective: يارم كون *yarîm gûn* half a day, يارم ساعت *yarîm sa'at* half an hour, يارم الما *yarîm élma* half an apple.

Bouchouq is always used in connexion with a number. Ex.: ايكى بوچوق *iki bouchouq* two and a half, اوچ بوچوق ساعت *úch bouchouq sa'at* three hours and a half, آلتى بوچوق كون *altî bouchouq gûn* six days and a half.

§ 76. The English phrase "there is, there are" etc. is expressed in Turkish by [1] وار *var* 'there is, exists': its negative being يوق *yoq* 'there is not' (§ 126 a).

وار، وار در *var, var dir* there is,

يوق، يوقدر *yoq, yoq dour* there is not.

وار ايدى *var idi, varîdi* there was,

يوق ايدى *yoq idi* there was not.

بر كتاب وار (در) *bir kitab var (dir)* there is a book,

بر كتاب وار ايدى *bir kitab var îdi* there was a book.

بر كتاب يوق، بر كتاب يوقدر *bir kitab yoq, bir kitab yoq dour* there is not a book,

بر كتاب يوق ايدى *bir kitab yoq idi* there was not a book.

§ 77. The *Locative case* is made by the addition of ده *dé, da* to the end of the word (§ 84). Ex.: اوده *évdé* in the house, كتابده *kitabda'* in the book,

---

[1] The word *var* is called the Verb of Existence and Non-existence, or Verb of Presence and Absence by some European Grammarians, but there are no such *verbs* in Turkish.

باغچهده *bah'-jé-dé* in the garden. *Evdé bir adém var, —dir*, there is a man in the house.

او کتابده تصویرلر وار در   *o kitabda tasvirlér' var dir*, there are pictures in that book.

باغچهده چیچك یوقدر   *Bah'-jéde chichék yoq' dour*, there are no flowers in the garden.

باغچهده بر كل وار ایدی   *Bah'-jédé bir gûl' var idi*, there was a rose in the garden.

بر كوزل وَ بویوك اوده ایدك   *Bir gûzél vé beôyûk' évdé idik*, we were in a nice [and] big house.

§ 78. In asking the hour, it is said:

ساعت قاچدر؟   *sa-at qach'dir?* What o'clock is it?

ساعت ایکیدر   *sa-at iki'dir*, it is two o'clock.

But قاچ ساعتدر   *qach' sa-at dîr?* means: How many hours are there?

ایکی ساعتدر   *iki' sa-at dir*, there are two hours.

Sa-at means also 'a watch': اسکی بر ساعت *és-gi' bir sa-at* an old watch, بر آلتون ساعت *bir altoun' sa-at* a gold watch.

<h2 style="text-align:center">Words. لغتلر</h2>

p. سیاه	*si-yah'* black	a. بیاض	*béyaz* white
ایری	*i-ri* large, big	اوفاق	*oufaq* small
یکی	*yé-ñi* new	اسکی	*és-gi* old
چوق	*choq* much, many	آز	*az* few, *bir az* a little
صاری	*sarî* yellow	کیم؟	*kim?* who?
قاچ؟	*qach?* how many?	بر قاچ	*bir qach* some
سود	*sûd* milk	a. شراب	*sharab* wine
p. میوه	*méyvé* fruit	a. مکتب	*méktéb* school
Prop. names. a. حسن	*Hasan*	a. کریم	*kérim* Grace.

<h2 style="text-align:center">Exercise 5. تعلیم ٥</h2>

۱ باغچهده ایری آغاجلر وَ آغاجلرده كوزل میوهلر وَ یشیل یاپراقلر وار در ۰ ۲ اَوده بویوك برکدی وَ اوفاق برکوپك وار ایدی ۰

۳ کوچوك چوجوقلر باغچهده وبیوك چوجوقلر اوده درلر. ٤ چالیشقان اوغلانلر مکتبده وَ تنبللر طاغده درلر. ٥ دوستلره دوست ايز وَ دشمنلره دشمن ايز. ٦ پدر، والده وَ خصملر اوده دکللر می؟ (دکامیدرلر؟). — خیر افندم! پدر وَ والده اوده درلر. خصملر اوده دکلدرلر. ٧ ايو دکللر، ايو دکل درلر. ايو دکامیدرلر؟ ايو ايدیلر. — خیر! ايی دکل ايدیلر. ٨ قهوه سياه، سود بياض وَ شراب قیرمیزی در. ٩ کوچوك کدی سياه میدر؟ — خیر افندم! بیوك کدی سياهدر، کوچوك کدی صاری در. ١٠ باغچهلرده صاری، بياض، قیرمیزی چیچکلر واردرلر. ١١ اوَده کیم وار؟ — اوده آدم یوقدر. ١٢ ساعت قاچدر؟ — ساعت بر بوچوقدر. ١٣ ساعت درت دکل می ايدی؟ — خیربکم! درت بوچوق ايدی، درت دکل ايدی. ١٤ بو ساعت ايی میدر، کوتو میدر؟ خیربکم! بو ساعت کوزل بر آلتون ساعت در.

ترجمه ٦   Translation 6.

1. Was he sick? — No, Sir (*Bé-yim*), he was not sick; the soldier was very sick. 2. Is Ahméd Béy at home? — No, Sir, he is in the garden. 3. Who is there at home? — Hassan Effendi is at home. 4. Seven days and nine hours. Eight and [a] half days. 5. Was the coffee hot? — Yes, Sir, the coffee and the milk are hot; they are not cold. 6. Who is this young gentleman? — He is Kérim Effendi. 7. Three and seven are ten; five and six are eleven. 8. There are twelve hours in a day. 9. Aq-Shéhir, Esgi-Shéhir and Yéñi-Shéhir are large [and] fine cities. 10. How many islands are there in the Mediterranean Sea? 11. How many islands are there in the Black Sea? — There are two [or] three bad islands.

To be corrected.

١ آق دکیزده چوق یوق وار بیوك کار وَ کوزلر آطهلر. ٢ بش یاریم ساعت در. ٣ ساعت قاچ وار؟ — ساعت اون ايکی یاریم وار.

ساعت بوچوقدر . ٤ در بر ایی چوجوق اوده ؟ ٥ باغچه ده در یوق
سوك بر آغاج . ٦ سن دكلسين بر ایی چوجوق .

مكالمه Conversation.

سلام Sélam Salutation

Sabah´lar khayr´ olsoun!	Good morning!
Akh´shamlar khayr´ olsoun!	Good evening!
Vaqîtlar khayr´ olsoun!	Good day!
Na´sîl siñiz, éyi´mi siñiz?	How do you do?
Eyi´yim, téshék´kûr édérim.	I am well, thank you!
Siz na´sîl siñiz, éyi´mi siñiz?	How are you? are you well?
Choq´éyiyim efféndim.	I am very well, Sir!
El-ham´dûl-lah´ éyi´yim.	Thank God, I am very well.
Rija´édérim, otourouñouz´.	Please take a seat.
Théshék´kûr édérim.	Thank you!
Bouyou´rouñ efféndim,otou´rouñ.	Come in, Sir; take a seat.
Hassan´ Effendi, nérédé siñiz?	Mr. Hassan, where are you?
Bouyou´rouñ éfféndim!	Yes, Sir.
Géjélér khayr´ olsoun!	Good night!
Hosh´ géldiñiz.	You are welcome.

درس ٤ Lesson 4.

احوال اسم Declension of Nouns.

§ 79. There are two numbers in Turkish: Singular and Plural; and six cases, expressing the different relations of words to each other; namely: the Nominative, Genitive, Dative, Accusative, Locative and Ablative cases.

§ 80. The Nominative case (or the Subject) answers to the questions: *who?* or *what?* كيم kim? نه né? as the subject of the verb; as: Who is learning? — The boy اوغلان ogh´lan.

§ 81. The Genitive (or Possessive) case answers to the questions: *whose?* or *of which?* كيمك kimiñ? نه نك

néniñ. Ex.: Whose book? — The boy's book اوغلانك *oghlaniñ*[1] *kitabî.*

§ 82. The Dative answers to the questions: *to whom? to which?* كيمه *kimé?* نه يه *né-yé?* Ex.: To whom shall I give it? — To the boy اوغلانه *oghlana.*

§ 83. The Accusative (or Objective case) marks the object of an action, and answers to the questions: *whom?* or *what?* كيمى *kimi?* نه يى *néyi?* Ex.: Whom or what do you see? — I see the boy, the house اوغلانى *ogh-lanî*[1], اوى *évi*[1].

§ 84. The Locative answers to the questions: *where? wherein?* نره ده *nérédé?* Ex.: Where is the boy? — He is in the school مكتبده *méktébdé.*

§ 85. The Ablative answers to the questions: *from whom? from what?* كيمدن *kimdén?* نه دن *nédén?* Ex.: From whom did you take this book? — From the boy اوغلاندن *oghlandan.*

§ 86. There is only one declension in Turkish, with four variations:

First Form.

§ 87. The first form comprehends all nouns ending in consonants (except ك *k*, and ق *q*):

a) Nouns ending in soft syllables.

Singular مفرد *Mûfréd'*		Plural جمع *Jém'*	
N. پدر *pédér'*		پدرلر *pédérler'*	
G. پدرك *pédériñ'* of	} the father	پدرلرك *pédérleriñ'* of	} the fathers
D. پدره *pédéré'* to		پدرلره *pédérléré'* to	

---

[1] The Genitive and the Accusative do not always take the terminations *-iñ*, *-i*. These are required only when the noun in

A.   پدرى *pédéri'*   پدرلرى *pédérléri'*

L.   پدرده *pédérdé'* in   پدرلرده *pédérlérdé'* in

A.   پدردن *pédérdén'* from   پدرلردن *pédérlerdén'* from

(the father.)   *(the fathers.)*

b) Nouns ending in hard syllables.

N.   طاش *tash'*   طاشلر *tashlar'*

G.   طاشك *tashiñ'* of   طاشلرك *tashlariñ'* of

D.   طاشه *tasha'* to   طاشلره *tashlara'* to

A.   طاشى *tashi'*   طاشلرى *tashlari'*

L.   طاشده *tashda'* in   طاشلرده *tashlarda'* in

A.   طاشدن *tashdan'* from   طاشلردن *tashlardan'* from

(the stone.)   *(the stones.)*

c) Nouns ending in syllables which have the hard vowels *ou* or *o* in them.

N.   موم *moum'*   موملر *moumlar'*

G.   مومك *moumouñ'* of   موملرك *moumlariñ'* of

D.   مومه *mouma'* to   موملره *moumlara'* to

A.   مومى *moumou'*   موملرى *moumlari'*

L.   مومده *moumda'* in   موملرده *moumlarda'* in

A.   مومدن *moumdan'* from   موملردن *moumlardan'* from

(the candle.)   *(the candles.)*

d) Nouns ending in syllables which have the soft vowels *eô* or *û* in them.

N.   سود *sûd'*   سودلر *sûdlér'*

G.   سودك *sûdûñ'* of   سودلرك *sûdlériñ'* of

D.   سوده *sûde'* to   سودلره *sûdléré'* to

A.   سودى *sûdû'*   سودلرى *sûdléri'*

L.   سودده *sûddé'* in   سودلرده *sûdlérdé'* in

A.   سوددن *suddén'* from   سودلردن *sudlérdén'* from

(the milk.)   *(the milks.)*

---

the Genitive or Accusative is definite. When the -*iñ* or -*i* is omitted, the Genitive or Accusative is the same as the Nominative in form (§§ 109, 251). When the Indefinite form of these two cases is to be described, it is styled by some Orientalists the Nominatival form of the Genitive or Accusative. But the indefinite forms of those two cases are called by the native grammarians simply Nominative.

Second Form.

§ 88. The second form of declension comprises all consonants ending in ق *q*. The difference from the first declension is this, that ق *q* is changed into غ *gh*, whenever it is followed by a vowel (§ 52, 2). Ex.: بالق *ba-līq*: here ق *q* is not followed by a vowel, because it stands at the end of the syllable. بالقَه *ba-lī-qa*: here the third syllable begins with ق *q* and is vowelled, therefore it changes into غ *gh*, thus we have بالغَه *ba-lī-gha*. This change takes place in the Genitive, Dative and Accusative cases: in the Locative and Ablative cases and in the plural the ق *q* remains unchanged, because in those cases *q* is not followed by a vowel.

Note. In Arabic and Persian words and in all words borrowed from foreign languages, the ق *q* remains unaltered.

Singular مفرد *Mûfréd'*		Plural جمع *Jém'*	
N.	بالق *ba-līq*	بالقلر *ba-līq-lar*	
G.	بالغك *ba-lī-ghiñ* of	بالقلرك *ba-līq-la-riñ* of	
D.	بالغَه *ba-lī-gha* to	بالقلره *ba-līq-la-ra* to	
A.	بالغى *ba-lī-ghi*	بالقلرى *ba-līq-la-ri*	
L.	بالقده *ba-līq-da* in	بالقلرده *ba-līq-lar-da* in	
A.	بالقدن *ba-līq-dan* from	بالقلردن *ba-līq-lar-dan* from	

(the fish. / the fishes.)

The fire-place

اوجاقدن   اوجاقده   اوجاغى   اوجاغَه   اوجاغك   اوجاق

o-jaq-dan   o-jaq-da   o-ja-ghi   o-ja-gha   o-ja-ghiñ   o-jaq.

The boy

چوجوغى   چوجوغَه   چوجوغك   چوجوق

cho-jou-ghou   cho-jou-gha   cho-jou-ghouñ   cho-jouq

چوجوقدن   چوجوقده

cho-jouq-dan   cho-jouq-da.

Third Form.

§ 89. The third form contains all the soft syllabled nouns ending in ك *k*. The letter *kéf* is changed into *yaf*, because it is vowelled: that is, when the syllable would otherwise begin with كَ *k*, the *k* is changed into *y*. Ex.: اوردك *eôr-dék:* here ك *k* is not vowelled, it is at the end of the second syllable. اوردكه *eôr-dé-ké* is wrong, for the last syllable would begin with ك *k*; therefore the *k* must be changed into *y*, اوردگه *eôr-dé-yé* (§ 52, 2). This is noticed only in the pronunciation, as there are no different forms for *kéf* and *yaf* (§ 34).

In the plural and in the Locative and Ablative cases *k* is unchangeable, as a vowel does not immediately follow the *k* (§ 88).

Singular مفرد *Müfréd*

N.   اوردك   *eôr'-dék* the duck

G.   اوردكك   *eôr'-dé-yiñ* of the duck

D.   اوردگه   *eôr'-dé-yé* to the duck

A.   اوردكى   *eôr'-dé-yi* the duck

L.   اوردكده   *eôr'-dék-dé* in the duck

A.   اوردكدن   *eôr'-dék-dén* from the duck.

Plural جمع *Jém*

N.   اوردكلر   *eôr'-dék-lér* the ducks

G.   اوردكلرك   *eôr'-dék-lériñ* of the ducks

D.   اوردكلره   *eôr'-dék-lé-ré* to the ducks

A.   اوردكلرى   *eôr'-dék-lé-ri* the ducks

L.   اوردكلرده   *eôr'-dék-lér-dé* in the ducks

A.   اوردكلردن   *eôr'-dék-lér-dén* from the ducks.

The bread

اكمكدن   اكمكده   اكمكى   اكمگه   اكمكك   اكك

ék-mék-dén   ék-mék-dé   ék-mé-yi   ék-mé-yé   ék-mé-yiñ   ék-mék.

The whistle

دودوكی	دودوكَه	دودوكك	دودوك
dû-dû-yû	*dû-dûyé*	*dû-dû-yûn*	*dû-dûk*

	دودوكدن	دودوكده	
	dû-dûk-dén	*dû-dûk-dé.*	

Note. يوك *oq* arrow, طوق *toq* satiated, قرق *qirq* forty, اوق
yûk load, كوك *keôk* a root, are exceptions to the above rules, as
they do not change *q* into *gh*, and *k* into *y*.

Fourth Form.

§ 90ᵃ. The fourth form comprises all nouns
ending in the vowel letters ا و ه ى. In the singular,
the Genitive is formed by adding نك *-nin*; in the Dative
ه *-yé* is added to the Nom., in the Acc. ى *-yi* (§ 53).
No change takes place in the remaining cases or in
the plural (§§ 88, 89).

§ 90ᵇ. When a word ending in a vowel receives
a grammatical ending beginning with a vowel, a hiatus
results, which is practically a difficulty in pronunciation.
This is very common in Turkish (§ 53). To avoid this
difficulty it is usual to insert a consonant ى *y* (and only
in the Genitive ن *n*. This is really the retention of
part of the original genitive termination *-nin*).

Singular مفرد *Múfréd'*		Plural جمع *Jém'*	
N. آنا *a-na*		آنالر *a-na-lar*	
G. آنانك *a-na-nin* of		آنالرك *a-na-la-rin* of	
D. آنايه *a-na-ya* to	the mother.	آناله *a-na-la-ra* to	the mothers.
A. آنای *a-na-yî*		آنالرى *a-na-la-rî*	
L. آناده *a-na-da* in		آنالرده *a-na-lar-da* in	
A. آنادن *a-na-dan* from		آنالردن *a-na-lar-dan* from	

The cat

كدیدن	كدیده	كدیی	كدیه	كدینك	كدی
ké-di-dén	*ké-di-dé*	*ké-di-yi*	*ké-di-yé*	*ké-di-nin*	*ké-di.*

The well

قويوڭ	قويويه	قويونك	قويو
qou-you-you	*qou-you-ya*	*qou-you-noun*	*qou-you*

قويودن	قويوده
qou-you-dan	*qou-you-da.*

The hill

دپەدن	دپەده	دپەيى	دپەيه	دپەنك	دپە
de-pé-dén	*dé-pé-dé*	*dé-pé-yi*	*dé-pé-yé*	*dé-pé-nin*	*dé-pé.*

The water

صودن	صوده	صويى	صويه	صويك	صو
sou-dan	*sou-da*	*sou-you*	*sou-ya*	*sou-youn*	*sou.*

Note 1. Singulars ending in the vowel ه *-é* do not join this letter to the sign of the plural or the endings of cases (§ 32 b).

Note 2. The word صو *sou* forms its Genitive irregularly.

تعليم ٧ Exercise 7.

Decline the following words, writing them in Turkish characters: and also indicate their pronunciation in English characters, with their meanings.

بابا ، قارداش ، طاغ ، باش ، آغاج ، باغچه ، قيز ، آخشام ، دَره ، افندى ، آغا ، بك ، بوجوق ، قهوه ، چوق ، كوچوك ، بوبوك ، ياپراق ، قره ، صيجاق ، صغوق ، *franq* a franc فرانق ، *déymék* a stick دكنك ، كوى *kêoy* village

Translate into English.

١ اوچ كون ، اوچ كوندن ، بش فرانقه ؛ آلتى آغاجى . ٢ يدى اخشامده ، ايو بر باغچه‌يى ، كوزل بر قيزه . ٣ كوچوك بر كدى‌يى ؛ يوكسك بر دپەده ؛ آق دكيزى ؛ قیرميزی چيچكلرى . ٥ چوقلردن ؛ چوغى . آزدن ؛ آزه . ٦ كوزلرى ، كوتولردن ؛ قويوڭوزده . ٧ قهوه‌يى ؛ قهوه‌دن ، قيزلرده . ٨ چوجوقلره ، كتابى ، كتابدن . ٩ (*sovou-gha*) صغوغه ، صيجاغه ؛ كوچركى . ١٠ اوقه ، اوقدن ؛ اَلدن ،

الى ۰ ۱۱ كویه ، كویده كویلردن ۰ درهدن ، دپهدن ، یاپراقلردن ،
یاپراقلری ۰

ترجمه ۸ Translation 8.

1. The mountains; of the mountains; to the mountains; from the mountain. 2. Four [or] five trees; on the three trees; of the good tree, of the good trees, from the good trees. 3. Give the book (acc.) to the big [one]. From the big [one]. 4. In the valley, to the valleys. The valleys are green. 5. ₆I saw ₂the green hills, ₃the black mountains ₄and ₅the white flowers ₁from the village. 6. In the hot, to the hot; the hot (acc.); the hot (nom.). 7. ₂I saw ₁the gentlemen (acc.); to the gentleman; of the gentlemen; on the gentleman. 8. The green leaf (acc.); on the green leaves; on many green and nice leaves. 9. Of the coffee; in the coffee; from the coffee. To the coffee-houses (qah'véléré). 9. From the hot; from the cold; from the little and on the great. 10. To the great men. 11. To the white and the black (acc.). 12. To five francs.

Correct the following words.

۱ صونك ؛ آنانه ؛ بابایدن ؛ بیوغدن ؛ كوچوكی ku-chu-kû ؛
صویدن ۰ ۲ آغایك ؛ قرداشیك ؛ صیجاغلر ؛ یاپراغدن ۰ ۳ یاپراقك ،
قونشویك ۰ اوغی ، the arrow ، طوغه ۰ ٤ فرانغه ، فرانغی ؛ بوچوقه ؛
درهنی ، درهیك ۰

مكالمه Conversation.

Hoshja qaliñ éfféndim.	Good bye, Sir!
Hosh géldiñiz, séfa géldiñiz.	You are welcome.
Sélam seôylé.	Give my salutations (to the home circle).
Pédéré choq sélam seôylé.	Give my salutations to your father.
Bash ûstûné éfféndim.	Very well, Sir.

درس ٥ Lesson 5.

كنايات The Pronouns.

§ 91. Turkish Pronouns are divided into seven classes:

1. Personal, 2. possessive, 3. adjectival, 4. demonstrative, 5. reflexive, 6. indefinite and 7. interrogative pronouns.

1. Personal Pronouns. ضمير شخصى

§ 92. They are: بن *bén,* سن *sén,* او *o,* كندى *kéndi.* They are declined as follows:

First Person.

Singular مفرد *Múfréd'*		Plural جمع *Jém'*	
N.	بن *bén* I	بز *biz* we
G.	بڭم *bénim* my	بزم *bizim* our
D.	بكا *ba-ña* to me	بزه *bizé* to us
A.	بنى *bé-ni* me	بزى *bizi* us
L.	بنده *béndé* in me	بزده *bizdé* in us
A.	بندن *béndén* from me.	بزدن *bizdén* from us.

Second Person.

N.	سن *sén* thou	سز *siz* you
G.	سنك *sé-niñ* thy	سزڭ *siziñ* yours
D.	سكا *sa-ña* to thee	سزه *sizé* to you
A.	سنى *sé-ni* thee	سزى *sizi* you
L.	سنده *sén-dé* in thee	سزده *sizdé* in you
A.	سندن *sén-dén* from thee.	سزدن *sizdén* from you.

Third Person.

Singular مفرد *Múfréd'*

N.	او *o*	he she, it
G.	اونك آنڭ *onouñ, aniñ*	his, hers, its

D. اوکا ، آ کا o-na´, a-na´ ⎰ to him, him
⎱ to her, to it

A. اوڭی ، آنی o-nou´, a-ni´ him, her

L. اونده ، آنده on-da´, an-dé´ in him

A. اوندن ، آندن on-dan´, an-dén´ from him.

Plural جمع Jém´

N. اونلر ، آنلر onlar, anlér them

G. اونلرك ، آنلرڭ onlariñ, anlériñ of them

D. اونلره ، آنلره onlara´, anléré´ to them

A. اونلری ، آنلری onlari´, anléri´ them

L. اونلرده ، آنلرده onlarda´, anlérdé´ in them

A. اونلردن ، آنلردن onlardan´, anlérdén´ from them.

Reflexive form of the Third Person.

Singular مفرد Mûfréd'   Plural جمع Jém'

N. کندی kéndi		کندیلر kéndilér	
G. کندیڭ kéndiniñ of		کندیلرڭ kéndilériñ of	
D. کندینه kéndiné to	himself.	کندیلره kéndiléré to	themselves.
A. کندینی kéndini		کندیلری kéndiléri	
L. کندنده kéndindé in		کندیلرده kéndilérdé in	
A. کندندن kéndindén from		کندیلردن kéndilérdén from	

§ 93. The English conversational form of address is 'you'; in Turkish, however, there are two forms: *sén* and *siz*. **Sén** is employed in addressing parents, near relatives, children, servants, pupils, and intimate friends, such as would be addressed by their Christian names in England. **Siz** is used in addressing strangers, or mere acquaintances (§ 494).

§ 94. Instead of *biz* and *siz* their double plural بزلر ، سزلر *bizlér, sizlér* are sometimes used in all the six cases. This cannot be expressed in English. They are even used, out of politeness, instead of *bén* and *sén*.

2. Possessive Pronouns. ضمير اضافى

§ 95. The Possessive Pronouns of the Turkish language do not really correspond to those of the English, but are merely possessive affixes. Possessive affixes are used instead of the English possessive pronouns. They consist of syllables added at the end of nouns. They have the value of pronouns, and cannot stand alone.

§ 96. The possessive affixes are the following:

م‍ Sing. I. person my   مز‍ Plur. I. person our

ك‍ » II. » thy   كز‍ » II. » your

ى‍ » III. » his.   لرى‍ » III. » their.

Ex.: Sing. الم *élim*   الك *éliñ*   الى *é-li*
              my hand,   thy hand,   his hand;
      Plur. المز *é-limiz*   الكز *é-liñiz*   اللرى *él'-léri*
              our hands,   your hands,   their hands.

§ 97. The pronunciation of the Possessive Affixes varies in the following way (§ 52):

1. If the word to which they are added end in a consonant, the affixes are pronounced: *im*, *iñ*, *i*; *imiz*, *iñiz*, *léri*, as in the above.

2. If the preceding predominant vowel in the word be *ou* or *o*, although written in the same way, they are pronounced: *oum*, *ouñ*, *ou*; *oumouz*, *ouñouz*, *lari*. Ex.: قوشلرى ، قوشكز ، قوشمز ، قوشى ، قوشك ، قوشم *Qoushoum*, *qoushouñ*, *qoushou*; *qoushoumouz*, *qoushounouz*, *qoushlari*. My bird etc.

3. If the word end in a vowel, they have then only the value of the letters *m*, *ñ*, *si*; *miz*, *ñiz*, *léri*. Ex.: آنالرى ، آناكز ، آنامز ؛ آناسى ، آناك ، آنام *Anam*, *anañ*, *anasi*; *a-namiz*, *a-nañiz*, *a-nalari*. My mother etc.

4. If the predominant vowel in the word be *eô*, *û*, the vowel of the affix is pronounced *û*, to agree with it; as: كوزلرى ، كوزكز ، كوزمز ؛ كوزى ، كوزك ، كوزم *Geô-zûm*,

gêô-zûñ, gêô-zû; *gêô-zû-muz, gêô-zû-ñûz, gêôz-lé-ri.*
My eye etc.

§ 98. In the third person singular, when the word ends in a vowel, a س *s* is inserted for euphony, as: باباسی *ba-ba-si* (and not باباى *ba-ba-i*). The only exception to this rule is the word صو *sou*; as: صویم ، باباك soú-youm, sou-youñ, sou-you; sou-you-mouz, *sou-you-ñouz, soulari*. My water etc.

§ 99. If the word ends in one of the connected letters (§ 24) the suffix ی is not written when declined in Singular cases, but the sound *i* is retained; as: كتابندن ، كتابنده ، كتابنی ، كتابنك ، كتابی *Kitabi,* *-bî-niñ, -bî-na, -bî-nî, -bîndan, -bînda.*

§ 100. If it ends in one of the unconnected letters (د ر ز و) the ی *i* is retained; as: اوی ، اوینك ، اوینه ، اوینی ، اویندن ، اوینده *é-vi, é-vi-niñ, é-vi-né, é-vi-ni* etc.

§ 101. If the final vowel of the substantive is ه *é*, it is never joined on to the possessive in writing (§ 32); as: ددهسی ، ددهك ، ددهم *dé-dém, dé-déñ, dé-dési* not ددهٔ ، ددهم My grandfather etc.

§ 102. The genitives of the Personal pronoun are used, when required, to emphasize and corroborate the possessive affixes of the same number and person. They are never used alone, without their equivalent possessive affixes to corroborate them; thus قارداشم *qardashim* my brother (not my sister etc.), بنم قارداشم *bénim qardashim* my brother (not your brother or his brother) (§ 120).

§ 103. A final ق *q*, in a polysyllable, as in declension, changes into غ *gh* before the possessive

affixes, singular or plural, excepting that of the third person plural; so also كـ *k* changes into *y* in like cases (§ 53). Ex.: قوناق ، قوناغِم ، قوناغِك ، قوناغى ، قوناغِمز ، قوناغِكز *Qo-naq, qo-na-ghîm, qo-na-ghîñ, qo-na-ghî; qo-na-ghî-mîz, qo-na-ghî-ñiz*. My mansion etc. اينك ، اينكم ، اينككز ، اينكمز ، اينكى ؛ اينكى ، اينكك *I-nék, i-né-yim, i-né-yiñ, i-né-yi; i-né-yi-miz, i-né-yi-ñiz*. My cow etc.

With Singular Nouns.

بنم آتم *bénim a-tim* my horse

سنك آتك *séniñ a-tiñ* thy horse

اونك آتى *onouñ a-ti* his horse

بزم آتمز *bizim a-tî-mîz* our horse

سزك آتكز *sîziñ a-tî-ñiz* your horse

اونلرك آتلرى *onlariñ at-la-ri* their horse.

With Plural Nouns.

بنم آتلرم *bénim atlarim* my horses

سنك آتلرك *séniñ atlariñ* thy horses

اونك آتلرى *onouñ atlari* his horses

بزم آتلرمز *bizim atlarîmîz* our horses

سزك آتلركز *sîziñ atlariñîz* your horses

اونلرك آتلرى *onlariñ atlari* their horses.

§ 104. In some words the vowel of the last syllable is eliminated when the possessive affix is added, except in the third person plural.

كوكل ، كوكلم *géö-ñûl, geoñ-lûm* heart, my —.

آغز ، آغزك *a-ghîz, agh-ziñ* mouth, thy —.

بويون ، بوينى *bo-youn, boy-nou* neck, his —.

اوغل ، اوغلمز *o-ghoul, ogh-lou-mouz* son, our —.

بورون ، بورنكز *bou-roun, bour-nou-ñouz* nose, your —.

4*

a. عقل · عقلم *a-qîl,* *aq-lîm* mind, sense, my —.

a. وقت · وقتك *va-qît.* *vaq-tiñ* time, thy —.

a. قسم · قسمی *qi-sîm,* *qis-mi* part, his —.

a. اسم · اسممز *i-sîm,* *is-mi-miz* name, our —.

p. شهر · شهركز *she-hir',* *shéh'-ri-ñiz* city, your —.

But in the third person *geô-ñul-léri, a-ghîz-lari, bo-youn-lari, oghoul'lari, bourounlari, aqîl'lari* etc.

§ 105. As it has been seen, the possessives are affixed to the substantives they qualify, and form one word with them. That compound word is then declined like a simple substantive; as:

1. Affixes of the First Person.

Singular مفرد *Mûfréd'*		Plural جمع *Jém'*	
N.	كتابم *kitabim*	كتابمز *kitabimiz*	
G.	كتابمك *kitabimiñ* of	كتابمزك *kitabimiziñ* of	
D.	كتابمه *kitabima* to	كتابمزه *hitabimiza* to	
A.	كتابمی *kitabimi*	كتابمزی *kitabimizi*	
L.	كتابمده *kitabimda* in	كتابمزده *kitabimizda* in	
A.	كتابمدن *kitabimdan* from	كتابمزدن *kitabimizdan* from	

(my book. / our book.)

2. Affixes of the Second Person.

N.	كتابك *kitabiñ*	كتابكز *kitabiñiz*	
G.	كتابكك *ki-ta-bi-yiñ* of	كتابكزك *kitabiñiziñ* of	
D.	كتابكه *kitabiña* to	كتابكزه *kitabiñiza* to	
A.	كتابكی *kitabiñi*	كتابكزی *kitabiñizi*	
L.	كتابكده *kitabiñda* in	كتابكزده *kitabiñizda* in	
A.	كتابكدن *kitabiñdan* from	كتابكزدن *kitabiñizdan* from	

(thy book. / your book.)

3. Affixes of the Third Person.

N.	كتابی *kitabi*	كتابلری *kitablari*	
G.	كتابنك *kitabiniñ* of	كتابلرينك *kitablariniñ* of	
D.	كتابنه *kitabina* to	كتابلرينه *kitablarina* to	

(his book / their book)

A.	كتابنى *kitabini*	كتابلرينى *kitablarini*	
L.	كتابنده *kitabinda* in	كتابلرنده *kitablarinda* in	
A.	كتابندن *kitabindan* from	كتابلرندن *kitablarindan* from	

his book.   *their book.*

Vaqtim, vaqtîmîñ, raqtîma, vaqtîmi, -timda, -dan My time ...
Eviñ, é-vi-yiñ, é-viñé, éviñi, é-viñdé, éviñdén Thy house ...
Qapousou, qapousounouñ, -souna, -sounou, -soundan, -da His door ...
Ba-li-ghî-mîz, -mîzîñ, -mîza, -mîzi, mizda, -mîzdan Our fish ...
Ek-mé-yi-ñiz, -ñiziñ, -ñizé, -ñizi, -ñizdé, -ñizdén Your bread ...
Ormanlari, -larîñîñ, -larîna, -larîni, -larinda, -dan Their forest ...

§ 106. The Accusative Singular of a noun agrees in form and in pronunciation with the third person singular possessive affix added. The noun with this affix, however, is always the subject in a sentence, while the other similar form is always object. Ex.:

عالينك كتابى بوراده در *Aliniñ kitabi bourada dir* The book of Ali [Eli] is here.

عالينك كتابى غائب اولدى *Aliniñ kitabi ghayb oldou* The book of Ali [Eli] has been lost.

كتابى عالى بولدى *Kitabi Ali bouldou* Ali has found the book.

In the first and second examples the word كتابى means 'his book' (Nom. third person), and is the subject of the sentence: in the third example the word is the objective case of the word كتاب.

لغتلر Words.

چيزمه	*chiz'mé* (out of door) boot	چاريق	*chariq* sandal
f. فوطين	*fotin* boots	چوراب	*chorab* stockings
f. قوندورا	*qoundoura* shoe	جزوه	*jézvè* { a little coffee-pot
p. پابوج	*pabouj* slipper	فنجان	*finjan* coffee-cup
f. قالوش	*qalosh* over-shoe, galoche	چوبان	*choban* shepherd
آياق	*a-yaq* foot	f. چاى	*chay* tea (Chinese)
دكنك	*déy-nék* stick	چاى	*chay* brook.

تعليم ٩ Exercise 9.

١ بزم ؛ بنده ؛ بزلردن ؛ اونلرده ؛ سزك ؛ سزده ، سزه ؛ اوكا ؛
اونده . ٢ اوندن ، كندييى ، كندندن ؛ اونك ؛ سزلره ؛ ٣ اونلرك

سوُدی ؛ اونلرك سودینی ؛ بزم قهوه مزده ؛ سزك اُویکزدن . ٤ اُویندن
évindén ؛ اُوندن ondan ؛ اوُنك ؛ اَوِینك ؛ اوی . ٥ چایم ' چایکز '
چایلری ؛ چایزی ' چایلرینی ' چاییی' چایی (acc.) . ٦ بزه وَسزه '
بزدن وَ سزدن ' اونلردن وَ سزاردن . ٧ باغچه لرنده ' باغچه مزده
وَ باغچه کزده ایری وَ کوزل آغاجلر وار . ٨ بنم آیاغمده چزمه یوقدر .
سزك آیاغکزده پوطین وار . ٩ آیاغکز ' آیاقلری ' آیاقلرنده . ١٠ صویم '
صویده ' صویکز ' صولرنده . ١١ بزم صویمز چوق ایی در . سزك
صویکز کوتو وآز در . ١٢ ایکیمز ' اوچمز وَ دردمز deôrdûmûz
چالیشقان ایز ' اونلر تنبل درلر . ١٣ چوجوقلر کز شو اوده درلر . چوجوقلرمز
اویزده évimizdé درلر . ١٤ قوندورام و فوطینم ؛ چوبانك چاریغی
و دکنکی . ١٥ قیزیکزك قیرمیزی پابوجی و سیاه چورابی . ١٦ اونك
جزوه سی ؛ اونلرك جزوه سنده ' جزوه لرنده قهوه یوقدر . ١٧ بر فنجان
قهوه ؛ ایکی فنجان سود . ١٨ اوغلکز ؛ اوغلکزی ' اوغلمزده '
افندیکزده ؛ افندیزده ؛ کوز کزده .

ترجمه ١٠ Translation 10.

1. Me, he, they, you, thou, my, her, his, thy, ours, yours, their. 2. To me; to thee; to you; on thee; in you; on me; from me. 3. Him, himself; to him; in him; from him. 4. The cat (acc.), the cat (nom.); his cat (nom.), his cat (acc.); his cats (nom.), his cats (acc.); their cats, their cat (nom.). 5. His daughter (nom.); his daughter (acc.), the daughter (acc.), your daughter (acc.). 6. In their valley, in our house, to your garden, to your horse. 7. My son, to my son, to his son; his children (pl. nom.). 8. In your time; from your time; to his time. 9. His nose, of his nose; to your nose, their noses. 10. In the city, in your city, to your city, from our city. 11. On my head, on his head, my head (nom.), my head (acc.). 12. The tea (acc. and nom.),

his tea (acc. and nom.); in our brook. 13. The shepherd, their shepherd, their shepherds (nom. and acc.). 14. My over-shoes, thy shoes; his sandals; her stockings and boots; our coffee-cup, your coffee-pot.

To be corrected.

۱ اوغليسى و ‘ *oghoulouñouz* ‘ *oghoulou* ۲ · آناى ‘ قپوى ‘ كدىى (third pers.) · ۳ آياغلرى ‘ آياقكزده · ٤ كديسيمز ‘ موميسى ‘ دره سيلرى · ٥ بالقى ‘ بالغدن ‘ كوزيسى · ٦ چورابيسڭك ‘ چورابيڭك ·

مكالمه Conversation.

S. Haftaniñ gûnlérini séöylé!	*Q.* Tell me the days of the week.
J. Pazar, Pazar'-értési, Salî, Char'shamba, Pér'shémbé, Jouma-a', Jouma-a értési.	*A.* Sunday, Monday, Tuesday, Wednesday, Thursday, Friday, Saturday.
S. Sénéniñ déört mévsimlérini séöylé!	*Q.* Tell me the four seasons of the year.
J. Bahar, Yaz, Gûz, Qîsh.	*A.* Spring, Summer, Autumn, Winter.
S. Gûnûñ taqsimlérini séöylé!	*Q.* Tell me the divisions of the day.
J. Shafaq, Sabah', Qoushlouq, Eoylén, Ikindi, Akhsham, Géjé, Yat'sî, Géjé yarîsî or Yarî géjé.	*A.* The Dawn, Morning, Fore-noon (9 a. m.), Noon, After-noon, Evening, Night, Bed-time (two hours after sunset), Mid-night.

درس ٦ Lesson 6.

اضافت The Izafét.

§ 107. The possession or connexion of one thing or person with another is called in Turkish, *Izafét*, which means 'addition or annexation'.

One substantive is governed by another in three different ways:

§ 108. I. By juxtaposition, without change. This is used to shew the relation between a material and the thing composed of it. The name of the material

is simply put, like an adjective, before the other substantive. Ex.:

آلتون قوطو *altoun qoutou* a golden box.

ایپك مندیل *i-pék méndil* a silk handkerchief.

كوموش ساعت *gû-mûsh sa'at* a silver watch.

Or the noun expressing the material is put in the ablative case; as:

آلتوندن كوستاك *altoundan kêôstêk* a chain of gold.

الماسدن بیاهزیك *élmasdan bilézik* a bracelet of diamond.

یوندن چوراب *youndan chorab* woollen stockings.

§ 109. II. By placing the first substantive in the nominative or unaltered form, and adding to the second the pronominal affix of the third person (ی or سی -**i** or -**si**). This is used to indicate not only possession but also genus and species, the name of the species coming first (§ 81, Note). Ex.:

اَو قپوسی *év qapousou* a house-door (indefinite).

قویو صویی *qouyou sou-you* well water.

آرمود آغاجی *armoud a-gha-ji* pear tree.

آماسیه الماسی *Amasiya élmasî* Amassia apple.

§ 110. The names of countries, rivers, mountains, cities etc. are formed in this way, the first of the two nouns remaining unchanged; as:

عثمانلی دولتی *Osmanlî dévléti* The Ottoman government.

انكلیز قرالیچهسی *In-gi-liz qralichasî* The queen of England.

سیواس شهری *Sivas shéh'ri* The city of Sivas.

ارمنی ملتی *Erméni mil'léti* The Armenian nation.

ارجیاس طاغی *Er-ji-yas da-ghî* Mount Argeas.

طونه نهری *Touna néh'ri* The river Danube.

مایس آیی *Mayis a-yi* The month of May.

§ 111. III. By placing the first in the Genitive, and adding to the second the pronominal affix of the

third person (ى or سى ‑*i* or ‑*si*). This indicates the relation of possession and is essentially d e f i n i t e, and is generally used when the article 'the' would be put before the first noun in English.

The name of the possessor is placed first, as when the possessive case is used in English. Ex.:

اَوك قپوس *é‑viñ qapousou* The door of the house (definite).

الْمانڭ آغاجى *élmaniñ a‑ghaji* The tree of the apple.

قويونك صوىٰ *qou‑younouñ souyou* The water of the well.

§ 112. When the two nouns come together in English, with the word *of* between them, the first expressing the quantity of the second, the phrase is translated into Turkish by simply putting the name of the quantity before the other noun and omitting 'of' as in German they say Eine Flasche Wein, 'a bottle of wine'.

بر قدح چاى *bir qadéh chay* a cup of tea.

اوچ اوقه شکر *úch oq'qa shé‑kér* three okes of sugar.

اون آرشين بز *on arshîn béz* ten yards of cloth.

يوز اولچك بوغداى *yúz êôlchék boughday'* a hundred bushels of wheat.

بر سورو قويون *bir súrú qoyoun* a flock of sheep.

§ 113. The following construction is frequent between a noun and a cardinal number.

كتابك دردى or كتابلردن دردى *kitabiñ déôrdú* or *kitablardan déôrdú* four of the books, or four books.

اوطهنك ايكيسى or اوطهلرك ايكيسى or اوطهلردن ايكيسى *o‑da‑niñ ikisi* or *odalariñ ikisi* or *o‑dalardan ikisi* two of the rooms, or two rooms.

§ 114. These constructions are declined:

Eviñ qapousou, ‑nouñ, ‑na, ‑nou, ‑sounda, ‑soundan.

§ 115. There are two words ده — (‑*dé*, ‑*da*) in Turkish; one is used with the nouns to form the Locative case, and is always accented (§ 84): اوده *év‑dé'*, باغده *baghda'* in the house, in the vineyard.

§ 116. The other *-dé* is a conjunction, meaning 'also, and': it is never connected with the noun, nor is it accented; that is, the accent is at the end of the preceding word; as: باغ ده او ده ' *év' dé* ' *bagh' da* ' پدرم ده *pédérim' dé* ' بنم ده *bénim' dé*; meaning 'The house also, the vineyard too, my father also, mine also'.

بنده ده وار ' سنده ده وار *béndé' dé var, séndé' dé var* 'There is in me and in you'. i. e. 'I have and you have' (§ 477).

§ 117. *Da-khi* دخى is also used with the same meaning ('also, too'); as: بنده دخى ' سنده دخى *béndé' dakhi, séndé' dakhi* 'in me also, in thee too' (§ 477).

لغتلر Words.

Familya فاميليا The Family.

آنا بابا *a-na baba*	parents	قيز قارداش *qiz qardash*	sister
a. والدين *validéyn*		p. همشيره *hémshiré*	
بابا *baba*	father	اوغل *oghoul* son	
p. پدر *pédér*		اوغلان *oghlan* boy	
آنا *a-na*	mother	چوجوق *chojouq* child	
a. والده *validé*		قيز *qîz* girl, daughter	
آننه *an'-né* mamma		a. كريمه *kérimé* daughter	
بويوك بابا *béôyûk baba*	grand father	قارى *qari* wife, woman	
دده ' ددده *dédé*		a. عمى *ém'mi*	uncle (father's brother)
ننه ' نهنه *néné*	grand mother	عموجه *a-mou-ja*	
ابه *é-bé*		تيزه *téy'zé*	aunt (mother's sister)
بويوك آنا *béôyûk ana*		خاله *khala*	
طورون *toroun* grand child		a. عمه *é-mé*	aunt (father's sister)
قارداش *qardash*	brother	داىى *da-yi*	uncle (mother's brother)
قارنداش *qa-rindash*		قاين *qa-yin*	brother-in-law
p. برادر *biradér*		قاين برادر *qa-yin birader*	

قاین آتا *qayîn ata* { father-in-law	باجاناق *bajanaq* { brother-in-law (wife's sister's husband)
قاین آنا *qayîn ana* { mother-in-law	قوجه *qoja* husband
كلين *gélin* { the bride; the daughter-in-law	آبلا *ab'la* elder sister
كوه كى *gûréyi* { the bride-groom	چهچه *chéché* eldest sister
داماد *damad* the son-in-law	a.p. خدمتكار *khîzmétkiar* } servant
انیشته *énishté* { sister's husband	a.t. خذمتجی *khizmétji* }
بالدیز *baldîz* wife's sister	خانم *hanim* Lady, Miss, Mrs.
التى *élti* { husband's brother's wife	صایی *sa-yî* number
كورومجه *geôrûmjé* { husband's sister	اوبر، اولبر *obir, olbir* the other
دوكور *dûñûr* { relative (by intermarriage)	a. خلائق *khala-yiq* } maid servant
یكن *yéyén, yégén* { a nephew; niece	a. جاریه *jari-yé* }
p. عموجه زاده *amja zadé* }	افندی *éfféndi* gentleman, Sir
p. خاله زاده *khala zadé* } cousin	a. مسافر *mûsafir* guest
p. دایی زاده *dayi zadé* }	قفس *qafés* cage.

تعليم ۱۱ Exercise 11.

۱ فامیلیامزك صاییسی اون آلتی در : پدرم وَ والدهم ایکی ،
اوچ برادرلوم بش ، برادرلرمك اوچ كاینلری سكز ، بیوك قارداشم عالی
بكك بالدیزی طقوز ، درت یكنلرم اون اوچ ، خلائق و بر خدمتكار
اون بش وَ بن دخی اون التی . ۲ والدهمك اوطهسنده ایكی قفسی
وار ؛ بو قفسلرك برنده بیوك و كوزل بر قوش واردر . ۳ دون بزده ایكی
مسافر وار ایدی : بونلردن بری كوچوك قارداشمك باجاناغنك برادری
ایدی . اولبری قوكشومزك كوه كیسی ایدی . ٤ كتابلرك صاییسی اون
ایدی : بشی اوده وَ بشی ده مكتبده در . ٥ شو افندی خالهمك اوغلی
واهان افندی در . ٦ او كوچوك اوغلانك آنهسی چوق خسته در .
۷ بیوك والدهمك التیسی بابامك عموجهسنك قاریسی در وَ بزه خصم در .

‏٨ دوكور انشته‌نك آناسى و باباسى وَ كاينك قاين آنا و قاين آتاسى در .

‏٩ داماد قيزك قوچه‌سى ودوكورك اوغلیدر . ١٠ عموجه‌زاده‌یه عموجه

‏اوغلى ده دیرلر (derler is called) ؛ دایى زاده‌یه دایى اوغلى وَ تیزه

‏زاده‌یه تیزه اوغلى ده دیرلر . ١١ كوروجه : قوجه‌نك قیز قارداشى

‏وَ التى : قوجه‌نك قارداشینك قاریسیدر . ١٢ قیز قارداشك اوغلنه

‏یكن وَ قارداشك اوغلنه ده یكن دیرلر . ١٣ دكز صویى' الما صویى'

‏الما شرابى .

Translation 12. ‏ترجمه ١٢

1. Coffee-pot, coffee-cup; an oke of coffee of Yémén (‏یمن). 2. Cow's milk; the milk of the cow; in cow's milk, in the milk of the cow. 3. Three of them; two of the oxen; the ten (of the) gold watches. 4. Two bottles of wine; a glass of water. 5. Three pounds (okes) of tea; three and a half yards of cloth. 6. The children of the village; the village children. 7. Both of them; my father and my grand father. 8. The English government; the English nation. The city of Paris. 9. The door of the garden; a garden door. 10. Two of those children; two of your children. 11. Four of my cousins. 12. The number of the books of my brother's son is great. 13. Am I not your son, and are you not my parents? — Yes, my son! thou art my son, I am your father and she is your mother. 14. Néjibé Hanîm is my sister and Miss Mary is her sister-in-law. 15. A city-door; the door of the city; the door of a city; a door of a city; a door of the city.

To be corrected.

‏١ او كتاب در بو چالیشقان چوجوغك ؛ ٢ بر صو قدحك ؛ بر قهوه‌نك

‏فنجان . ٣ چیچكلرم یكنم ؛ قپوى مكتبك . ٤ ایكیسى اونلرك ؛

‏٥ برى سزدن . ٦ اونك او بویوك در ؛ باغچه‌سى اوَك ؛ اوغل اونك

‏در خسته .

مكالمه Conversation.

والدَيْن كيمه ديرلر؟ — آنا بابايه والدَين ديرلر.

التى كيم در؟ — قوجه‌نك قارداشنك قاريسى در.

كوچك كيم در؟ — تازه كينك قوجه‌سيدر.

دايى زاده‌نك اسمى نه در؟ — نجيب افندى در.

آننه اوده مى؟ — اوده دكلدر، ابهم اوده‌در.

آغوب افندى قاين برادركز مى در؟ — اوت افندم! قاينم در.

ننه‌ك نره‌ده در؟ — همشيره‌مك آونده در.

ددك باغچه‌ده ميدر؟ — خير افندم! باغچه‌ده دكلدر.

احمد افندى سنك عميك ميدر؟ — خير افندم! داييمدر.

چه‌چه وَ آبلا كيمه ديرلر؟ — كوچوك چوجوقلر بيوك همشيره‌يه ديرلر.

درس ٧ Lesson 7.

The verb 'To Have'.

§ 118. The English verb 'To Have' is expressed in Turkish in two ways, according to the object of the verb.

If the object is indefinite the adjectives وار *var* 'present: existent' and يوق *yoq* 'absent: non-existent' are used to express that sense. These may be followed by the verbal particle of affirmative در *dir*, which in this case, as in many other cases may be omitted in conversation (§ 76).

If the object is definite the Substantive verb is employed (§ 127).

1. The verb To Have with an Indefinite Object.

§ 119. In such phrases as: I have a book, he has a dog, it is expressed in two ways.

I. By putting the subject in the Genitive, followed

by the object with the possessive affix and the verb

وار ' در وار ، وار *var, var dir*; يوق ' يوقدر *yoq, yoq dour*; as:

بنم بر كتابم واردر *bénim bir kitabim vardir* I have a book.

بابامك بر كتابى يوقدر *babamin bir kitabi yoqdour* My father has not a book.

Literally: of me there is a book, of my father there is no book.

§ 120. Sometimes the subject, when a pronoun, is omitted, especially when the subject is not accented or emphasized: then the affix of the object indicates the subject (§§ 70. 102); as:

بر كتابم وار در *bir kitabim var dir* I have a book.

The affix shows the person of the subject.

§ 121. When the subject is a noun it is always considered as in the third person, therefore the object must end with the pronominal affix of the third person,

ى or سى (*i* or *si*).

افندينك بر اوى واردر *Efféndiniñ bir évi vardir* The gentleman has a house.

چوجوغك بر الماسى وار *Chojoughouñ bir élmasî var* The boy has an apple.

The words افندى ' چوجوق being substantives, are of course in the third person.

§ 122. II. The verb To HAVE with an indefinite object is rendered in Turkish in another way also. In the first way the subject was in the Genitive case; in the second, the subject must be put in the Locative; as:

بنده بر كتاب وار در *béndé bir kitab var dir* I have a book.

پدريمده بر قلم وار در *pédérimdé bir qalém var dir* My father has a pen.

§ 123. Although it is not very correct grammatically, there is a custom among the common people not to append to the noun the possessive affixes of the first and second persons plural. Instead of saying correctly *Siziñ atîñiz, bizim évimiz,* they say *Siziñ at, bizim év* just as in English. *Bizim éviñ pénjérési* the window of our house, for *Bizim évimiziñ pénjérési. Bizim pédér* our father, for *Bizim pédérimiz,* or merely *pédér*; as:

بزم پدرمز اوده در ' پدرمز اوده در ' بزم پدر اوده در ' پدر اوده در

§ 124. The Plural Locative forms of the Personal Pronouns sometimes give the sense of 'house, home'. *Bizdé bir i-nék var* means both 'We have a cow' and 'There is a cow in our house'. *Lit.:* 'in us'.

§ 125. But the rendering for nouns is different: 'at my father's' or 'in my father's house', 'the people of my father's house', are expressed by adding كيل *gil;* as:

بابام كيل   *babam gil* The people of my father's house, my father's family.

باجاناغم كيلده   *bajanaghîm gildé* at my brother-in-law's house.

همشيره‌م كيله   *hémshirém gilé* to my sister's.

دايم كيل بزده در   *dayîm gil bizde dir* The family of my uncle is in our house.

§ 126. 'There is, there are' is rendered by the Locative with وار در ' يوق در *var dîr, yoq dour* (§ 76). But *onda var, béndé var,* denote possession; as: *Evdé bir at var* There is a horse in the house. But *Béndé bir at var* I have a horse. In the first sentence it expresses location and in the second possession.

§ 126a.   *Hal* حال Present.

بنم وار در ' بنده وار در   *bénim var dir, béndé var dir,*

سنك وار در ' سنده وار در   *séniñ var dir, séndé var dir,*

اونك وار در ' اونده وار در   *onouñ var dir, onda var dir,*

بزم وار در ' بزده وار در   *bizim var dir, bizdé var dir,*

سزك وار در ' سزده وار در   *siziñ var dir, sizdé var dir,*

اونلرك وار در ' اونلرده وار در   *onlariñ var dir, onlarda var dir.*

I have, thou hast, he has a — etc.

The Negative Form.

بنم يوقدر ' بنده يوقدر   *bénim yoqdour, béndé yoqdour.*

I have not a — etc.

§ 126b.   *Mazi* ماضى Past (Preterite).

بنم وار ايدى ' بنده وار ايدى   *bénim var îdî, béndé var îdî,*

سنك وار ايدى ' سنده وار ايدى   *séniñ var îdî, séndé var îdî,*

اونك وار ايدى ' اونده وار ايدى   *onouñ var îdî, onda var îdî,*

بزده وار ایدی ، بزم وار ایدی ، *bizim var îdi,*   *bizdé var îdi.*

سزده وار ایدی ، سزك وار ایدی ، *siziñ var îdi,*   *sizdé var îdi,*

اونلرده وار ایدی ، اونلرك وار ایدی ۰ *onlariñ var îdi, onlarda var îdi.*

I had, thou hadst, he had a — etc.

The Negative Form.

بنم یوغیدی or بنم یوق ایدی ، *bénim yoq' idi* or *-yo'ghoudou,*

بنده یوغیدی or بنده یوق ایدی ۰ *béndé yoq' idi* or *-yo'ghoudou.*

I had not a — etc.

The Interrogative Forms.

بنم یوقمیدر ؟ بنم وار میدر ؟ *bénim var' midir? bénim yoq' moudour?*

وار می ایدی ؟ or سنده وار میدی ؟ *séndé var' miyidi?* or *var' mi idi?*

Have I a —? Have I not a —? hadst thou not a —? etc.

2. The verb To Have with a Definite Object.

§ 127. When the object of the verb To Have is definite, it is rendered in Turkish by the substantive verb در *dir* (§ 118).

§ 128. The order of the construction is this: first comes the object, then the subject, and the verb in the third place.

§ 129. This is a general rule in the Ottoman-Turkish language. In every case when the object is indefinite, the subject comes first; and when the object is definite the object comes first; Ex.:

بنم بر کتابم وار در *bénim bir kitabîm' var dir* I have a book.

کتاب بنده در *kitab béndé' dir* I have the book.

In the first instance the object (a book) is indefinite, therefore the subject comes first; in the second the object (the book) is definite, therefore the object comes first and the subject follows it.

§ 130. *Remarks:* The English Conjunction but is expressed either by putting the Arabic words لکن ، امّا

فقط *ém'-ma* or *am'ma, lakin, faqat* or the Turkish ایسه ده *i-sé' dé,* all meaning 'but' (§ 239, 476); as:

پاره‌م وار اما آز در ؛ پاره‌م وار لكن آز در ؛ پاره‌م وار فقط آز در ؛
پاره‌م وار ايسه ده آز دز *param var am′ma az dîr; param var lakin
az dîr; param var faqat az dîr; param var i-sé dé az dîr* I have
but a little money.

§ 131. "Any" is expressed in Turkish in two ways:
one by p. هيچ *hich,* and the other without using that word,
but by simply using the object of the verb (§ 188); as:
سنده هيچ اكمك وار ميدر؟ سنده اكمك وار می ؟
Have you any bread? اونك هيچ پاره‌سی يوقدر. اونك پاره‌سی يوقدر
He has not any money

§ 132. "Not any, not at all" is expressed by هيچ *hich.*
هيچ پاره‌سی يوقدر ؛ هيچ ايو دكل چوق خسته در *hich parasî yoqdour; hich é-yi déyil choq hasta dir.* He has not any money; He
is not at all well: he is very sick.

§ 133. "How many?" is expressed by قاچ *qach?*
(§ 174). Ex.:

How many piastres have you?   قاچ غروشك وار در ؟

How many books has he?   قاچ كتابی وار در ؟

§ 134. "How much?" is expressed by نه‌قدر، نقدر
né qadar? (§ 179); as:

How much sugar have you?   نه‌قدر شكرك وار ؟

How much bread have we?   نه‌قدر اكمكمز وار ؟

§ 135. "Some" is expressed by بر آز *bir az* 'a little,
a small piece of anything', in reference to inanimate
objects (§ 182); as:

بر آز اكمك *bir az ékmék* some bread.

But in reference to animate objects بعض *ba′zi,* بر قاچ
bir qach is used (§ 181); as:

بعض آدملر *ba′zi adémlér* some people.

بر قاچ افنديلر *bir qach′ éfféndilér* some gentlemen.

بعض حيوانلر *ba′zi hayvanlar* some animals.

§ 136. "Both" is rendered by p. هم هم *hém — hém*
(§ 469); as:
بنده هم اكمك و هم طوز وار
I have both bread and salt.

خاله‌مك هم كاغدی وهم قلمی وار در
My aunt has both paper and pen.

Turkish Conv.-Grammar.   5

§ 137. "Either ... or ..." is rendered by p. يا يا *ya-ya-*; "Neither ... nor ..." is rendered by نه نه *né--né* (§ 472); as:

I have neither bread nor salt. بنده نه اكمك وار نه طوز

You have either pen or paper. سنده یا قلم وار یا كاغد

§ 137a. *Hal* حال Present.

بنده در *béndé dir,*   بزده در *bizdé dir,*

سنده در *séndé dir,*   سزده در *sizdé dir,*

اونده در *onda dir.*   اونلرده در *onlarda dir.*

I have **the** —, thou hast **the** —, he has **the** — etc.

Negative Form.

اونده دكلدر ، سنده دكلدر ، بنده دكلدر *béndé déyil dir, séndé déyil dir, onda déyil dir* etc. I have not the — etc.

§ 137b. *Mazi* ماضى Past (Preterite).

بنده ایدی *béndé idi,*   بزده ایدی *bizdé idi,*

سنده ایدی *séndé idi,*   سزده ایدی *sizdé idi,*

اونده ایدی *onda idi.*   اونلرده ایدی *onlarda idi.*

I had **the** —, thou hadst **the** —, he had **the** — etc.

Negative Form.

اونده دكل ایدی ، سنده دكل ایدی ، بنده دكل ایدی *béndé déyil idi, séndé déyil idi, onda déyil idi* etc. I had not **the** — etc.

Examples.

كتاب بنده در ؛ كتاب سنده در ؛ كتاب اونلرده در I have the book etc.

كتاب بنده میدر؟ كتاب سنده میدر؟ كتاب اونده میدر؟ Have I the book? etc.

كتاب سزده دكل میدی ؟ *kitab sizdé déyil miyidi?* Did you not have the book? etc.

لغتلر Words.

الما *élma* apple   قایصى *qa-yî-sî* apricot

آرمود *armoud* pear   p. شفتالى *shéf-ta-li* peach

اریك *é-rik* plum   اوزوم *û-zûm* grapes

كيراز *kiraz* cherries

قويون *qoyoun* sheep

چوبان *choban* shepherd

يومورطه *youmourta* egg

سيركه *sirké* vinegar

پينير *péy-nir* cheese

كستانه f. *késtané* chestnuts [Gr.]

ويشنه f. *vishné* (commonly *fishné*) the morella cherry (Slavonic)

پورتوقال f. *portouqal* oranges

ليمون f. *limon* lemon

پاتاتس f. *patatés* potato

طوماتس f. *tomatés* tomato

تره ياغی *tèré yaghî* butter.

[1]Exercise 13.   تعليم ١٣

‎I. ١ باغچه مزده چوق آغاجلر وار در: الما ، آرمود ، اريك ، قايصی
وَ شفتالی . الما آغاجنده كوزل قيرميزی المالر وار . آرمود آغاجنده پك آز
آرمود وار در ، لكن قايصی آغاجنك هيچ ميوه‌سی يوقدر . ٢ اونلرده
نه وار؟ — اونلرده اوچ اوقه اوزوم ، درت اوقه آرمود وَ براز ويشنه
وار در . ٣ كستانه آغاجنده ايری كستانه‌لر وار . كستانه آغاجنك ايری
كستانه‌لری وار در[1] . ٤ عالينك اونبش غروشی وار ايدی: سزك قاچ
غروشكز وار ايدی ؟ ٥ باغده اوزوم وار می ايدی ؟ — خير افندم !
اوزوم يوغيدی ؛ لكن شفتالی ، پورتوقال وَ ليمون وار ايدی . ٦ كوچوك
قيزده بر چيچك وار در . كو چوك قيزك النده بر چيچك وار ايدی .

‎II. ٧ سنك پاره‌ك وار می ؟ — اوت ! بنده اون غروش اون
پاره وار ، لكن خدمتكاريكزك هيچ پاره‌سی يوقدر . ٨ افندينك بر
آلتون قلمی وار ؛ سزك ده وار می ؟ — بنده يوغيسه‌ده ، باجاناغمده
كوزل بر آلتون قلم وار در . ٩ چوجوغك كتابی وار ميدر ؟ — اوت !
كتب چوجوقده در . ١٠ عموجه‌كده پاره وار ميدر ؟ پاره‌ك وار می ؟
پاره وار می ؟ — پاره بنده دكلدر ، عموجه‌مده ده دكلدر . ١١ كاغد

---

[1] Student must practice using both the Locative and Genitive forms (§§ 119, 122).

قلم سنده ميدر ؟ — خير ! بنده نه كاغد وار نه قلم وار . لكن بزم برادرده

هم كاغد وار هم قلم وار در . ١٢ اكك سزده ميدر ؟ ١٣ قاره قويونلر

نجيب چوباننده در . ١٤ يومورطهلر و سيركه خلايقده در . ١٥ پينير

سزده دكامىدى ؟ — خير افندم ! پينير بزده دكل ايدى ؛ تره ياغى

بزده ايدى .

ترجمه ١٤ [1]Translation 14.

I. 1. I have an apple; thou hast some cherries; he has the oranges. 2. My brother has the dog; your aunt has a cat; they have three horses. 3. How much money have you? — I have seventeen piasters. 4. Have you any sugar? — No, Sir, I have not any. 5. I had no pen. I had the pen. I had not the pen. 6. Give me some bread and grapes. — Have you any bread and grapes? 7. How many children has your grandson? — He has two children; one a boy, the other a girl.

II. 8. Have I a dog? — Yes, Sir, you have a dog, and my brother has a horse. 9. Has he the pen? — No, Sir, he has no pen. 10. Where is your book? — It is at my uncle's. 11. Who has my money? — I have your money. 12. Is there any servant in the kitchen? Is the servant in the kitchen? 13. The servant is in the kitchen. There is a servant in the kitchen. 14. Who has the pen and the paper? — Your father had the pen and I have the paper. 15. Are there any eggs? Yes, Sir, there are plenty of them.

مكالمه Conversation.

Mat-bakhda né var?	Bir az tomatés vé patatés var.
Siziñ birader nasîl dîr?	Hich é-yi déyil, choq hasta dîr.
Onoun atî kimdé dir?	Babam gildé dir.
Gûzél qoush qardashiñda mi?	Khayr, chojoughouñ qafésindé dir.
Qafésdé né var?	Bir yéshil, bir siyah vé bir béyaz qoush var.
Ekmék séndé mi dir?	Khayr, ékmék béndé déyil dir.

---

[1] See the Note page 67.

درس ۸ Lesson 8.

کنایات The Pronouns. (Continued.)

3. Adjectival Pronoun. ضمیر وصفی

§ 138. The Adjectival Pronominal affix is the word
کی -*ki*, signifying 'the — which, that which',
according as it is a noun or an adjective. It is attached
to nouns and pronouns in two ways; by putting them
either in the Genitive or in the Locative case.

§ 139. In the first instance it is used always like
a substantive, and signifies 'that which belongs to'.
In the second case, it is sometimes used substantively
and signifying 'that which exists': when it is attached to a substantive, it is an adjective, signifying
'the — which exists'. Ex.:

بابا *baba'* father; بابانك *babaniñ* of the father; بابانکی
babaniñ-ki that or the one which belongs to the father.

بابادﻩ *babada* in the father; بابادﻩکی *babadaki* that or the
one which exists in (the possession of) the father.

بندﻩکی *béndéki* that which I have, or is in my possession.

§ 140. The separate possessive pronouns corresponding to those of the English language are formed
in the first way; as:

بنمکی *bénimki,* سننکی *séniñki,* اونکی *onouñki* mine, thine, his.

بزمکی *bizimki,* سزنکی *siziñki,* اونلرکی *onlarinki* { ours, yours, theirs.

Both of these forms, when used as substantives,
have plurals and declensions as usual; but the last ی
is eliminated, retaining the sound *i* (§ 99).

Note. کی -*ki* never varies in pronunciation for the sake
of euphony (§ 54).

Declension of -*ki* with the Genitive preceding.

N.	بنمكی	*bénimki*		بنمكيلر	*bénimkilér*		
G.	بنمكنك	*bénimkiniñ* of		بنمكيلرك	*bénimkilérin* of		
D.	بنمكنه	*bénimkiné* to	mine	بنمكيلره	*bénimkiléré* to	those of mine.	
A.	بنمكنی	*bénimkini*		بنمكيلری	*bénimkiléri*		
L.	بنمكنده	*bénimkindé* in		بنمكيلرده	*bénimkilérdé* in		
A.	بنمكندن	*bénimkindén* from		بنمكيلردن	*bénimkilérdén* from		

Declension of -*ki* with the Locative preceding.

N.	بنده كی	*béndéki'*		بنده كيلر	*béndékilér'*		
G.	بنده كنك	*béndékiniñ'* of	mine, the thing I possess.	بنده كيلرك	*béndékilériñ'* of	those of mine, those things which I possess.	
D.	بنده كنه	*béndékiné'* to		بنده كيلره	*béndékiléré'* to		
A.	بنده كنی	*béndékini'*		بنده كيلری	*béndékiléri'*		
L.	بنده كنده	*béndékindé'* in		بنده كيلرده	*béndékilérdé'* in		
A.	بنده كندن	*béndékindén* from		بنده كيلردن	*béndékilérdén* from		

Examples.

خواجهنك *hojañ'* of the teacher. خواجهنككی *hojaninki* that of the teacher. خواجهنككيلر *hojaniñkilér* those of the teacher. خواجهلرمككی *hojalarîmíñki* those of my teachers.

سنده بنم قلم می وار يوخسه خواجهلرمككی می وار؟ *séndé bénim' qalémim mi var, yokh'sa hojalarîmíñki mi var?* have you my pen or that of my teachers?

بنده نه سنك قلملك وار نه ده خواجه كزككيلر *béndé né séniñ' qalémiñ var, né dé hojanîzíñkilér* I have neither your pen, nor those of your teacher.

سنده كی پاره *séndéki para* the money you have.

قارداشم كيلده كی قوش *qardashim gildéki qoush* the bird which is at my brother's.

Bah'jédéki aghajlar the trees which are in the garden. *E'vdékiler* those at the house. *Shimdiki* the present. *Soñraki* the latter. *Ev'vélki* the former.

4. Demonstrative Pronouns. اسم اشارت

§ 141. The Demonstrative Pronouns are:

بو *bou* used for things which are near the speaker, This.

شو ، شول *shou, shol* used for things which are near the person spoken to, This.

او ، اول *o, ol*   »   »   »   »   are some distance off, That (yonder).

اشبو *ish'bou* This present (person or thing).

§ 142. The Demonstratives when they modify a noun, are regarded as adjectives. شول ، اول ، اشبو are used only as adjectives, and they never undergo any change.

Declension of Demonstrative Pronouns.

Singular مفرد *Mûfréd'*

N.	بو	*bou* this	شو	*shou* this
G.	بونك	*bounouñ* of this	شونك	*shounouñ* of this
D.	بوكا	*bouña* to this	شوكا	*shouña* to this
A.	بونى	*bounou* this	شونى	*shounou* this
L.	بونده	*bounda* in this	شونده	*shounda* in this
A.	بوندن	*boundan* from this.	شوندن	*shoundan* from this.

Plural

بوندن بولرده بولرى بولاره بولرڭ بولر

شوندن شولرده شولرى شولاره شولرڭ شولر

bounlar, -iñ, -a, . . .   shounlar, -iñ, -a, . . .

Note. The declension of او *o* that, is the same as that of the third person of the Personal Pronoun, page 47.

§ 143. Other Demonstratives:

بويله ، بويلهسى *beôy'lé, beôylési'* such, such as this.

شويله ، شويلهسى *sheôy'lé, sheôylési'* »   »   as this.

اويله ، اويلهسى *eôy'lé, eôylési'* »   »   as that.

§ 144. Adverbial Demonstratives:

بورا *boura'* here, this place (contracted from بوآرا).

شورا *shoura'* here, this or that place (»   »   شوآرا).

اورا *ora'* there, that place (»   »   اوآرا).

نره *né'ré* where? what place (»   »   نهآرا).

Examples.

بورادن، شورادن، اورادن from here, from there.

بوراده، شوراده، اوراده here, in this spot; there.

بویله بر کونده *beôylé bir gûndé* on such a day.

بویلهسی بر آدمدن *beôylési bir adémdén* from such a man.

اویلهسی کوتو بر چوجوق *eôylési keôtú bir chojouq* such a bad boy.

شول افندیدن *shol éfféndidén* from that gentleman.

اول ذاتك آونده *ol zatíñ érindé* in the house of that gentleman.

5. Reflexive Pronouns. ضمیر تأکیدی

§ 145. The English words myself, himself, yourself etc. are termed Reflexive Pronouns, when they represent the same person as the subject or the nominative. They are expressed in Turkish by the pronoun کندی *kéndi*:

I myself	بن کندم *bén´ kéndim.*
Myself	کندم *kéndim´.*
Thou thyself	سن کندك *sén´ kéndiñ.*
Thyself	کندك *kéndiñ´.*
He himself	او کندیسی *o´ kéndisi.*
Himself	کندیسی *kéndisi´.*
We ourselves	بز کندیمز *biz´ kéndimiz.*
Ourselves	کندیمز *kéndimiz´.*
You yourselves	سز کندیکز *siz´ kéndiñiz.*
Yourselves	کندیكز *kéndiñiz´.*
They themselves	اونلر کندیلری *onlar kéndiléri.*
Themselves	کندیلری *kéndiléri´.*

Also: کندی کندم، کندی کندك، کندی کندیسی I myself...

کندی کندیمز، کندی کندیکز، کندی کندیلری We ourselves...

§ 146. The English word "**own**" is also expressed by کندی; as:

My own book   بنم كندى كتابم   *bénim kéndi kitabîm.*

With his own hand   كندى الى ايله   *kéndi éli ilé.*

§ 147. ***Kéndi*** is usually employed after the subject to emphasize it, or to limit or specialize the meaning; as:

Bédros kéndi' bashînî yîyqayor   بدروس كندى باشنى ييقايور
Peter is washing **his own** head.

Bédros onouñ' bashînî yîyqayor   بدروس اونك باشنى ييقايور
Peter is washing **his** head, denotes another person's head.

Efféndi kéndi' odasînda dîr The master is in **his own** room.

Efféndi onouñ' odasînda dîr The master is in **his** room (some one else's).

لغتلر Words.

Ûst bash اوست باش Apparel.

a. اثواب	*ésrab* clothes	f. روبا	*rouba* clothes [It.]
f. پانتالون	*pantalon* pants	f. فستان	*fistan* gown [Gr.]
كوملك	*gêomlék* shirt	f. میسو	*miso* petticoat [Gr.]
ايچ دونى	*ich' donou* drawsers	f. شابقه	*shapqa* hat [Slav.]
سترى	*sétri* frock-coat	f. باستون	*baston* stick, cane [It.]
يلك	*yélék* waistcoat	كیسه	*késé* purse
آستار	*astar* lining	دوكمه	*dûymé* button
الديون	*éldivén* gloves	چوقه	*chouqa* broad cloth
a. منديل	*méndil* handkerchief	باصمه	*basma'* print, calico
بيچاق	*bichaq* knife	اكمكجى	*ékmékji* baker.

Prop. Nouns يوسف *yousouf* Joseph.   احمد *Ahméd.*

تعليم ١٥ Exercise 15.

١ اثوابكز نره ده در ؛ — اثواب لريز سزك اوده در ؛ فقط پدرمك كيلر عوجهم كيلده ايدى · ٢ اليكزده كيلر نه درلر ؛ — بر باصمه یلك ' چوقه دن بر پانتالون ' بر سترى در · ٣ سنده كى بيچاق ' شابقه وَ باستون كيمكدر ؛ — بنده كى شابقه كوچوك يكنمك ' باستون بنم

وَ بيچاق آشجينك در . ٤ چوبان احمد فقير بر آدمدر؛ «كوملكنك
آستارى يوقدر»[1] . ٥ كيملك بيچاغى سنده در؟ — نه يوسفك بيچاغى
بنده در؛ نه ده اككجينككيلر بنده در . ٦ بو شابقه وَ باستون
كيمكدرلر؟ — بونلربنم كنديمك درلر؛ افندينككيلر بوراده دكلدر .
٧ قيز قارداشمك فيستانى قيرميزى يوندن در وَ منديلى ايپكدن در .
٨ كندى روبهسى پك اسكى ايدى . ٩ بونك اوى شونككندن
تازه در . ١٠ شول چوجوغك اوستى باشى پك تميز در . ١١ اشبو كتابدهكى
تصويرلر پك بويوكدرلر . فقط داييلريككيلر كوچوكدر . ١٢ شوراده
برميسو وَ اوراده بر شابقه وار .

ترجمه ١٦   Translation 16.

1. Of that; those of that; those of those [men].
2. That which is in this; that which is there; that
which is here. 3. Have you our coats or those of our
neighbours? — I have not your coats; I have those of
my father. 4. That of my sister; those of my mother;
from those of my uncle. 5. The oxen which are here;
the cows which are there. 6. These houses are large;
that house is little; from that house. 7. Where are my
overshoes, and where are those of my aunt? 8. Yours
are here and those of your aunt are there. 9. To yourself;
from himself; in ourselves. 10. My mother is in her
garden; my sister is in her house; my sister is in his
house. 11. My own cane; his own book; in his own room.

مكالمه   Conversation.

بنم قلمم نرده ده در؟	اوراده در .
سنك كندى كتابك بوراده ميدر؟	خير افندم! بوراده دكدر .
احمد بك يوسف افندينك برادرى ميدر؟	خير افندم! احمدبك بنم كندى قارداشمدر .
سزك كندى آتكز باغچهده ميدر؟	اوت افندم! اوراده در .

---

[1] All sentences enclosed by quotation marks are either
idiomatic sayings or proverbs.

خواجه‌نك كندی آتی در .   اوده‌كی آت كیمك در ؟

اونك كندی اوغلیدر .   شوراده‌كی چوجوق كیمك اوغلیدر ؟

كندی اوطه سنده در .   ماری خانم نره‌ده در ؟

اونك اوطه سنده در .   والده خانم نره‌ده در ؟

درس ۹   Lesson 9.

صفت   The Adjective.

§ 148. The Turkish adjective whether used as
a predicate or as an attribute, remains unchanged, as
in English (§ 79):

او كوچوك در *év kûchûk dûr* the house is little.

بویوك بر آدم *beôyûk bir adém* a great man.

المالر طاتلی در *élmalar tatlî dir* the apples are sweet.

بویوك آدملر *beôyûk adémlér* the great men.

The Derivative Adjective.

§ 149. The derivative adjective which is called
in Turkish اسم منسوب [1], is made by the addition of the
following particles to the nouns.

§ 150. I. لو ‘ لی *-li, -lî, -lou* indicates possession
of the thing designated by the noun; as:

صو *sou* water,   صولو *soulou* watery, fluid.

یر *yér* place,   یرلی *yérli* fixed in a place; native.

او *év* house,   اولی *évli* that has a house; married.

آت *at* horse,   آتلی ‘ آتلو *atlî, atlou* horseman.

a. عزت *iz'zét* honour.   عزتلو *iz'zétlou* honorable.

§ 151. With the proper names of men or places,
the same affix indicates a native or an inhabitant of
those places or connexion of those persons; as:

آمریقا *Amériqa*,   آمریقالی *Amériqalî* American.

---

[1] *Is'mi Ménsoub* Noun (or adjective) of relationship.

عثمان *Osman* عثمانلى،عثمانلو *Osmanli* Ottoman.

تركيا *Tûrkiya* تركيالى *Tûrkiyali* an inhab. of Turkey, Turk.

مرذيفون *Mérzifoun* مرذيفونلى *Mérzifounlou* a native of Merzifoun.

§ 152. The names of some European nations are formed differently, as they were introduced by the Venetians or Genoese; as:

انكليز *ingiliz* Englishman.   جنويز *jiniviz* Genoese; Roman.

فرانسز *fransiz* Frenchman.   اسپانيول *ispanyol* Spaniard.

نمچه *némtsé, némché* Austrian.   تاليان *talyan* Italian.

موسقوف *mosgof'* Russian; Muscovite. فيلهمنك *filéméng'* Dutch.

§ 153. II. جه *-jé* added to the names of nations forms the names of their languages; as:

آلمان *alman* a German: آلمانجه *almanja* the German language.

تورك،ترك *tûrk* Turk: تركجه *tûrkjé* the Turkish language.

ارمنى *érméni* Armenian: ارمنيجه *érménijé* the Armenian language.

§ 154. جه *-jé* if added to nouns (except the names of nations), expresses relation; as:

ملتجه *mil'létjé* national.   اوجه *évjé* household.

كيسهجه *kilisejé* ecclesiastical.   لسانجه *lisanja* linguistic.

§ 155. III. جه *-jé* added to the adjectives and nouns forms the Diminutive, expressing rather, somewhat, slightly, -ish; as:

حيوانجه *hayvanja* brutal. چوجوقجه *chojouqja* childish.

بياضجه *béyazja* whitish.   قولايجه *qolayja* rather easy.

§ 156. جق؛جك *-jîq, -jik; -jaq, -jék, -jûk.* This is a modification of the above form, dictated by the principal of euphony (§ 52). If the word ends in ق or ك these letters are omitted; as:

قيصهجق *qisajîq* rather short. كوزلجك *gûzéljik* beautiful little thing.

آزاجق *azajîq* just a little.   بريجك *birijik* only (begotten).

يومرو *youmrou* globular; tumour: يومروجق *youmroujaq* the plague.

بو يوك *béôyûk:*   بو يوجك *béôyûjék* rather large.

كوچوك *kûchûk:*   كوچوجك *kûchûjék, -jûk* smallish, tiny.

§ 157. IV. جى *-ji, -jî, -jou* added to a noun indicates the individual who exercises a trade or calling connected with the first noun; as:

اكمكجى *ékmékji* baker   توفنكجى *tûfénk'ji* gun maker.

صوجى *soujou* water seller   بكمزجى *békmézji* treacle seller.

§ 158. جى *-ji* is also used for making adjectives or nouns designating persons who practise something expressed by the noun to which it is appended; as:

دعاجى *douvaji* who prays.   يالانجى *yalanji, -chî* liar.

شقاجى ، لطيفهجى *shaqaji, latiféji* joker, storyteller.

§ 159. V. لك ، لق *-lîq, -lik* added to a noun, denotes a condition, nature or quality of the thing denoted by the original noun; as:

كيجهلك *géjélik* (night) gown.   كونلك *gûnlûk* daily (pay).

اونلق *onlouq* a coin of ten paras.   يللق *yîl'lîq* yearly (pay).

يوزلك *yûzlûk* a coin of 100 paras. پانتالونلق *pantalonlouq* (stuff for) pan-talons.

بكلك *béylik* belonging to the state, government.

Yirmi adamlîq yémék. Food sufficient for 20 persons.

§ 160. VI. سز *-sîz, -siz, -souz,* is a privative adjectival suffix, meaning without, void of, lacking, free from, -less; as:

پاره‌سز *parasîz* moneyless.   اتسز *étsiz* fleshless, thin.

صوسز *sousouz* waterless, thirsty.   يوزسز *yûz'sûz* who has no face; shameless.

يولسز *yolsouz* roadless; impolite.   صاغسز *saghsîz* unhealthy, weakly.

Derivative Nouns.

§ 161. Derivative nouns are made by the addition of the following particles to the nouns; as:

§ 162. I. لك ، لق *-lîq, -lik.* Joined to nouns it expresses a place peculiar to the thing named, or a place where it abounds; as:

پابوجلوق *paboujlouq* the place where the slippers or boots are left.

آغاجلق *aghajliq, aghachliq* a place where the trees abound.

كومورلك *kêomûrlûk* a place where coal is deposited.

طاشلق *tashliq* a place where stone abounds, stony; stone-pit.

§ 163. This *-lik, -liq* added to an adjective, forms its abstract noun; as:

قيزيللق *qizil'liq* redness; rouge.　ايبلك، *éyilik* kindness.

چوجوقلق *chojouqlouq* childishness, childhood.　فقيرلك *faqirlik* poverty.

§ 164. Names of trades or professions are also formed by adding *lik, liq* to the words denoting the persons who exercise them. Ex.:

اكمكجيلك *ékmékjilik* the occupation of a baker.

آشجيلق *ashjiliq* the occupation of a cook, cooking.

§ 165. II. تاش، داش *-dash, -tash* a fellow, a companion.

آدداش *ad'dash, adash* namesake.　ياشداش *yashdash* of the same age.

قارداش، قرنداش *qarîndash, qardash* (womb-fellow) a brother.　قارینداش

بكتاش *bég'tash, bégdash* the fellow of a prince.

آرقه‌داش *arqadash* companion, comrade.

صنفداش، درسداش *dérsdash, sinifdash* a class-mate.

§ 166. III. جق، جك؛ جغز، جك، جق *-jîq, -jik; -jîghaz, -jiyéz*. Diminutive nouns are made by the addition of these particles to the nouns.

اوجك، اوجغز، اوجكز *évjik, évjiyéz, évjîghaz* a little house.

كتابجق *kitabjîq* booklet.　اوطه‌جق *odajîq* a little room.

§ 167. Some Diminutives are terms of endearment; as:

باباجق، باباجغز *babajîq, babajîghaz* papa.

آناجق، آناجغز، آناجكز *anajîq, anajîghaz, an'néjiyéz* mama.

قيزجغز *qizjîghaz* poor little girl.

لغتلر Words.

Mil'létlér ملتلر Nations	*Shéhirlér* شهرلر Cities
a. عرب a'rab Arab.	استانبول istambol Constantinople.
كرد kûrd Kurd.	وندیك vénédik Venice.
چرکس chérkés Circassian.	اسكندریه iskéndériyé Alexandria.
آرناود arnavoud Albanian.	مونجسون mounjousoun Pontusa.
a. عجم ajém Persian.	ازمیر izmir Smyrna.
روم roum Greek.	حلب haléb Aleppo.
بولغار، بلغار boul'ghar Bulgarian.	قدس qoudous Jerusalem.
چین chin China.	كیرید girid Crete.
ماجار، مجار majar Hungarian.	ویانه viyana Vienna.

§ 168. *Note.* Surnames are formed in Turkish by adding اوغلی *oghlou* to the name of the father, family and often to the name of the trade or occupation: as: حسن اوغلی عالی *Hasan oghlou Ali*, Ali the son of Hassan, قایقجی اوغلی احمد *Qayîqji oghlou Ahméd.* But for the dignitaries p. زاده *zadé* is used; as: كمال پاشا زاده *Kémal Pasha zadé*, son of Kemal Pasha. (§ 668, *Note*).

چلبی *chélébi* a non-Moslem gentleman.	a. اجنبی *éjnébi* a foreigner.
f. موسیو *mûsû* Gentleman (Monsieur) [Fr.].	a. تجّار *tuj'jar* merchant.
a. اصناف *ésnaf* artisan, trademan.	a. عقل *a-qîl* sense, wisdom.
a. صنعت *san'at* vulg. *zénahat* art, craft.	a. غریب *gharib* stranger, poor.
f. چزار *chézar* Caesar.	a. شیطان *shéytan* Satan.
صاتار *satar* he sells.	یاپار *yapar* he makes.
a. دكان *dûk'kian* shop.	a. بقّال *baq'qal* grocer.

تعلیم ١٧ Exercise 17.

١. لوندره‌لی ، بوستونلی ، نیویورقلی ، پاریسلی . 2. A Constantinopolitan, a native of Amassia, of Smyrna, of Aleppo,

of Alexandria, of Japan, of China, of Montenegro, of
Pontusa, of Jerusalem; a Viennese, a Cretan, a Hungarian,
a Roman. 3. The Kurdish, German, Circassian, Italian,
Arabian, Albanian, Persian, Greek, Bulgarian, Armenian
languages; Chinese, Turkish. 4. رومجه ' دینجه ' ملکتجه'

صنفجه ' آدمجه ' مکتبیجه .5. Pertaining to the country, trade,
craft, artisan, wisdom; devilish. 6. Slightly sweet;
quite well; coldish; rather warm; rather high; fleshy.
7. A stationer; a mender of old things; mule-driver,
donkey-driver, horse-rider. 8. One who sells oil; who
keeps a vineyard, a garden; one who sells bread, coffee,
sugar, tomatoes, potatoes, milk, tobacco. 9. Stuff
for a cloak, shirt, girdle, shoe, handkerchief. 10. Ten
paras' worth; 1000 piastres' worth; 500 piastres' worth;
a piastres' worth; one para's worth; changes [small
pieces of money] (smallness). 11. Without house, horse,
books, donkey, coffee, tea; coffee without milk, coffee
with milk. 12. Rather white, black, high, much, pretty,
well. 13. Humanity; height; blackness; the profession of
a teacher, cooking; boatmanship. 14. Fellow-traveller;
co-religionist; sharer of the same room. 15. Beautiful
little hands; a little pen; my dear grandmother.

تعلیم ۱۸ Exercise 18.

۱ او آدم کیمدر ؟ — آمریقالی برچلبی در . اسمی نه در ؟ —
اسمی مستر هنری ریکز در . ۲ شو اوزون بویلو اجنبی کیم در ؟
فرانسز ملتندن بر موسیو در . ۳ جزار کیم ایدی ؟ — اسکی جنیویزلرك
بیوك بر ایمپراطوری ایدی . ٤ روما شهری نرده در ؟ — ایتالیاده
در ؛ تالیانلرك مملکتنده در . ٥ شکرجی اوغلی احمد اغا غریب
برآدمدر . کندی صنعتی شکرجیلکدر ؛ باباسی و باباسنك باباسی ده
شکرجی ایدی . شکرجی اصنافندن ایدی . ٦ بو یازیجینك[clerk]آیلغی
ایکی یوز غروش در . ۷ کتابجی کتاب صاتار ؛ بکمزجی بکمز صاتار .
۸ بن بوشهرك یرلیسی دکلم ؛ غریب برآدم ایم . ۹ سنك آدك ده عالی

بنم آدم ده عالى ؛ ايكيمز آدداش ايز ٠ ١٠ اوجكزم پك كوچوك ايسه ده باشنده فتيرالك وار ٠ ١١ سنك قارداشك بكا صنفداش و ياشداش در ٠ ١٢ پاره‌سز آدم فقيردر؛ پاره‌لى آدم زنكين در ٠ ١٣ اوراسى آغاجلق بر ير ايسه ده ؛ صوسز در : صو يوقدر ٠ ١٤ آرقه‌داشكزك صنعتى نه‌در ؟ ١٥ آرقه‌داشم طاشجى در ؛ باباسى اككجى ايدى ٠

ترجمه ١٩ Translation 19.

1. Do you know French? — No, Sir, I know a little English. 2. I am a Constantinopolitan; I know Turkish well. 3. What does that shopkeeper sell? — He sells to the villagers and citizens grapes, sugar, coffee; there are many such shops and shopkeepers in the villages and cities. 4. O grocer! give me 20 paras' worth of bread, 10 paras' worth of cheese, 15 paras' worth of grapes and 2 piastres' worth of sugar. 5. Give me five piastres' worth of paper; this paper is rather yellow. 6. Where is the salt-cellar? — It is here (bourada). 7. There is no coal in the coal-seller's shop, the trade of coaling is not a clean one. 8. "Art thou moneyless? thou art friendless". 9. You are a very wise man; you have sense, but your servant is a fool (without sense). 10. Who is this cheesemonger and who is that iron-monger? — They are my friends.

مكالمه Conversation.

بالجى زاده يوسف افندى در ٠	بو آدم كيم در ؟
بن نئچه ملتندن ايم ٠	سن نره‌لى سين ؟
آيلغم اوچ فرانسز ليره‌سيدر ٠	آيلغك قاچ غروش در ؟
بر عثمانلو ليره‌سى پاره‌م وار ٠	چوق پاره‌ك وار مى ؟
فرانسزلرك برامپراطورى ايدى ٠	ناپوليون كيم ايدى ؟

درس ۱۰ Lesson 10.

كنايات The Pronouns. (Continued.)

6. Interrogative Pronouns. ضمير استفهامى

§ 169. The Interrogative Pronouns are the following. [The Interrogative sign مى -*mi* is never used with them.]

§ 170. كيم *kim?* who? whoever?

This is applied to persons, and is declined alone and with possessive affixes.

سن كيم سين ؟ *sén kim sin?* who art thou?

كيم در او ؟ كيم او ؟ او كيم او ؟ *kim dir o? kim o? o kim o?* who is it?

§ 171. Sometimes when there is no question, **kim** expresses the meaning of 'some'.

كيمى كلدى كيمى كيتدى *kimi géldi kimi gitdi,* some came others went,

كيمم وار ؟ كيمك وار ؟ كيمى وار ؟ *kimim' var? kimiñ' var? kimi' var?* whom have I? whom hast thou? whom has he?

كيمسهسى يوق *kimsési yoq* he has nobody.

كيمكى ؟ *kimiñki'?* whose?

§ 172. نه *né?* How? (with adjectives); what? (with nouns).

It is applied to inanimate object and is declined alone and with possessives.

نه در او ؟ نه او ؟ *né' o? né' dir o?* What is it?

نه ايسترسكز ؟ *né istérsiñiz?* What do you want?

نهلرى = نكز ، نه كز ، نمز = نهمز ، نسى = نهسى ، نك = نهك ، نم = نهم
ném'? néñ'? nési'? némiz'? néñiz'? néléri?

Ném' var? néñ' var? nési' var? What have I? What hast thou? What has he?

Némiz' dir? néñiz' dir? What thing, part or belonging to us, to you, is it?

نده = نهده ؟ *nédé'?* at or in what?

نهدیمك ؟ *né'démék?* What does it mean?

نهلر = نلر *nélér'!* What things! What wonderful things!

نهایچون = نیچون ؟ *né'ichin? ni'choun? ni'chin?* For what? Why?

§ 173. ؟ هانکی ؟ قنغی[1] *han'gi? han'ghi?* Which?

It is applied to persons and to inanimate objects without distinctions. It may be used either alone or with possessives, and is declined:

هانکیسی ؟ *han'gisi?* Which?

هانکیمز ؟ *han'gimîz?* Which of us?

هانکیکز ؟ *han'giñîz?* Which of you?

هانکیلری ؟ *han'gilari?* Which of them?

هانکیسدن ؟ هانکیسك ؟ هانکیسی ؟ Which? of —? from —?

هانکی کتاب ؟ *han'gi kitab?* Which book? ؟ هانکی آدم *han'gi* Which man?

§ 174. ؟ قاچ *qach?* How many?

It is applied to pronouns and to inanimate objects, and may be used either alone or with possessives, and it is declined:

قاچیمز ؟ قاچیکز ؟ قاچی ؟ قاچ *qa'chimîz? qa'chiñîz? qa'chi'?* How many of us, of you, of them?

قاچ کونده ؟ *qach' gûndé?* In how many days?

آیك قاچنده ؟ *ayiñ qachinda'?* On what (day) of the mouth?

§ 175. ؟ نصل *na'sîl?* How? What sort of a thing? What kind?

نصل سکز ؟ *na'sîl siñiz?* How are you?

نصل بر آدم در ؟ *na'sîl bir adém dir?* What sort of a person is he?

هر نصل ایسه *hér na'sîl isé* In whatever way it may be.

§ 176. ؟ نیجه *nijé?* What kind? How?

بو آدم نیجه آدمدر ؟ *bou adém nijé adémdir?* What kind of a man is this (man)?

بو آغاج نیجه آغاجدر ؟ What sort of a tree is this (tree)?

§ 177. It is also used indefinitely: it then means how much? how many?

---

[1] *Qanghi* is the old form, now it is obsolete.

نيچه دفعهلر *ni'che* or *ni'jé déf'alar!* How many times!

نيچهيهدك *nijéyé'dék? nichéyé'dék!* Till how many times!

نيچه آدملر، نيچهلر *ni'jélér? ni'chélér? ni'ché adémlér?* How many
peoples?

7. Indefinite Pronouns. ضمير مبهم

The Indefinite Pronouns are:

§ 178. كيمسه، كيمسنه *kimsé, kimésné* anybody.

These are applied to persons only, and are declined
alone and with possessives.

اوراده بر كيمسه وارمى *orada bir kimsé var'mî?* Is there anybody
there?

كيمسه يوق، كيمسنه يوق *kim'sé yoq, ki'mésné yoq.* There is nobody.

كيمسهسز *kimsésiz'* without anybody, without patron;
friendless.

§ 179. قدر *qadar.*

Expresses quantity or number (§§ 199, 229).

نه قدر اكمك؟ *né' qadar ekmék?* How much bread?

نه قدر كون؟ نه قدر؟ *né' qadar? né' qadar gûn?* How many days?

بو قدر، شو قدر، او قدر، اول قدر So much.

يتيشهجك قدر، يتهجك قدر، يتر قدر *yétér' qadar, yétéjék' qadar, yé-
tishéjék' qadar* So much as will suffice, enough.

آيى قدر، اشك قدر *éshék' qadar, ayî' qadar* As (big) as an ass as a bear.

پارمق قدر *parmaq' qadar* As (small as a little) finger.

§ 180. p. هر *hér* each, every, -soever.

Hér is always an adjective and is used with all
other indefinite pronouns.

هر كس، هر كيمسه، هر آدم *hér' kés, hér' kimsé, hér' adém* everybody.

هر نه *hér né'* whatsoever.

هر هانكى *hér ha'ngî* whichever.

هر بر *hér' bir* each, every.

هر بريمز *hér' birimiz* every one of us.

هر يرده *hér' yérdé* every where.

هر كيم *hér' kim* whoever, whosoever.

هر كيميكز *hér ki′miñiz* whoever of you.

هر برى *hér′ biri* every one of them.

هر ايكيسى *hér′ ikisi* both, each, either.

§ 181.   a. بعض ، بر آز ' *bir az, ba′zî* some (§ 135). *Ba′zî* means a certain number of persons or things.

بعض آدملر ، بعض كيمسهلر ' *ba′zî adémlér*, *ba′zi kimsélér* Some people.

بعض دفع ، بعض كره ' *ba′zî défa, bazî kér′ré* sometimes.

بعضارى ، بعضيكز ، بعضيمز ' *ba′zimîz, ba′ziñîz, ba′zîlarî* some of us, of you, of them.

بعضيسى *ba′zîsî* some people, some of them.

§ 182.   *Bir az* expresses a small quantity, a few (§ 135).

بر آز صو ، بر آز اكمك ' *bir′ az ékmék, bir′ az sou* a little bread, water.

بر آز پاره *some money*; بر آزى *bir′ azî* some of it.

§ 183.   بر قاچ *bir qach* a few, several (§ 135).

بر قاچ غروش *bir qach′ ghouroush* a few piastres.

بر قاچ آدم *bir qach′ adém* a few persons.

بر قاچ كون اول *bir qach′ gûn év′vél* several days ago.

§ 184.   ديكر p. ' آخر ، بشقه a. ' or باشقه *bashqa′*, *a-khér′, digér′* other, another; as:

ديكر بر آدم ' آخر بر آدم ' بشقه بر آدم *another man.*

بشقهجه *bashqa′ bashqa′* separately. بشقهجه *somewhat apart.*

بشقهلرى ، آخرلرى ، ديكرلرى ' *bashqalarî, akhérléri, digérléri* others.

§ 185.   a. فلان *filan* a certain (definite or indefinite person or thing), so-and-so.

فلان آدم *filan′ adém* so-and-so, such a one.

فلان شى *filan′ shéy* such a such a thing.

فلان وقتده *filan′ vaqîtda* at such and such a time.

§ 186.   a. كافه ' a. جله : هپ *kîaf′fé, jûmlé, hép* all.

كافهٔ عالم ، جله عالم ' *kîaf′féyi além, jûm′lé além* all the world.

هپ آدملر، جمله آدملر hép adémlér, jûm'lé ádémlér all men.

كافەمز، جملەمز، هپيمز kîaf'fémiz, jûm'lémiz, hé'pimiz all of us.

كافەسى، جملەسى، هپيسى kîaf'fési, jûm'lési, hé'pisi all of it.

§ 187. بوتون، اولانجه olanja, bûtûn whole.

بوتون كون bûtûn' gûn the whole day.

بوتون دنيا bûtûn' dûnya the whole world.

پاره نك اولانجەسى paraniñ olan'jasi all the money.

اولانجەم بو در olan'jam bou dour this is all I have.

اولانجه پارەم all my money. بوتون اكمك the whole loaf (acc.)

§ 188. هيچ hich nothing, [never] (§§ 131—132).

هيچ برى hich' biri none. هيچ بر كيمسه hich' bir kimsé nobody.

هيچ بر وقت hich' bir vaqit not at any time, never.

مطالعات Mûta-la-at Remarks.

§ 189. a) The English pronoun **one** [pl. ones] after an adjective is not expressed in Turkish; as:
Have you the fresh loaf? — No! I have the old one.
Tazé somoun séndé'mi?. — *Khayr! bayati' béndé dir.*
Two old lions and two young ones. The little ones.
Iki ikhtiyar vé iki génj arslanlar. Kûchûklér.
The great ones of the world. *Dûnyaniñ beôyûklérí.*

§ 190. b) **Somebody** is expressed by برى، بريسى *biri, birisi.*
Somebody is asking for you. *Biri séni chaghîrîyor.*
Somebody is knocking at the door. *Qapouyou vourouyorlar.*

§ 191. c) **Each other, one another,** are expressed

by p. بربرى، بربرى، يكديكرى *yékdigéri, birbiri, birbirléri.*
They love each other. *Birbirini sévérlér.*
We will help each other. *Birbirlérimizé yardîm'édéjéyiz.*
You see one another. *Yékdigériñizi geôrûr'sûñûz.*

مثالر Misal'lér Examples.

Chiftjiniñ béyaz qoyounlari var'mî?	Has the farmer the white sheep?
Khayr', siyahlar onda dir.	No! he has the black ones.
Hojaniñ beôyûk oghlou bourada' mî dir?	Is the teacher's elder son here?

Khayr' éféndim! ol biri bou-
   rada dir.   No, Sir, that one (= the other)
                          is here.
Bou qalémlériñ hér han'gisi.   Either of these pens.
Han'gisini istérsiñiz?   Which will you have?
Han'gîsi oloursa olsoun.   Either, whichever it may be.
Dostlarimin hich'birisi évdé déyil   Neither of my friends was at
   idi.   home.
Né onou' istérim, né ol'birini.   I will have neither.
Né'var? dérdiñ né'?   What is the matter?

لغتلر Words.

ایشجی *ishji* workman.	یتکین *yétgin* ripe.
دولو، طولی *dolou* full.	p. خام *kham* unripe.
a. جنس *jins* kind.	پوکار *pouñar* fountain.
a. قیمت *qiymét* value.	آرا *ara* relation.
a. ماعدا *ma'da* except.	چیفت *chift* pair.
p. شاکرد *shayird* pupil.	خیرسیز *khirsiz* thief.

٢٠ تعلیم Exercise 20.

١ بو چوجوقار کیمدر ؟ — شوزادهکی آیشجیلردن بعضیارینك
اوغلاری در ٠ هپسیده اوغلان می ؟ — خیر افندم ! کیمی اوغلان
کیمی قیز در ٢ بندهکی قلملردن بعضیلری سزده کیاردن چوق ایودر٠
لکن برادرکز ککیار هپیسی ده ایو در ٣ ٠ نهقدر پارهك وار ؟ —
کیسهم پاره ایله طولیدر ٠ نه جنس پاره ایله طولیدر ؟ — بعضیسی آلتون
بعضیسی کوموش پاره ایله طولیدر ؟ — ٤ بو میوهلردن هانکیلری خام
وَ هانکیلری یتکین در ؟ — کیراز وَ طوتاردن ماعدا المالر' آزمودلر'
وَ بوتون باشقه میوهلر خام درلر ٠ ٥ بربرکز ایله آراکز نصلدر' ایومیدر ؟
— یکدیکریز ایله آرامز هر وقت ایو در : هیچ کوتو دکلدر٠ ٦ اوده
نهکز وار ؟ — ایپکدن بر چیفت مندیلم وار ٠ ٧ خسته شاکردلر نیجه
درلر ؟ — بعضیسی ایو ایسه ده' دیکرلری هیچ ایو دکلدرلر٠

ترجمه ۲۱ Translation 21.

1. How many lessons have the boys? They have five lessons every day. 2. There are many thieves in these mountains. 3. God is the father of all men. 4. What kind of a young man is he? — He is a man sometimes good, sometimes bad. 5. "Everything has its time". "Everything has its place". 6. Who were with Mr. Joseph? — His wife and some of his grandchildren. 7. There were two thieves: one on one side, the other on the other side. 8. Are Mary and Ann here to-day (this day)? -- Neither of them is here. 9. Have you any friend in this village? — Yes, several of the rich families in this village are my friends. 10. Has Néjibé a white rose? — No, but she has a red one. 11. Are there many mosques and churches in this country? — Yes, Sir, every city and village has some churches or mosques.

مكالمه Conversation.

خير! بعضيلر ايو بعضيلر كوتو در.	هر آدم ايو ميدر ؟
بالديز يمك بر قاچ قلمى وار ايسه ده ؛ بنم هيچ يوقدر.	قلمك وار ميدر ؟
ايو دكلدر؛ بوتون او صوغوقدر.	اويكز نصلدر ؟
هيچ بر كيمسه دكلدر.	او كيم او ؟ (Qui vive?)
كيمسه يوقدر.	اوراده كيم وار ؟
هيچ برى ده غيرتلى دكلدر ، ايكيسى ده تنبلدر.	هانكيسى غيرتلى در مارى مى ، آنا مى ؟
يكنم مارى خانك قيزى در.	پوكار باشنده كى قيز نه كز در ؟
ابلامك اسمى قاطارينا در.	آبلا كك اسمى نه در ؟
چه چه مك اونده در.	بيوك والدهك نره ده در ؟

۱۱ درس   Lesson 11.

اسماء اعداد   Numeral Adjectives.

§ 192. The numerals are of four kinds: Cardinal, Fractional, Ordinal and Distributive numbers [اعداد اصليّه،

اعداد وصفيّه ، اعداد كسرّيه ، اعداد توزيعيّه].

1. Cardinal numbers. *Adadî asliyé.*

1	بر	*bir*	١	30	اوتوز	*otouz*	٣٠
2	ایکی	*i-ki*	٢	40	قیرق	*qîrq*	٤٠
3	اوچ	*ûch*	٣	50	اللی	*él'li*	٥٠
4	درت	*déôrt*	٤	60	آلتمش	*altmish*	٦٠
5	بش	*béʂh*	٥	70	یتمش	*yétmish*	٧٠
6	آلتی	*altî*	٦	80	سكسان	*séksén*	٨٠
7	یدی	*yédi*	٧	90	طقسان	*doqsan*	٩٠
8	سكز	*sékiz*	٨	100	یوز	*yûz*	١٠٠
9	طقوز	*doqouz*	٩	200	ایکیـوز	*iki yûz*	٢٠٠
10	اون	١٠		300	اوچیـوز	*ûch yûz*	٣٠٠
11	اونبر	*on bir*	١١	1000	بیك	*biñ*	١٠٠٠
12	اون ایکی	*on i-ki*	١٢	10000	اون بیك	*on biñ*	١٠٠٠٠
13	اون اوچ	*on ûch*	١٣	100000	یوز بیك	*yûz biñ*	١٠٠٠٠٠
20	یكرمی	*yirmi*	٢٠	million	ملیون	*milyon*	
21	یكرمی بر	*yirmi bir*	٢١	milliard	ملیار	*milyar*	

بو سنه خریستوسك بیك طقوز یوز ایکی سنهسیدر
Bou séné Kristosoun biñ doqouz yûz iki sénesi dir
This is the year 1902 (of Christ). A. D.

هجرتك بیك اوچیوز یكیرمی سنهسنده
Hijrétin biñ ûch yûz yirmi sénésindé
In the 1320th year of the Hejira.

§ 193a. A hundred, one hundred; a thousand, one thousand are in Turkish simply یوز ، بیك *yûz, biñ.*

It is not common in Turkish to say twelve hundred, twenty five hundred, but simply *biñ iki yúz, iki biñ bésh yúz*.

§ 193b. For the sum of 100,000 piastres in financial circles the word *yûk* یوك load, burden is used, and in the olden times the sum of 500 piastres was called کیسه *késé* bag, purse.

اون یوك *on yûk* one million. بش کیسه پاره *bésh késé para* 2500 piastres.

§ 194. The hours of the day and night are expressed as follows (§ 78):
Sa'at qach dir? What o'clock it is? — *Sa'at yarîm dir.* It is 12.30 o'clock.
Sa'at deôrt dûr. It is 4 o'clock. — *Sa'at yédi bouchouq dour.* It is 7.30 o'clock.

§ 195. Minutes are reckoned as follows:
Béshé on' var بشه اون وار Ten minutes to five.

Ikiyi bésh' géchmish ایکیی بش کچمش Five minutes past two.

§ 196. A person's age is expressed thus:
قاچ یاشنده سیڭ؟ *qach yashinda siñ?* How old are you?

قرق یاشنده ایم *qîrq yashindayîm.* I am 40 years old.

§ 197. **Numeral Adverbs** are formed by joining دفعه ، که *déf'a, kér'ré* to the cardinals; as:
Bir déf'a once; *iki déf'a* twice; *úch kér're* thrice. *Deôrt déf'a besh yirmi édér* four times five makes twenty.

§ 198. The **Variative numerals** are formed by adding چشید ، چشیددن ؛ جنس ، جنسدن *jins, jinsdén; chéshid, chéshid'dén.*
Bir jinsdén of one kind; *iki chéshid'dén* of two kinds; *úch jins, úch jinsdén* three sorts.

§ 199. Some thirty, some forty is expressed by قدر *qadar;* as (§§ 179, 229):
Otouz qadar, qîrq qadar. Some fifty persons *El'li adém qadar.*

§ 200. The word **or** between two numbers in English is omitted in Turkish.
Iki úch gûn some two or three days. *Bésh on adém qadar* some five or ten men. *Deôrt bésh ghouroush* some four or five piastres.

§ 201. The **Multiplicative numbers** are generally formed by the addition of قات *qat* fold to the cardinals; as:

تك *ték* simple, single.   يوزلرجه *yûzlérjé* hundreds of.

يالكز *yaliñiz* only, single.   بيكلرجه *biñlérjé* thousands of.

بريجك *birijik* only (begotten).   مليونلرجه *milyonlarja* millions of.

ايكي قات *iki qat* twice.   درت كوشه *déôrt kéôshé* ⎞

اوچ قات *ûch qat* triple.   چام چارشى *cham charshi* ⎠ square.

درت قات *déôrt qat* quadruple.   يوز قات *yûz qat* a hundred fold.

§ 202. The **Collective numbers** are:

p. چيفت *chift* a pair of (boots).   طاقم *taqîm* a set, lot.

p. چيفته *chifté* paired, double.   چيفته توفنك *chifté* double-barrelled gun.

f. دوزينه *douzina* a dozen [It.].   f. غروسه *grosa* a gross [It.].

اش ، تك *ésh, ték* mate; one of the pair.   سورو *sûrû* a flock.

§ 203. When using a numeral with a noun, the Turks frequently introduce a second noun between the two, which is quite superfluous in European languages, but occasionally employed in English, as 'ten head of cattle, six sail of ships' etc. This noun varies according to the nature of the things defined by the numeral. For men it is نفر *néfér* individual; for beasts it is رأس *rés* head; for bulbs it is باش *bash*; for ships, gardens, fields, letters, maps it is قطعه *qît'a* piece; for cannons, ships and villages, it is پاره *paré, para*; for things usually عدد ، دانه *dané, tané, adéd*; as:

ايكى نفر عسكر *iki néfér askér* two soldiers; *déôrt rés bargir* four pack-horses; *ûch qît'a méktoub* three letters; *alti qît'a tarla* six pieces of ground; *yédi bash soghan* seven bulbs of onions; *on paré kéôy* ten villages; *sékiz adéd tûféng* eight guns; *bir bab maghaza* a magazine (store); *bir qita arzouhal* a petition.

The common people uses the word دانه for all these different words; as: *iki dané asgér, déôrt dané bargir* etc.

لغتلر Words.

طوغدی	*doghdou* was born.	a. الحمرا	*él-hamra* Alhambra.
پنجره	*pénjéré* window.	p. سرای	*séray* castle, palace.
یازدیم	*yazdîm* I wrote.	a. عصر	*asr* century.
f. غزته	*gazéta* newspaper.	a. درم	*dîrhém* dram.
فرون	*fouroun* oven.	p. خان	*khan* inn.
a. حمام	*hamam* bath.	p. دكرمان	*déyirman* mill.
تارلا	*tarla* field.	چایر	*chayîr* pasture.
آخور	*akhor* stable.	a. صفر	*sîfîr* zero.

تعالیم ۲۲ Exercise 22.

۱ قاچ یاشنده سکز ؟ — اوتوز یاشنده یم · — برادر افندی قاچ
یاشنده در ؟ — اوتوز یدی یاشنده در · خرستوسك ۱۸٦۳ سنه سنده
طوغدی · ۲ آخورمزده قرق رأس صغیر وار · چایرلقده اون رأس آت ٬
یوز رأس قویون ٬ اللی رأس اینك و سورولرده اوچ درت یوز باش قدر
كچیلریز وار · ۳ اشبو ۱۹۰۲ سنه سنده مرزیفون شهرنده ۱۱۷۹
قطعه دكان ٬ ۳٥ قطعه فرون ٬ ۱٥ عدد خان ٬ ۱٤ دانه دكرمان ٬ ۳۰۹۱
قطعه باغ ٬ ۱۱۲۸ قطعه تارلا ٬ ۱۳۹ قطعه باغچه ٬ ۱ دانه چایر ٬
٤٥ باب جامع ٬ ۲٦ باب مكتب ؛ ۱۱٤ قطعه پوكار ؛ ۳۲۱۰ باب اَو
وَ ٥ باب كلیسه وار ایدی · ٤ آناطولیا قوله جینك اشبو ۱۹۰۲ سنه سنده
۲٤۰ نفر اركك وَ ۱٦۰ نفر قیز شاكردی وار ایدی · ٥ اوچ قطعه
عرضحال و ایكی قطعه مكتوب یازدیم · ٦ درت قطعه خاریطه م
وار در · ۷ بر عصرده یوز سنه ٬ بر سنه ده ۳٦٥ كون ٬ بر كونده
۲٤ ساعت ٬ بر ساعتده ٦۰ دقیقه و بر دقیقه ده ٦۰ ثانیه وار در ·
۸ یوز: اونك اون قاتی در · اون دفعه اون یوز ایدر · ۹ ۱,۰٥۰,۹۳٤ ٬
۲,۳٤٥,٦۷۸ ٬ ٦۸۷,٤۹٥

ترجمه ۲۳   Translation 23.

1. An oke is 400 drams; a batman is six okes.
2. My father is 70 years old, my mother 62, my brother
40 years old. 3. Take 200 (units) eggs, 500 walnuts,
50 pounds of apples and three batmans of pears.
4. What is the name of that book? — It is the Thousand and One Nights. 5. The palace of Alhambra has
999 windows. 6. Here are two sets of cloths. 7. There
were two kinds of handkerchiefs, a blue one and a black
one. 8. This cloth has three folds. 9. There are 40
loads of money in the bank. 10. I have three dozen
pencils. Twelve dozens make a gross. 11. The shoemaker has three pairs of shoes. 12. How many paras
make a piastre?

مكالمه   Conversation.

ساعت دردی اون ایکی کچمشدر.	ساعت قاچدر؟
یوز اللی پاره كويی وار.	مونجسونك قاچ پاره كويی وار؟
یوزلرجه و یکلرجه آدملر وار ایدی.	خانده چوق آدم وار می ایدی؟
اوت! بر عدد چیفته توفنكم وار.	توفنكك وار میدر؟
ساعت اوچ بوچوق ایدی.	دون بو وقتده ساعت قاچ ایدی؟
بش بیك غروش ایدر.	اون كیسه پاره قاچ غروش ایدر؟
شورادهك قوندوراجی دكاننده در.	قوندوراملك تكی نرهده در؟
عالی افندینك بریجیك اوغلیدر.	یوسف افندی كیمدر؟
نجیبه خانم در.	بو اویونده اشیكز كیم در؟
كیمسنه یوقدر، یالكز ایم.	اوطهده كیم وار؟
چام چارشی در.	اوطهكز نصلدر؟
اون ایكی دانه در.	بر دوزینه قاچ دانه در؟
یوز قیرق درت دانه وار.	بر غروسهده قاچ دانه وار؟
آوروپا خاریطهسیدر.	الیكزدهك خاریطه نه خاریطهسی در؟
ایكی باش صوغان یهدی.	چوجوق قاچ باش صوغان یهدی؟
چوق! بر قاچ یوز پاره وار.	انكلترانك قاچ قطعه كمیسی وار؟
آلتی قالِب صابونم وار در.	نقدر صابونك وار در؟

درس ١٢ Lesson 12.

اسماء اعداد Numeral Adjectives. (Continued.)

2. Fractional numbers. *Adadî késriyé.*

§ 204. The Fractional numbers are derived from the Cardinals; the denominator is put in the locative and the numerator in the nominative, and the latter follows the former.

اونده بر *onda bir* one tenth, بشده ایکی *beshdé iki* two fifths,

$$^1/_{10} = {}^1/10, \quad ^2/_5 = {}^2/5.$$

Yuzdé iki, $2\,^0/0 = ٢^0/_0$

بیکده یکرمی *biñdé yirmi* $20\,^0/00 = ٢٠^0/_{00}$

یوزده آلتی *yûzdé alti* $6\,^0/0 = ٦٠^0/_0$

§ 205. Sometimes one of the words p. پای *pay,* a. جز *jûz,* a. حصّه *his'sé,* a. قسم *qîsim,* all meaning 'a portion'; is introduced:

Dêôrt payda biri, dêôrt jûzdé biri, dêôrt hissédé biri, $^1/4 = {}^1/٤$

Yirmi parchada on dêôrdû, $^{14}/20 = {}^{١٤}/٢٠$

§ 206. Other fractional numbers are as follows:

یاری ، یاریم ، بوچوق ، a. نصف ، p. نیم *yari, yarim, bouchouq, nîsif, nim* half.

توم ، تم a. *tûm* whole (number).

چیرك p. *chéyrék* a quarter.

ربع a. *roub, ouroub* one fourth.

مطالعات. *Mûta-la-at* Remarks.

§ 207. There are three Turkish, one Arabic and one Persian word used for half (§ 75). **Yarîm** is used before a noun, like an adjective: *yarim sa'at, yarim élma.* **Bouchouq** is always used in conjunction with a cardinal number: *iki bouchouq gûn.* **Yarî, nîsif** are used like a noun: *élmanin yarîsî, kitabin nîsfi* the

half of the apple, the half of the book. The use of **nim** is very rare in Osmanli-Turkish: *nim résmi* half official (sources, papers).

§ 208. The Persian fractional number چاريك *char'yék* a quarter, commonly spelt چيرك *chéyrék* is used for a quarter of an hour or of a méjidiyé: f. قارت *qart* is used also for a quarter of a méjidiyé: a. ربع *roub*, *ouroub* is used to express one fourth of an arshîn (yard) and sometimes of a piastre.

Sa'at biré chéyrék var.   It is a quarter to one.
Bir arshîn ûch ouroub.   One and three quarter yards.
Elmanîn oqqasî deôrtdén roub éksiyé dir | One oke of apples is worth
المانك اوقهسى درتدن ربع اكسيكه در | 3 ³/₄ piastres.
Ûch méjidiyé qartî.   Three quarters of a méjidiyé.
Besh méjidiyé chéyréyi.   Five quarters of a méjidiyé.

3. Ordinal numbers. *Adadî vasfiyé.*

§ 209. These are formed from the cardinals by adding the termination نجى -*inji, -înji, -ounjou, -ûnjû.* The first has, however, an irregular form also, which is ايلك *ilk*, which is corrupted from اولكى *év'vélki* 'first'

1st	برنجى *birinji.*	8th	سكزنجى *sékizinji*
2nd	ايكنجى *ikinji.*	9th	طقوزنجو *doqouzounjou.*
3rd	اوچنجى *ûchûnjû.*	10th	اوننجى *onounjou.*
4th	دردنجى *deôrdûnjû.*	20th	يكرمنجى *yirminji.*
5th	بشنجى *béshinji.*	100th	يوزنجى *yûzûnjû.*
6th	آلتنجى *altînji.*	1000th	بيكنجى *biñinji.*
7th	يدنجى *yédinji.*	the last	صوك *soñ.*

Ingiliz Qiralî yédinji Edward. Edward VII, king of England.

مطالعات *Mûta-la-at* Remarks.

§ 210. In compound numbers, only the last unit assumes the ordinal form; all the others remain cardinals, as:

بيك دوقوز يوز اون آلتنجى *Biñ doqouz yûz on altînji* 1916th.

§ 211. The date is expressed as follows:

*Bou gûn ayîñ qachinjî gûnû dâr? Bou gûn ayîñ qachî dir?
Ayîn qachî' dir?* What day of the month it is to-day?
Bou gûn ayîñ sékizi dir. To-day is the 8th of the month.
Mayisîñ yirmi déôr'dûnjû gûnû dâr. It is the 24th of May.

§ 212. **Distinctives.** There is no special form for
the distinctive adverbs, the ordinals are used directly
without any alteration:

Firstly *Birinji*; Secondly *Ikinji*; Tenthly *Onounjou*.

4. Distributive numerals. *Adadî tévziyiyé.*

§ 213. Distributive numerals are formed by the
addition of ر ـَـ *-ér, -ar* to the cardinal numbers ending
in consonant, and شـ *-shér, -shar* to those ending
in ى *yé*.

برر *birér'* one each; برر برر *birér' birér* one by one.

ايكيشر *ikishér'* two each; ايكيشر ايكيشر *ikishér' ikishér* two by two.

اوچر *ûchér'* three each; اوچر اوچر *ûchér' ûchér* three by three.

دردر *déôrdér'* four each; دردر دردر *déôrdér' déôrdér* four by four.

التيشر *altishar'* six each; آلتيشر آلتيشر *altishar' altishar* six at a time.

يوزر *yûzér'* 100 each. بيكر *biñér'* a thousand each.

§ 214. When there are hundreds or thousands
in the number, the *ar* or *shar* comes after the numeral
expressing the number of hundreds, or thousands, and
nothing is put after *yuz* or *biñ*.

يوز الليشر بيك *yûz él'lishér biñ* 150000 each.

ايكيشر يوز *ikishér yûz* 200 each.

اوچر بيك *ûchér biñ* 3000 each.

§ 215. **The Ottoman-Turkish Calendar.** There
are three principal calendars or reckonings of time in
Turkey. The Christians usually observe the Christian
calendar, which is called either تاريخ ميلاد *tarikhi meelad*
the date of the Birth (of Christ) [*meelad* meaning birth-
day, Christmas-day], or *Kristosoun tarikhi* the date of
Christ. In this are used the Latin months: January,
February etc. (*Hounvar, Pédîrvar*).

Table of the Months.

Sacred months.		Civil months.		Popular names.	English.
محرّم	Mouhar'rém	مارت	Mart	Mard	March
صفر	Séfér	نيسان	Nisan	Abril	April
ربيع الاول	Rébil év'vél	ماييس	Mayis	Mayis	May
ربيع الاخر	Rébil akhîr	حزيران	Haziran	Oraq ayî	June
جمادى الاول	Jémazil év'vél	تمّوز	Tém'mouz	Témiz	July
جمادى الاخر	Jémazil akhîr	اغسطس	Avosdos	Avosdos	August
رجب	Réjéb	ايلول	Ey'loul	Gûz ayî	September
شعبان	Sha'ban	تشرين اول	Tishrini év'vél	Orta gûz ayî	October
رمضان	Ramazan	تشرين ثاني	Tishrini sani	Soñ gûz ayî	November
شوّال	Shév'val	كانون اول	Kianounou év'vél	Qara qîsh	December
ذى القعده	Zil qadé	كانون ثاني	Kianounou sani	Zam'harir	January
ذى الحجة	Zil hijjé.	شباط	Shoubat.	Gûjñk.	February.

§ 216. Among the Ottoman Turks there are two calendars, the Sacred and the Civil. The lunar year is adopted for the sacred and the solar for the civil. The Sacred year is dated from the Hejira or Flight, the first year of which Era began with the new moon of the 15th of July A. D. 622. The lunar year is 10 days shorter than the solar year, it is used in religious chronology and religious Law (sher'i). The months are reckoned differently from ours; they run thus: Mûhar'rem, Séfér etc.; and *shérif* 'sacred' is always added to their names; as: Shabanî shérif.

§ 217. The other is the Civil or the Financial calendar: the first day of which coincides with the first day of March O. S., and is now two years behind the Sacred. It is commonly used in all matters except those pertaining to religion. The months are: March, Nisan etc. —, the old Arabic and Syrian calendar, with slight changes. The year 1902 corresponds to the year 1320 of the Hejira and 1318 of the Financial or Civil year.

§ 218. The common people have a different reckoning of the months, running thus: Zamharir etc. (See the Table.)

§ 219. There is another popular division of the year into two parts: the summer and the winter divisions:

قاسم *Qasîm*, St. Demetrius' Day, the 26th Oct. O. S., is popularly reckoned as the beginning of the winter season, this has 180 days. خضر الياس *khîdir-él'léz*, St. George's Day, the 23rd April O. S., is celebrated as the beginning of the summer season, which lasts for 185 or 186 days.

§ 220. The New Style calendar is called in Turkish *alafranqa* and the Old Style *roumi* (Greek).

§ 221. The Ottoman Turks commence their reckoning of time from sunset. This is with them the twelfth hour, an hour later it is one o'clock, and so on till the twelfth hour in the morning (6 a. m.), when they begin again. This is called *alatourqa* (Turkish), to distinguish it from European time, which is called *alafranqa* (French, European).

لغتلر Words.

a. تاريخ *tarikh* date.   a. وفات ايتدى *véfat étdi* died.

a. مساوى *mûsavi* equal.   آلندى *alîndi* was taken.

آطه ، آدا *ada* island.   قره ، قاره *qara* land.

a. متصادف *mûtésadîf* corresponding.   p. بخشيش *bakh'shish* present.

تعليم ٢٤ Exercise 24.

١ استانبول شهرى ميلادك ١٤٥٣ نجى سنه‌سى آلافرانقه مايسك ٢٩ نجى كونى آلندى . بو تاريخ هجرتك ٨٥٧ نجى سنه‌سى جماذى الاول يكرمى برينه متصادف در . ٢ بو كونكى تاريخ نه‌در؟ — ١٩٠٠ سنه‌سى كانون اولك آلافرانقه يكرمى ايكى وَ رومى طوقوزى در . بو كون قاره قيشدر . ٣ درت و قيرق : قيرق درده مساويدر . ٤ ساعت قاچدر؟ — ساعت آلافرانقه درت و آلاتورقه اونبر بوچوقدر . ٥ كوچوك برادرم صنفده برنجى در : سز قاچنجى سكز؟ — بن ده صنفده اوچنجى ايم . ٦ سزه نقدر بورجاو ايم؟ سزه اولان بورجم نه‌قدر در؟ — بر عثمانلو ليراسى بر ليرا چيرگى وَ اوچ چيديه قارتى بورجك وار در . ٧ رمضان شريف بو سنه كانون اولك برنجى كونينه متصادفدر . ٨ اككك نصفى بكاآز در ؛ تومى ده چوقدر . ٩ چوجوقلره اوچر غروش بخشيش وير . ١٠ دنيانك درتده اوچ پايى صو وَ بر پايى ده قره در .

ترجمه ٢٥ Translation 25.

1. April is the fourth month of the year, October the tenth and December the twelfth. 2. He is in his sixtieth year; and my father is in his 68th year. 3. Give them each 10 piastres. Give those children a present of five piastres each. 4. A para is one fortieth of the piastre. A month is one twelfth of the year. 5. Come six by six. In the middle of the year. 6. Six per cent,

50 per thousand. 7. We are in the third year of the twentieth century. 8. Is Ali a good man? — No, Sir! he is in prison four fifths of the time. 9. At twelve o'clock, or a quarter to twelve, I shall be here (I am). 10. ₄Leon VI., the ₂last ₃king of ₁Cilicia, died at Paris in 1393, Nov. 19th, in the 60th year of his age.

مكالمه Conversation.

آلتمش يتمش غروش قدر پاره‌سی وار.	پدرکزك نقدر پاره‌سی وار؟
بابامك پاره‌سنك اوچ درت قاتی قدر در.	سنك پاره‌ك نقدر در؟
يدی يوز نسخه قدر وار در.	سزده بو كتابدن قاچ نسخه وار؟
آلتی يوزه مساوی در.	درت دفعه يوز اللی قاچه مساویدر؟
يوزبیكلرجه و مليونلرجه آدملر وار در.	آوروپاده چوق آدم وار می؟
چام چارشو یكبر میشر آرشوندر.	او باغچه نقدر اوزون در؟
كونلكلری اوچر بوچوق غروشدر.	ايشجيلرك كونلكی قاچر غروشدر؟
يوز اون پاره‌يه آلدم.	بو باصمه‌نك آرشونی قاچ پاره‌يه آلدك؟
اوچدن ربع اكسيكه مساويدر.	يوز اون پاره قاچه مساویدر؟

۱۳ درس Lesson 13.

درجات وصف Degrees of Comparison.

§ 222. In Turkish, as in English, there are three degrees of comparison, the Positive, the Comparative and the Superlative.

§ 223. The Comparative degree is generally expressed by putting the word with which the comparison is made in the ablative case, and leaving the adjective unaltered. The word دها *daha* 'more' is sometimes put before the adjective, for the sake of emphasis, or to prevent ambiguity; as:

بن سندن بۆيوگ'ۆم (بۆيۆ'يۆم)   *bén séndén bĕŏyûg'ûm (bĕŏyû'yûm)* ⎫
بن سندن دها بۆيوگ ۆم   *bén séndén daha' bĕŏyûg ûm* ⎭   } I am older than you.

بو كون هوا دونكيندن صغوقدر؛ بو كون هوا دونكندن دها صغوقدر

Bou gûn hava dûnkindén sovouq dour, Bou gûn hava dûnkindén daha' sovouq dour. To-day the weather is colder than yesterday.

§ 224. The Superlative degree is in general expressed by the word الك *éñ*, prefixed to the adjective; as:

اك يوكسك طاغ   *éñ' yûksék dagh* the highest mountain.

اك صوغوق هوا   *éñ' sovouq hava* the coldest weather.

§ 225. The word *éñ* is sometimes omitted:

آدمارك قباسى   *adamlariñ qabasi'* the rudest of men.

حيوانلرك بۆيوكى فيلدر   *Hayvanlariñ bĕŏyûyû fil'dir.* The largest of [all] the animals is the elephant.

Elmalariñ éyisini' séch   Choose the best of the apples.

§ 226. The words پك *pék* very, a. زياده *ziyadé*, آشيرى *a'shîrî* 'exceedingly' are used to signify an excess of any quality above what is requisite, as it is done in English by prefixing the adverbs 'too' or 'very' to adjectives; as:

پك يورغوندر   *pék' yorghoundour* he is very tired.

زياده بهاليدر   *ziyadé' bahalidir* it is too expensive.

آشيرى صغوقدر   *a'shîrî sovouqdour* it is too cold.

§ 227. Other superlatives are formed in a way peculiar to Turkish, by prefixing to certain adjectives a syllable somewhat similar in sound, commencing with the same vowel and consonant, or the same vowel, and ending with ب 'م 'س; as:

بم يـاض   *bém' béyaz* very white, exceedingly white.

ap' achîq very open.	*qap' qara* quite black.
yam' yassî very flat.	*sip' sivri* very sharp.
sap' saghlam very healthy, sound.	*sim' siyah* very black.
tas' tamam very complete.	*dop' dolou* quite full. [right.
bĕŏs' bĕŏyûk very big, great.	*dos' doghrou* quite straight, quite

ملاحظات *Mûlahazat* Observations.

§ 228. Spoken Turkish has the singular usage

of repeating nouns, adjectives and verbs, substituting in the repetition an **m** for the first letter of the word, if it begins with a consonant, and prefixing an **m** if it begins with a vowel, for the purpose of generalizing the idea contained in the word so repeated [compare the English shilly-shally, the French pêle-mêle, etc.]; as:

Kitab mitab boul'madîm. I sought for books or anything of the kind, but found nothing.

Dûk'kiăn mûkiăn év mév bir' shéy qal'madî. Not a shop or anything like one remained.

Eviñiziñ qouyousou mouyousou yoq'mou? Has your house a well, a cistern, a fountain? etc.

Ekméyi gétir, qourou mourou né'oloursa olsoun. Bring the bread, no matter if it be somewhat dry or crumbled.

Sachî machî yoq'dour. He has not a hair nor anything like one.

Further: *Oufaq téféy.* Little trifling matters.

Eyri bûyrû. Zigzag, serpentine.

§ 229. Certain idiomatic English phrases used in expressing comparison are expressed in the following way (§ 179).

as ... as ... is expressed by قدر *qadar,* which is not repeated as in English.

as much as —	قدر چوق —	— *qadar choq*
as little as —	قدر کوچك —	— *qadar kûchûk*
as few as —	قدر آز —	— *qadar az*
as far as —	قدر اوزاق —	— *qadar ouzaq*
as near as —	قدر یاقین —	— *qadar yaqîn*
as long as —	قدر اوزون —	— *qadar ouzoun*
as short as —	قدر قیصه —	— *qadar qîs'sa*

Shékérim qadar qah'vém var. I have as much coffee as sugar.

Shékér bal qadar tatlî dîr. Sugar is as sweet as honey.

Ol qadîñiñ qîzlarî qadar [choq] oghlanlarî var dîr. That lady has as many boys as girls.

Atîmiz bou at qadar éyi deyil dir. Our horse is not good as this.

Ingiltérra qadar ouzaq bir mahalé gitdi. He went to a place as far as England.

Gûnlér shimdi qishdaki qadar qîs'sa dîr. The days are now as short as in the winter.

Eshék qadar iri idi. It was as big as an ass.

Ol vaz Béôyûk Perhiz qadar ouzoun oudou. That sermon was as long as Lent.

Words. لغتلر

a. صادق *sadîq* loyal, true.	a. فائده *fay'dé* use, advantage.
آغير *aghîr* heavy.	سيركه *sirké* vinegar.
a. خفيف *hafif* light (in weight).	a. اعلا *a'la* best, excellent.
a. معدن *ma'dén* metal.	كيفلي *kéyfli* gay.
f. پيلاتين *platin* platinum.	a. كامل *kîamil* sober, grave.
a. ظالم *zalim* cruel.	a.t. قوتلو *qouv'rétli* strong.
a. فاره *faré* mouse.	قاقهرق *baqaraq* looking, in compa- [rison with.
قورشون *qourshoun* lead.	a. البته *élbét'té* of course.
كسكين *késkin* sharp.	بوى *boy* stature.

Proper Names هارون *Haroon* Aaron.   هانرى *Hanri* Henry.

نورى *Noori* Luke, Lucas.   نوريه *Nooriyé* Lucy.

Exercise 26. تعليم ۲٦

۱ هارون افندى كيمدر؟ — الك صادق دوستلرمدن بريدر.
۲ الك آغير معدن هانكيسى در؟ معدنلر اغيرلقده هپ بر ايسه‌ده؛
پيلاتين الك آغيردير. فقط الك فائده‌ليسى دميردر. صوكره‌كى اولكندن
خفيف در. ۳ او سيركه ايو ميدر؟ — خير اغام! بالدن طاتلو در.
سزده دها ايوسى وار ميدر؟ — اوت افندم! قيرميزى سيركه‌مز
سزككندن چوق اعلا در. ٤ الك اعلا دوستكز كيمدر؟ — عوجه‌مك
الك بويوك اوغلى هازرى افندى در. ٥ سزده الك ياشليسى كيمدر؟ —
الك ياشليمز وَ الك زنكينمز نورى افندى در. ٦ كدى فاره‌يه باقهرق
آرسلان در؛ لكن آرسلانه باقارق فاره در. ۷ بغداد قدر اوزاق برشهره
كيتدى. ۸ بنم بويم سزككى قدر اوزوندر. ۹ پارمق قدر كوچوك
بر قلمى وار. ۱۰ ال قدر ايزى بركاغدلرى وار. ۱۱ دون هفته‌نك
الك صوغوق كونى ايدى، فقط اولكيلردن صوغوق دكل ايدى.

ترجمه ۲۷   Translation 27.

1. Mr. Luke is taller than I am, but he is not the best in the class. 2. To-day is hotter than yesterday. 3. Iron is heavier than stone. Gold is more precious than silver, but iron is the most useful metal in the world. 4. Which is lighter: a pound of wool or a pound of lead? — Of course a pound of wool is as light as a pound of lead. 5. Your knife is as sharp as mine: but it is not as long as mine. 6. This young gentleman is much gayer than his friend. 7. The last week has been the worst of the year; it was very cold. 8. What kind of a man is Mr. Joseph? — He is a very good and useful man. 9. That mountain is higher than the other mountains of the country. 10. Henry is rich, Hassan is richer, and Ali is the richest of all.

مکالمه   Conversation.

آویكز نصلدر بویوكمیدر؟	اویمز سزككینه باقهرق چوق كوچوكدر .
اك بویوك قلم بو میدر؟	بنده بوندن بویوك بر دانه وار .
ددهكز پك اختیار می؟	اوت؛ فقط صاپ صاغلامدر .
سنده پاره وار می؟	بنده پاره ماره بر شی یوقدر .
كتاب اونده میدر؟	اونده كتاب میتاب بر شی یوقدر .
قورشون قلمك نصلدر؟	ایودر؛ اوجی سیپ سیوری در .
قدحده چای وار می؟	اوت؛ طوپ طولی در .
باغچهنك قپوسی آچیق می؟	اوت؛ آپ آچیقدر قپالی دكلدر .
ترجمهك طوغری میدر؟	اوت افندم ! طوس طوغریدر .
درسكز حاضر میدر؟	اوت ! تاس نمام حاپ حاضر در .
اوده اشكدن آتدن برشی وار می؟	آت مات اشك مشك بر شی یوقدر .
چارشیدن نه آلدك ؟	بعض اوفاق تفك شیلر آلدم .

دَرْس ١٤ Lesson 14.

حرف جرّ ايله اسم Noun with Prepositions.

§ 230. In the Turkish language there are no prepositions, properly so called, but their place is supplied by words or syllables, called post-positions, placed after the words which they govern.

§ 231. Post-positions, as well as prepositions, are particles which serve to show the relation which exists between two words. These relations being of different kinds, the post-positions indicating them are used with different cases, namely the Genitive, Dative or Ablative, and also with the uninflected form of the noun.

§ 232. **1. Post-positions appended to the uninflected form or stem.**

ه ‘ ه -é, -a to. (Sign of Dative case.) (§ 82.)

ايله ‘ له -ilé, -lé with, by. (Sign of Instrumental case.) (§ 82.)

ايچون îchîn, ichoun for, in order to, for the sake of.

كبى ‘ كى gibi like. so that.

ى -i, -î. (Sign of Acc. case.) (§ 83.)

ده -dé in, on. (Sign of Locative case.) (§ 84.)

دن -dén from. (Sign of Ablative case.) (§ 85.)

ظرفنده zarfînda during, in the space of.

§ 233. But when the object, which the post-positions govern is a Pronoun (personal or demonstrative), it must be in the genitive case, except اونلر onlar.

مثاللر Misal'lér Examples.

بنم ايچون bénim' ichin for me.   اونلر ايچون onlar' ichin for them.

پاره ايله para' ilé with money.   سينك كبى sinék' gibi like a fly.

سزك ايله sizin' lé with you. or سزكله   قوتده qouv'vétdé in the strength.

§ 234.   2. Post-positions with the Dative case.

دك *dék* | until, till, as
دكين *déyin* | far as.

طوغرى *doghrou* towards, straight.

a. دائر *dayir* concerning.

قدر *qadar* until, as much as.

ياقين *yaqîn* near.

قارشى *qarshi* against.

كوره *géôré* according to, after.

مثاللر *Misal'lér* Examples.

استانبوله‌دك ، دكين ، ـقدر *Istambolá'dék, Istambolá'déyin, -qadar* up to Constantinople, as far as Const.

عقلمه كوره *aqlima' géôré* according to my judgement.

Bizé qarshí against us.   *Shéhré' doghrou* towards the city.

„*Sénden ouzaq' Al'laha yaqîn*" far from you, near to God.

Kitaba' dayir concerning the book.

§ 235.   3. Post-positions with the Ablative case.

اوزاق *ouzaq* far.

طيشارى ، ديشارى *dîshari* out of.

a. ماعدا *ma'da* |
باشقه *bashqa* | except, besides.

اول *év'vél* before.

صوكره *soñra* after.

اوتورو *éôtûrû* | regarding,
طولايى *dolayi* | about.

برو ، برى *bérou, béri* since.

ايسه *i-sé* instead of, rather than.

اوته *éôté* on the other side of, beyond.

مثاللر *Misal'lér* Examples.

Shéhirdén' ouzaq far from the city.
Îrmaqdan éôté beyond the river.
Sizdén' ma'da, onlardan bashqa except you, them.
Yirmi bésh' sénédén bérou for the last 25 years (25 years ago).
Bou ishdén' dolayi, -'éôtûrû concerning this business.
Béndén' év'vél before me.   *Béndén soñra* after me.
Gélmésindén' i-sé gél'mémési éyi dir his not coming is better than his coming.

§ 236.   4. Declinable Post-positions requiring the Genitive.

اوزره *ûzré* on, upon.

طيشارى ، ديشارى *dishari* out of.

آلت *alt* under.

ايچرى ايچهرى *ichéri* inside.

آرقه *arqa* behind.

ايچ *ich* in

اوك *éôñ* before.

يان *yan* by, near.

اوزرینه ، اوزرکه ، اوزرمه *ûzérimé, ûzériñe, ûzériné* | on me,

اوزرنده ، اوزرکه ، اوزرمده *ûzérimdé, ûzériñdé, ûzérindé* | thee, him or it.

ایچلرینه ، ایچیکزه ، ایچیمزه *ichimizé, ichiñizé, ichlériné* | in us, in you, in them.

ایچلرنده ، ایچیکزده ، ایچیمزده *ichimizdé, ichiñizdé, ichlérindé* | among us, you, them.

یانیمده *yanîmda* at, by my side.   یانیمه *yanîma* to my side.

§ 237. These eight post-positions, when in the locative case, indicate a state of location or rest, and answer to the question نرهده *nérédé?* **where?** They require the dative after the question **whither?** or **where to?** نرهیه *néréyé?* with a verb denoting direction or motion from one place to another.

Examples with the Locative [rest].

1. کتاب صفرانك اوزرنده در *Kitab sofraniñ ûzérindé dir.* The book is on the table.

2. قوشك یاوروسی یووانك ایچنده در *Qoushouñ yavrousou youvaniñ ichindé dir.* The birdling is in the nest.

3. شهرك دیشاریسنده اوطوردیلر *Shéh'riñ dîsharîsînda otourdou-lar.* They dwelt [on] [the] out-side [of] the city.

4. چوجوق آغاجك آردنده صاقلاندی *Chojouq aghajîñ ardinda saq-landî.* The boy hid himself behind the tree.

5. پدرك اوکنده طوردم *Pédériñ éôñûndé dourdoum.* I stood in front of my father.

6. بالیق کولك ایچنده در *Baliq géôlûñ ichindé dir.* The fish is in the lake.

Examples with the Dative [motion].

1. کتابی صفرانك اوزرینه آتدم *Kitabî sofraniñ ûzériné atdîm.* I threw the book on the table.

2. قوش یاوروسنی یووانك ایچینه قویدی *Qoush yavrousounou youvaniñ ichiné qodou.* The bird put its young into the nest.

3. شهرك دیشاریسنه چیقدیلر *Shéh'riñ disharisîna chîqdîlar.* They went [to the] out[side] of the city.

4. چوجوق آغاجك آردینه قاچدی *Chojouq aghajîñ ardina qachdi.* The boy ran behind the tree.

5. پدرك اوکنه دوغری کیتدم *Pédériñ éôñûné doghrou gitdim.* I went towards the father.

6. باليق كولك ايچينه آتلدى *Baliq géôlûñ îchiné atildi.* The fish jumped into the lake.

Motion, where to? whither? *néréyé?* شهره ' استانبوله ' قاره يه

قاپونك يانينه ' اوك ايچريسنه ' صويك ايچينه ' باغه ' باغچه يه ' اوه ' دكيزه ' ابر ماغه .

Location, where? *nérédé?* باغده ' باغچه ده ' كتابده ' دكيزده

اوده ' صوده ' قپونك ياننده ' اوك ايچريسنده ' صويك ايچينده ' تارلاده ' آغاجده ' كتابده .

تعليم ۲۸ Exercise 28.

۱ اوطه دن طيشارى . اوطه نك طيشاريسنده . اوطه نك ايچريسنده . اوطه نك قپوسنه ' اوطه نك قپوسنده . ۲ باغه ياقين . اوه ياقين . ال ايله . آياق ايله . الى ايله = اليله . آياق ايله ' آياغم ايله ' آياغى ايله = آياغيله . ۳ كوز ايله ' كوزم ايله ' كوزيكز ايله = كوزيكزله ؛ كوزى ايله = كوزيله . ٤ اورمانك ايچينده ' اورمانده . اورمانك ايچينه ' اورمانه ' اورماندن . ٥ آغاج ايچون ' آغاجى ايچون = آغاجيچون . كتابم ايچون . كتابى ايچون = كتابيچون . ٦ كتابلريمك آرقه سنده كوزل آلتون يازيلر وار . بو سوزلرى كتابكه ياز . ۷ الكى بنم اوزريئه قوى ! الك بنم اوزريده در . ۸ قوش آغاجده در . قوش آغاجه اوطوردى . ۹ قدحى صويه قوى . قدح صوده در . ۱۰ قدحلر يچون .

ترجمه ۲۹ Translation 29.

1. Towards the mountains: on the mountains; by the mountains (rest), by the mountains (motion). 2. From the door: by the door; with the door; for the door. 3. For me, for him; like you, like them; with me, with him. 4. As far as Sivas; as far as London; until

[1] If ايله ' ايچون are added to nouns to which the pronominal affixes of the 3rd person Sing. and Pl. are attached, the ى is omitted, but the sound *i* is retained.

to-day. 5. There is nobody except us. 6. What have you in your purse? — There is nothing in my purse except ten paras. 7. After to-morrow come at half past eleven. 8. He went ten days earlier than my father. 9. There is a thief among you. 10. Come among us (motion).

مكالمه Conversation.

كوزل تصويرلر وار در.	كتابكزده نلر وار؟
اك قيصه آى شباط آيى در.	اك قيصه آى هانكيسيدر؟
خير افندم! حلب قدر اوزاق دكلدر.	استانبول چوق اوزاق ميدر؟
فقير بر قارى وار.	اوطهنك اوكنده كيم وار؟
خير خانم افندى! هيچ يوقدر.	باغچهدهكى آغاجلرده ميوه وار مى؟
اوت بكم! پك چوقدر.	ايرماقده باليق چوق ميدر؟
خير آغام! چوق ياقين ايز.	شهردن پك اوزاق ميز؟
آلتيمزدهكى حيوان آت ايدى.	آلتيكزدهكى حيوان نه ايدى؟

۱۵ درس Lesson 15.

The Substantive Verb. (Continued.)

§ 238. We have already treated of the Present and Past (Preterite) tenses of the substantive verb. (§§ 65, 73.) The Perfect and Conditional tenses of the verb remain to be spoken of.

The Conditional.

isém = ايسهم ايسم		*isék* = ايسهك ايسك	
isén = ايسهك ايسك		*iséñiz* = ايسهكز ايسكز	
isé = ايسه ايسه		*isélér.* = ايسهلر ايسلر	

If (or though or perhaps) I am, if thou art, if he is —. etc.

The Negative Conditional.

déyilsém = دكل ايسهم = دكلسم	*déyilsék* = دكل ايسهك = دكلسك
déyilzén = دكل ايسهك = دكلسك	*déyilséñiz* = دكل ايسهكز = دكلسكز

دكل ايسه = دكسه *déyilsé*   دكل ايسه لر = دكلسار *déyilsélér*.

If I am not, if thou art not, if he is not —, etc.

Perfect (Dubitative).

ايشم *imishim*	ايشيز *imishiz*	(They say that)
ايشسين *imish-siñ*	ايشسكز *imish-siñiz*	I was or I have been, etc.
ايش *imish*	ايشلر *imishlér*	

This tense, which is also called in Turkish Dubitative, denotes mere hearsay or report, founded on the authority of others (§ 312). The Negative is دكل ايشم *déyil imishim* (They say that) I have not been.

مطالعات Remarks.

§ 239. a. When ده *-dé* is added to the Conditional tense of the substantive verb, it expresses the meaning of "but" or "yet":

ايسه لر ده ، ايسكز ده ، ايسك ده : ايسه ده ، ايساك ده ، ايسم ده

isém dé, iséñ dé, isé dé; isék dé, iséñiz dé, isélér dé

If (or though) I am —, yet —; thou art —, yet —; he is —, yet —.

§ 240. b. By the addition of the 3rd person sing., to the Past tense (§ 73), the Past Conditional is obtained:

ايديلرسه ده ، ايديكزسه ده ، ايدكسه ده : ايديسه ده ، ايدكسه ده ، ايدمسه ده

idimisé dé, idiñsé dé, idiysé dé; idikisé dé, idiñizisé dé, idilérisé dé

Though I was —, yet —; thou wast —, yet —; he was —, yet —.

مثاللر Examples.

Pédériñ évdé isé, gilsiñ.	If your father is at home, let him come.
Pédérim évdé isédé géléméz.	My father is at home, but he cannot come.
Biradériñ néré dé imish?	Where is your brother?
Evdé imish.	(I heard that, they say that) he is at home.
Chojouqlar hasta´mî imishlér.	Were the children ill? (Did you hear anything?)
Ev´vét, hasta´ dîrlar.	Yes, they are ill (I know).
Qonshoumouz zéngin´ isé dé, éyi bir adém déyil´ imish.	Our neighbour is rich, but they say that he is not a good man.
Bén génj´im, sén isé ikhtiyar´ sîñ.	I am young, but thou art old.

The Conditional and Dubitative tenses
of the verb To HAVE.

§ 241.   The Conditional and Dubitative tenses of the verb To HAVE are obtained by the addition of ايسه *isé* and ايمش *imish* to وار *var*.

§ 242.   **The Conditional of To HAVE** [with an indefinite object][1].

بنده وار ايسه	بنم وار ايسه	*béndé var isa*	*bénim var isa*	etc.
سنده وار ايسه	سنك وار ايسه	*séndé var isa*	*séniñ var isa*	
اونده وار ايسه	اونك وار ايسه	*onda var isa*	*onouñ var isa*	— a have I If
بزده وار ايسه	بزم وار ايسه	*bizdé var isa*	*bizim var isa*	
سزده وار ايسه	سزك وار ايسه	*sizdé var isa*	*siziñ var isa*	
اونلرده وار ايسه	اونلرك زار ايسه	*onlarda var isa*	*onlariñ var isa*	

The Negative.

بنده يوغيسه	بنم يوغيسه	*béndé yoghousa*	*bénim yoghousa*	etc.
سنده يوغيسه	سنك يوغيسه	*séndé yoghousa*	*séniñ yoghousa*	
اونده يوغيسه	اونك يوغيسه	*onda yoghousa*	*onouñ yoghousa*	— a not have I If
بزده يوغيسه	بزم يوغيسه	*bizdé yoghousa*	*bizim yoghousa*	
سزده يوغيسه	سزك يوغيسه	*sizdé yoghousa*	*siziñ yoghousa*	
اونلرده يوغيسه	اونلرك يوغيسه	*onlarda yoghousa*	*onlariñ yoghousa*	

§ 243.   *Note.*   a. The abridged form of يوق ايسه *yoq isé* is يوغيسه *yoghousa* which is much used.

b. يوق ايسه *yoq isé*, يوغيسه *yoghousa* or يوخسه *yokhsa*, when used without object or subject, is considered as a conjunction: meaning or, otherwise; as:

كتاب سنده مى ' يوخسه قارداشكده ميدر؟ *Kitab séndé mi, yokhsa qardashiñda' midir?* Who has the book, you or your brother?

§ 244.   **The Conditional with a definite object.**

اونلرده ايسه ' سزده ايسه ' بزده ايسه ؛ اونده ايسه ' سنده ايسه ' بنده ايسه
béndé isé, séndé isé, onda isé; bizdé isé, sizdé isé, onlarda isé
If I have the —, if thou hast the —, etc.

----
[1] Vide §§ 119, 122, 127.

اونلرك ايسه ، سزك ايسه ، بزم ايسه ؛ اونك ايسه ، سنك ايسه ، بنم ايسه

bénim isé, séniñ isé, onouñ isé; bizim isé, siziñ isé, onlariñ isé

If the (book) is mine, thine, his, etc.

The Negative.

اونلرده دكلسه ، سزده دكلسه ، بزده دكلسه ؛ اونده دكلسه ، سنده دكلسه ، بنده دكلسه

béndé déyilsé, séndé —, onda —: bizdé déyilsé, sizdé —, onlarda —

سنك دكلسه ، بنم دكلسه — *bénim déyilsé, séniñ déyilsé*, etc.

If I have not the —, etc. If the — is not mine, etc.

§ 245. *Remark.* When ده *-dé* is added to the conditional of the verb To Have, it expresses the sense of but.

بنده وار ايسه ده	*béndé var isé dé,*	I have a —, but —
بنده يوغيسه ده	*béndé yoghousada,*	I have not a —, but —
سنك ايسه ده	*séniñ isé dé,*	It is yours, but —
سنك دكلسه ده	*séniñ déyilsé dé,*	It is not yours, but —
اونده ايسه ده	*onda isé dé,*	He has the —, but —
اونده دكلسه ده	*onda déyilsédé,*	He has not the —, but —.

§ 246. **The Dubitative tense of To Have** [with a definite object].

اونلرده ايمش ، سزده ايمش ، بزده ايمش ؛ اونده ايمش ، سنده ايمش ، بنده ايمش

béndé imish, séndé—, onda —; bizdé imish, sizdé—, onlarda —.

اونلرك ايمش ، سزك ايمش ، بزم ايمش ؛ اونك ايمش ، سنك ايمش ، بنم ايمش

bénim imish, séniñ —, onoun —; bizim imish, siziñ —, onlariñ —.

I have the —, thou hast the —; (That) was mine, thine, his —.

§ 247. **The Dubitative tense of To Have** [with an indefinite object].

اونده وار ايمش ، سنده وار ايمش ، بنده وار ايمش *béndé var imish* etc.

اونك وار ايمش ، سنك وار ايمش ، بنم وار ايمش *bénim var imish* etc.

(They say that) I have a —; thou hast a —, etc.

مثاللر Examples.

Séniñ parañ varîsa.	If thou hast money.
Inéyiñiz varîsa.	If you have a cow.
Parañ varîsa, baña bésh ghouroush vér.	If you have money, give me five piasters.
Param var'isa da vérmém.	I have money, but I will not give.

Ekméyiñiz yoghousa aliñ.	If you have not bread, take some.
Kitablarî yoghousada —	They have not books, but —
Qalém béndé isédé vérmém.	I have the pen, but I will not give it.
Ati var'idi isé —	If he had a horse —
Eshéyi yogh'oudou isédé —	Though he had not a donkey, yet —.

لغتلر Words.

واريمز يوغمز *varimiz' yoghoumouz'* all that we have.

آلمام *almam'* I do not take.   a. لسان *lisan* language.

كسكين *késkin* sharp (knife).   آز *az* less.

آغير باشلى *aghîr bashlî* sedate (man).   a. كامل *kiamil* sober, wise.

Proper Names: آرسلان *Arslan* Leon.   a. صادق *Sadiq* Justin,
Justus.   a. نوريه *Nooriyé* Lucy.

تعليم ٣٠ Exercise 30.

١ آرسلان مى كيفليدر يوخسه برادرى حَسَن مى ؟ هانكيسى
كيفلى در ؟ — آرسلان كندى قارداشى حَسَندن كيفلى ايسه ده ؛
حَسَن پك كامل وَ آغير باشلى برچوجوقدر . ٢ واريز يوغيمز هپيسى درت
غروشدر ' زياده بر پارهمز يوقدر . ٣ آرسلان قوهدهكى حيوانلرك الك
قوتليسى ايسهده ' پك ظالمدر . ٤ بزم آتيمز بياض آتيكزدن كنج
ايسهده ' اوندن قوتلى دكلدر . ٥ هانكى لسان دها قولايدر ' تركجه
مى يوخسه انكيليزجه مى ؟ — تركجه انكيليزجه قدر قولايدر ' اوندن
زور دكلدر ؛ فقط روسجه چوق زور ايمش . ٦ كاغدك يوغيسه بندن آل !
— تشكر ايدرم ؛ كاغدم يوغيسهده كيمسهدن آلمام . ٧ «پارهك وار
ايسه هر كس دوستك ؛ پارهك يوغيسه هر كس دشمنك در» .
٨ «دوستك دوستى دوست ايسه ' دوستك دشمنى ده دشمن در ؛
دشمنك دوستى دشمن در وَ دشمنك دشمنى دوستِ, در» . ٩ كتابلر
سزده ميدر ؟ — كتابلر بزده دكللرسه ده ؛ قلملر بزده در .

ترجمه ٣١ Translation 31.

1. The apples are sweet; the pears are sweeter; the grapes are the sweetest. 2. Your maid servant is diligent, but [I heard that] my neighbour (woman) is more diligent than she. 3. Though Mr. Justus is a rich man, yet [they say that] he has not a good name. 4. Miss Lucy is the handsomest girl in town, but she is sick. 5. The strength of the strongest man is far less than that of an elephant. 6. I am as tall as you, but my brother Leon is not so tall as you. 7. Is your fruit as fresh as ours? — Yes, Sir, it is as good as yours, but it is too little [in quantity]. 8. Your knife is as large as mine, but it is not as sharp as mine.

مكالمه Conversation.

يوقدر افندم : وار ايسه ويريرم .	سنده اكمك وار ايسه بر آز وير !
واريكز يوغيمز اوشبش غروشدر .	واريكز يوغيكز قاچ غروشدر؟
باغچه‌ده ايمش .	پدر افندى نره‌ده ايمش؟
اون سنه اول چوق زنكين ايمش .	آرسلان بك بك زنكين مى ايمش؟
خير اوستمده دكلدر .	پيچاغك اوزركده ايسه وير !
آوده دكله باغده در .	والده خانم آوده ميدر؟
خير افندم قفسده ايمش .	قوش آغاجده دكل مى ايمش؟
خسته ايدم ايسه‌ده كلدم .	خسته دكاميديكز؟
بك ايى افندم !	آتلرى يوغيسه ، بنمكنى آل !

درس ١٦ Lesson 16.

مصدر The Infinitive of Verbs.

§ 248. The Infinitive (or the Masdar) is the basis of the Turkish verb[1]. It ends either in مق -*maq* or مك

---

[1] The Turkish verb is the most highly organised part of the language, being most minutely subdivided, most extensively

-mék: -maq is peculiar to roots with hard and -mék to roots with soft vowels. When we remove the ending maq or mék we get the stem or the root of the verb, which is also the 2nd person Sing. of the Imperative; as:

آلمق almaq′ to take: آل al′ take thou.

ويرمك vérmék′ to give: وير vér′ give thou.

§ 249. The Negative form of the verb is obtained by adding مه ‘ م -mé- to the root when it has a soft vowel and له -ma- when it has a hard vowel; as:

آلمامق al′mamaq not to take: آلمه or آلما al′ma do not take.

ويرمملك or ويرمه vér′mémék not to give: ويرمه vér′mé do not give.

Different kinds of verbs.

§ 250. There are six kinds of verbs in Turkish: Transitive, Intransitive, Causal, Passive, Reciprocal and Reflexive.

§ 251. I. Transitive (or Active) verbs indicate such an action as cannot be completed without something else becoming directly affected thereby. They always require a direct object taking the nominatival form of the noun, if the object is indefinite and the full accusative form if the object is definite (§§ 83 note, 291).

صو ايچمك sou ichmék to drink some water (indefinite).

صوىى ايچمك souyou ichmék to drink the water (definite).

يازمق ايستهمك yazmaq istémék to wish to write (indefinite).

§ 252. II. An Intransitive (or Neuter) verb indicates such an action of the agent as is complete in itself without directly affecting anything else. When an action is implied, an Intransitive verb requires an indirect object in the dative case, if motion is implied: if rest is denoted, it requires its indirect object to be in the locative (§ 237); as:

---

developed, and at the same time most simple and regular in its formation and in the modification of the signification of its various branches. It is a perfectly symmetrical system, through all the ramifications of which the eye or mind can run with ease.

اوه كيتمك *é-vé gitmék* to go home (motion).

اوده اوطورمق *évdé otourmaq* to sit in the house (rest).

يازمغه باشلامق *yazmagha bashlamaq* to begin to write (motion).

§ 253. III. Causal or Causative verbs. This form of the verb is not much used in English, but it is very common in Turkish. It implies an order or command from the speaker to a second or third person. The action is performed not by the agent or speaker but by the person to whom the order is given. These verbs are translated into English by adding to cause, to make, to have, to get, to allow and to let, to the simple verb according to the sense[1]; as:

قالفهيه بر اَو ياپديره جغم *Qalfaya bir év yapdîrajaghîm.* I shall cause the architect to build a house.

مكتوبى اوحانـه يازديره جغم *Méktoubou Ohan'nésé yazdîrajaghîm.* I shall get John to write the letter.

آرتينه بر چيفت قوندوره ياپديردى *Artiné bir chift qoundoura yapdirdî.* He got Pascal to make a pair of shoes.

Ol tasvirli kitabî chojouqlara bou' gún oqoudajaghîm. I shall allow the boys to read that book full of pictures to-day.

Bénim ichin bir sétri yapdîrabilir'misiñ? — Yarîn bir danésini gétirdébilirim. Can you get (or have) a coat made for me? — I shall have one brought to-morrow.

§ 254. IV. Passive verbs. The English and Turkish languages have this peculiarity, that they can form passive verbs from Intransitive, as well as from Transitive verbs; as:

باقمق *baqmaq* to look at (intrans.): باقيلمق *baqilmaq* to be looked at.

آلمق *a'lmaq* to take (trans.): آلينمق *alînmaq* to be taken.

§ 255. V. Reciprocal verbs express an action performed together with or against each other. They are translated by adding to the infinitive the words one another, each other, together; as:

سويشمك *sévishmék* to love each other.

---

[1] The meaning and use of the Causal verb are seen by comparing the verb raise with the verb rise, of which the former is the Causal, in English. So also we may call to set the causal of to sit, the former meaning to cause to sit. Similarly to lay is the causal of to lie, the former (to lay) meaning to cause to lie.

قوشوشسونلر *qoshoushsounlar'* let them run together.

ووروشه‌جقلر *vouroushajaqlar'* they will beat each other.

§ 256. VI. Reflexive verbs. When the action of a verb returns to the subject from which it proceedes, the verb is called Reflexive. These verbs are translated into English by the reflexive pronouns (§ 145); as:

اورتونمك *êörtûnmék'* to cover himself.

صویوندیلر *soyoundoular'* they undressed themselves.

ییقانه‌جغم *yiyqanaja'ghim* I shall wash myself.

تعلیم قرائت Reading Exercise.

کدی ایله دوه حکایه‌سی
The Story of the Cat and the Camel.

برکون دوه صیرتنده آغیر بر یوك ایله كیدركن ' كدی‌یه راست كلدی . كدی صیرتنی قانبورلاده‌رق دوه‌یه دیدی:

كدی — اوغورلر اولسون : دوه قارداشلق ! نره‌یه بویله ؟

دوه — اللّٰه امانت اول ! امّا بن ناصل سنك قارداشك ایشیم ؟ سن نره‌ده ؟ بن نره‌ده !

كدی — اڭا شبهه یوقدر ! البتّه بن سنك قارداشكیم . باق هله ! سنككی قدر ایری وبیوك قانبورم یوقمیدر ؟

دوه — بلكه ! لكن عجبا بنمكی قدر ده قوتلی می ؟

كدی — وای ! نه بوش سوز ! شو صیرتكده یومروق قدر كوچوك بر شی وار ایسه ' عجبا سوزك اونك ایچون میدر ؟

دوه — امّا ایو باق ! بو یوك سنك ایچون پك بیوك دكلمی ؟

كدی — بوش سوزلر سویله‌مه ! شونی بكا ویر ' تنبل هریف !

دوه — پك اعلا ! براٰز بری كل ! هوپ بالا ! دیمش وَیوكنی كدینك صیرتینه یوكلتمش !

كدى — آمان! آمان! آمان! نه آغير ايش! ايشيم بيتدى! واى!
واى! واى!

دوه — ايشته بلاكى بولدك! كيت بويوك سوز سويلهمكى اوكرن!
قصّهدن حصّه — بويوك لقمهيه' بويوك سوز سويلهمه!

Talimi Qîra'at.
Kédi ilé dévé Hik*ÿ*ayési.

Bir gûn Dévé sîrtînda[1] aghîr bir yûk ilé gédérkén[2], Kédiyé rast géldi[3]. Kédi sîrtînî qambourladaraq[4] dévéyé dédi[5]:

Kédi — *Oughourlar olsoun[6], dévé qardashlîq[7]! néréyé béôylé?*

Dévé — *Al'laha émanét ol[8]! am'ma bén na'sîl séniñ qardashîñ imishim? sén' nérédé? bén' nérédé?*

Kédi — *Oña shûb'hé yoqdour[9]! Elbét'té[10] bén séniñ qardashîñ im. Baq hélé[11]! séniñki qadar iri vé béôyûk qambouroum[12] yoq'mou dour?*

Dévé — *Bélki[13]! lakin ajéba[14] bénimki qadar' da qouv'vetli' mi?*

Kédi — *Vay! né' bosh séôz[15]! shou sîrtîñda youmrouq[16] qadar kûchûk bir shéy var îsa, ajaba séôzûñ onouñ' ichoun mou dour?*

Dévé — *Am'ma éyi baq! bou yûk séniñ ichin pék béôyûk deyil' mi?*

Kédi — *Bosh séôzlér séôylémé! Shounou baña vér! témbél hérif[17]!*

Dévé — *Pék a'la! bir az béri[18] gél! hop'bala[19]! — démish[20], vé yûkûnû kédiniñ sîrtîna yûklétmish[21].*

Kédi — *Aman! aman! aman[22]! né' aghîr imish! ishim bitdi[23]! vay! vay! vay[24]!*

Words. 1. on his back. 2. while going. 3. he met. 4. arching (making hunch-back). 5. said. 6. good speed! 7. half brother, good brother. 8. thank you! (I commit you to the charge of God). 9. there is no doubt about it. 10. of course. 11 look here! 12. hunch. 13. perhaps. 14. I wonder. 15. what a useless word. 16. as large as a fist. 17. villager, rude man (lazy fellow!). 18. nearer. 19. Heyday! (hoop po loo!) 20. he said. 21. he burdened, he placed (leaded). 22. O dear! O dear! 23. my work is finished, i. e. I am lost, it is all up with me. 24. Oh! Alas!

Dévé — Ishté bélañî bouldouñ²⁵! git'. béôyúk séôz séôy-
léméyi eôyrén'²⁶!

    Qîs'sédén hîs'sé²⁷ — Béôyúk loqma²⁸yé, béôyúk
séôz séôylémé!

    25. you have got (found) your punishment. 26. go and learn the [calamity of] speaking conceited (haughty) words. 27. moral from the story. 28. morsel (of food).

مكالمه Conversation.

بر كوزل حكايه در .	بو قرائت درسى نه در؟
«دوه ايله كدينك حكايه‌سى» در .	بو حكايه‌نك ماذه‌سى نه‌در؟
كدى‌يه راست كلدى .	دوه كيدركن كيمه راست كلدى ؟
غايت آغير بر يوك وار ايمش .	دوه‌نك صيرتينده نه وار ايمش ؟
دوه ايرى بر يوك حيوانى در .	دوه نه‌در؟
كدى دوه‌يه باقه‌رق پك كوچكدر .	كدى مى بويوك؟ دوه مى بويوك ؟
«اوغورلر اولسون قارداشلق» ديدى .	كدى دوه‌يه نه ديدى ؟
يولجيلره ديرلر افندم !	اوغورلر اولسون كيمله‌ره ديرلر؟
بلكه بغداده طوغرى يولجى ايدى .	دوه نره‌يه يولجى ايمش عجبا ؟
خير افندم ! بو پك بوش بر سوز ايدى .	كدى دوه‌نك قارداشى مى ايدى ؟
شو كوچوجك يوككى بكا وير ديدى .	كدى صوكره دوه‌يه نه ديدى !
پك اعلا افنديجكزم !	يور ! بو حكايه‌يى صوكنه قدر سويله !

درس ١٧ Lesson 17.

Primitive and Derivative Verbs.

مجرّد وَ مزيدْ فيه مصدرلر¹

    § 257. Simple or Primitive Verbs are those which have no letters or syllables inserted after the root: for instance يازمق *yazmaq* to write, سومك *sévmék* to love. اوقومق *oqoumaq* to read, are simple verbs, because there

---

¹ *Mûjér'réd vé Mézeedún feehi masdarlar.*

are no letters added to the roots $\sqrt{\text{یاز}}$ *yaz*, $\sqrt{\text{سو}}$ *sév*, $\sqrt{\text{اوقو}}$ *oqou*.

§ 258. But if I say یازدیرمق ٬ سویشمك ٬ اوقونمق *yaz-dirmaq, sévishmék, oqounmaq*: these are derivative verbs, the new or secondary roots are یازدیر ٬ سویش ٬ اوقون *yazdîr, sévish, oqoun*. These are formed by inserting certain letters between the simple roots and the infinitive termination, and thus changing the meaning of the verb, more or less.

سومك *sévmék*; $\sqrt{\text{سو}}$ *sév* to love:

سویشمك *sévishmék*; $\sqrt{\text{سویش}}$ *sévish* to love each other.

یازمق *yazmaq*; $\sqrt{\text{یاز}}$ *yaz* to write:

یازدیرمق *yazdîrmaq*; $\sqrt{\text{یازدیر}}$ *yazdîr* to cause to write.

اوقومق *oqoumaq*; $\sqrt{\text{اوقو}}$ *oqou* to read:

اوقونمق *oqounmaq*; $\sqrt{\text{اوقون}}$ *oqoun* to be read.

§ 259. The so-called servile letters are those letters, which, when added to the roots, change, more or less, the meaning of the verb. They are: ت *t*, در *dir*, ر *r*, ن *n*, ل *l*, ش *sh*.

§ 260. These letters or syllables have each their own special signification when inserted to form a new root. Each alters the meaning of the verb in a regular manner. 1, 2, 3. ت *t*, دیر *dir*, ر *r* have the power of making verbs Transitive, if the original root is Intransitive; and Causal, if the original verb is Transitive. 4, 5. A verb is made either Reflexive or Passive by adding ل *l* or ن *n* to the root of a primitive verb. 6. Reciprocal verbs are formed by adding ش *sh* to the root of primitive verbs.

§ 261. There are six measures [باب *bab*, وزن *vézn*], as they are called in Turkish, which serve as formulas

to enable the student always to remember the addition and the changes of meaning caused by the insertion of the servile letters.

1. Oqoutmaq اوقوتمق [Transitive and Causal].

§ 262. This form is obtained by adding ت *t*, (*it*, *ût*, *out*) to the stem (§§ 52, 56).

The effect of the insertion of this letter is twofold:

1. If the original primitive form is intransitive, it is made transitive; as:

اوطورمق *otourmaq* to sit: اوطورتمق *otourtmaq* to make to sit, seat.

باقمق *baqmaq* to look: باقيتمق *baqitmaq* to make to look, to show.

2. If the original simple form be transitive, it changes to causal; as:

اوقومق *oqoumaq* to read: اوقوتمق *oqoutmaq* to cause to read.

ييقامق *yiy'qamaq* to wash: ييقاتمق *yiy'qatmaq* to cause to wash.

Note. This ت *t* is added, generally, when the root of the verb ends in a vowel, or in one of the semivowels ل *l*, ر *r*, ن *n*.

تعليم ٣٢ **Exercise 32.**

Change the following verbs into the first measure and give their meanings.

Transitive verbs. 1. سويلهمك *seôylémék* to speak. دوشهمك *deôshémék* to floor, to carpet. 2. چاغيرمق *chaghir-maq* to call. باشلامق *bashlamaq* to begin. 3. قازيق *qazi-maq* to dig, to engrave. آرامق *aramaq* to seek. 4. آقمق *aqmaq* to flow. بيلهمك *bilémék* to sharpen (a knife). 5. يوكلهمك *yûklémék* to load. ديكلهمك *diñlémék* to listen.

Intransitive verbs. 6. صيچرامق *síchramaq* to jump. اريمك *érimék* to be melted. 7. اوشومك *ûshûmék* to feel cold, shiver. صوغومق *sovoumaq* to become cold, cool. قوقمق *qoqmaq* to smell, to have a smell. 8. اويومق

آغلامق *agh-* onyoumaq to sleep. ياشامق *yashamaq* to live.
lamaq to cry, to weep.

2. *Yazdîrmaq* يازديرمق [Transitive and Causal].

§ 263. This measure is formed by adding دير (*dir,
dîr, dûr, dour*) to the root (§§ 52, 56).

The effect of this syllable on the root is just the
same as that of the first measure:

1. If the primitive verb is intransitive, it is made
transitive; as:

اولمك *ôlmék* to die (intrans.): اولدرمك *ôldûrmék* to kill (trans.).

اویانمق *ouyanmaq* to awake (intrans.):

اویاندیرمق *ouyandîrmaq* to awaken (trans.).

2. If the primitive verb be transitive, it is changed
into a causal; as:

آچمق *achmaq* to open (trans.): آچديرمق *achdîrmaq* to cause to open.

يازمق *yazmaq* to write (»): يازديرمق *yazdîrmaq* to cause to write.

Note. This دير *dîr* is added generally to those verbs whose
stem ends in a consonant other than those mentioned above.

There are some exceptions:

كورمك *geôrmék* to see: كوردرمك، كوسترمك *geôstermék, geôrdûrmék*
to make to see,
[to show.

كلمك *gélmék* to come: كتیرمك *gétirmék* to bring.

كیتمك *gitmék* to go: كوتورمك *geôtûrmék* to carry.

قالقمق *qalqmaq* to rise: قالدیرمق *qaldîrmaq* to raise, to lift up.

تعلیم ۳۳ **Exercise 33.**

Change the following verbs to this measure and
give the meanings.

Intransitive verbs. 1. كزمك *gézmék* to walk.

كولمك *gûlmék* to laugh. 2. اوصانمق *osanmaq* to become
tired of. اوتانمق *outanmaq* to be ashamed. 3. اینمك *énmék* to come down. بینمك *binmék* to ride on. 4. اولنمك
évlénmék to marry. چالیشمق *chalishmaq* to work.

Transitive verbs. 5. بولمق *boulmaq* to find. بيلمك *bilmék* to know. 6. آلمق *almaq* to take. ويرمك *vérmék* to give. 7. سومك *sévmék* to love كسمك *késmék* to cut.

3. Ichirmék ايچيرمك [Transitive and Causal].

§ 264. This measure is formed by adding ر (-*ir*-, -*îr*-, -*our*-, -*ûr*-) to the stem (§§ 52, 56).

It changes the Intransitive into Transitive and the Transitive into Causal; as:

طوغمق *dogh'maq* to be born (intrans.): طوغورمق *doghourmaq* to give birth.

پيشمك *pishmék* to be cooked (intrans): پيشيرمك *pishirmék* to cook.

ايچمك *ichmék* to drink (trans.): ايچيرمك *ichirmék* to give to drink.

Note. This form is a modification of the second form, losing the د *d*; therefore its derivatives are very limited, and almost all are here given.

تعليم ٣٤ **Exercise 34.**

Change the following verbs into the third measure and give the meanings.

Intransitive verbs. 1. اوچمق *ouchmaq* to fly. ياتمق *yatmaq* to lie down. 2. آرتمق *artmaq* to be increased. باتمق *batmaq* to sink. 3. دوشمك *düshmék* to fall. شاشمق *shashmaq* to miss one's way. 4. بيتمك *bitmék* to be finished: طاشمق *tashmaq* to overflow. 5. دويمق *douymaq* to hear of. طويمق *doymaq* to become satiated. 6. قاچمق *qachmaq* to flee. كچمك *géchmék* to pass. ييتمك *yitmék* to be lost.

4. Taranmaq طارانمق [Reflexive, Passive].

§ 265. This measure is formed by adding ن *n*, (*in*, *ûn*, *oun*) to the root of the verb (§§ 52, 56).

It changes the Transitive into the Reflexive and Passive; as:

طارامق *taramaq* to comb : طارانمق *taranmaq* to be combed, to comb himself.

اورتمك *eôrtmék* to cover : اورتونمك *eôrtûnmék* to be covered, to cover oneself.

اوقومق *oqoumaq* to read : اوقونمق *oqounmaq* to be read.

بولمق *boulmaq* to find : بولونمق *boulounmaq* to be found.

§ 266. In spelling there is no difference between the reflexive and the passive, as both are formed by adding ن *n*. The difference is in the meaning. If the verb deals with the subject, it is reflexive; if the verb refers to the logical object, it is passive, because passive verbs have no grammatical object; as:

Efféndi yîyqandî The Master washed himself (reflexive).
Qadéhlér yîyqandî The cups have been washed (passive).

تعليم ٣٥ Exercise 35.

Change the following verbs into the fourth measure.

1. چالمق *chalmaq* to steal; to knock at (the door); to play (a tune). 2. دوكمك *deôkmék* to pour. *deôymék* to beat. 3. صويمق *soymaq* to undress, strip. 4. قيلمق *qîlmaq* to do, to perform. طيقامق *tîqamaq* to plug, stop. 5. كزمك *gézmék* to walk about. ييقامق *yîyqamaq* to wash. 6. باقمق *baqmaq* to look. سومك *sévmék*. 7. طيامق or دايامق *dayamaq* to prop up. سويلهمك *seôylémék* to speak.

5. *Yazîlmaq* يازيلمق [Passive].

§ 267. The measure is formed by the addition of ل *l*, (*il*, *ûl*, *oul*) to the root (§§ 52, 56).

It changes the primitive verbs into passives; as:

يازمق *yazmaq* to write : يازيلمق *yazîlmaq* to be written.

كسمك *késmék* to cut : كسيلمك *késilmék* to be cut.

Note. a. The passive of those verbs which end in a vowel, or liquid letter, is never formed according to this measure, but according to the fourth.

b. The passive form of the verbs ايتمك ' ايلهمك *étmék, éyl-émék* to do, perform is ايديلمك *édilmék*.

تعليم ٣٦ Exercise 36.

Change the following verbs into this measure and give the meanings.

1. ويرمك ' سومك .2 قيرمق ' وورمق .3 كيتمك ' آچمق

4. ايچمك ' چاغيرمق *chaghîrmaq* to call. 5. اوطورمق ' بينمك

6. باقمق ' ديكمك to plant. كورمك ' بويورمق

6. *Géôrûshmék* كورشمك [Reciprocal].

§ 268. This measure is formed by adding ش *sh*. (*ish, oush, ish*) to the root of the verb (§§ 52, 56).

It changes the meaning of the verb into a reciprocal one; as:

كورمك *géôrmék* to see: كوروشمك *géôrûshmék* to see one another.

اورمق *vourmaq* to beat: اوروشمق *vouroushmaq* to fight with one another.

تعليم ٣٧ Exercise 37.

Change the following verbs into the sixth form.

آغلامق *aghlamaq* to cry. weep.   كولمك *gûlmék* to laugh.

دورتمك *dúrtmék* to poke.   اوينامق *oynamaq* to play.   سومك

sévmék. بوزمق ' بوزمق *bozmaq* to ruin, to disconcert.

مطالعات *Múta-la-at* Remarks.

§ 269. a. The meaning of the Negative form is, of course, in general perfectly clear; but the negative form of the causal verbs, besides its ordinary signification, sometimes expresses a prohibition or prevention of the action being done. Thus *oqout'mamaq* means 'not to cause to read', but also 'to prevent some one from reading'; *yazdir'mamaq* 'not to cause to write', and also 'to prevent from writing'.

§ 270. b. A Transitive verb, or a verb which has been converted into one, according to the rules mentioned above, may become doubly, and even triply, transitive, causative, or passive; as:

اوقومق *oqoumaq* to read: اوقونغق *oqoun'maq* to be read.

اوقوتغق *oqout'maq* to cause to read: اوقونلمق *oqounoul'maq* to be read.

اوقوتديرمق *oqoutdour'maq* to cause to cause to read:

اوقوتديرتغق *oqoutdourt'maq* to cause to cause to cause to read.

تعليم قرائت Reading Exercise.

The Divisions of Turkey. ممالك محروسهٔ شاهانهنك تقسيملرى

ممالك محروسهٔ شاهانه ولايتلره ٠ ولايتلر لوا ياخود سانجاقلره ٠ سانجاقلر قضالره ٠ قضالر ناحيهلره ٠ ناحيهلر دخى قريهلره تقسيم اولنور ٠ — ولايتدن مسؤل اولان ذات والى ٠ سانجاقدن مسؤل اولان متصرف ٬ قضادن مسؤل اولان قائمقام ٬ ناحيهدن مسؤل اولان مدير وَ قريهلردن مسؤل اولانلر اختيار مجلسلرى و مختارلر در ٠

ممالك محروسهٔ شاهانه ۲۹ ولايته تقسيم اولنور ٠ بونلردن آلتيسى آوروپاده ٬ يكرمى برى آسياده ٬ برى آفريقاده وَ برى دخى آق دكيزده در ٠

Mémaliki Mahrouséyi Shahanénin taqsimléri.

₂*Mémaliki* ₁*Mahrouséyi* ₃*Shahané*[1] *Vilayétléré, Vila-yétlér*[2] *Liva*[3] *yakhod*[4] *Sanjaqlara, Sanjaqlar*[3] *Qazalara, Qazalar*[3a] *Nahiyéléré, Nahiyélér*[5] *dakhi Qaryéléré*[5a] *taqsim olounour*[6]. — *Vilayétdén mé'soul*[7] *olan*[8] *zat*[8a] *vali*[9]*, Sanjaqdan mé'soul olan Mûtésar'rif*[10]*, Qazadan mé'soul olan Qayim'maqam*[11]*, Nahiyédén mé'soul olan Mûdir*[12] *vé Qaryélérdén mésoul olanlar*[13] *Ikhtiyar méjlisléri*[14] *vé moukhtarlar*[15] *dir.*

Words. 1. The Protected Countries of His Majesty (Royal). 2. province. 3. a county, arrondissement 3a. a district, canton. 4. or. 5. a sub-district (parish or commune). 5a. village. 6. are divided. 7. responsible. 8. who is (who governs). 8a. person. 9. governor general. 10. governor. 11. sub-governor. 12. a governor of a sub-district, mûdir. 13. who are. 14. bailiff courts. 15. bailiffs.

*Mémaliki Mahrouséyi Shahané 29 vilayété taqsim
olounour. Bounlardan altisî Avropada, yirmi biri Asiyada,
biri Afriqada vé digér biri dakhi Aq dénizdé dir.*

مكالمه Conversation.

يكرمى طقوز قطعه ولايتاره تقسيم اولنور.	ممالك شاهانه نهيه تقسيم اولنور؟
آلتى قطعهسى آوروپاده در.	بو ولايتلرك نقدرى آوروپاده در؟
يكرمى بر قطعه در. [در.	آسياده بولنان ولايتلر قاچ قطعه در؟
برى آفريقاده وَ ديكرى آق دكيزده	ديكر ايكيسى نره لرده در؟
ولايتدن آشاغى اولان تقسيمدر.	لوا وَ ياخود سانجاق نه در؟
ولايتك اداره سنه مسؤل اولان ذاتدر.	والى كيمدر؟
متصرفلر مسؤلدرلر.	لوانك اداره سنه كيم مسؤلدر؟
بر قضانك اداره سنه مسؤل اولان	قائممقام كيمدر؟
مديرلر مسؤلدر. [ذات در.	ناحيه نك اداره سنه كيم مسؤلدر؟
كوى ديمكدر.	قريه نه ديمك در؟
اختيار مجلسلرى وَ مختارلر مسؤلدرلر.	قريه لرك اداره سنه كيم مسؤلدر؟
افندم! لوالرك عددى ۱۱۹ در.	ممالك شاهانه ده كى لوالرك عددى قاچدر؟
افندم! قضالر ۵۵۰ قطعه در.	قضالرك عددى قاچدر؟
ناحيه لرك عددى ۱۳۹۰ وَ قريه لركى ايسه ۶۰۳۰۷ در.	قاچ ناحيه و قاچ قريه وار در؟
متصرفلق ده درلر. [ده ديرلر.	لوايه دها نه ده ديرلر؟
قضايه قائممقاملق وَ ناحيه يه مديرلك	ديكرلرينه نه ديرلر؟

Lesson 18. درس ۱۸

Compound Verbs. مركب فعلار

§ 271. Compound verbs are formed by employing
Arabic, Persian and Turkish words with the Turkish
auxiliary verbs, or by affixing certain particles to nouns
and adjectives in order to turn them into verbs.

1. Compound verbs, formed by using nouns with auxiliary verbs.

§ 272. I. Compound Transitive verbs are constructed by uniting with nouns and adjectives (generally of Arabic and Persian origin) one of the four purely Turkish synonymous auxiliary verbs ايتمك ' ايلمك or ايلهمك ' قيلمق ' بويورمق *étmék, éylémék, qilmaq, bouyourmaq*, all meaning to do, to perform; but the first is most frequently used.

a. سوال *sival* question: سوال ايتمك ' سوال ايلمك ' سوال قيلمق ' سوال بويورمق to question.

p. آزاد *azad* free: آزاد ايتمك · آزاد ايلمك ' آزاد قيلمق ' آزاد بويورمق to free.

t. صوص *sous* silent: صوص ايتمك to still, to hush.

t. ياش *yash* moisture; wet: ياش ايتمك to moisten; to wet.

Note. The original meaning of بيورمق *bouyourmaq* is to command, to deign, to be kind enough, but as an auxiliary it is used when the agent is a person of rank or is politely treated as such.

§ 273. II. Compound Intransitive verbs are formed by uniting Arabic or Persian adjectives and active and passive participles (*ismi fayil, méfoul*) to the intransitive verb اولمق *olmaq* "to be, to become"; as:

p. خسته *hasta* sick: خسته اولمق *hasta olmaq* to be sick.

a. ممنون *mémnoun* glad: ممنون اولمق *mémnoun olmaq* to be glad.

t. صوص *sous* silent: صوص اولمق *sous olmaq* to be silent.

§ 274. III. Compound Passive verbs are constructed with the same kind of words and with the passive form of the auxiliaries ايدلمك ' قيلنمق ' بيورلمق *édilmék, qilinmaq, bouyroulmaq*, or more frequently with the passive forms of the verb اولمق *olmaq*; viz. اولنمق *olounmaq* to become, to which there is nothing to correspond in English; as:

a. سوال *sival*: سوال ايدلمك · سوال اولنمق ' سوال قيلنمق ' سوال بيورلمق to be asked.

p. آزاد يورلق ، آزاد قيانمق ، آزاد اونمق ، آزاد ايدلك :azad
to be free.

§ 275. IV. Compound Causal verbs are constructed with the same kind of words and with the causal forms of the auxiliaries يورتمق ' ايتدرمك *étdirmék, bouyourtmaq*, to cause to do.

p. فروخت *firoukhté* sale: فروخت ايتدرمك *firoukht' étdirmék* to cause to sell.

a. قتل *qatl* slaughter: قتل ايتدرمك *qatl étdirmék* to cause to kill.

a. احسان *ihsan* grant: احسان يورتمق *ihsan bouyourtmaq* to help to be granted.

Exercise 38. تعليم ۳۸

Form verbs from the following words:

1. a. كرم *kerem* kindness.   a. رجا *rija* request.

2. a. ايجاد *ijad* invention.   a. تشريف *téshrif* honour, visiting. 3. p. شاذ *shaz* glad. a. تبديل *tébdil* change.

4. a. عزيمت *azimét* departure.   a. عودت *avdét* return.

5. a. تعليم *talim* instruction. a. ترجمه *térjémé* translation.

6. a. ظهور *zouhour* appearance.   a. بنا *bina* building.

7. a. وعظ *vaz* sermon. p. كور *kéôr* blind. 8. a. حفظ *hifz* keeping. a. غيرت *ghayrét* labour.   a. هديه *hédiyé* present, gift.

2. Verbs derived from Nouns and Adjectives.

§ 276. I. Transitive verbs are formed from nouns and adjectives by the addition of لامق *lamaq* to those containing hard vowels, and لهمك *lémék* to those containing soft vowels. When this termination is added to a noun, it has the meaning of to provide with, and when added to an adjective signifies to render; as:

كوز	*gêöz* eye:	كوزلهمك	*gêözlémék* to watch.
باش	*bash* head:	باشلامق	*bashlamaq* to begin.
قره	*qara* black:	قرهلامق	*qaralamaq* to blacken.
تميز	*témiz* clean:	تميزلهمك	*témizlémék* to clean.

§ 277. II. Intransitive and Passive verbs are formed by the addition of لنمك ، لانمك *lénmék, lanmaq* to nouns or adjectives; as:

اولنمك *évlénmék* to marry. كوزللنمك *gûzéllénmék* to grow pretty.

خرصلانمق *khirslanmaq* to be angry. حاضرلانمق *hazirlanmaq* to be ready.

§ 278. III. By adding simply مق -*amaq*, مك -*émék*, المق -*almaq*, لمك -*élmék*, to the adjectives or nouns, another kind of Intransitive or Passive verbs is obtained; as:

قان	*qan* blood:	قانامق	*qanamaq* to bleed.
قوجه	*qoja* old:	قوجهمق	*qojamaq* to become old.
باش	*yash* age:	ياشامق	*yashamaq* to live.
چوق	*choq* much:	چوغالمق	*choghalmaq* to increase.
آز	*az* little:	آزالمق	*azalmaq* to diminish.

§ 279. IV. Some Intransitive verbs are formed from adjectives by the addition of لشمك ، لاشمق -*léshmék*, -*lashmaq*, meaning to grow, to become, to get (gradually).

a. فنا *féna* bad: فنالاشمق *fénalashmaq* } To become worse
كوتو *kêötû* bad: كوتولشمك *kêötûléshmék* } (gradually).

ايو *éyi* good: ايولشمك *éyiléshmék* To grow better (grad.).

§ 280. The same termination, however, added to nouns produces reciprocal verbs; as:

a. مكتوب *méktoub* letter: مكتوبلاشمق *méktoublashmaq* to correspond.

خبر *khabér* information: خبرلشمك *khabérléshmék* to communicate (intelligence).

§ 281. V. Causal compound verbs are obtained by inserting ت *t* in the first and 3rd forms and در *dir* in the 2nd and 4th forms.

1. باشلاتمق *bashlatmaq* to let be begun.

2. اولندرمك *evléndirmék* to make marry.

3. چوغالتمق *choghaltmaq* to make abound.

4. ايولشدرمك *éyiléshdirmék* to make grow gradually better.

§ 282. VI. There are some exceptions to the above-mentioned rules; as:

يان *yan* side: ياناشمق *yanashmaq* to approach.

صارى *sarî* yellow: صارارمق *sararmaq* to grow yellow.

اوزامق *ouzamaq* to elongate.   صوصامق *sousamaq* to thirst.

پارلامق *parlamaq* to shine.   آجيقمق *ajîqmaq* to be hungry.

تعليم ٣٩ **Exercise 39.**

Form verbs from the following words.

I., II., V. 1. آو *av* game. 2. p. مهر *mộhúr* a seal. 3. a. حاضر *ḥazîr* ready. 4. قات *qat* fold, p. پاره ، پارچه *paré, para, parcha* piece. 5. طوپ *top* ball, قيش *qîsh* winter, ياز *yaz* summer, كوز *gúz* autumn. 6. طاش *tash* stone, ياغ *yagh* oil, باغ *bagh* bind, tie. 7. طوز *touz* salt, كاغد؛ پول *poul* postage stamp. III. قورو ، اسكى *qourou* dry, بوش *bosh* empty, بكز *béñz* countenance, اكشى *ékshi* sour, كنج *génj* young. IV. پاى *pay* portion, قوجاق *qoujaq* bosom, كوج؛ اَل *gúj* hard, ايرى *iri* big. VI. يشيل *red* ، قيزيل ، كوچوك.

The Potential Verb.

§ 283. To be able to do an action is expressed by the verb بيلمك *bilmék* 'to know, to be able' put after

9*

the root of any verb, with و *hé* joined to it. This is called in Turkish the Potential verb. It somewhat resembles the Potential mood of the English verb. But this is a class of verbs in the Turkish language, which has all the moods, tenses and modifications which the regular verbs have; as:

يازه يلمك : يازه ، يازمق *yazmaq* ، *yaze* : *yazabilmék* to be able to write, i. e. to know how to write.

سوه يلمك : سوه ، سومك *sévmék* ، *sevé* : *sévébilmék* to be able to love, i. e. to know how to love.

بيله يلمك : بيله ، بيلمك *bilmék* ، *bilé* : *bilébilmék* to be able to know, i. e. to know how to know.

§ 284. If the root of the verb end in a vowel, a *yé* is inserted between the stem and *hé* (§ 53); as:

سويله يه يلمك : سويله ، سويلمك *seôylémék* : سويلهمك *seôyléyébilmék* to be able to speak.

§ 285. The negative which expresses inability or impossibility, is made by adding مامق *-mamaq* or مهمك ، مك *-mémék* to the stem of the verb instead of *bilmék*; as:

يازه يهمامق *yaza'mamaq* not to be able to write (not يازهمهمك

اوقويهمامق *oqouya'mamaq* not to be able to read.

كيدهمهمك or كيدهمك *gidémémék* not to be able to go.

Accelerative Verbs.

§ 286. By adding the verb ويرمك *vermék* to the root of any verb, another verb is formed which expresses doing the same action, but in a very off-hand way. This verb is called by native grammarians فعل تعجيل *Fec-li Tajil* Accelerative verb or Verb of Facility.

§ 287. If the root of the original verb end in a consonant it takes a vowel ى *yé* after it; and if it end in a vowel the syllable يى *-yi* must be added to it (§ 53); as:

يازمق : $\sqrt{}$ ياز : يازى ويرمك *yazi vérmék* to write quickly.

اوقومق: $\sqrt{}$ اوقو : اوقويى ويرمك *oqouyou vérmék* to read quickly.

تعليم ٤٠ Exercise 40.

Change the following verbs into the affirmative and
negative forms of the Potential and Accelerative verbs.

1. كلمك ‘ كورمك ‘ قيرمق ‘ اورمق ؛ .2 آچمق ‘ ايچمك ‘

3. دوكمك *deôymék* ‘ دوكمك *deôkmék* : 4. كسدرمك ‘ كوسترمك ‘

5. اورتونمك *eortúnmék* ‘ كچيرمك ‘ سويلتمك ‘ ايتمك وعظ ؛

6. ترجمه ايتمك ؛ 7. آلامق ‘ هديه اوننمق ‘ باشلامق ؛ 8. مهرلتدرمك ‘

9. باشلامامق ‘ باشلانق ‘ باشلانق.

مكالمه Conversation.

١ اولنمك نيتنده¹ ميسكز ؟ — خير افندم ! بن اولنمك نيتنده

دكلم . آنام بابام بنى اولندرمك نيتنده درلر. ٢ شو قدحلرى ييقامق

لازم مى ؟ — اوت افندم ! هپسنى ده تميزلمك لازمدر . ٣ آرسلان

اولامق قولاى ميدر ؟ — خير ! كوجدر ؛ همده چوق تهلكه ليدر² .

٤ بو سنه نره يه كيتمك مرامنده¹ سكز ؟ — صامسونه عزيمت وَ عودت

ايتمك نيتنده يم . ٥ بو درسى ترجمه ايتمك بولاييدر ؟ — پك قولايدر

1. *niyét, méram* intention.   2. *téhliké* danger.

تعليم قرائت Reading Exercise.

ولايتلر The Provinces.

ممالك محروسهٔ شاهانهنك آوروپا قطعه سنده بولنان ولايتلرى

شونلر در: ادرنه ‘ سلانيك ‘ قوصوه ‘ يانيه ‘ اشقودره ‘ مناستر.

آسیا قطعه سنده بولنان ولایتلر: حجاز ' یمن ' بصره ' بغداد ' موصل '
حلب ' سوریه ' بیروت ' خداوندکار ' قونیه ' آنقره (انکورو) ' آیدین '
آطنه ' قسطمونی ' سیواس ' دیاربکر ' بیتلیس ' ارضروم ' معمورت العزیز '
وان ' طربزون .

افریقا قطعه سنده: طرابلس ' آق دکیزده: جزائر بحر سفید .

بونلرك مرکزلری شونلر در : حجازککی جدّه ' سوریه نککی
شام ' خداوندکارککی بروسه ' آیدینککی ازمیر ' معمورت العزیزککی
خربوت ' وَ دیکرلرککی هنامارى اولان شهرلر در .

Vilayétlér.

Mémaliki Mahrouséyi Shahanéniñ Avropa qit'asînda[1]
boulounan vilayétléri shounlar dir: Edirné[2], Sélanik[3],
Qosova, Yan'ya, Îshqodra, Monastîr.

Asiya qit'asînda boulounan vilayétlér: Hijaz, Yémén,
Basra, Baghdad, Mousoul, Haléb[4], Sûriya[5], Béyrout,
Khúdavéndigiar, Qonya[6], Anqaré (Engûrû)[7], Aydîn,
Adana[8], Qastamouni, Sivas, Diyarbékir, Bitlis, Erzroum,
Mamourétûl-Aziz, Van, Trabzoun.

Afriqa qit'asînda: Tarablous[9]; *Aq-Dénizdé:* ₁Jézayiri
₃bahrî ₂séfid[10].

Bounlariñ mérkézléri[11] *shounlar dîr:* Hijaziñki Jid'dé;
Sûriyaniñki Sham[12], Khúdavéndikiariñki Brousa, Aydi-
niñki Izmir[13], Mamourétûl-Aziziñki Kharpout, vé digér-
lériñki hémnamlari[14] olan[15] shéhirlér dîr.

Words. 1. part, segment. 2. Adrianople. 3. Thessalonica.
4. Aleppo. 5. Syria. 6. Iconium. 7. Galatia. 8. Cilicia. 9. Tripoli.
10. (the islands of the White Sea) Archipelago, Rhodes. 11. centre,
central city of the province. 12. Damascus. 13. Smyrna. 14. having
the same name, homonymous. 15. which are.

درس ۱۹   Lesson 19.

The Derivative forms of the Infinitive.

§ 288. There are three formations of verbal Substantives derived from the Infinitive: By appending to the Infinitive the syllables لك ، لق -*lîq*, -*lik*, and by affixing to the root of the verb the terminations مه -*ma*, -*mé*; ش ، یش -*ish*, -*îsh*, the three derivative forms of the Infinitive are obtained; as:

سومك *sévmék* to love: 1. سومكلك *sévméklik* Loving, the action of loving.

یازمق *yazmaq* to write: 1. یازمقلق *yazmaqlîq* Writing, the action of writing.

2. $\sqrt{}$ سو *sév:* سومه *sévmé* Loving, the action of loving.

3. $\sqrt{}$ سو *sév:* سویش *sévish* Loving, the mood of loving.

§ 289. Turkish Infinitives and verbals are frequently used substantively, and when so used they can be declined like substantives, with or without the pronominal affixes.

Declension of the Infinitive.

N. سومك *sévmék* loving   A. سومكی *sévméyi*

G. wanting   L. سومكده *sévmékdé* in

D. سومكه *sévméyé* { for loving, to love }   A. سومكدن *sévmékdén* from } loving.

Declension of the first Derivative form.

N. سومكلك *sévméklik* loving

G. سومكلكك *sévmékliyiñ* of loving

D. سومكلكه *sévmékliyé* to loving

A. سومكلكی *sévmékliyi* loving

L. سومكلكده *sévméklikdé* in loving

A. سومكلكدن *sévméklikdén* from loving.

Declension of the second and third Derivative forms.

N.	سومه *sévmé*		سویش *sévish*		
G.	سوممنك *sévméniñ* of		سویشك *sévishiñ* of		
D.	سوممیه *sévméyé* to		سویشه *sévishé* to		
A.	سوممیی *sévméyi*		سویشی *sévishi*		
L.	سوممده *sévmédé* in		سویشده *sévishdé* in		
A.	سوممدن *sévmédén* from		سویشدن *sévishdén* from		

loving, the action or the mood of loving.

Note. The Plurals are not in common use.

§ 290. The first, second and third forms of these Verbal Derivative nouns are often used with the pronominal affixes; as:

1. یازمقلغم *yazmaqlighim* my
   یازمقلغك *yazmaqlighiñ* thy
   یازمقلغی *yazmaqlighi* his *writing.*

   یازمقلغمز *yazmaqlighimiz* our
   یازمقلغكز *yazmaqlighiñiz* your
   Not used *writing.*

2. یازمهم *yazmam* my
   یازمهك *yazmañ* thy
   یازمهسی *yazmasi* his *writing.*

   یازمهمز *yazmamiz* our
   یازمهكز *yazmañiz* your
   یازمهلری *yazmalari* their *writing.*

3. یازیشم *yazishim* my
   یازیشك *yazishiñ* thy
   یازیشی *yazishi* his *writing.*

   یازیشمز *yazishimiz* our
   یازیشكز *yazishiñiz* your
   یازیشلری *yazishlari* their *writing.*

§ 291. Turkish Infinitives govern nouns and pronouns, which are always put before them; the object is to be put in the nominatival form, if indefinite; and in the accusative if definite. This is the case also for Verbal nouns and Participles (§§ 83, Note, 251); as:

كتابی آچمق *kitabi achmaq* to open the book.

كتاب اوقومقلق *kitab oqoumaqliq* reading a book.

صو ایچمه *sou ichmé* drinking some water.

§ 292. The logical subject of the Infinitive is to be put in the Genitive case: or to use another expression,

the infinitive or verbal noun, if considered as a substantive, requires a noun or pronoun before it in the genitive. In the case of Pronouns this is not always necessary, as the affixed pronoun represents the logical subject; as:

كلمم ، بنم كلمم *bénim gélmém, gélmém* my coming.

ـسنك كلمكلكك *séniñ gélmékliyiñ* your coming.

افندمزك كلشى *eféndimiziñ gélishi'* the coming of our Lord.

§ 293. If the Infinitive is to be used as the object, it may be put in three different cases: With neuter verbs following it is always in the dative; with active verbs, if the object is definite, in the accusative; if indefinite, it assumes a nominatival form (§ 83, Note); as:

اوقومغه باشلامق *oqoumagha bashlamaq* to begin to read.

يازمه يلمز *yazma bilméz'* he does not know how to write.

يازمقلغى يلمز *yazmaqlighi bilméz* he does not know the writing.

§ 294. The first Derivative formed from the Infinitives denotes the act, the action. The negative of this form is composed in two ways:

يازمامقلق *yaz'mamaqliq* and يازمامزلق *yaz'mamazliq*

Méktoubon yazmamazliq étmé Don't fail to write the letter.

§ 295. But the negative, dative and ablative forms when used with some verbs mean to behave as if:

Gêôr'mémézlikden géldi, geôr'mémézliyé vourdou He pretended not to see.

Tanîmamazliq étmék To behave as if not acquainted.

§ 296. The second Derivative of the Infinitive is

يازمه ، سومه *sévmé', yazma'* the mode of writing, the manner of loving; loving, writing. Always accent the last syllable.

§ 297. The pronunciation and the spelling of this second form is just the same as that of the second person Imperative negative singular; but the accent is decisive. The second Derivative has the accent on the last syllable, while in the Imperative the penultimate (the syllable before the negative suffix) is accented:

يازمه *yazma'* writing, to write: *yaz'ma* don't write (thou).

سومه *sévmé'* loving, to love: *sév'mé* don't love (thou).

§ 298. The English Impersonal verbs and those verbs whose objects are not mentioned, but understood, are rendered in Turkish as follows. The subject of the Impersonal verb and *the object must be mentioned*; as:

yazî yazmaq to write.
geök gürlémék to thunder.
dikish dikmék to sew.
tütün ichmék to smoke.
yémék yémék to eat (food).
yaghmour yaghmaq to rain.
qar » to snow.
dolou » to hail.
shimshék chaqmaq to lighten.
ish ishlémék to work.

The Infinitive used as a Substantive.

§ 299. It has been several times mentioned that the Infinitive is regarded as a noun, and that, like a noun, it is liable to every kind of change which the noun undergoes (§ 289). The student will understand these peculiarities from the study of the following examples.

يازمق ايچون، يازمق اوزره *yazmaq ichin, yazmaq ûzré* for the purpose of writing.

يازمقسزين، يزمقسز *yazmaqsîzîn, yazmaqsîz* without or before writing.

يازمقله · آلمقله *yazmaq'la, almaq'la* by writing, by taking.

يازمه‌يه نيتى يوق *yazmaya niyéti yoq* he has no intention to write.

يازمقدن مقصدم *yazmaqdan' maqsédim* my intention in writing.

يازمقدن ايسه *yazmaqdan' isé*
يازمه‌دن ايسه *yazmadan' isé* } instead of writing.

دشمنى سومكده *dûshméni sévmékdé'* in loving the enemy.

كه‌مه‌دن، يازمه‌دن *gél'médén, yaz'madan* without, before coming, writting.

بزه كه‌مه‌دن كيتمه *bizé gél'médén git'mé* do not go before you come to see us.

دعا ايتمه‌دن *douva ét'médén* before prayer [praying].

يازمقده ايكن *yazmaqda' ikén* while I was writing.

كه‌مه‌سى اوزرينه *gélme'sî ûzériné* on his coming.

كه‌مه‌سيله كيتمه‌سى *gélmésiy'lé gitmési* his coming and going.

سويله‌يشى *séöyléyishi* his manner of speech.

§ 300. **The Continuative** tenses are formed from the Infinitive as in the following examples:

یازمقده‌درلر، یازمقده‌سکز، یازمقده‌یز، یازمقده‌در، یازمقده‌سین، یازمقده‌یم

yazmaqda'yim.   -'sin.   -'dir,   -'yiz,   -'siniz,   -'dirlar.
I am writing ...

یاغمور یاغمقده ایدی   *yaghmour yaghmaqda' idi* it was raining.

یمك یمکده ایمش   *yémék yémékdé' imish* I heard that) he was eating.

دیکیش دیکمکده ایسه   *dikish dikmékdé isé* if he is sewing.

قار یاغمقده   *qar'yagmaqda* it snows.

§ 301. Some of the derivatives of the second and third forms are used as common nouns (§ 443): as:

اوچورمه *ouchourma* a kite.	یاكیش *yañlish* a mistake.
ایصیتمه *isîtma* malaria.	طوغش *doghoush* birth.
باصمه *basma* print, calico.	یاپمه *yapma* made up.
بولمه *béôlmé* partition.	دوندورمه *dondourma* ice-cream.
دونانمه *donanma* { illumination. a fleet.	قزمه *qazma* a pickaxe.
شکرلمه *shékérlémé* sugar-plums.	یرمه *yarma* crushed wheat.
آلیش وریش *alish vérish* business transaction, trade.	قیزارتمه *qizartma* roasted meat.
قاوورمه *qavourma* fried meat.	اصمه *asma* hanging, a vine.

لغتلر Words.

p. روزگار *rûzgiar* wind.	اسمك *ésmék* to blow.
a. كاتب *kiatib* clerk.	كوجبلا *gûjbéla* hardly.
یتیشمك *yétishmék* to reach.	at. خیرلی *khayrli* better.
a. قادر *qadir* able.	a. تكلیف *téklif* proposition.
بکلمك *béklémék* to wait.	آنجق *anjaq* only.
پوسته‌خانه *posta-hané* post office.	a. مراد *mûrad* intention.
a. سبب *sébéb* reason.	a. تحصیل *tahsil* learning.

Proper Names: شاهین *Shahin.* احسان *Ihsan* Grant.

تعليم ٤١ Exercise 41.

۱ بنم مكتبه كيرمهم ٬ آنجق اوقومه يازمه تحصيل ايتمك ايچوندر ·

۲ بنم بو قلمی كسمهم ٬ سنك ايو يازی يازمقلغك ايچوندر · ۳ نيچون برادركزك مكتبدن كلمهسنی بكلهمكده سكز؟ اونك مكتبدن كلمهسنه دها برساعت وار در · ٤ سزی بو كون بوراده بكلهمهمزدن مرادمز آنجق سزكله كوروشمك ايچوندر · ٥ قوزوم ! بن بوراده يوغيكن ٬ آنجق سنك درسلرك چالشمهكی آرزو ايتمكدهيم · ٦ بو ايشی بكا يأپدرمقدن مقصديكز نه در؟ — بنم نيتم سزه پاره قازاندرمق در · پك اعلا ! قازان قازان وير قازانه · ۷ يككی يمدن مكتبه كيتمه ! چوق يه ٬ آزيه ! — ايش ايشلهمكسزين اكك يك هيچ طوغری دكلدر · ۸ اخشاملری نه ياپقدهسكز؟ — بن بر كتاب اوقومقده ٬ والدهم ديكيش ديكمكده ٬ پدرم توتون ايچمكده ٬ كوچول همشيرهم ده اويون اوينامقده در · ۹ بو كون پادشاهمزك طوغش كونی در · بو كيجه شهرمزده بيوك دونانمه وار در ·

ترجمه ٤۲   Translation 42.

1. Giving is better than taking. 2. Every ascent has its descent and every going has its coming. 3. I have no intention of [to] writing a letter to the father; have you? 4. To mount a donkey is a shame, to dismount another (two). 5. Nobility is [gained] by giving, bravery by killing. 6. The wind is blowing very hard. 7. Which is better, smoking tobacco or drinking coffee? — Neither of them is [not] useful for health. 8. Are those sugar-plums nice? — Yes, Sir! 9. This ice-cream is made of milk, ice and lemon. 10. This cup is made (*yapma*) in Germany. 11. Seal the letters and send them to the post-office; don't forget to seal them, seal and tie. 12. Why are these children crying? — I don't know the reason. 13. Don't go to see the teacher without

taking me.   14. To begin to read his lesson.   15. The days began to grow shorter.

مكالمه Conversation.

س) بر ترجمه‌یی حاضرلامق ایچون قاچ ساعت لازمدر؟

ج) افندم ! بو ترجمه او قدر قولای دكلدر · بونی حاضرلامق ایچون اوچ ساعت لازمدر.

س) بو چوجقلرك درس وقتنده كوزل جواب ویرمه‌لرینك سببی نه‌در.

ج) درسلرینه ایو چالشمه‌لری در.

س) اكر مرادك بكا ایولك ایتمك ایسه‌ ، بو ایشی بكا تكلیف ایتمه !

ج) بو تكلیفم زور بر شی دكلدر · سن اونی ایتمكه قادر سین.

س) آیش ویریشلر بو سنه نصالدر؟

ج) چوق ایی در.

س) پازار اخشامی هوا نصل ایدی ؟

ج) پك فورطونه‌لی ایدی · یاغمورلر یاغمقده ، كوكلر كوره‌مكده ، شیمشكلر چاقمقده وَ روزكارلر اسكده ایدی.

س) سز اولوقت نره‌ده ایدیكز؟

ج) باغده ایدك ! اخشام ساعت یاریده كوجبلا اوه یتیشمكه قادر اولدق.

درس ۲۰ Lesson 20.

The Finite Verb.

§ 302. Turkish verbs, like nouns, have two numbers: the singular and the plural. They have three persons, which do not vary for gender as they do in Arabic.

§ 303. **The Moods of the Verb.** In Turkish the verbs have six moods[1]: the Infinitive[2], the Imperative, the Indicative, the Assertive, the Narrative and the Conditional. The Infinitive, the Imperative and the Indicative are common to almost all languages; but the Assertive, Narrative and Conditional are peculiar to the Turkish.

---

[1] صورت *souret.* — [2] مصدر *masdar,* امریه *émriyé,* اخباریه *ikhbariyé,* شرطیه *shartiye.* روایت *rirayét,* حكایه *hikiayé,*

§ 304. **The Conjugation of Verbs.** All the Turkish verbs are conjugated in the same way, these being no irregular Verbs, except the Substantive defective verb 'to be'; but there are certain modifications required by the law of euphony which hold good in the inflections of the verbs as in those of other parts of speech. We employ as examples in each mood and tense the verbs سومك and يازمق, verbs which are generally used as models for the conjugation of all verbs, soft or hard.

§ 305. The Indicative mood has eight tenses and the three other moods seven each: they are as follows.

1. Present حال [1]   4. Dubitative ماضئ نقلى   7. Necessitative وجوبى

2. Aorist مضارع   5. Future مستقبل [2]   8. Suppositive فرضیه

3. Past ماضئ شهودى   6. Optative التزامى

§ 306. Of the six moods of the verb, the Infinitive has been fully described in the previous chapters.

§ 307. **The Indicative mood** is the simple conjugated form of the verb and is the basis of the other three compound moods. It has eight tenses.

§ 308. **The Compound moods,** the Assertive, Narrative and Conditional are formed by the aid of the three tenses of the substantive verb, which latter is called in Turkish the Auxiliary verb[3].

§ 309. **The Substantive verb** in general corresponds to the English verb 'to be', but it is defective. It has been mentioned several times in the previous chapters[4]; but it is useful to bring it in again here (§§ 65, 72, 73, 238).

---

[1] *Hal; Muzari, Maziyi shouhoudi; Maziyi naqli; Mûstaqbél; Iltizami, Vûjoubi; Farziyé.* — [2] The Imperative, Optative and Necessitative are really moods according to the European Grammarians. But they are not considered as moods according to the Turkish idea; they are *variations of the Future tense.* The Turkish language acknowledges only four moods as has been mentioned. — [3] فعل اعانه *Fiy'li-Ia'né.* — [4] *vide* §§ 65, 73, 238.

	Present	Past	Dubitative	Conditional
Terminations	م -im	دم = ايدم	ايمشم	سم = ايسهم
	-sin سين	دك = ايدك	ايمشـين	سك = ايسهك
	(در) -dir	دى = ايدى	ايمش	سه = ايسـ
	ز -iz	دك = ايدك	ايمشيز	سهك = ايسهك
	-siñiz سكز	ديكز = ايديكز	ايمشـكز	سهكز = ايسهكز
	-dirlér درلر	ديلر = ايديلر	ايمشـلر	سهلر = ايسهلر

§ 310. The Assertive mood, is used when the fact mentioned is asserted by the knowledge of the speaker; or it is stated on the authority of the speaker; he knows it of his own experience or knowledge, without depending upon hearing it from others; as:

كوچوكلكمده دائما اوقور ايدم *kûchûklûyûmdé dayima oqour idim* In my childhood I was always reading.

§ 311. This mood is obtained by adding to the third person singular of the tenses of the Indicative mood the past tense of the substantive verb. It has all the tenses of Indicative.

§ 312. **The Narrative Mood** is employed when a fact is stated, but not on the authority of the speaker. It is a hearsay or report founded on the statement of others (§ 238); as:

كوچوكلكمده چوق اوينار ايمشم *kûchûklûyûmdé choq oynar imishim.* (It is said that) I was playing much in my childhood.

دون مكتوبى يازمالى ايمشـكز *Dûn méktoubou yazmalî imishsiñiz* You ought to have written the letter yesterday (it is said).

§ 313. This mood is obtained by adding to the third person singular of the tenses of the Indicative mood the Dubitative or Perfect tense of the Substantive verb. It has all the tenses of Indicative save the Past.

§ 314. **The Conditional Mood.** This states the condition on which another action takes place, has taken place, or will take place. It corresponds to what is called in European languages the Subjunctive; as:

كلسه‘ ممنون اولورم *gélsé, memnoun olouroum* If he comes I shall be glad.

پاره‌م اولورسه‌ایدی سکا برایرا ویریرایدم *param oloursayidi saña bir lira vériridim* If I had money I would give you a pound.

§ 315. This mood is formed by adding to the third person singular of the tenses of the Indicative, the Conditional tense of the substantive verb.

It has all the tenses of the Indicative, except the Imperative.

§ 316. **The Imperative Mood.** صورتِ امريه

    Per. 1.   wanting

      2.   سو   *sév́* love thou

      3.   سوسون ، سوسین   *sévsin´* let him love

      1.   سوه‌لم   *sévélim* let us love

      2.   سویکز ، سویك   *séviñiz* } love you
                            séviñ }

      3.   سوسونلر ، سوسینار   *sévsinler* let them love!

    Per. 1.   wanting

      2.   یاز   *yaz´* write

      3.   یازسین ، یازسون   *yazsiñ´* let him write

      1.   یازه‌لم   *yazalim* let us write

      2.   یازیکز ، یازیك   *yaziñiz* } write you
                            yaziñ }

      3.   یازسونلر ، یازسینلر   *yazsînlar* let them write!

§ 317.   **The Negative.** نفیِٔ امر

Per. 1.   wanting

      2.   سومه   *sév́me* don't love

      3.   سومه‌سون ، سومه‌سین   *sév́mésin* let him not love

      1.   سومه‌یه‌لم   *sév́meyélim* let us not love

      2.   { سومه‌یك   *sév́méyiñ* }
               { سومه‌یكز   *sév́méyiñiz* } don't love

      3.   سومه‌سونلر ، سومه‌سینار   *sév́mésinlér* let them not love!

§ 317 a. The first person Singular is wanting. The root of the verb is the second person Imperative Singular, the plural of which is formed in two ways: *séviñ, yaziñ* is very common in speech; *séviñiz, yaziñiz* is used in literature and among literary people.

لغتلر Words.

f. غزته *gazéta* newspaper   at. ! زواللى *zéval'li!* poor!

a. ! كرم ايت *kérém ét!* please!   ! هايده *haydé!* Now then!

! هايدهك *haydéñ!* (used as pl.)   Let us go! Come along!

تعليم ٤٣ Exercise 43.

١ پدركه سويله ؛ بو كون بزه كلسون ٠ ٢ چوجوقلر مكتبه
كيتسونلر ٠ ٣ درسلركزى ايوجه اوكرنمكه چاليشيك ' بوش طورمهيك ٠
٤ هايده افنديلر ! آتلره بينهلم ' كزمكه كيدهلم ٠ ٥ كلمهسندن
كلمهمهسى خيرليدر ٠ بر آدم كوندهريكز كلمهسين ٠ ٦ كيت ' سؤال
ايت ' باقالم ساعت قاچدر ؟ كليسهيه كيتمك وقتى ميدر' دكلميدر ؟
اكر كليسه وقتى ايسه ' شاكردلرك هپيسى ده كليسهيه كيتسونلر ٠
٧ هايدهك برادرلر ' براز چابوق يورويهلم ٠ ٨ بوجهديهيى دكيشديريكز '
ايودكيلدر ٠ ٩ اوزومك اوقهسنى اوتوز پارهيه صاتيك ' زيادهيه صاتمهيك ٠

ترجمه ٤٤ Translation 44.

1. Where are you going? — I am going to the
doctor. — Why are you going to the doctor? — I have
malaria. I am going to show myself to the doctor.
2. What is the price of this calico? — It is four piastres
a yard. 3. It is raining: let us go home and read the
day's newspapers. 4. The flesh of those cattle is not
good for the health: let nobody eat it. 5. What are
the children doing? — They are reading their books.
6. Please call the maid-servant. 7. Bring me a little
fried meat and a piece of roast meat. 8. There is a
knife on the table.

مكالمه Conversation.

آغوب افندى ! نه ياپمقدهسكز ؟   بوكونكى درسمى حاضرلامقدهيم ٠

درس اوقومقدن خوشلانغقده ميسكز ؟   اوت افندم ! فقط پك يورغونم ٠

باشم پك زياده آغريمقده در .   بوش بوش نيچون اوطورمقده سين ؟

سيزى چاغيرمقده در افندم ' بويورك !   بو قيز چوجوغى كيمى چاغيرمقده در ؟

اوت افندم ! سايهٔ پادشاهيده اوقومغه وَ   عثمانليجه اوقومغه وَ يازمغه قادرميسكز ؟

يازى يازمغه قادرم .

اوت افندم ! سايهگزده قادرم .   تركجه سويلهيه بيلمكده ميسكز ؟

عزيز كتابدن هركون اوچ باب   پدر افندى شيمدى هانكى كتابى قرائت

اوقومقده در .   ايتمكده در ؟

يوقاريكى اوطهده درسمى اوكرنهكده   نرهده ايدك ؟ قارداشك ايكى ساعت در

ايدم .   سنى آرامقده در .

تعليم قرائت   Reading Exercise.

دينلر وَ مذهبلر   The Religions and Denominations.

ممالك شاهانهده بولونان دينلر: اسلاملق ' خريستيانلق و يهوديلك

ناملريله اوچدر . اسلاملر درت مذهبه آيرلمشلردر : حنفى ' حنبلى '

شافعى وَ مالكى . اسلاملرك بويوك قسمى حنفى مذهبندن در : تركلر

و كردلردن بعضيلرى حنفى درلر . عجملر ' قيزلباشلر وَ كردلردن بعضيلرى

شافعى درلر . عربلردن بعض قبيلهلر حنبلى وَ بعضيلر مالكى درلر .

هر كويده وَ شهرلرده جامعلر و اماملر وار در .

ممالك محروسهده بولونان خريستيانلر دخى باشليجه درت بويوك

مذهبلره آيرلمشلردر : پروتستان ' قاتوليك ' ارمنى وَ روم . هر خريستيان

كويلرده وَ شهرلرده كليسهلر وَ پاپاس وَ واعظلر وار در . يهوديلر پك

آز در . انجق استانبولده وَ ممالك شاهانهنك بعض شهرلرنده بولنورلر .

Transliteration.

Mémaliki Shahanédé boulounan[1] dinlér[2] Islamliq[3],
Khristiyanliq[4] vé Yéhoudilik[5] namlari[6] ilé uch dûr. Is-

Words.   1. found, existing.   2. religions.   3. Islamism.
4. Christianity.   5. Judaism.   6. names.

lamlar deôrt mézhébé[7] *ayrîlmîshlar dîr*[8]: *Hanéfi*[9], *Hanbali*[10], *Shafiyi*[11] *vé Maliki*[12]. *Islamlariñ beôyûk qîsmî*[13] *Hanéfi mézhébindén dir: Tûrklér vé Kûrdlérdén bazîlarî Hanéfi dirlér. Ajémlér*[14], *Qîzîl-bashlar*[15] *vé Kûrdlérdén bazîlarî Shafiyi dirlér. Arablardan bazî qabilélér*[16] *Hanbali vé bazîlar Maliki dirlér. Hér keôydé vé shéhirlérdé jamilér*[17] *vé imamlar*[18] *var dîr.*

Mémaliki Mahrousédé boulounan Khristiyanlar dakhi bashlîja deôrt beôyûk mézhébléré ayrîlmîshlar dîr: Protéstan, Qatolik, Erméni vé Roum. Hér Khristiyan keôylérdé vé shéhirlérdé kiliséler vé papas[19] *vé vayizlér*[20] *var dîr. Yéhoudîlér pék az dîr. Anjaq Istanbolda vé Mémaliki shahanéniñ bazî shéhirlérindé boulounourlar.*

7. denomination, sect; religious opinion; one of the four orthodox schools of opinions in Islam. 8. are divided. 9. the Hanéfi sect or school of Sunni Moslems, founded by Imam Ebou Hanifé. 10. The Hanbali sect, founded by Imam Ahméd ibni (son of) Hanbal. 11. The Shafiyi school or sect, founded by the great lawyer Muhamméd son of Idris, called Imam Shafiyi. 12. The school founded by Imam Malik. 13. part. 14. Persians. 15. Redheads: the non-Sunnite Turks (said in contempt as though worshipping the round red stone in Kérbéla, on which were beheaded Hassan and Hûséyin, the two sons of Caliph Ali; they are also called Alévee: i. e. followers of Ali, while the Hanéfees are called Sunnites). 16. tribes. 17. mosques. 18. a leader in public worship of Islam. 19. priest. 20. preacher.

---

٢١ درس Lesson 21.

زمان حال The Present Tense.

§ 318. In the formation of the tenses, the third person singular is first made by the addition of some suffix to the root of the verb. The other persons are made by the addition of the present tense of the Substantive verb. Every tense has its characteristic suffixes.

§ 319. The characteristic sign of the Present is the syllable يور *-yor* or ييور *-iyor*, which, added to the root of the verb, makes the third person singular of this tense (§ 54). The other persons are obtained by simply adding the present tense of the Substantive verb to the stem thus formed (§§ 309, 522).

yazîyor. يازىيور: ياز√، يازمق *oqouyor.* اوقويور، اوقو√: اوقومق

§ 320. *Note.* This tense is often called by English Grammarians the Present Progressive or Second Present Tense. It indicates that the action is going on *at the present moment*, while one is speaking; whereas the Aorist of the Indicative indicates that the action is *going on* but *is not over*, and is habitual. Hence the Aorist of the Indicative has often been regarded as the Present Tense of that mood; but it is not really so, as it expresses the action in an indefinite way, referring both to the present and the future (§ 328). Thus *yazîyoroum* means 'I write at the present moment, I am writing', just like the Continuative Present (§ 300) *yazmaqda'yim;* whereas *yazarim* means 'I write in general as a habit', or it conveys a promise, and then corresponds to 'I will write'.

§ 321. **1. Indicative Present.** حال اخباريه

سويپورم	*séviyoroum,*	I am loving,
سويپورسين	*séviyorsoun,*	thou art loving,
سويپور	*séviyor.*	he is loving,
سويپورز	*séviyorouz.*	we are loving,
سويپورسكز	*séviyorsoûnouz,*	you are loving,
سويپورلر	*séviyorlar.*	They are loving.

Potential Present. حال اقتداری

سوه بيليورم	*sévébili'yoroum,*	سوه بيليورز	*sévébili'yorouz,*
سوه بيليورسين	*sévébili'yorsoun,*	سوه بيليورسكز	*sévébili'yorsoûnouz,*
سوه بيليور	*sévébili'yor,*	سوه بيليورلر	*sévébili'yorlar.*

I am able to love etc. (lit. I know how to love).

The Negative Present. حال منفى

سومهيورم *sév'méyoroum* I am not loving, etc.

سوه مهيورم *sévé'méyoroum* I am not able to love, etc.

Interrogative Present. حال استفهامى

سويپورميسين؟ سويپورميم *sévi'yormouyoum? —mousoun?* Am
I loving?

سومه‌يورميم *sév'méyormouyoum?* Am I not loving?

سوه‌مه‌يورميم *sévé'méyormouyoum?* Am I not able to love?

---

§ 322.

2. Assertive Present (Imperfect). حال حكايه

The Assertive Present, which corresponds to the
Imperfect tense of the English, indicates that an action
had begun, but was not finished at the time spoken
of; as:

سويپور ايدم *sévi'yor idim,*   سويپور ايدك *sévi'yor idik,*

سويپور ايدك *sévi'yor idiñ,*   سويپور ايديكز *sévi'yor idiñiz,*

سويپور ايدى *sévi'yor idi,*   سويپور ايديلر *sévi'yor idilér.*

I was loving, thou wast loving, etc.

سومه‌يور ايدم *sév'méyor idim,* or —*oudoum* . . . I was not loving.

§ 323. 3. Narrative Present. حال روايت

سويپور ايعشم *sévi'yor imishim,*   سويپور ايعشيز *sévi'yor imishiz,*

سويپور ايعشسين *sévi'yor imish'sin,*   سويپور ايعشسكز *sévi'yor imishsiñiz,*

سويپور ايعش *sévi'yor imish,*   سويپور ايعشلر *sévi'yor imishlér.*

It is said that I was loving (I may have been loving).

§ 324.

4. Conditional (Subjunctive) Present. حال شرطى

سويپورسم *sévi'yorsam,*   سويپورسك *sévi'yorsak,*

سويپورسك *sévi'yorsañ,*   سويپورسكز *sévi'yorsañiz,*

سويپورسه *sévi'yorsa,*   سويپورسه‌لر *sévi'yorsalar.*

If I am loving, etc.

§ 325. Further:

يازيپورسه‌مده *yazi'yorsamda* I am writing, but —

يازمايور ايسه‌مده *yaz'mayor isémdé* I am not writing, but —.

Words. لغتلر

آفرين ! *aférin!* well done!   p.   چارشو ، چارشى *charshi* market   p.

قارين *qarîn* abdomen, stomach   قارنم آج *qarînm aj* I am hungry

طوق *toq* satisfied   صوسز *sousouz* thirsty

شدّتلى *shid'détli* violent   at.   عجله *ajélé* hasty, pressing   a.

قلم *qalém* a (government)   a.   نظامسز *nizamsîz* irregular   at.
office [(money)

بوزمق *bozmaq* to change   شمسيه *shémsiyé* umbrella.   a.

Exercise 45. تعليم ٤٥

۱ احمد افندى نره‌دن كلمكده سكز ؟ — مكتبدن كليورم
افندم ، سز نره‌دن كليورسكز ؟ — بن ده باغلار آراسنده كزمه‌دن
كليورم . ۲ اى كوچوك چوجوقلر ! اوراده نه ياپييورسكز ؟ — درس
اوكره‌نيورز ، افندم ! بوش اوطورمايورز . — آكر درسلركزه چاليشيور
ايسه‌كز ، آفرين سزه . ۳ كيمى آرايورسكز ؟ كيمه باقيورسكز ؟ —
چارشويه كوندرمك ايچون خدمتجى‌يى آرايورم . ٤ دون ساعت درتده نه
ياپييور ايديكز ؟ — هيچ برشى ياپمىورايدك ، آج ايدك يمك يه‌يور ايدك .
٥ شدتلو ياغمور ياغيور ، آكر شيمدى كله‌مه‌يور ايسه‌كز ، بر آزدن كليك !
ايشم پك عجله دكلدر . ٦ بنى مى چاغرييور ايديكز ؟ — اوت ، سنى
چاغرييوردم . چابوق كل وشو مكتوبى پوسته‌خانه‌يه كوتور . ۷ كاتب
افندى نره‌ده در ؟ — قلمده در چاليشيور . ۸ مملكتدن خبر
آلييورميسكز ؟ اورالر بو سنه ناصل ايمش ؟ — اوت ، افندم ! پدر افنديدن
هر هفته مكتوب آلييورم . هوالر چوق نظامسز ايمش . هر كون بوزيلييور
ايش . هر كون يا ياغمور ياغيور ايش يا قار .

Translation 46. ترجمه ٤٦

1. I am eating bread and drinking water; what art thou doing? — I am preparing myself to go to Iconium. 2. Thou art reading thy lesson: but thy classmates are not studying (working); they are lazy. 3. No, Sir, why do you say so? How hard they are working! But it is very difficult, they cannot do better. 4. Are they coming to our house to-morrow? — If they are coming tell them to bring my umbrella. 5. He was thirsty; you are hungry. — No, Sir, I am satisfied. 6. I wish to go to Smyrna, do you wish to see that city? 7. Can you change a mejidiyé for me? — I cannot change it; but if you can give me ten paras, I can give you four quarters. 8. The bread is very cheap now; they are giving an oke of it for 23 paras.

Conversation. مكالمه

خير افندم ! قارنم طوق ايسهده	نه ايستهيورسكز، قارنكز آج می؟
بن اونك قوقشوسیم. [صوسزم.	قواص مصطفی اغا سن میسین؟
اوت ؛ بعض دفعه آدم آدمه بكزهيور.	بربريكزه چوق بكزهيورسكز؟
اعلا صامسون توتونی ايچييورم.	نه جنس توتون ايچييورسكز؟
كونده بش سغارهدن زياده ايچمهيورم.	كونده قاچ سيغاره ايچهبيليورسكز؟
كله بيلير ايسهده، كلمك ايستهمهيور.	واعظ افندی سزه كلمهيورمی ؟
مطبخده بوش اوطوريور ايش.	خدمتجی نرهده ايدی؟
اويقوم كوزلرمدن آقيور، هيچ طورهمايورم.	نيچون بوقدر ارکن ياتييورسكز؟
كوتورهمم! ايكی حمال لازمدر.	بو ماللری چارشيدن اوه كوتوره بيليورميسكز؟
اويله بر نيق وار ايديسهده، شيمدی صاقايور، بابادن قالمه بر باغچه ايش.	مصطفی اغا باغچهسنی صاتيور می؟

Reading Exercise. تعليم قرائت

The Use of Animals. حيوانلرك بزه اولان فائدهلری

حيوانلرك بزه چوق فائدهسی وار در.

ایلك یرده حیوانلرك برچوغی بزم ییه‌جكلرمزی تدارك ایدییورلر ·
صیغیر ، طانه ، قویون ، كچی ، قوزو وَ اوغلاق كبی حیوانلرك ؛ وَ طاوق ،
قاز ، اوردك كبی قوشلرك اتلرینی یه‌یورز · آو اتلریله بالیقلر دخی بعض
لذیذ طعاملر یاپمغه قوللانیلیور ·

اینك ، كچی ، قویون وَ جاموس كبی حیوانلرك سودندن سودلی
قهوه ، سودلی چای ، سودلاج ، یوغورت وَ بونلر كبی بعض لذیذ طعاملر
یاپیلیور · بونلردن بشقه بونلرك سودیله تره یاغی وَ پینیر یاپیلمقده در ·
دیشی اشك سودینی ده حكیملر خسته‌لر ایچون پك چوق قوللانیورلر ·

Hayvanlariñ bizé olan ba'zî faydéléri.

Hayvanlariñ bizé pék choq faydési[1] var dir.

*Ilk yérdé hayvanlariñ bir choghou bizim yéyéjéklérimizi[2]
tédarik[3] édiyorlar. Sighir[4], dana[5], qoyoun, kéchi, qouzou
vé ovlaq[6] gibi hayvanlariñ; vé tavouq, qaz[7], eôrdék[8] gibi
qoushlariñ étlérini yéyorouz, av etlériylé baliqlar dakhi ba'zi
léziz[9] ta'amlar[10] yapmagha qoul'lanîliyor.*

*Inék, kéchi, qoyoun vé jamous[11] gibi hayvanlariñ
sûdûndén sûdlû qah'vé, sûdlû chay, sûdlaj[12], yoghourt[13]
vé bounlar gibi ba'zi léziz ta'amlar yapîliyor. Bounlardan
bashqa bounlariñ sûdûylé téré yaghî[14] vé péynir yapîlmaqda
dîr. Dishi[15] éshék sûdûnû dé hékimlér hastalar ichin pék
choq qoullaniyorlar.*

Words. 1. use, benefit. 2. food. 3. to prepare, procure.
4. cattle. 5. calf. 6. kid (§ 36). 7. geese. 8. duck. 9. delicious.
10. foods, *qoul'lanmaq* to use. 11. buffalo. 12. rice-milk. 13. thick
curds of milk, madzoun. 14. butter. 15. female.

---

۲۲ درس Lesson 22.

مضارع The Aorist.

§ 326. The characteristic sign of the Aorist of the
Indicative is the letter ر *ré* added to the root of the
verb, which forms the third person singular. The other

persons are formed by simply adding the abbreviated present of the Substantive Verb (§§ 52², 309).

§ 327. The vowel sound between the *re* and the root of the verb varies, being either *-ar, -ér; -ir, -îr; -our, -ûr*, and can only be learnt by practice or from a good dictionary. Ex.:

يِمك ، يَهمك	*yémék* to eat:	يِر	*yér* he eats
ديمك	*démék* to say:	ديِر	*dér* he says
اوتمك	*eôtmék* to sing (the bird):	اوتِر	*eôtér* he sings
باقمق	*baqmaq* to look:	باقار	*baqar* he looks
كلمك	*gélmék* to come:	كلِر	*gélir* he comes
آلمق	*almaq* to take:	آلِر	*alîr* he takes
اوطورمق	*otourmaq* to sit:	اوطورور	*otourour* he sits
اولمك	*eôlmék* to die:	اواور	*eôlûr* he dies.

§ 328. 1. Indicative Aorist. مضارع اخباريه

سَوَهرم	*sévé'rim*,	I love (habitually)	I shall love
سورسين	*sévér'sin*,	thou lovest »	thou wilt love
سَوَر	*sévér'*,	he loves »	he will love
سوهرز	*sévé'riz*,	we love »	we shall love
سورسكز	*sévér'siñiz*,	you love »	you
سورلر	*sévérlér'*,	they love »	they } will love.

The Potential Aorist. مضارع اقتدارى

سوهيلرم	*sévébili'rim*,	سوهيلرز	*sévébi'liriz*,
سوهيلرسين	*sévébilir'sin*,	سوهيلرسكز	*sévébilir'siñiz*,
سوهيلر	*sévébilir*,	سوهيلرلر	*sévébilirlér'*.

I am able to love, I can love ... I know how to love.

The Negative Aorist. مضارع منفى

سومم	*sévmém'*,	سومهيز	*sévmé'yîz*,
سومزسين	*sévméz'sin*,	سومزسكز	*sévméz'siñiz*,
سومز	*sévméz'*,	سومزلر	*sévmézlér'*.

I do not love or I shall not love ...

سوه‌مم *sévé'mém,*   سوه‌مه‌يز *sévé'méyiz,*

سوه‌مزسين *sévé'mézsin,*   سوه‌مزسكز *sévé'mézsiñiz,*

سوه‌مز *sévé'méz,*   سوه‌مزلر *sévé'mézlér.*

I am not able to love, I cannot love . . .

Interrogative Aorist. مضارع استفهامی

سومزميم؟ *sévméz'miyim?*   سومزميز ؟ *sévméz'miyiz?*

سومزميسين؟ *sévméz'misin?*   سومزميسكز ؟ *sévméz'misiñiz?*

سومز می ؟ *sévméz' mi?*   سومزلر می ؟ *sévmézlér' mi?*

Do I not love? dost thou not love? etc.

سورميم؟ سورميسين؟ *sévér'miyim?* -'*misiñ?* Do I love?

سوه‌مم می ؟ سوه‌مزميسين؟ سوه‌مز می ؟ } Am I not able to
sévé'mem mi? sévé'mézmisin? sévé'méz mi? } love?

مطالعات *Mûta-la-at* Remarks.

§ 329. I. The formation of the Negative Aorist is irregular, as is seen above.

§ 330. II. The use of the Aorist among the common people varies; as:

sévérim, **sévéñ,** *sévér;*   **sévérik,** *sévérsiñiz, sévérlér.*
sévmém, **sévméñ,** *sévméz;* **sévmézik,** *sévmézsiñiz, sévmézlér.*

§ 331. **The First Gerund.** When جه‌سنه *jésiné* is added to the third person singular it gives the meaning 'as if, intending to do'.

اويورجه‌سنه كوزلريني قاپادی *ouyour'jasîna gêôzlérini qapadî.* He shut his eyes pretending that he was sleeping.

سسی آليرجه‌سنه باغردی *sési alîr'jasîna baghîrdî.* He shouted out as loud as he could (take his voice).

§ 332. This *jésiné* is sometimes added to nouns, and signifies 'after the manner of, as, like'.

مردجه‌سنه طاورانيور ايدی *mérd'jésiné davranîyor oudou.* He was behaving himself in a manly way.

Eshék'jésiné baghîrdî. He cried out like an ass.

§ 333. **The Second Gerund.** Such English phrases as 'before coming, before going' etc. consisting of 'be-

fore' with a gerund, are rendered in Turkish in two ways: one by the use of the second derivative from the Infinitive, as has been mentioned above (§ 299). The other by appending دن -*dén* or دن اول -*dén évvél* to the third person singular of the Aorist, negative form; as:

بن كلمهدن كتمه *bén gélmédén gitmé* } Don't go before my

بن كلمزدن كتمه *bén gélmézdén gitmé* } coming.

بن سنى چاغيرمزدن اول كلمه *bén séni chaghîrmazdan év'vél gélmé.*
Don't come before (my calling you) = I call you.

§ 334. **The Third Gerund.** When the third person affirmative and negative come together a gerund results:

يازار يازماز *yazar yazmaz.* As soon as I (you, he) wrote.

gélir gélméz chaghîrdî. He called me as soon as he came.

2. The Assertive Aorist (Conjunctive). مضارع حكايه

§ 335. The Assertive Aorist, which is called by English scholars Past Habitual (corresponding to the Imparfait and Conditionnel tenses of French) indicates that one was formerly, in the habit of doing an action or that one would do it on condition of something else happening. Thus كلير ايدم *gélir idim* signifies either 'I used to come or I would come (if something else happened)'.

Baña bir lira vérirséñ choq mémnoun olour idim. If you would give me a pound, I should be very glad.

يازار ايدم *yazar idim*

يازار ايدك *yazar idiñ*

يازار ايدى *yazar idi*   } I used to write, I should write.

يازار ايدك *yazar idik*   I should have written, etc.

يازار ايديكز *yazar idiñiz*

يازار ايديلر *yazar idilér*

Negative and Interrogative.

سومزدم or سومزايدم *sévméz'idim, sévméz'dim; sévméz'idiñ* . .
I used not to love or would not love or would not have loved, etc.

سور‌میدم؟ *séver´miyidim?*   سومزمیدم؟ *sévméz´miyidim?*

Used I not to love? etc.   Did I not use to love? etc.

---

§ 336.

3. The Narrative Aorist. مضارع روايت

سور ایشم *sévér´ imishim,*   سور ایشیز *sévér´ imishiz,*

سور ایشسین *sévér´ imishsiñ,*   سور ایشسکز *sévér´ imishsiñiz,*

سور ایش *sévér´ imish,*   سور ایشلر *sévér´ imishlér.*

(They say that) I used to love. (Perchance) I love . . .

---

§ 337.

4. The Conditional Aorist. مضارع شرطی

سورسهم *sévér´sém,*   سورسهك *sévér´sék,*

سورسهك *sévér´séñ,*   سورسهکز *sévér´séñiz,*

سورسه *sévér´sé,*   سورلرسه *sévérlér´sé.*

If I love, If thou lovest, etc.

سومزسهم *sévméz´sém, -'séñ.* If I do not love . . .

§ 338. *Note.* The Conditional Aorist is abbreviated sometimes by omitting the characteristic *ré*, and then resembles greatly the Suppositive tense § 378; as: *sévsém, sévséñ, sévsé.*

§ 339. Further:

سورسه‌مده *séver´sémdé*   Though I love, yet —

سومزسه‌کده *sévméz´séñdé*   thou dost love, but —

هر کیم کایرسه *hér kim´ gélirsé*   whoever comes.

هر نه ائلورسه *hér né´ oloursa*   whatever it may be.

کایرسه‌ده کلمزسه‌ده *gélir´sédé gélméz´sédé* whether he comes or not.

§ 340. When two or more verbs follow one another in the same tense, number and person, the personal ending is generally omitted in all but the last:

یر ایچر و کزهرم *yér, ichér vé gézérim* for *yérim, ichérim vé gézérim.* I eat, drink and promenade.

Pédér hér akh'sham sizé gidiyor vé yarî géjéyédék otourou-
yoroudou, for *gidiyoroudou.* My father used to go every night
to your house and stay there till midnight.

Words. لغتلر

p. که *ki* that

a. مسافر *mûsafir* guest

p. اکر *éyér* if

a. تکرار *tékrar* again

a. طرف *taraf* place, side

اويله يا ! *eôylé ya!* certainly!

a. سنبل *sûnbûl* hyacinth

صاچمق *sachmaq* to spread

a. موسم *mévsim* season

سورمك *sûrmék* to plough

اکمك *ékmék* to sow

يازين *yazin* in the summer.

تعليم ٤٧   Exercise 47.

۱ خواجه افندی ساعت قاچده مکتبه تشریف ایدر؟ — هرکون
آلافرانقه ساعت طقوزده کلییور ایدی ایسه ده ٔ بیلمم که : بوکون
کایر می کلمز می؟ اونده بر مسافری وار ایمش ٠ ۲ اکر خواجه کز اول
وقت کلیرسه ٔ کم ایت شو کتابی کندیسنه ویر ٠ اما اکر کلمزسه ٔ
تکرار بکا کوندر ٠ — پك اعلا ! خواجهم کلیر کلمز ٔ کتاب کزی
ویریرم ٠ لکن کلمزسه سزه کونده ریرم ٠ ۳ بن ترکجه بیلیرم ٔ هم یازار هم
اوقورسه مده چابوق سویله یه مم ٠ سن هم صو کبی اوقویه بیلییور هم
کوزل سویله یه بیلییورسین ٠ ٤ بن سنی اوچ یاشنده ایکن بیلیرم ٠ هیچ
طورماز آغلار ٔ چاغیریر ٔ باغیریر ایدك ٠ ٥ شو بهار موسمی نه کوزل بر
موسمدر ! هر طرف کوکر ٔ آغاجلار چیچکله نیر ٔ کللر ٔ سنبللر و بشقه
چیچکلر آچیلیر ٔ هر طرفه کوزل قوقولر صاچارلر ٠ ٦ چیفتجیلر بهارین
و کوزین سوردرلر و اکرلر ٠ اکر سورمزلر و اکزلرسه ٔ یازین و قیشین اللرینه
بر شی کچمز ٠ ۷ «یاره یی آلمازدن کیمسه کیمسه یه مال ویرمز» ٠

ترجمه ٤٨ Translation 48.

1. I know Armenian. Thou knowest German. Does he know Greek? 2. Before you came here, you did not know us (assertive). 3. Before seeing the property (*mal*), I cannot give the money, but if I see and approve, I will give the money. — Well, Sir, if I can make you like it, then I hope you will pay. — 4. At what o'clock do you go to bed? — I eat at 12 o'clock Turkish time, and lie down at 3 o'clock, in summer, but in winter I eat at one o'clock and go to bed at five. Sometimes, if I have guests, I sit up until six o'clock. 5. I do not do so! I eat early and I retire early. I rise early in the morning. While others are sleeping, I read and write my lesson. Sometimes in the fresh morning air I take a walk in the field. 6. Well done! my boy; you do well. 7. Can you ride on horseback? — Yes, I can (ride), but you cannot ride. 8. What do they call this boy? — They call him Néjib.

مكالمه Conversation.

بو كويه بوياجى كوبى ديرلر ·	بو كويه نه ديرلر؟	[ايش؟]
اون كونه قالماز كلير ايش ·	قوكشوكز حجازدن نه وقت كلير	
كلمز دييورلر ·	اون كوندن اول كلمز مى؟	
اون لبرادن اشاغىيه ويره مزلر ·	شو آتى قاچه صاته بيلبرلر؟	
اوقورلر ، يازارلر ، درس ويريرلر ·	چوجوقلر مكتبده نه ياپارلر؟	
پك اىى افندم ! كونده ريرم ·	خدمتجى كلير كلمز بكا كونده رير	
	نيسين؟	[ايديكيز؟]
شو قارشيده كى اوده اوطورمقده ايدك ·	سز بو آوه كلمزدن نره ده اوطورور	

تعليم قرائت Reading Exercise.

حيوانلرك سسلرى Voices of Animals.

بوتون حيوانلرك كنديارينه مخصوصى سسلرى وار در ، وَ اول سسى
كوسترمك ايچون ده برر تعبيرلرى وار در : مثلا —

آت كيشنر' اشك آكيرير' اينك بوكورور' آرسلان كوموردَر'
آيو خوموردار' قورد اولور' كوپك حاولار' تيلكى اينجه بر سسله
سيكيلر' قويون وَ كچى مهلر' كدى مياولر' خروس اوتر' طاوق
غيداقلر' پيليجلر وَ اوفاق قوشلر جيويلدر' هند طاوغى غولوغولو ايدر'
پاپاغان لاقيردى ايدر' كوكرجين دم چكر' بلبل شاقير' اوردك واق
واق ايدر٠

Hayvanlariñ sésléri.

Bûtûn hayvanlariñ kéndîlériné makh'sous[1] sesleri var dîr, vé ol sési géostérmék ichin dé birér ta'birléri[2] var dîr; Méséla.[3] —

At Kishnér[4], éshék añîrîr[5], inék béôyûrûr[6], arslan géômûrdér[7], ayî khomaurdar[8], qourd oulour[9], kéôpék havlar[10], tilki injé bir séslé siñilér[11], qoyoun vé kéchi mélér[12], kédi miyavlar[13], khoros éôtér[14], tavouq gîdaqlar[15], pilijlér vé oufaq qoushlar jivildér[16], hind tavoughou[17] goulou goulou édér[18], papaghan[19] laqîrdi édér[20], géôyérjin[21] dém chékér[22], bûlbûl[23] shaqîr[24], éôrdék vaq vaq édér[25].

Words. 1. Especial. 2. term. 3. for instance. 4. *Kishnémék* to whinny. 5. *añîrmaq* to bray. 6. *béôyûrmék* to moo. 7. *géômûrdémék* to roar. 8. *Khomûrdamaq* to growl. 9. *ouloumaq* to howl. 10. *havlamaq* to bark. 11. *siñilémék* to squeak. 12. *mélémék* to bleat. 13. *miyavlamaq* to mew. 14. *éôtmék* to crow. 15. *gîdaqlamaq* to cackle. 16. *jivildémék* to chirp. 17. turkey (Indian) hen. 18. to gobble. 19. parrot. 20. to chatter. 21. pigeon. 22. to coo. 23. nightingale. 24. *shaqîmaq* to warble. 25. to quack.

درس ٢٣ Lesson 23.

ماضيلر The Past Tenses.

§ 341. There are two tenses denoting the Past.

§ 342. One is the Categorical Preterite called by the natives *Maziyi shouhoudi* 'eye-witness past', which depicts the speaker as having been present or as having witnessed something with his own eyes, so as to know it for certain without any doubt. Hence it corresponds

with the compound tense formed with the Past Participle and the auxiliary verb 'To have'. For instance *yazdî*, not only means *he wrote* (in the presence of the speaker), but also *he has written*.

It may also be translated by the English Past, formed with *did*; as: *yazdî mî?* Did he write? — *yazdî*, he did write.

§ 343. The other is the Dubitative Past, *Maziyi naqli* implying or expressing doubt. The speaker is not sure about the matter, he may have heard it from others. This tense can be correctly used only when the truth of an assertion is not guaranteed, and when the speaker means to state that he believes what he says, but cannot vouch for it; as: *yazmish* 'he wrote (as others say) he has written (I believe), I am not sure about it'. This tense is used in telling stories of the past or anecdotes which the speaker has heard from others or read in books.

1. Indicative Past. ماضئ شهودى

§ 344. The characteristic sign or suffix of the Past tense is دى -*dî, -di* in the third person. For the first person plural it is دك -*dik* for the soft vowels and دق -*diq* for the hard ones.

يازدم *yazdîm'*,	سودم *sévdim'*,	
يازدك *yazdîñ'*,	سودك *sévdiñ'*,	
يازدى *yazdî'*,	سودى *sévdi'*,	I wrote, I did write, I have written . . .
يازدق *yazdîq'*,	سودك *sévdik'*,	I loved, etc.
يازديكز *yazdîñiz'*,	سوديكز *sévdiniz'*,	
يازديلر *yazdîlar'*.	سوديلر *sévdilér'*.	

Potential Past. ماضئ اقتدارى

سوه يلدم *sévébildim'*,	سوه يلدك *sévébildik'*,	
سوه يلدك *sévébildiñ'*,	سوه يلديكز *sévébildiñiz'*,	I was able to love . . .
سوه يلدى *sévébildi'*,	سوه يلديلر *sévébildilér'*.	

Negative and Interrogative.

سومهدم *sév'médim* I did not love.   سوههدم *sévé'médim* I was not able to love.

يازدم مى؟ *yazdîm' mî?* Did I write?   سودم مى ؟ *sévdîm' mî?* Did I love?

yaz'madîm mî? Did I not write?   *yaza'madîm mî?* Was I not able to write?

§ 345. **The Fourth Gerund.** A very common expression is formed by adding ده *-da, -dé* to the first person plural of the Past, thus indicating when an action is performed.

چان چالندقده هركس اوطورسون يازدقده *yazdîqda* when he wrote. *chan chalîndîqda hér kés otoursoun* when the bell is rung every body must sit down.

§ 346. **The Fifth Gerund.** By adding وجه *-jé* to the same person, another kind of gerund is made, which corresponds to *in proportion as, the more — the more:*

كتابى اوقودقجه سويبورم *kitabî oqoudouq'ja séviyoroum.* The more I read the book the more I like it.

اثوابك كيدكجه خوشلانهجقسين *esvabîñî géydikjé hoshlanajaqsin.* The more you weare your dress the more you will like it.

§ 347. **After** with a Participle, is rendered in Turkish by the addition of دن صوكره *-dén soñra* to the same person as:

بن اولدكدن صوكره *bén êôldûkdén soñra* after my death.

بن يازدقدن صوكره *bén yazdîqdan soñra* after I wrote.

Méktoubou yazdî, vé yazdîqdan soñra méôhûrlédi. He wrote the letter, and after writing he sealed it.

§ 348. **Further:**

Eoyrénémédik gitdi. At last we were not able to learn.
Séôylédim gitdi. At last I have spoken.

2. Assertive Past. حكايهٔ ماضئ شهودى

§ 349. The Assertive Past, which is called in English the Pluperfect, is made in two ways, one by adding the Past tense of the Substantive Verb to the

third person of the Past tense and the second by adding the third person of the Past of the Substantive Verb to the Past tense.

سودم ايدى *sévdim idi,*	سودى ايدم *sévdi idim,*
سودك ايدى *sévdiñ idi,*	سودى ايدك *sévdi idiñ,*
سودى ايدى *sévdi idi,*	سودى ايدى *sévdi idi,*
سودك ايدى *sévdik idi,*	سودى ايدك *sévdi idik,*
سوديكز ايدى *sévdiñiz idi,*	سودى ايديكز *sévdi idiñiz,*
سوديلر ايدى *sévdilér idi,*	سودى ايديلر *sévdi idilér.*

I had loved (I am sure), Thou hadst loved.

Note. The Narrative Mood is wanting.

---

§ 350.

3. Conditional Past. ماضئ شهودئ شرطى

It is made in two ways, as in the Assertive Mood.

يازدم ايسه *yazdĭm isé,*	يازدق ايسه *yazdiq isé,*
يازدك ايسه *yazdiñ isé,*	يازديكز ايسه *yazdiñîz isé,*
يازدى ايسه *yazdĭ isé,*	يازديلر ايسه *yazdilar isé.*

If I have written, If thou hast written ...

Further:

سودم ايسهده *sévdim isédé*	I loved, but —.
آلهمادم ايسهده *alamadim isédé*	I was not able to take, but —.
كيم يازدى ايسه *kim yazdi isé*	whoever may have written.

The Dubitative Past. ماضئ نقلى

§ 351. The characteristic sign or suffix of this tense is مش *-mîsh, -mîsh, -mûsh, -moush,* according to the dominant vowel. The formation of the persons is regular.

§ 352. **1. Indicative Dubitative.** نقلئ اخباريه

سومشم *sévmi'shim,*	سومشيز *sévmish'iz,*
سومشين *sévmish'sin,*	سومشكز *sévmish'siñiz,*

سومش در *sévmish' (dir)*,   سومشلردر *sévmishlér' (dir)*.

I loved, I have loved (it is said) ...

Potential Dubitative.   نقلئ اقتدارى

يازه يلمشم *yaza bilmish'im*,   يازه يلمشيز *yaza bilmish'iz*,

يازه يلمشسين *yaza bilmish'sin*,   يازه يلمشسكز *yaza bilmish'siñiz*,

يازه يلمش در *yaza bilmish' (dir)*,   يازه يلمشلردر *yaza bilmishlér' (dir)*.

(They say that) I was able to write ...

Negative and Interrogative Forms.

يازمامشم *yaz'mamishîm*, سومهمشم *sévmémishim* I did not write,
                 ... love

يازهمامشم *yaz'amamishîm* I was not able to write

يازمش ميم *yazmishmiyim?* -*'misin?* .. Did I write?

يازهمامشميم *yaza'mamishmiyim?* Was I not able to write?

as it was said or reported.

§ 353. 2. Assertive Dubitative.   نقلئ حكايه

سومش ايدم *sévmish idim*,   سومش ايدك *sévmish idik*,

سومش ايدك *sévmish idiñ*,   سومش ايديكز *sévmish idiñiz*,

سومش ايدى *sévmish idi*,   سومش ايديلر *sévmish idilér*.

I had loved (I am sure), Thou hadst loved.

§ 354. 3. Narrative Dubitative.   نقلئ روايت

سومش ايمشم *sévmish' imishim*,   سومش ايمشيز *sévmish' imishiz*,

سومش ايمشسين *sévmish' imishsin*,   سومش ايمشسكز *sévmish' imishsiñiz*,

سومش ايمش *sévmish' imish*,   سومش ايمشلر *sévmish' imishlér*.

(They say that) I have loved, etc.

§ 355. 4. Conditional Dubitative.   نقلئ شرطى

سومش ايسهم *sévmish' isém*,   سومش ايسهك *sévmish' isék*,

سومش ايسهك *sévmish' iséñ*,   سومش ايسهكز *sévmish' iséñiz*,

سومش ايسه *sévmish' isé*,   سومش ايسهلر *sévmish' isélér*.

If I loved (as they say), (as others say).

Yaz'mamish isém, -*iséñ* If I had not written (as others say).

11*

§ 356.   Further:

يازمش اولسهم   *yazmish olsam* If I had written.

آلمش اولسهلر   *almîsh olsalar* If they had taken.

لغتلر   Words.

سوپورمك	*sûpûrmék* to sweep	سعادتلی a.t.	*sa'adétly* happy
اعلاج a.	*ilaj* medicine	تلغراف f.	*télégraf* a telegram
اوكسورمك	*eôksûrmék* to cough	درد p.	*dérd* affliction,
يوله چيقمق	*yola chîqmaq* to start, to set out, to sail.		sickness
		گری	*géri* back
دكيرمن	*déyirmén* mill	دیو'دی	*déyi* saying

ايصيتمه طوتمق   *îsîtma* or *sitma toutmaq* to suffer from malaria.

تعلیم ٤٩   Exercise 49.

١ نجيب افندی بو كون استانبوله كيتمك ايچون يوله چيقدی · ٢ عجبا شاكر افندی نه وقت كيتدی ' بيليرميسكز ؟ — دون كيتمش در ديو ايشيتدم · ٣ دون درسكی چوق كوزل اوقومش سين ! ايشيتدم ده پك شاذ اولدم · ٤ بو نه قدر ضعيفلنمش سين ؟ دردك نه در ؟ — خستهيم ايكی كوندن برو ايصيتمه طوتيورم · ٥ نه ياپدك اعلاج آلدك می ؟ — خير ! حكيمه خبر كوندردم ' چوجوقلر كيتمشلر ' آرامشلر ' آرامشلر ' بولهمامشلر · ٦ بو اوطهيی كيم سوپورهمشدر ؟ — نه وار كه ؟ — كيم سوپورمش ايسه هيچ ايی سوپورهمهمشدر · — اويله ايسه خدمتجی قيز كلسون وَ تكرار سوپورسون · — باش اوستنه افندم · ٧ پدرم والدهمدن تلغراف آلمش ' ايكی كوندن كلييور ايمش · — والده خانم نره يه كيتمش ايدی ؟ — مايس آينده ازميره كيتمشدی · ٨ نوازل اولمشم · حكيم تره ديدی · تره لهمك ايچون چوق چاليشدم ايسهده تره لهيهمهدم كيتدی · ٩ يه ! يدكجه اشتاهك كاير ·

ترجمه ٥٠   **Translation 50.**

1. What has he planted in the garden? — He
has planted there some lilies, potatoes and tomatoes.
2. Whose brother has two small knives? 3. It is reported [they say] that a man was killed yesterday in
the town. 4. [They say] some one has been killed
this week at the mill. 5. When did the ship sail? —
She sailed on the first day of the month. 6. The mail
from Samsoun arrived this morning. 7. Did you see
my father? No, Sir, I waited for him in the market
but I could not see him. My brother James saw him
yesterday. 8. The more you learn the happier you
are. 9. The more you advise him the angrier he gets.
10. When your brother comes from the town, please
let me know.

مكالمه   **Conversation.**

س) استانبول شهری میلادك هانكی تاریخنده¹ وَ کیمك واسطه‌سیله² فتح³
اولونغشدر؟

ج) میلادك ١٤٥٣ تاریخنده فاتح⁴ سلطان محمد الی اوچ کونلك بر
محاصره‌دن⁵ صوكره فتح ایله‌مشدر . بونی جیبونك «رومانك زوالی⁶»
نام⁷ تاریخنده اوقودم .

س) عثمانلیلر ویانه‌یی قاچ دفعه وَ هانكی تاریخلرده محاصره ایتمشلر در؟
بیلیرمیسكز؟

ج) عثمانلی تاریخنده کوردم که : ایكی دفعه محاصره ایتمشلر: بری قانونی
ساطان سلیمانك⁸ قوماندهسی⁹ آلتنده ١٥٢٩ ده ، وَ دیكری وزیر¹⁰
قره مصطفی پاشانك قوماندهسی آلتنده ١٦٨٣ تاریخنده محاصره ایتمشلر در.
موی الیه¹¹ مرزیفوندن یاریم ساعت اوته‌ده بولونان مارینجه قریه‌سی
اهالیسندن¹² بر اودونجینك اوغلی ایدی .

Words. 1. a. *tarikh* date, history. 2. a. *vasita* hand, means.
3. *fet-h étmék* to conquer. 4. *fatih* conqueror (§ 601). 5. *mouhaséré* siege (§ 618). 6. *zéval* fall. 7. p. *nam* name. 8. *Qanouni
Soultan Suléyman* Sultan Suleyman, the Lawgiver (1520—66). 9. *qomanda* commandership. 10. *vézir* vizier. 11. *moumayiléh* His Excellency [the person refered to, i. e. the latter]. 12. *éhali* inhabitants.

س) سلطان سليمانك نه قدر عسكرى وار ايدى وَ اولوقت غِجه ايمپراطورى كيم ايدى ؟

ج) سلطان حضرتلرينك ١٣ ٢٥٠ بيك عسكرى وار ايدى . اول وقت غِجه ' (يعنى آلامانيه وَ آويستريا ايمپراطورى) مشهور بشنجى قارولوس ايدى . قارولوسك اسمندن عثمانلولر خرستيان حكمدارلرينه ١٤ قرال نامنى ٧ ويرديلر .

س) اينجيل شريف ١٥ تركجه‌يه ايلك دفعه نه وقت وَ نرده‌ه ترجمه وَ طبع ١٦ اولونغشدر؟

ج) اون يدنجى عصرك صوكلرنده ١٧ استانبولده مهتدى ١٨ على بك ترجمه ايتمش وَ ١٨١٩ ده پاريسده انكليز كتابِ مقدّس شركتنك ١٩ همّتيله ٢٠ طبع اولونغشدر .

13. *hazrétléri* His Majesty. 14. *hukûmdar* ruler. 15. *Injili Shérif* the Holy Gospel. 16. *tab* printing. 17. towards the end of the 17th century. 18. a pervert to Islam. 19. *Ingiliz Kitabî Mouqad'dés shirkéti* B. & F. B. Society. 20. *him'métiylé* through the assistance, by.

Proper Names: Jibon Ed. Gibbon. *Qarolos* Charles V.

درس ٢٤ Lesson 24.

مستقبل The Future Tense.

§ 357. The Future tense in Turkish corresponds to that of the English language; with this difference, that it simply asserts what will happen, without making a promise, which is always rendered by the Aorist.

§ 358. The Categorical Future is made by adding ه ، ـه -*é*-, -*a*- to the verbal root, if it ends in a consonant; and يه -*yé*-, -*ya*- if it ends in a vowel; and afterwards جك -*jék* is added if the verbal root is soft and جق -*jaq* if *it* is hard (53):

اوطوره‌جق ، اوطوره√ ، اوطور√ ، اوطورمق   *otourajaq*

ايسته‌يه‌جك ، ايسته‌يه ، ايسته√ ، ايسته‌مك   *istéyéjék*

كيده‌جك ، كيده ، كيت√ ، كيتمك   *gidéjék.*

§ 359. *Note.* The radical endings تْ *-t*, ق *-q*, كْ *-k*, are changed into د *-d-*, غ *-gh-*, -*y*-, when followed by a vowel: § 52², 88.

§ 360. 1. Indicative Future. مستقبل أخباريه

يازه‌جغم *yazaja'-ghîm,*	ايسته‌يه‌جكم *istéyéjé'-yim,*
يازه‌جقسين *yazajaq'-sîn,*	ايسته‌يه‌جكسين *istéyéjék'-sin,*
يازه‌جق در *yazajaq' (dîr),*	ايسته‌يه‌جك در *istéyéjék' (dir),*
يازه‌جغز *yazaja'-ghîz,*	ايسته‌يه‌جكز *istéyéjé'-yiz,*
يازه‌جقسكز *yazajaq'-sîñîz,*	ايسته‌يه‌جكسكز *istéyéjék'-siñiz,*
يازه‌جقلر در *yazajaq-lar' (dîr).*	ايسته‌يه‌جكلر در *istéyéjék-lér' (dir).*

I shall write, thou will —.   I shall ask, thou will ask ...

Negative and Interrogative.

يازمايه‌جغم *yaz'mayajaghîm,-sîn...*	I shall not write...
يازه‌مايه‌جغم *yaza'mayajaghûm...*	I shall not be able to write...
يازه‌جق‌ميم؟ *yazajaq'mîyîm?*	Shall I write?
يازمايه‌جق‌ميم؟ *yaz'mayajaqmîyîm?*	Shall I not write?
يازه‌مايه‌جق‌ميم؟ *yaza'mayajaqmîyîm?*	Shall I not be able to write?

§ 361. 2. Assertive Future. مستقبل حكايه

Assertive Future or Imperfect Future signifies that an action was going to take place in the past, Present, or future.

يازه‌جق ايدم *yazajaq idim,*		يازه‌جق ايدك *yazajaq idik,*	
يازه‌جق ايدك » *idiñ,*		يازه‌جق ايديكز » *idiñiz,*	
يازه‌جق ايدى » *idi,*		يازه‌جق ايديلر » *idilér.*	

I was about to write, (yesterday, to-day or to-morrow).

Note. This tense is often written and pronounced in the following manner:

يازه‌جقدم ، سوه‌جكدك *yazaja'ghîdim, séréjé'yidiñ...*

§ 362. 3. Narrative Future. مستقبل روايت

سوه‌جك ايشم *sévéjék imishim,*   سوه‌جك ايشز *sévéjék imishiz,*

سوه‌جك ايشسين » *imish'sin,*   سوه‌جك ايشسكز » *imishsiñiz,*

سوه‌جك ايش » *imish,*   سوه‌جك ايشلر » *imishlér.*

[They say that] I was about to love . . .

---

§ 363. 4. Conditional Future. مستقبل شرطى

سوه‌جك ايسه‌م *sévéjék isém,*   سوه‌جك ايسه‌ك *sévéjék isék,*

سوه‌جك ايسه‌ك » *iséñ,*   سوه‌جك ايسه‌كز » *iséñiz,*

سوه‌جك ايسه » *isé,*   سوه‌جك ايسه‌لر » *isélér.*

or *sévéjéyisém, sévéjéyiséñ; yazajaghîsaq, yazajaghîsañiz* . . .
If I shall love, If I am to love . . .

§ 364. Further:

يازه‌جق ايسه‌مده *yazajaq isémdé* I shall write, but —.

كوره‌مه‌يه‌جك ايسه‌كده *geôréméyéjék isékdé* We shall not be able to see, but —.

يورويه‌مه‌يه‌جك ايسه‌كزده *yeôrûyéméyéjék iséñizdé* You will not be able to walk, but —.

Words. لغتلر

كيفلنمك *kéyflénmék* to be delighted

ييل باشى *yil bashi* New-Year's-Day

واعظ .a *vayiz* preacher

بيك باشى *biñ bashi* major

ميرآلاى *miralay* colonel

يايلا *yayla* summer-residence

صيق *siq* thick

هانيا؟ *haniya?* where is it?

يعنى .a *yani* that is to say

يالديزلى *yaldîzlî* gilt

سيرك *séyrék* sparse

كوپرى *keôprû* bridge

كوروشمك *geôrûshmék* to visit

فاميلياجق *familyajaq* with the whole family.

Exercise 51. تعليم ٥١

۱ يارين باغلر آراسينه كيده‌جكز . باغلرى كورورسه‌ك چوق كيفلنه‌جكز . ۲ يارين ييل باشى‌ يعنى ١٩٠٣‌ سنه‌سنك كانون

ثانيسنك بری در ۰ واعظ افندی بزلره برر يالديزلی انجيل شريف و ايكيشر تصوير ويرهجك در ۰ ۳ بن شيمدی اوه كيدييورم ٬ سز نه يه كيدهجكسكز ؟ ٤ بز بو سنه يازين فاميلياجق بريره چيقمق ايستهيورز — هانكی طرفه طوغری كيتمك ايستهيورسكز ؟ ٥ شو قارشيدهكی قارلی بوزلو طاغلره و صيق اورمانلقلره طوغری كيتمك نيتنيندهيز۰ اورالرده اولر پك سيرك در ۰ ظن ايدهرم بيك باشی و ميرآلای افنديلر دخی فاميلياجق اورايه كيدهجكلر ۰ ٦ بز اورمانلقلره كيدهميهجك ايميشيز۰ بابام بشقه يره كيتمكه سوز ويرمش ۰ ٧ اكر يادين بزم اوه كلهجك ايسهكز٬ اوده قالهجق و سزی بكلهيهجكم ۰ ٨ ايشيتديكز می ؟ دون آق كوپری ييقلمش ۰ بزم برادر آز قالمش صويه دوشهجك بوغولهجق ايمش ۰ ٩ آج ميسين؛ صوسز ميسين٬ اويقوسز ميسين ؟

ترجمه ٥٢   Translation 52.

1. Who will come to visit us to morrow? — I believe that my sister Eliza will pay us a visit. 2. In the Psalms (مزمورلر *mézmourlar*) David says: Thou will show me the path of life. 3. Mrs. Mary loved her children and is loved by them. 4. As soon as I hear, I shall let you know. 5. You shall not go to the gardens. I will not allow it. 6. I shall write a few lines before I go to supper. 7. Shall I give him so much? No, Sir, he is asking too much. 8. Would Anna read such a dirty paper? — She could read others more dirty than that. 9. If I could (give), I would give you five pounds, but I cannot give [it]. 10. Where will he go? — If he finds a horse, he will go to the summer-residence.

مكالمه   Conversation.

س) بو كون پدر افنديدن مكتوب آلهبيلهجكميسكز ؟

ج) استانبول پوستهسی كايرسه ظن ايدهرم بر مكتوب آلهجغم ۰

س) صرّاف اون ليرهيى بردن بوزهبيلهجكمى ؟

ج) اوت افندم ! بوزهرم ديوخدمتجى ايله خبر كوندرمش .

س) بورادن چيقارسه كز ؛ نرهيه كيدهجكسكز ؟

ج) هيچ بر يره كيدهمهيهجكم ؛ اوطهجغمه كيدهجك وَ درسمى حاضرلايهجغم .

س) عموجهك شمدىيهدك كويه يتيشهبيلدى مى ؟

ج) اوت افندم ! شمدىيه قدر چوقدن يتيشمش اولهجقدر .

س) عجبا بو اخشام آى ساعت قاچده طوغهجقدر !

ج) هوا بولوطلى در ؛ يوخسه چوقدن طوغمش اولهجقدى .

تعليم قرائت   Reading Exercise.

نصر الدينك بر وعظى   *A Sermon of Nasr-éd-din.*

نصر الدين خواجه افندى[1] امثالسز[2] بر واعظ ايدى . اونك
كبى بر واعظ نه كلمش نه ده كلهجكدر . عمرنده[3] هيچ بر دفعه[4] بوش
بر لاقيردى[5] سويلهمهمشدر . هر سوزندن بر حصّه آلينير ؛ يا اشتاهله
كولونور[6] . شمدى شو حكايهيى دكلرسه كز[7] ، بكا حقّ ويرهجكسكز[8] .
بر كون خواجه افندى جامعه كيتمش ، كرسىيه[9] چيقمش ، يوزينى
جماعته[10] چويرمش[11] وَ يوكسك سسله شويله ديش : «اى جماعت !
اى مسلمانلر ! بوكون ، بوساعتده ، سزه نهلر دييهجكم ، بيليرميسكز ؟»
— جماعت تعجّب ايتمش[12] وَ «خير خواجه افندى ! سن ديزدن بز ناصل
بيلهبيليرز» ديش .

خواجه افندى جواباً[13] : «يا سيز بيلمزسه كز بن سيزه نه سويلهيهيم[14] ؟
واريك ! اوكونك ! كليك !» ديش .

Words. 1. *Nasréd'din Hoja Efféndi* the reverend teacher
Nasreddin. 2. *émsalsiz* unique. 3. *ômrûndé* in his life. 4. *hich'bir
défa* not at all. 5. *laqîrdî* a word. 6. *ishtahla gûlûnmék* to laughed at heartily. 7. *diñlémék* to listen. 8. *haqq vérmék* to approve.
9. *kûrsû* a pulpit. 10. *jéma'at* congregation, people. 11. *chévirmék* to turn (his face). 12. *té-aj'jûb ét.* to wonder. 13. *jévabén*
in answer. 14. *séôyléyéyim* I may speak.

ایرتـه‌سی ¹⁵ جمعه کونی خواجه افندی تکرار ¹⁶ وعظه باشلار وَ

اولکی سوالی تکرار ایدر ٠ بو دفعه جماعت کویا عقللی ^{16ª} داورنق ¹⁷

مقصدیله : «اوت خواجه افندی٬ بیلیرز! بیلیرز!» دیو هپیسی بر

آغیزدن باغریشیرلر ¹⁸ ٠

خواجه افندی اونلرك بو تربیه‌سزلکلرینه ¹⁹ پك زیاده کوجه‌نیر ²⁰

وَ «مادام که ²¹ بیلیریز دییورسکز٬ سیزه نه سویله‌یه‌یم ٠ هایدی کیدك !

کوزم کورمه‌سون !» دیر٬ کرسیدن اینر وآلیر یورویی ویرر ²² ٠

15. *értési* the following. 16. *tékrar* again, repeating. 16ª. *aqîl'li* wise. 17. *davranmaq* to behave. 18. *baghrîshmaq* to shout, to call out together. 19. *térbiyésizlik* rudeness. 20. *gûjénmék* to be angry. 21. *madam ki* since. 22. *yéôrûyû vérmék* (to depart and) go quickly.

Lesson 25.   درس ٢٥

The Optative Tense.   الترامی

§ 365. The Optative tense expresses a desire or wish that some action may be performed. Its characteristic sign is ـه -é, -a (or یه -yé, -ya, when the root ends in a vowel) added to the root of the verb. This forms the third person singular. The first person plural is formed by adding لم -lim, -lîm to this.

§ 366. **1. Indicative Optative.** الترامیٔ اخباریه

سوه‌یم *séréyim'*,	سوه‌لم *sévélim'*,
سوه‌سین *séré'sîn*,	سوه‌سکز *séré'siniz*,
سوه٬ سوسون! سوسین *séré'*, *sévsin'*,	سوه‌لر *sévélér'*.

That I may love, that thou mayest love, etc.

Negative.   منفیٔ الترامی

سومه‌یه‌یم *sév'méyéyim*, *sév'méyim*.	سومه‌یه‌لم *sév'méyélim*,

سومهيهسين sév'méyésin,   سومهيهسكز sévméyésiñiz,

سومهيهلر sév'méyé, sév'mésin,   سومهيه ، سومسون ، سومهسين sév'méyélér.

That I may not love, etc.

استفهامئ التزامی Interrogative.

§ 367.   The interrogative forms are generally in use only for first and third persons, they are used to ask permission for something, and are rendered by *shall* or *may:*

Person 1:   یازهیم می yazayim' mî?   یازهلم می yazalim' mî?

  »   3:   یازسون می yazsîn' mî?   یازسونلر می yazsînlar' mî?

May I write, may he, we, they write?

Person 1:   آلمایهیم می al'mayayim mî?   آلمایالم می al'mayalim mî?

  »   3:   آلماسون می al'masîn mî?   آلماسونلر می al'masînlar mî?

Shall I not take?

مطالعات *Múta-la-at* Remarks.

§ 368.   The third person of the Optative is used to form some important gerunds:

§ 369.   **The Sixth Gerund.** By adding لی *-li, -lî* or لیدنبرو *-lidén bérou*, a gerund is obtained, called the Primitive, meaning 'since'; as:

بورایه کهلی ، بورایه کهلیدنبرو *bouraya gélélidén bérou, bouraya géléli.* Since he came here.

بوچوجوق طوغهلی خسته در *bou chojouq doghali,* (or *doghalîdan bérou*) *hasta dîr.* This boy is sick ever, since his birth.

§ 370.   **The Seventh Gerund.** By repeating the third person singular another gerund is formed which denotes repeated action:

قوشه قوشه کلدی *qosha qosha géldi.* He came running continually.

§ 371.   **The Eighth Gerund.** Another Gerund is produced by adding رق رك *-raq, -rék* to the same part of the verb; it expresses the *manner* of a subordinate

action which takes place at the same time as that stated by the verb it accompanies:

سوينه‌رك مكتبه كيديبور *sévinérék méktébé gidiyor.* He is going to school joyously.

قوشه‌رق كلدى *qosharaq géldi.* He came running.

§ 372. **The Ninth Gerund.** This is obtained by the addition of سى ، سيجه '*-si,* or *-sîja* to the third person, and is used for cursing and blessing:

اوجاغى ياناسى *ojaghî yanasî* or *yanasîja!* May his hearth be alight! (i. e. may he be prosperous!)

اوجاغى باتاسيجه *ojaghî batasîja!* May his fireplace be sunk! (i. e. may his offspring be annihilated!)

كور اولەسيجه *kêôr olasîja!* May he be blinded!

2. The Assertive Optative. الترامى حكايه

§ 373. The Assertive Optative either expresses a wish that some action may take place, although one scarcely expects it, or indicates regret that some action has not taken place in the past:

يازه ايدم *yazay´idîm,*	يازه ايدك *yazay´idiq,*
يازه ايدك *yazay´idiñ,*	يازه ايديكز *yazay´idiñiz,*
يازه ايدى *yazay´idî,*	يازه ايديلر *yazay´idîlar.*

That I might write! *or* That I had written!

§ 374. The Dubitative Past third person singular of any verb is compounded with the Assertive Optative of the verb **olmaq** اولمق 'to become', to express just the same meaning:

يازمش اولايدم *yazmîsh olayidîm,*	يازمش اولايدك *yazmîsh olayidiq,*
يازمش اولايدك *yazmîsh olayidîñ,*	يازمش اولايديكز *yazmîsh olayidiñiz,*
يازمش اولايدى *yazmîsh olayidî,*	يازمش اولايديلر *yazmîsh olayidilar.*

That I might write! That I had written!

مطالعات *Műta-la-at* Remarks.

§ 375. a. Words which express a wish require the verb which follows to be in the Optative: such words are:

نولايدى (نه‌اوله ايدى) *no'layidî!* Would that!

p. كاشكى *kîash'ki* vulg. *késh'gé!* Would that it were so!

الله ويره ده ! الله ويرسون كه ! *Al'lah' vérsin ki! Al'lah véré dé!* God grant that!

الله ويريدى ده ! *Al'lah véré'yidi dé!* Would to God that!

مثاللر *Misal'lér* Examples.

Kîash'ki bourad'a olayîdî! Would that he had been here!
Kiash'ki, or, *no'layidi véré'yidim!* Would that I had given!
Al'lah vérsin'ki or *Al'lah véré'yidi dé,* or *Al'lah vérédé éyi bir yaghmour géléyidi!* Would that God would grant a good rain!

§ 376. b. Sometimes the meaning approaches much closer to that of the Suppositive Past (§ 379): ويرمش

ويرمش اولسيديم ، اوله‌ايديم *vérmish olayîdîm* or *vérmish ol-sayîdîm* are the same.

لغتلر Words.

صاتون آلمق *satîn almaq* to buy   صاتمق *satmaq* to sell

كوڭول *géôñûl* heart   مرتك *mérték* post, beam

صانمق *sanmaq* to suppose, take   a. اذن *izin* permission

a. صداقه *sadaqa* alms   p. برابر *bérabér* together.

عافيت اولسون ! ـ اوله ! *afiyét' olsoun,* or *ola!* May that be health to you! [§ 490].

تعليم ۵۳ Exercise 53.

۱ كاشكى پاره‌م اوليدى ده ، شو قوناغى صاتون آلايدم ! ۲ هايده‌اك آرقه‌داشلر ! ديشارى كيده‌لم ده درسلريزى برابر اوكوه‌نه‌لم ، ايو اولرز مى ؟ ۳ پك كوزل اولور ! كيده‌يم خواجه افنديدن اذن آلايم ده كله‌يم . ٤ وارايم شو فقيره بش اون پاره صداقه ويره‌يم . كاشكى پاره‌م اولايدى ده ، برقاچ پاره زياده ويره ايدم . اوجاغى ياناسيجه پك بيچاره در ! ۵ بن ده برقاچ پاره اولسون (even) ويرمه‌يى ايستر ايدم ؛ لكن

كوكولده وار الده يوق · ٦ اكر سنك يكن اغا اوقومغى يازمغى بيلمش
اولايدى! شيمديـيه قدر چوق پاره قازانير ايدى · فقط ايشك كوترسى
شو در كه ' النى كورورسه مرتك صانير ' بابى كورسه چاناق · ٧ بو كون
چوق چاليشدم ؛ يازى يازه يازه اوصاندم · ٨ صو مى ايچديكز؟
عافيت اولسون! — عمرك چوق اولسون افندم · ٩ سوينه سوينه
مكتبه كيدييورم · ١٠ اوقويه اوقويه كوزم يورولدى·

ترجمه ٥٤ Translation 54.

1. Shall I read it? what shall I say? 2. How shall
I have patience? 3. May his hand be broken! 4. Since
I began my lessons I have not missed a day. 5. O
that I knew a little French! 6. Oh! that he might
come. 7. It is well that I did not offer it to you, for if
I had given it you would not have taken it. 8. Would
that he had been here! 9. Shall we go to see the
lion? — It is hot now, I cannot go. 10. May God
keep you in good health! 11. What shall I do now?
— You cannot do anything now. Go to your room
until I call you. 12. You must not go to your uncles'
house, unless you are invited. 13. By asking continually you can find [the way to] Bagdad. 14. By
studying continually you will learn fast.

مكالمه Conversation.

س) ربّانى دعايى١ بيلىرميسكز؟ اكر بيلىرسەكز سويلەيكز! ممنون اولەجغم ·
ج) «اى سماواتده٢ اولان پدريمز! اسمك مقدّس٣ اولسون! پادشاهلغك
كلسين! ارادتك٤ سماواتده اولديغى كبى٥ بر اوزرنده دخى اجرا
اولونسون٦ ···» بو قدرينى بيلىرم · كاشكى هپيسينى ده بيله ايدم ده
سويلەيەبيله ايدم·
س) ربّانى دعايى اوكرەنەلى نەقدر اولدى؟

Words. 1. *Rab'bani douva* Lord's Prayer. 2. *sémavat* heavens. 3. *mouqad'dés* holy. 4. *iradét* will. 5. *oldoughou gibi* as
it (was). 6. *ijra olounmaq* to be done.

ج) اوچ كون اولدى ؛ وقتم چوق يوقدر . اولايدى هپيسنى بردن
اوكرهنه بيلير ايدم .

س) ايشيتدم كه قارداشكزه امرِحقّ وقوع بولش[7] ؛ چوق اسف ايتدم[8] .
باشكز صاغ اولسون !

ج) تشكر ايدرم . سز صاغ اولك ! الله سيزلره اوزون عمرلر وبرسون ! الله
بزم برادرك عمرينى سزلره باغيشلاسين[9] !

س) احمد اوستهكيله كيدييورميسين ؟

ج) سن بكا اونلره كيتمه دييهلى اولرينه آياق باصمادم .

س) سز مرذيفونه كلهلى قاچ سنه اولدى ؟

ج) افندم بن بوشهره كلهلى اون سكز سنه اولدى .

س) ددهك اولهليدنبرو قاچ آى اولدى ؟

ج) آى دكل يكرمى طقوز سنه اولمشدر . بنم عقلم يتمز[10] .

7. *emri haqq rouqou boulmaq* the decree of the True one
happened, he died. 8. *éséf ét.* to be sorry. 9. *baghîshlamaq* to
grant. 10. *aqlîm yétméz* I cannot comprehend (my reason do not
reach [so far] i. e. I was a child).

درس ۲٦ Lesson 26.

The Suppositive Tense [Subjunctive].

§ 377. The Conditional Optative, which is called
by many Grammarians simply the Suppositive tense,
is formed by adding the Conditional terminations to the
hé ه of the third person Singular of the Optative.

§ 378. **1. Suppositive Present.** حال فرضيه

يازسهم *yaz'sam,*	يازسهق *yaz'saq,*
يازسهك *yaz'sañ,*	يازسهكز *yaz'sanîz,*
يازسه *yaz'sa,*	يازسهلر *yaz'salar.*

If I write, If I were to write, etc.

منفئ حال فرضيه **Negative.**

يازمسهم or يازماسهم ، يازمسهك ، يازمسه | If I do not write.
yaz'masam,   yaz'masañ, yaz'masa, etc. | If I were not to write.

§ 379. 2. Suppositive Past. ماضئ فرضيه

The Suppositive Past states the condition on which, if something had happened, some other action would have taken place, or would still take place. It casts doubt on the performance of some condition.

يازسه‌ايدم ، يازسيدم *yaz´sayîdim*,   يازسيدق *yaz´sayîdiq*,

يازسه‌ايدك ، يازسيدك *yaz´sayîdiñ*,   يازسيديكز *yaz´sayîdiñiz*,

يازسه‌ايدى ، يازسيدى *yaz´sayîdi*,   يازسيديلر *yaz´sayîdilar*.

If I had written, etc.

§ 380. 3. Narrative Suppositive. روايت فرضيه

يازسه ايشم *yaz´sa imishim*,   يازسه ايشيز *yaz´sa imishiz*,

يازسه ايشسين *yaz´sa imishsin*,   يازسه ايشسكز *yaz´sa imishsiñiz*,

يازسه ايش *yaz´sa imish*,   يازسه ايشلر *yaz´sa imishler*.

If I had written (as others say) . . .

مطالعات *Mûta-la-at:* Remarks.

§ 381. a. The Conjunction p. اكر *éyér'* 'if', is, so to speak, included in the Suppositive Tense, as the characteristic sign of this tense سه -*sé* has the meaning if, but it can be and often is used together with it, especially for the sake of emphasis; as:

اكر چاليشمه‌سڭ *éyér chalîshmasañ*, or *chalîshmasañ* If you do not try.

§ 382. b. If the Suppositive tenses are used with كاشكى *kîaski*, they are regarded as Optative. If they are used with اكر *éyér'*, they become Suppositive; as:

Kîashki on ghouroushoum´ olsa! O that I had ten piastres!
Eyér´ on ghouroushoum ol´sa. If I had ten piastres.
Kîashki érkén´ gélséyidim! O that I had come earlier!
Eyér érkén gélsé´yidim. If I had come earlier.

§ 383. c. The Optative of the auxiliary verb اولمق *olmaq* 'to become, to have' is used with the third person Dubitative and Future of any verb, to express the Suppositive; as:

يازمش اولسه ، يازمش اولسه‌ك ، يازمش اولسه‌م

yazmîsh ol'sam, — ol'sañ, — ol'sa, etc.

} If I had written.

يازمش اولسيدى ، يازمش اولسيدك ، يازمش اولسيدم

yazmîsh olsa'yîdim, — olsa'yîdiñ, — olsa'yîdî, etc.

يازه‌جق اولسه‌ك ، يازه‌جق اولسه‌م

yazajaq ol'sam, yazajaq ol'sañ

} If I am about to read.

يازه‌جق اولسيدك ، يازه‌جق اولسيدم

yazajaq olsa'yîdim, yazajaq olsa'yîdiñ

مثال‌لر *Misal'lér* Examples.

Dûn bizé gélmish olsayîdinîz, amoujamî georûrûdûnûz.
If you had come to us yesterday, you would have seen my uncle.
Ma'ashînîzî alajaq olsañîz, borjouñouzou vériñiz.
If you receive your salary, pay your debts.

لغتلر Words.

a. سلام *sélam* salutation

a. دقيقه *daqiqa* minute

طاريلمق *darîlmaq* to be offended

ديويت *divit* inkstand

بيله *bilé* even, though

نه ديك *né démék!* certainly

تعليم ٥٥ Exercise 55.

۱ اويكزه كلسه‌م ، بنى اچه‌رى آليرميسكز ؟ نه ديرسيكز
كله‌يم مى ؟ كلمه‌يه‌يم مى ؟ ۲ يارين صباح سزك اوه كله‌جك اولورسه‌م
بنمله برابر حكيمه كيده‌بيليرميسكز ؟ — كيده‌بيليرم ظن ايده‌رم .
لكن بو كون اخشام اوستى ده كله‌جك اولسه‌ك كيده‌بيليرم . ۳ بو
قوناغى كچن سنه صاتون آلمش اولسيديكز ، دها اوجوز آليز ايديكز .
٤ المدن طوته‌لرايدى ؛ دوشمه‌يه‌جك ايدم . ٥ برسودلى قهوه پيشيرتسه
ايديكز ، كوزلجه ايچر ايدك . ٦ واهان افندى كله‌جك اولسه ، بن
يوقاريده‌يم بكا خبر ويز . ٧ كاشكى وقتم اوزون اولسيدى ده ، سيزكله
برابر اوطورسه‌ق وَ قونوشسه ايدك . ٨ خاله‌زاده‌م پاره آرتيرمش
اوله ايدى ، بزم ايله برابر استانبوله كيده‌بيلير ايدى . ٩ «اوقومه يازمه

اوكزنسهك بك اولورسين افندى اولورسين · اوكزنسهك حمال اولورسين» ·

۱۰ كاشكى او اعلاجى ايچسه ايدم ' اكر ايچسه ايدم شمدىيه چوقدن ايلهشير ايدم ·

ترجمه ٥٦ Translation 56.

1. Where will he go? — If he finds a horse he will go to the forests. 2. Had we been walking in the street, we should have been seen. 3. May I bring my ink-stand here? 4. If you write to your mother, give her (say to her) my compliments (salutations). 5. Had we stayed there for a minute, we should have seen the Governor-general and the governor. 6. Although you bring the grapes, I may not eat them. 7. Should you want money, take them to the city and sell them. 8. Were the merchant to send the goods now, I should use them to-day. 9. I believe that, if they were here now, we could sell them here. 10. If I take your pen for a moment, will you be offended? — No, Sir, you may use it as long as you wish. 11. May he bring his younger brother with him? — Certainly; if he brings him, my children will be very glad.

مكالمه Conversation.

پاره‌م اولسیدی آلیردم ·   شو اشكی صاتون آلمق ایسته‌رمیسكز؟

ساعت دردی بش كچه‌رك اوده اولورم ·   سزی یارین نه وقت كوره‌بیلیرم؟

كیتسیدیكز ابو یاپار ایدیكز ·   عجبا چارشویه كیتسه‌م می كیتمه‌سه‌م می؟

كیتسه ایدم ؛ كوتورور ایدم · اما   سزه برمكتوب ویرسیدم پوسته‌خانه‌یه كیده‌مه‌یه‌جكم ·   كوتورور میدیكز؟

اكر آوه باشقه بر كیمسه كلمه كلیرم ·   یكككیزی یسه‌كز بزه كلیرمیسكز؟

تعلیم قرائت Reading Exercise.

A Sermon of Nasr-éd-din. نصر الدينك بر وعظى (مابعد[1])

عجبا خواجه افندى نه سويله‌يه‌جك ايدى ديو جماعته بويوك

Words. 1. a. *ma'bad* continued.

12*

بر مراق² اولور . خواجه‌نك سوزی آغزیندن ناصل آله‌بیلیرز دیو دوشونه‌رك قرار ویریرلر³ که : اگر بردها کرسی یه چیقار وَ سوال ایدرسه «کیمیمز بیلیرز ٬ کیمیمز بیلمه‌یز» دیو جواب ویرسونلر .

خواجه حضرتلری اوچنجی دفعه اوله‌رق کرسی‌یه چیقار وَ «ای فارداشلرم ! بیلیرمیسکز ؟ بو کون بن سیزه نه سویله‌یه‌جکم ؟ » دیو صورار . جماعتك هپیسی بر آغیزدن «کیمیمز بیلیرز ٬ کیمیمز بیلمه‌یز» دیو باغریشیرلر .

خواجه افندی : «نه کوزل ! مادام که بیلیور ایشسکز ؛ اویله ایسه بیلنلریکز⁴ بیلمه‌ینلریکزه اوکرتسونلر ! » دیمش و طاریله‌رق کرسیدن اینمش ٬ براقمش ٬ کیتمشدر .

2. *méraq* curiosity. 3. *qarar vérmék* to decide. 4. *bilénlériñiz* those who know among you (§ 407).

درس ۲۷ Lesson 27.

The Necessitative Tense.

§ 384. The Necessitative Tense indicates necessity, obligation and duty, that an action must or ought to take place.

The characteristic sign of this tense is ملی ٬ مه‌لی -*méli* with the soft and مالی -*malî* with the hard verbs. This termination is added to the root.

سومك ٬ سو√ : سومه‌لی *sévméli'* He must love (if is necessary).

یازمق ٬ یاز√ : یازمالی *yazmalî'* He must write (that is his duty).

§ 385.

1. Indicative Necessitative. وجوبئ اخباریه

سومه‌یز *sévméli'yiz,*   سومه‌لیم *sévméli'yim,*

سومەلیسین *sévméli'sin,*   سومەلیسكز *sévméli'siñiz,*

سومەلی در *sévméli' dir,*   سومەلیدرلر *sévméli'dirler.*

I must love, *or,* ought to love, *or,* am to love, etc.

Negative and Interrogative.

سومەمەملیدر ، سومەمەملیسین ، سومەمەملیم } I must or ought not
sév'mémeliyim, sév'mémelisin, sév'mémelidir }   to love.

سومەلی میم *sévméli' miyim?* Ought I to love? Must I love?

سومەمەلی میم *sév'mémelimiyim?* Ought I not to love? Must I not love?

§ 386. *Note.* In some regions of Turkey the people make a wrong use of the third person plural as *sévmélilér,* instead of the regular *sévméli dirlér.*

2. Assertive Necessitative. حكايهٔ وجوبى

§ 387. The Assertive Necessitative (which is called by some grammarians Past Necessitative) expresses that it was necessary or right that an action should have taken place, or that one was forced to perform some act; as:

دون كەلمەلیدك *dûn' gélméliyidiñ* You ought to have come yesterday.

مكتبه كیتمەلیدیكز *méktébé gitméli'yidiñiz* 1. You ought to have gone to the school. 2. You were obliged to go to the school. 3. You were to go to the school. 4. You should have gone to the school.

§ 388. It is the Past tense of m u s t, which is wanting in English, and corresponds to the German musste.

یازمالیدم *yazmalí'yîdim,*   یازمالیدك *yazmalí'yîdiq,*

یازمالیدك *yazmalí'yîdiñ,*   یازمالیدیكز *yazmalí'yîdiñiz,*

یازمالیدی *yazmalí'yîdi,*   یازمالیدیلر *yazmalí'yîdilar.*

I ought to have written. It was necessary that I should write.

یازمامالیدم *yaz'mamaliyîdim* I ought not to have written.

§ 389.

3. Narrative Necessitative. روایت وجوبى

یازمالی ایمیشم *yazmalí' yîmîshîm,*   یازمالی ایمیشز *yazmalí' imishiz,*

يازمالى ايمشسين *yazmalí imíshsin,* يازمالى ايمشكز *yazmalí imíshsiñiz,*

يازمالى ايمش *yazmalí imish,* يازمالى ايمشلر *yazmalí imishlér.*

(They say that) I ought to have written.

§ 390.

4. Conditional Necessitative. شرطى وجوبى

يازمالى ايسم *yazmalí isém,* يازمالى ايسهك *yazmalí isék,*

يازمالى ايسهڭ *yazmalí iséñ,* يازمالى ايسهكز *yazmalí iséñiz,*

يازمالى ايسه *yazmalí isé,* يازمالى ايسهلر *yazmalí isélér.*

If it is necessary for me to write, etc.

مطالعات *Mûta-la-at:* Remarks.

§ 391. a. Instead of using this Necessitative form, some words may be used to denote obligation and necessity together with the Substantive verb, such words are:

a. لازم *lazîm'* necessary.   كرك *gérék'* necessary, requisite.

a. مجبور *méjbour'* obliged.   a. اقتضا *iqtiza'* requisite.

a. واجب *vajib'* necessary.   a. مقتضى *mouqtazi'* necessary.

Yazmalí'dir, is expressed by *yazmasí lazîm', gérék', vajib', mouqtazi'dir;* or, *yazmagha méjbour'dour; yazmasí iqtiza'édér.*

§ 392. b. When one verb follows another on which it depends and with which it is connected by that, expressed or understood, the use of the conjunction ك *ki* between them is frequently avoided by employing the word ديو *déyi* 'saying'.

It is used also after all kinds of quotations.

كلسون ديو امر ايتدى or امر ايتدى كه كلسون *émr étdi ki gélsin,* or, *gélsin déyi émr étdi.* He ordered him to come.

اوطورسون ديو ير كوستردى or ير كوستردى كه اوطورسون *yér geôstérdi ki otoursoun,* or, *otoursoun déyi yér geôstérdi.* He showed him a place to sit.

باباك سنى "كل" ديو چاغيرييور *babañ séni gél déyi chaghîriyor.* Your father is calling you to come (i. e. saying Come!).

§ 393. c. The English verb 'To Have' when followed by an infinitive, expresses an obligation or necessity:

therefore the two verbs together are translated into Turkish by the Necessitative tense or by the obligatory words (§ 391).

I have to write a letter. *1. Bén bir méktoub´ yazmalîyim. 2. Bir méktoub´ yazmagha méjbouroum. 3. Bir méktoub´ yazmaq-lighîm iqtiza´ édér.*

I have to learn my lesson. *1. Dersimi êôyrénméli´yim. 2. Dérs´ êôyrénmékliyim lazim dir, gérék´dir, vajib´dir, iqtiza´édér, mouqtazi´dir etc.*

§ 394.   d. When the object of the finite verb in such sentences comes before the infinitive, the sentence does not denote obligation, but possession. It must therefore be rendered in Turkish either by the Future Participle (§ 408) or by the Infinitive Dative or Nominatival with ايچون *ichin* 'for'; as:

He has a book to read. *1. Oqouyajaq bir kitabî´ var. 2. Oqoumagha bir kitabî´ var. 3. Oqoumaq ichin bir kitabî´ var.*

لغتلر Words.

كيمك	*géymék* to put on	بوش بوشينه	*bosh boshouna* in vain
دسته p.	*désté* quire (of paper)	بسلهمك	*béslémék* to feed
قوطو	*qoutou* box	مطلقا a.	*mout´laqa* absolutely
يامهلامق	*yamalamaq* to mend	يامه	*yama* patch
تذكره	*tézkiré* a note	مانع a.	*mani* obstacle.

تعليم ٥٧ Exercise 57.

۱ پدرم بو هفته كلهرم ديو يازمش ايدى ايسه ده كلهمدى ٠ مطلقا بر مانعى اولمالى ٠ ٢ مارقوس ايى بر شاكرد در ديو ايشتمش ايدم؛ اما ياكليش اولمالى ٠ ٣ چوجوقلار چاليشمالى؛ هم ده چوق چاليشمالى درلر ٠ ٤ نه يابهجق ايسهكز بر ساعت اول ياپماليسكز ٠ ٥ آدم خسته اولمامق ايچون نه چوق يمهلى نه ده چوق ايچمهلى (ايچملى) ٠ ٦ هر نه امر ايتسهم ياپماليسين؛ يازهجقسين ديو نه سويلهسهم چارچابوق ياپماليسين؛ دويدك مى ؟ ٧ نه ياپمالى ايدك ؟ — قوندوراكى چابوق كيمهلى و كيتمهلى

ایدك ٠ ٨ نه صاتون آلماليديلر ؟ — ایکی دیویت ' بر دسته كاغد وَ بر
قوطو قورشون قلم صاتون آلمالى ایدیلر ٠ ٩ دوستكزك ایده‌جك بر ایشی
وار می ؟ — یازه‌جق بر مكتوبی وار در ٠ ١٠ صاته‌جق بر آتم وار ٠
اوقویه‌جق بر غزته‌سی وار (۴۰۸ ' ۳۹٤ §§) ٠

٥٨ ترجمه   Translation 58.

1. You must have come to us as soon as you had
heard this news. 2. What shall I do? — If you have
not learnt your lesson, you should learn it now. 3. What
had your wife to do? — She had to write a note. 4. Have
they to go this way? — No, Sir, they are to go the
other way. 5. Who has to work all the day? — The
poor man has to work all the day. 6. Who had to give
all his money. — The baker had to give all his money.
7. What have you to do to-day? — I have to write a
letter. 8. What has the shoemaker to do? — The
shoemaker has to mend my shoes. 9. Am I obliged
to come here? — Yes, you must come, your coming
is necessary. 10. The teacher called the pupils, saying,
Come.

مكالمه   Conversation.

س) سویله باقالم ! قوشلر بهارین نه یاپاچالیدرلر ؟

ج) قوشلر بهار موسمنده یووالرینی یاپمالی ' یومورطه‌لرینی یومورطلامالی '
یاورولرینی چیقارمالی ' اونلری بسله‌مه‌لی وَ اوچورمالی درلر ٠

س) عجبا همشیره‌كز خانم بنی كورسه طانیه‌جق میدر ؟

ج) طانیه‌مایدر ٠ كورمشم دیو چوق دفعه لاقیردی‌كزی ایدر ٠

س) اثوابلریمی كیم دیكه‌جك ؟ وَ چورابلریمی كیم یامالایه‌جقدر ؟

ج) بن یاپاجفم اما یلم كه : چورابلرك پك اسكی در ؛ یامالامالیمی ؟
یامالامامالیمی ؟

س) بر تذكره یازه‌جق كاغدیكز وار میدر ؟

ج) بویورك افندم ! بر تذكره‌لك دكل آ ؛ ایشته سیزه اون تذكره‌لك كاغد ؛
كاغدم یوقدر دیو یازمامازلك ایتمه‌یكز (§ ۲۹۷) ٠

Reading Exercise. تعليم قرائت

The Marriage of the Teacher. خواجه‌نك اولنمه‌سى

نصرالدين خواجه افندينك باشى بوزولمش ؛ ايكنجى دفعه اوله‌رق
اولنمك آرزوسينه دوشمش . اسلاملر آراسينده عادتدن درکه ' ارککلر
قاريلرك يوزلريني کورمزلر . قاريلر يابانجى ' بر ارکك کورورلراينه '
چارچابوق يوزلريني اورترلر . خواجه‌نك دوستارى کنديسينه غايت
چيرکين برقارى بوله‌رق کوزل در ديو يوتدورمشلر . قارى اوه کلير
کلمز خواجه يوزينك اورتوسينى قالديرمش باقمش که ؛ نه ديك !
پك چيرکين برشى ! عادتا بر کومور ! جانى چوق صيقيلمش ايسه ده
هيچ سس چيقارمامش .

ايرته‌سى کون بزم خواجه اودن چيقارکن ' قارى در: «آمان خواجه
افندى ! سن کيدييورسين ' سويله ! کيمه کورونه‌يم ؟ کيمه کورونمه‌يم »
ديو بر ادا ايله سوال ايتمش . — خواجه «بره قارى ! جانيکى
سورسه‌اك ' بکا کورونغه ده کيمه کورونورسه‌اك کورون ! » ديمش
وَکوچبلا ياقانى قورتارمش .

> *Words.* 1. *bashî bouzoulmaq* (to be put out of order) = to
> be a widower. 2. to be anxious. 3. *adétdén ol.''* to be usual.
> 4. *yabanjî* stranger. 5. to veil. 6. to cause to swallow, to deceive.
> 7. *ôrtû* veil. 8. *né déñ!* (what do you say) = what wonder! 9. *adéta*
> simply; really. 10. his soul was oppressed = he was angry.
> 11. to unveil (her face). 12. to veil. 13. *éda* arrogance. 14. *bîré
> qarî* now then, woman! 15. *diniñi sévérséñ* if you love your soul
> = please! 16. he could scarcely get rid of her.

Lesson 28. درس ٢٨

The Participles. فرع فعل

§ 395. There is no Relative Pronoun in Turkish
corresponding to the English who, which, or that.

These are always accompanied by a verb in English. In Turkish the Subjective and Objective Participles of the verb take the place of both the Relative and the verb.

§ 396. *Note.* This peculiarity is the most characteristic, and at the same time the most beautiful feature in the Turkish language, though foreigners and even natives of Turkey, whose mother-tongue is not Turkish, are often guilty of infringing it, and are frequently in utter ignorance of its value and meaning. For instance, *béni sévén adém* 'the me-loving man'; *ot yéyén at* 'the grass-eating horse': are equivalent to 'the man who loves me' and 'the horse which eats grass'. The great number of Participles derived from the Turkish verb enables a very great degree of precision to be given to this construction.

§ 397. The only Relative Pronoun in Turkish *ki*, که meaning 'who, which, that, what' is not Turkish in origin, it is Persian. This word, *ki*, is never used in correct Turkish, though employed in translated Persian and Arabic sentences. It is also used by foreigners.

§ 398. The Participles may be divided into two classes or moods: Subjective and Objective.

1. Subjective Mood.

§ 399. The Subjective Participles are those which are composed of the subject, (the nominative case of *who, which, that, what*) and the verb. They are derived both from active and from neuter or passive verbs. In the first case they are called Active Participle (*Ismi Fayil*) and in the second Passive Participle (*Ismi Méfoul*). The Active Participle corresponds to the Present Participle and the Passive Participle to the Past Participle of the English Grammar.

§ 400. The Subjective Active and the Subjective Passive Participles have seven tenses each:

§ 401. Subjective Active Participle. اسم فاعل

Present: یازان *yazan* who writes, writer, writing (adjectival).

Aorist: یازار *yazar* one who writes, writing »

Past: یازدق *yazdiq* one who wrote.

Dubitative:	يازمش	*yazmîsh*	one who has written.
Pluperfect:	يازمش اولان	*yazmîsh olan*	one who had written.
Future:	يازه‌جق	*yazajaq*	one who will write.
Past Future:	يازه‌جق اولان	*yazajaq olan*	one who is (about) to write.

§ 402. Subjective Passive Participle. اسم مفعول

Present:	يازيلان	*yazîlan*		is being
Aorist:	يازيلير	*yazîlîr*		may be
Past:	يازلدق	*yazîldîq*		is
Dubitative:	يازلمش	*yazîlmîsh*	That which	has been
Pluperfect:	يازلمش اولان	*yazîlmîsh olan*		had been
Future:	يازيله‌جق	*yazîlajaq*		will be
Past Future:	يازيله‌جق اولان	*yazîlajaq olan*		is (about) to be

written.

The Negatives are: يازمايان *yazmayan,* سومه‌ين *sévméyen,* يازلمايان *yazîlmayan,* سويلمه‌ين *sévilméyén,* etc.

مطالعات *Múta-la-at:* Remarks.

§ 403. I. The Present Active Participle is applicable either to the present or to the past; as:

يازان آدم *yazan adém,* means either 'the writing man, the man who writes, the man who is writing', and 'the man who wrote'.

§ 404. II. The Aorist Participle means 'whose nature or business is to write' or 'who is willing to write'; as:

اوقور يازار بر آدم *oqour yazar bir adém* 'a man who can read and write, a literary man'.

كورونور كورونمز شيلر *géôrúnûr géôrúnméz shéylér* 'things which can be seen and cannot be seen, i. e. visible and invisible things'.

§ 405. III. The Negative of the Past Participle is more used than the Affirmative:

سز ايو بر ادم سكز، سزى سومه‌دك كيمسه يوقدر *siz éyï bir adém siñiz, sizi sévmédik kimsé yoq dour.* You are a good man, there is nobody who does not love you.

§ 406. IV. Only the Present, the Pluperfect and the Past Future tenses are used either as the subject or as the adjective qualifying the subject of a sentence. The remaining four tenses are always used as adjectives qualifying the subject (§§ 71, 417, 423).

bou بومكتوبى يازان ' يازهجق اولان ' يازمش اولان ذات كيم در؟ *méktoubou yazan, yazajaq olan, yazmîsh olan zat kim´ dir?* Who is the person who wrote this letter? or ' بومكتوبى يازان ' يازهجق اولان *bou méktoubou yazan, yazajaq olan, yazmîsh* يازمش اولان كيمدر *olan´ kim dir?* Who is the writer of this letter?

§ 407. V. Therefore, these three tenses, when used as subjects, are declined like substantives, either alone or with pronominal affixes.

N. يازان *yazan*   A. يازانى *yazani*

G. يازانك *yazaniñ* of —   L. يازانده *yazanda* in —

D. يازانه *yazana* to —   A. يازاندن *yazandan* from —

The person writing, the writer.

Also: يازانلرى ' يازانكز ' يازانغز ⎰ The writer among us,
yazanîmîz, yazanîñîz, yazanlarî ⎱ you, them.

§ 408. VI. In English, when the object of the verb falls between the verb 'to have' and the Infinitive, it may be rendered into Turkish by the Future Participle (§ 393).

ييهجك اكمكى يوقدر *yéyéjék ékméyi yoq dour.* He has no bread to eat.

§ 409. VII. The Aorist, Past, Dubitative and Future Participles are the same in spelling and pronunciation with those of the Indicative Mood. It is very easy to distinguish them, and there is one absolute rule: If it is Indicative Mood, it must always stand at the end of the sentence, because verbs are always put at the end of the sentence. If it is a Participle, as a subject or a modifier of the subject, it must precede the verb in any case:

بو اوده كيم اوطورهجق؟ *bou évdé kim´ otourajaq?* Who will dwell in this house?

بو اوده اوطوره‌جق كيمسه كيم در؟ *bou évdé **otourajaq** kimsé kim dir?* Who is the man, who will dwell in this house?

تطبيقات *Tatbiqat:* Comparison.

§ 410. The order of construction in Turkish is just the opposite of English. In English the Antecedent (subject) begins the sentence, then comes the Relative Clause and thirdly the Verb (or predicate); or the Verb, Antecedent and Relative Clause. But in Turkish the order is always the same: first Relative Clause, then the Antecedent, and third the Verb.

         antecedent   relative clause   verb
1. The man who came now is blind.
     relative clause   antecedent   verb
     Shimdi gélén   adém   keôr' dúr.
      verb   antec.   relative clause
2. These are the boys who did not learn their lessons.
      relative clause   ant.   verb
    Dérslérini eôyrénméyén chojouqlar bounlar' dir.
3. There is nobody (who does not love you).
    (Sizi sévmédik) kimsé yoq'dour.
4. (Those who have gone to and come) from India.
    Hindistana (gitmish vé gélmish olanlar).
5. I saw the man (whose house is big).
    (Evi beôyúk olan) adémi geôrdúm.
6. A woman (whose eyes are blind).
    (Geôzléri keôr olan) bir qarî.
7. A horse (that runs fast).
    (Chapouq séyirdir) bir at.
8. A man (who is not fit for anything).
    (Bir ishé yaramaz) bir adém.
9. A letter (the address of which is not written).
    (ústú yazilmamish [or yazilmadiq]) bir méktoub.
10. There was a man there (whose hand was withered).
    Orada (éli qouroumoush olan) bir adém var idi.
11. The merchant (who has to come [or will come] to-morrow).
    (yarîn géléjék [or géléjék olan]) túj'jar.

12. [Those who know among us], will teach (those
who do not know among you).
[*Bilénlérimiz*] (*bilméyénlériñizé*) *eôyrédéjéklér*.

13. Who is the man (who will call the servant?)
(*Khîzmétkiāri chaghîrajaq olan*) *adém kim dir?*

14. I have (nothing to be afraid of).
(*Qorqajaq bir' shéyim*) *yoq dour*.

Words. لغتلر

بالطه	*balta* an axe	a. بلا	*béla* evil
كسر	*késér* adze	بلّی	*bél'li* known, perceptible
دپه ، تپه	*dépé* hill, top	كچیله‌جك	*géchiléjék* passable, fordable
a. مكافات	*mûkiafat* prize	الندن كلمك	*élindén gélmék* to be able to do
اوله‌جق	*olajaq* hopeful	اولمق	*olmaq* to become
ینمك	*yénmék* to be eaten	یتمك	*yétmék* to ripen
قاینار	*qaynar* boiling	ایش كوج	*ish gûj* occupation.

تعليم ٥٩ Exercise 59.

١ عقلی باشنده اولان آدملری سوه‌رم · ایشه یاراما‌یان آدملردن
خوشلانغام · ٢ ایشنی كوجینی براقان ' هر وقت تنبل تنبل كزن
كیمسنه‌لردن كیم خوشلانیر؟ ٣ باباسینه اطاعت ایدن ' آناسنی سوَن
بر چوجوق هر وقت سَویلیر · ٤ سویلیر طبیعتی اولانلری هر كس سور
ایسه ده ؛ سویلمز ' چیركین طبیعتلی اولانلردن ده هیچ بر كیمسه
خوشلانماز · ٥ اوله‌جق چوجوق كوچوكلكندن بللی در · اوله‌جق آت
طای ایكن بللیدر · ٦ كچن سنه نره‌یه كیتدیكز و كله‌جك سنه یازین
نره‌یه كیده‌جكسكز؟ — كچن سنه مردیفونه یاقین بولنان یكیجه
قریه‌سنه كیتدم و بو سنه دخی كیده‌جك باشقه بر یرم یوقدر ·

تعليم ٦٠ Exercise 60.

١ بو سوزی سزه سویله‌ین كیم ایدی؟ — دونكی كون بورایه

۲ باغده میوه‌لر ایله دولو اولان   كامش اولان قیصریه‌لی برتجار ایدی ۰

۳ یتمه‌مش میوه‌لری   بر آغاج كوردم ؛ فقط میوه‌لری ینمز حالده ایدی ۰

كین چوق چوجوقلر بیلیرم كه ، خسته یاتیورلر ، ایصیتمه طوتیورلر ۰

٤ الدن كله‌جك بر ایش ایسه یاپارم ؛ یوخسه یاپه‌مام ۰ ٥ بزی كورونور

وَ كورونز بلاردن صاقلایان الله تعالی حضرتلری در ۰ ٦ بیچاغك

كسر می ؟ — كسر بر بیچاغم ، كسمز بر بالطه‌م وَ كسكین بر كسرم

وار در ۰ ٧ ایرماقدن كچیله‌جك یری بكا كوستره‌جك اولسه‌كز چوق

ممنون اولورم ۰ ٨ ایچیكزده خسته اولانكز وار می ؟ ٩ ییه‌جكه

براز قاینار صو قو ۰ ۱۰ كچمشلریكزك جانیكه رحمت اولسون !

۱۱ نوری بك نك نصل بر آدم در ؟ — هیچ ! بوش كزنلرك باش

قالفه‌سیدر ۰

ترجمه ٦۱ Translation 61.

     1. The man who died yesterday morning, was your neighbour. 2. What have you? — I have a book, on the cover of which there is a beautiful yellow picture. 3. What do you see? — 4. I see the baker who bakes bread. 5. If you have seen the horse one of whose eyes is blind, it is not ours. 6. The adze cuts the wood. 7. Boys! do not be afraid, there is nothing to be feared. 8. It is a statement which cannot be believed. — No, Sir, it is a credible statement. 9. Have you anything to say to me? — I have nothing to say to you. 10. Whoever knows himself, knows a great deal (many things). 11. Is this the lady whose sister is sick? — No, she is the lady whose father is sick. 12. This villager is not a man who does not know anything, he is a man who reads and writes.

مكالمه Conversation.

بو كوملكلری كیمه كوندره‌جكسكز ؟   فقیر وخسته اولانلره كوندره‌جكم ۰

هیچ بر شیئی اولمایانلره نه دیرلر ؟   فقیر دیرلر ۰

شمدی كندی مغازه‌سنده اولمالی .   اوی داغلك دپه‌سنده اولان تجار نره‌ده در ؟

كوچك همشیره‌م نازك خانم در .   بوسنه مكتبده برنجی مكافاتی آلان كیم ایش ؟

اوكلام‌قدیمك هدیه‌سی ۱۲۰ غروشدر .   شو صاتیلان كلام قدیمك هدیه‌سی قاچ غروشدر ؟

بیلم ! عالمده برمسافر اولسه .   بویله كیج وقت قاپیی چالان كیم در عجبا ؟

پك پك اوچ كوندن ویره‌برم .   بو پاره‌یی نه وقت ویره‌بیلیرسكز ؟

آه ! اللّٰه شكرلراولسون ! كولدوره‌جك قدر دكلسه ده ؛ آغلایه‌جق قدر ده دكل .   موس كیا ! بوسنه آكینلر نصلدر ؟

تعلیم قرائت Reading Exercise.

ایپه اون سرمك To hang flour on a line.

ویره‌جكنی ویرمز ' حدینی طانیماز[1] كوتو قونشونك بری ؛ بر دفعه خواجه حضرتلرینه مراجعتله[2] : « جانم خواجه افندی ! بزم چوجوقلر[3] بو كون چاماشیر[4] ییقایورلر . چاماشیر سرمك[5] ایچون شو سزك چاماشیر ایپینی[6] ویره‌بسه‌كز نه اولور[7] ! » دیو یالوارمش[8] . — « پك اعلا اوغلم اما ؛ كل كله‌لم[9] كه بزمكیلر[3] ده بو كون ایپه اون سرمشلر ؛ یوقسه قضاكی آلسون[10] ' نه واركه[11] » دیو جواب ویرمش . اوته‌كی[12] حالا[13] مسئله‌یی[14] اكلامایه‌رق — « نه دیوك[15] خواجه ' هیچ ایپه اون سریله‌یرمی ؟ »

Words. 1. Who does not pay his debt. Who does not know his limits i. e. conceited. 2. *múraja-at ét.''* to appeal. 3. our children, the woman of the household (these names are applied to the women in the Harém). 4. *chamashîr* household linen. 5. *sérmék* to hang up in full length and breadth on a line. 6. clothes-line. 7. *né olour?* a common term for 'If you please'. 8. to implore. 9. let us come that = unfortunately. 10 *qadañî alsîn* may your misfortune befall on it! = nothing at all! 11. *né olour ki!* not worth mentioning. 12. the other one. 13. yet. 14. the case. 15. *né déyoñ?* for *déyorsoun.* What are you saying?

ديو اصرار ¹⁶ ايتديكنده : خواجه افندى «به حريف ! آكلاسه‌ك نه¹⁷ !
ويره‌جك كوكلم اولمه‌سه : ايه اون دكل يا ' صو بيله سرده‌رم» ديه‌رك باش
آغريسنى دفع ¹⁸ ايتمشدر .

16. *israr ét."* to insist. 17. *añlasañ' né?* why do you not
understand? 18. *déf ét."* to repel, expel.

دلس ۲۹   Lesson 29.

The Participles. (Continued.)

2. Objective Mood. صيغهٔ صله *Sîyghéyi Sîlé.*

§ 411. The Objective Participles are those which
combine the meanings of the oblique cases of the
Relative Pronouns (i. e. 'whom, which, that, what', governed
by the words **of, to, on, in, out of, from, by, with)**
and **where** with that of the verb. They are derived
from every kind of verbs, whether Active, Neuter or
Passive.

§ 412. The Objective Participles are formed by the
addition of possessive suffixes to the Past, Pluperfect,
Future and Past Future tenses of the Subjective Participle (§§ 401—402). These are used as objects or as
adjectives qualifying the objects.

Subjective Participle.

Past: يازدق *yazdiq*

Pluperfect: يازمش اولان *yazmîsh olan*

Future: يازه‌جق *yazajaq*

Past Future: يازه‌جق اولان *yazajaq olan*

The **person** who wrote; who had written ...

Objective Participle.

Past: يازديغم *yazdighîm*

Pluperfect: يازمش اولديغم *yazmîsh oldoughoum*

Future: يازه‌جغم *yazajaghîm*

Past Future: يازه‌جق اولديغم *yazajaq oldoughoum*

The **thing** which I wrote, which I shall write ...

§ 413.   Objective Past Tense.   ماضئ صله

Per. 1.	يازديغم *yazdighim'*,	يازدقلرم *yazdiqlarim'*.	
2.	يازديغنك *yazdighiñ'*,	يازدقلرك *yazdiqlariñ'*,	
3.	يازديغى *yazdighi'*,	يازدقلرى *yazdiqlari'*,	
1.	يازديغمز *yazdighimiz'*,	يازدقلريمز *yazdiqlarimiz'*,	
2.	يازديغكز *yazdighiñiz'*,	يازدقلريكز *yazdiqlariñiz'*,	
3.	يازدقلرى *yazdiqlari'*,	يازدقلرى *yazdiqlari'*.	

That which I, he, we, you, they wrote. Those which I, you ... wrote.

§ 414.   Pluperfect.   حكايةٔ ماضئ صله

يازمش اولديغم   *yazmish' oldoughoum.*   }   That which I, you,

يازمش اولدقلرى   *yazmish' oldouqlari.*   }   they ... have written.

§ 415.   Future.   مستقبل صله

Per. 1.	يازه‌جغم *yazajaghim'*,	يازه‌جقلرم *yazajaqlarim'*,	
2.	يازه‌جغك *yazajaghiñ'*,	يازه‌جقلرك *yazajaqlariñ'*,	
3.	يازه‌جغى *yazajaghi'*,	يازه‌جقلرى *yazajaqlari'*,	
1.	يازه‌جغمز *yazajaghimiz'*,	يازه‌جقلريمز *yazajaqlarimiz'*,	
2.	يازه‌جغكز *yazajaghiñiz'*,	يازه‌جقلريكز *yazajaqlariñiz'*,	
3.	يازه‌جقلرى *yazajaqlari'*,	يازه‌جقلرى *yazajaqlari'*.	

That which I shall write ...   Those which I shall write ...

§ 416.   Past Future.   حكايةٔ مستقبل صله

يازه‌جق اولديغم   *yazajaq' oldoughoum.*   }   That which I, we shall

يازه‌جق اولديغمز   *yazajaq' oldoughoumouz.*   }   have written ...

مطالعات   *Múta-la-at* Remarks.

§ 417.   I. The plural forms (*yazdiqlarim'*, *yazajaq-larim'*) are never used as adjectives in the plural to

qualify plural nouns, since adjectives when they qualify nouns do not take the plural termination (§§ 71, 423).

§ 418. II. The Objective Future Participle first person and the Indicative Future first person are the same in spelling, but in pronunciation and use are different. If the word is a participle, it is never found at the end of the sentence, and it is accented on the last syllable, but if it be the Indicative, it must be put at the end of the sentence and is accented on the penultimate.

Bir mektoub yazaja'ghîm.   I shall write a letter.
Yazajaghîm' mektoub.   The letter which I shall write.

Comparison. تطبيقات

1. This is (the book which I read).
 (Oqoudoughoum kitab) bou dour.
 Note. The verb is first person, the Past Part. is first person.
2. The cook will bake (the food which you like).
 Ashjî (sévdiyiñ yéméyi) pishiréjék.
3. Where is (the letter which I have written) yesterday.
 Dúnki (yazmîsh oldoughoum méktoub) nérédé dir?
4. This is (the word which they spoke).
 (Seôylédikléri seôz) bou dour.
5. (The money which he gained) is ten piastres.
 (Qazandîghî para) on ghouroush dour.
6. The medicine [acc.] (which the sick person drank).
 Ol hastanîñ (ichdiyi ilají [acc.]).
7. The house (in which you are dwelling) now (loc.).
 Shimdi (otourdoughouñouz) év.
8. The man (whose house [acc.] we rented), is dead
 (E'vini kiraladîghîmîz) adém eôlmúsh dúr.
9. The lesson (which I shall [or have to] learn).
 (eôyrénéjeyim' [or eôyrénéjék' oldoughoum] dérs.
10. Do you know (the road [acc.] which we shall go) to-morrow?
 Yarîn (gidéjéyimiz [or gidéjék oldoughoumouz])
 yolou bilir' misîñiz?
11. (The water with which [Inst.]) the master washed himself.
 Efféndinîñ (yîyqandîghî) sou.

13*

12. The Teacher cut (the branch on which [loc.] he
    was sitting).

Hoja (otourdoughou dalı) késdi.

The Declinable Objective Participles.

§ 419. If the Substantive which is the object in
the sentence is omitted and the participle is used alone
as an object, then the four tenses of the Objective Participle are declined according to the case and person
of the object and the person of the verb in the Relative
clause (§ 410).

§ 420. For instance بنم يازديغم مكتوبى كوندر *bénim
yazdighim' méktoubou geônder*, 'send the letter which I
wrote', here the object *(méktoubou)* is in the Accusative,
the subject first person *(bénim)* and the tense past *(yazdighim)*. But if I say بنم يازديغمى كوندر *bénim yazdighimi'
geônder*, 'send what I wrote', the meaning is the same,
but the Participle takes the accusative termination,
because the noun is omitted.

§ 421. The case is just the same with the adjectives also; I can say ايى آدملرى سوەرم *éyi adémléri' sévérim*, I like the good people: It is possible again to say
ايیلری سوەرم *Eyiléri' sévérim* I like the good (ones), omitting the Substantive.

§ 422. The addition of the possessive endings
implies a possessor. The possessor is put in the Genitive case and forms the Subject in the English sentence.
It is not always inserted, the terminations of the Objective participle being substitutes for it. بنم يازديغم
bénim yazdighim' is equal to يازديغم *yazdighim'*; the ending showing the person and the number (§ 102).

§ 423. The singular nominative is used both as an
object and as an adjective qualifying the object, but the
other cases, as well as the plural nominative of Past
and Future Objectives, are never to be used as adjectives,
but as Substantive object: it is not permitted to say

بثم يازدقلرم *bénim yazdighîmî méktoubou* or بنم يازديغمى مكتوبى

بنم يازديغم *bénim yazdiqlarîm méktoublarî*; but مكتوبلرى

bénim بنم يازديغمى and بنم يازديغم مكتوبلرى or مكتوبى

yazdighîmî or بنم يازدقلرىى *bénim yazdiqlarîmî* (§§ 406, 417).

Past Tense.   ماضى صله *Maziyi Sîlé.*

First Person Singular.   متكلم *Mûtékél'lim.*

N.	يازديغم	*yazdighîm'*	
G.	يازديغمك	*yazdighîmîñ'* of —	
D.	يازديغمه	*yazdighîma'* to —	That which I wrote, what
A.	يازديغمى	*yazdighîmî'*	I wrote, my writing.
L.	يازديغمده	*yazdighîmda'* in —	
A.	يازديغمدن	*yazdighîmdan'* from —	

First Person Plural.

N.	يازديغمز	*yazdighîmîz'*	
G.	يازديغمزك	*yazdighîmîziñ'* of —	
D.	يازديغمزه	*yazdighîmîza'* to —	That which we wrote,
A.	يازديغمزى	*yazdighîmîzî'*	what we wrote,
L.	يازديغمزده	*yazdighîmîzda'* in —	our writing ...
A.	يازديغمزدن	*yazdighîmîzdan'* from —	

Second Person.   خاطب *Moukhatab.*

N.	سوديكك	*sévdiyiñ*	سوديككز *sévdiyiñiz*
G.	سوديككك	*sévdiyiyiñ* of —	سوديككزك *sévdiyiñiziñ* of —
D.	سوديككه	*sévdiyiñé* to —	سوديككزه *sévdiyiñizé* to —

That which thou lovedst, you loved; their, your loving ...

Third Person.   غائب *Ghayib.*

N.	اوقوديغى	*oqoudoughou'*	اوقودقلرى *oqoudouqlarî'*

G. اوقودوغونك *oqoudoughounouñ'* of –   اوقودوقلرينك *oqoudouqlariniñ'* of –

D. اوقودوغونه *oqoudoughouna'* to –   اوقودوقلرينه *oqoudouqlarina'* to –, etc.

That which he read.   What they read, their reading ...

Future Tense. مستقبل صله *Mustaqbéli Sîlé.*

First Person. متكلم

N.   يازه جغم *yazajaghîm'*   يازه جغمز *yazajaghimiz'*

G.   يازه جغمك *yazajaghîmiñ'* of —   يازه جغمزك *yazajaghîmîziñ'* of —

D.   يازه جغمه *yazajaghîma'* to —   يازه جغمزه *yazajaghîmiza'* to —

A.   يازه جغمى *yazajaghîmî'*   يازه جغمزى *yazajaghîmîzî'*

L.   يازه جغمده *yazajaghîmda'* in —   يازه جغمزده *yazajaghîmîzda'* in —

A.   يازه جغمدن *yazajaghîmdan'* from -   يازه جغمزدن *yazajaghîmîzdan'* from —

That which I shall write, what I shall write; My writing ...

Second Person. مخاطب

N.   بيله جككك *biléjéyiñ'*   بيله جككز *biléjéyiñiz'*

G.   بيله جككك *biléjéyiyiñ'* of —   بيله جككزك *biléjéyiñiziñ'* of —

D.   بيله جككه *biléjéyiñé'* to —   بيله جككزه *biléjéyiñizé'* to —

A.   بيله جككنى *biléjéyiñî'*   بيله جككزى *biléjéyiñizi'*

L.   بيله جككده *biléjéyiñdé'* in —   بيله جككزده *biléjéyiñizdé'* in —

A.   بيله جككدن *biléjéyiñdén'* from —   بيله جككزدن *biléjéyiñizdén'* from —

What thou, you will know.   Thy, your knowledge ...

Third Person. غائب

N.   يازه جغى *yazajaghî'*   يازه جقلرى *yazajaqlari'*

G.   يازه جغينك *yazajaghîniñ'* of —   يازه جقلرينك *yazajaqlariniñ'* of —

D.   يازه جغينه *yazajaghîna'* to —   يازه جقلرينه *yazajaqlarina'* to —

A.   يازه جغينى *yazajaghîni'*   يازه جقلرينى *yazajaqlarini'*

L.   يازه جغينده *yazajaghînda'* in —   يازه جقلرنده *yazajaqlarinda'* in —

A.   يازه جغيندن *yazajaghîndan'* from -   يازه جقلرندن *yazajaqlarîndan'* from -

What he, they will write.   His, their writing ...

§ 424. Four important gerunds are obtained from the Declinable Objective Participles.

§ 425. **The Tenth Gerund.** The Dative case of the Objective Future Participle is used as a gerund: it then corresponds to the phrases 'instead of, rather than'; as:

بن آته بینه‌جکمه اشكه بینه‌رم *bén ata binéjéyimé éshéyé binérim.* I would rather ride a donkey than a horse.

§ 426. **The Fourth Gerund.** The Locative case of the Objective Past Participles, when used as a gerund, indicates the time of an action, when an action is performed.

مسافرلر كلديكنده یه‌مکیمزی یه‌دك *mûsafirlér géldiyindé yéméyi-mizi yédik.* When the guests arrived we dined; or, the guests having arrived we dined; or, the guests arriving we dined; or, on the arrival of the guests we dined.

§ 427. **The Twelfth Gerund.** The Ablative case of Past and Future Participles is used as a gerund, and indicates the reason why some other action is performed? The doer of the first is indicated by the possessive affixes; as:

پدرم مکتوب یازه‌جغندن کلمه‌دی *pédérim méktoub yazajaghîndan gélmédi.* My father did not come, because he was about to write a letter.

او ایشیتمه‌دیکندن جواب ویرمه‌دی *o ishitmédiyindén jévab vérmédi.* Owing to his not having heard he did not answer.

§ 428. **The Third Gerund.** If کبی *gibi* is added to the nominative of the Objective Participle, another gerund is obtained, which means 'as soon as'.

قارداشك كلديكی کبی بنی چاغیر *qardashîñ gél'diyi gibi béni chaghîr.* Call me as soon as your brother comes (§§ 334, 431).

§ 429. As we have already seen, the Dative, Ablative and Locative cases of the Objective Participles have two meanings: one as a participle, the other as a gerund. This identity must not escape the student. But it is very easy to distinguish them, as the subject of the gerund is always in the *nominative*, while that

of the participle is in the *genitive*. Therefore confusion is scarcely possible when the words are used in a sentence. (See the examples 5—8.)

تطبيقات Comparison.

1. Give me the account (of whatever you have bought).
   (*Sizin* satin aldighiniziñ) hisabini baña vériñiz.

2. The guest does not eat (what he expects), but eats (what he finds).
   Músafir (oumdoughounou) yéméz, (bouldoughounou) yér.

3. Put in the bag (whatever you [will] find).
   (*Boulajaghiñizi*) torbaya qoyouñ.

4. Have you anything to say ([of] what the boy wrote)?
   Chojoughouñ (yazdighina) bir déyéjéyiñiz' var mî?

5a. I have no doubt (that you will do) this nicely.
   Séniñ bounou gûzéljé (yapajaghiña) shûb'hém yoq.

5b. (Instead of doing) the wrong, do the best.
   Sén kéôtúyû (yapajaghiña), éyiyi yap.

6a. There is no deficiency (in what I sold).
   Bénim (satdighîmda) bir' qousour yoq dour.

6b. (Whenever I sell) your property, I will give you your money.
   Bén maliñi (satdighîmda) parañî véririm.

7a. I had no news (of his being ill [that he was ill]).
   Onouñ hasta (oldoughoundan) habérim yoghoudou.

7b. My mother could not come here (because she was ill).
   Validém hasta (oldoughoundan) bouraya gélémédi.

8a. My father did not know (that you were about to come) here.
   Sizin bouraya (géléjéyiñizdén) babamiñ habéri yoghoudou.

8b. We could not go there (because we had to come here).
   Biz bouraya (géléjéyimizdén) oraya gidémédik.

لغتلر Words.

اوكوتمك *ûyûtmék* to grind   a. روح *rouh* Spirit

a. تعجب ايتمك *téaj'jûb ét''* to marvel   a. علامت *alamét* sign

a. معلومات *malûmat* knowledge   ¹ جورباجی *chorbaji* Mr.

a. خاطر *khatîr* memory   t. p. بكزاده *béyzadé* nobleman.

¹ A conventional title applied to Christian notables, bankers, merchants, etc.

Exercise 62. تعلیم ۶۲

۱ ویرمش اولدیغکز ساعت · بنم اوكوتمش اولدیغم بوغدای · اوکرده نه جك اولدیغم درس · آغالرك ایچه جك اولدقلری قهوه ۰ ۲ جورباجیلرك صاته جق اولدقلری خانه · بکزاده لرك صاتون آلمش اولدقلری آت · ۳ کتیرمش اولدیغی قهوه فینجانی صفرا اوزرنده ایدی ؛ آله كز اولدی می ؟ ٤ حسین قالفه نك بکا سویله یه جك اولدیغی سوزك نه اولدیغنی بیلیرمیسین ؟ — خیر افندم ! نه دیه جکندن معلوماتم یوقدر · ۵ شاکردم اولدیغکز ایچون · شاکردم اولدیغکزدن · شاکردم اولدیغکز سببیله · ٦ ویره مدکلری ایچون · ویره مدکلرندن · ویره مدکلرندن طولایی · ویره مه دکلری سببدن حبس اولوندیلر · ۷ شاکردلر درسلرینی سویله یه مه دکلرندن · سویلمکه قادر اوله مادقلری سببدن تکدیر اولوندیلر · ۸ « یتیشه مه دیکك كویك بری یاننده یاتی ویر » (§ ۲۸٦) ·

Exercise 63. تعلیم ۶۳

۱ کلدیکنی کوزه مه دم · کزدکلری باغچه قاین آنامکدر · ۲ یاتاجقلری یاتاق اوتدن ایمش · ۳ سن بنم دیدیکمی خاطردن چیقارمه · ٤ ات کسدیکم بیچاق نرده در ؟ — اتك اولدیغی دولابده در · ۵ كله جك هفته بزه كله جك اولان مسافرلری طانیرمیسکز ؟ ٦ یارین

بن كلديكمده هر ايشى بيتمش كورمك ايسته‌رم · ۷ بويله كوتو
آرقه‌داشلر ايله كزه‌جككه ، ايى آرقه‌داشلر ايله كز قونوش ·
۸ مكتبده چان چالينديغنده هر كس يرينه ياتار ايدى · ۹ يانار طاغلره
ياقين ياپيلان شهرلر ذلذله‌دن پك قورقارلر · ۱۰ كورديككز
وَ كوره‌جككز شيلرى كيمسه‌يه سويله‌مه‌يه‌سكز · ۱۱ دايىكده
اولان آلاجغمى آلديغم كبى سكا اولان ويره‌جكمى ويره‌جكم ·

ترجمه ٦٤   Translation 64.

1. I received the letter which you sent me, dated
7th July 1902. 2. The house to which I am now going is
my father-in-law's. 3. I wrote all the words you spoke
to me. 4. The greatest of the cities which Alexander
the Great built [made], was Alexandria. 5. The physician of whom you speak is in Europe. 6. Mr. Jacob
is the man of whom we have read in the newspapers.
7. Do you know what I want? — I don't know what
you want, if you do not tell me. 8. Let no one change
that which I have written. 9. Do you know that I lost
my purse full of money? 10. When I was in Constantinople I saw the goods in the shops changed every day.
11. Learn this from what you see. 12. I did not know
that he went to Trebizond.

ترجمه ٦٥   Translation 65.

1. He that hath an ear, let him hear what the
Spirit saith unto the churches. 2. For he knew what
was in man. 3. They marvelled that he talked with
the woman. 4. What shall be the sign of thy coming?
5. Let not thy left hand know what thy right hand
doeth. 6. Have you not read what David did, when he
was hungered, and they that were with him? 7. We heard
of their having become soldiers. 8. I do not object to
your going there. 9. The baker is not an honest
(*doghrou*) man: he writes what is due to him [his
credits] and does not write his debits (what he owes).

تعليم قرائت Reading Exercise.

Translate and tell the following story in Turkish fully.

1. This is the house that Jack built.
2. This is the malt, That lay in the house that Jack built.
3. This is the rat, That ate the malt, That lay in the house that Jack built.
4. This is the cat, That killed the rat, That ate the malt, That lay in the house that Jack built.
5. This is the dog, That worried the cat, That killed the rat, That ate the malt, That lay in the house that Jack built.
6. This is the cow with the crumpled horn, That tossed the dog, That worried the cat, That killed the rat, That ate the malt, That lay in the house that Jack built.
7. This is the maiden all forlorn, That milked the cow with the crumpled horn, That tossed the dog, That worried the cat, That killed the rat, That ate the malt, That lay in the house that Jack built.
8. This is the man all tatter'd and torn, That kissed the maiden all forlorn, That milked the cow with the crumpled horn, That tossed the dog, That worried the cat, That killed the rat, That ate the malt, That lay in the house that Jack built.
9. This is the priest all shaven and shorn, That married the man all tatter'd and torn, That kissed the maiden all forlorn, That milk'd the cow with the crumpled horn, That tossed the dog, That worried the cat, That killed the rat, That ate the malt, That lay in the house that Jack built.
10. This is the cock that crowed in the morn, That waked the priest all shaven and shorn, That married the man all tatter'd and torn, That kissed the maiden all forlorn, That milked the cow with the crumpled horn, That tossed the dog, That worried the cat, That killed the rat, That ate the malt, That lay in the house that Jack built.

11. This is the farmer sowing his corn, That kept the cock that crowed in the morn, That waked the priest all shaven and shorn, That married the man all tatter'd and torn, That kissed the maiden all forlorn, That milk'd the cow with the crumpled horn, That tossed the dog, That worried the cat, That killed the rat, That ate the malt, That lay in the house that Jack built.

Translation.

11. *Jackiñ yapdighi évdé saqlanan, Arpayî yéyén, Faréyi êôldûrén, Kédiyi ûrkûdén, Kêôpéyi bouynouzlayan, Eyri bouynouzlou inéyi saghan, Bicharé qîzî êôpén, Esgi bûskû roubalî adémi nikiâhlayan, Daz qafalî (shaven), tûysûz (shorn) papazî ouyandîran, Sabah'layîn êôtén horozou saqlayan, Boughdayî ékén chift'ji [ishté] bou dour.*

مكالمه Conversation.

س) يعقوب كهيانك ياپديرديغى اوده صاقلانمش اولديغى آرپهيى يهين كيمدر ؟

ج) اكرى بوينوزلى اينهكك قاقديغى كوپكك قورقوتديغى كدينك يديك فاره در .

س) اول اكرى بوينوزلى اينهكى صاغان قيز ايله نكاحلانان كيمدر ؟

ج) اول اوكسوز قيزى اوپن اسكى پوسكو روبالى بر چوبان ايدى .

س) اول اوكسوز بيچاره قيزى شول پريشان چوبان ايلهكيم نكاحلادى ؟

ج) صباحلاين اوتن خروسك اويانديرمش اولديغى داز قافالى توسيز پاپاس نكاحلادى .

س) داز قافالى پاپاسى اويانديرمش اولان خروسى صاقلايان هريف كيمدر ؟

ج) شويشيلدكلرنه اورتولمش اولان طاغارى درهلرى اكن رنجبر هارو اغا در .

درس ۳۰ Lesson 30.

رابطه صيغهلر Gerunds.

§ 430a. The number of purely Turkish Conjunctions is very limited, only six in number: and these too are

derived from Verbs or Adverbs (§ 475). The place of
Conjunctions is supplied by Gerunds, which are called
Conjunctive Moods or Words, *Rabîta Siyghéler*. They
are mere combinations of Conjunctions with the verbs,
appended at the end of sentences (§ 230). The Gerunds,
like the Conjunctions, serve the purpose of connecting
sentences and parts of sentences. They have the same
power of government as their verbs, but they are never
used alone as governing words.

§ 430b. There are thirteen gerunds in Turkish,
some of which we have already met with in the course
of the previous lessons. Here we shall give them in
order. (See the Table.)

§ 431. **The Third Gerund.** This is formed by adding the termination ينجه ' نجه *-injé, -înja* to the root,
(and *-yinjé, -yînja, -younja* if the root ends in
a vowel). It means 'as soon as' or 'on'; ex.:

يازنجه كتدى *yazinja gitdi* as soon as he wrote, he went out.

اوقويونجه اوطور *oqouyounja otour* on your reading sit down.

The meaning is also expressed in two other ways (§§ 334, 425).

§ 432. But the Negative form has a wholly different meaning.

يازماينجه كتمه *yaz'mayinja git'mé.* Don't go unless you write.

§ 433. **The Eleventh Gerund.** The third form of
the Gerund when annexed to يهدك ' يهدكين ' يهقدر
-yé dék, -yé déyin, -yé qadar, means until.

بن كلنجهيهدك اوطور *bén gélinjéyédék otour.* Sit until I come.

§ 434. **The Fourteenth Gerund.** By adding ايكن or
كن *-ikén, -kén* to the Aorist, Present, Dubitative,
Future and Necessitative third persons, another gerund-
like expression is obtained, which is rendered by while.

Gitmish ikén. Now that the act of going has occured.
Yazayaq ikén. While just about to write.

No.	Gerunds		Meaning	Derived from	Section §
1	يازارجسنه	yazar'jasına	As if —, intending to —	Aorist	331
2a	يازمدن	yaz'madan	Anteriorly to —	Infinitive	299
b	يازمدن اول	yaz'madan év-vél		»	»
c	يازمازدن	yaz'mazdan	Before —	Aorist	333
d	يازمازدن اول	yaz'mazdan év-vél		»	»
3a	يازنجه	yazın'ja	As soon as he —	Root	431
b	يازار يازماز	yazar' yazmaz		Aorist	334
c	يازدغى گبى	yaz'dığı gibi		Obj. Participle	428
4a	يازدقده	yazdıq'da	When the — occurred, whenever, when the —, on the —	Past	345
b	يازدغنده	yazdıghında'		Obj. Participle	426
5	يازدقجه	yazdıq'ja	The more — the more —	Root	346

6a	يازالي	*yazalí*	Since the act of — occurred,	Optative	369
b	يازالدن برو	*yazalídan bérou*	since he —, ever since he —	»	»
c	يازدى يازالى	*yazdí yazalí*		Opt., Past	»
7	يازه يازه	*yaza' yaza*	— on steadily, keeping on —	Optative	370
8	يازه رق	*yaza'raq*	continuing to —	»	371
9	يازسه	*yazasí*	May he —!	»	372
	يازسه جه	—'ja		»	»
10	يازه جغنه	*yazajaghí'ña*	Instead of —, Rather than —	Obj. Participle	425
11	يازنجه	*yazín'ja*	Until he —	Root	433
	يازه جغه قدر	—ya qadar		»	»
12	يازديغندن	*yazdíghín'dan*	Because he —	»	427
	يازه جغندن	*yazajaghín'dan*	by the act of —	Obj. Participle	»
13	يازوب	*yazíp'*	Having —	Root	435
14	يازاركن	*yazar'kén*	While, during	Present, Aorist, Dubit., Future, Necessitative.	434

§ 435. **The Thirteenth Gerund** is a conjunctive inflexion of the verb equivalent to a verb (generally of the same tense and frequently with the same object) found at the end of the phrase, followed by the conjunction 'and'. The sense may be such as to require the words 'also' and afterwards to be supplied, according as the succession of the two actions is intended. It is characterized by the termination وب— *-oup, ip*, (or يوب— *-youp* if the root ends in a vowel [53]). § 17; as:

يازوب *yazîp* having written.　اوقو يوب *oqouyoup* having read.

اوطوروب اوقودیلر *otouroup oqoudoular*. They sat and (afterwards) read, or having sat down they read: equivalent to *otourdoular vé oqoudoular*.

کیدوب کوره جکم *gédip gêôréjéyim*, equivalent to *gédéjéyim vé gêôréjéyim*. I shall go and see [him also] (having gone I shall see).

لغتلر Words.

f. آبانیز *abanîz* Ebony		a. محجوب *mahjoub* humble
داملامق ، طاملامق *damlamaq* to drop		a. مغرور *maghroor* proud
صورمق *sormaq* to ask		a. او راضی *razi ol″* to be content
قورباغه *qourbagha* frog		کنیش *génish* wide
کچینمك *géchinmék* to subsist		a. جاهل *jahil* young people
پیره *piré* flea		تکری ، تاکری *tañrî* God
بت *bit* louse		اوروملك *ûrûmék* to bark
دوه قوشی *dévé qoushou* ostrich		باطلامق *patlamaq* to burst.

تعلیم ٦٦ Exercise 66.

Douroubou émsal. ضروب امثال Proverbs.

۱ آغاج صوده طوره طوره اولور آبانیز ؛ اوشاق اوده طوره طوره اولور بابا کزـ ۲ طاملایه طاملایه کول اولورـ ۳ صوره صوره بولنور بغدادـ ٤ قالین اینجه لینجه یه دك اینجه نك جانی چیقارـ ٥ کوله صو کلنجیه قدر قورباغه نك کوزی باطلارـ ٦ زنکینك کوکلی اولنجیه یه دك فقراتك

ایشی بیتر· ۷ قارینجه قدرنجه· ۸ اولومی کورونجه خسته‌لغه راضی
اولدی· ۹ کنیش وقتکده دار کچین که دارلق کلدیکنده کنیش
کچینه بیله‌سین· ۱۰ پیره ایتده بولنور؛ پاره یکیتده· ۱۱ جاهلك
تکریسی اولماز· ۱۲ آتالو سوزی سسسز توفنکه بکزر اوردیغی کبی
یاتیریر· ۱۳ آنبال دوه قوشینه بکزر: یوکه کلدیکنده «قوشم» دیر
یه کلدیکنده «دوه‌یم»· ۱٤ ایت اورور کروان کوچر· ۱٥ اوله‌جغه چاره
یوق؛ ایش اوله‌جغنه واریر· ۱٦ دیوارك قولاغی وار· ۱۷ قورقولی
دوش کورمه‌دن اویانیق یاتمه‌سی ایی در·

ترجمه ٦۷   Translation 67.

1. When the teacher began speaking, every one
stopped his talk. 2. Until the teacher entered the school-
room, all the pupils were talking together. 3. Since
I came to Merzifoun I have three times visited Mounjousoun. 4. As soon as Eli goes, I will call you. 5. I
read and write. He came and went afterwards. 6. He
mounted his horse and went into the country. 7. The
teacher Nasréd-din, taking an axe, mounted the tree
and began to cut the branch on which he sat. 8. A man
saw him and said that he would fall down from the
tree. As soon as the man spoke the teacher fell down.
9. He ran after the man and caught him by his collar
and said: As you knew that I would fall down from
the tree, of course you must also know the time when
I will die. 10. The man said: When your ass brays
three times, you will die. 11. Do not go until I come.

مکالمه   Conversation.

س) قونشوکز عالی بابا ناصل بر آدم در؟

ج) فقیر ایکن محجوب ایدی ایسه‌ده زنکینلند کجه مغرورلانیور·

س) برادرکز شیمدی‌یه قدر قاچ مکتوب یازمشدر؟

ج) برادر افندی استانبوله کیتدی کیده‌لی اوچ مکتوب یازمشدر·

س) خسته‌کز شیمدی ناصلدر؟

ج) حکیمك ویردیکی علاجی ایچه‌لیدنبری خسته ایولشمکه یوز طوتدی .

تعلیم قرائت Reading Exercise.

انسانك حیواندن فرقی

The Distinction between Man and Beast.

انسانك حیوانلردن فرقی سوز سویله‌مك وَ اوقویوب یازمق ایله در .

انسان یارادیلیشده¹ حیوانلردن چوق عالی² در . حیوانلرده حِسّ³ وار در .

مثلا⁴ : کوپك افندیسنی کوردیکی کبی ' طانیه‌رق ' سوینوب قویروغینی

صاللامغه⁵ باشلار . — بن سوز سویله‌یه بیلدیکم ایچون حالی⁶ بر آدمه

آکلاده‌بیلیرم ؛ فقط بیچاره⁷ کوپك وَ سائر⁸ حیوانلر نطقدن⁹ محروم¹⁰

اولدقاری جهتله¹¹ ' حاللرینی بنم کبی افاده¹² ایده‌مزلر .

بن بویم طوغری اولدیغی حالده¹³ یورورم . باشمی هر طرفه

چویره‌بیلدیکم کبی¹⁴ کوکه طوغری ده قالدیره‌بیلیرم . لکن سائر

حیوانلر اویله یاپه‌مازلر . انسانده کورمك ' ایشیتمك ' ال وَ سائر

اعضا¹⁵ ایله طوقونغق ' طاتمق¹⁶ ' قوقلامق حسّاری وار در .

Words. 1. creation. 2. high, noble. 3. *hiss'* instinct (of animals). 4. for instance 5. to wag. 6. *hal* condition, case, situation. 7. poor. 8. a. *sayir* other. 9. a. *noutq* speech. 10 a. *mahroum* destitute. 11. *oldouqlari jihétlé* = *oldouqlarindan*. 12. *ifadé ét.'* to explain, to state. 13. being (being in the state of). 14. since I can turn. 15. *aza* members. 16. *tatmaq, datmaq* to taste.

مابعد mab'ad Continuation.

بو حسّار حیوانلرده ده واردر . حتّی¹ بعض حیوانلر انساندن دها

زیاده کوزور وَ قوقو آلیر . بن آیاقلرم ایله یوروبه‌بیلدیکمی ' قوللرقلرم ایله

ایشیده‌بیلدیکمی ' آغزیم ایله ییه‌بیلدیکمی ؛ بورینم ایله قوقو آله‌بیلدیکمی

بیلیرم ؛ انجاق² حیوان بیلمز ' هر شیئی بیلمه‌یه‌رك اجرا³ ایدر . بن

Words. 1. *hat'ta* even. 2. *anjaq* only, but. 3. *ijra ét.'* to do, to perform.

ادراکه⁴ مالك اولدیغم ایچون⁵ هر بر شی ایچون دوشونه بیلیرم · مثلا :

بر خانه یه نیچون قاپو ، پنجره ، اوجاق⁶ لازِم⁷ اولدیغنی ؛ پنچره لره

جامك⁸ نیچون طاقیلدیغنی⁹ ؛ بر قابه¹⁰ نیچون قولپ¹¹ قونولدیغنی

آکلاریم · بر چیزمه¹² یاپق ایچون دمیر یاخود پاچاوره¹³ قوللانیلمایوب ده

نیچون مشین¹⁴ قوللایلدیغنی فرق ایده رم ·¹⁵

کندی هوسمه¹⁶ ، فکرمه اویعایوب آنامه ، بابامه ، خواجه لریه

اطاعت¹⁷ ایتمکلکم لازم اولدیغنی بیلیرم ·   ⟨معلم ناجی¹⁸⟩

4. *idrak* intellect.   5. = *malik oldoughoumdan: malik ol."* to possess.   6. *ojaq* a hearth.   7. necessary.   8. *jam* glass.   9. *daq-maq* to put, affix.   10. *qab* vessel.   11. *qoulp* handle.   12. *chizmé* out of door shoes.   13. *pachavra* a clout, rag.   14. *méshin* leather.   15. *farq ét."* to distinguish.   16. *hévés* a mania, wrong desire.   17. *ita-at' ét."* to obey.   18. *Mou-al'lim Naji.* Professor Naji (a distinguished Turk author 1850—94).

درس ۳۱ Lesson 31.

Nouns and Adjectives derived from Verbs.

صفت مشبهه Verbal Adjective.

§ 436. The regular form of the Verbal Adjectives (*Siféti Mûshéb'bihé*) ends in یجی *-iji*, *-îjî*, *-oujou* and it is derived from every kind of verbs, except Passive and Reciprocal verbs; as (§ 53):

یازمق *yazmaq* to write: $\sqrt{}$ یاز ؛ یازیجی *yazîjî* one whose business is to write, a clerk.

صاتمق *satmaq* to sell: $\sqrt{}$ صات ؛ صاتیجی *satîjî* one whose business is to sell, a seller, a dealer.

اوقومق *oqoumaq* to read; $\sqrt{}$ اوقو ؛ اوقوییجی *oqouyoujou* one who to invite: habitually reads, a reader; inviter.

سیلمك *silmék* to wipe, to rub out: $\sqrt{}$ سیل ؛ سیلیجی *siliji* a professional scrubber of floors.

§ 437. This form resembles the Subjective Present Participle in meaning (§ 401). The difference is that, while

yazan, satan, oqouyan, pishirén mean 'one who *occasionally* writes, sells, reads, or cooks', the Verbal Adjectives *yazîjî, satîjî, oqouyoujou, pishiriji* respectively mean 'one who *habitually* does so, whose *occupation* is to write, to read, to cook', that is to say 'clerk', 'reader' and 'cook'.

§ 438. There are other forms of verbal nouns and adjectives which do not always occur, not being formed from all roots, but they can be divided into classes as: —

§ 439. I. If the verbal root ends in a vowel, a verbal noun or adjective is obtained by omitting the *mim* of the Infinitive termination.

چوروملك *chûrûmék* to rot: چوروك *ckûrûk* rotten.

صوغومق *sovoumaq* to be cold: صوغوق *sovouq* cold (§ 36).

ايشلهملك *ishlémék* to work: ايشلك *ishlék* that works well, smoothly.

§ 440. II. If the verbal ends in a consonant, the *mim* of the Infinitive is changed into *vav*, or *yé:*

آچمق *achmaq* to open: آچيق *achîq* open.

بوزمق *bozmaq* to spoil: بوزوق *bozouq* spoilt.

§ 441. III. By removing the Infinitive ending مك ، مق and adding غون ، قين ، قون -*qoun, -qîn, -ghoun* or كين ، كون -*gûn, -gin* to the root, another class of verbals is formed; as:

سورملك *sûrmék* to banish: سوركون *sûrgûn* an exile.

پيشملك *pishmék* to become cooked: پيشكين *pishgin* well baked.

جوشمق *joshmaq* ⎫
طاشمق *tashmaq* ⎬ to overflow:
جوشقون *joshqoun* ⎫
طاشقين *tashqîn* ⎬ overflowing.

يانمق *yanmaq* to be burut: يانغين *yanghîn* fire, conflagration.

§ 442. IV. Sometimes لى -*li*, لو -*lou* or ى -*i, -î, -ou, -û* is added to the root:

قاپامق *qapamaq* to shut: قاپالى *qapalî* shut.

كيزلهملك *gizlémék* to hide: كيزلى *gizlî* hidden.

So also: صاقلى *saqli'* hidden;   آصيلى *asili'* hung.

طولى *dolou* full;   اولو *ôlû* dead.

§ 443. V. The second and third forms of Derivative Infinitives are regarded as regular verbal nouns, as we have seen (§ 301):

دوكمه *dêôkmé* cast.   باصمه *basma* printed.

الويريشلى *élvérishli* sufficient.   آصمه *asma* suspended.

§ 444. VI. Some of the verbal nouns are formed by the addition of م ٔ يم *-im, -îm, -oum* to the root:

يمك ٔ يه‌مك *yémék* to eat: يم *yém* food.

اولمك *ôlmék* to die: اولوم *ôlûm* death.

ايچمك *ichmék* to drink: ايچيم *ichim* a draught.

§ 445. VII. Others are made by the addition of ى ٔ و ٔ كى *-i, -î, -ou, -gi* to the stem:

يازمق *yazmaq* to write: يازى *yazî* writing.

قورقمق *qorq'maq* to fear: قورقو *qorqou* fear.

ايچمك *ichmék* to drink: ايچكى *ichgi* intoxicating liquid.

§ 446. VIII. Another class of verbals is obtained from the passive verbs, by adding ج *j* to the stem (§ 265):

سوينمك *sévinmék* to be joyful: سوينج *sevinj* joy.

اودنمك *ôdénmék* to be paid: اودونج *ôdûnj* vulgar *ôn'dûj* a loan.

Similarly: كولونج *gûlûnj* laughable;   اوصانج *osanj'* tiresome.

قازانج *qazanj* profit;   قيصقانج *qîsqanj'* jealous.

§ 447. IX. By adding دى ٔ تى ٔ ندى *-indi, -ti, -di*, another class of verbals is obtained:

يورلمق *bouyroulmaq* to be ordered: يورلتى *bouyroultou* an order.

آقمق *aqmaq* to flow: آقيندى *aqîntî* a current.

ييقمق *yîqmaq* to pull down: ييقينتى *yîqintî* débris.

سوپورمك *sûpûrmék* to sweep: سوپرونتى *sûprûntû* sweepings.

كورولتى ، ايكيلتى ، چاتيرتى ، جاييرتى ، پاتيرتى *patîrtî, jayîrtî,*
chatîrtî, iñilti, gûrûltû all mean a continuous or repeated clattering,
noise, roar, hissing, creaking, crackling, rending and tearing of
the sea, wind, lion etc.

§ 448. X. **The Noun of Excess** is formed by the
addition of غيـج ، غان ، قان -*qan*, -*ghan*, -*ghîj* to the stem:

چاليشمق *chalîshmaq* to work: چاليشقان *chalîshqan* assiduous.

ايشيتمك *ishitmék* to hear: ايشيتكن *ishitgén* quick to hear.

Similarly: اونوتغان ، اونوتقان *ounoutqan', ounoutghan'* forgetful.

ياپيشقـان *yapîshqan* sticky. سوزكج *sûzgéj* a strainer.

يوزكج *yûzgéj* a skilful swimmer. طـالغيـج *dalghîj* diver.

صولوغان *souloughan* shortness of breath, roaring.

§ 449. XI. **The Noun of Location** derived from
the verb is obtained by adding ق -*q* to the root, if it
ends in *élif*, and اق -*aq* if it does not end in that letter:

ياتـق *yatmaq*: $\sqrt{\text{يات}}$ ، ياتاق *yataq* bed.

اوتلامـق *otlamaq*: $\sqrt{\text{اوتلا}}$ ، اوتلاق *otlaq* a pasture.

يايلمـق *yayîlmaq* to pasture: يايلاق *yay'laq, yayla* a summer-residence, or pasturage.

قيشلا *qîshla* winter quarters, military headquarters, barrack.

§ 450. XII. **Instrumental Nouns** obtained from
the verb, are formed irregularly:

الهمك *élémék* to sift: الك *élék* a sieve.

طراق ، طاراق ، طارامق *daramaq* to comb: طاراق *daraq* a comb.

سوركى *sûrgû* sliding bar of a door. اوراق *oraq* a sickle.

So also:

بيچاق *bîchaq* a knife. بيچقى *bîchqî* gardener's knife.

ياصتيق *yastîq* a pillow. صارغى *sarghî* bandage.

باصقى *basqî* press. چالغى *chalghî* musical instrument.

سوپورکه *sûpûrgé* broom. آصقى *asqî* braces.

بيلهكى *bîléyi* a whetstone, from بيلهمك *bilémék* to sharpen.

Exercise 68. تعليم ٦٨

Change the following verbs into verbal nouns or adjectives:

I. ايصلامق *islamaq* to wet; ايستهمك to desire, to wish; ديلهمك *dilémék* to ask, to make a request; بودامق *bouda-maq* to lop; اوركمك *úrkmék* to startle.

II. آرتمق *artmaq* to remain over; اويانمق *oyanmaq* to awaken; ايلمك *ilmék* to tie with in a loop; باريشمق *barîshmaq* to make peace; صارمق *sarmaq* to wrap round; يانمق *yanmaq* to be burnt; سيلمك *silmék* to wipe; ايليمق *ilimaq* to grow luke-warm; قورقمق *qorqmaq* to fear; قاچمق *qachmaq* to flee; اورتمك *eôrtmék* to shut; كسمك *késmék* to cut; قيرمق *qir-maq* to break.

III. يورمق *yormaq* to weary; دولمق *dolmaq* to be filled; دالمق *dalmaq* to become plunged in thought; اولمق *olmaq* to be ripe; شاشمق *shashmaq* to be stupid; كسمك *kés-mék* to cut; يلمق *yilmaq* to be frightened.

VI. آلمق *almaq* to take, buy; صاتمق *satmaq* to sell; آتمق *atmaq* to throw; يودمق *youdmaq* to swallow; بيچمك *bichmék* to cut, to shape; ديلمك *dilmék* to cut into slices; سومك *sévmék* to love; اوچورمق *ouchourmaq* to cause to flee, to let fall from a hight; يلديرمق *yildîrmaq* to flash.

VII. ياپمق *yapmaq* to build; اولمك *eôlmék* to die; اولچمك *eôlchmék* to measure; بيلمك *bilmék* to know; ويرمك *vér-mék* to give, to pay tribute; اورتمك *eôrtmék* to cover; قاپامق

qapamaq to shut; چیزمك *chizmék* to scratch, to draw a line; طوغمق *doghmaq* to rise (the sun); باتمق *batmaq* to set (the sun).

XI. يالامق *yalamaq* to lick; يونمق *younmaq* to wash one'sself; باتمق *batmaq* to sink down; اوطورمق ، قونمق *otour-maq, qonmaq* to halt, to rest.

تعليم ٦٩ Exercise 69.

١ كونشك طوغديغى طرفه كون طوغنى و باتديغى طرفه كون باتى ديرلر . ٢ بيچاغكزى بيله‌دیكز می‌؟ — اكر بزده بر بيله‌كى طاشى اولسيدى ، بيله‌ر ايدم . ٣ اولومدن قورقوكز وارمى؟ بو عمردن اوصانج كلديسه ده ؛ ينه اولمك ايسته‌مم . ٤ چارشيده ايشلر ناصلدر؟ — هيچ ايو دكلدر . آلیم صاتیم يوق ، قازانج يوق . كيمسه كيمسه‌دن اون پاره اودونج آلاميور . ٥ بوكون چوق سوينجلى كورونويورسكز ؛ سزده نه وار؟ — سوكيلو بر دوستمدن بر مكتوب آلدم . اونك ايچون چوق سوينجده‌يم . ٦ روباكزى بكنمه‌دم . هيچ بيچيمى يوق بيچيمسز برشى ، كيم بيچمش كيم ديكمش . ٧ دون برشى يه‌يه‌مه‌دم ؛ بر ديليم اكمك يه‌ديم و ايكى يودوم صو ايچدم . ٨ ايچديككك توتونك ايچيسى ايى ايسه برايچيم توتون وير . ٩ ايچكى ايچمه‌يك ! بر سرخوش بيليرم كه بر اوچورومدن كنديسنى دكيزه آتدى ، آقينتى كنديسنى آلدى كوتوردى . صوكره اولوسنى چيقارديلار . ١٠ بر آتيم باروتكز وارمى؟ — چوق اونوتقان سكز ؛ براز اول يوق ديدم ايدى .

ترجمه ٧٠ Translation 70.

1. My beloved son, I have read your letter with great joy. Now I shall give you some (an) advice. Don't bor-

row money from others: if your profit (income) is less,
your expenses must be less. 2. Death is such a black
camel, that it kneels before every door. 3. The divers
plunge in the depth of the sea: they are also good swim-
mers. 4. That old man is not deaf, he is quick to
hear. 5. Your uncle's horse is short in breath (broken-
winded). 6. You are very forgetful; you forget everything. 7. He was sunk in the marsh, and was obliged
to make a halt there. 8. The children are very fond
of kites. 9. I ordered from the market three sieves,
two combs, four suspenders, five musical instruments,
ten iron bolts and one filter. 10. The soldiers were in
the winter-quarters. 11. We shall go this summer to
the pasturage of Télli-Oghlou.

مكالمه Conversation.

ايتو دكلدر . صاتيجى چوق ، آليجى يوقدر .	آليش ويريشلر ناصلدر؟
پك ايشلك بر يولدر . كيديجى كليجى پك چوقدر .	صامسون يولى ناصل بر يولدر؟
پيشكين بر اكمك و اولغون بر الما اولسه ، يهرم .	بو كون يهمك ييكه ايستككز وارمى؟
قاپو آچيق دكل ، اورتوك در .	قاپويى اورتوكز : رجا ايده‌رم .
خير ! دائما پاكت ايچه‌رم .	قاچاق توتون ايچرميسكز؟
بيتمش باريشيق اولمش .	محاربه‌دن نه‌خبر واردر؟
اصلا ! سيلك بشلكلر وَ قيريق كسيك اونلقلر ايله قاريشيقدر .	ويرديكم پاره‌يى قبول ايتديكزمى؟
خير افندم ؛ ايرماق شيمدى پك جوشقون و طاشقين در . شيمدى كچمك شاشقينلقدر .	قيزيل ايرماقدن كچه‌بيله‌جكميز .
آياقلرينده زنجير اوله‌رق درت سوركون وار ايمش .	يانغين چيقان اوده كيم وار ايمش؟
باشينده صاريق اولان شو افنديده وار در .	كيمده بر كسكين قلم تراش وار در؟

دالـغـين دورمايك ! پالتولريكـزى   پك ايى ! ايليكلرى ايليكله‌ديك .
ايليـكله‌يك ! صوغوق آلير‌سيكيز .

صاقلى كيزلى بر شيئيكز آچيقدن   خـير افنـدم ! هر شيئيكز وارميدر ؟
آچيغه در .

خـسته‌كز بو كون ناصل ايدى ؟   عقلى باشنده دكل ايدى ! اخشامه‌دك
بايغـين ايدى .

يارى كيجه‌ده بوبكجيلر نه‌چاغير‌ييورلر ؟   «يانغين وار !» ديو باغير‌ييورلر . آمان !
بنم كوزم يانغيندن پك ييلغين در .

Reading Exercise.   تعليم قرائت

Lateefé An Anecdote.   لطيفه

بر كون قونشو‌لقدن بر آدم خواجه افندى‌يه كلـوب : «كَرَم ايت
خواجه ! اشكى ويرده يوره‌كيل¹ قريه‌سنه كيده‌جكم ، كيدوب كله‌يم»
دیمش . — خواجه افندى «برشى دكل² ، اوغل ، اما اشك اوده دكلدر ،
داغه اودون كتيرمكه كيتدى» دير . حريف قاپيدن ديشارى چيقه‌جق
ايكن ، اشك در آخوردن آكيرماسون مى ؟ — «يا اشك آخورده
آكيرييور³ خواجه !» دير قونشو . خواجه كنديسنى هيچ بوزمه‌يه‌رق⁴
بر حِدَّتله⁵ — «سن نه تحاف⁶ آدم ايمشسين ؟ آخورده‌كى اشكك
آكيرمه‌سنه ايتا‌نييورسين ده ، آق صقالم ايله بنم سوزيمه ايتانمايورميسين ؟»
دیمش .

Words. 1. *Uréyil qaryési* the village Urégil (at Cæsarea).
2. nothing at all, you are welcome. 3. *añîrmaq* to bray. 4. *kén-disini hich' bozmayaraq* indifferently. 5. *hid-dét* anger. 6. *touhaf*
queer, funny, strange.

درس ٣٢ Lesson 32.

Prepositions. (Continued.)[1]

4. The Declinable Postpositions.

§ 451. Postpositions of this class are generally used as nouns in connection with other nouns and pronouns to supply the place of prepositions. Their use will be best understood from examples. These prepositions take possessive affixes and are used with the genitive case. Thus آرا *ara* means 'the midst'. آرامیزده *aramîzda* 'in our midst' i. e. 'between us'.

§ 452. The words thus employed and the English prepositions the place of which they supply are as follows (§ 236):

آرد *ard*	The back, the space behind.	Behind.
آرقه *arqa*		
آلت *alt*	The space under.	Under.
دیب *dib*	The bottom of anything.	Under.
آرا *a-ra*	The midst.	Between, among.
اوڭ *eôñ*	The front.	Before, in front of.
اوست *ûst*	The space over,	Over, upon, on.
اوزره *ûzré*	the upper part.	
دیشاری *dîsharî*	The outer part of anything.	Out of, outside.
ایچه‌ری *ichéri*	The inside, interior,	In, inside.
ایـچ *ich*	the inner part.	
ایله‌ری *iléri*	The front part.	Forward.
یوقاری *yoqari*	The top or upper part of anything.	Above.
آشاغی *ashaghi*	The lower part.	Below, under.
یان *yan*	The side.	By, near, by the side of
یر *yér*	Place.	Instead of . . .

---

[1] See Lesson 14, page 106, §§ 230—237.

گری *géri*	The hinderpart.	Back (backwards).
اطراف *étraf* a.	Surroundings.	Round, around.
اوته *ôté*	The farther side.	Beyond.
برابر *bérabér* p.	Even with, breast to breast with.	Together with.
یاقین *yaqîn*	The space near.	Near, by.
حق *haqq* a.	A respect, regard, relation.	About, concerning.
اوزاق *ouzaq*	The space far away.	Far.
قارشی *qarshî*	The space opposite.	Against.
واسطه *vasîta* a.	A means, a go-between.	By means of.

مثاللر *Misal'lér* Examples.

آرقه‌سیندن کیت *arqasindan gét*	Go after him.
آردیمدن کل *ardimdan gél*	Come after me.
قهوه آلتی *qahvé altî, qahyalti*	After the coffee *i. e.* breakfast
آلت قات *alt qat*	Lower story (of the house
اوستینه چیقمق *ûstûné chiqmaq*	To go to the top.
صندیغك دیبینده *sandighiñ dibindé*	At the bottom of the box
حقمده ، حقكده ، حقینده *haq'qimda, haq'qiñda, haq'qinda*	About me, thee, him.
یاقینمزده ، یاقینلرنده *yaqinimizda, yaqinlarinda*	Near us, them.
یانیمزده در ، یانیمزه کل *yanîmizda dir, yanîmiza gél*	It is near us, come near u
اونك واسطه‌سیله *onoun vasitasiyila*	By means of him.
اوزه‌رمه ، اوزه‌رکه *ûzérimé, ûzériñé*	On me, on thee.

5. Turkish equivalents for some English Prepositions.

§ 453. All the English Prepositions, which indicate a state of location or rest must be translated by the **locative**: all others which indicate a direction or motion from one place to another are to be rendered by the **dative** case (§ 237).

We entered the city before five o'clock and remained there five days. *Sa'at béshdén év'vél shéhré girib ora**da** bésh gûn dourdouq.*

§ 454. Study and compare the following sentences: The fight lasted **above** five hours. *Ghavgha (or qav'ga) bésh sa'-atdan **ziyadé** sûrdû.*

Above the knee	*Dizlérindén **yoqarî**.*
Those who were **about** him	***Etrafînda** olanlar.*
I have no change **about** me	*ûzérimdé oufaqliq yoq dour.*
I am **about** to go	*Gitmék ûzré yim.*
About noon	*Eoyléné **doghrou**.*
She laughed **at** him	*ûzériné gûldû.*
I wonder **at** what you have said	*Dédiyiñizé té-aj'-jûb édiyoroum.*
We were **at** your aunt's	*Halañ gildé idik.*

Mrs. Mania is loved **by** every body. *Manya Hanîm hér késdén sévilir* or *Hér kés Manya Hanimî sévér.*

Cæsarea was taken **by** the Persians. *Farisilér Kayséríyéyi zabt étdilér* or *Kayséríyé Farisilérdén alîndî.*

Translated **by** a priest	*Bir papas **marifétiy'le** térjémé olounmoush.*
He sent it **by** him	*Onoûñ **rasîtasîyla** géôndérdi.*
He came **by** sea	*Qaradan géldi.*
Sit **by** me	***Yanîmda** otour.*
After the Turkish fashion	*Tûrk ousoulou ûzré, alatourqa.*

لغتلر Words.

طاوس *tavous* peacock. a.	طولانمق *dolanmaq* to go round about
يوزمك *yuzmék* to swim	مردیون *mérdivén* stairs
زینب *Zéynéb* Zenobia. a.	تعطیل *ta'til* vacation. a.
قوشاتمق *qoushatmaq* to encircle	حصار *hisar* wall. a.

تعلیم ٧١ Exercise 71.

۱ بعض قوشلار قیشدن اول بزی براقوب ایلك بهارده ینه بزه
کلیرلر · ۲ بوتون قوشلار آراسینده طاوس قوشیندن کوزلی یوقدر ·
۳ عثمانلیلر اسکی استانبول شهرینك اوکنده اللی آلتی کون قالدیلر ·
٤ کیجه ظرفنده دشمن قاچدی · ٥ ایچلرینده برچوق یارهلیلر وار ایدی
٦ بنی غایت یوکسك بر طاغ دپهسینه چیقاروب بر طاش اوزرینه
اوطورتدی · ۷ خیرسیز اوك اطرافنی طولاندی وَ بزی کوردیکی کبی
دیوارك آرقهسینده کیزلندی · ۸ سکز کوندن بری سزی آرایورم ·
۹ انکلیز اوردوسی دشمنه طوغری آغیر آغیر یورومکده ایدی ·

۱۰ فقیرلر حقینده مرحمتلی اولوکز ٬ اونلر هر وقت یانیکزده درلر ·
۱۱ خدمتجی آرمود یرینه الما کتیرمش · ۱۲ سویلدیکی یالاندن طولایی
(دولایی) خواجه افندی زینبه چوق داریلدی · ۱۳ عسکرلر اونی طوتوب
اوکندن ٬ یانندن وَ آرقهسندن قوشاتدیلر · ۱٤ محاربهیه دائر هیچ
بر شی ایشیدهمهیورز · ۱۵ مزارك اوتهسینده پادشاه ایله دیلنجی
آراسینده هیچ فرق یوقدر · ۱٦ مانیه خانمك سویله دیکینك کچك
اولوب اولمادیغینه دائر بر دیهجككـز وارمی ؟

ترجمه ۷۲   Translation 72.

1. That package is for me: how much did you pay
for it? 2. I have a great deal (*choq shéylér*) to tell you
concerning this boy. 3. I have fallen (*youvarlandim*)
down the stairs. 4. I shall read that book during the
vacation. 5. The child threw the ring into the well: all
the servants gathered around the well to take up the ring
from the well. 6. Within a year. All the houses within
the wall were burnt. Within some days. 7. Can you
swim round the ship? 8. He must wait till five o'clock.
9. He spoke about his mother. 10. One sat above, the
other below me. 11. The inn is without the town, but
the hospital is within the walls of the town. 12. Nobody came yesterday to our house except Haji Hassan
Effendi. 13. Your house is among the trees, my house
is in front of the church.

ترجمه ۷۳   Translation 73.

1. My father was not above twenty years old when
he was married. 2. My uncle's house is very handsome,
but it cost him (*mal oldou*) above 500 pounds. 3. It is above
a year since my friend started for America. 4. Yozgad
was built by Chapan Oghlou. 5. The poor man was
driven out of his house by his creditors. 6. I shall
get up to-morrow at six o'clock. 7. Were you at
Dr. Tracy's last night? 8. He had no money about

him (*yanînda*). 9. At noon. In the summer: at night.
10. The dog sprung out from under the table. 11. Now
we turn towards the East.

مکالمه Conversation.

قهوه‌نك اوكونده اوطورمغه كیدییورم .	نره‌یه كیدییورسكز اسماعیل افندی !
هیچ ! ها بر ناركیله ایچه‌جكم .	اوراده نه یاپه‌جقسیكز؟
پك ایی افندم بویورك كیده‌لم .	بنی ده برابر كوتورورمیسكز؟
جانم نه اوله‌جق ! الله كریم ، برشی	قهوه پاره‌سنی كیم ویره‌جك ، یانكده
یاپارز هایدی .	پاره‌ك وارمی ؟
اوت ! كوزل ساز چالارم .	چالغی چالمق بیله‌رمیسین؟
بیچقیم كسمه‌یور ، بودایه‌مادم .	بو آغاجی بودادك می ؟
بنم ایتم در .	یالاقدن صو ایچن كیمك ایتی در؟
آتیجی ، اوروجی ، قاپیجی آدملردرلر .	خیرسیزلر نه چشید آدملر درلر؟
اوراق ایله بیچه‌جكم .	باغچه‌ده‌كی اونلری ناصل بیچه‌جكسكز؟

تعلیم قرائت Reading Exercise.
كوی اوطه‌سی *Kēoy Odasî* The Village Room.

قیش كلنجه ؛ ممالك محروسهٔ شاهانه‌نك هر طرفنده اولدیغی كبی١ ، قیصریه‌یه یاقین بولنان مونجسون٢ قریه‌سنده دخی ؛ هراخشام ؛ قرانلق٣ باصار باصماز٤ ، كویلولر اوجاغك دوماننی٥ كوردكلری كبی٦ ، كهیانك٧ اوطه‌سنه طوپلانیرلر ؛ وچرق دفعه یاری كیجه‌یه‌دك اوطورورلر . قهوه ، توتون ، ناركیله٨ و چوبوق٩ ایچرلر . حكایه‌لر سویلرلر ، اكله‌نیرلر١٠ : توتونك ، ناركیله‌نك و چوبوغك دومانی اورته‌لغی١١

Words. 1. as it is [custom] (429). 2. *Mounjousoun* a village near Caesarea, the ancient Pontusa. 3. *qaranliq* darkness. 4. *basmaq* to set in, to prevail (darkness) [334]. 5. *dûman* smoke. 6. as soon as they see [428]. 7. *kéh'ya* the bailiff of a village (p. 126). 8. *nargilé* a hookah. 9. *choubouq* tobacco-pipe. 10. *éylénmék* to amuse one's self. 11. *ortaliq* the space, the whole room.

قابلار¹² ، كوز كوزى كورمز¹³ اولور ؛ فقط كيف¹⁴ ده ايشته اورادن
چيق۔ار .

كوتوكلر¹⁵ اوجاقده ايكيل ايكيل يانار¹⁶ ؛ اوجاغك صيجاقلغى
بر طرفدن ، آخورك صيجاقلغى ديكر طرفدن ، لاقيردينك¹⁷ صيجاقلغى ده
او بر طرفدن گوكوللرى ايصيندير.ير¹⁸ · ديشاريكى صوغوغى هيچ دويمازلر ·
بعض دفعه هر ناصل ايسه¹⁹ لاقيردينك صوكى در كلير · اول وقت هپ بر
آغيزدن «جانم ! بو كون بو نه قدر صوغوق وار در» ديرلر · قيش نه قدر
شدتلى²⁰ اولورسه ، كوياولر ده او قدر كيفلى²¹ اولورلر · صيجاجق²²
آخور اوط۔ه۔سينده برينك جاموسنى²³ ، ارلبرينك آتنى ، برباشقه۔سينك
اوكوزينى ، اينكينى اوكرلر²⁴ · بعض دفعه ده ه۔وا مساعده۔لى²⁵
اولورسه ، ايچلريندن برى شهره²⁶ كيدر ؛ كون دوغيدن ، كون باتيدن ، قبله-
دن²⁷ و پويرازدن²⁸ تازه تازه حوادثلر²⁹ خبرلرله يوكله۔نير كلير ·

(مابعدى وار)

12. *qaplamaq* to cover, to fill. 13. unable to see (404).
14. a. *kéyf* pleasure. merriment. 15. *kûtûk* root of the trees.
16. *iñil iñil* with a clashing or crashing sound [447, 502]. 17. *la-qîrdî* talk, chattering. 18. *îsindîrmaq* to warm. 19. *nasilisa* in
some way or other. 20. *shid-détli* severe. 21. *kéyfli* merry, jolly
(150). 22. *sîjajîq* rather warm, snug (156). 23. a. *jamous* buffalo.
24. *êŏymék* to praise. 25. a. *mûsa-a-déli* favourable. 26. *shéhir*
(*shéh'ré*) the city *i. e.* Cæsarea. 27. a. *qib-lé* south. 28. f. *por'yaz*,
poy'raz north. 29. a. *havadis* intelligence, news (651).

---

۳۳ درس Lesson 33.

ظَرْف ياخود حال Adverbs.

§ 455. Adverbs are words modifying verbs, adjectives or other adverbs. They therefore denote manner, place, time, quantity, affirmation, doubt, negation, interrogation and order.

§ 456. Almost all Turkish adjectives may also be used as qualifying adverbs, with all the changes which the adjectives undergo. Ex.:

Choq séôy'lémék. To talk too much or intrusively.

بنم مكتوبم سنڭكندن ايو يازيلمشدر *Bénim méktouboum séniñkindén éyi yazîlmish dir.* My letter is better written than yours.

1. Adverbs of Manner. حال

§ 457. The Adverbs of Manner answer to the question ناصل ‘ نچه *ni'jé? na'sîl?* How? The adverb of manner is generally obtained by the addition of some particle or word to the adjective, and is expressed in English by the corresponding adjectives with the addition of the termination *-ly*.

§ 458. The adverb of manner is obtained in three ways: by repeating the adjective, by the addition of جه *-jé*, or of صورتده *sourétdé*, to the adjective:

آغير آغير *aghir aghir,* آغيرجه *aghirja,* آغير صورتده *aghir sourétdé.* Heavily. طاتلى طاتلى ‘ طاتليجه ‘ طاتلى صورتده Sweetly.

§ 459. This جه or جهسنه is also added to nouns and pronouns, and thus we obtain an adverbial expression (§§ 155, 331):

بنجه ‘ كنديسينجه *bénjé, kéndisinjé* according to me, to him.

آدمجه ‘ آدمجهسينه *adamja, adamjasîna* in a manly way;

also: آدمجيلاين ‘ آدم عقللى *adamjîlayin, adam aqîlli.*

§ 460. The 4th and 8th Gerunds are also used as adverbs of manner (pp. 206, 207):

هديه اولهرق *hédiyé olaraq* as a gift.

ايستهمهيهرك كيتدى *istéméyérék gitdi* he went unwillingly.

سويلهديكنده *séôylédiyindé* when he spoke.

§ 461.   1. Adverbs of Manner.

يكيدن *yéñidén* newly, anew.   بريول *biryol, biyol* once.

ینه yiné, yéné ⎫
کینه giné, géné ⎬ again, never-theless.
a. تكرار tékrar ⎭

یكین yégin´, yéyin´ strongly.
بویلهجه beôyléjé thus, in this way.
بوشینه boshouna in vain, idly.

§ 462.　　2. Adverbs of Time.

بو كون bou gûn to-day.

یارین yarin to-morrow.

دون dûn yesterday.

ایرتهسی كون értési gûn the following day.

اوته كون eôté gûn ⎫ the day before yesterday.
اولكی كون év´vélki gûn ⎭

شیمدی shim´di now.

نه زمان né zéman ⎫
نه وقت né vaqit ⎬ when (§§ 345, 426).
قاچان ha´chan ⎭

دمین démin´ ⎫ a few minutes ago.
بایاقدن bayaqdan´ ⎭

چاپوجق cha´poujaq ⎫ quickly.
او ساعت o´ sa-at ⎭

بردن بره birdén´biré ⎫ suddenly.
آپ آنسز ap´ansîz ⎭

بر آزدن bir azdan´ soon, after a while.

ار، اركن ér, ér´kén early.

كیج géj late.

آرا صیره ara´ sîra ⎫ now and then.
ایكیده برده ikidé´ birdé ⎭

كچن سنه géchén séné ⎫ last year.
بیلدیر bîldîr´ ⎭

a. اول év´vel before.

صوكره soñ´ra afterwards.

a. دائما da´yima always.

a. نهایت niha´yét at last.

كچنده géchéndé´ ⎫ lately.
كچن géchén ⎭

§ 463.

3. Adverbs of Affirmation, Doubt and Negation.

اوت ! év´vét, é-vét ⎫
هه ! hé, hî-î! ⎬ yes!
p. بلی bé´li ⎭

p. هیچ hich´ ⎫ never.
a. اصلا as´la ⎭

a. واقعا vaqa´a truly, in fact.

كرچكدن gérchékdén truly, really.

نهدیمك ! né´démék! ⎫ of course, no doubt! certainly!
شبههسز ! shûb´hésiz ⎭

یوق yoq´ ⎫ no!
خیر kha´yir ⎭

یله bilé´ even.

a. عجبا ajé´ba ⎫ I wonder! Is it so?
اولا ! ola´ ⎭

§ 464. 4. Adverbs of Interrogation.

نيچون *ni'chin?*

نه‌ديو *né'déyi?* } why? wherefore?

نه‌يه *néyé'?*

نه سببدن *né' sébébdén?*

ناصل *na'sil?* } how? by what manner?

نيجه *ni'jé?*

نه‌قدر *né'qadar?* how much?

نه *né?* what?

§ 465.

5. Adverbs of Quantity and Comparison.

نيته‌كيم *nitékim* as, in the manner as.

تك توك *ték' túk* here and there.

هيچ اولمازسه *héch' olmazsa* } at least.
بارى *ba'ri*

اولسه اولسه *ol'sa olsa* at the most.

اولدقجه *oldouq'ja* } pretty well.
اپ ايى *ép'-éyi*

كرك كبى *géréyi' gibi* properly, duly.

آنجق ، انجاق *an'jaq* only.

بوسبوتون *bûs'bûtûn* } entirely.
a. كاملاً *kia'milén*

a. جداً *jid'dén* seriously.

a. قصداً *qas'dén* intentionally.

p. بادهوا *ba'dihava* } gratis, freely.
a. مجاناً *méj'janén*

طولاييدن *do'layidan* indirectly.

صايكه *say'ki, san'ki* almost, nearly (§ 478).

صالت *salt'* only.

Note. There are also a great many more adverbs which can easily be learnt by practice and reading (§ 212).

§ 466. 6. Adverbial Expressions of Time.

In adverbial expressions denoting time of day the word in is expressed by the addition of لاين ، له‌ين *-léyin, -layîn*, and for the seasons by adding ين *-în, -ûn* (p. 55):

بهارين *baha'rîn* in spring.

كوزين *gû'zûn* in autumn.

قوشلقلاين *qoushlouq'layin* at 9 o' clock A. M.

كيجه‌له‌ين *géjé'léyin* at night.

اخشاملاين *akhsham'layin* in the evening.

ايكينديله‌ين *ikindi'léyin* in the afternoon.

لغتلر Words.

a. مأذون *mé'zoun* graduate.

آواره *avara* useless.

15*

a. وعد *vad* promise.

a. شقا *shaqa* joking

p. بیهوده *bihoudé* in vain

یاتسو ، یاتسی *yatsi* bed-time, curfew.

Exercise 74. تعلیم ٧٤

١ بیلدیر آناطولیه قولجدن چیقان مأذونلرك عددی قاچ ایدی ؟ —
٢ پنجشنبه کونی آماسیه‌یه یتیشوب ایرتهسی کون توقاده یولجی اوله‌جغم ·
٣ بر آرالق ایشیمز چوق اییی کیتدی ایسه‌ده چابوجق بوزولدی ·
٤ ایکیده برده بنی چاغیریورسکز ، نه دییه‌جكسکز ؟ ٥ حسن
افندینك آدم عقللی بر ایشی یوقدر ، هر ایشی ده آواره در ·
٦ آخشامه‌دك بوش بوشینه اوطورویورسكز ؛ وقتاری بیهوده‌یه
كچیریورسكز · ٧ دمین بورایه كلن افندی نه‌لی ایدی · ٨ هركون
شفقلاین اویانیر وَ یاتسولاین یاتارم · ٩ صباح ایله اوكان اورته‌سینه
دوشن وقته قوشلق ، اوكان ایله اخشام آراسینه دوشن وقته ایكیندی
وَ كونشك باتمه‌سیندن ایكی ساعت صوكره‌كی وقته یاتسو دیرلر ·
١٠ شقا سویله‌مه‌یورم جدّی اوله‌رق سویله‌یورم ایشیدییورمیسكز ؟
١١ یاغمورلر كره‌كی كبی یاغیورلر · ١٢ «جاناً آلدیكز جاناً ویریكز» ·
١٣ بورجكزی نهایت ویره‌جكمیسكز ؟ — نه دیك ! سویله‌ییك !
البتّه ویره‌جكم ·

Translation 75. ترجمه ٧٥

1. When will you set out, to-morrow or the day
after to-morrow? 2. He has been here at least three
·times. 3. That is beautiful indeed! 4. How much do
you charge for it? — It will cost you 20 méjidiyés at
most (*éñ choghou*). 5. At present (*shimdilik*) I want nothing else. 6. If we have given a promise, let us keep
it; else we shall certainly· lose our good name. 7. I
could find him nowhere. 8. The preacher's house is

very far off. 9. The one came hither, the other went
thither. 10. I could open the door neither from within
nor from without. 11. Act as if you were (olmoush-
jasina) at your home. 12. Did you know him formerly?
13. Yes, I have long known him. 14. She is better
to-day than yesterday. 15. The next time I shall be
here betimes.

مكالمه Conversation.

طانيه‌جغم ظن ايتدم اما ؛ طانيه‌مادم .	بزم اوه كان مسافری طانیدیکز می ؟
اوبركون عموجه‌كه ايتديكم بروعدی	اوطوردیغکز بردن بردن بره نیچون
اجرا ايتمك ايچون عجله ايله	قالدیکز ؟
کیتدم .	
بر سنه قالدم ؛ ايرته‌سی سنه چورومه	يوزغادده نه قدر قالديکز ؟
کیتدم .	
بردن بيره مكتوبی كسديکز ؛ پك ايی ! هر هفته بر مكتوب يازمغه	بردن بيره مكتوبی كسديکز ؛ صیق
سوز ويربرم .	صیق يازيك رجا ايده‌رم !
هيچ بوش طوردیغی يوق ؛ ويره	اوحانس افندی نه ياپيیور ؟ نه ايش
يازار .	كورويور ؟

تعليم قرائت Reading Exercise.

كوی اوطه‌سی (مابعد) The Village Room. (Continued.)

اول اخشام شهره كيده‌نی اوجاغك باشينده اوطورديرلر .

ناركيله‌نك الك اعلاسنی وَ قهوه‌نك كوپوكليسنی¹ اوكا اکرام² ايدرلر .

او ده آرتيق³ اوزه‌نه⁴ اوزه‌نه نقل ايتمكه⁵ باشلار ؛ هر كس صوص
اولوب آغزيندن آصيلیرلر قالیرلر .

كونارده بركون⁶ كویلولردن ايكيسی بردن كويدن چيقارلر .

بريسی قيصريه‌يه كيدر وَ ديكری ده قيصريه‌دن بر ساعت بَريده⁷

Words. 1. *kêopûklû* foamy, creamy. 2. *ikram ét''.* to serve.
3. therefore. 4. *êozénmék* to do carefully (§ 370). 5. *naql ét''.* to
relate. 6. one day. 7. on this side.

بولنان تلاس[8] قریه‌سینه کیدر · بونلردن اولکیسی کویدن درت ساعت
وَ صوکره کیسی ده درت بوچوق ساعت اوزاقلقـده درلر · ایرته‌سی کون
اخشام؛ هر کس دیبه کك[9] سـسنی آلیر آلماز، قوشدیلر وَ غیجی[10]
کهیانك اوطه‌سنی طولدردیلر · اوطه خینجا خینج[11] طولی ویردی ·

8. *Talas*, the classical Mutalassi. 9. *dibék* a wooden mortar,
in which coffee is pounded. 10. *Ghiji* a very common proper
name, Sticky. 11. *khinja khinj dolou vérmék* to become brim-full
quickly (§ 286).

---

۳٤ درس Lesson 34.

حَرفِ عطف Conjunctions.

§ 467. Conjunctions are particles which serve to
connect words and sentences, bringing them into a
certain relation with one another.

§ 468. There are very few conjunctions of Turkish
origin, the nature of the language being such that it
scarcely requires them (§ 430). Many Persian and Arabic
conjunctions, however, are used in the language.

§ 469. **1. Copulative Conjunctions.**

a. p. وَ *vé* ⎫
ایله ، له *ilé, lé* ⎭ and.

a. حتّٰى *hat'ta* ⎫
بیله *bilé* ⎭ even.

p. هم ـ هم *hém— hém—* both, also.

p. هم *hém* and, also.

دخی ، ده *dé, dakhi* also, and
(§§ 116, 117).

p. t. هم ده *hém dé* and moreover.

§ 470. وَ *vé* is Arabic or Persian originally. The
common people never use it in speech; its use is proper
to books and educated people.

a) ایله ، له *ilé*, *lé* takes the place of وَ *vé* for nouns
and pronouns, as بن ایله سن ، پدر ایله اوغلی *bén ilé sén*,
pédér ilé oghlou, i. e. *bén vé sén*, *pédér vé oghlou*; also:
Anam babam = anam ilé babam = anam vé babam (§ 232).

b) But in place of 'and' between verbs the gerunds are used, as: آلوب ویردی *alîp vérdi* = آلدی وَ ویردی (§§ 371, 435).

§ 471.   حتی *hat'ta* introduces a phrase which corroborates what precedes it, it is generally accompanied by ده *dé* or بیله *bilé*:

حتی برادرك بیله كلهمدی *hat'ta biradériñ* **bilé** or **dé** *gélémédi.* Even your brother could not come.

§ 472.   **2. Disjunctive Conjunctions.**

p. یا ، وَیا *ya, vé ya* ⎫ or   كرك ـ كرك ـ *gérék – gérék –* ⎫
p. یاخود *yakhod*   ⎭   ایستر ـ ایستر ـ *istér – istér –* ⎬ whether – or –
a. اِلّا *il'la* very rather   ها ـ ها ـ *ha – ha –* ⎭

p. یا ـ یا ـ *ya – ya –* either – or –   p. نه ـ نه ـ *né – né –* neither – nor –

یوق ایسه ، یوغیسه ، یوخسه *yokhsa, yoghousa, yoqisé* or, otherwise. (§ 243.)

§ 473.   **Gérék, istér, ha** are put before two opposite words or phrases to state an alternative:

Istér gélsin istér gélmésin.   Whether he choose to come or not; let him come or not. (I do not care!)
Gérék bêôyûk gérék kûchûk.   Whether great or small.
Ha almish ha almamish.   Whether he has taken it or not.

§ 474.   **Il'la** contradicts some words of the previous clause; it can be used only, if the antecedent clause contains a negation: it means *but on the contrary, nay rather.*

Bén déyil, il'la pédérim' hasta dir.   I am not ill but my father.
Qizînî déyil, il'la yégénini' sévérim.   I do not love his daughter, but his niece.

§ 475.   **3. Contracting Conjunctions.**

ایسه ، ایسهده ، فقط . a ، وَلكن . a ، لكن . a ، اِمّا . a
i-sé; isédé; faqat; vélakin; lakin; am'ma, ém'ma ⎬ but, yet.

كرچه p. ، اكرچه p. ، هر نه قدر p. ⎫
gérchi; ég-, éyérchi; hér né qadar ⎬ although.

§ 476.   **Amma, lakin, vélakin, faqat** are put at the beginning of the sentences, while **isé, isé dé** comes at the end (§§ 130, 239—240, 241, 245, 325, 339).

§ 477. *Gérchi*, *éyérchi*, *hér né qadar* are followed by *isédé* 'yet'.

كرچه فقير ايسهده *gérchi faqir isé dé.* Although he is poor, yet . . .

4. Miscellaneous Conjunctions.

§ 478. The remaining conjunctions are as under:

p. اكر *éyér*, *égér* if (§§ 238, 381—382).

صانكه، صايكه *san'ki*, *say'ki* ⎫
سوزده *seôzdé* ⎬ as if, as though (as was promised).
p. كويا *gúya* ⎭

a. يعنى *yani* that is to say, i. e.

p. زيرا *zira* ⎫
p. چونكه *chûnki* ⎬ because.

a. p. مادامكه *madam ki* since.

a. ظن اعلم، الله اعلم *zann' édérim*, *al'lahalém* vulg. *al'léhém* I think.

a. فرضا *faraza* ⎫
طوتالم كه *toutalim ki* ⎬ supposing that.

ايمدى *imdi* ⎫
اونك ايچون *onouñ ichin* ⎬ therefore.

اول سببدن *ol sébébdén* therefore.   p. مكر *méyér* ⎫ unless, and
a. بعده *badéhou* then, after-   p. t. مكرسه *méyérsé* ⎬ still, but.
           wards.
آنجق، انجاق *anjaq* however, only.   ديو، ديه *déyi* in order that (§ 392).

p. كه *ki* that, for.   p. شايد *sha'yéd* ⎫
p. تا *ta* until; so that.   p. بلكه *bél'ki* ⎬ perhaps.

قالدى كه *qaldi ki* there remains (to us) that.

p. تا كه *ta ki* in order to; (before negatives) lest.

5. Turkish equivalents for some English Conjunctions.

§ 479. Some English idiomatic conjunctional phrases are given below, with their Turkish equivalents.

As — so. As is the mother, so is the daughter آناسى ناصل ايسه قيزى ده اويله در *Anasî nasîl isa*, *qizî da éôylé dir.*

As — so. As the stars in multitude, so shall thy seed be نسلك
چوغاله‌جقدر قدر يلديزلر *Nésliñ yildizlar **qadar** chogha-
lajaq dir.*

As — as. I am as tall as you بن سنك قدر اوزونم *Bén séniñ **qadar**
ouzounoum* (§ 229).

Both — and. Both good and bad were left to his choice. *Eyi vé
kéôtû **ikisé dé** onouñ kéndi keyfiné (ikhtiyarina) braqildi.*

Either — or. Either he or I will do it يا او يا بن بوني ياپه‌جغز *Ya
o' ya bén' bounou yapajaghîz.*

Neither — nor. Neither you nor I can go. *Né sén', **né** bén' gidé-
biliriz or Sén'**dé** bén'**dé** gidéméyiz.*

Whether — or. I care not whether you go or stay. *Gitséñ **dé** git-
méséñ **dé** oumouroumda déyil dir.*

If — then. If you will take this, then I will take that. *Sén bounou
alirsañ bén **dé** ol birini alirim.*

So — that. It was so late that I could not come. *Ol qadar géj
idi **ki** gélémédim.*

Not only — but also. She was not only poor, but also very sick.
*Hém faqir vé hém or hém **dé** hasta idi* (§ 474).

Though — yet. Though he live many years, yet his life is a
failure. *Choq' sénélér yashadî **isé dé**, eômrû boshouna'
gitdi.*

Therefore — because. Therefore doth my father love me, because
I lay down my life. *Bén eômrûmû féda étdiyim **ichin**
or étdiyimdén pédérim **dé** béni sévér.*

لغتلر Words.

چالمق *chalmaq* to play		عفو .a *afv'* pardon	
a. صنعت *san'at* profession		كل *kél* bald-head	
ديكيلمك *dikilmék* to stand up directly		قاميش *qamish* reed	
a. نقد *naqîd* money		ايكيلمك *éyilmék* to bend, to curve.	
a. مركب *mérkéb* donkey; *mûrékkéb* made, composed of; ink.			

تعليم ٧٦ Exercise 76.

١ كاغد وَ قلم. آت ايله مركب. اشك وَ قاطير. ٢ نه اوقويه‌بيلير
ايشسكز نه يازه‌بيلير ايشسكز؟ اويله مى! — خير افندم! سكا
ياكليش آكلادثشلر؛ هم اوقورم هم يازارم. ٣ قاپونك اوكنده ديكيلوب

طورمه ؛ یا ایچهری کل یا دیشاری چیق • ٤ چوق فقیر در ؛ حتی جیبنده
بر اوئلغی بیله یوقدر • ٥ یارین ساعت قاچده سزه کلهیم ؟ — ایستر
آخشـام کل ایستر صباح ؛ آخشامهدك اودهیم • ٦ كزك سن كزك
قارداشك دون مكتبه كلمهمش سكز ؛ نزده ایدیکز ؟ ۷ هرنهقدر
كلمك ایچون حاضرلاندق ؛ حـتی یوله بیله چیقدق ایسهده ، آپ آنسز
بابام خستهلاندی • ۸ اكرچه سزه اون لیرا قدر بورجم وار ایسهده ، پارهم
یوق که ویرهیم • ۹ مادامکه پارهك یوقدر ؛ بر سند ویر •

تعلیم ۷۷ Exercise 77.

۱ برادر افندی ! اگر اركن كلسيدم ، سوزده بكا هدیه اولهرق
بر كتاب ويرهجك ايديكز ؛ اما ويرمهديكز • ۲ پدركز دون بزه
كلدی ، براز اوطوردی ؛ بعده آننهم ايله كليسهيه كيتدی • ۳ چاغيردم
چاغيردم كلمهدی ؛ مكرايسه (مكرسه) خسته ايش • ٤ بن ايستهديكم
قدر ايو دكلم ؛ سن ده بشقهلرك ديديكی قدر كوتو دكلسين • ٥ بن
جاهل ايسمده جاهلمكمی بيلیرم • وَ لكن سن جاهل اولدیغكی بيله
بيلمك (bilmén) • ٦ بن قهوه‌ئی ايچرکن سن ده درسكی حاضرلا •
۷ چای انكلترهده قوللانيلديغی قدر آلمانيهده ده قوللانيلماز • ۸ سن
دها دقتلی اولغی وعد ايتدیکك ايچون سکا عفوايدهجکم • ۹ نه سن
بزه کل ، نه بن سزه کلهیم • ۱۰ «ها کل حَسَن ؛ ها حَسَن کل ؛ ایکیسی
ده بر در» • ۱۱ كزك زنكين كزك فقير ، كزك عالم كزك جاهل ؛ جملهسی
ده بر کون اولهجکدر • ۱۲ بونی کیمسه بیلمز ، انجق بن بیلیرم •

ترجمه ۷۸ Translation 78.

1. Your sister and my niece. 2. We have written
a long exercise, but we have not learnt it. 3. You
must go home directly, or you will get wet; for it

will soon rain. 4. «The reed bends, but does not break.» 5. You ought to speak to your children, for they are very naughty. 6. Do not waste your time, for life is made up of it. 7. «Time is money.» 8. The horse may be very strong, nevertheless *(yiné)* it does not please me. 9. He was very tired, nevertheless he continued working. 10. I feared lest *(déyi)* he should die. 11. As [since] he does not work, I shall give him nothing. 12. I wish you to wait till I have done my exercise. 13. After I had breakfasted, I took a walk, although it was raining a little.

ترجمه ٧٩   Translation 79.

1. Give me your letter that I may send it to the post-office. 2. He says he will not marry until he has a profession. 3. Read it twice, lest *(yokhsa)* you forget it (Aor.). 4. The lady must be careful, lest she fall (Fut.). 5. The more frequently you practice (what you learn in) your music lesson, the better you will play it. 6. Unless the Lord build the house, their labour is in vain, who build it. 7. Ask him when he will come. 8. Why did you sleep so long? — I slept so long, because I was very tired. 9. The more I study Turkish, the more I like the language. 10. I do not know whether he is rich or poor.

مكالمه   Conversation.

استانبوله كيتديككزده بنى ده بلك ايدِ؛ كيدرسم كوتورورم •   كوتورورميسكز؟

شايد بزى صوران اولورسه؛ سلام سويله!   آته نيچون بينمه‌يورسكز؟

دوشه‌رم دييو قورقويورم •

بو باغى نيچون صاتون آلماديكز؟   مادام كه امر ايدييورسكز، باش اوستنه!

بوخسه بكنمديككزدن مى آلماديكز؟   چونكه پاره‌م يوغيدى •

پاره‌كز اولسيدى آلير مى ايديكز؟   خير بكندم؛ آنجق پاره‌م يوق •

طوالم كه يارين پاره‌كز اولسه گينه آلير ميسكز؟   باغى دكل حتّى باغچه‌يى ده برابر آليردم •

شبهه‌سز آليرم، هيچ ديكله‌مم •

تَعليم قرائت   **Reading Exercise.**

(مابعد) كوى اوطەسى **The Village Room.** (Continued.)

قیصریه یه كیدن كونس چاوش¹ اوجاغڭ صاغ طرفنده وَ تلاسه

كیدن قوبور³ اوستە⁴ ایسه⁵ اوجاغڭ صول طرفنده اوطورویور؛ بری چبوق

ایچیپور دیكرى ٹارکیله چكیپور ایدى ٠ هر كس قهوەسنى سیغارەسنى

ایچدكدن ٬ كیفلارینى⁶ چاتندقدنصوڭره ٬ اوطە صاحبى غیجى كهیا ٬

فوق العاده بر حرمتله : — «اى جانم كونس چاوش ! خوش كلدڭ !

صفا كلدڭ ! سویله باقالم ؛ شهرده نه وار نه یوق ٠ یدیكلڭ ایچدیكلڭ

هپ سنڭ اولسون ؛ نه كوردكسه اونى سویله!» دیەرك چاوش

آغایه خطاب⁷ ایتدى ٠

— «جانم غیجى كهیا ! دون شهرده نه كورسم ؟ هیچ⁸ عقلدن

فكردن كچمەدك⁹ برشى كوردم» دیدى كونس چاوش ٠

— «خیر اولە¹⁰ ! عجبا نه ایش ؛ اوشاق¹¹ ! سسكزى كسیڭ ؛

دیكلەیڭ» دیه¹² كهیا امر ایتدى ؛ هر كس كوز قولاق اولەرق¹³ ٬ یوزینه

باقدیلر ٠

(مابعدى وار)

Words. 1. *Kêônés* prop. name, Star (Slavonic). 2. *chavoush* a sergeant in the army. 3. *Qoubour* prop. name, a holster. 4. *ousta* a captain (of Janissaries). 5. *isé* while. 6. *kéyf chatmaq* to be in complete merriment. 7. *khitab ét".* to address. 8. never, absolutely. 9. See § 405. 10. *khayr ola* what is the matter! Good news, let us hope. 11. *oushaq!* children! boys! 12. *déyi* § 392. 13. *géôz qoulaq ol".* to be all eyes and ears, to pay full attention.

---

۳۵ درس Lesson 35.

حَرفِ ندا The Interjections.

§ 480. Interjections are words which are used to express a sudden or violent emotion of the mind.

Sometimes they are used alone, and sometimes accompanied by the word to which they refer, which in Turkish is generally put in the dative:

آفرين سکا ! *aférim* ! آفرين ! *aférin, aférim!* Bravo! Well done!

saña! Good for you! وای سزه ! *vay sizé!* Woe unto you!

ای ! هی ! *éy! héy!*		واخ ! *vakh!*		
شیش ! *shish!*	O! eh! halloo!	ایواه ! *éyvah'!*	Alas!	
اوغلان ! *oulan!*		جانم ! *janim!* My dear!		
یاهو ! *ya'hou!*		یازیق ! *yaziq!* What a pity!		
بره ! به ! *biré, bré; bé!*	Fellow!	آفرین ! *aférim!* Bravo! Capital!		
به هریف ! *bé hérif!*		آمان ! *aman!* O dear! Oh! Pity!		

باقسانا ! *baqsa'na!* Look! I say!   عجائب ! *ajayib!* Wonderful!

هایده ! *haydé!* Come! Hie thee!   ییقیل ! *yiqil!* ⎫

وای ! *vay!* Woe!   دفع اول ! *déf'ol!* ⎬ Begone!

صوص ! *sous!* Hush!   ای والله .a ! *éy'vallah!* Thank you!

والسّلام ! .a ! *vés'sélam!* All right! All correct, O. K.

ماشاالله ! .a ! *ma'shallah!* Beautiful! How strange!

انشاالله ! .a ! *in'shallah!* If God will! Please God! I hope so!

معاذالله ! .a ! *ma'zallah!* God forbid! Shocking!

الله کریم ! .a ! *Al'lah kérim!* God is gracious! Let us hope!

الحمد لله ! .a ! *élhamdû-lil'lahi* com. *élhamdûl'lah!* Thank God!

تعلیم ٨٠ Exercise 80.

١ اگر ترجمه کزی حاضرلادیکزایسه ، بیك آفرین سزه ! حاضرلامادیکزایسه وای سزه ! ٢ شیش ! چوجوق ! یولدن اوته کیت ! آتلرسنی دپه لرلر . ٣ دستور ! یولدن گچه یم . ٤ واردا ! آتلرك اوکندن کیدك . ٥ اولان حسن ! بورایه کل . سویله باقالم شو قاری کیمدر ؟ ـــ شو کویلونك عورتی در . ٦ بره هریف ! بو قدر ارکندن چارشوده ایشك ندر ؟ چین صباح کوزیکه چوپ می دوشدی . ٧ باقسانا علی !

كيت امام افندىيى چاغير · ٨ دون مكتبه كيتمشدم · ماشاالله !
سزك چوجوقلر چوق ايلهرى كيدىيورلر · ٩ عجائب ! ناصل اولدى ده
كيتدىكز ؟ ممنون اولدم · انشاالله دعاكز بركتيله دها ايلهرى كيدرلر ·
١٠ انشاالله ! بعض چوجوقلر ده كوردم كه · معاذالله ! هيچ آدم اوله‌جقلرى
يوقدر · ١١ آمان حكيم باشى ! چابوق كل · والدم پك راحتسزدر ·
١٢ يازيق ! خسته‌لغى نه‌در ؟ ١٣ بيلمه‌يورم ؛ آمان آمان دىيه‌رك ياتدى.
١٤ الله كريمدر ! چوق تلاش ايتمه · ١٥ جانم افندم ! شيمدىيه‌دك
نره‌لرده ايدىكز ؟ ١٦ به چوجوق ! بر دها سنى بورالرده كورمه‌يه‌يم ·
ييقيل كيت شوندن !

تعليم قرائت   Reading Exercise.

كوى اوطه‌سى (مابعد)   The Village Room. (Continued.)

كونس چاوش اوچ دفعه اوكسوردى[1] · درت دفعه آقصيردى[2]
و سوزه باشلادى : — «دون قوشلق وقتلرينه طوغرى شهره ينيشدم ·
بر تاوه[3] ايله بر تنجره[4] آلمق ايچون قازانجيلار چارشوسينه[5] كيتدم · باقدم
كه اوراده هيچ سس شماطه[6] يوق · شاشدم[7] قالدم · اوته برى
دوشدم · بونلر نره‌يه كيتمشلر دىيو صوروشدردم · دىدىلر كه : شهرك
ديشاريسنده‌كى تارلالرده ايشله‌يورلر ·

«قوپدم[8] كيتدم كه · نه كوره‌يم ! بن دىيه‌يم ايكىيك ؛ سن دى
اوچىك قازانجيلر · قالايجيلر[9] الرنده برر چكيج[10] · كوروك[11] اوله‌رق ؛
قوجه ! قوجه[12] ! بر قازانك ايچينه كيرمشلر · تاقور توقور تاقور توقور[13]

Words. 1. *êôksûrmék* to cough. 2. *aqsirmaq* to sneeze.
3. *tava* pan. 4. *ténjéré* cauldron, saucepan. 5. *Qazanjilar Char-
shîsi* (The market of) Boiler-Makers. 6. *shamata* an uproar.
7. to be astonished. 8. *qopmaq* to run. 9. *qalayji* an artisan who
tins copper vessels. 10. *chékij* hammer. 11. *kêôrûk* a pair of
bellows. 12. *qoja! qoja!* tremendous. 13. *taqour touqour* a repeated
tapping and knocking noise.

سس شماطه اورته‌لغی ¹⁴ آلمش ، هر كس قولاقارينه پاموق طيقامش ¹⁵

قازانك بر طرفيندن آغزينه ¹⁶ قدر بر مرديون قورمه‌شلر • ﴿مابعدى وار﴾

14. *ortaliq* the whole (field). 15. *tiqamaq* to plug. 16. *aghzina* to the brim. (They have placed a big ladder on the outside of the cauldron from the bottom to the brim.)

مابعد   Continued.

«مرديوندن چيقدم ، قازانك ايچينه باقدم كه ، نه ديك ¹ ! بر كومه ² آدم قازانك بر كوشه‌سينده ، قوچه بر كومه بر باشقه طرفينده ، بيوك بر غلبه‌لك ³ ده ديكر بر طرفده ؛ كيمى چكيجلار ⁴ ، كيمى كينتلر ⁵ كيمى لهيملر ⁶ ، كيمى قالايلار ⁷ ، اورته‌لق آنا بابا كونى ⁸ ، قيامت قوپويور ⁹ ، بو نه اوله‌جق ، ديو يانئده كيلردن برينك قولاغينه باغيردم • چوق زورلقله كوجبلا كوچ ايشيتديره‌بيلدم • نهايت هريف قولاغيندن پاموغى چيقاردى و ينه باغيره‌رق ديدى كه : ‹سلطان مراد ¹⁰ افنديمز ايكييوز اللى بيك عسكرله بغداد سفرينه ¹¹ كيدييور ده ، اوردونك پيلاوى چورباسى بو قازانده پيشه‌جكدر ›•

«بونى ايشيتديكمده تعجب ايتدم ¹² ؛ قازانى ، تاوايى اونوتدم ، براقدم كلدم • عمرمده بويله بر شى نه ايشيتمش ايدم نه ده كورمش • حالا قازانك تاقيرتيسى ¹³ قولاغمك ديبيندن كيتمه‌يور» — ﴿مابعدى وار﴾

Words. 1. *né déñ!* what do you say! what a wonder! 2. *kéômé* group. 3. *ghalabaliq* crowd. 4. *chékijlémék* to hammer (§ 276). 5. *kinétlémék* to clamp together. 6. *léhimlémék* to solder. 7. *qalaylamaq* to tin. 8. a day when father and mother both are at home; hence, a state of noise and confusion. 9. *qiyamét qopouyor* a commotion is occuring: *lit.* the Day of Judgement is breaking. 10. *Soultan Mourad* Amurath IV. 11. *Baghdad séféri* the Baghdad campaign (A. D. 1638). 12. *té-aj-jûb ét".* to be astonished. 13. See § 447.

مابعد   Continued.

كونس چاوشك نقليتى ¹ پك زياده مراق ² جلب ايتدى • اوطه

Words. 1. *naqliyét* story. 2. *méraq jélb ét".* to arouse the interest.

خلقندن بعضیسی ایناندی٬ بعضیسی ایناناٴدی ٠ فقط غیجی کهیا دیدی
که — «اوشاق! اینانیلمایهجق بر شی یوقدر ٠ بزم مرحوم۳ پدر
شاهنامه‌ده۴ بوندن غریب۵ شیلر اوقومشدر ٠ چوجوقلغمزده بزه نقل
ایدر دورور ایدی».

حاضر اولانلردن قواس۶ اغا — «سوزکی بال ایله کسدم۷ ٬ کهیا!
امر ایت۸ ده بزه قوبور اوسته ده نقل ایتسون؛ باقالم اونهلر کورمشدر؟»
دیدی ٠

— «بویور باقالم قوبور اوسته! سویله٬ سن نه‌لر کوردك؟» دیدی
اوطه صاحبی ٠

— «جانم! دیدی قوبور اوسته بیغینی بوره‌رق۹ ؛ اولکی کون
تلاس اووه سندن۱۰ کچییور ایدم؛ تا اوزاقدن قوجه جویز آغاجی کبی
بر شی کوردم ٠ اما کورسه کز۱۱! غایت هیبتلی بر شی ایدی ٠ یاقلاشه
یاقلاشه کوردم که عقلدن فکردن کچمز۱۲ درجه‌ده ایری۱۳ بر لهنه۱۴
(لاحانه) ایمش ٠

(مابعدی وار)

3. *mérhoum* deceased, blessed. 4. *Shah'namé* 'The Book of Kings', the celebrated work of the Persian author Firdousi. 5. *gharib* wonderful. 6. *Qavas* prop. name. 7. 'I cut your speech with honey' (a polite expression used when one is obliged to interrupt the talk of another). 8. *émr ét.* allow, permit (him). 9. *biyighini bourmaq* to twist his mustache. 10. *ova* field. 11. *gêor-séñiz* if you had seen. 12. See § 404. 13. *i-ri* large. 14. *lahana* cabbage.

مابعد وَ خَتام   Continued.

«لهنه‌نك بر یاپراغینك آلتنده خنکیار۱ اوردو قورمش۲ ٬ بیکارجه
چادیرلر۳ وار٠او بر یاپراغینك آلتنده اون بیکارجه آتلی عسکرلر جرید
اوینایورلر۴ ٠ اولبر یاپراغینك آلتنده ایسه٬ صاییلماز۵ عسکرلر تعلیم

Words. 1. p. *hûn-kiar* the Fortunate One, a title of the Ottoman sovereigns (§§ 535, 556). 2. to form a camp, to encamp. 3. tent. 4. *jirid* is a certain game played on horseback, in which a stick is used as a dart. 5. innumerable (§ 404).

ايدييورلر · ʼبونلر نه‌در ʼ ديو صوردم ايسه ʼسلطان مراد افنديمزك

اوردوسى در ʼ عجم سفرينه⁶ ʼ كيدييورلر ʼ ديديلر · »

بوقدر مبالغه‌لى⁷ بر نقليته هر كس كوٴلمكه باشلادى · لكن

اك چوق كولن كونس چاوش ايدى — « جانم ! ديدى ؛ اويله بر يالان

سويله كه ʼ يالانه اويسون⁸ · او قوجه لخنه بيتمز⁹ ʼ قوپماز¹⁰ · هم او قوس

قوجامان¹¹ لخنه‌يى نه ياپه‌جقلر ايمش » ·

— « قوزوم كونس چاوش ! بر آز اول قيصرى اووه‌سينده سنك

كورديكك قازانك ايچينده پيشيروب ʼ عسكره ويره‌جكلر » ديدى

قوبور اوسته ·

بو سوزك اوزرينه اوطه خلقى¹² هپ بر آغيزدن اول قدر شدتلى

كوٴلديلر كه ʼ بعضيلرى باييلديلر¹³ قالديلر ·

كونس چاوش ايسه بو پاتيرتينك¹⁴ آراسينده جوبوغينى آلديغى

كبى سيويشى ويردى¹⁵ · ‹ و . آ . ٠ ›

6. *Ajém séféri* the Persian expedition. Baghdad was then in the hands of the Persians. 7. *mûba-laghali* exaggerated. 8. *ouymaq* to fit, to match. 9. *bitmék* to grow (plant). 10. *qopmaq* to pluck out. 11. *qos qojaman* very big, gigantic. 12. *khalq* people. 13. *bayilmaq* to faint. 14. See § 447. 15. *sivishi vérmék* to slip away quietly (§ 286).

ختام   *Khitam* End.

درس ٣٦   Lesson 36.

علاوهِ Appendix.

§ 481. The method in which to address and salute people always requires considerable attention. The Ottomans themselves are very careful about such matters, especially in writing. Every class of people has its especial title by which its members must be addressed.

I. Salutation. سلاملامق *Sélamlamaq.*

§ 482. The Moslems salute one another with the address *Sélamún aléykúm* 'peace be unto you', the answer is *Vé aléykúm sélam* 'unto you be peace'. And when necessary to return the salutation, the one saluted says *Mérhaba* 'you are welcome!', to which is answered *Ey'vallah'* 'Thank you'.

§ 483. Christians salute Christians and non-Christians, and Moslems Christians in the morning by saying *Sabah'lar khayr olsoun!* 'May the mornings be good' = 'Good morning!' At noon-time or in the middle of the day, *Vaqitlar khayr olsoun!* 'Good day'. In the evening they say: *Akhshamlar khayr olsoun!* 'Good evening!' When it is necessary to return the salute, the person saluted says: *Khosh géldiñiz* 'you are welcome'; or, *Sabah'lar khayr olsoun, Vaqitlar khayr olsoun, Akhshamlar khayr olsoun,* according to the time of day.

§ 484. At parting, Moslems and Christians say *Qal sagh-líqla, Khoshja'qal; Qa'liñ saghlíqla, Khoshja'qaliñ,* all meaning 'Good-bye': the reply to which is *Khosh' géldiñiz, séfa' géldiñiz* 'you are welcome'.

§ 485. But at night when taking leave they say *Géjélér khayr' olsoun* 'Good night': to which the answer is *Khayra qarshî* 'Toward the good one (morning)' which extends the idea of the salutation to the morning light.

II. Congratulations. تبریکات *Tébrikiāt.*

§ 486. Returning after an absence, one is greeted with *Khosh' géldiniz* 'Welcome!': to which he replies *Khosh' geôrdúk!* which may be rendered 'I am happy to see you'.

§ 487. If the new comer has entered the room in the absence of the person whom he comes to visit, the latter, on coming in, makes use of the same salutation, only substituting the Dubitative for the Past tense *Khosh'gélmishsiñiz.*

§ 488. In the East it is considered polite, in meeting a person, to ask after the health of absent parents or

friends. In answering such questions, it is necessary to consider the age of the person who asks:

a) If he is junior, the answer given is *Choq sélamlar édér* 'He offers you many salutations'. Then the younger man replies *El'lérini eôpérim, makhsous sélam seôylé* 'I kiss his hands, give (him) my compliments'. If the person regarding whom he has asked is of high rank, much superior to his own, he says, *Etéklérini eôpérim, makhsous sélam seôylé* 'I kiss his skirts, many compliments'.

b) If the person who enquires about the health of the absent person is aged and of good position, it is customary to answer *Ellériñizi eôpér* 'He kisses your hands', or with more formality *Etéklérinizi eôpérlér* 'They (he) kiss your skirts'.

§ 489. The person who is to convey these greetings assumes the responsibility by saying *Bash' ûstûné* 'on my head' = 'with pleasure!' and acquits himself of it when he meets the person to whom the greetings are sent by saying *Filan éfféndi choq' choq' sélamlar seôylédi, éllériñizi eôpér* 'Mr. S. offers you many salutations and kisses your hands'. To which the other replies a) *Téshék-kûr' édérim* 'Thanks!'; b) *Sagh' olsoun* 'May he be well!'; c) *Gétirén geôndérén' sagh olsoun* 'May he who brings and he who sends the sélam be well!'; d) *El eôpén' sagh olsoun* 'May he who kisses hands be well!' As we say, 'I am much obliged both to you and to him' (§§ 365, 375).

§ 490. When somebody drinks something, or washes his hands or comes from the bath or shaves himself or is shaved by a barber, it is usual to say *Afiyét' olsoun!* 'Health be to you!': to which the other replies *Eomrûñ choq' olsoun!* 'May your life be long!'. Which may be rendered 'Thank you!' (§ 365.)

§ 491. At the beginning of the new year they say *Yéni sénéñiz mubarék' olsoun! Salî jédidiñiz mûbarék' olsoun!* 'A happy new year to you!': the answer to which is *Choq' sénéléré* 'For many years!' (§ 365.)

§ 492. Among the Moslems on both their festivals (Ramazan and Qourban) the form of congratulation

is *Bayramiñiz mûbarék' olsoun,* or *eediñiz sayid' olsoun*
'May your festival be blessed'.

§ 493. Besides the above, which are for set times,
there is a great variety of occasional salutations and
congratulations, such as (§ 365):

1. *Géôzûñûz aydin' olsoun!* or more learnedly, *Chésh-
miñiz roushén' olsoun!* 'May your eye be bright', addressed
to one whose daughter or son have just married, to
parents on the birth of a child, or to those who have
just welcomed a new relative or dear friend from
abroad, or even received a letter from a distant friend.
The reply to this is: *Aydinliq' ichindé ol!* 'May you
enjoy the light' or *Darosou éviñizé' olsoun!* 'The same
(millet) to your house!' or if addressed to a bachelor.
Darosou bashiñiza' olsoun! 'May your turn come next!'

2. To one who enters a new dwelling the salutation
is *Saghlijaq' ilé otourasin!* 'May you dwell in it in good
health!'

3. To one who puts on a new garment *Saghlijaq'
ilé géyinésiñ!* 'May you wear it with health!'

4. To one who is commencing an enterprise *Allah
ish' achiqlighî vérsin!* 'May God give you success!'

5. To one who is convalescent after an illness
Géchmish' ola! 'May it be past and forgotten!' (§ 365).

6. To one who has lost a friend, or to imply the
death of a friend enquired after *Bashiñiz sagh' olsoun!*
'Life to you!': the answer is *Allah sizé ouzoun êômúrlér'
vérsiñ!* 'God grant many years of life to you!'

7. When somebody receives any sum of money,
he usually says, *Bérékét vérsiñ!* 'May God give you a
blessing (blessed increase)' = 'Thank you!': the reply
to which is *Bérékétini' géôrésin!* 'May you experience its
increase!'

8. *Téshékkûr' édérim, Mémnoun'oum,* are expressions
in imitation of the European phrase, 'Thank you!' and
their usage is confined to educated circles. The common
people express the same meaning by such terms as:
Sagh' ol! Eliñé saghliq'. When addressed to a child
or an inferior 'Thank you!' is expressed by *Choq' yasha,
A'férim oghloum!* ('Very good!, Well done my boy!')

9. When speaking of a disease from which the speaker has suffered in the past, he must add the expression *Shéytan' qoulaghîna qourshoun!* 'Lead into Satan's ear' = 'May Satan's ears be stopped that he shall not hear what is now spoken!'

10. One who is obliged to use an impolite expression, or to name an unclean animal (as for instance the dog, donkey or pig which are considered unclean among the Moslems), he must add *Séôzûm oña'! Séôzûm yabana'! Ha'sha houzourdan!* 'My word to him! My word to the desert! Be it warded off from your honour' = 'Pardon the expression' or 'Excuse me for saying so!'

11. *Inayét' o-la! Al'lah vérsin!* 'May God's favour be upon you!' 'Let God give you': to the beggars, by way of refusing them alms (§ 365).

12. When somebody is going on a journey, in bidding farewell he says *Khoshja qalîñ!, Allaha sîmarladîq!, Bizi douvada ounoutmayîñ!*, 'Good bye! Remember us in your prayers!': to which the answer is *Allaha émanét oloun!, Rab'bim bilénizjé olsoun!* 'We command you to God!', 'The Lord be with you'; or *Oughourlar olsoun!* 'God speed!', Good bye!, 'Good luck attend you!'

13. *Ziyadé olsoun!* 'May it be too much' = 'No, thank you!' Formula used in declining an invitation to partake of food.

14. 'Pardon the omission', 'Don't pay attention to my shortcomings!' and 'I beg your pardon!' are rendered in Turkish by *Qousoura qalmayîñ!, Afv édérsiñiz!*

III. Modes of Address.

§ 494. The word سن *sén* 'thou' is not used except with reference to a child, an intimate friend, a servant or a pupil: at other times سز *siz* 'you' is used to one's equals, unless for politeness' sake one of the words now to be explained takes its place (§ 93).

§ 495. In addressing superiors, the words ' افندم ذات عالیکز ' ذاتکز *Éfféndim, zatîñiz,* or *za'ti alîñiz* are used meaning 'Sir', 'Your Honour', or 'Your Lordship'.

Other such terms are خاكپايكز ، خاكپايلرى *kha'kipayiñiz,*
kha'kipayiléri 'the dust of your feet': that is, the speaker
addresses the dust of the foot of the other, out of
humility (§ 69).

§ 496. *Note.* The word *Efféndimiz* has two different
meanings: If it is used alone, among the Christians, it
means 'Our Lord' (the Saviour). If it is connected with
the word *shévkétmé-ab'* 'Imperial', as *Shévkétméab Effén-
dimiz,* it means 'H. I. M. our Sultan'.

Among the innumerable titles of H. I. M. the Sultan,
the following: *zatî shahané, zatî hazréti padishahi* 'His
majesty the Emperor' are very common.

§ 497. The words *hazrétléri, jénabléri* 'his (lit.
their) majesty, excellency, highness' are titles equivalent
to 'his majesty, his lordship, his excellency', but they
are placed after titles and names and not before them,
as in most European languages:

Imperator hazrétléri	H. I. Majesty.
Ingiltér'ra qralichasî hazrétléri	H. M. the Queen of England.
Vali pasha hazrétléri	H. E. the Governor.
Qaymaqam béy hazrétléri	H. Honour the Qaymaqam.
Hoja éfféndi jénabléri	The respected teacher.

§ 498. It is considered more polite to address
superiors in the third person plural: *Za'tî alilériné khay'lî
zahmét vérdim* 'I have given your Excellency much
trouble'.

§ 499. In high and polite circles the speaker cannot
speak of himself as 'I', or others as 'he, we, they'.
He must say:

Béndéñiz, qoulouñouz, ajizléri I (your servant).

Béndéléri, qoul'larî I or we (your servant or servants).

Dayiléri I, he, we (who pray for you) used by and
of clergymen.

Jariyéñiz, jariyéléri I, we (your maid servant) used
by and of ladies.

§ 500. Generally the word *hazrét* before a single
name indicates one of the prophets, saints or patriarchs
of old; as: *Hazré'ti Ibrahim* 'the patriarch Abraham'.
Hazré'ti Davoud 'the prophet David'. *Hazré'ti Souléy'man*

'the prophet (King) Solomon'. *Hazré'ti Isa (ee-sa) Effén-dimiz* 'Our Lord Jesus'. *Hazré'ti Méryém, Méryém Ana* 'Saint Mary' (the virgin Mother). *Hazré'ti Méseeh'* 'the Holy Anointed One' (Christ).

IV. Honorific Titles. القاب رسميه *Elqabî Résmiyé.*

§ 501. Titles of Honour also are of great importance, as every person of position must be addressed by his own proper title.

شهامتلو *shéha'métlou* 'valorous and successful', is used for the Shah of Persia.

حشمتلو *hash'métlou* 'royal, imperial' for Christian sovereigns.

اصالتلو *ésa'létlou* 'noble' for the ambassadors and consuls.

رتبتلو *rût'bétlou* 'honorable, venerable' (His Grace) for clergymen of high rank, patriarchs, archbishops, bishops and missionaries.

فضيلتلو *fazi'létlou* 'reverend' for judges, priests, pastors and preachers.

فخامتلو دولتلو *fékha'métlou dév'létlou* 'illustrious and magnificient' for the Khîdive of Egypt and Presidents of Republics.

دولتلو عطوفتلو *dévlétlou atoufétlou* 'illustrious and munificient' for Grand Viziers.

دولتلو *dévlétlou* for *Valis* (Governors-General).

سعادتلو *sa-a'-detlou* 'prosperous' for the Mûtésar'rîfs.

عزتلو *iz'zétlou* 'honorable' for the Qaymaqams.

رفعتلو *rif'atlou* 'eminent' for other officials.

مروتلو ' حمتلو *mûrûv'vétlou, hûr'métlou* 'generous, respected' to merchants, teachers, etc.

عصمتلو *is'métlou* 'virtuous' for married ladies.

عِفّتلو *if'fétlou* 'chaste' for unmarried ladies.

مثاللر *Misal'lér* Examples.

Dún dévlétkhanéyé[1] *géldim, ém'ma za'tî alînizi géôrémédim.* I came to your house yesterday, but you were not at home.

Faqirkhanéyé[2] *né vaqit téshrif édéjéksiñiz?* When you will honour (visit) my house?

Hémshiré hanîm nasîl dîr? — *Hémshirém jariyéléri choq hasta dir.* How is your sister? — My sister is very sick.

Béndéléri pék faqirim, zatî alîniz isé pék zéngin siñiz. I am very poor, but you are very rich.

Amériqa jümhouriyéti réyisi fékhamétlou dévlétlou Mc Kinley hazrétléri. His Honour Mc Kinley, the President of the Republic of America.

Dayiléri Anatolia Collegi mûdiri yim. I am the President of Anatolia College.

Jariyéléri Protéstan méktébi mou-al'limési yim. I am the teacher of the Protestant School.

Words. 1. *Dévlétkhané* the abode of prosperity, i. e. your house, used as a term of politeness. 2. *Faqirkhané* the house of your poor servant, i. e. my house.

تعليم ٨١ Exercise 81.

۱ بوكون ذاتِ عاليكزى زيارته¹ كله بيلير ميم ؟ — اكر فقيرخانه يه تنزّل² ايدرسكز ، خوش كلديكز صفا كلديكز ! بويوزاك افندم ٠ ٢ سلام عليكم احمد افندى ! — وعليكم سلام مراد³ بك ، بويوراك اوطوراك ٠ مرحبا ! انشا الله ايوسكز ٠ ٣ محدوم⁴ بكدن مكتوب آلييورميسكز ؟ — چوقدن برو مكتوبك آرقه سنى كسمش ايدى ، لكن الحمد لله بو هفته برمكتوب آله بيلدك — كوزكز آيدين اويله ايسه ٠ نه وار نه يوق ؟ نه يازييور ؟ ٤ آيدينلق ايچنده اول ! داروسى سزه ٠ چوق ايو ايشلر ٠ سزه چوق چوق سلاملر ايتمش ، الله ريكزى اوپر ٠ ٥ ال اوپن صاغ اولسون ! مكتوب يازارسه كز بنده كزدن مخصوص⁵ سلاملر يازيكز !

Words. 1. a. *ziyarét* to go on a visit. 2. a. *ténéz'zúl* to condescend. 3. a. *Mourad* prop. name. 4. a. *makhdoum béy* your son Master ... 5. a. *makhsous* especial.

— باش اوستنه افندم ! سزنصلمسكزِ؟ حالكزِ ديرلككزِ⁶ ايو ميدرِ؟
٦ اوزريكزِه شفالر اولسون⁷ ! دون برآز خسته‌جه ايدم · فنا بر صوغوق
آلمشم · لكن شيطان قولاغنه قورشون ! الحمدلله بوكون ايي ايم ·
هيچ آراماز ' عجبا شو دوستمزِ نصلدر نصل دكلدر ديو صورمازسكزِ ·
بزه تنزل² ايتمزسكزِ كه ! ٧ استغرالله افندم⁸ ! حقيقةً هيچ خبرم
يوغيدى · عفو ايدرسكزِ · پدر افندى صامسوندن عودت ايتديلر مى ؟
— اوت افندم ' دون برادر بنده‌لرى ايله برابر تشريف ايتديلر ·
٨ لطفاً⁹ احترامات فانقه‌مى¹⁰ تقديم¹¹ ايديكزِ ' اتكلريى اوپه‌ريم ·
٩ باش اوستنه افندم ! خوشجه قالكِ ! — سعادت ايله¹² افندم ' خوش
كلديكزِ صفا كلديكزِ ' تكرار بويوريكزِ !

6. *haliñiz dirliyiñiz* the circumstances of your life. 7. *uzeriñizé shifalar olsoun!* may it be health to you! 8. a. *éstagh'firoul'lah* lit. 'I ask pardon of God' = Not in the least, I have no such pretensions. 9. *loutfén* be kind enough! 10. *ih'tiramatî fayiqa* (my) highest respects. 11. *taqdim ét."* to present. 12. a. *sé-a-dét ilé!* Go in happiness (said to a departing friend).

تعليم ٨٢   Exercise 82.

١ شوكتماٌب افندمز شهرمزك فقراسنه¹ اون بيك غروش احسان²
بويورمشلر · ٢ شهامتلو ايران شاهى حضرتلرى درسعادتى³ تشريف
ايتمشلر · ٣ آوروپا حكمدارلرينك الك قدملى‌سى⁴ انكلتره قراليچه‌سى
حشمتلو ويقتوريا حضرتلريدر · ٤ فرانسه جمهوريتى رئيسى فخامتلو
دولتلو موسيو لوبه حضرتلرى ' سلطنت سنيه‌نك⁵ پارس سفيرى دولتلو
عطوفتلو منير⁶ پاشا حضرتلريى حضورلرينه⁷ قبول بويورمشلر⁸ · ٥ سيواس

Words. 1. a. *fouqara* poor people. 2. a. *ih'san bouyourmaq* to grant, to bestow. 3. *Dér'sa-a-dét* Constantinople (§ 519). 4. *qidémli* senior. 5. *Saltana'tî séniyé* The Ottoman Government. 6. *Mûneer* prop. name, Lucian. 7. *houzour* presence. 8. a. *qaboul bouyourmaq* to accept.

واليسى دولتلو عطوفتلو حاجى حسن پاشا حضرتلرى ، توقاد متصرفى
سعادتلو بكـر پاشا حضرتلرى وَ مرذيفون قائمقامى عزتلو محمود بك
حضرتلرى آماسيهيه تشريف ايتمشلر · ٦ ذاتكـز بو ايشه نه دييورسكـز؟
— بندهكـز بيلمم ، ذات عاليلرى دها ايى بيليرسكـز · ٧ همشيرهم
جاريهلرى غيرتله مكتبه دوام⁹ ايدييور · ٨ جاريهكـز آرتين افنديك
والدهسيم · ٩ ذات عاليلرى شيمدى نرهده اقامت¹⁰ ايدييورسكـز؟ —
بندهكـز شيمدى صوفيلر محلهسنده¹¹ اقامت ايدييورم · ١٠ بو كون
خاكپايكزه يوز سورمك ايچون دولتخانهيه واردق ايسهده تَشَرُّفْ¹²
ايدهمهدك ·

9. a. *dévam* to continue. 10. a. *iqamét ét.''* to dwell. 11. *Sofoular
mahal'lési* the street called Sofoular (in Merzifoun). 12. a. *téshér'rûf*
to be honored (we could not see you).

٨٣ ترجمه Translation 83.

1. H. I. M. the German Emperor, William II. 2. His
Grace the Armenian Patriarch. 3. His Excellency the
Governor of Angora. 4. His Eminence, the Mûtésarrif
of Samsoun, Qadri Pasha. 5. H. E. the English Am-
bassador Sir Nicholas O'Connor. 6. H. E. the American
Ambassador at Constantinople, Dr. Angel. 7. Rev. Charles
Tracy, President of Anatolia College. 8. Rev. Carabet
Kapriélian; Rev. Kéropé Yakoubian. 9. I request your
Excellency to give me permission to go to England.
10. Under the shadow of His Majesty *(sayé'yi padi-
shahidé)* we are all safe. 11. H. H. Artin Pasha, the
Ambassador of the Ottoman Government in London. 12. I
have received your letter. 13. I was for two hours waiting
for you at my house, but you did not come: afterwards
I went to your house, but you were not at home.
14. Please give me to-day's newspapers. 15. How is your
father's health? 16. Thank you, Doctor, he is very well,
through your kind assistance *(sayé'yi aliñizdé)*. 17. My
sister is the wife of Kémal Béy. 18. When did you
come here? — I came three days ago with your son.

V. Onomatopoeia.

§ 502. Is the term applied to words or phrases, the sound of which conveys some idea of or resemblance to the thing signified.

It is customary in common language to use some onomatopœic expressions. For instance, they say in Turkish:

Sou kharîl kharîl aqîyor. The water flows violently.

Taq taq qapouya vourdou. Tap tap he knocked at the door.

Jombadaq (or *jomb déyi*) *souya atîldi.* He threw himself suddenly (with noise into) the water.

These words *kharîl kharîl, jomb* are intended to represent the sound of the water when flowing or splashing, just as *taq taq* does that of knocking at the door.

Sa-at tiq tiq tiq édiyordou. The watch was ticking, = 'going tick, tick'.

Kiliséniñ chañi dañ douñ êôtûyordou. The church bell was ringing, ding-dong.

Ellérini shapour shoupour birbiriné vourdoular. They loudly clapped their hands.

Qoushlar jivil jivil êôtûyorlar. The birds are singing tweet tweet.

VI. اذان *Ezan.*

§ 503. Is the notification, announcement, call to divine worship, proclaimed from a minaret or any other place, five times a day, by the *mû-éz'-zin* (chanter). The following is the formula:

1. First of all الله اكبر *Al'lahou ékbér.* 'God is Most Great' four times repeated, turning the face towards the four directions of the world.

2. اشهد ان لا اله الّا الله *Esh'-hédû én'né la ilahé illal'lah.* I bear witness that (there is) not a god, save God [twice repeated].

3. اشهد ان محمداً رسول الله *Esh-hé-dû énné Mouhammédén ré-soul oullah.* I bear witness that Mouhammed is the apostle of God [twice].

4. حى على الصلوة *Hay'yé alés'sélat.* Hasten to divine worship [twice].

5. حى على الفلاح *Hay'yé alél félah.* Hasten to permanent blessedness [twice].

6. الله اكبر *Allahû ékbér.* God is great [twice again repeated].

7. لا اله الا الله *La ilahé illal'lah.* [Once more repeated.]

The call chanted at daybreak has this addition after the fourth clause:

الصلوة خير من النوم *Es'-sélatû khay'rûn min én' névm.* Prayer is better than sleep.

In great and imperial mosques, the *mû-éz'-zins* sometimes make optional additions to the fifth clause; as:

الصلوة والسلام عليك ياحبيب الله ! يا نورعرش الله ! يا سيد الاوابن و الاخرين !
يا رسول الله ! *Es'sélatû vés'sélamû aléyk, yá Habee ballah!* or *Ya nooré arshillah!* or *Ya séy'yidûl év'véleen vél a-khîreen!* or *Ya résoul oul'lah!* May blessing and peace be upon thee, O Beloved one of God! or O Light of the throne of God! or O Prince of the former and later (prophets)! or O Prophet of God!

Inside the place of worship also, this call is uttered when worship begins; but then with this addition after the fifth clause:

قد قامة الصلاة *Qad qamétis'salat.* Divine worship has already been entered on (begun) [twice].

VII. The Christian Services. عبادَتِ مَسيحيه

§ 504. The Benediction:

Rabbîmiz Hisous Kristosoûñ [or *Isa-él-Mésihiñ*] *inayéti, Pédér Allahîmizin mouhab'béti vé Rouhoul Qoudsoûñ mûsharékéti jumléñiz ilé bérabér olsoun; Amin.*

The Lesson:

Oqouyajaghîm mahal Tékvee'nûl Makhlouqat Kitabiniñ birinji babîñiñ birinji ayétindén 16inji ayétiné qadar dir.

Mat-téosoûñ tahreer éylédiyi Injiliñ altînji babîniñ iptidasîndan soñounadék oqouyajaghîm.

Pavlos Résouloûñ Romalilara yazdîghî résaléñiñ on ikinji babîndan oqouyajaghîm.

Onounjou Mézmourou oqouyajaghîm.

The Text:

Louqasiñ tahreer éylédiyi Injiliñ sékizinji babîñiñ yirmi birinji ayéti haq'qînda mûta-la-a' édéjéyim.

Youhan'na Injiliniñ birinji bab yirmi doqouzounjou ayétiniñ ikinji qismî ûzériné vaz édéjéyim.

Esa'si Kélamîmîz Amali Rousoul Kitabîniñ deôrdûnjú bab on ikinji ayétindé boulounour or *mérjoud dour.*

The Hymn:

Maqam Kitabînîn altînjî sahifésindé boulounan oni-kinji ilahiyi térén'-nûm édélim.

Yûz otouz yédinji ilahiyi térén'-nûm édélim.

Téshék'kûr ilahisini térénnûm édélim.

The Baptismal formula:

Laura Eupheme, séni Pédériñ, Oghoulouñ vé Rouhoul Qoudsouñ namîna [or *bismil Eb vél Ibn vél Rouhoul Qouds*] *vaftiz édérim.*

The Ending of Prayers:

Rabb vé Khélaskîarîmîz Hisous Krisdosouñ ismi shéri-findé dilériz, ih'san éylé, Ameen!

انتهاى قسم اوّل

قسم ثانى

لسان رسمى وادبى

بِسْمِ اللهِ الرحمن الرحيم

Second Part.

The Elements of Arabic and Persian Grammar

as

they are used in Ottoman-Turkish.

Introductory Remarks.

§ 505. The Arabic and Persian languages and literature have for many centuries exercised a very extensive influence upon the Ottoman. Therefore there are very many Arabic and Persian words and phrases used in Ottoman. In order to be able to understand and use them correctly, it is necessary to have an elementary knowledge of Arabic and Persian Grammar.

§ 506. The following points should be noted:

a. All such Arabic and Persian words taken singly are declined according to the grammatical system of the Turkish language.

b. All such Arabic words taken singly may be used in accordance with the rules of Persian Grammar. But genuine Turkish words cannot be treated in this way.

c. Only genuine Arabic words are used according to the Arabic grammatical system, Turkish and Persian words cannot be so dealt with.

§ 507. There are, however, some very much used Turkish and Persian words which are treated according to the rules of Arabic Grammar, because they are supposed to be Arabic. Such words are called غلطات مشهوره *ghalata'tî mésh'houré* 'barbarisms' or 'manifest errors' (§ 583).

Note. There are some orthographic signs which are peculiar to Arabic; but as mention has been made of these in the Introduction, they do not require to be dealt with again here (§§ 35—48).

---

٣٧ درس Lesson 37.

جمع فارسی The Persian Plural.

§ 508. In the Persian language there are only two numbers: the Singular and the Plural.

§ 509. Persian plurals are formed in two ways:

a. If the noun be the name of an **animate** being, it may form its plural by taking the termination ان -*an*; as:

مرد *mérd* a man	مردان *mérdan* men.
برادر *biradér* a brother	برادران *biradéran* brothers.
شیر *sheer* a lion	شیران *sheeran* lions.

b. If the Persian noun be the name of an **inanimate** object, it becomes plural by the addition of ها -*ha*; as:

سال *sal* a year	سالها *sal'ha* years.
دریا *dérya* a sea	دریاها *déryaha* seas.

§ 510. If the animate nouns end in a vowel *hé* (-*a*, -*é*), their plural is made by changing that letter into ك *giaf* (-*g*-) and adding ان -*an*; as:

بنده *béndé* a servant	بندكان *béndégian* servants.
خواجه *khajé, khoja* a teacher	خواجكان *khajégian* teachers.
a. طلبه *talébé* student	طلبكان *talébégian* students.

§ 511. The following nouns, though denoting inanimate objects, may form their plurals in ان -*an*; as:

اختر *akh'tér* a star	اختران *akhtéran* stars.
هزار *hézar* a thousand	هزاران *hézaran* thousands.

So also: روزان *rouzan* days, شبان *shéban* nights, چشمان *chésh-man* eyes, دراختان *dirakhtan* trees.

تعلیم ۸٤ Exercise 84.

Change the following nouns into the Persian plural.

باغ[1] ، قهرمان[2] ، پهلوان[3] ، فرشته[4] ، مرده[5] ، مادر[6] ، زنده[7] ،

ضابط[8] a. ، یاور[9] ، دیو[10] ، خانه[11] ، خان[12] ، شاه[13] ، پادشاه[14] ،

شاکرد[15] ، اصلزاده[16] ، دختر[17] معتبر[18] a. ، فریق[19] a. ، خواهر[20] ،

خسته[21] ، کس[22] ، بیچاره[23] ، تجّار[24] a. ، طلبه ، مسلم

Words. 1. vineyard. 2. *qah'riman* hero. 3. *péh'livan* wrestler. 4. *firishté* angel. 5. *mûrdé* a corpse. 6. *madér* mother. 7. *zindé* alive. 8. *zabit* officer. 9. *yavér* attendant. 10. *deer, dév* a demon; a giant. 11. house. 12. inn, tavern. 13. *shah'* king. 14. *padishah* a great king. 15. *shagird* pupil. 16. *asîlzadé* nobleman. 17. *dûkhtér* daughter. 18. *mûtébér* a notable (man). 19. *fériq* a general of Division (in the Army). 20. *khahér* a sister. 21. sick. 22. *kés* person. 23. poor. 24. *tûj'jar* merchant [*tûj'jaran, tûj'jarlar*].

§ 512. *Note.* 1. a. مسلم *muslim* 'one who submissively obeys God = Moslem'. Persian pl. مسلمان *mûsliman* 'moslems; an orthodox believer', which is used as singular in Ottoman and Persian; and مسلمانلر ، مسلمانان *mûslimanan, mûslimanlar* is considered as the double pl. of it.

2. So also a. طلبه ، تجار *talébé, tûj'jar* 'students, merchants', which are the Arabic plurals of طالب ، تاجر *talib, tajir* 'student, merchant', but are used in double pl. form in Ottoman and Persian: طلبكان ، طلبه لر *talébégian, talébéler*. (See the Double Plurals of Arabic, Lesson 51.)

3. There is another word in use *mûsûlman, mûsélman, mûsûr-man* meaning 'a moslem', which is of Syriac origin, but never admitted into the correct language, it is used in the Southern regions of Turkey among the common and uneducated people.

تعلیم قرائت Reading Exercise.

کبریتجی قیز The Match Girl.

»افندیار ، کبریت کبریت[1] ! اوچ قوطوسی اون پاره !

»مرحمتلی[2] بك افندیار ! آننهم خسته ا ک کسز . . . .

Words. 1. a. *Kibrit! kibrit!* Matches! matches! 2. a. t. *mér-hamétli* gracious.

«آليڭ بوني ، قوزوم ! بكا اون پاره‌جق ويريڭ سز .»

ياوروجغڭ³ او صاريجه ، كور⁴ صاچلري طاغينيق⁵ !

كوزلرينڭ آلتى ماوى⁶ ؛ يوزى كيرلى و يانيق⁷ ؛

اوستى⁸ اسكى ، آياغينده قوجه⁹ بر چيفت قوندوره .

شو زوالّى قيزجيغاز ده بر لقمه¹⁰ اكمك ايچون

سوقاق سوقاق¹¹ «كبريت !» ديو طولاشييور¹² بوتون كون .

نيچه چيركين¹³ ، ياره پاره¹⁴ يوزلره :

«بنم كوزل بكم !» دييور ، بلكه كونده يوز كره .

— «قيزم ! سنڭ بابا‌ڭ كيم در ؟ سنڭ اوڭ نرده ؟

«باق ، قيرق پاره ويره‌جكم ، صورديغمى سويله ده :

«با‌باڭ يوق مى ؟ بيلمز ميسين اوني سن ؟» —

— «بنم بابام يوقدر ! اوت ، بيلمه‌يورم اوني بن ! . . . .»

زوالّى قيز هريرده غريب¹⁵ در ؛

هر كس اوني «پيج !»¹⁶ دييه‌رك اينجيدير¹⁷

اونڭ ضعيف وجودينڭ¹⁸ اوستنه

بر كيمسه‌جك قاناد¹⁹ كروب²⁰ طورمايور ؛

اونڭ ايچون هيچ بر يوره‌ك اورمايور .

بوكونه‌دڭ بيلمه‌مش كه : بابا نه ؟

چاليشييور ، چاليشماسين نه ياپسين ؟

چاليشمه‌دن باشقه يول يوق كه صاپسين²¹ .

3. *yavroujouq* that little creature. 4. *gêor!* see! 5. *daghiniq* untidy. 6. *mavi* blue. 7. *yaniq* burnt. 8. *ûst* clothes. 9. *qoja* big. 10. a. *loqma* slice. 11. from street to street. 12. *dolashmaq* to wander. 13. *niché!* how many! *chirkin* dirty, ugly. 14. *yara para* wounded. 15. *gharib* stranger. 16. *pij* bastard. 17. *injitmék* to hurt. 18. a. *vûjoud* body. 19. *qanad* wing. 20. *gérmék* to spread the wings. 21. *sapmaq* to swerve.

كنديسيچون چابالايان²² كيمى وار ؟

كيمى وار كه ؟ بر آكسكى «آل ! يه ! » دير ،

بر شى ويرن ، اوندن ده بر شى ايستر ،

آه يوقسوللق²³ ! . . . . آه باباسز چوجقلر ! . . . . (م . امين²⁴)

22. *chabalamaq* to struggle. 23. *yoqsoullouq* poverty. 24. *Mé-hémméd Emin* a living Turk poet (1860).

مكالمه Conversation.

س) فارسيده بر اسمى مُفْرَدْ حالیندن جمع حالینه گتیرمك ایچون قاچ قاعده وار در ؟

ج) ایكی قاعِده وار در : بو ایكی قاعدهدن اولكیسی مُسَمَّاسی ذیروح¹ یعنی جانلی اولان اسملرك جمعیدر در كه ، مفردلرینك صوكینه (ان) علاوه قیلینهرق حاصِل³ اولور ؛ مثلا : پَدَرْ ، پدران ؛ زَنْ ، زنان .

س) فارِسی اسملری جمع حالینه گتیرمك ایچون مَوْضوع⁴ اولان ایكینجی قاعده نهدر ؟

ج) بو قاعدهلرك ایكینجیسی مُسَمَّاسی جانسز اولان اسملرك جمعیدر : بوده مفرد بر اسمك صوكینه (ها) علاوه ایتمكدن عِبارَتْ⁵ در ؛ مثلا : باغْ ، باغها .

س) مُسَمَّاسی ذیروح اولمایان كَلِمات⁶ فارسیه ، عِبارات تُرکیه آراسینده (ها) اداتی⁷ ایله جمعلهنیر می ؟

ج) اَلْیَوْم⁸ ایرانده⁹ جانلی وَ جانسز اولان اسملری علی العموم¹⁰ (ها) ایله جمعلندیرمك عادَت اولمش ایسه ده ، عِبارات تُرکیه آراسینده مُسْتَعْمَل¹¹ اولان جانسز اسملر (لر) اداتی⁷ ایله جمعلهنیر .

س) بونی لطفاً¹² برقاچ مثاللر ایله ایضاح ایدرمیسككیز¹³ ؟

ج) اوت افندم ! مثلا : «باغهام وَ خانههام وار در ؛ یولجیلر كوی خانهسینده راحَتْ ایدهمزلر» تعبیرلری¹⁴ یرینه .«باغلریم وَ خانهلریم وار در ؛ یولجیلر كوی خانهلرینده راحَتْ ایدهمزلر» یازیلیر .

س) تركى وَ عربى اسملر فارسى قاعده‌لر ايله جمعله‌نه‌بيلير مى؟

ج) افندم ' تركى وَ عربى اسملر قاعده‌لر ايله اصلا جمعلنمز . فقط
مصدرى[1] ذيروح[2] اولان عربى كلمه‌لردن بعضيلرى لسانِ عثمانيده (ان)
ايله جمعله‌نير : 'ضابطان ' فريقان ' معتبران ' تجاران ' صرافان ' منشيان '
راويان ' شهيدان ' مديران ' پاپاسان ' مختاران[15]' كبى .

س) خُسْرَوْ[16] افندى ! دون مكتبگزى زيارته كلن ذواتِ كرام[17]
كيملر ايدى؟

ج) مشيرانِ عِظامدن[18] دولتلو يوسف پاشا وَ فريقانِ كرامدن سعادتلو
عالى پاشا حضراتى[19] ايدى .

س) مُرْدگان وَ زِنْدگان نه معناده در؟

ج) مردگان اولولر وَ زندگان ديريلر ديمكدر : مرده‌لرك مكانى مزارستان '
زندكانك مكانى ايسه باغِ عالمدر[20] .

س) اقامت ايتديكيگز[21] رَمْزى افندينك خانه‌نك مستأجرى[22] مسلمان مى
خرستيان مى؟

ج) اصنافِ كاندن وَ صرافانِ معتبراندن عزتلو الحاج عثمان افندى[23] در .
مرحوم[24] پدرلرى خواجكاندن ايدى .

س) طلبگانك وظيفه‌سى نه‌در؟

ج) پدر وَ مادرانه اطاعت ' خواهرانى صيانت[25] وَ خواجكانه حرمت ايتمكدر .

س) شهِ شهيدان[26] نه صورتله ارتحالِ دارِ بقا[27] ايله‌ديلر؟

ج) شاهِ شهيدان حضرتِ حسين رضه[28] (رَضِىَ اللهُ عَنْهُ) باشى كسيله‌رك
شهيد اولوب كربلاده مشهدِ مخصوصنده[29] دفن اولونغشدر . نيته‌كيم
مُنشيان‌دن مشهور ضيا پاشانك ترجيع بندنده ده مُحَرَّر[30] در :
بيت : * مَسْمُوماً ايتدى ذاتِ حَسَنْ عَدَنه انْتِقال *
* مَظْلوماً اولدى شاهِ شهيدان بُريده‌سَرْ *

س) فَرْهاد كيم در؟

ج) پهلوانانِ قديمان‌دن[31] بر قهرمان ايدى ؛ ديوان كبى قوتلى اولديغنى راويان
اخبار وَ ثنا ايدرلر . شيرين ايله اولان معاشقه‌سى[32] مشهور در .

س) بو گونكی جریده‌لرده شایانِ دِقَّت³³ بر شی كورولدی می ؟

ج) اوت افندم ! یاورانِ حضرتِ پادشاهیدن سعادتلو سلیمان پاشا حضرتلری بیچار كان وَ خسته‌كانه اِعانه اولمق اوزره ٤٠٠ عدد لیرای عثمانی اعطا بویورمشلر³⁴ . كذا خیرخواهانِ سلطنتِ سنیهٔ عثمانیه‌دن³⁵ آلمانیه‌لی موسیو هوفمانه برنجی رتبه‌دن مجیدی نشانِ ذیشانی³⁶ احسان بویورلمشدر . بونی درسعادتده نَشْر اولونان «آخْتَرْ» نام غزته‌ده اوقودم .

س) القابِ رسمیه‌دن 'سعادتلو' عُنْوانی كیمله‌ره اعطا اولونور³⁴ ؟

ج) 'سعادتلو' عنوانی فریقانِ كرامدن¹⁷ اولان ذاتله‌ره ویریلیر .

س) 'سعادتلو' دولتلو' فضیلتلو' وَ 'سعادتلی؛ دولتلی' فتیلتلی ' كاضمه‌لرینك⁶ بربرلرندن فَرْقلری³⁶ نه در؟

ج) ایكی نوعی‌ده تركی اِسْمِ مَنْسوبدر: (لو) ایله اولانلر القابِ رسمیه‌ده مستعملدرلر³⁷ (باق صحیفه ۲٤۷) . 'سعادتلی' فضیلتلی' دولتلی' ایسه القاب مقامنده مُسْتَعْمَلْ اولمایوب³⁸ صفت مقامنده³⁹ مُسْتعملدرلر : «فضیلتلی زنان سعادتلی عائله‌لر تَشْكیل ایدرلر؛ یعقوب افندی دولتلی بر ذات در» كبی . (۱٤۹ §) .

س) عاكِفْ افندی ناصل بر آدمدر؟

ج) اوزی⁴⁰ سوزی دوغری' مسلمان (Mussulman) بر آدمدر .

س) هندستانده‌كی مسلمانلرك مقداری نه قدر در؟

ج) هندستانده بولونان مسلمانانك مقداری آلتمشبر ملیوندر .

س) ناحیه‌لرك⁴¹ اداره‌سیندن كیملر مسؤلدرلر؟ (صحیفه ۱۲٦) .

ج) ناحیه‌لرك اداره‌سیندن مدیران ' مختاران ' امامان وَ پاپاسان مسؤلدرلر .

Note. 1. For the words included in the Conversation see the Key.

2. For the sentences indicated by a, b, c, see more in the next Lesson; the letters show the order in the composition.

درس ٣٨ Lesson 38.

اضافت The Persian Izafét.

§ 513. In books and in conversation also, when elegance is studied, instead of the Turkish way of connecting noun with noun and noun with adjective, the Persian method is used, especially when the words employed are either Arabic or Persian.

I. The Construction, when two nouns are connected with one another as possessor and possession.

§ 514. The Turkish way is, as we have seen (§ 109), to put the possessor first and the thing possessed afterwards, just like the English possessive followed by the noun which governs it; as: پدرك كتابى *pédériñ' kitabî* the father's book.

§ 515. The Persian method consists simply in putting the thing possessed first and the name of the possessor after it, with an *ésré* between the two, if the first noun ends in a consonant. This corresponds to the ordinary English use of 'of' between two nouns:

كتاب پدر *kita'bî pédér.* The book of the father.

اعمال رُسُل *amal'î rousoul.* The Acts of the Apostles.

II. The Construction, when a noun is qualified by an adjective.

§ 516. The Turkish method is simply to put the adjective before the noun (§§ 107, 669); as:

مقدس كتاب *mouqad'dés' kitab* 'The Holy Book = The Bible'.

§ 517. The Persian method, when both words are either Arabic or Persian, is to put first the noun and afterwards the adjective, with an *ésré* between them:

كتاب مقدس *kita'bî mouqad'dés* the Book the Holy = the Bible.

سال جديد *sal'î jédid* 'the new year'.

§ 518. *Remarks:* 1. If the first member of the construction, *i. e.* the noun, end in *élif* or *vav* used as a vowel (-*a*, -*ou*), instead of the ordinary *ésré*, a *yé* (-*y*-) is inserted for the sake of euphony (§ 53).

Instead of پاشا بغداد *pasha-i-Baghdad*, we must write پاشای بغداد *pasha'yi Baghdad* 'the Pasha of Baghdad'.

بالای خانه *bala'yi khané.* The upper (part) of the house.

چارسوی کبیر *charsou'yi kébir.* The Grand Bazar.

Note. The original Persian word چارسو *charsou* (a square) is commonly spelt in Ottoman as چارشو ٬ چارشی *charshî*, *charshou'*.

§ 519. 2. If the first member of the construction, *i. e.* the noun, end in the vowels *yé* and *hé* (-*i*, -*é*), a *hémzé* (-*y*-) is placed over the final letter for the sake of euphony (§ 53):

Instead of خانه پدر *khané-i pédér*, it must be خانهٴ پدر *khané'yi pédér* 'the house of the father'.

قاضیٴ آماسیه *qadi'yi Amassia* the judge of Amassia.

باغچهٴ کبیر *bagh-ché'yi kébir* the great garden.

مثاللر *Misal'lér* Examples.

حرکت ارض *harékét'i arz* the movement of the earth, earthquake.

در سعادت *Dér'i Sa-a-dét* the door of Prosperity ⎫ Constan-

در علیه *Dér'i Aleeyé, Déraliyé* the lofty door ⎭ tinople.

باب عالی *Bab'î Alee* the Sublime Porte.

کرهٴ ارض *kûré'yi arz* the sphere of the earth, the Earth.

پادشاه عالم *padisha'hî além* the king of the world.

§ 520. In Turkish the pronominal suffixes corresponding to my, thy, his, etc., that of mine, yours, etc. are always put after the noun to which they refer. In Arabic and Persians constructions, if the noun be followed by an adjective, simple or compound, or by another noun with which it is conjoined, their suffixes

are put at the end of the last word. This is the case with declensional endings also:

كتاب مقدسك *kitab'i mouqad'désiñ* of the Holy Book.

آرزوی شدیدیمیزه *arzou'yi shédidimizé* to our strong desire.

خاكپايلرنده *khakipaylérindé* at the dust of your feet, with you.

آواز بلند ايله *avaz'i bûlénd ilé* with a loud voice.

تعليم ۸٥   Exercise 85.

1. زمين *zémeen* earth + رو *rou* face. 2. a. احمر *ahmér* red + a. بحر *bahr* sea. 3. سفيد *séfid* white. 4. a. بحر + a. محيط *mouheet* [Ocean]. 6. بحر + سياه *siyah'*. 5. بحر + a. محيط *mouheet* [Ocean]. 6. بحر + 7. (a. عهد *ahd* testament + a. جديد *jédeed* new.) 8. (a. عهد + a. عتيق *ateeq* old.) 9. (پا *pa* foot + تخت *takht* throne) [= the capital]. 10. (خاك *khak* dust + پا.) 11. (a. انجيل *injeel* Gospel + a. شريف *shérif* holy.) 12. (بلند *bûlénd* loud + آواز *avaz* voice.) 13. (a. شديد *shédeed* strong + آرزو *arzou* desire.) 14. (a. سلطنت *saltanat* government + a. سنيه *sénee-yé* sublime.) 15. (a. ذات *zat* person + a. عالى *a-lee* high.) 16. (ايران *ee-ran* Persia.) شاه + 17. (a. حرارت *hararét* + a. شمس *shéms* sun.) 18. (a. صرف *sarf* grammar + عثمانى *Osmanee* Ottoman.) 19. (a. لسان *lisan* language + عثمانى.) 20. (a. كثيره *késeere* many, great + a. فوائد *févayid* benefits.) 21. (a. ضابط + خانه.) 22. (a. كتاب چارسو.) 24. (= Palestine].) 23. (a. ارض + مقدس + a. شريف.) + a. مذكور *mézkûr* mentioned.) 25. (يوحنا *Youhan'na* John

+a. وحی *vahee* revelation.) 26. (a. امثال *émsal* proverbs +

سليمان *Souléyman*.) 27. (داود *Davoud* David +a. مزامير *mé-*

zameer Psalms.) 28. (a. اسما *ésma* names + a. اعداد *adad*

numbers.)

Key. زمينك رويى (ياخود) يوزى *zémeeniñ rouyi* (yakhod)

yûzû; روى زمين *rou'yi zémeen* the face of the earth; *yûz*

is Turkish and رو *rou* Persian, both meaning 'face'.

The Persian Numerals. اسمای اعداد

§ 521. The Persian numeral adjectives are also
sometimes used in written Turkish, and in gambling.
They are the following:

يك *yék* 1	چهار، چار *chîhar, char* 4	هفت *héft* 7
دو *dû* 2	پنج *pénj* 5	هشت *hésht* 8
سه *sé* 3	شش *shésh* 6	نه *nûh'* 9

صد *sad* 100; هزار *hézar* 1000; نيم *neem* half; يكانه *yégiané*

single; يكان يكان *yégian yégian* one by one.

§ 522. The terms used in backgammon, dominos
and other games are as follows; (*ou* means 'and'):

dû-shésh 6 × 6, *dû-bésh* 5 × 5, *deôrt-chîhar* 4 × 4, *dû-sé*
3 × 3, *dû-baré* 2 × 2, *hép-yék* 1 × 1; *shésh-bésh* 5 × 6, *shésh-*
chîhar 4 × 6, *shésh ou-sé* 3 × 6, *shésh ou-dû* 2 × 6, *shésh ou-yék*
1 × 6; *bésh-deôrt* 5 × 4, *pénj ou-sé* 5 × 3, *pénj ou-dû* 5 × 2,
pénj ou-yék 5 × 1; *chîhar ou-sé* 4 × 3, *chîhar ou-dû* 4 × 2,
chîhar ou-yék 4 × 1; *sé-ba-dû* 3 × 2, *sé-yék* 3 × 1, *iki-bir* 2 × 1.

§ 523. مثاللر *Misal'lér* Examples.

yékvijoud of one body.
yékparé of a single piece.
yék takhtadan at once.

yékdil of one heart.
yékchéshm one-eyed.
charpa a quadruped.

ششخانه *shésh-khané* a (six-celled) rifle, an arquebuss.

يكديكر *yékdigér* one another, each other.

نيم جزيره *neem jézeeré* (half island) peninsula.

نیم رسمی *neem résmee* semi-official (paper, etc.)

سه‌پا *sépa, sîpa* a tripod, a three-legged stool.

تعلیم ۸٦ Exercise 86.

۱ بحرِ احمر عربستان ایله مصر آراسنده در۰ ۲ درِ سعادتده
نشر اولنان ٔصباح ٔ غزته‌سی سلطنتِ سنیه‌نك نیم رسمی غزته‌سی درِ۰
۳ در علیه‌ده اسیرِ پازارنده رمزی افندی خاننده طلبهٔ علومدن
رفعتلو واهان افندی‌یه۰ ٤ انگلتره دولتنك پایتختی لوندره شهری در۰
٥ روی زمینده بنی آدمك مقداری ۱٦۱۰ ملیوندن زیاده در۰ ٦ كرهٔ
ارضده بر چوق دولتلر وملتلر وار در۰ ۷ چارشوی كبیردن برعدد ششخانه
توفنك آلدم۰ ۸ حاكمِ افندی آوازِ بلند ایله ذاتِ حضرتِ پادشاهی
نامینه بر دعای بلیغ قرائت ایتدی۰ ٩ معلّمِ افندی درسی
طلبكانه یكان یكان تعریف ایله‌دی۰ ۱۰ یكچشم اینجه كیانك
پارمغنده یكپاره الماس طاشلی بر یوزوكی وار در۰ ۱۱ افندیمز حضرتِ
مسیح ٔیكدیگری كری سویكز ٔ دیو امر بیوردیلر۰ بوآیت انجیلِ
یوحنّاده محرّر در۰ ۱۲ طالعك یاور ٔ زارك هر وقت دوشش
كلیور۰ ۱۳ زوالی هریف شاشیردی ششی بش كورویور۰

Words. 1. *Misîr* Egypt. 2. *néshr ét."* to publish. 3. *Esir-pazarî*
the street called Esir Pazarî (the Market of Slaves). 4. *Rémzi
Efféndi khanî* the inn named Rémzi Effendi. 5. *talébéyi ouloum*
students (the seekers after science). 6. *béni Adém* the children
of Adam, mankind (575). 7. *béleegh* eloquent. 8. *qra'at ét."* to read.
9. *mou-al'lim* teacher. 10. *tareef ét."* to explain. 11. *ayét* verse.
12. *mouhar'rér* written. 13. *tali'yiñ* your star, fortune. 14. *zar*
a die used in playing.

تعليم قرأت   Reading Exercise.

اسامیٔ¹ فضائِل² وتنبیهات³

A list of Moral Maxims (= Franklin's Principles).

حکیمِ⁴ مشهور⁵ فرانقلینك⁶ تنظیمِ⁷ حرکات⁸ و اصلاحِ⁹

نفس¹⁰ ضمننده¹¹ اتخاذ ایلدیكی¹² اون ایكی قاعدهلر¹³ :

ریاضت¹⁴ : — آغیرلانهجق¹⁵ صورتده یمه ! سرسام (سَرْسَمْ)¹⁶

اولهجق قدر ده ایچمه !

سكوت¹⁷ : — كندیكه و باشقهسنه برفائدهٔیی مفید¹⁸ اولمایهجق

سوزی سویلهمه !

انتظام¹⁹ : — خانهگده هر شیئنك یرینی و هر بر ایشك وقتنی

تعیین²⁰ ایله !

تخصیصِ²¹ مقصد²² : — یاپمغه مجبور اولدیغك²³ شیئی قرارلاشدیر²⁴

و بلا²⁵ قصور²⁶ اجرا ایله !

امرِ تصرّف²⁷ : — كندیكه و یا آخره²⁸ لزومِ²⁹ حقیقیسی³⁰ اولان

شیئدن ماعداسنه³¹ بر اقچه صرف ایتمه³² !

Words. 1. _é-sa'mee_ names, lists. 2. _fézayil_ virtues. 3. _ténbechat_ (commands), maxims. 4. _hakeem_ a philosopher. 5. _mésh'hour_ celebrated. 6. Benjamin Franklin. 7. _tanzeem_ to put in order. 8. _harékiat_ acts, conducts. 9. _islah' ét."_ reforming. 10. _néfs_ life; self, personality. 11. _zimninda_ for, regarding. 12. _it'tikhaz ét."_ to adopt. 13. _qayidé_ a rule. 14. _riyazét_ ascetic discipline. 15. to be heavy. 16. _sérsém_ stupified. 17. _sûkût_ silence. 18. _mûfeed_ profitable. 19. _intizam_ order, regularity. 20. _tayeen ét."_ to fix, appoint. 21. _takhsees_ to assign or specially appropriate. 22. _maqséd_ an aim, endeavor. 23. _méjbour ol."_ to be obliged. 24. to decide, to settle. 25. _bila_ without. 26. _qousour_ defect (= perfect, complete). 27. _emri tesar'rouf_ frugality, economy (_émr_ work). 28. _akhér_ other (people). 29. _louzoum_ necessity. 30. _haqiqi_ real. 31. _ma-a-da_ except. 32. _sarf ét."_ to spend.

سعى و عمل³³ : ــ وقتكى ضايع ايتمه³⁴ وَ دائما فائدهلى بر شيله

مشغول اول³⁵ ! ⟨معلم ناجى⟩

33. *say ou amél* labour and work. 34. *zay' ét."* to waste.
35. *méshghoul ol."* to be busy.

مكالمه Conversation.

Dérs haqqînda sivallar. درس حقنده سؤاللر

س) بنيامين فرانقلين كيم در؟ ــ آمريقالى مشهور بر فيلوسوفدر.

س) فرانقلين هانكى عصرك فيلوسوفلرندن در؟ ــ اون سكزنجى عصرك.

س) فيلوسوف نه ديمك وَ حكيم نه ديمك ؟ بونلرك آراسنده نه فرق وار ؟

ــ فرق يوقدر. ايكيسيده بر معناده. فقط حكيم اكرچه *hékim* اوقونورسه ؛

طبيب ديمكدر.

دَرس ٣٩ Lesson 39.

تَرْكيبِ تَوْصيفى Persian Compound Adjectives.

§ 524. The simple adjectives of the Persian language
are much used in Turkish; as: سياه *siyah'* black, آل *al*
red, بد *béd* bad, سفيد *séfid* white.

§ 525. The compound adjectives of the Persian
language are formed in two ways: either by the addition
of particles, or by joining two words together.

A. The Derivative Adjective, formed by the addition of particles to nouns.

§ 526. The most common derivative adjectives used
in Turkish are made by the addition of the following
particles to Arabic or Persian nouns (§§ 149, 579):

§ 527. I. The letter ى *yé* (-*i*), signifies relation. If
the word ends in the vowels ا ‘ ى ‘ ه (-*a*; -*i*; -*é*, -*a*), they
are changed into و (-*v*-), and afterwards the *yé* is added:

انكليز *ingliz* Englishman   انكليزى *inglizi* English.

افرنج *éfrénj* a European   افرنجی *éfrénji* European.

عقل *aql* mind a.   عقلی *aqli* mental.

چین *chin* China   چینی *chini* chinaware.

دنیا *dûnya* world a.   دنیوی *dûnyavi* worldly.

§ 528. II. انه -*ané* signifies relation and resemblance. If the word ends in the vowel *he* (-*é*), this is changed into ك (-*g*-): and if it ends in و vowel (-*ou*) a ى (-*y*-) is inserted between the word and particle; as:

شاه *shah* king   شاهانه *shahané* royal.

بنده *béndé* servant   بندكانه *béndégiané* as a servant.

عدو *adou* enemy a.   عدویانه *adouyané* as an enemy.

§ 529. III. The terminations وان ، بان ، كار -*ban*, -*van*, -*kiar*, -*giar* form nouns denoting 'doer, keeper', etc. باغبان *bagh-ban* keeper of vineyard. خدمتكار *khîdmétkiar* a servant.

خداوندكار *khûdavéndigiar* the sovereign, the Sultan.

پروردكار *pérvérdigiar* the Nourisher (God), Providence.

یادكار *yadgiar*, *yadigiar* a remembrance, memento.

§ 530. IV. The prefixes نا *na*-, بی *bi*- mean 'without', and denote the absence of something; *na*- is used with adjectives, *bi*- with nouns:

نامعلوم *nama'lûm* unknown.   ناپاك *napak* unclean.

بیچاره *bicharé* unfortunate.   ناخوش *nakhosh* unpleasant.

بیوفا *bivéfa* inconstant (friend), unreliable.

خواه ناخواه *khah'nakhah* willingly or unwillingly.

§ 531. V. هم *hém*- prefixed to a noun expresses companionship.

همشهری *hémshéh'ri* fellow-citizen. همجنس *hémjins'* homogeneous.

همشیره *hémsheeré* who sucks the same milk, a sister.

§ 532. VI. Adjectives are also formed by the

addition of اسا ، وش ، ين ، مند ، ناك ، ور or وار ‑*asa*, ‑*vésh*, ‑*een*, ‑*ménd*, ‑*nak*, ‑*vér* or ‑*var*.

نساسا *nisa-asa* womanlike.   مهوش *méh'vésh* like the moon = bright.

آتشين *atésheen* fiery.   حصهمند *his'séménd* partaker.

a.p. غمناك *ghamnak* sorrowful.   فرحناك *férah'nak* cheerful.

اميدوار *ûmmidvar* hopeful.   جانور *janvér* (wild) animal.

هنرمند ، هنرور *hûnérvér, hûnérménd* skilful.

§ 533. VII. By doubling some words and inserting an *elif* between them, fulness or multifariousness may be expressed:

برابر *bérabér* breast to breast; together; equal.

لبالب ، مالامال *lébaléb, malamal* (lip to lip) brimful.

رنكارنك ، كوناكون ، نوعانوع *réngiaréng, gûnagûn, névanév* varied in hue, variegated.

B. Compound Adjectives composed of two words.

§ 534. The compound adjectives obtained by the union of two words are generally formed either: 1. of a noun and a participle, or the root of a verb, 2. of an adjective and a noun, or, 3. of two nouns.

They may consist of two Persian words, or of an Arabic and a Persian word, or of two Arabic words.

§ 535. **a. Adjectives formed of a noun and a participle or the root of a verb.**

دل *dil* heart,   بر *bér* take, captivate: دلبر *dilbér* enchanting.

مدد *médéd* help, رس *rés* arrive: مددرس *médédrés* helper.

دلشكسته *dilshikésté* broken hearted. See also: § 556.

§ 536. **b. Adjectives formed of an adjective and a noun.**

بو *bou* odour   خوشبو *khosh'bou* sweet scented, odorous.

تهى *téhi* empty   تهيدست *téhidést* empty-handed, deprived.

§ 537. **c. Adjectives formed from two nouns.**

آهو *ahou* gazelle: آهوچشم *ahouchéshm* gazelle-eyed, attractive.

شیر *sheer* lion: شیردل *sheerdil* lion-hearted.

کلعذار *gûlazar* rosy-cheeked; Rose (pr. name). (گل + عذار .a +)

§ 538. Many such compound words lose their meaning as an adjective and are considered as compound nouns:

کلدسته *gûldésté* a bunch of flowers, a bouquet.

سرعسکر *séraskér* head of the army, a commander-in-chief.

قانوننامه ٬ نظامنامه *nizam'namé, qanoun'namé* a code of laws.

The Degrees of Comparison.

§ 539. The Comparative is obtained by the addition of تَر *-tér* to the simple form of the adjective, and the Superlative by adding ترین *-téreen*:

بد *béd* bad: بدتر *béd'tér* worse: بدترین *bédtéreen* worst.

بالا *bala* high: بالاتر *balatér* higher: بالاترین *balatéreen* highest.

تعلیم ٨٧ Exercise 87.

Change the following nouns into adjectives:

527. فرنك *fréng* European. ترك *tûrk.* a. شرق *sharq* the east. یهود *yéhoud* (Judah) Jew. ادرنه *Edirné* Adrianople. فرانسه *Fransa.* یابان *yaban* the wilderness. حلب *Haléb* Aleppo. خاك *khak* earth. a. صلیب *salib* a cross.

528. دیو *deev* a demon. مرد *mérd* man. دوست *dost.* a. خالص *khalis* sincere. a. عاجز *ajiz* humble. پدر *pédér.*

529. باغچه *baghché.* کناه *gûnah.* a. خلاص *khélas* deliverance. ساخته *sakhté* false. پاس *pas* watch (at night). کار *kiâr* profit. صندوق ٬ صندیق *sandouq, sandîq* a coffer. روز *rouz* day. دَر door. قَلَم pen, graver.

530. a. اَساس foundation.   t. صوچ *souch* sin, fault.

a. مقبول *maqboul* acceptable.   a. قدرت *qoudrét* power.

مرد *mérd* (brave) man.   a. مزاج *mizaj* state of health.

a. حضور *houzour* a becoming in repose, ease.   تاب strength.

531. a. مّلّت *mil'lét* nation.   a. مذهب *mézhéb* religion.

a. جوار *jivar* neighbourhood.   راه *rah* way, road.

535. (ره *réh* way + نَما *nûma* show), (شیر *sheer* +

خوار *khor* eat), (خان + بك *béy*, زاده *zadé* born).

536. (كِران *giran* heavy + بها *baha* price), (ساده *sadé*

simple + دل), (چشم *chéshm* eye + سیاه), (نان bread

+ كور *kêôr*) ، (بد + بخت) ، (دل + شاد).

538. (a. تبریك congratulation + letter), (روز day

+ letter), (نو *név* new + سال year), (a. اِذْن + letter).

539. خوش *khosh* nice, مه *mih'* great, به *bih* good.

تعلیم ۸۸   Exercise 88.

۱ خلاصكاریز حضرت مسیح افندیز ' كناهكارلرك خلاصی
ایچون بودنیایه تشریف بویوردی ۰ ۲ لسانِ انكلیزیبی وَ فرانسویبی
چوق سوه‌رم ۰ ۳ شوكتاب لسان تركی اوزره یازلمشدر ' تركیلری
و شرقیلری حاویدر' ۰ ٤ چینی طباقلری² چیندن كاربانلر واسطه‌سیله³
كلیر ۰ ۵ سزه دوستانه بر نصیحت ویره‌یم : دنیوی اوله‌یكز ۰
٦ خدمتكاركز دیوانه میدر نه در؟ برشی آكلادیغی یوقدر ۰ ۷ پاسبانلر
نصفِ لَیلده⁴ بنی چارشوده یاقالایوب⁵ بنده‌لرینه عدویانه سویله‌دیلر ۰
۸ كلعذارخانم دون نامزاج اولدقلرندن بك غمناك ایشلر ۰ یازه‌جقلری

Words. 1. a. *havee* containing. 2. *tabaq* plate. 3. a. *vasîta* hand,
means. 4. a. *nisf* half, a. *léyl* night. 5. *yaqalamaq* to collar, seize.

فرانسوی مکتوبی خواه ناخواه یازه‌مامشلر · ۹ همجواریزده بولنوب ده
نساآسا اولرنده نااومید برحالده اوطورانلره یاردیم ایتدیم ٬ اونلره مردانه
یاشامه‌لر یچون نصیحت ایله‌دیم · ۱۰ خانه‌مز اول قوناقدن بالاتر وهواسی
ایسه خوشتردر ·

۸۹ ترجمه Translation 89.

1. Richard I., king of England, was called[1] lion-hearted. 2. That ungrateful servant did not write a letter of congratulation on New Year's-Day. 3. That beautiful woman (*dilbér*) is very inconstant. 4. The gardener is not a coward, but he is a simple-hearted man. 5. To eat with unclean hands is very unpleasant. 6. Is your fellow-traveller a skilful man? 7. I was a partaker of the supper[2]. 8. I did not lose hope (hopeless), I am hopeful yet[3]. 9. He prayed to the Saviour sincerely and humbly. 10. A forger is a great sinner. 11. He is not an empty-handed person, he has a costly[6] gold watch in his hand. 12. The leader was a helper to me on the way[4]. 13. That caravan, which comes from China and India, was loaded with china-ware and odorous spices[5].

Words. 1. *tésmeeyé oloundou.* 2. *akhsham ta-a-mi.* 3. *hala.* 4. *ésnayi rahdé.* 5. p. *béhar, bahar.* (Ar. pl. *béharat.*) 6. *qiymét-dar* (§ 535).

تعلیم قرائت Reading Exercise.

حکیم مشهور فرانقلینك تنبیهاتندن مابعد وختام

استقامت[1] : — کذب[2] وحیله‌دن[3] حذر[4] ایت · دائما دیدیکك
کبی یاپ و دوشوندیکك کبی سویله !

حقّانیت[5] : — کرك وظیفه‌اك[6] داخلنده[7] وکرك خارجنده[8] اجراسنه
مجبور اولدیغك[9] حسناتدن[10] فرار[11] و هیچ برکیمسه‌یی اضرار ایله‌مه[12] !

Words. 1. a. *istiqamét* honesty. 2. a. *kizb* falsehood. 3. a. *heelé* cheating. 4. a. *hazér ét."* to beware. 5. a. *haq'qaneeyét* justice, equity. 6. a. *vazeefé* duty. 7. a. *dakhil* the inside. 8. a. *kharij* the outside. 9. a. *méjbour ol."* to be obliged, compelled. 10. a. *hasanat* good works, pious deeds. 11. *firar* to run away, to desert, flee. 12. a. *izrar ét."* to injure.

اعتدال[13] : — افراطدن[14] احتراز ایله[15] وَ حقسزدن عقلكجه

لایق كوردوكك[16] صورتده اخذِ ثاره[17] قیام ایلهمه[18] !

نظافت[19] : — كرك وجود وَ اثوابكجه وَ كرك خانه كجه نظافته

اهتمام ایله[20] !

حضورِ قلب[21] : — اوفاق تفك[22] شیلردن ، عادی[23] وَ یا خلاصی

ناقابل[24] اولان وقوعات[25] وَ صدماتدن[26] مضطرب[27] اوله !

عفت[28] : — كندك كبی باشقهسنك دخی امنیت[29] وَ صلاحِ[30]

حالِ وُشانِنی[31] تهلكه یه[32] قویمه !

(معلم ناجی)

13. a. *eetidal* moderation. 14. a *ifrat* excess. 15. a *ih'tiraz et."* to guard one's self. 16. a. *layîq geôrmék* to judge worthy. 17. a. *akhz* taking; *sar* vengeance = to revenge one's self. 18. a. *qiyam ét."* to set about. 19. a. *nézafét* cleanliness. 20. a. *ihtimam ét."* to be careful. 21. a. *houzour* ease, quietness; *qalb* heart. 22. trifles. 23. a. *a'dee* inferior, ordinary. 24. *naqabil* impossible. 25. a. *vouqou-at* events. 26. a. *sadémat* blows, misfortunes. 27. a. *mûztarib ol."* to suffer. 28. a. *if'fét* chastity. 29. a. *émneeyét* safety. 30. a. *salah'* peace, virtue. 31. *hal ou shan* position and honour. 32. a. *téh'liké* danger.

مكالمه   Conversation.

س) باغچه كزده نه وار ؟

ج) باغچه مزده رنكارنك خوشبو چیچكلر وار ایسهده ، باغچهبان بر دانهسنی

بیله بكا ویرمه یور ؛ سرعسكر پاشا حضرتلرینه تقدیم اتمك اوزره

بركلدسته یاپهجق ایمش .

س) بالاده كی فضائلِ مُحرَّرَهنی اكتساب و اعتیاد آرزوسنده اولانلر ذهنلرینی

عمومنه بردن می حصر ایتمه لی دررلر ؟

ج) خیر افندم ؛ حكیمِ موسی ایله علاوةً دیبورلركه «آنجاق برنده مَلَكَه پیدا

ایتدكدنصوكره ، دیكرینه تَشَبُّث ایتمه لی و بو صورتله اون ایكیسینی ده

موقعِ اجرایه قویمه یه چالیشمالی در» .

س) استقامت نه كلمه در ؟

ج) استقامت عربی بر كلمه اولوب معناسی طوغرولق در .

س) نظافت نه دیمكدر ؟

‫ج) بو دخی بر عربی كلمه اولوب تميزلك وَ پاكلك ديمكدر.‬

‫س) فرانقلينك آثارندن بو بالاده وَ اوكی درسده كوردیكمز تنبیهـاتی كیم‬
‫تركجهیه نقل ایتمشدر؟‬

‫ج) شاعر وَ مُنشئ مشهور مرحوم معلم ناجی افندی ترجمه ایتمشار در.‬

‫۶۰ درس‬ Lesson 40.

The Persian Derivative Nouns.

§ 540. Persian derivative nouns are of four kinds: Nouns of Location, Nouns of Instrument, the Abstract noun, and the Diminutive noun.

‫اسم مكان‬ The Noun of Location.

§ 541. The noun of Location is made by the addition of ‫ستان‬ -*istan*, ‫گاه‬ -*giah* 'place', ‫زار‬ -*zar* a plot or bed, ‫كده‬ -*gédé* hut, ‫خانه‬ -*khané* house (§ 162):

‫هندستان‬ *hindistan* India.

‫چمنستان‬ *chiménistan'* ⎫
‫چمنزار‬ *chiménzar'* ⎭ meadow.

‫اردوگاه‬ *ordougiah'* a camp.

‫گلستان‬ *gûlistan* ⎫ rosary, a garden
‫گلزار‬ *gûlzar* ⎭ of roses.

‫میكده‬ *méygédé* ⎫ wineshop,
‫میخانه‬ *méykhané* ⎭ drinking-saloon.

‫طوپخانه‬ *top-khané, top-hané* arsenal of ordnance and artillery.

‫كاركاه‬ *kiarkiah* vulg. *kérgéf* a work-frame. (‫كار‬ work.)

‫بزستان‬ *bézistan* vulg. *bédéstén* a covered market-place. (‫بَز‬ cloth.)

‫اسم آلت‬ The Noun of Instrument.

§ 542. The noun of Instrument is made by the addition of ‫دان‬ -*dan* 'a holder, receptacle, case':

a. ‫شمع‬ *sham* candle: ‫شمعدان‬ *shamdan'* a candlestick.

‫بخوردان‬ *boukhourdan'* a censer, incense-box.

p.t. ‫یاغدان‬ *yaghdan* an oil can.   p.t. ‫توكوردان‬ *tûkûrdan* a spittoon.

‫ریكدان‬ *reek'dan* vulg. *righdan* a sand-holder; *reek, rîgh* sand (to dry writings).

کلاب *gûlab* rose-water (§ 538): کلابدان *gûlabdan* a flask for sprinkling scented water.

The Abstract Nouns. اسم معنا *Ismi Mana.*

§ 543. Abstract nouns are made by the addition of ی -*i* at the end of adjectives. If the word end in *elif*, then the *yé* is doubled (-*yi* [§ 53]); if it end in a vowel *hé* (-*é*), it is changed into ك (-*g*-), but the sound *é* is retained (§§ 163, 581).

آسان *asan* easy, facile: آسانی *asani* facility.

بنده *béndé* slave: بندگی *béndégi* servitude.

روشنا *roushéna* bright: روشنایی *roushénayi* brightness.

Note. Yé added to a noun, changes it into an adjective (§ 526).

The Diminutive Nouns. اسم تصغیر *Ismi Tasghir.*

§ 544. Diminutives are made by the addition of چه -*ché*, -*jé* at the end of nouns. Some diminutives are terms of endearment, as in Turkish (§ 167).

مور *moor* ant: مورچه *moorché* a little ant.

پا *pa* foot: پاچه *pacha* trotters of sheep.

عم، عمو *amm, am'mou* uncle: عموجه *amja, amouja* dear uncle.

تعلیم ۹۰ Exercise 90.

Change the following nouns into Derivative Nouns:

541. فرنك *fréng* European. a. یهودی *yéhoudi* Jew. تاتار a Tartar. ترك Turk. a. عجم *ajém* a Persian. a. عَرَب Arab. 2. t. طاغ *dagh*, p. کوه *kûh'* mountain. بنفشه *bénéf'shé* violet. 3. a. سنبل *sûnbûl* hyacinth. a. قبر *qabr*, a. مزار *mézar* grave. آتش *atésh* + hut. 4. t. اوكسوز *ôksûz*, a. ایتام *éy'tam* orphans + house. a. دباغ *déb'bagh* vulg. *tabakh* tanner + house. کار *kĩar* manufacturing + house. 5. a. کتاب *kitab,*

18*

book + house. a. اجزا *éjza* (vulg. *éza*) a drug + house.
آش *ash* food + house. شكار *shikiar* game, prey + place.

542. جامه *jamé* cloth + holder. خامه *khamé*, a. قلم
qalém + case. تير *teer* arrow. نمك *némék* salt.

543. آشنا *ashina* poor. آسوده *asoodé* quiet. آشنا *ashina*
intimate. آزاده *azadé* free. خسته *khasté*. سزا *séza* worthy.
تنك *téng* narrow.

544. پاره *paré* piece. باغ *bagh*. بوغ *bogh* a square
wrapper for a bundle. كوروم *geôrúm* husband's sister.
t. آق كيمان *kéman* a violin. t. چكمه *chékmé* a drawer.

تعليم ۹۱ Exercise 91.

۱ قدس شريف¹ يهودستانك پايتختى ايدى · ۲ ميلادك اونبرنجى
وَ اون ايكينجى عصرلرنده فرنكلر فرنكستانك هر طرفندن طاقم طاقم
سوريه‌يه² يوروديلر · بونلره صليبى نامى ويريلمشدر · ۳ دون بزستانه
كيتديم وَ بر طوپ چوقه³ ايله ايكى طوپ آمريقان بزى⁴ اشترا
ايدوب⁵ بوغچه‌لايه‌رق · ايتاجانه‌يه ارسال ايلدم⁶ · ٤ هه‌مشيره‌م سنبلستانده
اوطوروب كارگاه ايشله‌يور · ٥ شيمدى مرذيفونده‌كى آمريقان
اوكسوزخانه‌سينده ۱٤۰ نفر ايتام موجود⁷ در · ٦ ريكدان وَ قلمدان
ماصه‌نك⁸ اوزرينده در · ۷ ماكينه‌يى ياغلايه‌جق ايدم آمّا ياغدانده
ياغ يوغيدى · ۸ شو قارشوكى قبرستانده كورديكم تربه⁹ كيمك در ؟
٩ طاغستانلى بر شيخك¹⁰ مزارى در · ۱۰ عمومجم ايله برلكده
بنفشه‌زارلرده وَ چمنزارلرده كزدك · هر يرده آسودكى وار ايدى ·

Words. 1. a. *Qoudsou Shéreef* Jerusalem. 2. *Souriya* Syria.
3. *chouqa, choukha* broad-cloth. 4. *ameriqan bézi* unbleached linen.
5. a. *ishtira ét.''* to buy. 6. a. *irsal* to send. 7. a. *mévjoud* existent.
8. f. *masa* table. 9. a. *túrbé* tomb. 10. a. *shéykh'* a head of a tribe.

ترجمه ٩٢   Translation 92.

1. The owner of that big tannery and the keeper of the prison [-house] are the friends of the saloon-keeper. 2. «The beer-seller[1] is the witness[2] of saloon-keeper.» 3. The orphans are in the orphanage. 4. That Tartar has come from Tartary. 5. There were 3000 soldiers in the camp. 6. The people who dwell[3] in mountainous regions are generally brave. 7. Daghistan is a great region in Russia. 8. Where is your donkey[4]? — He is always in the meadow. 9. Please stick[5] a candle into the candlestick. 10. There was a big rosary in the garden of the manufactory of the attar of rose[6]. 11. The Parsees[7] and the ancient Persians were worshipping[8] the fire in the fireplaces.

Words. 1. *biraji, bozaji* (157). 2. a. *shahid*. 3. a. *iqamét ét."*. 4. *chiménzarzadé* vulg. *chiméndérzadé* the son of the meadow = donkey. 5. *dikmék*. 6. *gûl yaghî*. 7. *parsee, giâvour, gébr* a Zoroasterian, a fire worshipper, a Guebre; (in Turkey) a non-Moslem [said in contempt]. 8. a. *ibadét ét."*

تعليم قرائت   Reading Exercise.

اشك ايله تيلكى حكايهسى The Story of the Donkey and Fox.

چيقدى بر باغاڭ ايچندن بر ياشلى حمار ' ،

نقل ' ايچون بلدهيه ' يوكلنمشيدى روى نگار ' ؛

ديركن ' ، آج قارنه بر تيلكى كورونجه ؛ كلدى ،

بويله بر تازه اوزوم حسرتى ' باغرين ' دالدى .

اوته كى چيفتهيى ' آتدى بو يازاشدجه برآز ،

صوكره لكن آرهدن قالقدى بوتون ناز وينياز ' .

تيلكى : — «كلسهم اولماز مى حضوره '' ؟ آ بنم آرسلانم !

Words. 1. a. *himar* donkey. 2. a. *naql* to carry. 3. a. *béldé* town. 4. *rouyi nigiâr* a kind of light pink colored grapes. 5. *dérkén* just then (while he was saying this). 6. a. *hasrét* desire, affection. 7. *baghrin'* for *baghrini* his heart, bosom. 8. *chifté atmaq* to kick with the hind legs. 9. p. *naz ou niyaz* graceful disdain. 10. a. *houzour* presence.

«تا یاقینیدن باقایم؛ حسنکزه¹¹ حیرانم¹² !

«دائم¹³ اولسون بکمك سایهٔ لطف و كرمی¹⁴ !

«گل بیتر¹⁵ باصدیغی یرلرده مبارك¹⁶ قدمی¹⁷ ،

«بكزور اول خوش قوقولی قویروغی اعلا¹⁸ میسكه¹⁹ ،

«قوقلارم؛ بورنومه وورمازسه افندی فیسكه²⁰ ؛

«ایلر عرفانتی²¹ ایما²² او سخنكو²³ كوزلر ،

«یاقیشیر آغزینه موزون²⁴ و مقفا²⁵ سوزلر . » —

اشك افراط²⁶ نشاطندن²⁷ آكیردی²⁸ ، دیر ایكن ،

صانكه قارپوز قابوغی كوردی یاخود تازه دیكن .

تیلكی : — «جانیمه ایشلهدی²⁹ كیتدی او فرحناك هوا³⁰ !

سز سكوت³¹ ایتسهكز اما ، كیمنه وار باشقه صفا³² ؛

چونكه بلبل³³ ایشیدوب نغمهكزی³⁴ سرقت ایدر³⁵ ،

چاغیریر³⁶ بلكه ، كلیر دیكلهینه حزن و كدر³⁷ . » —

تیلكی بویله نیجه دیلر دوكهرك ذوق³⁸ ایتدی .

اشكی بر قویونك باشینهدك سوق³⁹ ایتدی .

تیلكی — «بوراده⁴⁰ بر كوزل آخور ایله یمك وار در ،

«نیلهیم یوكله كیریلمز قاپیسی پك دار در ،

11. a. *hûsn* beauty. 12. a. *hayran im* I am confounded. 13. *da-yim olsoun!* Let it be long, eternal. 14. *sayéyi loutf ou kérémi* the shadow or protection of his kindness and mercy. 15. *bitmék* to grow. 16. a. *mûbarék* graceful. 17. a. *qadém* foot. 18. a. *a-la* excellent. 19. p. *misk* musk. 20. a. *fiské* a fillip with the middle-finger. 21. a. *irfan* wisdom. 22. a. *eema ét.* to express. 23. *sûkhén-gû* eloquent (§§ 535, 556). 24. *mévzoun* well proportioned. 25. a. *mou-qaf'fa* rhymed. 26. a. *ifrat* excess. 27. a. *néshat* mirth, joy. 28. *añirmaq* to bray. 29. *janima ishlédi gétdi* it pierced into my heart (§ 348). 30. a. *hava* air. song. 31. a. *sûkût* silence. 32. a. *séfa* pleasure. 33. a. *bûlbûl* nightingale. 34. a. *naghmé* song. 35. a. *sir-qat* stealing. 36. sings. 37. a. *huzn ou kédér* sorrow. 38. a. *zévq* mockery; pleasure. 39. a. *sévq* driving. 40. here (in this well); *néyléyim* for *né éyléyéyim* [what can I do?] alas!

«اوبورِوب یاقہ کیبی ذوق[38] وُ صفا چوق آنده ،

«صو ایچوب ، یم یهمهدن غیری[41] جفا[42] یوق آنده ،

«اونده ساکن دیشیلرده[43] او لطافت[44] باشقه ،

«هله[45] برکره باقك ؛ دوشمه یك اما عشقه[46] . »

یاقلاشنجه اشك آیینهٔ آبه[47] باقدی ،

یوزی عکسین[48] سزهرك[49] آغزی صویی پك آقدی :

اشــك : — «واقعا[50] کورمهدهیم دلـبَرِ وَ نازك[51] بر باش» .

تیــلکی : — «چاغیرك تیز اونی ، کلسین سزه اولسون اویناش[52]» .

«بورایه کل !» دیو فریاد[53] ایدهرك طاشدی[54] حمار ،

قویودن عکسِ صداسین[55] ایشیدوب شاشدی[56] حمار ؛

تیلکی : — «کوردوکكز می ؟ سزی شیمدی ایدییورلر دعوت[57] ؛

«بو ضیافتنده[58] عجب[59] یوقّی بكّا برخدمت[60] ،

«بونده قالسین یوکكز ؛ تك اینیكیز سز آشاغی

«آرقه کزدن کلیرم اولمهیه طاولا[61] اوشاغی» . —

اشك آتدی یوکنی یرلره ، کندین قویویه ؛

تیلکی میراث یدی[62] ، تا اوکا رحمت[63] اوقویه .

〈شناسی〉

41. a. *ghayri* other, than.   42. p. *jéfa* trouble.   43. *dishi* female.
44. a. *létafét* loveliness.   45. *hélé!* if you please!   46. a. *ashyа
dushmék* to fall in love.   47. p. *ayinéyi ab* the mirror of the water.
48. a. *aksin'* for *aksini* reflection (of image).   49. *sézmék* to see.
50. a. *vaqa'a* truly, really.   51. a. *nazik* delicate.   52. *oynash*
playmate, sweet heart (§ 165).   53. p. *féryad ét."* to scream, call out.
54. *tashmaq* to exceed the bound of moderation in joy.   55. a. *aksî
sédasin'* for — *sédasini* reflection of sound, echo.   56. *shashmaq*
to be surprised.   57. a. *davét ét."* to call, invite.   58. a. *ziyafét*
feast.   59. a. *ajéb* for *ajéba* I wonder.   60. a. *khîdmét* service.
61. *tavla oushaghi* stable boy.   62. a. *meeras yémék* to inherit.
63. a. *rahmét oqoumaq* to pray for the deceased.

مكالمه Conversation.

درس حقنده بعض سؤاللر

بو حكايهنك سرنامهسی ۱ نه در؟	اشك يله تياكی حكايهسی ٔ در .
بونك محرّری ۲ كيم در؟	عثمانلی اديبلرندن ۳ مشهور شناس ۴ افندی در .
شناسی افندی حياتده می بوخسه مرحوم در افندم ! مرحوم ۵ می ؟	۱۸۷۱ تاريخينده قيرقبر ياشـينده اولهرق وفات
اشك نه يوكلی ايدی ؟	اعلا اوزوم يوكنمشيدی . [ايتمشدر.
بونی كيم كوردی ؟	قارنی آج اولان خـٔـن ۶ بر تياكی .

تياكی قارداشلق نه ياپدی ٬ وَ نه سويلهدی ايسه ٬ بزه نقل ۷ ايديكز باقالم !
تياكی باقدی كه اشك كوكلی ايله اوزومدن يهديرمهيهجك ٬ اونك ايچون
بر چوق ديللر دوكهرك نه ياپدی ياپدی اشكه يوكنی براقديرهرق ٬ كندينی
قويويه آتديردی ٬ وَ اوزوملری صفای خاطِر ۸ ايله عافيت ايتدی ۹ .

Words. 1. *sérnamé* a heading (§ 538). 2. a. *mouhar'rir* a writer. 3. a. *édib* an author. 4. *Shinasee Efféndi* (1830—71). 5. a. *merhoom* deceased, dead. 6. a. *khayin* treacherous. 7. to tell. 8. heart. mind (*séfa'yi khatir* ease, peace of mind). 9. a. *afeeyét ét."* to eat [he helped himself].

درس ۴۱ Lesson 41.

The Persian Verb.

§ 545. The Persian Infinitive ends in دن -*dén* or تن -*tén*: كشادن *kûshadén* to open, پرستيدن *péréstidén* to worship.

§ 546. None of the tenses of the Persian Verb are used in Ottoman. The Roots of the verbs are very frequently employed in the formation of compound adjectives (§ 535); as: پرست *pérést*, root of *péréstidén*, پت پرست *pout pérést* idol-worshipper.

§ 547. Only one Derivative of the Infinitive and

three of the Verbal Roots are used in Ottoman, which are the following.

I. The Objective Participle. اسم مفعول

§ 548. The Objective or Past Participle is made by changing the last letter of the infinitive into *hé* vowel (-*é*) (§§ 402, 604):

دادن *dadén* to give: داده *dadé* given.

شکستن *shikéstén* to break: شکسته *shikésté* broken.

دیدن *deedén* to see: دیده *deedé* seen; eye.

II. The Subjective Participle. اسم فاعل

§ 549. The Subjective or Present Participle is made by the addition of ـنده *-éndé* to the Root. If the Root ends in an *élif* or *vav* vowel (-*a*, -*ou*), a *yé* (-*y*-) is inserted (§ 53).

خوان *khan* read, sing: خواننده *khanéndé* singer.

دار *dar* hold: دارنده *daréndé* bearer.

غا *numa* show: غاینده *numayéndé* who shows.

ساز *saz* make: سازنده *sazéndé* composer.

III. The Verbal Noun. اسم مصدر

§ 550. The Verbal Nouns are made by the addition of ش *-ish* to the Root. If the Root ends in *élif* or *vav* vowel (-*a*, -*ou*), a ی (-*y*-) is inserted for the sake of euphony (§§ 53, 288).

رو *rév* go: روش *révish* going.

دان *dan* know: دانش *danish* knowledge.

So also we have: آسایش *asayish* peace, غایش *numayish* a show, سپارش *siparish* ordering, order.

§ 551. There is another kind of verbal noun which is obtained by the removal of ن *-én* from the end of the Infinitive:

کشادن *kûshadén* to open: کشاد *kûshad* opening.

انداختن *éndakhtén* to throw: انداخت *éndakht* throwing, propelling.

فروختن *firoukhtén* to sell: فروخت *firoukht* selling.

§ 552. Verbal nouns are also formed by adding two shortened infinitives of different verbs or the shortened infinitive and the root of the same verb together:

کشت و گذار ، آمد شد *améd shûd, gésht ou gûzar* a coming and going.

کفت وکو *gûft ou gû* talk; chat; scandal.

داد و ستد *dad ou sitéd* selling and buying, trade.

IV. Verbal Adjectives. صفت مشبهه

§ 553. The Verbal Adjectives are formed by the addition of ان ، ا‍ -a, -an to the root of the verb; as:

دان *dan* know: دانا *dana* wise, savant (§§ 436, 606).

جوی *jouy* seek: جویان ، جویا *jouyan* that seeks.

رو *rév* go: روان ، رَوا *révan* that goes, fluent.

لرز *lérz* tremble: لرزان *lérzan* trembling.

The Persian Roots. فارسی امرِ حاضرلر

§ 554. The following table contains most of the Persian Verbal Roots, which are current in Ottoman. They are used only in compound words, and never used alone. Slightly changing their meaning in composition they help to form adjectives (§§ 535, 556).

آرا	*ara*	adorn	آلا	*a-la*	defile, soil
آزار	*azar*	torment	آمیز	*ameez*	mingle
آزما	*azma*	try, prove	انداز	*éndaz*	throw
آشام	*asham*	drink	اندوز	*éndouz*	collect
آشوب	*ashoub*	excite	انکیز	*éngeez*	excite
افراز	*éfraz*	raise	آور ، آر	*avér, ar*	bring
افروز	*éfrouz*	light. illuminate	آویز	*aveez*	hang
آفرین	*aféreen*	create	بار	*bar*	rain
افزا	*éfza*	increase	باز	*baz*	play

بر	*bér*	carry		ریز	*reez*	shed
بخش	*bakhsh'*	give		ربا	*rûba*	carry off; rob
بند	*bénd*	tie		زا	*za*	bear
بین	*been*	see		زن	*zén*	strike
پرور	*pérvér*	feed, nourish		ساز	*saz*	make; com- [pose
پذیر	*pézeer*	accept, receive		سپار	*sipar*	order
پرداز	*pérdaz*	engage in		ستا	*sita*	praise
پسند	*pésénd*	approve		سوز	*sooz*	burn
پیرا	*peera*	ornament		شتاب	*shitab*	haste
پرهیز	*pérhiz*	abstain		شکن	*shikén*	break
پوش	*poosh*	put on, wear		شمار	*shûmar*	count
پیما	*peema*	measure		شناس	*shinas*	recognize
تاب	*tab*	shine		شوی	*shouy*	wash
تاز	*taz*	rush		فرسا	*férsa*	rub, corrode
تراش	*trash*	shave		فرما	*férma*	command
جوی	*jouy*	seek		فروش	*firoush*	sell
چین	*cheen*	gather		فریب	*fireeb*	deceive
خراش	*khîrash*	scratch		گداز	*gûdaz*	melt
خوار	*khor*	eat		گذار	*gûzar*	pass
خوان	*khan*	read, chant		گزین	*gûzeen*	choose
خواه	*khah'*	wish		کش	*késh*	draw
خیز	*kheez*	rise		گیر	*geer*	seize, take
دار	*dar*	hold, keep		کشا	*kûsha*	open
دان	*dan*	know		کن	*kûn*	do, perform
دوز	*dooz*	sew, stitch		گو	*gû*	speak
ده	*dih*	give; grant		مال	*mal*	rub
ران	*ran*	urge, drive		نشین	*nisheen*	sit
رس	*rés*	arrive		نما	*nûma*	show
رسان	*résan*	cause to reach		نواز	*nûvaz*	caress
رو	*rév*	go		نویس	*nûvees*	write

نـكَـاه *nigāh* look | نِه *nih* place; put

یاب *yab* find.

§ 555. Persian Objective (Past) Participles.

آراسته	*arasté*	adorned	زاده	*zadé*	born
آزاده	*azadé*	free	زده	*zédé*	struck; suffered
آزموده	*azmoudé*	experienced	ساخته	*sakhté*	made; false
آماده	*amadé*	ready	سوخته	*soukhté*	burnt
آمده	*amédé*	come	شكسته	*shikésté*	broken
آسوده	*asoudé*	at rest, quiet	فرسوده	*férsoudé*	worn
آورده	*avérdé*	brought	فرستاده	*firistadé*	sent
آویخته	*avikhté*	hung	فرفته	*firifté*	deceived
افتاده	*ûftadé*	fallen	فرموده	*férmoudé*	commanded
افسرده	*éfsûrdé*	frozen	كذشته	*gûzéshté*	past; interest on money
ایستاده	*istadé*	standing, erect.	كرده	*kérdé*	made, done
بسته	*bésté*	tied; tune	كرفته	*girifté*	seized
پرورده	*pérvérdé*	nourished	كزیده	*gûzeedé*	choosen; best
خورده	*khordé*	eaten	كشاده	*kûshadé*	open
داده	*dadé*	given	كفته	*gûfté*	word
دیده	*deedé*	seen; eye	مانده	*mandé*	left
رنجیده	*rénjidé*	injured	مرده	*mûrdé*	dead
رسیده	*réseedé*	arrived; ripe	نهاده	*nihadé*	put
رفته	*réfté*	gone	یافته	*yafté, -ta*	found; label.

§ 556.   مثالها   Examples.

جهانكیر *jihangeer* world conquering, conquerer.

نورسیده *névréseedé* newly arrived, young.

پزمرده *pezmûrdé* vulg. *pézvarda* faded; untidy.

پرتوسوز *pértévsouz* » *pértafsîz* burning-glass.

جانباز *janbaz* » *janbaz* rope-dancer; a horse dealer.

دوربین *dourbeen* » *dûldûl* far seeing; telescope.

t. p. امكدار *émékdar* an old and faithful servant, veteran.

a. p. سلاحدار *silahdar* vulg. *zilifdar* armour bearer.

a. p. اصلزاده *asîlzadé* of noble descent, a noble.

a. p. قفادار *qafadar* an intimate friend.

a. p. آفترده *afétzédé* who has suffered misfortune.

a. p. طرفدار ، طرفكير *tarafdar, tarafgeer* a partisan.

تعليم ۹۳　Exercise 93.

Connect the following words with each other and give the meanings:

535. 1. (نام *nam* name + hold.)　2. (a. حكم *húkúm* authority + hold.)　3. (a. خزينه *khaziné* treasure + hold.)　4. (a. مقاس *maqas* a tailor's scissors + hold.)　5. (a. ضرر *zarar* injury + seen.)　6. (جهان *jihan* world + seen.)　7. (a. حريق *hariq* fire + struck, suffered.)　8. (t. بك *béy* prince + born.)　9. (شاه + born.)　10. (لنكر *léngér* anchor + throw.)　11. (نا *na* un- + know.)　12. (a. خير *khayr* good + wish.)　13. (بد *béd* evil + wish.)　14. (چوال *chouval* sack + sew.)　15. (سخن *súkhén* word + speak.)　16. (a. صلح *soulh* + nourish.)　17. (a. نعل *na'l* horse-shoe + tie.)　18. (a. مصلحت *maslahat* state affair + pass, do.)　19. (t. ايش work + pass, do.)　20. (f. موسيقى *mousiqi* music + engaged in.)　21. (خنك *khúnk* happiness, prosperity + bring [*khúnkîar* p. 240].)

550. Translate the following Participles into Persian.

Increase, augmentation; giving, present; a wishing, a desire; caressing, petting; praising; an act of opening, cheerfulness.

Exercise 94.   تعليم ٩٤

١ قواص اغا فاميليامزك امكدارى در ٤٠ سنه ددهمه وَ ٢٠
سنه بابامه خدمت ايتمشدر . ٢ يشيل ايرماق جوشمش وَ شهرك اوچ
محلهسنى سورمش . شهزادهلر مددرس اولوب آقتزدكانى صولرك ايچندن
خلاص ايتمشلر . برچوق اصلزادكان وبكزادكان دخى اكمك وَ البسه
يتيشديرمشلر . ٣ يارين سـاعت درتنده آماده اوله‌جغم ، كليرسكـز
سزكله‌برابر رسمِ كشادى اجرا اولنه‌جق اولان مكتبه كيده‌ريز ؛ ساعت
آلتيده اورايه رسيده اولورز . ٤ واپور قوشلق صيره‌لرنده صامسون ليمانه
لنكرانداز اولدى . ٥ افندى پك خيرخواه بر ذات ايـش ؛ تزينك
مقاصدازينه بول كيسـهدن يارى ليرا بخشـش ويرمش . ٦ ديده‌لردن
كوز ياشـلرى ريزان اولدى . ٧ ساخته سوزلر سويله‌مه ، پاره‌ى
كذشته‌سيله برابر وير . ٨ بو تَرَنّم اولنان مقامى پك بكندم ؛ دوغروسى
شايانِ ستايش در . عجبا كيم تأليف ايتمشدر ؟ ٩ كفته‌سنى شاعر
مشهور جورجى افندى وَ بسته‌سنى دخى موسيـقى پردازاندن حاجى
آرشاق افندى تنظيم ايله‌مشدر . ١٠ آسمان يوزنده بيشمار آختارلر وار
در . ١١ صنفنك الك كزيده‌سى نجيب افندى در .

Translation 95.   ترجمه ٩٥

1. Mehemmed II. was a great conqueror; he was
also a brave ruler. 2. The horsedealer was very untidy.
3. I had a small telescope, but I sold it; now I have
a burning glass. 4. The number of the sufferers from
the fire was more than 300. 5. The princes were among
the partisans of the king. 6. The steamer anchored
towards morning. 7. The treasurer distributed £ 400
to those who have suffered from the fire. 8. That man

is a very famous rope-dancer. 9. The armour-bearer of
the prince was very ungrateful. 10. Ali Effendi is my
intimate friend. 11. Who is Mr. Riddle? — He is the
Chargé d'affairs of the American legation at Constantinople.

تعليم قرائت   Reading Exercise.

مناجات مع التمجيد¹   A Supplication and Praise.

خالقِ العالمين³   سن جهان آفرين² سين يا رب !

سن یارب⁴ !

سن شعله افروزِ⁵ آسمانسين⁶ !   توشه بخشِ⁷ زمين سين يا رب !

كمك هپ جهانه شاملدر⁸ ؛   اكرم الاكرمين⁹   سين يا رب !

كيمه بيامم واروب فغان¹⁰ ايدهيم ؟ ارحم الراحمين¹¹   سين يا رب !

بن نه حاجت¹² كه عرضِ حال¹³ ايدهيم ؟ سينهده¹⁴ دلنشين¹⁵ سين يا رب !

ظاهرم¹⁶ باطنم¹⁷ سكا معلوم ،   حضرتك غيب بين¹⁸ سين يا رب !

⟨ديوان فاضل⟩

Words. 1. a. *Münajat ma ét'témjeed.* 2. *jihan* world, universe.
3. a. *khali'qûl-alémeen* creator of the universe. 4. a. *ya Rébb'!*
O Lord! 5. *shoulé éfrouz;* a. *shoulé* flame, light. 6. p. *asûman,*
asman heavens. 7. *toushé bakhsh; toushé* provisions. 8. a. *shamil* containing. 9. *ékrém' ûl ékrémeen* the most gracious of the gracious
ones. 10. *fighan* a moan, cry of distress. 11. a. *érhém ûr rahi-*
meen most merciful. 12. a. *hajét* need (what is the need?).
13. a. *arzihal* petition. 14. *seené* heart. 15. *dilnishin* seated in one's
heart. 16. a. *zahir* outside. 17. a. *batîn* inside. 18. *ghayib-been*
who see the invisible. *Divanî Fazil* (from) The Divan of Fazil
[† 1803].

Note. The Nos. 2, 5, 7, 15, 18 are Persian compound adjectives (§ 535) and the Nos. 3, 9, 11 are Arabic compound adjectives (§ 669).

مكالمه   Conversation.

شعرادن فاضل افندئ مرحوم در.   بالادهكِ شعرك محرّرى كيمدر؟

اشعار مجموعهسى ديمكدر.   ديوان' نه ديمكدر؟

ايچهريم ديشارم جناب اللهه آشكار   ظاهرم باطنم سكا معلوم' نه دمك ؟
در دمك در.

كوروبز اولان شيلرى كورن ديمكدر.   غائب بين نه معناده در؟

۲٬۵٬۷٬۱۵ وَ ۱۸ نومرولره مُرَقَّمْ   وَصفِ ترکیبی یاخود ترکیب تَوْصیفی
اولان کلماته صرف فارسیده نه دیرلر؟   دیرلر: وَصْفْ صفت دییکدر.
۳٬۹ وَ ۱۱ نومرولر نه در؟   اضافتِ عربیه در (§۶۶۹).

درس ٤۲ Lesson 42.

The Persian Prepositions.

§ 557. The Persian prepositions of frequent use in Ottoman are the following (§§ 236, 451):

a) از *éz* 'from': forms the Ablative case.

از جان وُ دل *éz jan ou dil* 'from soul and heart' = heartily, devotedly.

ازہر جہت *ézhér jihét* in every respect.

ازبر *ézbér* 'from breast' = by heart, committed to memory.

از جمله *éz jûmlé* 'from the number of' = as for example.

از قدیم *éz qadeem* from olden times.

b) بِ *bé* 'to, in': forms the Dative case.

رو برو *rou bérou* face to face.

بنام خدا *béna'mî khúda* in the name of God.

بہمه حال *béhémé hal* 'in every condition' = absolutely.

بہر سنه *béhér séné* every year. ماہبماہ *mah'bémah'* month by month.

کون بکون *gûn bégûn* day by day. t.

c) با *ba* 'with, by': forms the Instrumental case.

با علم و خبر *ba ilm ou khabér* by a receipt.

با صواب *ba savab* correct. با طاپو *ba tapou* with a deed.

با سند *ba sénéd* with a note.

با خصوص *ba khousous* especially.

با فرمان عالی *ba férma'nî ali* by an (Imperial) exalted edict.

با امتیاز *ba imtiyaz* with a privilege, privileged.

d) در *dér* 'in, at': forms the Locative case.

در دست *dér dést* at hand; arrested, seized.

در آنبار *dér anbar* in the; store, stored.

در حال ، در عقب *dér hal, dér aqab* immediately.

در خاطر *dér khatîr* in the mind, in heart.

در استانه *dér Asitané* in Constantinople.

e) بر *bér* 'on'.

بر عكس *bér aks* on the contrary.   بر طرف *bér taraf* aside.

بر قرار ، بر دوام *bér qarar, bér devam* continually, firmly.

بر موجب ، بر منوال ، بر وجه *bér véj'hi, bér minva'li, bér mouji'bi*
according as.

f) تا *ta* 'until, as far as'.

تا طاغك ديپه‌سنه قدر *ta daghiñ dépesiné qadar* as far as the top of
the mountain.

تا بصباح *ta bésabah* till the morning.

g) براى *bérayi* 'for, for the sake of'.

براى مصلحت *béra'yi maslahat* for a business.

براى امتحان   »   *imtihan* for the examination.

براى عبادت   »   *ibadét* for worship.

براى حرمت   »   *hûrmét* for the sake of respect.

مثاللر Examples.

در خاطر ايتمك *dér khatir étmék* to remember.

بر موجب بالا *bér mouji'bi bala* in the above-mentioned manner.

بر وجه آتى *bér vej'hi atee* in the following manner.

dér dést ét." to arrest.   *bér taraf ét."* to set aside.
dér anbar ét." to store.   *éz sér ta pa* from head to foot.

Substitution. ابدال *Ibdal.*

§ 558. Substitution of one letter for another rather
rarely occurs in the Persian language. This change
of one letter into another does not produce any change

of meaning: For instance, ب *b* is changed into و *v* in some words; as: بالا *bala* high = والا *vala* high, تابه *tabé* frying pan = تاوه *tava* frying pan.

§ 559. Substitution occurs often in the following letters:

ب to پ: *b* = *p*   بازار *bazar* market: پازار *pazar.*

د » ذ: *d* = *z* a. خدمت *khidmét* service: خذمت *khizmét.*

جادو *jadou* wizard: جاذو *jazou.*

شاد *shad* merry, joyful: شاذ *shaz.*

ب » و: *b* = *v*   باغچهبان *baghchéban* gardener: باغچهوان *bagh-chévan.*

ر » ل: *r* = *l*   پرکار *pérkiar* compass: پرگل *pérgél.*

پ » ف: *f* = *p*   کفچه *kéfché* skimmer: کپچه *képjé.*

ك » ج: *g* = *j*   کوهر *gévhér* jewel: جوهر *jévhér.*

س » ش: *sh* = *s*   مشك *mûshk* musk: مسك *misk, mûsk.*

خ » ح: *kh* = *h*   خنكار *khûnkiar* king: حنكار *hûnkiar.*

Omission. حذف *Hazf.*

§ 560. The Omission of letters is very frequent in the Persian language, without changing the meaning of the word:

The original word شاه *shah'* 'king' is written as شه *shéh'* 'king'. افغان *éfghan* 'lamentation' is written also فغان *fighan*. مه *méh* for ماه *mah* 'month', and گه *géh* for گاه *giâh* place.

§ 561. The following is a list of such words frequently used in Ottoman:

پای *pay* foot: پا *pa.*

چهار *chîhar* four: چار *char.*

بدتر *béd'tér* worse: بتر *bétér* or *béttér.*

استاد *oustad* master: اوسته ، اوستا *ousta.*

a. امیر *émeer* prince: میر *meer.*

يابان	*béyaban* desert:	يبان 'يابان	*yaban*.
خوشنود	*hoshnoud* content:	خشنود	*hoshnoud*.
خانه	*khané* house:	خان	*khan*.
سار	*sar* head:	سر	*sér*.
آزاده	*azadé* free:	آزاد	*azad*.
a. فقيه	*faqeeh'* student af Canon law:	فقى	*faqî*, vulg. *fakhî*.
كاروان	*kîarvan* caravan: (§ 529)	كروان	*kérvan*.

تعليم ٩٦   Exercise 96.

١ خنكاريمز سلطان عبد الحميد خان حضرتلرى در ٢٠ كريم افندى خواجهنك هر سؤالنه جواب باصواب ويرديكندن ٬ خواجه افندى ذحى ازجان و دل آفرين ديدى ٠ ٣ اختيار بر آدم كورديككگزده براى حرمت اياغه قالقيمگز ! ٤ آناطوليه قولهجى با فرمان عالى كشاده اولمشدر ٠ ٥ درسكگزى ازبر ايتمك ايچون بر دوام سعى و اقدام ايتمهليسكز ٠ ٦ خدمتجى درعقب عودت برله بر وجه آتى خبر كتيردى ٠ ٧ قوبور اوسته النده بر كفچه اولهرق خان قاپوسندن ايچهرى كيرمش ٬ هر كس بونى كورور كورمز شاذ و مسرور اولوب آفرين ديو ندا ايتمشلر ٠ ٨ ساعت بشده بهمهحال اوه عودت ايتمهليسكز ٠ ٩ بر موجب سند مَدْيون اولديغم اوتوز سكز عدد ليرايى بوكون با كذشته تأديه ايلهيوب سنديمى قورتاردم ٠ ١٠ با علم وخبر ٧٠٠٠ غروش آلدم ٠ ١١ تاوهده بولنان ياغ مسك كبى كوزل قوقويور ٠

ترجمه ٩٧   Translation 97.

1. From olden times he has been the friend of our family. 2. He was satisfied with me in every respect. 3. This mother loves her children devotedly. 4. He said this to me and immediately went out. 5. He sends me a present at the beginning of every

year: (for instance) this year I received a gold pen.
6. Day by day he was progressing in his lessons. 7. In
the name of God come quickly and help me! 8. He
is continually sick. 9. Kérim Effendi went to Salour
for business. 10. He climbed up to the top of the
mountain. 11. He cried incessantly until morning; because his body from head to foot was full of wounds.
12. Néjib Béy went to the mosque for worship. 13. He
spoke in the following manner. 14. The thief was arrested.
15. The wheat and the barley were stored. 16. The
caravan lost its way in the desert.

تعليم قرائت Reading Exercise.

آوجی (*) The Hunter.

— ۱ —

سزه ميلٌ؟ إيتمهسين می وجدانلر۳ ؟   قوشجيغزلر! سَويملی فَتّانلر۱ !

بو نه جُنْبُشْگهِ سرور آ کين۵ !   بو نه جمعيتِ سُرودِ آيين۴ !

چاليلـق صَوْتِكزله۸ پر آهنك۹ ؛   يريدر اولسه منشرح۶ دلِ تنك؟۷ ،

سسكِز خوش ، مَقامكز ده لطيف۱۲ ،   حاكزساده۱۰ ، شكلكِز ده ظريف۱۱ ،

بوزه جقدر بو انتظامی۱۴ هَمان .   لکن ، انديشه۱۳ ايلهيڭ که زمان

۱۵صوصيڭِز! قوشجيغزلرم! صوصيڭِز!

— ۲ —

دها يوق چانطهسنده سرچه بيله .   کليور ايشته آوجی سُرعَت۱۶ ايله ،

رحمی۱۸ يوقدر ،سزی كورورسه قيار۱۹ .   ۱۷نك طورورمی؟ الِنده چفتهسی وار ،

Words. (۱) 1. a. *fét'tan* naughty (boy [§ 609]). 2. a. *méyl*
incline. 3. a. *vijdan* heart; conscience. 4. *jémeeyé'ti sûroodakeen*
an assembly full of chants (§ 536). 5. *jûnbûshgé'hi sûrourakeen:*
junbûshgéh a place of pleasure (§§ 541, 560), *sûrourakeen* joyful (§ 536).
6. a. *münshérih'* cheerful; *yeri dir* it is lawful (just the place).
7. *dili téng: téng* poor, miserable; *chaliliq* bush. 8. a. *savt* chant.
9. p. *pûr* full; *ahéng* melody. 10. *sadé* simple. 11. a. *zareef*
graceful; a. *maqam* singing. 12. a. *latif* nice, beautiful. 13. *éndishé*
ét! take care! 14. a. *intizam* quietude, order. 15. *sousouñouz!*
be silent! *qoushjighazlarîm* my dear birdies (§§ 166—67).

(۲) 16. a. *sûr'at* speed; *chanta* bag. 17. *dék dourmaq* to keep
still, quiet; *chifté* double-barreled fowling piece. 18. a. *rahm* mercy.
19 *qîymaq* to kill (he will not spare you).

<hr>

(*) فرانسز شاعرِ مَشهوری «بَرانژه»نك بر مَنْظومهسندن مقتبسدر .

آوجيدن مرحمت اومارميسكز؟   كوزى وار سزده ، كوز بومارميسكز²⁰؟

شان دكل ، شين²¹ آدميتدر؛   بويله ايشلر سزاى لعنتدر²² .

جان ياقان شخصى خوش كورورمى الله ؟   كيمه آ كلاتغالى ؟ نه يا عالى ؟ آه !

صوصيكز ! قوشجيغزلرم ! صوصيكز !

— ۳ —

بر كون ايتمش ايدم شويبرده قرار²³ ،   ايكى قير لانغيج ايلهيوردى گذار .

اوتوشورلردى بختيارانه²⁴ ،   وبرمهسينلرى نشوه²⁵ انسانه؟

بنده عودتلرين ايدوب تبريك ،   اولدم آنارله ذوق وشوقه²⁶ شريك .

ناگهان²⁷ آتش ايتدى بر صياد²⁸ ،   اولدى بى چاره يولجيلر برباد²⁹ .

اوزاق اولمق ايچون بلايادن³⁰ ،   اتقا³¹ ايلهبك برايادن³² .

صوصيكز ! قوشجيغزلرم ! صوصيكز !

— ٤ —

بيليك انسانلرك خصائلنى³³ ،   كوركـ افكارينك دلائلنى³⁴ !

ضعفاسى³⁵ : وسيلهجوى ستيز³⁶ ،   اقوياسى³⁷ : بوتون بوتون خونريز³⁸ ؛

ايلهمشر جهانى ظلم آباد³⁹ .   بونلر انسانمى ؟ بر آلاى⁴⁰ جلاد⁴¹ !

اولهمازلر محبّ صادق وُ خير⁴² ،   بونلرك اك رحيمى⁴³ : قاتلِ طير⁴⁴ .

بيايريم كرچه ؛ وصف⁴⁵ لايقمى ؟   بكا سويلتمهيك ! حقايقمى⁴⁶ ؟

صوصيكز ! قوشجيغزلرم ! صوصيكز !

20. *yoummaq* to shut, close. 21. *sheeni adémeeyét: sheen* shame; a. *adémeeyét* humanity (§ 581). 22. *sézayi la'nét* detestable: *séza* subject; suitable, fitting; a. *la'nét* curse.

(۳) 23. a. *qarar ét."* to sit; *qirlanghij* swallow. 24. *bakhtiyarané* in a happy way (§ 528). 25. p. *nésh've* pleasure; a. *avdét* arrival; a. *tébrik ét."* to congratulate. 26. a. *zévqou shévq* pleasure and mirth (§ 696); a. *shérik* companion. 27. *nagéhan* suddenly. 28. a. *say'yad* hunter (§ 610). 29. *bérbad* ruined, lost (§ 557 e). 30. a. *bélaya* evils, misfortunes. 31. a. *it'tiqa ét."* (from *riqayé*) to be cautious. 32. a. *béraya* men.

(٤) 33. a. *khasayil* character; a. *éfkiar* opinion. 34. a. *délayil* tokens, proofs. 35. a. *zou-a-fa* the poor (ones). 36. *véseelé-jouyi siteez: vésiléjouy* who seeks for a pretext (to quarrel) (§ 535); *siteez* quarrel. 37. a. *aqveeya* the rich, the strong (ones). 38. *khoonreez* blood-shedder (§ 535). 39. *zoulm abad* a place of cruelty; hell. 40. *alay* troop. 41. a. *jél'lad* executioner (§ 609). 42. a. *mouhibbi sadiq ou khayr* (§ 696): *mouhibb'* friend; a. *sadiq* just, true; *khayr* good. 43. a. *raheem* merciful. 44. a. *qatil* murderer; a. *tayr* bird. 45. a. *vasf* praising, eulogy. 46. a. *haqayiq* right, just.

— ٥ —

قاناندن وورلدى بر ككليك .   دستِ صياده ياور اولدى تتيك⁴⁷'

آ كا وابسته⁴⁹ آولرك جلبى .   قوشوب آلدى آنى همان كلبى⁴⁸'

سفكِ دمدن⁵⁰ اولورمى آدم شاد؟   نه سوِيندك؟ نه كولدك؟ اى صياد!

ظالمه بندن زياده لعنت ايدر⁵² .   بوستمكر⁵¹ بو قانلى شيمدى كيدر'

نه در اغرب⁵⁴ جهانده؟ طبعِ بشر⁵⁵!   هم سور شرى' همده دشمنِ شرّ⁵³'

    صوصيكز! قوشجيغزلرم! صوصيكز!

— ٦ —

كوردى برباشقه آو شتاب ايدييور؛   قوشلرم! مژده! آوجيكز كيدييور'

شيمدى آهنكه باشلايك يكيدن؛   بركن يوق! تباعد⁵⁶ ايتدى كيدن؛

ويريكز مشربمجه⁵⁸ بر قونسر⁵⁹'   قالمادى شمديلك محلِّ حذر⁵⁷'

اوتك! اطرافى اوتديرك تكرار!   ويردى مهات⁶⁰ زمانه⁶¹ بر مقدار'

بورالردن يارن ايدرسه كذر؛   لكن! اول ظالم طمع⁶² پرور'

    صوصيكز! قوشجيغزلرم! صوصيكز!

     ⟨معلم ناجى⟩

(٥) 47. *yavér* helper; *tétik* trigger; *kéklik* partridge. 48. a. *kélb* dog. 49. *vabéste* appropriated; a. *jélb* bringing, fetching. 50. *séf'-ki dém* shedding of blood. 51. *sitémkér* unjust, cruel (§ 529). 52. a. *lanét ét."* to curse. 53. a. *shérr* evil. 54. a. *éghréb* wonderful. 55. a. *tab* heart, nature; a. *béshér* humanity.

(٦) 56. p. *múzhdé!* good news! a. *tébayûd* to disappear. 57. a. *mahélli hazér* place (= need) of caution, fear. 58. a. *mésh-rébimjé* as I like, according to my taste. 59. f. *qonsér* concert. 60. *múhlét vérmék* to grant a delay. 61. a. *zémané, zéman* Time; *bir míqdar* a little; a. *zalim* cruel. 62. *tama-pérvér* avaricious (§ 535).

درس ٤٣ Lesson 43.

كيفيت The Gender of Arabic Nouns.

§ 562. There is no gender in Turkish or Persian, but there is in Arabic. With respect to gender Arabic nouns are divisible into two classes: a) those which are only masculine; b) those which are only feminine. There is no neuter gender in the language.

§ 563. That a noun is of the feminine gender (*kéy-fiyét*) may be ascertained either from its **signification** or from its **termination**.

a. The feminine nouns which are such because of their **signification**, are all words denoting **females**; as:

خديجه ، زينب ، مانيه *Hadijé, Zéynéb, Manya* (fem. prop. names).

والده *validé* a mother, عروس *arous* a bride, بنت *bint* a daughter.

b. The feminine nouns and adjectives which are such by reason of their **termination**, are all substantives and adjectives ending in ه or ة ، ت ، ا (*-é, -ét, -at, -t, -a*), when those terminations do not belong to the root; as:

مملكت *mémlékét* a country, جنّت *jén-nét* paradise, محكمه *mah'kémé* a court, كبرا *kúbra* greater (§§ 29 c, 32 c, 610).

But ماء *ma* water, سكوت *súkút* silence, تنبيه *ténbeeh* warning, وقت *vaqít* time: are not feminine, because their terminations are **radical**; i. e. ا ، ت ، ه (*-a, -t, -h*) belong to the root (§ 587).

§ 564. Masculine nouns and adjectives are usually rendered feminine by the mere addition of the letters ة ، ه *hé, té* (*é, t*), which are called **feminine letters**:

عظيم *azeem* great:	عظيمه *azeemé* great (fem.).
جدّ *jédd* a grandfather:	جدّه *jéddé* a grandmother.
اخ *ékh, úkh* a brother:	اخت *úkht* a sister.
بن *bén, bin* a son:	بنت *bint* a daughter.

§ 565. *Note.* When the noun is feminine, the adjective must agree with it, and be also of the feminine gender (§ 656).

٩٨ تعليم   Exercise 98.

I Change the following masculine nouns into feminine ones:

‹ نجيب ⁸ ‹ وارث ⁷ ‹ متصرّف ⁶ ‹ معلّم ⁵ ‹ خال ⁴ ‹ عمّ ³ ‹ حفيد ² ‹ والد ¹ ‹ نبى

‹ ثالث ¹⁵ ‹ شاعر ¹⁴ ‹ مرحوم ¹³ ‹ غزّال ¹² ‹ فلان ¹¹ ‹ مومن ¹⁰ ‹ حامل ⁹

‹ كريم ‹ شهيد ‹ مَلِك ²⁰ ‹ صاحب ‹ باكر ¹⁹ ‹ اله ¹⁸ ‹ زوج ¹⁷ ‹ ثانى ¹⁶

Words. 1. *valid* a father (genitor). 2. *hafeed* grandchild. 3. *amm'*, vulg. *ém'mi* father's brother, uncle. 4. *khal* mother's brother, uncle. 5. *mou-al'lim* teacher. 6. *mûtésar'rîf* owner; governor. 7. *varis* heir. 8. *néjib* noble. 9. *hamil* bearer. 10. *mûmin* believer. 11. *filan* so and so (man). 12. *ghaz'zal* gazelle. 13. *mér-houm* the deceased. 14. *shayir* poet. 15. *salis* third. 16. *sanee* second. 17. *zévj* husband. 18. *ilah'* god. 19. bachelor. 20. King.

II. Ascertain whether the following words are feminine or masculine:

‹ مسرّت ⁷ ‹ فوت ⁶ ‹ موت ⁵ ‹ اخت ⁴ ‹ بنت ³ ‹ حبّه ² ‹ ظلمت ‹ نورى ¹

‹ نِعمَت ‹ ألطَف ‹ كَرَم ¹³ ‹ ابو ¹² ‹ نبات ¹¹ ‹ بيت ¹⁰ ‹ حديقه ⁹ ‹ مصلحت ⁸

1. *zoulmét* darkness. 2. *hab'bé* a grain. 3. *bint* daughter. 4. sister. 5. *mévt*, 6. *févt* death. 7. *mésér'rét* joy. 8. *maslahat* business. 9. *hadeeqa* garden. 10. *béyt* a house; a stanza. 11. *nébat* plant. 12. *ébou* father. 13. *kérém, loutf, nimét* kindness.

The Number of Arabic Nouns. كميت

§ 566. The Arabic language has three numbers (*kémiyyét*): Singular, Dual and Plural, and three cases (*hal*) in each number: Nom., Acc., and Genitive.

§ 567. *Note.* Of the three Arabic cases, only the Nom. and Acc. of the Singular and the Acc. of the Dual and Plural are in use in Ottoman, the Acc. of the Dual and Plural being used in place of the Nominative, and that too in a form shortened by the omission of the final short vowels. The Acc. Sing. is used only as an adverb in Ottoman (§ 682). In the following Lessons the short final vowels and everything else not used in Ottoman are omitted, but the student will find them in Arabic phrases adopted into the language as single words (§ 666—670).

Dual. تثنيه *Tésniyé.*

§ 568. The Dual indicates two things of the same kind and is formed by adding ان *-an* and ين *-éyn* to the singular. [Compare with the *-an* of Persian (§ 509)]; as:

ساحل *sahil* sea-coast:

ساحلان ، ساحلَيْن *sahiléyn', sahilan* two coasts.

ثلث *sûls* one third:

ثلثان ، ثلثَيْن *sûlséyn', sûlsan* two thirds.

قطب *qoutb* the Pole:

قطبان ، قطبَيْن *qoutbéyn', qoutban* the two Poles.

§ 569. If the word end in *hé* (-*é*) feminine (*hayi téénis*), it is changed into *té* feminine (-*t*-) (*tayi téénis*), before the dual termination is added (§ 32 c, 564, 592):

نسخه *nûskhé'* a copy: نسختين *nûskhétéyn'*.

سفينه *séfiné'* a ship: سفينتَيْن *séfinétéyn'*.

§ 570. The following duals are much in use, although they do not indicate two things exactly similar to one another:

والدَيْن ، ابوَيْن *validéyn', ébéréyn'* the parents. (Sing. والد ، ابو).

زوجَيْن *zévjéyn'* husband and wife.   (Sing. زوج).

قمرَيْن *qaméréyn'* the sun and moon.   (Sing. قمر).

حرمَيْن *haréméyn'* the sacred cities of Mecca and Medina.

Note that they do not mean 'two fathers', 'two husbands' and 'two moons'.

تعليم ٩٩   Exercise 99.

Change the following nouns into the dual:

مَنْزِل¹ ، جِهَت² ، صَحيفه³ ، ضَمَّه⁴ ، شَرْط⁵ ، بَلْدَه⁶ ، سُدْس⁷ ،
فِقْره⁸ ، شَريك⁹ ، وَارِث¹⁰ ، مَرقوم¹¹ ، جُمْلَه¹² ، طَرَف¹³ ، بَحْر¹⁴ ، بَرّ.

Words. 1. *ménzil* a halting place; a house. 2. *jihét* a side; a quarter. 3. *saheefé* page. 4. *zammé* the vowel *éôtré*. 5. *shart* condition. 6. *béldé* country. 7. *sûds* one sixth. 8. *fiqra* a sentence, paragraph. 9. *shérik* companion. 10. *varis* heir. 11. *mérqoum* the above said. 12. *jûmlé* clause. 13. *taraf* a side. 14. *bahr* a sea.

The Plurals in Arabic.   جمع *Jém.*

§ 571. There are two kinds of plurals in Arabic:

a. One of these has only two forms, and is called the r e g u l a r or s o u n d p l u r a l (pluralis sanus), because

all the vowels and consonants of the singular are retained in it (*Jémi Múzékké'ri Salim, Jémi Múénné'si Salim*); ex:

مأمور *mé-mour* an officer: مأمورين *mé-mou-reen'* officers.

b. The other which has various forms is called the b r o k e n or i r r e g u l a r p l u r a l (pluralis fractus), because it is more or less altered from the singular by the insertion or elision of consonants, or the change of vowels; ex.: سفينه *séfeené* a ship: سُفَن or سَفائن *súfén* or *séfayin* 'ships'. Here the form of the noun is broken.

So also شِى *shéy* a thing: اشياء *ésh'ya* things.

§ 572. The different ways of forming the irregular Arabic plurals are so numerous and complex that a separate chapter is requisite to explain them, which will be found further on (Lesson 51, § 637—652).

The Regular Masculine Plural. جمع مذكّر سالم

§ 573. The pluralis sanus of masculine nouns is formed by adding the termination ون -*oon* and ين -*een*; as: مسلم *múslim* a Moslem: مسلمون ٬ مسلمين *múslimeen', múslimoon'* Moslems. مؤمن *múmin* a believer: مؤمنين ٬ مؤمنون *múmineen', múminoon'* believers.

§ 574. This way of forming the plural is employed only in the case of names of r a t i o n a l beings, therefore اسد *éséd* 'a lion', مكتوب *méktoub* 'a letter' cannot be اسدين ٬ مكتوبون *ésédeen, méktouboon*: because they cannot reason or speak (§ 578).

§ 575. But the plurals of سنه ٬ عالم *séné* 'year', *a'lém* 'universe' are exceptions: they are سِنين *síneen, séneen*, عالمين *alémeen*. The plural of بن *bén* 'son, child' is بنون ٬ بَنين *benée* : but it becomes بنى *benée* when in con-

struction with a noun following; as: بنى آدم ، بنى اسرائل
bénee Israyél, bénee Adém 'the children of Israel', 'the
children of Adam, mankind'; the full form, however,
does not occur in Ottoman.

تعليم ١٠٠   **Exercise 100.**

Give, if possible, the regular plurals of the following nouns.

، مَشْهور ٦ ، مَظْلاوم ٥ ، طَيْر ٤ ، قارى ٣ ، مُعَلِّم ، مُدَرِّس ٢ ، كِتاب ١ ، نور

، رَسول ١٢ ، والِده ، بِنْت ، سارِق ١١ ، حَوارى ١٠ ، مُجْرِم ٩ ، سامِع ٨ ، رِياضى ٧

Words. 1. Book. 2. *mûder'ris, mou-al-lim* teacher. 3. *qaree*
reader. 4. *tayr* a bird. 5. *mazloum* poor, oppressed. 6. *mésh-
hour* remarkable (man). 7. *riyazi* astronomer. 8. *sami* hearer,
audience. 9. *mûjrim* criminal, sinner. 10. *havari* apostle (of our
Lord). 11. *sariq* a thief. 12. *résoul* an apostle, prophet.

The Regular Feminine Plural. جمع مونّث سالم

§ 576. The regular way of forming the plural of
Arabic feminine nouns and adjectives (*Jémi Mûénnési
Salim*) is by dropping the final ه *hé*, ت *té* (-*é*, -*t*, -*ét*) of
the singular (§§ 563—64) and adding ات -*at* to the word.

مسلمه *mûslimé* a female Moslem: مسلمات *mûslimat* Moslem women.

ثمره *séméré* a fruit: ثمرات *sémérat* fruits.

علامت *a-lamét* a sign: علامات *alamat* signs.

§ 577. If the word end in ات -*at*, the ت -*t* is
dropped and *élif* is changed into *vav* (-*v*-):

ذات *zat* person: ذوات *zévat*.

صلاة *salat* prayer: صلوات *salàvat*.

برات *bérat* an edict: بروات *béravat* edicts, firmans.

§ 578. Some of the masculine nouns denoting
things which have not reason or speech, form their
plurals by adding ات -*at*, as they cannot take the
regular masculine plural (§ 574):

‏تحرير‏ *tahreer* a writing: ‏تحريرات‏ *tahreerat* writings.

‏غلط‏ *ghalat* a mistake: ‏غلطات‏ *ghalatat* mistakes.

‏نبات‏ *nébat* a plant: ‏نباتات‏ *nébatat* plants.

‏تعليم ۱۰۱‏ Exercise 101.

Give the feminine plural of each of the following words:

‏تَسْلِيم۷ ، عَادَتْ٦ ، خِدْمَتْ٥ ، مُعْجِزَه٤ ، آلَتْ۳ ، حَيوَانْ۲ ، غَايَتْ۱ ، نَفَر‏

‏، زَكَاتْ۱۳ ، تَقْصِيرْ۱۲ ، تَأْلِيفْ۱۱ ، شِكَايَتْ۱۰ ، عِبَارَهْ۹ ، حَاجَتْ۸‏

‏سَبْزَه p.۱۹ ، تَعْمِيرْ۱۸ ، بَرَكَتْ۱۷ ، تَبْرِيكْ۱٦ ، مَعْلُومْ۱٥ ، تَعْرِيفْ۱٤‏

Words. 1. *ghayét* the end. 2. animal. 3. instrument. 4. *mûjizé* a miracle. 5. service (*khîdémat*). 6. *a-dét* custom. 7. a. payment. 8. *hajét* a need, want. 9. *ibaré* sentence. 10. *shikiāyét* a complaint. 11. *té-é-leef′* composition of a book; a book. 12. *taqseer′* deficiency. 13. *zékiāt* alms. 14. *tareef* explanation. 15. *maloûm* known; (knowledge). 16. *tébreek′* congratulation. 17. *bérékét* blessing. 18. *tameer′* repair. 19. *sébzé* vegetable.

‏تعليم ۱۰۲‏ Exercise 102.

‏۱ انكلترا بر مملكتِ عظيمه در. ۲ حفيده‌سی ، زوجی وَ ابوينی‏

‏ايله برابر حيوانات باغچه‌سنی كزمكه كيتدی. ۳ نوريه خانم نوری‏

‏افندينك اختِ كبراسيدر. ٤ علمِ نباتات: نباتات عالمندن ، علمِ حيوانات‏

‏ايسه ، حيوانات عالمندن بحث ايدرلر. ٥ ربّ عيسا افنديمز حضرتلری‏

‏عالمنك پادشاهی در. ٦ او مظلومين وَ مجرمينك يكانه اميدی در.‏

‏۷ مومنين ظلمت وُ موت درسندن مسرّتله كچرلر. ۸ بركاتِ الهيه‏

‏اونلره رهبر اوله جقدر. ۹ طرفينه كيسه‌نك ثلثانی تقسيم ايلدم.‏

‏۱۰ سارقينِ سنين وافردن برو محبوس درلر. ۱۱ رسولِين وَ حواريون‏

‏معجزاتِ كثيره اجرا ايلديلر. ۱۲ بكا تسليم ايله‌دكاری تحريراتی‏

‏كندی الله پوسته‌يه براقدم. ۱۳ مرحمتلی ذوات حيواناته ، حتی‏

‏نباتانه بيله مرحمت ايدرلر.‏

ترجمه ١٠٣   Translation 103.

1. Miss Gulistan is the heiress of the governess (teacher). 2. The owner of this house is Jémilé Hanim, the teacher. 3. Give the bearer of this letter five méji-diyés. 4. You must obey your parents. 5. Dr. Ch. Tracy has written a nice book for parents and for husbands and wives. 6. Paradise was in the land of Ararat. 7. The criminals were carried before the court. 8. The number of the hearers was 900, two thirds of whom were women. 9. Erase those two *eôtrés*. 10. The mother of the sovereign of the martyrs, Hûséyin, is the Princess of the women of the universe Fatima-Zéhra.

مكالمه   Conversation.

ايكي نوعدر: بري مُذَكَّرْ ديكرى مُؤَنَّثْ.	عريده كيفيت قاچ نوعدر؟
معناجه اركك عدّ اولنان كلمهلر در.	مُذَكَّرْ نه در؟
معناسنجه ديشى عدّ وُ اعتبار اولنان كلمهلر.	مُؤَنَّثْ نه در؟
اوچ جنسدر: مفرد، تثنيه و جمع.	عريده كميّت قاچ جنس در؟
بر جنسدن بر دانه كوستريرسه: او كلمهيه	بونلرك يكديكرندن فرقارى نهدر؟
مفرد ديرلر؛ ايكى دانه كوستريرسه: تثنيه	
و ايكيدن زياده كوستريرسه: اوكا ده	
جمع ديرلر.	
مفرد اولان كلمهنك آخرينه اوستونلى بر	تثنيه ناصل ياپيلير؟
١ين علاوه‌سيله اولور.	
اوچ: جمع مذكر سالم؛ جمع مونث سالم وَ	جمع قاچنوعدر؟
جمع مكسّر.	
مفرد مذكر كلمهنك آخرينه اسرهلى بر ١ين	جمع مذكر ناصل بنا ايديلير؟
علاوه‌سيله ياپيلير.	
مامورَيْنْ تثنيه اولوب: ايكى مأمورل	مامورَيْنْ نه ديمك وَ مامورينْ
معناسنده در. مامورينْ؛ ايكيدن زياده	نه ديمكدر؟
مامورل ديمك اولوب جمع مُذَكَّر در.	
شرق وَغرب ديمكدر.	مَشْرِقَيْن نه ديمكدر؟

تعليم قرائت   Reading Exercise.

تركيب بند *Térkibi Bénd.*   A Poem.

دهرك¹ نه صفا وار عجبا سيم و زرنده² ؟

انسان براغير³ هپسنی حينِ سفرنده⁴ .

بر رنكِ وفا⁵ وار می ؟ نظر قيل شو سپهرك⁶

نه ليل⁷ وُ نهارنده⁸ نه شمس و قرنده .

سير ايتدی هوا اوزره⁹ دينير تختِ سليمان¹⁰ ،

اول سلطنتك¹¹ يللر اسر شيمدی يرنده .

حرّ¹² اولمق اكر ايسترسك ؛ اوله جهانك

ذوقنده ، صفاسنده ، غمنده ، كدرنده¹³ .

خير اومه ! اكر صدرِ جهان¹⁴ اولسه ده بالفرض¹⁵ ،

هر كيم كه خساست¹⁶ اوله عرق وُ گهرنده¹⁷ .

ييلديز آرايوب كوكده نيجه طرفده منجم¹⁸ ،

غفلت¹⁹ ايله كورمز قويويی رهكذرنده²⁰ .

آنلركه ويرير لاف²¹ ايله دنيايه نظامات ،

بيك درلو تَسَيُب²² بولونور خانه لرنده .

آيينه سی ايشدر كشينك ، لافه باقيلماز ،

شخصك كورينور رتبهٔ عقلی²³ اثرنده²⁴ .

Words. 1. *déhr* world. 2. *seem* silver, *zér* gold. 3. *braghour* = *braqîr* leaves. 4. *séfér* journey; *heen* time. 5. *réngi véfa* permanent colour. 6. p. *sipihr* the sky, the sphere. 7. *léyl* night. 8. *nihar* day. 9. *héva úzré* in the air. [They say that Solomon's throne was in the air (Moslem tradition)]. 10. the throne of Solomon. 11. *saltanat* empire; magnificence. 12. *húrr* free. 13. *ghamm* anxiety; *kédér* grief. 14. *sadr* Grand Vizier, *jihan* world. 15. *bil-farz* for instance (§ 671). 16. *khasasét* baseness, vileness. 17. *îrq ou gihér* disposition and substance = character (§ 696). 18. *mû-nej'jim* astrologer. 19. *ghaflét* heedlessness. 20. *rahguzér* way (§ 535). 21. *laf* talk; word. 22. *téséy'yûb* lack of prudence; irregularities. 23. *rûtbé* degree; *aql* wisdom, sense. 24. *ésér* work, deed.

بن هر نقدر كوردم ايسه بعض مضرّات²⁵ ،

ثابت قدمم²⁶ ينه بو رأيك²⁷ اوزرنده:

«انسانه صداقت²⁸ ياقيشير كورسهده اكراه²⁹

ياردمجيسيدر طوغريلرك حضرتِ اه³⁰»   (ضيا پاشا)

25. *mazar'rat* injuries. harms (§ 576). 26. *sabit qadém* firm and steadfast in resolve (§ 636). 27. *réy* opinion; judgment. 28. *sadaqat* fidelity, honesty. 29. *ikrah* disgust; enmity (§ 619). 30. *Allah. Ziya Pasha* a distinguished Turkish author, poet, historian and statesman (1809—79). *Térkibi Bénd.* A poem in stanzas of similar metre but of different rhyme, the distichs of each stanza rhyme excepting the last distich.

Lesson 44. درس ٤٤

The Nisbé. النسبة

§ 579. The Noun of Relationship (*én Nisbé*, as it is called in Arabic), is formed by adding the termination ى -ee' to the noun, from which it is derived. It denotes that a person or thing belongs to or is connected therewith (in respect of origin, family, birth, sect, trade etc.) (Compare the Turkish and Persian *Nisbés* §§ 149, 526):

ارمن *Ermén* Armen (a fabulous Armenian hero):

ارمنى *Erménee'* belonging to Armen, Armenian.

شمس *shéms* the sun: شمسى *shémsee'* solar.

دمشق *dimishq* Damascus: دمشقى *dimishqee'* a native of Damascus.

مطالعات *Mûta-la-at:* Remarks.

§ 580. a. The feminine termination of nouns ه or ت is omitted before adding this termination; as:

مكّه *mék'ké* Mecca: مكّى *mék'kee'* a native of Mecca.

طبيعت *tabiyat* nature: طبيعى *tabiyee'* natural.

b. But if there is an *élif* preceding ت, it is retained:

ذات *zat* person: ذاتى *zatee'* personal.

حيات *hayat* life: حياتى *hayatee'* vital.

c. If at the end of foreign (non-Arabic) proper names there is a *hé* (-**a**), it is changed into *vav* (-***v***-):

فرانسه *Fransa* France: فرانسوى *Fransavee* French.

آمريقوى *Amériqavee* American: ادرنوى *Édirnévee* a native of Adrianople.

d. When any Arabic word ends in short or long *élif*, it is changed into *vav* (§ 29 c, d):

معنا (معنى) *man'a* meaning; spirit: معنوى *manévee'* spiritual.

دنيا *dûnya* world: دنيوى *dunyavee'* worldly.

بيضاء *Béyza* the town of Béyza: بيضاوى *béyzavee'* a native of Béyza.

عيسى *Isa* Jesus: عيسوى *Isavee'* Christian.

e. The *tens* of the numerals are made in the way which will soon be shown (§ 689).

f. There are other nouns of Relationship, the formation of which is irregular:

باديه *badiyé* a desert: بدوى *bédévee'* inhabiting the desert, a Beduin; a savage.

مدينه *médiné* a city: مدنى *médénee'* dwelling in the city, civilised. [urban.

سنه *séné* year: سنوى *sénévee'* yearly.

اخوت *oukhouv'vét* brotherhood: اخوى *akhavvee'* brotherly.

ماء *ma* water: مائى *mayee'* watery; fluid; blue.

g. Some nouns take an addition of ان before ى -*ee*:

روح *rouh* spirit: روحانى *rouhanee'* spiritual.

جسم *jism* body: جسمانى *jismanee'* corporal.

Other examples are:

عبرانى *ibranee'* a Hebrew: سريانى *sûryanee'* a Syrian.

كلدانى *kildanee'* a Chaldaean: نصرانى *nasranee'* { a Nazarene, a Christian.

h. A noun of Relationship is never formed from the plural, even when the sense might seem to demand it, but always from the singular: for instance words

like مأموريني ، تحريراتى *mémourinee, tahriratee* 'relative to officers or letters' are never used, but their singular is used مأمورى ، تحريرى *mémouree, tahriree* 'relative to an officer or letter i. e. official, literary'.

i. Although this rule is very strictly observed in Arabic, yet in recent Ottoman literature there are some terms in current use formed from plurals, but they are regarded as barbarisms:

قوهء جنوديه *qouvvé'yi jounoudeeyé* the military forces.

معاهداتِ دوليه *mou-a-héda'tî dûvéleeyé* the Treaties of the Powers.

جمعيتِ رسوميه *jémeeyyé'ti rousoumeeyé* the Taxation Committee.

The words *jounoud*, *dûvél*, *rousoum*, are the plurals of *jûnd* army, *dévlét* 'empire' and *résm* tax.

The Abstract Noun. اسم معنا *Ismi Mana*.

§ 581. Abstract nouns are formed by adding ت ، ه (*-yét*, *-yé*) to the end of Nouns of Relationship; or يت ، يه (*-iyét*, *-iyé*) to the end of nouns and adjectives (§§ 163, 541):

نصرانى *nasranee* a Christian: نصرانيت *nasraneeyét* Christianity.

مدنى *médénee* civilised: مدنيت *médéneeyét* civilisation.

حرّ *hûrr* free: حريت *hûr'riyét* freedom.

جمع *jém* collecting: جمعيت *jém'iyét* an assembly.

Also:

مجيديه *méjidiyé* the coin struck by Sultan Méjid.

بلديه *bélédiyé* the municipality, the city court.

دخوليه *doukhouliyé* admission fee, entrance-money.

§ 582. If ه ، ه (*-e*, *-yé*, *-a*) is added to the end of Arabic Derivative Adjectives and Participles, and used alone without any noun to modify. The feminine Adjectives and Participles thus formed are regarded as feminine substantives (§ 421):

خفىٰ *khéfee* secret: خفیه *khéfeeyé* detective.

مجموع *méjmou* collected: مجموعه *méjmou-a* collection.

مؤسّس *mû-és'sés* established: مؤسسه *mû-és'sésé* institution.

مانع *mani* hinder: مانعه *maniya* obstacle.

§ 583. The following abstract nouns are solecisms, being formed in the Arabic manner from Turkish, Persian or European words and not from Arabic words; (§ 507):

t. واريت *variyét* wealth: p. كرميت *gérmiyét* ardour, zeal.

p. سربستيت *sérbéstiyét* freedom: p. پريشانيت *périshaniyét* poverty.

f. قراليت *qraliyét* kingdom: p. ماهیه *mahiyé* (monthly) salary.

f. پوليتيقيه *politiqiyé* politics: t. اوتلاقيه *otlaqiyé* pasture-tax.

تعليم ١٠٤ Exercise 104.

Form Nouns of Relationship and Abstract nouns from the following words:

عادَتْ¹ ، بَيْضَه² ، بَيْت³ ، مَادّه⁴ ، نَبَات⁵ ، مَاء⁶ ، اِتِجَارَتْ⁷ ،

دَاخِل⁸ ، خَارِج⁹ ، مِلَّتْ¹⁰ ، بُوسْنَه¹¹ ، آنْقَره ، مَوْت ، بَحْر ، بَرْ ، زَمَان ،

سَوْدَاء¹² ، سَمَاء¹³ ، انكليز ، يونان ، مِرْدِيفون ، لَيْل ، نِهَار .

580 g. رَبْ¹ ، نُورْ² ، ظُلْمَتْ³ ، وَحْدَتْ⁴ ، تَحْتْ⁵ ، فَوْقْ⁶ ، حَقْ .

581. اِسْلَام ، طَبْع¹ ، ارض² (ard) ، شَمْس³ ، ضَبْط³ ، اَهَمّ⁴ .

مِلَّتْ ، مَسْرور ، مَمْنون ، مَحْزون ، مَأمور ، مَشْغُول .

582. رَابِط¹ ، لَطِيف² ، مُخْطِر³ ، مُقَدَّم⁴ ، مَنْظُوم⁵ ، ثَانی⁶ .

1. *adét* custom. 2. *béyza'* egg. 3. *béyt* family, house. 4. *mad'de* matter, subject. 5. plant. 6. water. 7. *tijarét* trade. 8. *dakhil* interior. 9. *kharij* outside, foreign. 10. *mil'lét* nation. 11. *Bosna* Bosnia. 12. *sévda* the spleen. 13. heaven.

580 g. 1. *rabb* the Lord. 2. *noor* light. 3. *zoulmét* darkness. 4. *vahdét* uniqueness, 5. *taht* the lower part. 6. *févq* over.

581. Islam. 1. *tab* disposition. 2. room (in Custom-House.) 3. *zabt* control. 4. *éhémm* important.

582. 1. *rabit* binding. 2. nice, amusing (story). 3. *moukhtir* who reminds. 4. *mouqad'dém* preceding, before. 5. *manzoum* written in rhyme and metre. 6. second (second).

Words. لغتلر

p. خدا *khûda, khoda* God	a. ايمان ايتمك *iman ét.''* to believe
a. نبى *nébi* prophet	a. نبويات *nébéviyat* prophecies
a. تزايد ايت *tezayûd ét.''* to increase	a. مدرسه *médrésé* seminary
a. قرآن *qour'an* Qoran	a. مفسّر *mûfés'sir* commentator
اكمال ايتمك *ikmal ét.''* to finish	a. حرارت *hararét* heat.

Proper Names: اشعيا *Ishaya, Eshaya* Isaiah.

Exercise 105. تعليم ١٠٥

۱ اسلاميّت دخى نصرانيّت كبى وحدانيّتِ خدايه ايمان ايدر. ۲ حرارتِ شمسيه شدّتلى اولورسه ، دائما بر شمسيه آليرم. ۳ بيضاوى قرآنك مفسّرلرندن مشهور بر ذات در. ٤ روحانىَ شيلر دائمى ؛ جسمانىَ شيلر ايسه زمانىَ درلر. ٥ عيسويلرك عبادتخانهسى شوراده ، موسويلركى ايسه شوقارشيكى سو قاغك ايچنده در. ٦ محمديّونك يوميَه بش وقت غازلرى وار در. ۷ ارضيه و اوتلاقيه مصارفى اولهرق ماهيه درت يوز غروش پاره ويريپورم. ۸ كچن اونطقوزنجى عصرده برچوق ملتلر بدوِيتك صوسز چوللرندن امرارله ، مدنيّتك چيچكلى صَحرالرينه داخل اولديلر. ۹ مادىَ ، معنوىَ و روحانىَ عالَمِرده پك چوق حقيقتلر وار دِر. ۱۰ تياترونك دخوليهسى بر چيرك مجيديه ايش ، ويرو وَ بنم ايچون بر بيلت آل. ۱۱ بلديه مجلسى شهرك تميزلكنه گرميتله چاليشيور. ۱۲ «آروسياق يونطوسى» نام غزتهده امورِ دينيّه ، علميّه ، پوليتيقيه ، بيّته و تجاريّهيه دائر پك چوق شيلر اوقودم.

Translation 106. ترجمه ١٠٦

1. The Old Testament is written in the Hebrew and Chaldæan languages and the New Testament in

20*

Greek. 2. Do you know the Lord's Prayer by heart. 3. The exchange of offices between two office-holders is done by the consent of the parties concerned. 4. Christians, Mahomedans and Jews believe in the Unity of God. 5. The military forces of the European powers are increasing every year. 6. He lost his wealth and fell into poverty. 7. Freedom is the life of a nation. 8. The Taxation Committee has raised the rate on rent. 9. I wrote a composition about the Treaties of the Powers. 10. The shape of my inkstand is oval. 11. Let us sing hymn number 51.

مكالمه   Conversation.

عبرانی، كلدانی وَ سریانی لســانلرینه آشنامیسكز ؟

پك آز ؛ بر سنه در اوقویورم .

برادریكز نه نقل ایدییور ؟

ظلمانی بر كیجه‌ده نورانی بر بولوط كورمش ؛ اونی سویله‌یور . [وار .

[وار ؟

بو تاره یاپیلان بیتكزك قاچ اوطه‌سی

فوقانی درت و تحتانی بش اوطه‌سی اوت افندم ؛

عیسا افندمز حقنده عهد عتیقده بولنان نَبَوِیاتی اوقومه‌كز اولدی می ؟

انبیای كبرادن نَبی اشعیانككنی اوقودم .

"قارداش محبتی" عربیده نه دیمكدر ؟

مُحَبَّتِ اَخَوِیَه دیمكدر .

فرانسزلر مُجرمینی طوته‌بیلدیلر می ؟

خفیه‌لر، ضبطیه‌لر هربری آرادیلر ایسه‌ده مجرمیندن بر اثر بولامادیلر .

حوادثات ملّیه، خارجیه و داخلیه‌دن شایانِ دقت بر شی وار می ؟

خیر افندم ؛ غزته‌لرده شایانِ اهمیّت بر شی یوقدر .

علمِ الهی اوقومش میسكز ؟

اوت افندم ! ۱۸۹۰ سنه‌سنده مرذیفون علمِ الهی مَدرَسه‌سنی اكمال ایله‌دم .

مذكور علمِ الهی مَدرَسه‌سنك مُدّتِ تَحصیلیه‌سی نه قدر در ؟

آوروپا وَ آمریقانك اكثری مُوسَّسه‌لرینده اولدیغی اوزره اوچ سنه در، افندم !

تعلیم قرائت   Reading Exercise.

قولومبوسك یومورطه‌سی   Columbus' Egg.

مشهور دركه¹ ، آمریقانك كاشفی² اولان قرستوف²ᵃ قولومبوس³ آمریقایی

Words. 1. *mésh'hour* well known: *mésh'hour dour ki* everybody knows = it is said. 2. *kiashif* discoverer. 2ᵃ. Christophorus.

كشف ایله³ عودتدن صوکره ٬ اَنْدُلُسْدهٔ⁴ بنی احمر دولتنی⁵ مغلوب⁶ ایدن قرال فردیناندك خوانِ ضیافتنده⁷ اوطورویورایمش · خُضّاردن⁸ وَ قرستوفك برِ جدیدی⁹ کشفندن طولایی مَظْهَرْ¹⁰ اولدیغی تلطیفاته¹¹ حَسَد¹² ایدن اسپانیا پرنسلرندن بری «مادامکه¹³ ٬ بو قطعه¹⁴ شو کرهٔ ارضْ اوزرنده موجود¹⁵ ایدی ٬ سز اولماسهکزده¹⁶ برکون اولوب¹⁷ یِنه بولونوردی» قوْلیله¹⁸ قرستوفك همّتِ معاوهمهسنی¹⁹ اِستِصْغار²⁰ ایتمك ایسته مش · قرستوف قولومبوس دخی «خیر پرنس حضرتلری! بر قطعه یومورطهیی سیوری طرفنده²¹ طوردورهبیلن آدمدن باشقهسی کشفه مقتدر²² دکلدر» جوابنی ویرمش.

       (ابو الضیا²³)

3. *késhf et.''* to discover; *ilé* for *vé* (§ 470 a) = *késhf édib.*
4. *Én'dúlûs* Andalusia. 5. *Béni Ahmér dévléti* the Moors (in Spain), the dynasty of Beni [children of] Ahmer. 6. *maghloub* defeated (§ 604). 7. *khanî ziyafét* the banqueting table. 8. *houz'zar* those who were present (*houz'zardan vé ... prénslérdén biri*). 9. *bér'ri jédid* the New World = America. 10. *mazhar ol.''* to be the object of, to enjoy. 11. *taltifat* favours, honours. 12. *haséd ét.''* to envy, to be jealous. 13. *madam ki* since, as. 14. *qît'a* part, segment (of the world). 15. *mévjoud ol.''* to exist. 16. *siz olmasañizda* even if you were not; *da* for *dakhi* (§ 117). 17. *bir gûn oloub* some day, one day. 18. *qavl* word. 19. *him'mét* effort, action; *malûm* known. 20. *istisghar* a making little of, belittling. 21. *sivri taraf* the smaller end (of the egg). 22. *mûqtédir* able. 23. *Ebûz'ziya* a celebrated living Turkish author.

درس حَقّنده مكالمه   Conversation about the Lesson.

اسئله *Ésilé.*	اجوبه *Éjvibé.*
اجوبه وَ اسئله نه معناده درلر؟	عربی جمع اولوب سؤَالرٝ وَحوابلر دیمكدر.
آمریقایی كیم كشف ایتدی؟	جنویز ملتندن قرستوف قولومبوس كشف ایتدی.
هانكی قرالك وقتنده كشف اولوندی؟	اسپانیا قرالی فردیناندك وقتنده كشف اولونمشدر.
قرستوفك بر یومورطه حكایهسی مشهور بر حكایهدر. اونی وار دٝر٬ بیلیرمیسكز؟	اوت افندم! مشهور بر حكایهدر. اونی بیلمهدك كیمسه یوقدر.

بوحكايه نره‌ده وقوع بولدى؟   قرال فردیناندك بر ضیاقتنده وقوع بولدى .

بوحكايه‌يه سَبَبِيَتْ ويرن خصوص نه ايدى ؟   مومى اليهك قرال طرفندن مَظْهَر اولديغى لطف وُ إكرامدن طولايى حُضَّاردن بر پرَنسك حَسَد ايتمه‌سيندن نشأت ايتمشدر .

بو پرنس قرسطوفك همّتنى استصغار ايتمك ضمننده نه سويله‌دى؟   قرستوف قولومبوسدن ماعداسى دخى بَرِّ جديدى كشــف ايده‌يله‌جكنى سويله‌دى .

قرستوف حضارك حيرت ومراقنى جلب ايده‌جك صورتده برشى تكليف ايتدى مى ؟   اوت افندم ! بر يوموره‌طه‌يى سيورى طرفنده طوردیره‌بيان آدم آمريقالى كشفه مقتدر اولديغنى جواباً بيان ايله‌دى .

بوحكايه‌يى كيم ترجمه ايتمشدر؟   عطوفتلو ابو الضيا توفيق بك حضرتلرى .

بوحكايه ختام بولديمى؟   خير افندم ! دها مابعدى وار در .

درس ٤٥ Lesson 45.

The Arabic Infinitive (Masdar).

§ 584. There is no limit to the number of words which the Ottoman language borrows from the Arabic. The number of Arabic words to be learnt would thus involve a great deal of study, if they were not derived from certain roots which are, of course, very much less numerous. If the student can master the system by which Arabic derivatives are derived from their roots (*mad'dé*, *mad'déyi asliyé*), his labour will be vastly diminished. After learning a certain number of roots, he will at once recognize and remember a large number of words formed from them. The Arabic system of derivation is extremely regular, logical and beautiful; although at first it appears somewhat complicated.

Almost every word in Arabic may be referred to

a significant root, consisting of either three or four letters, the triliterals being by far the more common.

In European languages, significant roots are irregular in form, and the grammar of those languages treats only of prefixes and affixes, by which the meaning of the word is modified. Thus in English we add the termination *-er* to express the agent of a verb, and *-ing* to express the Present Participle Active or the Gerund; as: make, mak*er*, mak*ing*. In Arabic, however, such modifications are obtained not only by prefixing or affixing, but by inserting letters between those of the root. The root فعل *faεl* signifying **action**, is taken as the typical root for exhibiting these modifications, and the formulae thus obtained are called 'the measures of words'. For instance, the insertion of an *élif* between the first and second radical, and the punctuation of the later with an *ésré*, give the sense of the Agent or Active participle: thus فعْل *faεl* becomes فَاعِل *fa-εil* 'one who does' and this word is the **measure** upon which all other "agents" of this kind are formed. It is in fact, a mere formula, like the letters used in Algebra; for as (a + b + c) may represent (2 + 3 + 4), (5 + 6 + 7), or any other number; so for the triliteral root فعل in فَاعِل, we may substitute any other triliteral root and obtain the same modification of meaning; as:

قتل *qatl* to kill: قَاتِل *qatil* a murderer.

علم *εilm* wisdom: عَالِم *εalim* wise;

where قَاتِل and عالِم are said to be the فَاعِل of the triliteral roots to which they respectively belong.

The Arab grammarians use this word فعل as a paradigm, and every change in and addition to the root is made on this model. But as the utterance of the second radical (ع) is very difficult for Europeans, therefore we adapt the word فقل *faql* as its equivalent, since it is easier to pronounce; using the 'measures' of فعل also when necessary:

حَرْف *harf* 'letter' is of the measure فَقْل *faql*, that is to say it is measured, weighed or balanced on the word فَقْل *faql*, having the same quantity of letters and the same vowel.

§ 585 a. The root فقل in Arabic is pointed with three *ústúns*, as: فَقَلَ *faqala*, which means 'he fanned', this being the third person singular Past tense; but for shortness' sake we always render it into English by the Infinitive or Verbal Noun[1] (§§ 272, 614).

§ 585 b. **The Arabic Infinitives** (= Masdar) are divisible, in respect of their origin, into two classes: Primitive or Simple and Derivative or Augmented.

§ 586. **The Primitive Infinitives** are those which have no servile letters in them, or even if they have the serviles do not change the meaning of the word; as:

نَظَر *nazar* to look; دَخْل *dakhl* 'to enter' are simple or primitive forms, because there is no augment or servile letter in them. But نَظَرَت *nézarét* to look, دُخُول *doukhoul* or دَخَالَت *dékhalét* 'to enter' also are called Primitives; because although there are servile letters (ت ‘ و ‘ ١), yet they do not change the meaning: they are only different forms of نَظَر and دَخْل.

§ 587. **The Servile Letters** are (١ ت س م ن و هى), which are also called 'changers or letters of augmentation', because they change or add to the meaning of the word.

§ 588. **The Derivative Infinitives** are those infinitives which have servile letters inserted in them,

---

[1] The second vowel of the third person Sing. Past tense is sometimes *i* = فَقِلَ *faqila*, sometimes *ou* = فقل *faqoula*, instead of being as here *a* = فَقَلَ *faqala*: but this does not concern the student of Ottoman.

which change the meaning of the word more or less. For instance the word اِنْتِظَار *intizar* 'to look after, to wait'; اِدْخَال *idkhal* 'to cause to enter, to insert', are derivatives; because their ground forms نَظَر *nazar* and دَخَل *dakl* mean 'to look' and 'to enter' respectively, and the augmentative letters ١ ' ١ ' ت have changed the meaning (§§ 259, 613).

A. The Primitive Triliterals. مصدر ثلاثى مجرد

§ 589. There are a great number of Verbal Nouns or Infinitives which are derived directly from the triliteral roots. Those that are most frequently used in Turkish belong to one of 23 "measures". The root فعل is taken as the 'measure' or formula (= وزن *véz̧n*), and we shall assume that all these 23 forms can be derived from it; although they are not all in use. Every root is supposed to have the power of producing all these derivatives, though, in fact, sometimes only a few such are actually formed from a given root.

مطالعات *Mûta-la-at* Remarks.

§ 590. If the third radical is و or ى, in the measures 15, 16 and 17 it is changed into (ء) at the end, which is often omitted (§ 705 d); as: فَنَاى ' جَزَاى ' دُعَاى ' بِنَاى are changed into جَزَا = جَزَاء ' فَنَا = فِنَاء ' بِنَا = بِنَاء ' دَعَو ' بَنَى ' فَنَى ' جَزَى the roots being √جَزَى ' فَنَى ' بَنَى ' دَعَو , دُعَا = دُعَاء.

§ 591. Those letters which have the mark of reduplication, are written twice in the root, without the mark (ّ); as: شِدَّت *shid-dét* severity, root √شَدَد *shédédé*.

§ 592. The feminine letters ت and ه ' ة are substituted for each other in the termination of nouns:

§ 593. The Measures of Primitive Triliteral Infinitives.

No.	وزن Measures		مثال Examples		مادّه Root	Meaning of Examples
1	faql	قَعْل	harf	حَرْف	√حرف	letter.
2	fiql	فِعْل	hîfz	حِفْظ	√حفظ	protection.
3	fouql	فُعْل	shûkr	شُكْر	√شكر	thanks.
4	faqal	فَعَل	talêb	طَلَب	√طلب	demand.
5	faqlèt [fem.]	فَعْلَت	rahmét	رَحْمَت	√رحم	mercy.
6	fiqlèt »	فِعْلَت	khêdmèt	خِدْمَت	√خدم	service.
7	fouqlèt »	فُعْلَت	nousrét	نُصْرَت	√نصر	victory.
8	faqalèt »	فَعَلَت	harakèt	حَرَكَت	√حرك	motion.
9	faqilèt »	فَعِلَت	ʾazimét	عَزِيمَت	√عزم	departure.
10	faqla »	فَعْلٰى	fètwa	فَتْوٰى	√فتو	decree.

11	قُقْلَ	fouqla »	بُشْرَى	bâshra	good tidings.
12	فِقْلَن	feqlan	حِرْمان	hêrman	disappointment.
13	فُقْلَن	fouqlan	غُفْران	ghoufran	forgiveness.
14	فَقْلَن	faqélan	هَيَجان	hêyéjan	excitement.
15	فَقَل	faqal	ذَهاب	zéhab	a going.
16	فِقَل	fiqal	كِتاب	kitab	book.
17	فُقَل	fouqal	سُؤال	souwal	question.
18	فُقَالَت	fuqalét [fem.]	صِحانَة	sahabét	protection.
19	فِقَالَت	fiqalét »	عِبادَت	'ibadét	worship.
20	فَقُول	faqoul	قَبُول	qaboul	acceptance.
21	فُقُول	fouqoul	دُخُول	doukhoul	entrance.
22	فُقُولَت	fuqoulét »	ضَرُورَت	zavourét	poverty.
23	فَقُولَت	fouqoulét »	سُهُولَت	souhoulét	facility.

such is the case in measures 5—9, 18, 19, 22, 23.

ثَمَرَه _séméré_ for ثَمَرَت _sémérét_ measure فَقْلَتْ ؛ مِعْلَتْ =

مِعَدَه measure فَقْلَتْ ؛ رَحْمَة = رَحْمَتْ ، رِفْعَة = رِفْعَتْ ، سَلَامَة

سَلَامَتْ ، غَلَبَه = غَلَبَتْ ٠

§ 594. When the letter ى is pronounced as ا with _ústún_, it is called _Short Elif_ (§§ 29 c, 610); therefore in such cases ا is substituted for ى: سُكْنَا _súkna_ for سُكْنَى root

$\sqrt{\text{شَكَوَ}}$ سَكَنَ ، شَكْوَا _shékva_ = شَكْوَى root $\sqrt{}$ 'habitation',

'complaint'; دَعْوَا = دَعْوَى ، كُبْرَا = كُبْرَى [measures 10—11].

§ 595. **The Quadriliteral Infinitives** have only one formula or measure; which is فَقْلَلَه _faqlélé_ the root being

considered $\sqrt{\text{فَقْلَلَ}}$; as: زَلْزَلَه _zélzélé_ 'earthquake', root

$\sqrt{\text{زَلْزَلَ}}$ _zélzélé_: شَعْشَعَه شَعْشَعَ $\sqrt{}$ دَبْدَبَه $\sqrt{\text{دَبْدَبَ}}$ ٠

تَعْلِيم ١٠٧   Exercise 107.

With the assistance of the Table of Verbal Measures given above find the measure and the root of each of the following words.

، مِلَتْ ٢ ٠ جِوَار ، كَمَال ، وَجْه ، حُضُور ، دِيَار ، حُبّ ، نَقْل ١

، نَبْعَان ، نَغْمَه ، تُرْك ، زَوْج ، نَصِيحَتْ ٣ ٠ لِسَان ، خَلَاص ، حَقِيقَتْ

٠عَلَامَتْ ، بَيْضَه ، نَبَات ، دُنْيَا ، آخَرَتْ ٤ ، رَسُول ، فَوْتْ ، طَرَف

، سُلْطَان ، سَمَاء ، فِقْرَه ٦ ٠سَفِينَه ، جِسْم ، قَلْب ، جَنَّتْ ، وَحْدَتْ ٥

٠إِلَه ، شُكْرَان ، إِنْسَان ، زِيَاده ، وَسْوَسَه ٧ ٠بُكَاء ، حَمْدْ ، قُوتْ ، رَبّ

Key. نَقْل _naql_ is measured on فَقْل, the root being نَقَلَ; because the first radical has an _ústún_, and the second, third radicals are quiescent. حقيقت _haqiqat_ is

measured on فُقِيَلَتْ *faqilét*, the root being √حَقَقَ ; because
the first and third radicals have an *ûstûn* and the second has
an *ésré*; after the second radical there is a servile ى and
after the third a servile ت. سَفِينه *séfiné* = فُقِيَلَتْ *faqilét*,
ا is substituted for ت. بكاء *bûkîa* = فُقَال (§ 591)

= *fîqra* فِقْرَه ، رَبَّ √ *faql* فَقْل √ رَبّ = *rabb* ، بَكَى √
فِقْلَتْ √ فَقَرَ ؛ قُوَّتْ = *fûqlat* قُوَّ √ نَبَات = *fâ'al* نَبَتَ √ ؛
تَقْوَى *fê'lâ* = فَيْلَى ، زياده = *fi'âlat* فِعَالَتْ ، سِيَرتْ = *fi'lat* فِعْلَتْ ؛ اِلَه = *fi'l* فِعْل .

تَعْلِيم قِرَأَت Reading Exercise.

۸٤ بِنْجِى مَزْمُور ؛ ٦ بِنْجِى اِلٰهِى Psalm 84; Hymn 6.

آرزولو بايغين⁸ جانم	١ نه كوزل مسكنلرِكْ¹ !
مومنلر جمهورِينى⁹ ،	نُور و حُبّ² دِيَارنده³ ،
قِبَال نوربخش¹⁰ ، كريم¹¹ رَبِّم !	نه لطِيف⁴ در حُضُورِكْ⁵ !
وجهكى¹² ، كَمَالكْثى¹³ .	درد⁶ ، كناه دريَاسِنده⁷ .

بكزه ديوب كوكرجينه ،	٢ بولديار ملجا¹⁴ قوشلر
زمِينده¹⁸ بولماز رَاحَتْ .	مذبحِكْ¹⁵ جِوَارنده ؛
صالت¹⁹ رِجْعَتْله²⁰ كمىيه	قول يورغون ، رَاحَتْ آرار
كَسْب ايدر²¹ نَجَاتْ²² ، حَيَاتْ²³ .	بَيْت الله¹⁶ حَوْلِيسِنده¹⁷ ،

Words. (۱) 1. *méskén* house, court (§ 578). 2. *nour* light;
houbb' love. 3. *diyar* land: it is the pl. of *dar* but used as
singular (Lesson 51). 4. *latif* pleasant. 5. presence. 6. *dérd* affliction,
woe. 7. p. *gûnah* sin; p. *déryâ'* sea. 8. *bay-ghîn* fainting. 9. *mûmin*
believer (*méfoul* of *iman* [§ 619]); *'jûmhour* congregation. 10. *nour-
bakh-sh qilmaq* to bestow the light. 11. *kérim* gracious (a. q. of
kérém [§ 606]). 12. *véjh* face. 13. *kémal* glory.

(۲) 14. *mélja* asylum (§ 598). 15. *mézbah* altar (n. l. of *zéb-h*
[§ 598]). 16. *Béy'toul-lah* the house of God. 17. *havli* court,
yard. 18. p. *zémin* earth. 19. t. *salt* only. 20. *rij-at* to turn back.
21. *késb ét."* to enjoy. 22. *néjat* salvation. 23. *hayat* life.

تقدّمله ³⁰ قوّتده	۳ بو بُكَا ²⁴ درسنده
تختكه ياقلاشانلر '	سيّاحلر ²⁵ نَغْمَه ²⁶ اوقور '
ديز چوكوپ عِبَادتده	صو نَبْعَان ²⁷ ايدر چولده '
اِسمكه حَمْد صونارلر ·	مَنّ ²⁸ كوكدن نازل ²⁹ اولور ·

لُطفكى ³³ دوك ³⁴ قَلبمه '	٤ رَبّ ! حادى ³¹ اول قولكه
شَمْس ³⁵ ، حَيَات ' ملجا سين سن ·	يول مشكل ' كثير ³² دشمن ؛
دُنيَاده وَ اَخْرَتده	سَمَادن نُورك اِيله
بولهيم سنده مسكن ·	طريقم ايله روشن ·

(۳) 24. *bûkiā* weeping. 25. *séy'yah* pilgrim. 26. *naghmé* song. 27. *nébᵧan ét.''* flow, to rise (water). 28. *ménn* manna. 29. *nazil ol.''* to descend. 30. *téqad-dûm ét.''* to progress, to grow (in strength).

(٤) 31. *hadi* guide; *mûshkil* hard, difficult. 32. *késir* abundant; p. *roushén*. 33. *loutf* grace. 34. *deôk* shower. 35. *shéms* sun.

Note. 1. This is a translation of the English hymn 'Pleasant are Thy courts above' by H. F. Lyte. 2. Find the measure and the root of each of the vowelled words contained in the above Reading Exercise.

درس ٤٦ Lesson 46.

Nouns derived from Primitive Triliteral Verbs.

§ 596. Certain nouns are derived from the Infinitives or from the roots of verbs, and may therefore be dealt with in connexion with the latter. The principal forms used in Ottoman are three; and the commoner measures for these three are seven in number. They all begin with a *mim* pointed by *ûstûn* or *ésré*.

1. Nouns with Mim. مَصْدَر ميمى

§ 597. Besides the simple forms already described above, another verbal noun almost equivalent to them in meaning is formed by adding a *mim* to the radicals. It has four forms:

I. مَفْقَل *méfqal*. By adding a *mim* with *ústún* to the first (*mé-*), and pointing the second radical with *ústún*:

قَصْد *qasd* purpose :   √أَصَدَ : مَقْصَد *maqséd* purpose.

II. The feminine of this form is مَفْقَلَتْ *méfqalét*.

رَحْمَتْ *rahmét* mercy :   √رَحَمَ ; مَرْحَمَتْ *mérhamét* mercy.

مِلْك *milk* country :   √مَلَكَ ; مَمْلَكَتْ *mémlékét* country.

III., IV. Some verbs, especially those commencing with و, take *ésré* on the second radical. Their measure is مَفْقِلَتْ ، مَفْقِل *méfqil, méfqilét* (§ 593):

وَعْد *vaɛd* promise :   √وَعَدَ ; مَوْعِدَه *mévɛidé.*

وَهَاب *véhab* gift :   √وَهَبَ ; مَوْهِبَه *mévhibé.*

رُجُوع *roujouɛ* returning: √رَجَعَ ; مَرْجِع *mérjiɛ.*

تَعْلِيم ١٠٨   **Exercise 108.**

Change the following Infinitives into the form beginning with *mim*:

I. ¹ذَهَاب .   II. ²حَمْد ; ³سَعَادَتْ ; ⁴نَفْع ; ⁵قُدْرَتْ ; ⁶فَسَاد ;
III. ⁷غُفْرَان .   IV. ⁸وَلَادَتْ ; ⁹عِرْفَان ; وَعْظ .

Words. 1. a going; road, way (religion). 2. praise. 3. happiness. 4. benefit. 5. strength. 6. sedition. 7. forgiveness. 8. birth. 9. knowledge, skill.

2. Noun of Location. اسم مكان

§ 598. This is formed precisely in the same manner as the Noun with Mim; the measures being the same; (§§ 162, 449, 541):

I.   طَبْخ *tabkh* to cook :   √طَبَخَ ;

مَطْبَخ (= مَفْقَل) *matbakh* a place where to cook, kitchen.

دَفْن *défn* to bury :   √دَفَنَ ;

مَدْفَن (= مَفْقَل) *médfén* grave.

II.   طَبَعَ *tabɛ* to print: √طَبَعَ:

مَطْبَعَة *matbaɛa* printing house. (مَفْقَلَة) =

III.   غُرُوب *ghouroub* to set: √غَرَبَ:

مَغْرِبْ *maghrîb* sunset, west. (مَفْقِلْ) =

شَرْق *sharq* to rise: √شَرَقَ

مَشْرِقْ *méshriq* sunrise, east. (مَفْقِلْ) =

تَعْلِيم ١٠٩   Exercise 109.

From the following words form Nouns of Location:

I.¹ رَعَى²؛ رُكِوبْ³؛ دُخُول⁴؛ خُرُوج⁵؛ سُكُون. II. ⁶نَظَارَتْ ؛ دَرْس ؛

⁷مِلْح؛ ⁸قَبِر؛ ⁹حِفْظْ؛ ¹⁰زِبِل؛ ¹¹حُكم. III. ¹²وَضْع؛ ¹³طُلُوع؛

¹⁴سُقُوط؛ ¹⁵سَجْدَه ؛ نُزُول ؛ وُقُوع ؛ جُلُوس.

Words. I. 1. *ray* to pasture. 2. riding. 3. entering. 4. going out. 5. to dwell. II. 6. looking (view). 7. salt. 8. tomb. 9. to keep. 10. manure. 11. judgment. III. 12. placing. 13. rising; of sun. 14. falling down. 15. worship.

3. Noun of Instrument. اسم آلت

§ 599. The most common measures of the Noun of Instrument are those which follow; (§§ 450, 542):

I.   مِفْقَل *mifqal:*

سطر *satr* a line: √سَطَرَ؛ مِسْطَر *mistér,* comm. *mastar* an instrument for drawing a line, a ruler.

ثَقَب *saqab, taqab* to pierce: √ثَقَبَ؛ مِثْقَب *misqab* comm. *matqab* anything that pierces, auger.

II.   مِفْقَال *mifqal:*

فتح *féth* to open: √فَتَحَ؛ مِفْتَاح *miftah* a key.

قرض *qard* to cut: √قَرَضَ؛ مِقْرَاض *mîqrad* comm. *maqraz,* *maqas* a cutting instrument, scissors.

III.   مَفْقَلَه *méfqalé:*

شُرْب *shourb* to drink: √شَرَبَ؛ مَشْرَبَه *mashraba* a cup.

شُعْلَه *shou‿lé* flame: ؛شَعَلَ√

مَشْعَلَه *mash‿ala* a torch.

تعليم ١١٠ Exercise 110.

آتالر سوزی Ancestors' Sayings = Proverbs.

١ طاتلی سوز پیلانی اینندن¹ چیقاریر؛ کوتو سوز انسانی دیننندن²
چیقاریر. ٢ کوره "مزم بهایه چیقدی³" دیشلر: "هیچ اُمورمده دکل⁴"
دیش. ٣ آلتین آتشده انسان محنتده⁵ تجربه⁶ اولونور. ٤ باشقهسنڭ
سوزندن زیاده سنڭ کوزڭه اینان. ٥ کپرودن کچنهقدر شیطانه بابا
دیهلی. ٦ اوکوزی بوینوزندن⁷ ، آدمی سوزندن طوتارلو. ٧ گل دیکنسز
اولماز؛ یار⁸ قصورسز. ٨ کچمز⁹ آقچه کوتو سوز صاحبنڭ. ٩ مغرور¹⁰
اولوب دیه "یوق بن کبی"؛ بر مخالف¹¹ روزکار آَسَر صاوورور¹² خرمان
کبی. ١٠ کوك یوزنده دوکون درنك¹³ وار دیرلرسه؛ قادینلر مردیون
قورمغه قالقیشیرلر. ١١ نه سال ایله در نه مال ایله در؛ بکم! اولولك
کمال ایله در. ١٢ قصورسز یار آرایان یارسز قالیر.

Words. 1. *in* den, cave. 2. *dindén, chiqmaq* to go out of
religion = to forget God, to be angry. 3. *bahaya chiqmaq* to rise
in price, to become dear. 4. *hich oumouroumda déyil* I do not
care a bit. 5. *mih'nét* affliction. 6. *téjribé ét."* vulg. *téjrûbé* to test.
7. *bouynouz* horn. 8. *yar* friend; sweetheart. 9. *géchméz* spurious.
10. *maghrour* proud. 11. *moukhalif* contrary. 12. *savourmaq* to
winnow; *harman* threshing floor. 13. *dûyûn dérnék* wedding, feast.

مكالمه Conversation.

اسئله *Ésilé.*	اجوبه *Éjvibé.*
بوكتاب هانكی مطبعهده طبع اولونغشدر؟	موسیو غروسك مطبعهسنده طبع اولونغشدر.
بو دلیك نه ایله دلدیكز؟	بر منقب ایله دلدم.
اوقهلق مشربه ایله نه شرابی نه ایله ایچدی؟	اوقهلق مشربه ایله اون دفعه ایچدی.

¹ *Bal Yéméz Oghlou* a celebrated drunkard.

مَشرقدن وَ مَغربدن بر چوق خبرلر قرائت ایله‌دیم.   غزته‌لرده نه اوقودیکز؟

بر مِسطَر وَ بر مِقراض آرایورم.   نه آرایورسکز؟

بریسی مَسجده چیقار دیکری مَقبره‌یه.   مَسکنکزڭ مَخرجی وَ مَدخلی نره‌ده در؟

مسقطم وَ مولِدم قیصریه در.   مملکتکز نره‌سیدر؟

افندم! چیمنزار زاده مزبله‌ده در.   مرکب نره‌ده در؟ مَرعاده می؟

مَملَحه‌یه طوغری در.   محکمه‌نڭ مَنظره‌سی نره‌یه طوغری در؟

اینجیلی ارمنی مَذهبندن ایم.   هانکی مَذهبدن سکز؟

خیر افندم! هوسم یوق؛ او بر مَوهبهٔ ربّانیه در.   مَقصدکز رَسّام (painter) می اولقدر؟

Reading Exercise. تعلیم قرائت

A Psalm of Life. نَغمهٔ حیات

١ بعض الحانِ محزونانه¹ ایله دیه که! حیات بر رویای واهیدر² وَ خوابیده اولان روح معدومدر. خیر! حیات جدّی³ در.

٢ خیر! حیات یاشاییجی در. قبر هیچ بر وقت اونڭ مَنزلِ مَقصودی اوله‌مایه‌جقدر. «سن طوپراق سین وَ طوپراق اوله‌جقسین!» کلامی جانه خطاب⁴ اولونمش دکلدر.

٣ صفا و جفا مقصد حیاتی تشکیل ایده‌مز.

٥ عُمر حربکاه‌نده⁵ وَ حیاتڭ مُوَقّت اوردوکاهنده چای کنارنده اوتلانان غیرِ ناطق حیوانلر کبی اوله! محاربه‌ده قهرمان⁶ اول!

٦ هر نه قدر خوش کورونسه ده استقباله⁷ قاپیلمه⁸! براق! ماضی⁹ کندی اولولرینی کومسون! سن زنده¹⁰ اولان زمانِ حالده یاشا! سنڭ قلبڭ کوکسکده وَ جنابِ حق ایسه باشڭ اوستنده در.

Words. 1. *élhan* numbers, songs; *mahzounané* mournful. 2. *rouya* dream; *vahee* nonsensical. 3. *jid'di* real. 4. *khitab olounmaq* to be addressed. 5. *harbgiah* battle-field (§ 541). 6. p. *qahriman* hero. 7. *istiqbal* future. 8. *qapilmaq* to be deceived (to rely). 9. *mazi* past (§ 601). 10. p. *zindé* living.

۷ ذوات كِراملك حياتى، بزم عمرلرمزكده اولوَجْهِله جَليل و جَميل اوله‌بيله‌جكنى تعليم ايدر ، اونلره إمتِثال ايله !

۸ دائماً بيتيره‌رك ، دائماً باشلايه‌رق ، حيات دكيزينى احاطه ايدن¹¹ قوملرك اوزرنده بر ايز¹² براقمغه چاليش ؛ بلكه كونك برنده ، قضازده¹³ اولان قارداشلرگدن بريسى ، يولنى بولمق ايچون بو ايزلردن استفاده¹⁴ ايله‌يه .

محرّرى — لونغفللو . (مترجمى — منيف پاشا)

11. *ihaté édén* surrounding (§ 620). 12. t. *iz* foot-print.
13. a. p. *qazazédé* shipwrecked (§ 535). 14. *istifadé ét.* to be benefited (§ 631). *Mûnif Pasha* a distinguished living Turkish author, poet and statesman; now in oblivion.

تعليمِ سابق حقنده مكالمه Conversation.

بالاده‌كى شِعرك مُحرّرى و مُترجمى محرّرى آمريقالى شاعرِ مشهور
كيم و مترجمى كيمدر؟ لونغفللو وَ مترجمى دولتلـو عطوفتلـو
  منيـف پاشا حضرتلرى در .

مادّه‌سى نه در؟ نغمهٔ حيات، در .

جاهللر حياتى نه تصوّر ايدرلر ايمش؟ بر رويای واهى كِبى تصوّر ايدرلر .

شاعرِ كنديسى حيـاتى ناصل تعريف حيات جدّى در، حيات ياشاييجى در،
ايدييور؟ دَيور .

سن طوپراقسين، عباره‌سى كيمه بوكلام جانه دكل، آنجاق تنه خطاب
خطاب اولندى؟ اولونمشدر .

عمر حَرْبكاهنده نه‌يه بكزه‌ملى؟ چـای كنارنده اوتلانان حيوانلر كِبى
  اولمايوب محاربه‌ده قهرمان اولمالى .

انسـان استقبالده مى يوخسـه حال خير افندم ! زنده اولان حالِ حاضرده
حاضرده مى ياشامالى؟ ياشامالى وَ ماضيِى اونوتمالى .

بحرِ مُحيطِ حياتى اِحاطه ايدن قوملر كونك برنده قضازده اولان قارداشلرمزه
اوزرنده ايزلر براقمغه نيچـون رَهْنُما اولمق اوزره بويوك ذاتلره
چاليشمالىيز؟ إمتِثالاً سعى واقْدام ايله‌مه‌لييز .

بوشعرده باشده‌كى رَقَمـلر نه كوستريـر؟ شعرك انكليزجه متنده اولان بيتلرينك
  نومرولرينى يان ايدرلر .

درس ٤٧ Lesson 47.

فـرع فعــل Arabic Participles.

§ 600. The Arabic Participles composed from the Primitive Triliteral verbs are much used in Ottoman; they are six in number (§§ 395, 548—549).

اسم فاعل Subjective Participle.

§ 601. The Subjective Participle of the Primitive Triliteral Verbs, also called the Noun of Agency, is formed of the measure فاقل *faqil*, i. e. by inserting an *élif* (-*a*-) between the first and second radical, and putting an *ésré* (-*i*-) under the second radical:

خَلْق *khalq* creation: √خَلَقْ : خَالِقْ *khaliq* creator.

سِرْقَتْ *sîrqat* theft: √سَرَقْ ؛ سَارِقْ *sariq* thief.

كتَاب *kitab* writing: √كَتَبْ ؛ كَاتِبْ *kîatib* clerk.

فِعْل *feel* work: √فَعَلْ ؛ فَاعِلْ *faعil* agent, doer.

§ 602. *Remarks.* a. If the second radical is ى or و, it changes into (ء, -*y*-) (§ 591).

دَوْر *dévr* to turn: √دَوَرَ ؛

دائر = داور *dayir* turning; about.

سَيَلَان *séyélan* to flow: √سَيَلَ ؛ ساپِل = سائل *sayil* flowing.

§ 603. b. When the first radical is *élif*, one of the *élifs* is omitted and a *médd* is put on the second *élif* (§§ 47, 701 d):

امر *émr* to command: √اَمَرَ ؛ اَامِرْ = آمِرْ *amir* a commander.

اتيان *ityan* to follow: √اَتَىَ ؛ اَاتِى = آتِى *ati* following.

تَعليم ١١١ Exercise 111.

Change the following Infinitives into Subjective Participles:

، جَرَيَان ٦ ، حِـكَـايَت ٥ ، نَظَارَت ٤ ، بُرُودَت ٣ ، جَهَالَت ٢ ، شَهَادَت ١

، (غزى) غَزَاء ١٣ ، بِنَاء ١٢ ، لُزوم ١١ ، عِلم ١٠ ، سَلَامَت ٩ ، رَغْبَت ٨ ، وُصُول ٧

. جِنَايَت ١٩ ، وَعْظ ١٨ ؛ عَلَى √ عُلُوّ ١٧ ، قَوْل ١٦ ، مَيْل ١٥ ، لِيَاقَت ١٤

Words. 1. testimony, witnessing. 2. ignorance. 3. coldness. 4. direction (director). 5. protection. 6. flowing, being current. 7. arrival. 8. desire (desirous). 9. safety (safe). 10. science, knowledge. 11. necessity. 12. building. 13. religious warfare, [against non-Moslems] (a champion of Mahometan religion). 14. worthiness. 15. inclination. 16. willingness. 17. elevation, grandeur (high). 18. sermon (preacher). 19. crime (criminal).

Objective Participle. اسم مفعول

§ 604. The Objective Participle of the Primitive Triliteral verb is always of the measure مَفْعُول *méfqoul*. It is formed by putting a *mim* with *ûstûn* (*mé-*) before the first radical and a و (*-ou-*) after the second (§§ 402, 548):

قتل *qatl* to murder: √فَتَلَ ؛ مَفْتُول *maqtoul* murdered, slain.

خَلْق *khalq* to create: √خَلَقَ ؛ مَخْلُوق *makhlouq* creature.

كَتْب *kétb* to write: √كَتَبَ ؛ مَكْتُوب *méktoub* written, letter.

خِدْمَت *khidmét* service: √خَدَمَ ؛ مَخْدُوم *makhdoum* one who is served; a son.

§ 605. When the second or third radical is ى, the و and *eôtré* of the measure مَفْعُول (*-ou-*), are removed and *esré* (*-i- -ee-*) is retained:

بِنَاء *bina* building: √بَنَى ؛ مَبْنُوى = مَبْنِي *mébni* built.

روَايَت *rivayét* to narrate: √رَوَىَ ؛ مَرْوُوى = مَرْوى *mérvi* told.

زِيَادَه *ziyadé* an increase: √زَيَدَ ؛ مَزْيُود = مَزْيِد *mézeed* increased.

تَعليم ١١٢ Exercise 112.

Change the following infinitives into Objective Participles:

بَعْث ٤ ، (رَدَدَ) رَدَّ ٣ ، جَرح ٢ ، رَغْبَت ١ ، جَهَاَت شَهَادَتْ عِلْم ، نَقْل

مُهْر p. ١١ ، خَفَاء ١٠ ، رِضَاء ٩ ، (مَنَنَ) مِنَّت ٨ ، مَنع ٧ ، قَبُول ٦ ، سُرُور ٥

Words. 1. desire (desirable, nice). 2. wound (wounded).
3. to reject (rejected). 4. sending (delegate). 5. joy (joyful).
6. accepting (acceptable). 7. forbid. 8. obligation (obliged, thank-
ful). 9. consent (pleased, satisfied). 10. to hide (secret). 11. seal.

Adjective of Quality. صفت مشبهه

§ 606. This is called by the native grammarians
'verbal adjective,' and implies the existence of an inherent quality. It is formed in accordance with various

measures, the most common of which is فقيل *faqeel,*
féqeel (§§ 437, 553).

ضَعْفْ *za'af* weakness: √ضَعَفَ ؛ ضَعِيف *zayeef* weak.

شَجَاعَتْ *shéja'at* bravery: √شَجَعَ ؛ شَجِيع *shéjee'* brave.

جَمَال *jémal* beauty: √جَمَلَ ؛ جَمِيل *jémeel* beautiful.

§ 607. There is another one in the measure فَقُول
faqoul, the derivative of which are:

صَبْر *sabr* patience: √صَبَرَ ؛ صَبُور *sabour* patient.

حَسَد *haséd* envy: √حَسَدَ ؛ حَسُود *hasoud* jealous.
                              [nignant § 40.

رَأْفَت *ré-é-fét* kindness: √رَأَفَ ؛ رَؤُف ، رَأُوف *ra'ouf* kind, be-

تعليم ١١٣ Exercise 113.

Change the following Infinitives into the Adjective
of Quality:

a. نَجَابَتْ ٦ ، صَغَرْ ٥ ، لَذَّتْ ٤ ، عَظَمَتْ ٣ ، سُهُولَت ٢ ، مَسْح ١

، كَرَامَتْ ، لَطَافَتْ ، شَرَفْ ، صِحَّتْ ١٠ ، كِبَر ٩ ، جَمَال ٨ ، قَرَابَتْ ٧

b. قِدَم ١١ ، عَجَلَه ، رَسَالَت ١٢ ، جَسَارَت ١٣ ، عَجْز ١٤ ، غَيْرَت ١٥

Words. 1. to anoint. 2. facility (easy). 3. greatness. 4. taste
(delicious, tasty). 5. youth (young). 6. nobility. 7. nearness.
8. beauty. 9. greatness, pride (great). 10. truth; health (true).
11. hurry, haste (hasty). 12. mission, legation (apostle). 13. bravery. 14. weakness (weak). 15. diligence (diligent).

Adjective of Colour and Defect. صفتِ الوان وُ عُيوب

§ 608. This is properly ranked with the Adjective of Quality, and is regular in its formation on the measure اَفْقَلْ *éfqal;* the Fem. Measure being فَقْلَاء.

حُمْرَت *houmrét* redness:	√حَمَرَ:	اَحْمَرْ	*ahmér* red.
بِيَاض *béyaz* whiteness:	√بَيَـضَ:	اَبْـيَـضْ	*ébyaz* white.
عَمْيَا *amya* blindness:	√عَمَى:	اَعْمَاء	*aᵎma* blind.
سَوَاد *sévad* blackness:	√سَـوَدَ:	اَسْـوَدْ	*ésvéd* black.
حَمَاقَت *hamaqat* folly:	√حَمَقَ:	اَحْمَقْ	*ahmaq* foolish.
صُفْرَت *soufrét* yellowness:	√صَفَرَ:	اَصْفَرْ	*ésfér* yellow.
سُمْرَت *sûmrét* brownness:	√سَـمَرَ:	اَسْـمَرْ	*ésmér* brown.

Noun of Superiority. اسم تفضيل

§ 609. This is formed by the measure اَفْقَلْ *éfqal.* The difference between this and the above mentioned measure of Colour and Defect is that, the latter is used especially to denote colour and defect. But this is used either for the superlative and for the comparative degrees of adjectives (§§ 222, 539):

كبير *kébeer* great:	√كَبَرَ:	اَكبر	*ék'bér* greater, greatest.
صغير *sagheer* little:	√صَغَرَ:	اَصْغَرْ	*esghér* less, lesser.

§ 610. The feminine of this form is فُقْلَا or فُقْلَى *fouqla:*

دنى لوkébeer: افقل = اَكْبَرْ : فُقْلَى = كُبْرَى *kûb'ra* greater.

دنى *dénee* low: √دَنَى : اَفْقَلْ = اَدْنَا *éd'na* lower, lowest.

دُنْيَا = فُقْلَا *dûn'ya* lower, lowest; the world.

تَعْليم ١١٤ Exercise 114.

Change the following words in accordance with the above-mentioned two measures:

‫قُصُو`¹ فَاضِل`² لَازِم`³ جَاهِل`⁴ رَحِيم`⁵ شَهِير`⁶ حُسْن`⁷ عَظِيم`⁸‬

‫عَلَى`⁹ وَسَط`⁹ً سَفِيل`¹⁰ قِدَم`¹¹ سَلَامَتْ`¹² صَحِيح`¹⁴ سَابِقَ`⁸√`‬

Words. 1. eminent; proud. 2. necessary. 3. ignorant.
4. merciful. 5. remarkable. 6. beauty. 7. great. 8. high.
9. middle. 10. poor. 11. priority. 12. safety. 13. true. 14. former.

The Noun of Excess. ‫مُبَالَغَهٔ فَاعِل‬

§ 611. The most common form is ‫فَقَّال‬ *féq'qal,*
formed by putting an *üstûn* on the first radical, by
doubling the second, and putting an *élif* after it:

‫دَوْر‬ *devr* to turn: ‫دَوَّرَ‬√ ‫دَوَّار‬ *dév'var* one who turns rapidly,
incessantly.

‫عِلْم‬ *ilm* knowledge: ‫عَلَّمَ‬√ ‫عَلَّام‬ *al'lam* All-Knowing, omni-
scient.

‫رَقْص‬ *raqs* to oscillate: ‫رَقَّصَ‬√ ‫رَقَّاص‬ *raq'qas* pendulum.

§ 612. If nouns of this measure are formed from
words denoting materials, they form nouns which denote
persons habitually engaged in certain occupations:

‫خَفّ‬ *khaff* a shoe: ‫خَفَّفَ‬√ ‫خَفَّاف‬ *khaf'faf* a shoe-seller.

‫بَقْلَهٔ‬ *baqla* { various kinds of grains: ‫بَقَّلَ‬√ ‫بَقَّال‬ *baq'qal* a grocer.

‫قَزّ‬ *qazz* silk: ‫قَزَّزَ‬√ ‫قَزَّاز‬ *qaz'zaz* a silk-merchant.

Exercise 115. ‫تَعْلِيم ۱۱٥‬

Change the following words into Nouns of Excess:

‫حَمُولَهٔ`¹ فَلَاحَتْ`² غُفْرَان`³ سِيَاحَتْ`⁴ عِطْر`⁵ بَزّ`⁶ صَرْف`⁷‬

‫خَلْق`⁸ جَبْر`⁹ مَدْح`¹⁰ دَلْك`¹¹ صَيْد`¹² مِنَتْ`¹³ شَمَس`¹⁴ رَسْم`¹⁵‬

Words. 1. burden. 2. husbandry (an [Egyptian] villager).
3. forgiveness, pardon. 4. journey (traveller). 5. rose-geranium
(perfumer). 6. cloth (linen-draper). 7. changing money (money-
changer). 8. to create (Creator). 9. force, tyranny. 10. joking.
11. shampooing the body in the bath (shampooer). 12. hunting
(hunter). 13. favour, bounty (All-Bounteous). 14. to serve (a
Christian deacon [Aramaic]). 15. picture (painter).

Exercise 116. تعليم ١١٦

Ascertain the nature, meaning and the measure of the following words:

كاتب' ، كاتبَين ، كاتبِين ، مكتوب² ، مكتوبات ، مكتوبَين :

سارق³ ، سارقِين ، سارقَين ، مسروق ، مسروقات ، آمِر⁴ ، امير :

معلومات ، عالم ، علّام ، عليم ، اعلم ، معلوم ، علم⁵ ، آمرون ، اميران :

عالِمين⁶ ، جاهل ، مجهول ، اجهل ، مجهولات : محهور⁷ ، مسيح⁸ ، رسولِين⁹ :

مرسول ، مرسولات ، عجز¹⁰ ، عاجز ، عجوزه ، اصغرِين¹¹ ، عطّارِين :

جمع¹² ، جامع ، مجموع ، مجموعه ، مجموعات ¹³: مِدحَت ، مادح :

ممدوح ، مدّاح ¹⁴: حمرا ، سَودا ، صَفرا ، اقدَم ، وُسطَى .

Translation 117. ترجمه ١١٧

Give the Arabic equivalents of the following words.
1. One who cuts, cut; 2. hearer, hearers, heard, things heard; 3. wounder, wounders, two wounders, wounded, wounded ones; 4. wisdom, wise, two wise men, wise peoples, known, knowledge, informations (Turkish pl.), wiser; 5. to sit, council; 6. to judge, judge, judges, court, condemned, condemned people; 7. greatness, great, greater, greatest; 8. to create, the Creator; 9. to cook, kitchen, cook; 10. ignorance, ignorant, unknown (doubtful), very ignorant, ignorant persons, unknown things. 11. The Anointed One, Messiah (Christ).

Exercise 118. تعليم ١١٨

١ الله تعـالى حضرتلرى اكبر' ارحم' غفّار ' وعلّام در٠٠ ٢ بو دنيانك وَ دنياده بولنان بتِرين موجودات وُ محلوقاتك خالقى جناب حقّ' در٠ ٣ كاتب افندىيه يازهجغى مكتوبه دائر بر امرِ كز وار ميدر؟ ٤ اوت! مكتوبى يازدقدنصوكره كوتورسون وَ اليله پوسته‌خانه مأمورينه تسليم ايلهسين٠ ٥ ايرماغك جريانى ناصلدر؟ — پك شديد در٠ ٦ «جاهل

ایله ضیافته کیتمهدن ، عالم ایله طاش طاشیمهسی اَحْسَنْدر» . ۷ آثار
جَهالتنی بیان جاهِل ؛ جاهل دکل عالِمدر: فقط جَهالتنی بیلمهین عالم ؛
عالِم دکل جاهِلدر، دیشار . ۸ «یك آدَما اولهكه سنی باصسینلر؛ یك
اَفْضَلْ اولهكه سنی آصسینلر». ۹ المانك اعلاسی وَ اَشْهری آسیای
صغراده واقع آماسیه شهرندن چیقار . ۱۰ چاپونیه اَقْصای شرقده در .

ترجمه ۱۱۹   Translation 119.

1. What are you doing? — I am writing a letter
to your son. 2. It was narrated by the ancients that
this bridge was built by the Romans. Is that certain?
— 3. No, Sir! it is doubtful, it is not certain. 4. Whatever you have told in secret, will be known to all the
world. 5. The Apostle says: 'Be glad and joyful'. 6. The
delegates were not accepted by the King. 7. God is
benignant and patient towards all his creatures. 8. All
the creatures in the world were created by God. 9. The
blind man was very foolish. 10. He is a brave man
but very jealous. 11. The pendulum of the clock is
broken.

مكالمه   Conversation.

اسئله Ésilé.	اجوبه Éjribé.
حمّال نرهدهدر؟	حمامده دلّاك ایله قونوشمقدهدر .
بو انكلیز سیّاحلر نرهدن كیور؟	اونلر سیّاح دكل واعظ درلر .
شو كیدن كیم وَ الندهكی آلت نه؟	برصیّاد در صیده كیدییور، الندهكیده بر ششخانه تفنكدر .
بو دكّان بقّال دكّانی میدر؟	خیر افندم؛ عطّار دكّانیدر .
مدّاح علی اوسته نه یاپیوردی؟	بر عرب فلّاحك نقلیتنی یاپیوردی .
شو یاقینلرده بر صرّاف دكّانی بولنورمی؟	خیر افندم! بوراسی بزّازلر چارشوسیدر صرّافلر قزّازلرك اوتهسنده درلر .
بورالردن بر چیفت قوندوره آلابیلیرمیم؟	اوت افندم ؛ خفّافلر چارشوسی یاقیندر .

كاغدك رنكى اسمر مى؟ بياض مى؟   أصْفَرْ در افندم .

شو اعما ديلنجى عاقل ميدر؟   يوق اغام يوق ، بر آز احمقجه در .

Reading Exercise. تعليم قرائت

A Litany of Praise to God. سنه باشنده تسبيحات[1]

— ۲ —   — ۱ —

جليلدر[12]، جميلدر[16]، لطفى فراوان[17]؛   كريمدر[2]، راحمدر[3]، عالمدر مولا'،

چولى چيمنه چويردى اول رحمان[18]؛   موجبِ حياتدر[4] الله تعالى:

خالقِ[19] عالمدر، درده او درمان[20]؛   هر بر احسانى نه لطيف[5]! نه اعلا[6]!

ينه برسنه تحمّل[21] ايلهدى . [ملك[24]   ينه[7] بر سنه ترحّم ايلهدى[8]:

عزيز[22] در عظيمدر[9]، نور[23] در اول   بونى بز عظيم[9] بر نعمت[10] بيله‌لم

حدّسز[25] قدرته[26] يالكزاو مالك[27]،   لطفى[5] بزلره كافيدر[11] ديه‌لم

فنا يوللره بز اولمشكن سالك[28]،   جليل[12] اسمنه تشكّر ايده‌لم[13]،

ينه بر سنه تأنّى ايلهدى .   اولسون عشقنه[14] عمرمز ده قربان[15]!

— ۳ —

حاضِر[29] در، ناظِر[30] در، موجود[31] در هر آن[32]،

شرّدن قومنى صاقلادى   اول منّان[33] .

Words. (۱) 1. *Tésbeehat'* fem. pl. of *tésbeeh'* (§ 615), lit. 'to say *sûbhan'allah'*, i. e. Praise ye the Lord. 2. *kéreem* gracious. 3. *rahim* compassionate. 4. *moujibi hayat* who grants the life: *moujib* causing, giver; *hayat* life; *Al'lah Ta-a-la* God the most High. 5. *ihsan* kindness; *lateef* All-Gracious (a. q. of *loutf* grace). 6. *'a-la* excellent. 7. *yiné*, *giné* again. 8. *térah'hûm ét."* to be merciful. 9. great. 10. *niymét* kindness, mercy. 11. *kiafi* sufficient. 12. *jéleel* All-Glorious. 13. *téshék'kûr ét."* to thank. 14. *ashq* love, loving-kindness. 15. *qourban* sacrifice.

(۲) 16. All-Gracious. 17. abundant. 18. *rahman* All-Merciful, Compassionate. 19. creator. 20. *dérd* affliction; *dérman* remedy. 21. *téham-mûl* patience, forbearance. 22. holy. 23. light. 24. *mélik* king. 25. *haddsiz* infinite. 26. *qoudrét* power. 27. *malik* possessor. 28. *salik* walking; *té-én-ni ét."* to wait patiently (§ 623).

(۳) 29. omnipresent. 30. All-Seeing. 31. present. 32. *héran* always (*hér* + *an* time). 33. *mén'nan* All-Bounteous.

حكمه ³⁴ مستحق ³⁵ كن ³⁶ بالجمله ³⁷ انسان ·

ينه بر سنه تحنن ³⁸ ايلهدى · ﴿آ. قونسطانطيان﴾

34. *hûkm* condemnation. 35. *mustahaqq'* deserving of. 36. '*kén* for *ikén* while. 37. *biljûmlé* all. 38. *téhan'nûn ét.''* yearning fondness; to love, to pity.

Note. The numbers 3, 19, 27—30 are Subj. Part.; No. 31 Obj. Part.; No. 2, 5, 9, 12, 16, 22 Adj. Qual.; No. 6 N. Excess.; No. 33 N. Superiority; No. 8, 13, 21, 28, 38 of the measure (*bab*) *téfaq'qoul* (§ 622).

درس ۴۸ Lesson 48.

The Derivative Triliteral Infinitives of Arabic.

مصدر ثلاثئ مزيدفيه

§ 613. The Derivative Triliteral Infinitives (*Masdarî Sûlasiyi Mézcedûn feehi*) are those words which are formed by the insertion or addition of servile letters to the root to form new verbs with certain changes of meaning. The meaning of the Simple or Primitive Infinitives may be extended or modified in various ways by the addition of one or more letters to the root (§ 288, 588).

§ 614. There are nine measures (*Bab*) of these Derivatives much used in Ottoman, the first of which is the second voice of Infinitives; the first voice being the Root of the Primitive Infinitives (§§ 272, 585 a).

تَفْعِيل = تَفْقِيل *téfqeel.* II.

§ 615. This measure is formed by prefixing the letter تَ *té* to the radical and putting a long ى *-ee-* after the second letter.

It intensifies the meaning of the root and makes the meaning, if intransitive, transitive:

خَوْف اِ ـ *khavf' ét.'* fear (intr.): خَوَفَ √ : تَخْوِيف *takh-veef* to terrify.

خِجَالَت *khéjalét* shame: خَجَلَ √ : تَخْجِيل *takh-jeel* to make ashamed.

شَكْل *shékl* form, shape: شَكَلَ √ : تَشْكِيل *tésh-keel* to form.

§ 616. If the last letter of the radical be a و or

ی it changes into ه ' ة -yé:

صَفْوَتْ saf'vét purity: √صَفْوٌ ؛ (تَصْفِيوْ) = تَصْفِيَهْ tasfeeyé to
                                           purify.

قَوَّتْ qouv'vét power: √قَوَوٌ ؛ (تَقْوِيوْ) = تَقْوِيَهْ taqveeyé to
                                        strengthen.

رِضَاء riza satisfaction: √رَضَیَ ؛ (تَرْضِی) = تَرْضِيَهْ tarzeeyé
                                        apology.

§ 617. Some other nouns also are formed in accordance with this measure:

    تجربه téjribé temptation: تفرقه téfriqa a feuilleton.

    تهلكه téhliké danger: تقدمه taqdimé offering.

    تذكره tézkiré memorandum; a short letter; note; a passport.

تَعْلِيم ١٢٠ Exercise 120.

Change the following Primitive Triliterals into the second voice of Derivative Infinitives:

سُكُونَتْ ٧ ، بُعْدْ ٦ ، بُرُودَتْ ٥ ، خَطَاءْ ٤ ، قَلَّتْ ٣ ، رِفَاقَتْ ٢ ، بُلُوغْ ١ ، نُور

كَدَرْ ١٣ ، بَيَاضْ ١٢ ، صَادِقْ ١١ ، خِفَّتْ ١٠ ، وَصِيَّت ٩ ، شَرَفْ ٨ ، حَرَكَتْ

بِشَارَتْ ١٩ ، بَرَكَتْ ١٨ ، جَدِيدْ ١٧ ، سِآوَتْ ١٦ ، رَبِّی ١٥ ، زِينَتْ ١٤ ، حَوَالَه .

Words. 1. reach (to communicate). 2. to accompany.
3. scarcity (to diminish). 4. fault (to cause to fail). 5. coldness (to make cold). 6. distance. 7. tranquility (to calm). 8. motion (to excite). 9. honour (to honour; to visit). 10. bequeathing, advice (to advise, recommend). 11. lightness (to lighten). 12. truthful (to affirm). 13. white (to copy fairly). 14. to refer, to confide (to change; a draft, a cheque). 15. ornament (to adorn) 16. to nourish (education). 17. condolence. 18. new. 19. good news.

III. مُفَاعَلَه = مُفَاعَلَهْ mûfaqalé.

§ 618. This measure is formed by prefixing a *mim* with êôtré (**mû-**, **mou-**) to the first radical, by inserting *élif* after the first (-a-) and a *hé* (-é, -ét) after the third of the radical letters. The noun thus formed conveys the idea of reciprocity. For some changes see §§ 705 c, 706 b.

ضَرْب darb to strike: √ضَرَبْ ؛ مُضَارَبَهْ mûdarébé to fight.

صُحِبَتْ souhbét conversation: √صَحِبَ ؛ مُصَاحَبَة mousahabét to converse.

قَتَلَ qatl to kill: √قَتَلَ ؛ مُقَاتَلَه mouqatélé to kill each other, massacre.

تعليم ۱۲۱ Exercise 121.

Change the following Primitive Triliteral Infinitives into the third voice:

' كَلَام ⁷ ' زِيَادَه ⁶ ' عِرْفَان ⁵ ' فُرْقَت ⁴ ' خُصُومَت ² ' عَهْد ³ ' قِيَاس ¹ ' بَدَل

' شِرْكَت ¹⁴ ' حَرْب ' جِهَاد ¹³ ' حُكْم ¹² ' تَرْك ¹¹ ' بَيْع ¹⁰ ' حِفْظ ⁹ ' نِزَاع ⁸

Words. 1. a measuring (to compare). 2. a covenant (treaty). 3. enmity (contention). 4. separation (to depart). 5. knowledge (a being mutually acquainted). 6. more (an auction). 7. speech (conversation). 8. quarrelling (to q. with each other). 9. to keep. 10. to buy. 11. to leave (armistice). 12. decree. 13. war. 14. partnership.

اِفْعَال = اِفْقَال *ifqal.* IV.

§ 619. This is formed by putting an ا with *esré* (*i*-) before the root, and another *élif* (-*a*-) between the second and third radicals. This gives a transitive sense to intransitive verbs and a doubly transitive or causal sense to those which are already transitive (§§ 262—263):

دُخُول *doukhoul* to enter (intr.): √دَخَلَ ؛ اِدْخَال *idkhal* to cause to enter, push.

مُرُور *mûrour* to pass » : √مَرَّرَ ؛ اِمْرَار *imrar* to cause to pass.

جُلُوس *jûlous* to sit » : √جَلَسَ؛ اِجْلَاس *ijlas* to seat.

§ 620. If the second radical be a و or ى, (-*v*-, -*y*-) it is omitted and a ه ' ه ' ة (-*é*) is added at the end:

عَوْن *avn* help: √عَوَنَ؛ (اِعْوَان =) اِعَانَه *iyané* to help.

طَيَرَان *tayran* to fly: √طَيَرَ؛ (اِطْيَار =) اِطَاَره *itaré* to cause to fly.

§ 621. If the first letter of radical be و (-*v*-), it is changed into ى (-*y*-):

وُصُول *rûsoul* to arrive: √وَصَلَ ؛ (اِوْصَال =) اِيصَال *iysal* to send.

تعاليم ١٢٢   Exercise 122.

Change the following Primitive Triliteral Infinitives into the fourth form of Derivative Triliteral Infinitives:

، طُهُور ٧ ، عُمْرَان ٦ ، شُغْل ٥ ، ضَلَاَت ٤ ، سُقُوط ٣ ، صُدُور ٢ ، بُلُوغ ، نُور ١
، وجُود ١٥ ، وُضُوح ١٤ ، دَوَر ١٣ ، طُول ١٢ ، دَيْن ١١ ، مَيْل ١٠ ، زَوَال ٩ ، فَيْض ٨
. عَوْدَت ٢٢ ، خُرُوج ، حَرِيق ٢١ ، تَام ٢٠ ، فُؤَاد ١٩ ، عَدَم ١٨ ، عَزْم ، ورُود ١٧ ، ١٦

Words. 1. arrival (reaching, arriving). 2. to go forth (to issue). 3. to fall. 4. to astray (to lead astray). 5. business (to occupy, to busy). 6. improvement (to improve). 7. to appear (to show). 8. bounteous gift (to pour out, to produce). 9. disappearance (to remove). 10. inclination (incline). 11. debt (to lend money). 12. length (to lengthen). 13. to turn (to manage; to economize [money]). 14. distinction (to explain). 15. existence (to invent). 16. to arrive (to put forward, to adduce). 17. resolution (to send). 18. annihilation (to murder, kill). 19. heart, mind (to explain to). 20. complete. 21. fire. 22. return.

تَفَعَّلْ = تَفْعَل   *téfaq'qoul.*   V.

§ 622. A class of verbs which are often Intransitive is formed by prefixing a تـ (té-) to the radical and doubling the middle letter with an *eôtré:*

صورت *sourét* image:	$\sqrt{}$ تَصَوَّرْ:صَوَرَ *tésav'vour* imagination.
تعليم *taleem* to teach:	$\sqrt{}$ تَعَلَّمْ : عَلَمَ *tée'al'lûm* to learn.
تسليم *tésleem* to hand over:	$\sqrt{}$ تَسَلَّمْ : سَلَمَ *tésél'lûm* to accept.

§ 623. If the third radical be و or ى (-*v*-, -*i*-) the *eôtré* of the measure is changed into *ésré* (-*i*):

بَنُو *bénou* son:	$\sqrt{}$ تَبَنَّى : بَنَوَ *tébén'ni* to adopt a son.
دَنَايَت *dénayét* meanness:	$\sqrt{}$ تَدَنَّى : دَنَى *tédén'ni* retrogression.
رِق *raqi* rising high:	$\sqrt{}$ تَرَقَّى : رَقَى *téraq'qî* progress.

تعليم ١٢٣   Exercise 123.

Change the following words into the fifth form:

، تَقْرِیر ٧ ، تَمْلِیك ٦ ، تَبْدِیل ٥ ، تَشْكِیل ٥ ، تَحْمِیل ٤ ، كِبْر ٣ ، تَكْثِیر ٢ ، نُور ١

، كَلَام ١٤ ، عَدُو ١٣ ، اَسَف ١٢ ، تَدْرِیس ١١ ، تَزْوِیج ١٠ ، تَأْدِیب ٩ ، نَصْرَانِی ٨

، شَكْوَی ٢٠ ، شُكْرَان ، ذِكْر ١٩ ، جَمْع ١٨ ، اَهْل ١٧ ، سَلْوَت ١٦ ، اُلْفَت ١٥

Words. 1. to increase (to be increased). 2. pride (to be proud).
3. to load (to support, to be patient). 4. to shape, to form (con-
formation). 5. to change (to be changed). 6. a giving possession
(to receive and take possession). 7. to render stationary; an official
report (to be stationary, established). 8. a Christian (to become
a Christian). 9. to chastise, punish (to be polite). 10. to marry
(to take a wife, marriage). 11. to teach (to learn). 12. sorrow
(to regret). 13. enemy (to persecute). 14. speech (to speak).
15. familiar intercourse (to unite in friendship; to compile). 16. comfort. 17. wife. 18. collection. 19. remembrance. 20. complaint.

لُغَتْلَر Words.

a. — اِبْراز ا *ibraz ét''.* to show.   a. — تَأْدِیه ا *té-é-diyé ét''.*⎫
a. — اِمْضاء ا *imza ét''.* to seal.   a. — اِیفاء ا *iyfa ét''.*⎭ to pay.
a. — اِرْسال ا *irsal ét''.* to send.   a. — اِعْطاء ا *ita ét''.* to give.

مَقاوَلات مُحَرِّری *mouqavélat mouhar'riri* Notary public.

تَعْلِیم ١٢٤ Exercise 124.

١ اون بِیكَار آراراتِك قارْلی بوزْلی طاغلَرِینی وَ چِیچَكْلی صَحْرالَرِینی
امْرار ایْله طَرَبْزونه واصِل اولْدِقْلَرِنْده ، دَرْیا ! دَرْیا ! ، دِیو نِدا اِیدوب
مَسَرَّتِ عَظِیمه اِبْراز اِیلَرْدِیلَر . ٢ مُعَلِّم اَفَنْدی دون اَخْشام بِر نُطْق اِیراد
اِیدَرِك بُجارِ ماكِینه‌سِنِك نِوَقْت و نَصورَتْله اِیجاد اولُنْدِیغِنی بَیان و اِیضاح
اِیلَدی . ٣ خاچَر اَفَنْدی وَصِیَّتْنی تَحْرِیر و تَمْیِیر اِیدَرِك مَقاوَلات مُحَرِّرِینه
تَصْدِیق اِیتْدِیرِدی . ٤ دَیِنِكْگِزی تَأْدِیه اِیتْدِیكِگِز می ؟ — بِر ماه مُرورِنْده
تَأْدِیه و اِیفا اِیتْمَك اوزْره بِر قِطْعه تَجْوِیل اَعْطا اِیلَدِیم . ٥ دَلِیقانْلِیلَرِك
غَیرَتی كَثِیر اَمّا تَجْرِبه‌سی ناقْصْدِر . ٦ دِرْت زائِد آلْتی ناقْص بِش : نه‌یه
مُساوی دِر ؟ — دِرْت زائِد آلْتی ، اون اِیدَر ؛ اون ناقْص بِش ؛ بِشه
مُساوِیدِر . ٧ یول تَذْكِره‌می حاضِرْلادِیكِگِز می ؟ — اِوَت اَفَنْدِم ! یارِین

قلمه تشریف ایدرسکز تسلّم ایدرسکز ۰ ۸ او سوزی سویلهمه ؛ چونکه
افندینك حِدّتنی تسکین ایدهجك یرده دها زیاده تحریك ایدییور ۰
۹ او قدر ضعیف ایدی که بر سوز تکلّمنه بیله قدرتی یوغیدی ۰
۱۰ تعلیم تعلّمی تأکید ایدر ۰ ۱۱ اِعتراض قولایدر ۰ لکن اِبداع کوجدر ۰

Translation 125. ترجمه ۱۲۵

1. The education of children is a very important
matter. 2. I adorned my room with the pictures of
my friends. 3. We are all invited to be the children
of God. 4. He was not progressing but retrogressing.
5. I have no complaint against him. 6. Many of the
people of China have become Christians. 7. Two more
pages were added to our lesson. 8. Be patient to all
complaints of the enemy. 9. I gave him possession of
the house and he possessed it. 10. I punished the boy
with great sorrow. 11. The pupil had no ability to
solve the question. 12. Nasréddin Efféndi was teaching
and the children were learning. 13. The birds are
flying in the air. 14. I have no money to help you with.
15. I am very sorry to have kept you waiting so long.

Conversation. مكالمه

Éjvibé. اجوبه	Ésilé. اسئله
بکا خجالت کتیرمزسه کز ویریرم ۰	هندی ! بنده کزه بر توصیه نامه
اعطاسنه همّت ایدرمیسکز ؟	
او رضاسنی تحصیل ایلدم ۰	ایتدیککز قصوردن طولایی ترضیه
اوت افندم !	ایتدیکز می ؟
خدمتکاری اِعزام ایلهدم ایسهده ، پك	قویومجی آلتونی کوزلجه تصفیه
مشغول اولدیغندن یاپهمامش ۰	ایلمشمی ؟
دینم ۷۰۰ غروشه بالغ اولدی ۰	دائنکز دَینیکزی قاچه اِبلاغ ایلهدی ؟
عفوایدرسکز ، مساعدم اولمدیغندن	مدیر افندینك تقریرینی قرائت
مطالعه ایدهمهدم ۰	ایلهدیکز می ؟
اوت افندم ! کاملاً تسلّم ایلهدم ۰	دکّانك اشیالرینی تسلیم آلدیکز می ؟

چين و ماچيندهكى محاربهدن برخبر اوت افندم ؛ دهشتلى خبرلر واردر ؛ وار مى ؟ محاربه دكل ، عادتا مقاتلهدر .

تعليم قرائت Reading Exercise.

دوستلق Friendship.

صادق دوست دنيانك بوتون خزينهلرندن[1] زياده قيمتليدر[2] ، فقط نادر[3] بولونور . چوق احبابى[4] وار ظن ايدهنك هيچ دوستى يوقدر ؛ زيرا هر دوست دوست دكلدر . چونكه دوستلق كوسترن آدم كيمسهيه دوست اولهمز . دوستلق نهقدر[5] اسكى اولورسه ، اوقدر قوتلى وَ پايدار[6] اولور . فاضل[7] وَ صادق بر دوست بولان آدم ايى بيلمهليدركه ، عظيم بر خزينه بولمشدر . دوست دوستنك كدرلى زمانسنده تسليَت[8] ايدهرك ؛ كدرلريني تقليل[9] وَ سُرورلى زمانننده مسرتنى تزييد[10] ايدر .

وولترك اقوالِ مشهورهسندن[11] برى ده «بر ناموسلى آدمك حسّ ايدهبيلهجكى الك بويوك مسرّت دوستلارينى مَسعود ايدهبيلمكدن كلير» سوزى در . دوستلغك شروطِ اساسيهسى[12] يكديكره حسنِ تَوَجُّه[13] ا يله كمالِ امنيت[14] ، خلوصِ قلب[15] ايله محبّت ، صداقت[16] وَ وفاكارلق وَ حينِ حاجتده[17] يكديكرى يولنده فداكارلق[18] ابراز ايتمكدر .

﴿معلم ناجى﴾

Words. 1. *khaziné* treasure. 2. *qîymétli* precious. 3. *nadir* rare. 4. *ahbab* friends. 5. *néqadar . . . olqadar* the more . . . the more . . . 6. *paydar* firm, enduring. 7. *fazîl* virtuous. 8 *tésliyét* comfort (§ 616). 9. *taqlil, takhfîf* to diminish, to lighten. 10. *tézyeed* to increase. 11. *aqval* words; *mesh'hour* remarkable, famous. 12. *shourout* conditions; *ésasi* fundamental. 13. *hûsn* good; *tévéj'jûh* sympathy. 14. *kémal* perfection; *émniyét* fidelity. 15. *khoulous* sincerity = a sincere heart. 16. *sadaqat* faithfulness. 17. *heen* time. *hajét* want = in case of necessity. 18. *féda-kîarlîq* self-denial.

تعليمِ سابق حقنده مكالمه Conversation.

سزك احبابكز وار مى ؟ اوت افندم ! بنم چوق دوستم وار در .

يلمم! بكا چوق آدم دوستلق و محبّت ابراز ايدر.   اويله ايسه هيچ دوستكز يوقدر!

اوت افندم! حتّی فاضل و صادق بر دوست بولان آدم عظيم بر خزينه بولش ايديكنی ده يلیرم.   حقيقی دوستلرك پك نادر اولديغنی بيلير ميسكز؟ عجبا فكرمی لايق وجه اوزره عرض ايده بيلديم می؟

كدرلی زماننده كدرينی تقليل ايدر.   فاضل و صادق بر دوست دوستنه نه ايلر؟

تَسْلِیَتْ ويرمكله تخفيف ايدر.   كدرينی نصورتله تقليل و تخفيف ايدر؟

البتّه! مَسْروريتنی تزيید ايتمك ايچون سعی و اقدام ايدر.   سُرورلی زماننده دخی فائده‌سی طوقونور می؟

اك بويوك مسرّتی استحصال ايدر.   ناموسلی بر آدم دوستلرينی مَسْعود ايتمكله نه استحصال ايده بيلير؟

وولترك اقوالِ مشهوره‌سندندر.   بونی كيم سويله‌مشدر؟

فرانسه‌نك اك مشهور فيلوسوفلرندن بری ايدی.   وولتر كيم ايدی؟

خير افندم! بوندن ۱۲۷ سنه مُقَدَّم (۱۷۷۸ ده) وفات ايتمشدر.   حكيمِ موی اليه¹ الان² حياتده ميدر؟

Words. 1. *hakee'mi mûmayiléyh* the above mentioned philosopher, he. 2. *él-an* now, at present.

درس ٤٩   Lesson 49.

The Derivative Triliteral Infinitives. (Continued.)

مصدر ثلاثی مزيد فيه

VI. تَفَاعُل = تَنَاقُل *téfaqoul.*

§ 624. Reciprocal verbal nouns are also formed by putting ت (*té-*) before the root and an *élif* (*-a-*) after its first radical:

صَحَابَتْ *sahabét* protection: $\sqrt{}$ صَحَبْ; تَصَاحُبْ *tésahoub* to protect.

22*

قَطْع qat to cut: √قَطَعْ : تَقَاطُعْ *téqatou'* to cut each other.

قُعُود qou'oud to rest: √قَعَدْ : تَقَاعُدْ *téqa'oud* being pensioned.

§ 625. If و or ى be found at the end of the root, it is changed into ى and the *êôtré* also into *ésré*:

عَطَاء 'ata giving: √عَطَى : تَعَاطِى *té'ati* delivering over to one another, to interchange.

وَلِى *véli* to be behind: √وَلَى : تَوَالِى *tévali* succession.

دَرْك *dérk* to attain: √دَرَكْ : تَدَارِكْ *tédarik* to procure; prepare.

تعاليم ۱۲٦ Exercise 126.

Change the following words into the sixth measure:

۰ نَقْض ۷ ، نَسْخ ٦ ، بُعْد ٥ ، صَدَمَهْ ٤ ، تَابِع ٣ ، نَسْل ٢ ، نُصْرَتْ ۱

Words. 1. aid, help (mutual help). 2. generation (genitary). 3. a servant (a becoming consecutive). 4. collision (collision, shock). 5. distance (to be distant). 6. to change, transform (metempsychosis, transmigration of soul). 7. to destroy, violate (contradiction).

VII. اِنْفِعَال = اِنْفِقَال *infiqal.*

§ 626. This measure is formed by prefixing اِن (*in-*) to the root and inserting an ا (*-a-*) after the second radical. It is necessarily Intransitive or Passive in signification:

قَطْع qat' to cut: √قَطَعْ : اِنْقِطَاع *inqîta'* to be cut, interrupted.

ضَم zamm to add: √ضَمَمْ : اِنْضِمَام *inzimam* to be added, addition.

قِسْمَت qîsmét portion, part: √قَسَمْ : اِنْقِسَام *inqîsam* to be separated, separation.

تعاليم ۱۲۷ Exercise 127.

Change the following Primitive Infinitives into the seventh measure of Derivative Triliteral Infinitives:

، جَذْب ۸ ، كَسْر ۷ ، حَل ٦ ، صَب ٥ ، قَبْض ٤ ، دَفْع ٣ ، قَيْد ٢ ، قَلْب ۱ فِصَال

٠ جَمَاد ، حَصْر ۱٤ ، عَكْس ۱۳ ، هَزِيمَتْ ۱۲ ، هَدْم ۱۱ ، عَقْد ۱۰ ، شَرْح ۹

Words. 1. change (changing, revolution). 2. binding (to be obedient). 3. to expel. 4. to grasp, hold (constipation). 5. a pouring (a stream's flowing). 6. solution (to be untied). 7. to break (to be broken). 8. attraction (to be attracted). 9. gladness (to be cheerful). 10. to tie (to be gathered). 11. to pull down (demolition). 12. defeat (to be crushed). 13. reflection. 14. restricting.

VIII. اِفْتِعَال = اِفْتِقَال   *iftiqal.*

§ 627. This measure is formed by prefixing an
ا (*i-*) to the first radical, and by inserting ت (*-ti-*) after
the first, and ا (*-a-*) after the second radical. It is
necessarily Intransitive or Passive in signification:

جَمْع *jém'* to collect: $\sqrt{\text{جَمَع}}$: اِجْتِمَاع *ijtima'* to be gathered,
                                                      collection.

فَخْر *fakhr* pride: $\sqrt{\text{فَخَر}}$: اِفْتِخَار *iftikhar* to be proud of,
                                                      to boast.

§ 628. According to the laws of euphony some
changes take place when the ت is inserted.

a. If the first radical be ض ، ص ، ط the letter ت
is changed into ط.

b. If the first radical be ز or د, the additional ت
is changed into د.

c. If the first radical be ا or و, it is changed into ت:

صَبْر *sabr* patience: $\sqrt{\text{صَبَر}}$: (اصتبار =) اِصْطِبَار *istibar.*

ضَرْب *zarb* a blow: $\sqrt{\text{ضَرَب}}$: (اضتراب =) اِضْطِرَاب *iztirab*
                                                      anxiety.

طُلُوع *toulou'* to appear: $\sqrt{\text{طَلَع}}$: (اطتلاع =) اِطِّلَاع *ittila'.*

زَحْمَت *zahmét* trouble: $\sqrt{\text{زَحَم}}$: (ازتحام =) اِزْدِحَام *izdiham*
                                                      a crowd.

دَعْوَى *dav'a* a law suit: $\sqrt{\text{دَعَو}}$: (ادتعاو =) اِدِّعَاء *iddi'a* to
                                                      maintain.

ذَخِيره *zakhiré* provision: $\sqrt{\text{ذَخَر}}$: (اذتخار =) اِدِّخَار *iddikhar*
                                                      to store up.

أَخْذ *akhz* taking: $\sqrt{\text{أَخَذ}}$: (اأتخاذ =) اِتِّخَاذ *ittikhaz*
                                                      to take, to adopt.

وَحْدَت *vahdét* unity: $\sqrt{\text{وَحَد}}$: (اوتحاد =) اِتِّحَاد *ittihad*
                                                      union.

Exercise 128.   ١٢٨ تَعْلِيم

Change the following Primitives into Derivatives:

، زَوْجَه ٨ ، مِحْنَت ٧ ، عَقد ٦ ، نَظْم ٥ ، رَدّ ٤ ، نَشْر ٣ ، خِيَار ٢ ، رَبْط ١ ، أَحَد

. (حَيِج) حَاجَت ١٥ ، حُرْمَت ١٤ ، خَلَل ١٣ ، رِخَاَت ١٢ ، أَصِل ١١ ، وَفْق ١٠ ، زِيَادَه ٩

Words. 1. to fasten, bind (connexion). 2. choice (to choose, prefer). 3. to scatter, to publish (to be spread). 4. to refuse (apostacy). 5. order (regularity). 6. to bind, tie (creed). 7. trouble (trial, examination). 8. wife (marriage). 9. many, much (growth). 10. to suit, agree (concord, alliance). 11. a root (to be united). 12. travelling (to travel; to die). 13. disorder. 14. honour. 15. need.

IX.   افْعِلَال = افْتِلَال   *ifqilal.*

§ 629. This measure of Derivative Infinitives is used to express a colour or quality, as the adjective أَفْقَل *éfqal* (§ 608). It is made from this form of adjective by doubling the last radical and inserting an *élif* between them.

أَحْمَر *ahmér* red: اِحْمِرَار *ihmirar* to become intensely red.

أَسْوَد *ésvéd* black: اِسْوِدَاد *isvidad* »   »   » black.

أَحْدَب *ahdéb* hump-backed: اِحْدِبَاب *ihdibab* to be hump-backed.

X.   اِسْتِفْعَال = اِسْتِفْقَال   *istifqal.*

§ 630. By putting the syllable اِسْت (*isti-*) before the root and an ا (-*a*-) after the second radical, a verbal noun is constructed which expresses asking for or demanding something designated by the primitive word:

نُطْق *noutq* speaking: √ نَطَق : اِسْتِنْطَاق *istintaq* interrogating.

رَحْمَت *rahmét* mercy: √ رَحَم : اِسْتِرْحَام *istirham* asking for mercy.

§ 631. If the first radical be ا or و, it changes into ى (-*y*-); and if the second radical be و, it changes into ه ، ة (-*é* -*ét* -*at*) at the end of the word (§§ 620—621):

أَذِنْ izn permission: √أَذَنَ ؛ (اِسْتِيْذَان =) اِسْتِوْذَان istiyzan
to ask for permission.

اِيْفَاء iyfa to pay: √وَفَى ؛ (اِسْتِيفَاء =) اِسْتِوْفَاى istiyfa
to receive.

رَاحَتْ rahat rest: √رَوَحَ ؛ (اِسْتِرَاحَتْ =) اِسْتِرْوَاح istirahat
to take rest.

وُضُوح vûzouh plain: √وَضَحَ ؛ (اِسْتِيضَاح =) اِسْتِوْضَاح istiyzah'
to explain.

تَعْلِيم ١٢٩   Exercise 129.

Change the following words into the tenth form:

فَهْم ٔ، اُخِرَتْ ٕ، رَدّ ٖ، عِلْم ٘، دَوَام ٙ، جَوَاب ٚ، خُرُوج ٛ، شُوَرَى ٜ.

1. understanding (to ask, interrogation). 2. hire, rent (to rent). 3. to return, refuse (to ask, to be restored). 4. knowledge (asking for knowledge). 5. continuation (perseverance). 6. answer (to question). 7. going out (to extract, to quote). 8. council.

مُطَالَعَات Mûta-la-at Remarks.

§ 632. It must be borne in mind that all Arabic roots of three letters cannot assume all the nine forms given above. Many have only a few of them: for instance علم 'ilm 'knowledge' can form the measures

مُعَالَمَه، إِعْتِلَام، اِسْتِعْلَام، تَعَلُّم، تَعْلِيم، اِعْلَام؛ but not such as

تَعَالُم، اِنْعِلَام.

تَعْلِيم ١٣٠   Exercise 130.

١ قلبكزك اضطرابى دفع اولدى مى ؟ — اوت افندم ! «صبر باشى سلامت» ديئلر؛ اضطراب اصطبار ايله اندفاع ايدر · ٢ ازدحامدن چوق زحمت چكديكز مى ؟ — اوت افندم ! ازدحامك اجتماعندن پك صيقيلدق · ٣ ذخيره‌نك ادّخارى ايچون نه تدبير اتّخاذ اولندى ؟ — افندم ! اتّفاق ايدوبده بر قراره كله‌مدك · ٤ سارقلر استنطاقلرنده قتل مادّه‌سنى ٔ اقرار ايتمشلر مى ٕ ؟ — اوت افندم ! اقرار ايتمشلر

Words. 1. mad'dé case. 2. iqrar ét.'' to confess. (VI. of qarar.)

وَ محاكَمهدنصوكه ده اِعدامه حكم اولونمشلر . ٥ جَدِّ عاليكُزِكُ اِرتحالى نه
وقت وقوع بولشدر ؟ — ١٨٧٢ تاريخنده استانبولده وقوعبولمشدر .
٦ اول خانهیی استیجار ایتدیکز می ؟ — خیر افندم ! متصرّفی ایله
مُعارَفهم اولمادیغی سببدن ایجار بدلی٣ حقنده اتّفاق ایدهمدك . ٧ ترجمهمی
اصلیه٤ مُقایَسه٥ ایدهمدیكمدن طولایی معلّم افندینك مساعدهسنی٦
استرحام ایلدم . ٨ درایت٧ وُ ذكاوت٨ صبر وُ اِجتهاددن٩ عبارت در .

3. *ijar bédéli* rent. 4. original. 5. to compare. 6. permission, pardon. 7. ability. 8. shrewdness. 9. endeavour.

ترجمه ١٣١ Translation 131.

1. He quoted[1] many passages[2] from the Old Testament. 2. Did any injury happen through the collision of the two steamers? — Yes, Sir, one of those two steamers sank in five minutes. 3. Is the war ended? — No, Sir, there is only an armistice[3] of two months. 4. I have the honour to present to you my brother-in-law Tahir Béy. 5. The Alévi Mohamedans and the Yézidees believe in transmigration of soul. 6. The treaty[4] was written, signed and interchanged[5] between those two powers. 7. Although there were five witnesses, yet there was contradiction in their testimony.

Words. 1. *istikhraj, iyrad étmék.* 2. *ayétler, ayatî kérimé.* 3. *mûtaréké.* 4. *mou-a-hédé.* 5. *ta-a-ti, mûbadélé ét.''*

مكالمه Conversation.

پاشانك قوناغنك اتّصالنده در .	اویکز نرهده در؟
اوت٬ چونكه طریقِ حقدن ارتداد ایتدیكز .	بنم ایچونی تأسف ایدییورسكز؟
افندم ! شیمدی مكتبده بویوك انتظام وَ ترقی مشاهده اولونمقده در .	مكتبك حالی شمدی نصلدر؟
مانیه خانم ایله تزوّج ایلدم .	كیم ایله عَقد ازدواج ایلهدیكز؟
اینجیلی كیسهلرك مركزیّ اتّحادی مرذیفوننده اِجتماع ایدهجكدر .	بوسنه اینجیلی ارمنلرك مركزیّ اتّحادی نرهده تَجَمّع ایدهجكدر؟

بوكون سزده بر اِنْشِراح وار : عجبا   چونكه خانهمك انشاسيچون اقتضا
سببى نه در؟   ايدن امرِعالى صدور ايتدى •

مكتبده بزم مخدوم نصالدر؟   اطاعتسز در' هيچ انقياد ايتمهيور •

نصل اولدى ده بزه تشريف ايتديكز ؟   افندم ! سزده اِنْجِذاب قوّتى واردردر •

تعليم قرائت Reading Exercise.

نجابت حقيقيه True Nobility.

كِرك مادّى١ وَ كِرك معنوى١ دوشونلسون' «انسان آناسندن بويوك
طوغماز» • عجبا انكلتره‌ده‌كى لوردلره' فرانسه‌ده‌كى پرنسلره' ماحاصلِ
دنيانك٢ هر جهتنده‌كى اصحابِ نجابته٣ صورولسه؛ نسلنى٤ مبدأى
خلقته٥ ايصال ايده‌بيله‌جك٦ كيمسه وار ميدر ؟

روايات وَ اساطيردن٧ قطعِ نظر٨ ' بزجه٩ تاريخاً١٠ ثابت١١ اولان
بعض وقايعى١٢ كوزومزك اوكونه آلالم ؛ وَ حتّى تطويله١٣ دوشمه‌مك
ايچون عرَب دولتلرينى دخى قاريشديرميه‌لم •

دولتِ صفّاريه‌يى١٤ تشكيل١٥ ايدن ذات بر حيدود١٦ ' دولتِ
غزنويه‌يى١٧ ميدانه كتيرن بر كوله ' دولت سلجوقيه‌يى١٨ او قدر عظمَت
وُ اجلاليله١٩ عالَمِ سياستده٢٠ برنجى دولتاردن معدود٢١ ايدن بر عشيرت
قوجه‌سى٢٢ دكلميدى ؟

Words. 1. *mad'dee, manévee, adee* physical; moral; ordinary,
inferior (§ 579). 2. *mahasal* total, all (the world). 3. *as-ha'bi
néjabét* the possessors of nobility = nobles. 4. *nésl* ancestors.
5. *mébdayî khîlqat* beginning of creation. 6. *iysal ét."* to carry,
to cause, to reach. 7. *rivayat* tradition, folk-lore; *ésateer* mythology.
8. *qat'i nazar* leave it out of consideration, except. 9. *bizjé* among
us *i. e.* Ottomans. 10. *tarikhén* historically. 11. *sabit* fixed, proved.
12. *vaqayi* events. 13. *tatvil* prolixity. 14. *dévléti Saffariyé* the
Saffari dynasty of Khorasan. 15. *téshkil édén* the founder. 16. *haydoud* a brigand. 17. *dévléti Ghaznévi* the Ghaznévide dynasty of
Persia. 18. *dévléti Séljouqiyé* the dynasty of the Seljuqs (in Central
Asia and in Asia Minor). 19. *azamét* grandeur; *ijlal* magnificence.
20. *alémi siyasét* the world of diplomacy. 21. *madoud* enumerated.
22. *asheerét* a nomadic tribe, clan. *qoja* chief.

نه حاجت۲۳ ! او دنیانك نصفنه حكم ایدن ، عالمِ انسانیتك۲۴

الڭ واسع۲۵ حكومتنی تشكیل ایلهین بر تاتار رئیسی۲۶ دكل می ایدی ؟

كثرتِ فتوحاتجه۲۷ جهانه هیچ مثلی۲۸ كلممش اولان تیمورلنك۲۹ ،

جنكیز خدمتكارلرندن۳۰ بر آدمك نسلندن كلمهدی می ؟

اتابكه۳۱ وَ ایوبیه۳۲ وَ ممالكه۳۳ كبی حكومتلری ، بر بابایكیت

عسكر۳۴ وَ یا بر غیرتلی اسیر۳۵ تأسیس ایتمهدیار می ؟

سلطنتِ عثانیهده بر معروف۳۶ خاندان۳۷ داحیی اولان ذواتدن :

جندرهلی قاره خلیل دادی۳۸ ، بر صوفته۳۹ ، كوپرولی محمد پاشا سرایده بر

آشجی ، محمد علی پاشا برچیفتجی زادهدن۴۰ باشقه بر شی می ایدیلر ؟

〈كمال بك〉

23. *né hajét!* what need is there? 24. *insaniyét* humanity (§ 581). 25. *vasi* vast. 26. *réyis* chief of a clan. 27. *késrét* abundance; *fûtouhat* victories (pl. of *fûtûh*). 28. *misl* equal. 29. *Timûrléng* Tamerlane. 30. *Jéngiz*; *nésl* children, progeny. 31. *Atabégé*, 32. *Eyoubiyé*, 33. *Mémaliké* the dynasties of Atabég, Eyyoubi and Memlooks in Persia and Egypt. 34. *baba yiyit* a young man of full growth and strength. 35. *éseer* slave. 36. *ma'rouf* remarkable. 37. *khanédan* race, line; Jéndéréli Qara Halil. 38. See the first word. 39. f. *softa* student of Canon Law (Gr. σοφιστής). 40. *chiftjizadé* the son of a farmer.

---

۵۰ درس Lesson 50.

The Participles of Derivative Infinitives.

§ 633. We have seen how the Subjective and Objective Participles are formed from the Primitive or Simple forms of the Infinitive (§§ 601, 604). We shall now consider the formation of both these Participles in the above mentioned nine Derivative Infinitives.

§ 634. There are four rules which govern the formation of all these Participles of the nine Derivative Infinitives.

a. The Participles óf the verbs of the measure تفقیل *téfqeel* are formed in the following manner: The

servile letters ت ' ى are dropped; a *mim* with *êôtré*

(م *mû-*, *mou-*) is prefixed to the remainder of the word: the second radical must be doubled by a *shéddé* (ّ), and the last syllable must have an *ésré*; this forms the Subjective Participle.

To find the Objective Participle change the *ésré* into *ûstûn*. (*Vide* No. II in the Table.)

b. The Participles of the derivatives of the measure

مفاقلة *mûfaqalé* are made as follows: Omit the last *hé* (*-é*) and put an *ésré* on the last syllable; this forms the Subjective Participle.

Change the *ésré* to *ûstûn* and you will obtain the Objective Participle. (*Vide* No. III in the Table.)

c. The Participles of the remaining two measures

beginning with ت (*té-*), are made in the following way. Prefix a *mim* with *êôtré* at the beginning and put an *ésré* on the last syllable; this is the Subjective Participle. To find the Objective Participle change the last *ésré* into *ûstûn*. (*Vide* Nos. V and VI in the Table.)

d. In those Infinitives which have an *élif* in the first and last syllables, the *élifs* must be dropped, a *mim* with *êôtré* must be prefixed to the remainder of the word and the last syllable must have an *ésré*. This forms the Subjective Participle of these derivatives. To form the Objective Participle change that *ésré* into *ûstûn*. (*Vide* Nos. IV, VII—X in the Table.)

§ 635. The Participles of the Quadriliterals are made simply by adding a *mim* with *êôtré* to the beginning and punctuating the last syllable with *ésré:* this forms the Subjective Participle. Change that *ésré* to *ûstûn*, you obtain the Objective Participle. (*Vide* No. Q in the Table.)

Note. Notice that *Mou-*initial is the sign of the measure *Mûfaqalé* (§ 618) and the Participles of Der. Inf.; while *Mé-*, *Mi-* is the sign of N. with *mim* and Méfoul (§§ 597, 604).

تعليم ١٣٢ Exercise 132.

Form the Subjective and Objective Participles of the following words at the beginning of p. 350:

Rule	No.	Measures	Voice	Examples	
	I.	The 23 measures in the pp. 314--315.		خلق *khalq*	to create
a	II.	تفعيل *téfqeel*	Transitive	تجليد *téjleed*	to bind
b	III.	مفاعله *mûfaqalé*	Reciprocal	محاربه *mûharébé*	to fight
c	V.	تفعّل *téfaq'qoul*	Intransitive Passive	تبدّل *tébéddûl*	to be changed
	VI.	تفاعل *tefaqoul*	Reflexive Intransitive	تجاوز *téjavouz*	to exceed
d	IV.	افعال *ifqal*	Transitive	ارسال *irsal*	to send
	VII.	انفعال *infiqal*	Reciprocal Passive	انقسام *inqisam*	to be divided
	VIII.	افتعال *iftiqal*	»	اكتساب *iktisab*	to earn, gain
	IX.	افعلال *ifqilal*	Excess	احرار *ihmirar*	to become intensely red
	X.	استفعال *istifqal*	Desire	استنطاق *istintaq*	to interrogate
	Q.	فعلله *faqlélé*	. . .	ترجمه *térjémé*	to translate

Remainder	Subjective Participle		Objective Participle	
فَقَلَ√	خَالِقْ *khaliq*	who creates, creator.	مَخْلُوقْ *makhlouq*	created, creature.
جالد	مُجَلِّدْ *mujél'lid*	who binds, binder.	مُجَلَّدْ *mûjél'léd*	bound (volume).
محارب	مُحَارِبْ *mouharib*	belligerent.	مُحَارَبْ *mûharéb*	engaged in war.
	مُتَبدِّلْ *mûtébéd'dil*	changer.	مُتَبدَّلْ *mûtébéd'dél*	changed.
	مُتَجاوِزْ *mûtéjaviz*	that exceeds.	مُتَجاوَزْ *mûtéjavéz*	surpassed.
رسل	مُرسِلْ *mûrsil*	sender, addresser.	مُرسَلْ *mûrsél*	an envoy, messenger.
نقسم	مُنْقَسِمْ *mûnqasim*	divider.	مُنْقَسَمْ *mûnqasém*	divided.
كتسب	مُكْتَسِبْ *mûktésib*	who earns.	مُكْتَسَبْ *mûktéséb*	earned.
حمرر	مُحْمَرّْ *mûhmerr'*	intensely red.		
ستنطق	مُسْتَنْطِقْ *mûstantiq*	interrogator (judge).	مُسْتَنْطَقْ *mûstantaq*	interrogated.
تَرْجَمَ√	مُتَرْجِمْ *mûtérjim*	translator.	مُتَرْجَمْ *mûtérjém*	translated.

، مُسَاقَوَتْ٦ ، اِرْتِفَاعْ٥ ، تَسْلِيحْ٤ ، تَعْطِيل٣ ، مُخَالَفَتْ٢ ، تَقَاعُدْ١ ، نَقْل

، تَفْتِيشْ١٢ ، تَعَدُّدْ١١ ، تَعَرُّفْ١٠ ، تَكَلُّم٩ ، مُنَازَعَه٨ ، بِنَاء ، اِعْتِبَار٧

، تَزْيِين١٨ ، اِسْتِعْجَال١٧ ، تَوَاضُع١٦ ، تَرْتِيب١٥ ، تَحْرِير١٤ ، اِسْتِنْطَاق١٣

، طَنْطَنَهْ٢٤ ، وَسْوَسَهْ٢٣ ، هَنْدَسَهْ٢٢ ، تَكْمِيل٢١ ، تَعْلِيم٢٠ ، تَصْحِيح١٩

. تَوَقُّف ، تَنْقِيد ، بُرهان ، صَيْقَل٢٧ ، عُنْوَان٢٦ ، جَوْهَر٢٥

Words. 1. to pension off (pensioned off). 2. to oppose (opposing, contrary). 3. to stop work, a vacation. 4. to arm (armed). 5. to become high. 6. sojourn (guest). 7. honour (honorable). 8. to quarrel (quarreling; disputed). 9. to speak (speaker, first person). 10. possession (possessor; governor). 11. to multiply (numerous). 12. to search, examine (inspector). 13. to question (a prisoner). 14. to write (writer; written). 15. to arrange, to compose (compositor). 16. humility (humble). 17. to hasten (pressing, important). 18. to ornament. 19. to correct (proof-reader). 20. to teach (teacher). 21. to finish (complete, perfect). 22. geometry (engineer). 23. anxiety (naturally suspicious). 24. magnificence (pompous). 25. a jewel, a pearl (set with pearls). 26. superscription (superscribed). 27. polish (polished).

تَعْلِيم ١٣٣ Exercise 133.

١ مرذيفونده مسافرتكزراڭ مدّتی١ نقدر در ؟ — اوكومزده كی آيلولده اون سكز سنه تكميل اوله‌جقدر. ٢ بو تاجرك اعتباری نصلدر ؟ — معتبر بر ذات در. ٣ سلاحارڭز اوزريڭزده ميدر ؟ — اوت افندم ! جمله‌مز ده مُسَلَّح ! ٤ بو سنه تعطيلده بر يره كيده‌جكميسڭز ؟ — خير ! مرذيفونده قالوب بعض ترجمه‌لر ايده‌رك؛ طبع اولونقی اوزره درسعادته كوندره‌جكم . و بَعْدَهُ٢ طبع اولونان قسملرينك تصحيحاتيله مشغول اوله‌جغم . ٥ اوراجه بر مُصَحِّح تدارك٣ ايتسه‌ڭز اولماز می ؟ — مُدَقِّق٤ بر مُصَحِّح بولمق پك مُشكلدر . ٦ وابور صامسونه پك كيج مواصلات ايتمشدر . عجبا روزكار مُخَالِف می ايش ؟ — اوت افندم !

Words. 1. *mud'dét* the length (of time). 2. *badéhou* afterwards. 3. to procure, to find. 4. *múdaq'qiq* (Sub. Part. of *tédqiq*).

روزكارك مُخالَفَتی اولمازسه ایكی كوندن واصل اوله‌بیلیر ایدی.
۷ انیشته‌كز تَقاعُد چیقدی می؟ — اوت، افندم! سایه پادشاهیده
بشیوز غروش مَعاش ایله متقاعِد اولدیلر. ۸ بو كتابك مُحَرّری كیمدر؟ —
مرذیفونده واقع آناطولیه قوله‌جی لسان عثانی مُعَلِّمی اوحانِس آغوبیان
افندی در. ۹ بو باغچه‌نك مُتَصَرّفی آماسیه متصرّفی سعادتلو بكر
پاشا حضرتلری درلر.

ترجمه ۱۳۴ Translation 134.

1. Who are your guests? — Mr. Gulian the Armenian
teacher of the College, and Dr. Nahad the translator of
'Hamlet'. 2. Who is the author of that remarkable
dictionary[1]? — It is the Rev. M. Aucher. 3. Have the
inspectors come whom the governor wished to send?
4. Though they have come, yet, having a very pressing[2]
engagement[3], they have not been able to do anything.
5. Who bound the book you have in your hand? —
Mr. Arshag, who is a very[4] skilful binder. 6. Are you
able to speak good Turkish? — Yes, I have attained[5]
the ability[6] to do so through your kindness[7]. 7. What
kind of a work[8] is the book which the engineer has
written? — It is translated from the Armenian: it is
an excellent (complete) work, illustrated[9] with numerous
pictures. 8. Are the compositors, who are setting up[10]
this book in Mr. Groos' printing-house, Armenians? —
No, Sir, all the compositors at Mr. Groos' are Germans.

1. *loughét kitabî.* 2. *músta'jél.* 3. *maslahat.* 4. *mahir, oustad.*
5. *késb ét."* 6. *iqtidar.* 7. *sayéyi aliñizdé.* 8. *ésér.* 9. *múzéy'yén,*
mousavvér (from *tézyin, tasveer*). 10. *tértib ét.", dizmék.*

مكالمه Conversation.

اجوبه *Éjvibé.*	اسئله *Ésilé.*
اعلا مجلَّد در افندم • بزم مكتب مجلّدخانه‌سنده دها چوق كوزللری تجلید اولونویور.	مُطالعه بویوردقلری كتاب جلدلی می جلدسز می؟
معلِّم موسیو هَریكك هَتیله مُكَمَّل صورنده عثمانلیجه‌یه ترجمه اولونغشدر.	كتاب مُقدَّس لسانِ عثمانیه‌یه كیم ترجمه ایتمشدر؟

مُطالعه بویوردقلری كتاب جلدلی می

مطبعهلردهکی مُصَحِّحک خِدمتی پك   نه دیتِك افندم ! مُرتَّبلرك یاپدِقلری
مُعْتَنَا می ؟   هزاران خطالری او تصحیح ایدر .

سَیّاحلر نه یاپدیلر ؟   مسلّح اولهرق اول مُرتَفع داغك
                           دیهسنهقدر چیقدیلر .

مُقَاوله سنداتی تحریر وتنظیم   ایكی قطعه اولهرق تنظیم اولِندقدنصوكره ؛
اولونهبیلدیلر می ؟   طرفَین امضالهرق تَعاطی ایلهدیلر .

"اقوال حکیمانه وجُمَل ادیبیهده" لِسان حقنده نه مُطالعه ایلهدیكز ؟

"دنیاده لِساندن اعلا نه تَصَوُّر اولونهبیلِیر ؟ لِسان رابطهٔ مَعیشَت و مَدَنیَت
مِفتاح عُلوم وُ معرِفت ، تُرجمانِ حکمت و حقیقتدر . اونك واسطهسیله شهرلر
بنا وَ قوملر اداره اولونور . تعلیم وُ تدریس وَ اِقناع وُ اِسکات اونكله
اجرا ایدیلیر . مَحاکِم وُ مَجالِسده اونك واسطهسیله حُکم ورَأی اعطا اولونور .
وَ وَظائفك اك مُقَدَّسی اولان عِبادات اونكله ایفا ایدیلیر" .   ﴿ازوب﴾

تعلیم قرائت Reading Exercise.

مَجالِسِ اداره* Administrative Councils.

هر ولایت وَ لوا وَ قضا مرکزلرنده بر مَجلِسِ اداره وار در . اِشبو
مَجلِس ، اعضای[1] طبیعیه[1] وَ اعضای مُنتَخَبهدن[1] مُرَکَّبدر[2] . اعضای
طبیعیه ؛ ولایتده : حاکِم[3] ، مُفتی[4] ، دَفتردار[5] ، مکتوبجی[6] ایله ولایت
مَرکزِندهکی مِللِ غیرِ مُسلِمه[7] رُؤَسای[8] روحانیهسندن[9] عِبارت در .
لواده کذلك : حاکِم[3] وَ مُفتی[4] وَ محاسبهجی[5] وَ تحریرات مدیری[6]
ایله مرکزِ لواده بولونان مِللِ غیرِ مُسلِمه[7] رؤسای[8] روحانیهسندن[9]
عبارتدر . قضاده دخی : نائب[3] وَ مُفتی[4] بلده وَ مال مدیری[5]

Words. * *Méjalisi Idaré* (pl. of *méjlis*). 1. *aza* members (pl.
of *ouzv*); *tabiyiyé* natural (§§ 580, 656); *mûntakhab* chosen, elected
(fayil of *intikhab*) 2. *mûrék'kéb* composed (fayil of *térkeeb*). 3. *hakim*
judge, a qadi (fayil of *hûkm*); *nayib* a judge-substitute (fayil of
niyabét). 4. *mûfti* the officer who answers questions in the Canon
Law of Islam (fayil of *ifta*). 5. *déftérdar, mouhasébéji, mal mûdiri*
the controllers of revenue and expenditure in Vilayét, Liva and
Qaza. 6. *méktoubjou, tahrirat mûdiri, tahrirat kîatibi* the Chief
Secretaries in Vilayét, Liva and Qaza. 7. *mûslim* Moslem (fayil
of *islam*); *ghayri-mûslim* non-Moslem (§ 695 [10]). 8. *roués'sa* heads,
chiefs (pl. of *réyis*). 9. *rouhanee* spiritual (§ 580 g).

وَ تَحرِيرات كاتبى⁶ ۰ وَ ملل غِـير مسلمه⁷ رؤساى⁸ روحانيه‌سندن⁹
عبارتدر¹⁰ ۰ خرِيستيانلر وَ يهوديلر ملل غيرِ مسلمه‌يى تشكيل ايدر ۰

اعضاى منتخبه : نصفى¹¹ مسلم⁷ وَ نصفِ ديگرى غيرِ مسلم اولمق
اوزره درت كـشيدن مركَّب² اولوب ؛ بونلرڭ انتخـابى¹² اهـالييه
عائد¹³ در ۰ مجالسِ اداره قضانڭ امور اداره‌سنه نظارت ايدر ۰

10. *ibarét* composed. 11. *nisf* half. 12. *intikhab ét."* to choose;
election (VIII. of *nûkhbé*). 13. *ayid* belonging (fayil of *avdét*).

Note. Consult the Reading Exercise, page 126.

درس ۵۱ Lesson 51.

جمع مكسر Broken or Irregular Plurals.

§ 636. The Regular or Sound Plurals are made
(as we have seen) by the addition of ين -*een* (m.) or
ات -*at* (f.) to the Singular, without any change in the
structure of the words. But in the case of Irregular
or Broken Plurals (*Jém'i Mûkés'sér*) the structure or the
form of the Singular is broken, as has been stated in
a previous lesson (§ 571).

It is impossible to give all the measures of Broken
plurals here, because they are very numerous. But
those which are in common use in Ottoman, may be
formed into the following groups.

§ 637. Nouns of the measures فقال ؛ فقله ؛ فقل form
their plural as follows:

§ 638. S. فَقْل *faql:* Plural = فُقُول *fouqoul:* as:
حَرْف *harf* letter: حُرُوف *hourouf:* حَدّ √حَدَدَ *hadd* boundary:
بَيْت *béyt* house: بُيُوت *bûyout:* نَقْد *naqd* cash:
حُدُود *houdoud:* نُقُود *nouqoud.* شَرْط a condition = شُروط ؛ حَقّ a right = حقوق

§ 639. S. a. فَقْل *faql* : b. فَقَل *faqal* : c. فِقْل *fiql* :
d. فُقْل *fouql*: Pl. = اَفْقَال *éfqal*: as:

a. وَقْت *vaqt* time: دَوْر *dévr* ' عَصْر *'asr* : اَوْقَات *évqat* :
century اَشْكَال: *édvar* ' عَصَار *'asar* : شَكْل *shékl* shape: اَدْوَار
ésh-krāl : لون *colour* : اَلْوَان ؛ نَوْع ؛ اَنْوَاع ؛ مَال (مَوَلَ) : اَمْوَال.

b. سَبَب *sébéb* reason: اَسْبَاب *ésbab* ؛ خَبَر *khabér* news:
اَخْبَار *akhbar* ؛ وَلَد *véléd* son: اَوْلَاد *évlad* ؛ عَدَد number: اَعْداد.

c. صِنْف *sînf, sinîf* class: اَصْنَاف *ésnaf* ؛ طِفْل *tîfl* child:
اَطْفَال *étfal', at'fal* ؛ شِعْر poem: اَشْعَار ؛ فِكْر : اَفْكَار opinion.

d. مُلْك *mûlk* property: اَمْلَاك *émlak* ؛ حُكْم *hûkm* decision:
a'za اَعْضَاء : عُضْو *ouzv* : موral اَخْلَاق : خُلْق ؛ *ahkiām* اَحْكَام.

§ 640. S. فُقْلَه *fouqlé, fouqlét*: Pl. = فُقَل *fouqal*: as:
نُسْخَه *nûskhé* copy: نُسَخ *nûsakh* ؛ صُورَت *sourét* manner, way;
picture: صُوَر *souvér* ؛ قُلَّه *qoul'lé* tower: قُلَل *qoulél* ؛ جُمْله : جُمَل.

§ 641. S. فِقْلَت' فِقْلَه *fiqlét*: Pl. = فِقَل *fiqal*: as:
نِعْمَت *niymét* favour: نِعَم *niyam* ؛ مِلَّت *mil'lét* nation:
مِلَل *milél* ؛ عِبْرَت *'ibrét* example: عِبَر *'ibér* ؛ بَلْده *béldé* : بِلَاد.

§ 642. S. فَقَال *féqal* and فِقَال *fiqal*: Pl. = اَفْقَلَه
éfqilé: as:
زَمَان *zéman* time: اَزْمِنَه *ézminé* times ؛ جَوَاب *jévab* answer:
اَجْوِبَه *éjvibé* ؛ طَعَام *ta-'am* food: اَطْعِمَه *et-'i'mé* ؛ مَتَاع' اَمْتِعَه.

§ 643. The plural of the Subjective Participles of
the Primitive Triliteral Infinitives are formed on the
following models; as: a. فَوَاقِل ' b. فُقَّال ' c. فَقَلَه ' d. فُقَلَا
févaqil, fouq'qal, féqalé, fouqala:

a. سَاحِل *sahil* sea-coast: Pl. = سَوَاحِل *sévahil* sea-shores ؛ جَامِع
jami' mosque: جَوَامِع *jévami'* ؛ جَانِب *janib* side: جَوَانِب *jévanib*.

b. تَاجِر *tajir* merchant: Pl. = تجار *tûj'jar* ؛ حَاكِم *hakim* judge:
حكام *houk'kiām* ؛ حَاضِر *hazir* present: حضّار *houz'zar*.

c. كَاتِب *kiâtib* clerk: Pl. = كتبه *kétébé* clerks ؛ تَابِع *tabi*ع follower, servant: تبعه *té-ba*ع*a* subjects ؛ وارث *varis* heir: ورثه *vérésé*.

d. عاقل *'aqil* wise: Pl. = عقلا *'ouqala* wisemen ؛ عالم *'alim* فَاضِل *fazil* learned ؛ علما ، فُضَلا *ouléma, fouzala* doctors of Canon Law ؛ شاعر *shayir* poet: شعرا *shou*ع*ara* ؛ جاهل = جُهَلَا ؛ صالح = صُلَحا .

The Subj. Participles which end in ى *-i*, form their plurals as follows:

S. والى *vali* governor: Pl. = ولاة *vûlat* ؛ قاضى *qadi* judge: عُصَاة = a rebel عاصى ؛ رُوَاة = historian راوى ؛ *qoudat* فُضاة .

§ 644. The plurals of the nouns derived from the Subjective Participle by the addition of ه or ة ، ت (-*é*, -*ét*) [§ 582], are formed according to the first measure *févaqil*: as:

a. لَازِمَه *lazîmé* necessity: Pl. = لَوَازِم *lévazim* necessities ؛ فَائِدَه *fayidé* benefit = فَوَائِد *févayid* ؛ قَاعِدَه *qayidé* a rule = قَوَاعِد *qavayid* ؛ عَاطِفَت *'atîfét* kindness = عَوَاطِف *'avatîf*.

b. مَادَّه *mad'dé* subject = مَوَادّ *mévadd'* ؛ حَاسَّه *has'se* sense = حَوَاسّ *havass'* ؛ خَاصَّه *khas'sé* peculiarity = خَوَاصّ *khavass'*.

§ 645. The plural of the Adjective of Quality (§ 606, model فَقِيل) is formed on the model of a. فُقَلَا ، b. فِقَال ، c. اَفْقِلَا *fouqala, fiqal, éfqila*:

a. فَقِير *faqir* poor: Pl. = فُقَرَا *fouqara* the poor ؛ وَزِير *vézir* a minister of state = وُزَرَا *vûzéra* viziers, viceroys ؛ حَكِيم *hakeem* sage, philosopher = حُكَمَا *houkéma* ؛ رَفِيق = رُفَقا .

b. كَبِير *kébir* great = كِبَار *kibar* grandees ؛ كَرِيم *kérim* noble = كِرَام *kiram* ؛ فَخِيم *fékhim* illustrious = فِخَام *fikham*.

c. قَرِيب *qarib* relative = اَقْرِبَا *aqrîba* ؛ حَبِيب *habib* friend = اَحِبَّا *ahîb'ba* ؛ طَبِيب *tabib* physician = اَطِبَّا *atîb'ba* ؛ نَبِى *nébee* prophet ؛ اَنْبِیَا *énbiya* ؛ صَدِيق = اَصْدِقا ؛ شَقِى = اَشْقِیا .

23*

§ 646. The plural of the nouns formed from Adjectives of Quality by the addition of ه or ة ، ت (-*é*, -*ét*, -*at*) [§ 582] is made on the model فَقَائِل *féqayil*; as:

جزره *jéziré* island = جزائر *jézayir* islands ؛ وظيفه *vazifé* duty = وظائف *vézayif* ؛ نصيحت *nasihat* advice = نصائح *nésayih*́ ؛ خزينه *khaziné* treasure = خزائن *khazayin* ؛ سفينه *séfiné* ship = سفائن *séfayin* ؛ صحيفه *séhifé* = صحائف *sahayif*; قبيله *qabilé* = قبائل *qabayil*; حقيقت *haqiqat* = حقائق *haqayiq*.

§ 647. The most important classes of nouns that form their plurals regularly are the Derivative Triliteral Infinitives and the Participles formed from those Infinitives. All these measures and their Participles take the plural in ين -*een* (m.) and ات -*at* (f.) [§§ 573—78].

The General Measure.

§ 648. All original Quadriliterals and most words in which the Triliteral root is increased by one or more letters[1], form their broken plurals on one and the same model, and this consisting of three syllables. The first of these syllables has an *ûstûn*, the second takes an *élif* and the third has an *ésré* for its vowel sound (— ٹ ١ ٹ ٹ = -*é* -*a* -*i*-). If there is an *élif* or *vav* in the last syllable, it is changed into *yé* (-*é* -*a* -*ee*); as:

Singular مفرد *Mûfréd*́	Plural جمع *Jém*́	
مملكت *mémlékét* country:	ممالك *mémalik*	Nouns with *mim.*
معرفت *ma'rifét* knowledge:	معارف *mé'arif*	
مكتب *méktéb* school:	مكاتب *mékĭatib*	
مكتوب *méktoob* letter:	مكاتيب *mékĭateeb*	Object. Partic.
مزمور *mézmoor* psalm:	مزامير *mézameer*	
مفتاح *miftah* key:	مفاتيح *méfateeh*́	N. of Loc.
تدبير *tédbeer* plan:	تدابير *tédabeer*	The measure *téf-qeel*.
تاريخ *tareekh* date; history:	تواريخ *tévareekh*́	
اصغر *ésghér* lesser:	آصاغر *ésaghir*	N. of Superiority.

---

[1] *i. e.* the Nouns with *Mim* (§§ 597—99), the Primitive Obj.

سلطان *soultan* Sultan: سلاطين *sélateen*   { The measure *fouqlan*.

جمهور *jûmhoor* republic: جماهير *jémaheer*

اقنوم *ûqnûm* a person (of Trinity):   اقانيم *éqaneem*

قانون *qanoun* law: قوانين *qavaneen*   } Quadriliteral nouns.

عسكر *askér* soldier: عَساكِرْ *'asakir*

ترجمه *térjémé* translation: تراجم *térajim*

مطالعات *Mûta-laɣat* Remarks.

§ 649. There are some nouns which form double plurals, these have often different meanings; the principal are:

حرف *harf* letter: حروف *houroof*:   حروفات *houroofat*.

دين *déyn* debt: ديون *douyoon*:   ديونات *douyoonat*.

اسم *ism* name: اسماء *ésma* names: اسامى *ésami* a list.

رسم *résm* a due: رسوم *rousoom* manners, custom:

رسومات *rousoomat* tolls, dues: مراسم *mérasim* ceremonies.

بيت *béyt* verse; house: بيوت *buyoot* houses;   ابيات *ébyat* verses.

شيخ *shéykh* chief: شيوخ *shûyoukh* old men.

مشايخ *méshayikh* chiefs.

راهب *rahib* a Christ. monk: رهبان *rouh'ban*:   رهابين *réhabeen'*.

§ 650. Other Arabic nouns which form their plurals irregularly occur in Ottoman. The chief of these are:

ام *ûmm* mother: امهات *ûm'méhat* mothers.

انسان *insan* man (homo):   ناس *nas* human beings.

قريه *qaryé* village: قرا *qoura* villages.

اسود *ésvéd* black: سودان *soudan* negroes; the Soudan.

اله *ilah'* god: آلهه *alihé* deities.

اهل *éhl* people: اهالى *éhali* inhabitants.

ارمنى *érméni* Armenian: آرامنه *araminé* Armenians.

سعى *say* labour: مساعى *mésayi* labours.

Participle (§ 604), the Noun of Superiority (§ 609), the measures *téfqeel*, *fouqlan*, etc.

§ 651. There are some very common Arabic plurals which are used in Ottoman as singular nouns and take a Turkish as well as an Arabic plural termination (§ 512); as:

معلوماتلر *malûmatlar* knowledge. تحریراتلر *tahriratlar* writings.

فیّاتلر *fiyatlar* prices. اعضالر *azalar* members.

وقوعاتلر *vouqou'atlar* events. اولادلر *évladlar* children.

اهالیلر *éhalilér* inhabitants. تجّارلر *tûjjarlar* merchants.

عملهلر *amélélér* labourers. اشیالر *ésh'yalar* furnitures.

دیارلر *diyarlar* countries. اصنافلر *ésnaflar* handicrafts.

§ 652. There are some Persian or Turkish nouns, which have assumed Arabic plural terminations. These are mere barbarisms or solecisms (§ 507):

چیفتلكات *chiftlikîāt* (Imperial) farms; (as چیفتلكات همایون t.

كیش *gélish* coming: كیشات *gélishat* talent, success. t.

سبزه *sébzé* vegetable: سبزوات *sébzévat* vulg. *zarzavat*. p.

خرده *khûrdé* small: خردوات *khourdavat* smallware. p.

فرمان *férman* firman: فرامین *férameen* edicts. p.

كیدیش *gidish* going: كیدیشات *gédishat* conduct. t.

تعلیم ۱۳٥ Exercise 135.

State the measure, the number and the meaning of the following words:

۱ كتاب ، كُتُبْ ، كاتِب ، مكتوب ، كتبه ، مُكاتَبَه ،
مَكاتَبْ ، مُكاتَبَات . ۲ خُروج ، اِخراج ، اخراجات ، خارج ، خارجیه ،
مَخرَجْ ، مُخرِج . ۳ نُزول ، نازِل ، مَنزِلْ ، اِنزال ، تَنزیل ، تَنزیلات ،
مَنازِل . ٤ ذِكْر ، مذكور ، تَذكِرَه ، مذكوره ، تَذَكُّرْ ، مُذاكَره ،
مُذاكَرات ، تَذَكُّرَات . ٥ قَتْل ، قاتِل ، قاتلَین ، قاتله ، مُقاتَلَه ، مقتول ،
مُقاتلات ، مَقتولِین ، مَقتولَین ، مَقتِلْ ، مَقتَلَهْ . ٦ جَبر ، مجبور ،
مجبوریت . ۷ عِلم ، عالِم ، مَعلوم ، معلومات ، اَعلَم ، عَلِیم ، عَلّام ، اِعلام ،
تعلیم ، تعلیمات ، مُعَلِّم ، مُعَلَّم . ۸ حُسْن ، اَحسَن ، اَحاسِن ، تَحسین ،

مَحَاسِنْ ، مُحَسَّنَات . ٩ وُصُول ، واصِل ، مَوصُول ، ايصال ، مُوَاصَلَتْ .
١٠ دُخُول ، اِدْخال ، اِدْخالات ، مَدْخَلْ ، مَدَاخِلْ ، مُدَاخَله ، مُداخلات ،
دُخُولِه . ١١ قُدس ، قُدُوس ، قُدسىّ ، قُدسِيَتْ ، تَقْدِيس ، مَقْدِسِى ،
مُقَدَّسْ . ١٢ ضَرب ، ضارِب ، مَضْرُوب ، اِضْطِراب ، مُضْطَرِبْ .
١٣ وَسْوَسَه ، مُوَسْوِسْ . ١٤ طَنْطَنَه ، مُطَنْطَن ، صَيقَل ، مُصَيقَلْ ،
عُنْوَان ، مَعْنَوْنْ . ١٥ مُسْتَشْرِقْ ، مُسْتَشْرِقِين (orientalists) ؛ اِتّصال .

ترجمه ١٣٦ Translation 136.

Form the derivatives of the following words:

1. The act of looking (نَظَر), who looks, looked at, to
wait (VIII), who waits, who is waited for. 2. Ignorance
(جَهالَت), ignorant; unknown; ignorant people. 3. The
act of sending (رَسالت), who is sent (apostle), two apostles,
apostles; to send (IV)؛ who sends؛ messenger. 4. To
burn (حَرق), fire (§ 606), to be burnt (VIII), burning, burnt.
5. To save (خلاص), to desire to save (X), saviour, saved.

6. To write (كَتب), book; clerk; written, letter; a place
where to write, school; schools, letters, two schools,
two letters; to correspond (IV). 7. News (خَبر); to give
news, to inform (IV), informer, informed; to communicate
(III), correspondent. 8. Change the word مِلْك into fayil,
méfoul; into noun with *mim*; to possess (I, X), to give
possession (II), to take possession (V), fayil of X, and Pl.

تعليم ١٣٧ Exercise 137.

١ سلطان حميد خان ثانى حَضرتلرى سلاطين عثمانيهنك اوتوز
اوچنجيسى در . ٢ عثمانلى ملتى مِلَلِ مُعظَّمهدن بريسيدر . ٣ بو قوناغك

املاك وير كيسى[1] ۷٤۰ غروشدر · ٤ وره ثه سنك جملهسى دخى تبعهٔ
دولت عليهدن ايديلر · ٥ ايران شعراسندن اك مشهورى حافظِ شيرازى در ·
٦ شهرك كبار اهاليسندن بعضيلرى بو هفته سواحله مُتَوَجِّهاً[2] حركت
ايلهديلر[3] · ۷ مأمورين كرامدن اكثريسى بنم احِبّامدن درلر · ٨ صَرف
قواعدينى[4] اَزبَر ايتديكز مى ؟ اكر ايتديكز ايسه بونك فوائدِ كثيرهسى
وار در · ۹ مكاتبك مُحَسّناتى پك چوقدر · اورادن مُنتهى چيقان فُقَرا
اولادلرى حُكَّاَ ، وُزَرا ، حُكَّام ، عُلَما و كَتَبَه سلكنه[5] داخل اولورلر[6] ·

Words. 1. *émlak vérgisi* property tax. 2. *mûtévéj'jihén*
toward (fayil of *térej'jûh* to turn, V. of *véjh'*). 3. *haréket ét."* to
start. 4. *qavayid* rules (pl. of *qayidé*). 5. *silk* career. 6. to enter.

ترجمه ۱۳۸ Translation 138.

1. This book contains[1] 320 figures[2]. 2. The eastern
boundaries[3] of Turkey are Russia and Persia. 3. I have
a gospel printed[4] in very small characters. 4. The
churches do not pay[5] property taxes. 5. The English
nation is one of the greatest nations of Europe[6]. 6. Are
those physicians among your relatives? 7. They made
a journey[7] towards the islands on board the ships. 8. It
is written in the Psalms "Lead[8] me to the rock that
is higher than I". 9. Where is the list of expenses?
— Here it is, the clothes bought from the merchants
are inserted[9] in this list with their prices. 10. The
success of the vegetables and flowers is perfect[10] this year.

Words. 1. *havi dir.* 2. *éshkial* (pl. of *shékl*). 3. *houdood*
(pl. of *hadd*). 4. *matbou'* (méfoul of *tab'-*). 5. *té-é-diyé ét."* (II. of
éda). 6. *Avropa.* 7. *séyahat.* 8. *ihda éylé* (IV. of *hidayét*). 9. *dakhil*
(fayil of *doukhoul*). 10. *mûkémmél* (méfoul of *tékmil*).

مكالمه Conversation.

Columbus' Egg. (Continued.) قولومبوسك يومورطهسى (مابعد)

بوجواب حضّاره[1] نه تأثير ايتدى ؟ 　　حضّارك حيرت[2] و مراقنى[3] جلب
(۳۰۸ صحيفهيه مُراجعَت يوريله) 　　و تحريك ايلهدى ·

Words. 1. *houz'zar* pl. of *hazir* (§ 643 b). 2. *hayrét* wonder.
3. *méraq* curiosity; *jélb ou tahreek ét."* to instigate and arouse.

بَرّ جَديدك كاشِفى عَلَيْهِنده عَداوتله
مَمْلو اولان پرنس موسى اليه ايله
مَدْعُوّينِ سائرين بو تكليفه نصورتله
مُوَفَّقَت ايله‌ديلر وَ نتيجه‌سى⁴ نه
اولدى؟

حُضّار بوڭا مُوَفَّق⁵ اوله يلديلر مى؟
قرستوف دوردوره‌يلديمى؟

[دیمش؟]

حُضّار بونى كورونجه قرستوفه نه
اويله دكل مى؟ قير دقدنصوكره هركس
دوردوره‌ماز مى؟ هُنَر و مَعْرفت
برشیئى قَبْلَ المُشاهَده مى يوخسه
بَعْدَ المْشاهده مى وُجوده كتير
مكده در؟

يومورطه‌نك حكايه‌سيله آمريقانك
كشفى بيننده نه مُنَاسَبَت¹² واردر؟

نتيجه‌سى شو اولدى كه ؛ بر سَبَت
يومورطه اِحضار اولنوب : قرالدن
باشلايه‌رك هپيسى ده يومورطه‌يى
سيورى طرفى اوزرينه دوردورمغه
چاليشديلر . [ايله‌ديلر.]

نه مُنَاسَبَت⁶! هركس اِظهار⁷ عَجز⁸
اوت افندم ! سيورى طرفنى قيرمقله
يومورطه‌يى دوردورمغه مُقْتَدِر⁹
اولدى .

دیشلرکه بو يولده هركس دوردوره‌يلير .
طوغرى ! ايشته معرفت¹⁰ اورايى،
ايلك آوّل دوشونوب ياپمقده در .
قولومبوس دخى بركرّه آمريقانك
يولنى ارائه¹¹ ايلدكدن صوكره هر
كس ده اورايه كيده‌بيلير .

آمريقانك يولى بولوندقدنصوكره ٬
هركس اورايه كمالِ سهولتله¹³
كيده‌بيلير .

4. *nétijé* the end, conclusion (§§ 582, 646). 5. *mouvaf'faq* successful (*méfoul* of *tév'feeq*). 6. *mûnasébét* connexion (III. of *nisbét*); *né-!* not at all! 7. *izhar* to show, confess (IV. of *zouhour*). 8. *ajz* inability. 9. *mûqtédir* able (VIII. of *iqtidar*). 10. *marifét* skill, talent (n. with *mim* of *irfan*); *ilk évvél* first of all, in the first place. 11. *irayé* to show (IV. of *rouyét*). 12. relation, connexion. 13. *kéma'li souhoulétlé* with the greatest ease (§ 695, 11).

---

٥۲ درس Lesson 52.

The Agreement of Adjectives with Nouns.

§ 653. The union of two Arabic nouns, or of an Arabic noun with an Arabic adjective (*Izafét*) according to the Persian system has been already mentioned. The examples given (§§ 517, 565) were all masculine and singular, both adjectives and nouns.

§ 654. When an Arabic adjective is placed before a noun, in Ottoman it generally remains invariable, whether the nouns which it qualifies are masculine or feminine, singular or plural; as:

خير دعا *khayr douva* a blessing: عالى حسيات *ali hissiyat* noble feelings.

§ 655. But when the Arabic noun is feminine or plural and the adjective follows the noun, then the adjective must agree with it in number and gender.

§ 656. Read carefully the following rules:

1. masc. sing. nouns require the adjective to be masc. singular.
2. fem. sing. » » » » » » fem. singular.
3. masc. dual » » » » » » masc. dual.
4. masc. plural » » » » » » {regular masc. plural or broken plural.
5. fem. plural » » » » » » fem. plural or sing.
6. broken plural » » » » » » {fem. sing. or broken plural.

§ 657. All broken plurals, the names of letters and cities are regarded as feminine.

§ 658. مثاللر *Misal'lér* Examples.

1. دعاى خير *douva'yi khayr* a good prayer; blessing.

بحر احمر *bah'ri ahmér* the Red Sea.

2. الف ممدوده *éli'fi mémdoudé* elongated Elif (§ 29 d).

قوة عظيمه *qouvvé'yi azimé* great power.

3. طرفين مرقومين *taraféy'ni mérqouméyn* those two parties.

حرفين متجانسين *harféy'ni mûtéjaniséyn* two homogeneous letters.

4. مورخين مشهورين *mûvérrikhee'ni méshhoureen'* the celebrated historians.

مأمورين فخام *mé-é-mouree'ni fikham* illustrious officers.

5. صفات الهيه *sîfa'tî ilaheeyé* the Divine attributes.

معلومات مهمه *malouma'tî mûhim'mé* important knowledge.

ذوات عاليات *zéva'tî aliyat* great personages.

6. امور مهمه *oumou'rou mouhim'mé* important affairs.

اجداد عظام *éjda'dî îzam* venerable ancestors.

مكاتب مليه *méktati'bi milliyé* national schools.

§ 659. متنوّعات *Mûténévviyat* Miscellaneous.

آيَتِ كَرِيمَه *ayé'ti kérimé* the sacred verse, the golden text.

دينِ مقدّس *din'i mouqad'dés* the Holy Religion.

دولَتِ عليه *Dévlé'ti Aliyé* the Sublime Government (Turkey).

سامعونِ كرام *samiyou'nou kiram* honorable hearers.

ازمنَهٔ قديمَه *ézminé'yi qadimé* ancient times.

تواريخِ عتيقه *tévarikh'i atiqa* ancient histories.

تبعَهٔ صادقه *téba-a'-yi sadiqa* loyal subjects.

سواحلِ بحريه *sévahil'i bahriyé* marine coasts.

اقصاى شرق *aqsa'yi sharq* the Furthest East.

§ 660. غلطاتِ مشهوره *Galatatî Mésh'houré* Barbarisms.

طوپخانَهٔ عامره *topkhané'yi amiré* Imperial Arsenal of Ordnance.

مطبخِ عامره *matba'khî amiré*   »   Kitchen.

ترسانَهٔ عامره *térsané'yi amiré*   »   Dock-yard.

قوّهٔ الكتريقيه *qouvvé'yi éléktriqiyé* electrical force.

آسياى صغرا *Asiya'yî soughra* Asia Minor.

تعليم ١٣٩ Exercise 139.

١ مرحوم¹ اولانلرى 'جنابِ الله جانلرينه رحمت ايلهسين' ديهرك
خير دعا ايله ذكر² ايتمهلى · ٢ مرذيفون قيزلر قولهجنك محترقْ اولان³
بناسنك مجدّداً⁴ انشاسى⁵ ضمننده⁶ ارادهٔ سنيه⁷ حضرتِ پادشاهى
شرفصادر⁸ اولمشدر · ٣ دنيانك قطعاتِ بعيدهسنده⁹ انكليزلرك
مستملكات¹⁰ متعدّدهسى واردر · ٤ مورّخينِ مشهورينك روايات

Words. 1. *mérhoum* deceased (mefoul of *rahmét*). 2. *zikr ét."*
to remember, to mention. 3. *mûh'téréq* burnt (mefoul of VIII.).
4. *mûjéd'dédén* newly (mefoul of *téjdid*). 5. *insha* to build.
6. *zimnînda* for. 7. *iradé* decree, command (VI. of *rivad; séneeyé*
sublime, exalted). 8. *shéréfsadîr* which has issued in honour.
9. *qita-at* parts of the world = countries (pl. of *qît-a*); *bayid*
distant (from *boud'* § 606). 10. *mûstémlikîat* colonies (pl. of *fayil*
of X. of *mûlk*); *mûtéad'did* numerous (fayil of *té-ad-dûd*, '*adéd* V).

و نقلیاتینه¹¹ نظراً¹² ، أزمنهٔ قدیمهده آسیای صغرا‌ده ملل متعدده میدانه

کلمشلر و ینه محو¹³ اولمشلر. ٥ حضرت ابراهم ؛ افندیمزك اجداد

عظامی آراسنده معدود در. ٦ دین مقدسمزك مکاتب ملیهده اولاد

و اطفال وطنه¹⁴ صورت لایقهده¹⁵ تعلیم و تدریسی ضمننده معلمون كرام

طرفندن كوكی كبی غیرت و همّت اولنمقده در. ٧ تدبیرده قصور ایدن

تقدیره بهانه بولور.

11. *rivayét, naql ét."* to narrate, to recount, to tell. 12. *nézarén* according (§ 682 b). 13. *mahv ol."* to disappear. 14. *atfal* children (pl. of *tîfl*). 15. *sourét* manner; *layiq* suitable.

ترجمه ١٤٠ Translation 140.

1. Some of the illustrious officers of the Turkish government were present at the commencement[1] exercises of the College. 2. You will find here all important[2] knowledge concerning the settlement[3] of the wretched immigrants[4] in South Africa[5]. 3. Dr. Carrington is one of the most eminent physicians. 4. Because of some important business[6] he was unable[7] to come here. 5. One of the loyal subjects began[8] to speak[9] and said 'Honourable hearers'. 6. I have Moses of Khorene's[10] and Agathangelos'[11] ancient Armenian histories[12].

1. *tévziyi mûktafat résmi* or *yévmi makhsous* = day of prizes. 2. *mouhimm'*. 3. *isktan* (IV. of *sûkûn*). 4. *mouhajiree'ni maghdoureen*. 5. *Afriqa'yi jénoubi*. 6. *mésali'hi mûhimmé sébébiylé*. 7. *mûqtédir olamamaq*. 8. *ibtidar ét."* 9. *kélam*. 10. *Mosés Khorini*. 11. *Aqatangélos*. 12. *mûvérrikhee'ni qadimé'yi Araminédén*.

مکالمه Conversation.

طوپخانه عامره‌یی كزمه كز اولمش میدر؟	خیر افندم ترسانه عامره‌یی كزدم.
بو یاز تعطیلنی نره‌ده امرار ایده‌جكسكز؟	آسیای صغراده بولنان متعدد بلاد
مقصدیكز بر سیاحت می ایتمكدر؟	قدیمه و برانه‌لرینی كزه‌جكم.
تلغرافلر نه ایله ایشله‌یورلر؟	قوهٔ الكتریقیه ایله ایشله‌یورلر.
بو كونكی درسك آیتِ كریمه‌سی نه‌در؟	"عیسایی كورمك ایسته‌ریز" آیتیدر.
بو آیت نره‌ده محرّردر؟	اناجیل اربعه‌دن انجیل یوحنّاك
	١٢ نجی باب ٢٢ نجی آیتنده موجود در.

'آر طوغرول، نه‌دیمکدر وَ کیمدر؟   عثمانلیلرك اجدادِ عظامندن بری اولوب
'جسور طوغرول، معناسنده در.

تعلیم قرائت   Reading Exercise.

دقتدن منبعث کشفیات*
Inventions Resulting from Observation.

تاریخِ۱ اختراعات۲ ، هر شیئه دقت ایتمکلکك لزومِ۳
حقیقیسنی۴ اثبات۵ ایدن امثالِ۶ کثیره‌یی حاوی۷ در ٠ اختراعاتك
اکثریسی۸ ؛ یا ذکیٰ۹ بر عمله‌نك۱۰ ، وَ یا۱۱ مُتفنِّن۱۲ بر عالِمك نظرِ
دقتنه۱۳ تصادف ایدن۱۴ صورتِ ظاهره‌ده۱۵ معناسز۱۶ بر شیئدن نشأت
ایدر۱۷ ٠ مثلا۱۸ :

دکیز، سواحله بر طاقِ اوتلرله برابر آورویاجه مَجهول بر نوع دکیز
یوصونلری۱۹ آثار ٠ اسمی جسمی۲۰ اول آنه۲۱ قدر هر کسجه نامعلوم۲۲
اولان بر گمیجی اونلری طوپلار۲۳ ؛ وَ دقتله مُعَاینه۲۴ و تدقیق۲۵
ایتدکدنصوکره ، بونلرك قِطَعَاتِ بعیده‌دن کلدیکنه حکم۲۶ ایدر ،

Words and Notes. * *diq'qat* careful observation; *mûnbayis*
caused (fayil of *inbiyas*); *késhfiyat* discoveries. 1. history (II. of
érékh). 2. *ikhtira̤at* (pl.; VIII. of خرع). 3. *louzoum* necessity.
4. real. 5. *isbat ét.* to prove (IV. of *sébt*). 6. *émsal* precedents,
examples (pl. of *mésél*). 7. *havi* containing (fayil). 8. *éksérisi* the
majority. 9. *zékee* sagacious (§ 606). 10. *amélé* labourers (used
as sing. § 651). 11. *ya — ya* either — or —. 12. *mûtéfén'nin*
versed in science (fayil of *téfén'nûn* § 622). 13. *nazarî diq'qat*
consideration. 14. *tésadûf ét.* to fall under (VI. of *sadéf*). 15. *sourét*
appearance; *zahir* external (fayil of *zouhour*). 16. *mana* meaning
(n. with *mim* of عَنَیٰ); *manasîz* unimportant. 17. *néshat ét.* to come
into existence, to originate. 18. *méséla* for instance (§ 683).
19. *yosoun* moss. 20. *jism* existence. 21. *an* time. 22. *namalûm*
unknown (§§ 530, 604). 23. *toplamaq* to gather (§ 276). 24. *mou-
a-yéné* to examine (III. of *'ayn* eye). 25. *tédqiq ét.* to scrutinize
(II. of *diq'qat*). 26. *hûkm ét.* to decide judicially.

و بونكله بحرِ مُحيطكِ اوته‌سنده يكى بر دنيا كشفنى تخيّل ايدر²⁷؛ بوكا ده موفّق اولور²⁸ .

مَناسترك²⁹ برنده ، قبّه‌دن³⁰ آصيلمـش اولان بر قنديل³¹ اورته‌ده صـاللانير . مشهور بر عالم ، بو قنـديلك عيـنى وقتنده³² ، دائمـا³³ مُطَّرِد³⁴ بر صـورتده كورولن حركتـلرينه⁴¹ دقّت ايله : بر ايكى ! بر ايكى ! ديه‌رك تعقيبنه³⁵ قويولور³⁶ . مُتَهَيِّج³⁷ خانه‌سنه عودت ايدر . حكمتِ طبيعيه‌نك³⁸ الك مِهم³⁹ قواعدندن برينى ، يعنى رقّاصك⁴⁰ حركت⁴¹ ياخود اِهتِزازاتِ مُطَّرِده‌سنى كشف ايله‌دى .

(مانيه خانيم)

27. tékhay'yûl ét." to imagine (V. of khayal). 28. mouvaf'faq successful (méfoul of tévfeeq). 29. manastîr monastery. 30. qoub'bé dome. 31. qandeel a lamp. 32. ayni vaqîtda at the very moment (§ 695, 13). 33. dayima continually (adverb). 34. mout'tarîd isochronous. 35. taᶜa-qeeb to follow. 36. qoyoulmaq to go on. 37. mûtéhéy'yij excited (fayil of téhéy'yûj, V. of héyéjan). 38. hikméti-tabiyiyé natural philosophy. 39. mouhimm' important (fayil of ihmam, III. of himmét). 40. raq'qas pendulum (§ 611). 41. harékét movement; vibration.

---

۵۳ درس Lesson 53.

حرف تعريف The Arabic Definite Article.

§ 661. In the Turkish and Persian languages there is no article either definite or indefinite; but in Arabic there are definite and indefinite articles (*Harfî Tarif*, *Ténveen*) which are used in Ottoman with Arabic terms. The Ind. Article or *Ténveen* is of three kinds: *-én, -in, -oun*, applied to the end of the words (§ 48); and they are used in Ottoman as adverbs. The definite article is ال *él* 'the':

الكتاب *él-kitab* the book, البيت *él-béyt* 'the house'.

§ 662. **The Arabic Letters** are 28 in number, (پ ، چ ، ژ ، گ being peculiar to Turkish and Persian): 14 of these are called lunar and the other 14 solar letters.

§ 663. **The Solar Letters** (حروف شمسیه *Houroufou Shémseeyé*) are: ن ل ظ ط ض ص ش س ز ر ذ د ث ت.

The Lunar Letters (حروف قمریه *Houroufou Qamé-reeyé*) are: أ ب ج ح خ ع غ ف ق ك م و ه ى.

§ 664. When the Arabic Article is added to a word beginning with a solar letter, to avoid harshness of sound, the *lam* is assimilated in pronunciation to the following solar consonant for euphony, and a *shéddé* (ˇ) is put over the latter: الصّبر *és'-sabr* the patience; الدّین *éd'-din* the religion; السّلام *és'-sélam* the salutation: and not *el-sabr, él-din, él-sélam*; also:

السمت *és-sémt* zénith: pl. السموت *és-sûmout* azimuth.

§ 665. But the pronunciation of the *lam* is retained when the Article is attached to a word beginning with a lunar letter:

الحقّ *él-haqq* the right.   الجبر *él-jébr* Algebra.

الكحل *él-kûhûl* alcohol.   القلى *él-qali* alkali.

الكيا *él-kimya* alchemy.   الانبیق *él-inbiq* alembic.

العضاده *él-idadé* alidade.   الغول *él-ghoul* the thief (Algol, the star).

الحمراء *él-hamra* the Red (castle), Alhambra.

المنقح *él-mûnaqqah* almanack.

§ 666. Almost all Arabic words properly end in a vowel: *ûstûn* (-*é*) is the sign of the Accusative, *ésré* (-*i*) is the sign of the Genitive, and *éôtré* (-*a*) the sign of the Nominative; also these are left in Ottoman, yet they are retained in Arabic sentences used in Ottoman.

When a word having the Article ال is preceded by a word, that word keeps the original final vowel (-*é*, -*i*, -*ou*); the *élif* of the Article is not pronounced but slurred over, and *lam* is connected with the last vowel of the preceding word; as:

رَأْسُ ٱلْحِكْمَةِ مَخَافَةُ ٱللهِ *résû'l hikméti mékhafétou 'llahi*
the beginning of knowledge is the fear of the Lord.

كَلَامُ ٱلْمُلُوكِ مُلُوكُ ٱلْكَلَام *kélamû'l mûlouki mûloukû'l kélami* the words of kings are the kings of words.

خَلِيلُ ٱللهِ *khalilou 'llahi* the chosen friend of Good (Abraham).

Not *Résû él hikméti, mékhafétou allahi, kélamû élmûlouki.*

Note. The word ٱلله is contracted from ال 'the', إِلَه *ilah* god,

ٱلله = ٱلْ إِلَهْ *Allah* the God.

§ 667. When the *élif* of the Article is absorbed by the final vowel of the preceding word, the elision is marked by the sign ـٰ, written over the *élif* and called وصلة *vaslé* 'union'; because it unites the vowel with *lam* directly; as: خَلِيلُ ٱللهِ ، رَاسُ ٱلْحِكْمَتِ ، كَلَامُ ٱلْمُلُوك .

The Arabic Izafét and Compound Adjective.

§ 668. The Arabic Definite Article is used for the following purposes:

I. To form the Arabic *Izafét:* as when an Arabic noun is united with a second noun; the last letter of the first vowel, being Nominative, has generally *eôtré* (-*ou*, -*û*) as its vowel (while it was *ésré* [-*i*] in the Persian system [§ 515]), and the second noun has the article:

امِيرُ ٱلْمُومِنِين *émirû'l mûmineen* the commander of the believers.

عبدُ ٱلْمَجِيد *abdû'l Méjid* the servant of the Most-Glorious.

مِيزانُ ٱلْحَرَارِه *mizanû'l hararé* the balance of warmth, thermo-meter.

دارُ ٱلسَّعَادت *darû's'sa*ع*adét* the house of prosperity, *i. e.* the Imperial Harém.

II. To form the Arabic Compound Adjective, formed of a Participle (*i. e.* fayil, méfoul, adj. of Quality, N. of Excess, [§§ 601—606]), and a Noun. The Participle precedes the noun and ends with *eôtré* (-*û*), while the noun has the Article.

خَالِقُ ٱلْأَرْض وَ ٱلسَّمَا *khaliqû'l arz vé'sséma* the creator of earth and of heaven.

وَلِيُّ ٱلنِّعَم *véleeyû'n'niam* protector of benevolence, benefactor.

سُلْطَانُ ٱلسَّلَاطِين *soultanûs sélateen* the Sultan of Sultans.

مَفْرُوضُ ٱلْآدَا *méfrouzou'l éda* the performance of which is assigned, incumbent, canonical (prayer).

أَكْبَرُ ٱلْأَكَابِرِ *ékbérû'l ékiabir* the great one of the greats.

Note. The word سُلْطَان is the Adj. of Quality of سَلَاطَتْ *sélatat* domination, rule.

III. To unite the nouns with the preposition. The prepositions are voweled generally at the end with *ûstûn* (-*é*, -*a*) and *ésré* (-*i*); (see more in the next section):

ب *bi-* 'by': ٱلذَّات *éz-zat* the person: بِٱلذَّات *bi'z-zat* in person, personally.

بين *béyné* between: ٱلْمِلَل *él-milél* the nations: بَيْنَ ٱلْمِلَل *béyné'l milél* between the nations, international.

§ 669.

Notes. 1. All these examples end in Arabic with *ésré* (-*i*), being in the Genitive case and meaning of; as: *Emirûl mûmineeni, Abdûl méjidi, Darûs séa-déti, Véliyûn niyami* etc.

2. Surnames or patronymics in Arabic [كنيه *kûnyé*] are composed with the words ابو *ébou* father; ام *ûmm* mother; ابن *ibn, bén,* (pl. بني *béni*); ولد *véléd* son; بنت *bint* daughter (§ 168). The Arabs have the custom of calling the parents by the name of their firstborn children; as: ابوبكر *ébou-Békir* the father of Békir, the surname of the first Caliph. ابوالفرج *Ébûlféraj* the father of Faraj, Abulfaragius. ام كثوم *ûmmû Kûlsoum* the mother of Kûlsoum, Mouhammed's youngest daughter. ابن سيناء *Ibni Sina* the son of Sina, Avicienna.

3. If the name of the person precedes the surname, then *élif* is left out and بن *bén, bin* is used. ولد *véléd* is used for non-Moslems; as: محمد بن عبدالله *Mouhamméd bén Abdoullah'* Mouhammed the son of Abdoullah. يوسف ولد ذكريا *Yousouf vélédi Zékérya* Joseph the son of Zechariah. بني احمر *béni Ahmér* the children of Ahmér.

مثاللر *Misal'lér* Examples.

مَلِكُ ٱلْمُلُوك *mélikûl-mûlouk* the King of Kings.

رَبُّ ٱلْأَرْبَاب *rab'bûl-érbab* the Lord of Lords.

رَئِيسُ ٱلْآبَا *réyisûl-aba* the chief of the fathers', patriarch.

عِيسَى ٱلْمَسِيح *Eesa-él-méseeh'* (among Christians), *Eesél-méseeh* (among the Moslems) Jesus the Anointed; the Messias.

(بِأَسْمِ) بِسْمِ اَللَّهِ اَلرَّحْمَنِ اَلرَّحِيم *bismil-lahir' rahmanir' raheem* in the name of God the All-Compassionate, the Most-Merciful.

§ 669a. The Declension of Arabic Nouns.

Nom. كِتَابٌ *kitabûn* a book.   اَلْكِتَابُ *él-kitabû* the book.

Gen. كِتَابٍ *kitabin* of a book.   اَلْكِتَابِ *él-kitabi* of the book.

Acc. كِتَابًا *kitabén* a book.   اَلْكِتَابَ *él-kitabé* the book.

تَعْلِيم ١٤١   Exercise 141.

Form from the following words Izaféts and Compound Adjectives:

I. 1. (إبن ' رُوح ' عَبْد ' بَيْت ' كَلِمَة ' رَسُول ' نُور ' رَحْمَت +

2. (اللّه). فيض ' عطا• *ata, féyz* gift; سعد *sa'd* felicity; سيف *séyf* sword + - (اللّه). 3. (عباد *îbad* servants + اللّه [men]).

4. (قدس *qouds* holy + اقداس *aqdas* holies). 5. (كليم *kéleem* interlocutor + اللّه [Moses]). 6. (سلطان + برين *bérréyn* two continents, Asia and Europe). 7. (*f.* خاقان *khaqan* emperor [Chinese *hu-hang*] + بحرين *bahréyn* two seas, the Black Sea and the Mediterranean). 8. (دار *dar* house + فنون *fûnoun* sciences; خير *khayr* benevolence; شفقة *shéfaqa* charity; سعادت *séadét* prosperity; طباعة *téba-at* printing; تحصيل *tahsil* learning; خلافت *khilafét* caliphate). 9. (بنت + عنب *inéb* grapes [wine]). 10. (أمّ + خبائث *khabayis* evils).

11. (عبد + رحمن *rahman* merciful, كريم *kérim* gracious; حميد ' مجيد ' عزيز *hamid, méjid, aziz* All-praise-worthy; ستار *séttar* forgiver; مسيح *méseeh* Christ). 12. (نُور ' شَرَف ' جمال; ناصر *nasîr* help; نصر ' عزّ *izz'* glory; برهان ' شمس

jémal beauty; مُظَفَّرْ *mouzaffér* successful + دِين *deen*, *din* religion).

Note. The nouns preceding دين end in *ûstûn* (-*é*).

II. 13. (عظيم *azeem* great, جليل *jélil* illustrious + ذكر' بيان *béyan* mention). 14. (سالف *salif* above + (شان. 15. (نادر *nadir* rare + استعمال *istimal* usage). 16. (سريع *séree* quick + حركت *haréket* motion). 17. (مرعى *méree* observed + خاطر *khatîr* [honorable]). 18. (كريه *kérih'* bad + صوت *savt* voice). 19. (مقبول *maqboul* acceptable + شهادت *shéhadét* testimony). 20. (ارحم *érhém* + راحمين *rahimeen* [the most compassionate of the compassionate]).

§ 670. الرشد ' رشد *rúshd, érrúshd*؛ خالدون + ابن) [Averrhoes]). (داود + ابن) *Davoud* David); (Jacob the son of Isaac); (Aliyé عاليه the daughter of Nayima نعيمه). (Carabét the son of Artin); (the father of Ziya).

The Arabic Prepositions.

§ 671. The Arabic Prepositions are much used in Ottoman, but only in connexion with Arabic words. Those most frequently met with are the following:

a.   اِلَى *ila*-, *iléy*- towards, as far as, until, to (§ 676 [6]).

اِلَى ٱلْاَبَدْ *ilél-ébéd* to all eternity, eternally.

اِلَى آخِرِهِ ' اِلَى نِهَايَهْ *ila akhirihi, ila nihayé* to the end thereof; et cætera, etc.

b.   ب *bi*- by, with, in (§ 676 [3]).

بِالذَّاتْ *biz'zat* in person. بِالْجُمْلَهْ *biljûm'lé* all, everyone. بِالْاِتِّفَاق *bil-it'tifaq* with agreement, unanimously.

c.   بَعْدَ *badé*-, *bad*- after (§ 676 [4]).

24*

بَعْدَالطَّعَام *badét'ta-am* after dinner.

بَعْدَمَا *badéma* after which.   بَعْدَهُ *badéhou* afterwards.

d.   بِلَا *bila* without (used with nouns).

بلا خوف *bila khavf* without fear.

e.   بَيْنَ *béyné-*, *béyn-* between, among.

بَيْنَ ٱلنَّاس *béynén-nas* among the people, among men.

f.   عَلَى *ala-*, *alé-*, *aléy-* upon (§ 676 5).

عَلَى ٱلدَّوَام *aléd-dévam* perpetually.

عَلَى حَالِه *ala halihi* in the former state.

g.   عَنْ *an* from.   عنه *anhou* from him.

عَنْ أَصْلْ *an asîl* originally.   عَنْ قَصْدٍ *an qasdin* on purpose.

h.   فَوْقَ *févqé-*, *févq-* upon, over (§ 676 9).

فَوْقَ ٱلْعَادَه *févqél adé* extraordinarily.

i.   فِى *fi-* in, at; on (of dates); at, for (of price) pl. فِيآت.

فِى ٱلْوَاقِع *fil-vaqî* in effect, really.   فِى ٱلْحَال *fil'hal* instantly.

فِى بش غروش *fi* or *fiyatî bésh ghouroush* per, at 5 piasters.

فِى ۲۳ آغستوس ۱۳۱۸ on the 23 August 1318 (1902) O. S. [§ 217].

j.   كَ *ké* like.   كَٱلْأَوَّلْ *kél év'vél* as it was before.

k.   ل *li-*, *lé-*, *léy-* in favour of, to; for (§ 676 7).

لِمَصْلَحَة *limaslahat* for the sake of business.

l.   مَعَ *ma-*, *ma-é* with (§ 676 9).

مَعَ ٱلْمَمْنُونِيه *ma-él mémnouneeyé* with pleasure.

مَعْ مَافِيه *ma mafihi* notwithstanding, yet.

m.   مِنَ *miné-*, *min-* from.

مِنَ ٱلْقَدِيم *minél qadim* from ancient times.

منه *min-hou*, *minhi*, *minh'* from him.

مِنْ غَيْرِ حَدٍّ *min ghay'ri haddin* without any right = I dare not.

n.   بابنده ، خصوصنده ، حقّنده ، ضمننده *zimnînda*, *haq'qînda*, *khousousounda*, *babînda* (partly Turkish) about, for.

Note. ل ' على ' الى connected with pronouns is pronounced as *iléy-, aléy-, léy;* but with nouns as *ila, ala, li* (§ 676 [5], [6], [7]).

Exercise 142. تَعْلِيم ١٤٢

١ اُلُوهِيتده¹ اقانيمِ ثَلَثَه² وار در: اَبْ ' اِبن وَ روحُ اَلقدس .

٢ جَنابِ واجبُ اَلوُجود حضرتلرى³ ربُ اَلارباب ' مَلِكُ اَلمُلوك وَ خالقُ اَلارض وَ اَلسَّما در . ٣ عِيسى اَلمسِيح افنديمِز حضرتلرى هم ابنُ اَللّه وَ هم ابنُ اَلانساندر⁴ . ٤ روحُ اَلقدس قُلوبِ انسانيهٔىٔ⁵ تطهِير ايدر⁶ . ٥ رئيسُ اَلآبا حضرتِ يعقوب عيسى اَلمسِيح افنديمِزك اجداد عظامندن در . ٦ ايشه باشلامازدن ' يمك يه‌مزدن ' اوقومازدن وَ صو ايچمزدن اوّل دائما بسمِ اَللّه ديه‌لى . ٧ وَ اَلحاصل مرقومه⁷ افاقت⁸ بوله‌مدى : اويله مى ؟ — اوت افندم ' ذاتُ اَلجَنبدن وفات ايله‌دى ٨ بِاِذنِ اَللّه⁹ يارين قيصريه‌يه مُتَوَجِّهاً حركت ايده‌جكم . ٩ كَاَلسَّابِق¹⁰ ايشيكه غيرت اِيله دوام اَيله . ١٠ قبلَ اَلطَّعام حاضرلاندى وَ بَعدَاَلطَّعام سندِ تحرير و تمهير اولوندى . ١١ عَلَى اَلعَادَه¹¹ بعدَ اَلطَّعام تنزّهه¹² چيقارم .

Words and Notes. 1. *oulouheeyét* Godhead. 2. *Eqaneem'i sélésé* three persons, Trinity. 3. *vajibûl vûjoud* God (whose existence is necessary, self-existent). 4. *ibnûl insan* the Son of Man. 5. *qoulou'bou insaneeyé* human hearts. 6. *tat-heer ét."* to purify. 7. *mérqoumé* she (§ 677); *zatûl jénb* vulg. *satlîjan* pleurisy. 8. *ifaqat boulmaq* to recover (§ 619). 9. *biznillahi* by the permission of God = if God wills. 10. *kés'sabiq* as it was before (§ 671 j). 11. *alél adé* (عادَت or عاده custom § 671 f) usually. 12. *ténéz'zûh'* to take a walk (V. of *nûzhét*).

Translation 143. ترجمه ١٤٣

One day Hoja Effendi, losing his donkey, enquires of a man about him. The man answering said: "I saw your donkey in the court of Iconium¹; he was acting as

Words and Notes. 1. *Qonya méhkémésindé … qadíliq idiyor.*

judge there." Hoja Effendi said: "Well[2]! I already knew that he would be a Cadi[3]; because when I was teaching (giving a lesson to) Khîléz, my son, that donkey sticking up his ears[4] was listening attentively." He immediately started[7], and after some weeks reached Iconium. He went directly[5] to the court. He saw the Cadi from afar. He took a bunch of grass from the bag of the donkey and showed it to him saying *gïâh! gïâh! gïâh! gïâh!*[6] The Cadi laughed at what the Hoja was doing. The Hoja said: "Well, he recognizes me. In a few moments he will come cheerfully to eat the fresh grass. I will wait for him." And he is still waiting there.

2. *pék ala.* 3. *onoun qadî* (fayil of قَضاء) *olajaghîni bén zatén bilir idim.* 4. *qoulaqlarîni dikérék diq'qatla dinlér idi.* 5. *dogh-roudan doghrouya méhkéméyé gitdi.* 6. means 'hay or straw,' used to call the donkeys and horses 'come, come, come!' 7. *filhal Qonyaya mútévéjjihén harékét édib . . .*

مكالمه Conversation.

لسان عثمانيده حروفاتك عددى قاچدر؟

اوتوز بر در : ا ، ب ، پ ، ت ، ث الى اخره . (الخ etc.)

شاهباز افندى بالجُمْلَه احبّاسنى باّلذّات ساحلده بولنان قوناغنه دعوتله مُكَمَّلْ بر ضيافت كشيده ايلهدى . بَعْدَ الطّعَام قايقلرله تَفَرُّجَه چيقدق . مع مافيهِ ذات عاليكز اوراده بولنمدينيغينيكزدن كيفمز حرام اولدى .

فى الواقع كوزل بر كيف ايتمشكز ، ايشيتدم . اكرچه بر قاچ كون اوّل خبرم اوليدى ؛ مع الممنونيه بنده كزده دعوته اِجَابَتْ ايدردم . لكن لمصلحة اِبِكْ ساعت اوته ده بولونان برقريه يه كيتمكه مجبور اولديغمدن مَعَ التَّأَسُّفِ عظيم كله مه دم .

اكر مسئله فى الحقيقه ديديككز كبى ايسه ؛ اعلا ! ديبه جك يوق . فقط بنده كز بعضيلرندن ايشيتدم كه ؛ ذاتكز كلمه مك ايچون عن قصدٍ اول قريه يه كيتمشكز .

حاشا افندم ! بين الناس سويله نيان هرسوزه ايناغمه يكز ! بنده كز الى الابد دوست كزم . بعدما چوق فُرْصَتْلره بونى بالذّات مشاهده و تقدير ايده جكسكز .

Words and Notes. 1. *téfér'rûj* diversion. 2. *haram ol."* to become unlawful; to be unhappy. 3. *ijabét ét."* to reply in the affirmative, accept (IV. of *jévab* § 620). 4. *hasha!* Heaven forfend! 5. *mayét'té-és-sûfú azim* with the greatest regret. 6. *foursat* opportunity.

تعليم قرائت **Reading Exercise.**

لطيفه **An Anecdote.**

بر مجلسِ الفتده¹ قاين والدهلرك² مناسبتسزلكلرندن³ بحث
ايديلديكی⁴ صيره‌ده ، دلی قانلينك بری: "بن اوَلنديكم زمان قاين
آنام بكا اذيته قالقيشيرسه⁵ ، ايكی بر ديم⁶ درحال⁷ بوغارم⁸" ديديكنی
خواجه حضرتلری ايشيديكنده ، ياننده بولونان بر دوستنك قولاغنه
اكيله‌رك شويله‌جه دردينی يانمش:

— آه! ايشته شو دليقانلی كوزومه كيردی ؛ بر قيزم اولسه‌ده ، شو
قهرمانی⁹ بكا داماد¹⁰ ايده‌بيلسه‌يدم ، ياقه‌می شو خنزير¹¹ قاريدن
قورتارير كيدردم والسلام¹² !

> *Words and Notes.* 1. *méjlisi ûlfét* social party. 2. mothers-in-law. 3. *mûnasibétsizlik* absurdity. 4. *bahs ét."* to speak about. 5. *éziyété qalqîshmaq* to trouble, tease. 6. without hesitation. 7. immediately. 8. *boghmaq* to strangle, to kill; *dérdini yanmaq* to confide his woes to another. 9. brave man. 10. son-in-law. 11. a. *khînzîr* pig; nasty. 12. *véssélam.*

درس ٥٤ Lesson 54.

Arabic and Persian Pronouns.

§ 672. The Arabic Pronouns are occasionally employed in Ottoman. They are used only in certain Arabic expressions adapted by the Ottomans. They are as follows.

§ 673. **The Possessive Pronouns:**

ى -*i* My.   نا -*na* Our.

ك -*ké* Thy (masculine). ك -*ki* Thy (feminine). كُمْ -*kûm* Yours.

ه ‘ -*hû,* -*hi* Him, it; his, its.   ها -*ha* Her.

هما -*hûma,* -*hima* Them [two] (dual).

هم -*hûm,* -*him* Them (masc.).   هن *hûn'né* Them (fem.).

§ 674. The Demonstratives:

ذا ' هذا za, *haza* This. ذالك ' ذلك *zaliké, zalik* That.

§ 675. The Relative Pronoun:

ما -*ma, ma-* Who, which.

§ 676. مثاللر *Misal'lér* Examples.

1. رَبّ *rébb* (among the Moslems), *rabb* (among the Christians) Lord. ربّى *réb'bi, rab'bi* My Lord, Lord, God. يا ربّى *ya'rébbi! ya'rabbi!* O my Lord! ربّنا *réb'béna!* Our Lord; Rabboni!

2. مولا ' مولى *mévla* (N. w. mim of ولى) Lord; sir. حضرت مولا *hazréti mévla* God. مولانا *mévlana!* My sir! His grace.

3. بِ *bi-* with : لطف *loutf* ' من *ménn* grace : بلطفه ' بمنده *bilout'fihi, bimén'nihi* by His grace : بمنه تعالى *bimén'nihi Taɛa-la* by the grace of God Most High. به *bihi', bih'* by him, on it.

4. بعد *badé* after : بعده *badé'hou* after it, after that.

5. على *ala-, aléy-* on, against : عليه *aléyhi* against or on him : سلام عليك عليك *aléyké* on or upon thee : عليكم *aléykûm* on you : عليهالسلام *sélamûn aléykûm!* Peace be on you! Hail! God bless you! *aléhis'sélam!* Upon him be peace! (said of any of the prophets). عليهمده *aléyhimdé* against me (partly Turkish). مدعى *mûd'dayi* the accuser : مدعى عليه *mûddaɛa aléyh'* com. *mûd'dayi aléyh* the accused. بناءً عليه *binayén aléyh* consequently.

6. الى *ila-, iléy-* to: اليه *iléyhi* to him : اليها *iléyha* to her : اليهم *iléyhim* to them : مشار ' مومى *mouma, mûshar* (the méfoul of *iyma* and *isharét*) said, mentioned : مشاراليهم ' مومىاليه ' مشاراليه *mûshariléyh, moumayiléyh, mûshariléyhim* (pl.) to whom allusion has been made, the said; he, they. مشاراليها ' مومىاليها *moumayiléyha, mûshariléyha* she. مرسل *mûrsél* one which is sent (or addressed): [the méfoul of *irsal*]: مرسلٌ اليه *mûrsélûn iléyh* one who is addressed.

7. ل *li-, lé-, léy* for, in favour of: له *léhou, léhi* for him, in favour of anybody : لهمده *léhimdé, léyhimdé* in favour of me, for me.

8. كـ *ké-* like: كذا *kéza* ، كذلك *kézaliké, -lik* like that; thus. هكذا *hakéza* so for thee this = so also. مع هذا *ma haza* in spite of this, with this. مع ذلك *ma zaliké* with this, notwithstanding this.

9. مافوق *ma- mabaqî* that which remains, the remainder. مافوق *mafévq* that which is above؛ مافوقنده *mafévqindé* above him. مابين *mabéyn* that which is between, between. ماشالله *ma'shallah* what has God willed; May God bless him! كماكان *kémakîan* as it was before. مع مافيه *ma mafîhi'* with that which is in it (mas.), yet. مابعد *mabad* that which is after, the remainder: مابعدى وار *mabadi var* there is its remainder = to be continued. ماعدا *ma'-a-da* which is over; besides, except.

مطالعات *Mûta-la-at:* Remarks.

§ 677. In writing, the use of pronouns in the third person is avoided by repeating the noun for which they stand accompanied by one of these words, which all mean The same, the said, the above mentioned:

مشارُاليه ، مومىاليه ، مرقوم ، مسطور ، مذكور ، مزبور *mézbour, mézkûr, méstour, mérqoum, moumayiléyh, mûshariléyh* or *mûsharûn iléyh.*

§ 678. *Mézkûr, mézbour, mérqoum* are used when speaking of persons of inferior position. *Moumayiléyh* to the people of the middle class. *Mûshariléyh* is applied to persons of high rank. When speaking of inanimate objects *mézbour* and *méstour* are used.

§ 679. In case of a person first mentioned by name, or by a common substantive, these words may be used as substantives, or, — we might say —, as a kind of Personal or Demonstrative Pronoun, in all the cases of declension. But, in case of a thing, they must be used as adjectives, repeated each time.

§ 680. **The Persian Pronouns** are rarely used in such expressions. They are: اين *een* this ؛ آن *an* that ؛ چه *chi* what? ؛ چند *chénd* some ؛ خود *khod* self, one's self; as:

غافل این و آن ghafi'li een ou an ignorant of this and that, inexperienced.

چه فائده chi fayidé! what is the use! Alas!

چند دفعهلر chénd défalar several times.

خود بخود khod bé khod personally, by himself.

تعلیم ۱٤٤ Exercise 144.

١ بِنَّهِ تعالی دون ساعت بر بوچوق رادّهلرنده یکیجه قریهسنه¹ مواصلت ایدوب² ٔ افندیٔ مومیالیه ایله ملاقات³ شرفتنه⁴ نائل بیوریلدقٔ⁵ ٔ دوغریسی مشارالیهك حقِّ عاجزانهمده ابراز بیوردقلری توجُّهدن⁶ دولایی فوق العاده منتدار قالدم⁷ ٔ ٢ افندیٔ مشارالیه لَهْ و عليهكزده واقع اولان⁸ مفتریاتدن⁹ دولایی بر شی بیان ایتدیلرمی¹⁰ ؟ — خیر افندم ! بر شی سویلهمدیلر؛ مع هَذا حقمده کوستردکلری مُحَبّتدن علیهمده سویلهنن سوزلره قطعاً¹¹ اهميت ویرمهدکاری¹² آقلاشیلیور ٔ ٣ دونکی مُحاكَهده¹³ فصل اولونان¹⁴ دعوا¹⁵ نه حقنده ایمش ؟ بر شی آقلاشیله بیلدی می ؟ — اوت افندم ! بر حقوق¹⁶ دعواسی ایمش ٔ مدّعی مدّعی علیهدن اون بیك غروش ادعا¹⁵ ایدییورمش ٔ ٤ دینیکزك ماباقیسنی بوکون تأدیه¹⁷ ایدهبیلیر میسکز افندم ؟ — آمان افندم ! چندهفته مساعده بیورمهلرینی تَمَنّی ایدهرم ٔ بوکونلرده تأدیه ایتمك قدرتمك مافوقنده در ٔ

Words and Notes. 1. To the village Yénijé (near Mérzifoun). 2. mûvasélét ét." to arrive, reach (III. of vasl). 3. mûlaqat interview (VII. of لقاء liqa an encounter). 4. shéréf honour. 5. nayil ol." to obtain, attain. 6. tévéj'juh sympathy. 7. min'nétdar qalmaq to be under obligation, grateful (§ 535). 8. vaqî ol." happening, occurring (fayil of vouqou'). 9. mûftériyat calumnies (pl. of iftira [§ 650]). 10. béyan ét." to express. 11. qat'an absolutely, not at all. 12. éhém'miyét vérmék to give importance (§ 582). 13. mouhakémé a tribunal's hearing a case and giving a legal decision, law-suit (III. of hûkm). 14. fasl olounmaq to be decided, judged (a case). 15. dava a case; id'da-a, id'di-a to claim (VIII. of dava [§ 628]). 16. houqouq rights, dues (pl. of haqq, used as sing.). 17. té-é-diyé to pay (II. of éda ادا [§ 616]).

عظيم مضايقهده¹⁸يم ٠ ٥ هكذا بنده‌كزڭ دخى مضايقهٔ نقديه‌سى¹⁸

دَرَجهٔ فوق العاده ده در ٠ مع مافيه چند كون دها مساعده ايده‌بيليرم ٠

اولان مطلوباتمدن¹⁹ ماعدا ديكرلرنده دخى واردر ٠

18. *mouzayaqa* distress (§ 618 of *zeeq*); *naqdeeyé* pecuniary (§ 579). 19. *matloubat* dues (*méfoul* of *taléb* [§ 578]).

ترجمه ١٤٥ Translation 145.

1. Jesus said unto her: Mary. She turned herself, and said unto him, Rabboni. 2. Will you say anything against or in favour of him? 3. I have nothing to say against him, but I have much to say in favour of him. 4. The accuser and the accused were before the judge. 5. The said gentleman also was sick. 6. What is written on the postal cards[1]? 7. Is this article[2] to be continued? 8. There was nobody in the school, except your son. 9. I cannot read those Arabic sentences, it is above my ability to read them. 10. Where is the residence of Habib Efféndi? — It is that blue-coloured house.

1. *achîq moukhabéré varaqasî* = correspondence card. 2. *bénd.*

مکالمه Conversation.

Hassan Efféndi. حسن افندى	*Houséyn Efféndi.* حسين افندى
و عليكم السّلام ! مولانا حسين افندى ٠	سلام عليكم ! حسن افندى ٠
ابوالله ! اللّٰه امانت اولك !	مَرْحبا اَهلاً وَ سَهلاً ٠
افندم ! دون تَشَرُّف ايده‌جك ايدم	ماشاالله ! ناصل اولدى ده بنده‌خانه‌يه
اَما ٬ حضرت يتجيا عليه السلامك يوم	تشريف ايده‌يلديكز ؟
مخصوصى اولمق مناسبتيله اوده قالوب	
طاعت وعبادتله مشغول اولدم ٠	
آمين ! ادعيهٔ خيريه‌لرى بركتيله	پك اعلا ايتمشسكز ! جناب الله شفاعت
انشاالله ٠ عجبا ذات عاليلرى نه‌ايله	مبـاركه‌لرندن اهل ايمانى محروم
مشغول ايديكز ؟	ايتمه‌سين !
اوت افندم ! تاريخ مقدس مطالعه‌سنه	افندم ! كماكان "قِسَسْ أُلْاَنْبِيآ" نام
فوقَ الْعَاده مراقكز اولديغنى يلرم ٠	اثرِ مُحْتَرَمى مطالعه ايله مشغول

ايدم . معلوم سنيه‌تري اولديغي اوزره
داعيلري بويله آثارك مطالعه‌سندن
پك زياده متلذّذ اولورم .

اَسْتَغْفِرُاللّه افندم ! تقديراتكزدن
دولابي فوق العاده منتداريكزم .
دون معلّم شهير آغوب افندي
دولتخانه‌يه تشريف ايتمشلرديو
ايشيتدم . ايلك دفعه اولهرق مي
تشريف ايلهديلر ؟

اوت افندم ! مومی الیهك قيمتنی بنده‌كز
دخی تقدير ايده‌رم . بزم كبی عالمِ
مدنيتجه غافلِ اين وَ آن اولان
كسان ايچون افندئ مومی اليه بر
رهبرِ يهَمتا در .

افندم او بويورديغيكز : "مرسلْ اليهك
نام وُ شهرت وَ محلّ اقامتی بالايه
يازيله‌جقدر" عباره‌سيدر .

بنده‌كز دخی پك هوسكار ايسه‌مده ،
حالا اويله آثاردن اِستفاده ايده-
يلمك قدرتك مافوقنده در .

خير افندم ! معلم موميالیه چند دفعه‌لر
دنی تشريف ايتمشلر در . من
الْقديم بَيْنَاده حُبّ و مَوَدّت
موجود در . لكن چه فائده كه
كثرت مشاغلدن ناشی پك آز
دفعه‌لر تشريف ايديبورلر .

بو يورديغيكزی تصديق ايده‌رم . اكرچه
مساعده‌لری اولورسه ، افنديزه بر
سؤال تقديم ايدهم . آچيق مخابره
ورقه‌لری اوزرنده قيرمزی حروفاتله
محرّر اولان عباره نه در ؟

پك اعلا ! فَوْقَ الْعَاده متشكّرم .

<table>
<tr><td>تعليم قرائت</td><td>Reading Exercise.</td></tr>
</table>

درياده سفائنك منع	Regulations and rules of
مُصادَمه‌لری ضمننده ياپيلان	the road, for preventing
قوانين و نظامات .	collisions at sea.

— ۱ —   — 1 —

مُخالِف قُونطره‌ده بولونان ايكی سفينه
بربرلرينه تصادف ايله‌دكاری حالده :
قونطره‌لری اسكله‌دن اولان ، سانجاقدن
اولانه دائمًا يول ويره‌جكدر ؛
(يا چوبره‌رك وَيا آچيقده طوره‌رق) .

When close-hauled on opposite
tacks, the ship on the port
tack is always to give way if
necessary, either by keeping
away or going about.

— 2 —

With the wind free, give way
to those on the wind.

— ۲ —

روزکاری قولای قوللانان کمی ،
روزکار اوزرنده کنه یول ویره جکدر.

— 3 —

Two ships meeting under
(having) full sail are to pass
on the port side of each other.

— ۳ —

باش باشه تصادف ایدرك مصادمه وقو-
عی ملحوظ اولان ایکی کمی ؛ بربرینك
اسکله طرفندن مرور ایده جکلردر.

— 4 —

Under steam and nearly end-on
to each other, both cast to
starboard and pass on the port
side of each other.

— ۴ —

ایستیم اوزرنده بولونان ایکی کمی بربرینه
تصادف ایتدکده ؛ منع مصادمه ایچون
ایکیسی ده دومنلرینی سانجاغه
قیره رق ، بربرینك اسکله سندن کچرلر.

— 5 —

A steamer always gives way
to a sailing vessel : and it must
be remembered that every vessel
under sail, with steam ready,
though not using it, is considered a steamer, in the event
of collision.

— ۵ —

واپور سفائنی ، یلکن سفائننه یول
ویرمکه مجبور اولدیغی کبی ؛ ایستیمی
حاضر اولدیغی حالده ، یلکن ایله سیر
ایدن سفائن دخی حین ِ مصادمه ده :
واپور کبی عدّ اولونه جقلری خاطردن
دُور طوتیلمامالیدر.

— 6 —

Every vessel underweigh is to
carry a green light on the starboard and a red light on the
port side.

— ۶ —

ده کیزده کزن هر سفینه سانجاق
جهتنه یریشیل ، اسکله جهتنده قیرمیزی
فنار (فَنَر) وضع ایتمکه مجبور درلر.

— 7 —

Steamers, in addition, carry a
white light at the fore-masthead
(*prova*). [*Worda* the broadside.]

— ۷ —

فضله اولهرق واپور سفائنی (بورده
فنارلرندن ماعدا) پرووه سُتوننه یاض
بر سیلیون فناری کشیده ایدرلر.

— 8 —

Vessels towing, carry two white masthead lights (*siliyon*).

— ٨ —

يدك چكن سفائن ايكى سيليون چكرلر.

— 9 —

During fogs, vessels under steam are to sound a steam whistle; vessels under sail, to use a fog horn: at anchor, to ring a bell.

— ٩ —

سيس زماننده واپور سفائنى دودوك ، يلكن سفائنى ده سيس بوينوزى ولنكرانداز اقامت بولوندقلرى حالده چاك چالارلر.

— 10 —

These signals to be sounded once, at least, every five minutes.

— ١٠ —

بونلر ده لا اقل بش دقيقهده بركره چالينمالیدر.

٥٥ درس Lesson 55.

The Arabic and Persian Adverbs.

§ 681. The simple Arabic Adverbs are rarely used in Ottoman, but the compound ones are very common. These are made by the addition of a tenveen of ûstûn together with an *élif* or *té* (-*én*, -*tén* § 48); as:

شرق *sharq* east: شرقاً *sharqén* eastward.

ذات *zat* origin: ذاتاً *zatén* originally, already.

شفاه *shifah* lips: شفاهاً *shifahén* orally.

§ 682. There are two rules which govern the pointing of tenveen of ûstûn[1]:

a. If the word ends in *hémzé* (§ 590), or short *élif* (§ 594), or servile *hé* or *té* (§ 592), only a double *ûstûn* is put at the end, provided that *té* and *hé* (ت ، ه ، ٥) must change into round *té* (ة ، ة -*tén*) and short *élif* (ى -*a*) must change into simple *élif* (أ -*én*):

جزاء *jéza* punishment: جزاءً *jéza'yén* as a punishment.

هديه *hédiyé* present: هدیةً *hédiyé'tén* as a gift.

---

[1] Which is the sign of the Accusative case (§ 670).

مرحمت *mérhamét* mercy: مرحمةً *mérhaméten* kindly.

معنى *man'a* meaning: معناً *ma'nén* in truth, virtually.

ماده *maddé* material: مادةً *maddéten* materially.

b. But if the final ت be radical, or if the word end with any other letter than those mentioned above, an *élif* with double *ûstûn* (اً *-én*) is added to the end; this *élif* is never pronounced:

موقت *mouvaq'qat* temporary: موقتاً *mouvaqqa'tén* temporarily.

نظر *nazar* a glance: نظراً *naza'rén* in respect of.

ثالث *salis* third: ثالثاً *sali'sén* thirdly.

بعضاً *bazén* sometimes: مؤخراً *mou-akhkha'rén* subsequently.

مثاللر *Misal'lér* Examples.

متمادياً *mûtémadi'yén* continually.   مجدداً *mûjéd'dédén* newly.

دفعةً *défa'tén* repeatedly.   فجةً *fûj'jétén* suddenly.

قضاءً *qaza'yén* by accident.   قصداً *qas'dén* designedly.

خفياً *khéfi'yén* secretly.   علناً *alé'nén* openly.

عوماً *oumou'mén* generally.   تقريباً *taqri'bén* nearly.

براً *bér'rén* by land.   بحراً *bah'rén* by sea.

جماً *jéman, jém'én* as a total.   مجاناً *méjjan'én* freely, gratis.

تحريراً *tahri'rén* written.   كلياً *kûl'liyén* totally.

جبراً *jéb'rén* by force.   جملةً *jûm'létén* wholly.

§ 683. Sometimes the tenween is not pronounced:

اولاً *év'véla* firstly.   عادتا *a'déta* simply.

حالا *hal'a* yet, now.   دائما *da'yima* always.

غالبا *gha'liba* most probably.   مطلقا *mout'laqa* absolutely.

واقعا *vaqa'-a* in fact, surely.   مثلا *mé'séla* for example.

عجبا *a'jéba, aja'ba* I wonder! strange! Really!

§ 684. **The Persian Adverb.** The Persian Derivative Adjectives, which are made by the addition of انه *-ané* (§ 528), are used as adverbs:

دوستانه *dosta'né* friendly.   برادرانه *biradera'né* brotherly.

جانسپارانه *jansipara'né* devotedly; bravely.

محرمانه *mahréma'né* intimately, confidentially.

Exercise 146.   تعليم ١٤٦

١ امتحانلریکز بو سنه تحریراً می اوله‌جقدر یوخسه شفاهاً می ؟
— اولا تحریراً اوله‌جغی معلّم افندی طرفندن اعلان¹ اولونشیدیسه‌ده ،
مؤخراً هیئت معلمین² شفاهاً اجرا اولونمه‌سنه قرار ویرمشدر³ . ٢ دشمن
براً و بجراً هجوم⁴ ایله‌دی . ٣ افندیمز حضرتِ عیسی عَلیهِ‌السلام ‏"خفیاً
سویله‌دکلرمی علناً وعظ ایده‌جکسکز‏" دیوبیورمشدر . ٤ مصطفی
دایم بنده‌کزه هدیةً بش لیرا ارسال ایله‌مش ؛ ذاتاً ده اون لیرا
کوندرمشیدی : جمعاً اون بش لیرا کوندرمش اولدی . ٥ درونده
اقامت ایله‌دیکمز قوناق بزم دکلدر . موقتاً اوطورویورز . ٦ ایشیتدیکمزه
نظراً آوّ صاحبکز نحةً⁴ وفات ایله‌مش ؛ اویله‌میدر عجبا ؟ — اوت
افندم ، حقیقت در . فقط بَدَناً⁵ اولقدر صاغلام ایدیکه ، وفاته حالا
ایناننعم کلمه‌یور . ٧ اویله‌در ؛ لکن مُسکراته⁶ مبتلا⁷ اولانلر ، عموماً
بویله‌جه وفات ایدرلر . بنم بیلدیکم متوقای مرقوم متمادیاً ایچکی⁶
ایچردی . ٨ واقعاً سزک ایچون بر مکتوب کلمش اما ؛ صوکره ده قضاءً
ضایع اولمشدر ، عفو ایدرسکز ، ٩ مکتوب ضایع اولامشدر ؛ بنی عادتا
اِغفال ایدییورسکز⁸ ، اِرادَتکز⁹ ایله ویریکز ؛ ویرمزسکز جبراً آلیرم .

Words and Notes. 1. *ilan ét."* to announce (IV. of *aléni*).
2. *hiyé'ti mou-al'-limeen* the Faculty. 3. *qarar vér."* to decide.
4. *hújoum* to attack; *fûj'jétén* for فجائتاً *suddenly.* 5. *bédénén* bodily.
6. *mûskirat, ichki* any intoxicating liquid (pl. of *mûskir*, which is
the méfoul of IV. *sékér*). 7. *mûbtela* addicted to (méfoul of *ibtila*).
8. *ighfal ét."* to deceive. 9. *iradét* will (IV. of √رَوَدَ [§ 620]).

ترجمه ۱٤۷ Translation 147.

1. "I will give unto him that is athirst of the fountain of the water of life freely." 2. He has not yet come. 3. The school house was newly built. 4. Nearly 500 persons were present. 5. He took the money by force. 6. They were treating[1] each other like brothers. 7. He was serving his Master devotedly. 8. I cannot reveal[2] to you that matter[3]; it was told to me in confidence. 9. He told me again and again (repeatedly). 10. It is most probable that he will never be able to come. 11. Really! That is my opinion[4] too.

Words and Notes. 1. *mou-amélé ét."* 2. *béyan ét."* 3. *mad'dé.* 4. *éfkiar. (Béndéniziñ dé éfkiari héman héman o mérkézdé dir.)*

تعليم قرائت Reading Exercise.

Newton. بر عالم مشهورك افعال سياسيهسى

علوم طبيعيه[1] علماسندن[2] مشهور نيوتون[3] يكرمى سنه انكلتره پارلامنتوسنده[4] مبعوث[5] صفتيله[6] بولونديغى حالده ٬ بركون نه[7] بر نُطق ايراد ايتمش[8] ٬ نه ده برتكليف[9] وُ اعتراضده[10] بولونغشدر · نهايت خارقُ اَلعَاده اوله‌رق[11] بركون قيام ايدوب ٬ وَقارلى بر صورتده[12] اداره‌ٔ كلام[13] ايده‌جكٔى اعضاى مجلس كوردكارنده : غايت تعجب ايدرلر[14] · وَاول آنه قدر پك چوق مسائل مهمه‌ده[15] اختيار سكوتله[16] ٬ هيچ بر سوز تكلُّم ايتمه‌مش[17] اولان بو ذاتك حركتنى مُطلقا مهم بر مسئله

Words and Notes. *éf'al* actions (pl. of *fiyl*); *siyasiyé* political (§ 579). 1. *ouloumou tabiyiyé* natural sciences. 2. *ouléma* scientists (pl. of *alim* [§ 643 d]). 3. *Névton* Newton. 4. *parlaménto* parliament. 5. *méb'ous* delegate, P. M. 6. *sifatiyla* with the title. 7. *né — né —* neither — nor —. 8. *iyrad* to deliver (§ 620); *noutq* speech. 9. *tékleef* proposition (§ 615). 10. *itiraz* opposition (VIII. of *arz*). 11. *khariqûl adé olaraq* extraordinarily (Turk. adverb). 12. *vaqarli' bir sourétle* in a serious manner, seriously (§ 458). 13. *idaréyi kélam ét."* to deliver a speech (§ 621). 14. *té-aj'jûb ét."* to be astonished. 15. *mésayil* questions (pl. of *mésélé* [§ 597]), *mouhimm'* important (*fayil* of *ihmam* [§ 619]). 16. *ikhtiyar ét."* to prefer, choose (§ 627); *sûkûtlé* for *sûkût édérék* remaining silent (= keeping silence). 17. *tékél'lûm ét."* to speak (§ 622).

الجاسیله ¹⁸ اولدیغـــنه حکم ایدرك ¹⁹ ؛ هیئتِ مجلس كمالِ دقتله ²⁰
مشارالیهك ²¹ بحث ایده‌جکی ²² مسئله‌یی استماعه ²³ حاضرلانیر •
اول علّامهٔ دوران ²⁴ نه دیسه ایی ²⁵ ! — "افندیلر ! صاغ جهتمده ²⁶
مشاهده بویوردیغینیکز ²⁷ شو پنجرهنك جامی قضاءً قیریلمش اولدیغندن ٬
جریان هوانك ²⁸ حدوثنی موجب اولویور ²⁹ ٬ وَبو ده بنم صحتمی
إخلاله ³⁰ باعث اولویور ²⁹ : بناءً علیه ³¹ ؛ بو قیریق جامك یرینه بر یکیسنك
طاقدیریلمهسنی تکلیف ایده‌رم" دیوب اوطوری ویرمشدر ³² • ﴿ابو الضیا﴾

18. *ilja* compelling (§ 619). 19. *hûkm ét.''* to judge, think.
20. with great attention. 21. see § 678. 22. *bahs ét.''* to discuss.
23. *istima ét.''* to hear. 24. *al'lamé* exceedingly learned (§ 582 of
al'lam, this is exceptionally masculine); *dévran* the century.
25. What do you think that he said? 26. *jihét* side. 27. *mûsha-
hadé* to see. 28. *jéréyanî hava* current of air. 29. *houdous ét.''*
to occur, happen; *moujib* causing (méfoul of *ijab* [§ 619]); *bayis
ol.''* to cause. 30. *sîh'hat* health; *ikhlal* to spoil, break. 31. *binayén
aléyh* therefore (§ 676 ⁵); *téklif ét.''* to propose, to move. 32. he sat
down quickly (§ 286). *Ebûz Ziya* the father of Ziya (§ 669², p. 369).

مكالمه Conversation.

To Thank. تشکر ایتمك	*Téshék'kûr étmék.*
I thank you very much for your kindness.	*Loutfouñouza pék ziyadé téshék-kûr édérim.*
Pray don't mention it.	*Estagh'firoul-lah!*
I feel very grateful to you.	*Zatî aliñizé min'nétdarîm.*
I am very much obliged to you.	*Min'nétdarinîzîm.*
I shall never forget your kindness to me.	*Qoulouñouza olan loutfou hich ounoutmayajaghîm.*
I return you a thousand thanks.	*Biñlérjé arzî téshék'kûr édérim.*
I beg you will accept my most grateful thanks.	*Min'nétdarané olan téshék'kûra-tîmî qaboul bouyourmañizî istirham édérim.*
Thank you, Sir.	*Téshék'kûr édérim éfféndim.*
I am sorry to give you so much trouble.	*Zatî alinizé bou qadar zahmét vérdiyim ichin mûté-és'sifim.*
You overwhelm me with your kindness.	*Loutfounouz qoulonouzou mah'-joub édiyor.*
No trouble at all.	*Hich zahmét déyil. Bir shéy déyil.*
I shall be most happy to return you the favour.	*Loutfounouzou iyadé édéjéyim ichin pék més'-oud oum.*
You are really too kind.	*Haqiqatén pék nazik siñiz.*
I hope I shall some day be able to get out of your debt	*Inshal-lah bir gûn olour bor-joumou éda édérim.*

I am delighted to have been use-ful to you.	*Khîdmétiñizdé bouloundoughoum ichoun pék mémnounoum.*
I am extremely glad to see you.	*Sizi geôrdûyûmé déréjéyi niha-yédé mémnoun oldoum.*
Nothing at all! Not at all!	*Bir shéy déyil.*
No ceremony between friends.	*Téklif yoq dour éfféndim!*

۵٦ درس Lesson 56.

اسماء اعداد Arabic Numerals.

§ 685. The Arabic Numeral Adjectives are fre-quently used in Ottoman, especially in writings, in official terminations, in speeches and sermons.

§ 686. I. Cardinal Numbers. اعداد اصلیه

واحد' احد *vahid* or *ahad* one; fem. واحده احدی *îhda, vahîdé.*

اثنین *ésnéyn* two.   سبعه *séb'-é* seven.

ثلثه *sé-lé-sé* three.   ثمانیه *sémaniyé* eight.

اربعه *érba'-a* four.   تسعه *tis'-é* nine.

خمسه *khamsé* five.   عشر' عشره *ashéré, ashér* ten.

سته *sit'té* six.   صفر *sifîr* zero.

احد عشر *ahadé ashér* 11, اثنا عشر *isna ashér* 12, ثلثة *sélését* ashér 13, اربعة عشر *érba-at ashér* 14, خمسة عشر *khamsét ashér* 15, ستة عشر *sittét ashér* 16, سبعة عشر *séb'ét ashér* 17, ثمانية عشر *sémani-yét ashér* 18, تسعة عشر *tis-ét' ashér* 19.

عشرین *îshreen* 20, ثلثین *séléseen* 30, اربعین *érba-yeen* 40, خمسین *khamseen* 50, ستین *sit'teen* 60, سبعین *séb'een* 70, ثمانین *sémaneen* 80, تسعین *tis'een* 90. (عشرون' ثلثون etc. is not used in Ottoman.)

مائه *miyé* 100, مأتین *miyétéyn* 200, ثلثمائة *sélésou miyétin* 300, الف *élf* 1000, الفین *élféyn* 2000, ثلثة آلاف *sélését alaf* 3000.

§ 687. II. Ordinal Numbers. اعداد وصفیه

اول حادی' *év'vél, hadi* 1st; fem. اولی *oula.*

ثانی *sani* second; fem. ثانیه *saniyé* second ($\frac{1}{60}$th of a minute).

25*

ثالث *salis* third. fem.	ثالثه	سابع *sabi* seventh.
رابع *rabi* fourth. »	رابعه	ثامن *samin* eighth.
خامس *khamis* fifth. »	خامسه	تاسع *tasi* ninth.
سادس *sadis* sixth. »	سادسه	عاشر *ashir* tenth.

§ 688. By the addition of an *élif* with a tenveen, they are changed into adverbs (§§ 681, 683):

اولا *év'véla* firstly.	سادساً *sadisén* for the 6th time.
ثانياً *saniyén* secondly.	سابعاً *sabiyén* » » 7th »
ثالثاً *salisén* thirdly.	ثامناً *saminén* » » 8th »
رابعاً *rabiyén* fourthly.	تاسعاً *tasiyén* » » 9th »
خامساً *khamisén* fifthly.	عاشراً *ashirén* » » 10th »

§ 689. The Nisbé of the units is made by the measure فُعَالى (§ 580 f.):

ثنائى *súnayi* composed of two letters, bi-literal.
ثلاثى *súlasi* » » three » triliteral.
رباعى *rúbayi* » » four » quadriliteral.

§ 690. **Fractional Numbers.** اعداد كسريه

نصف *nîsf, nîsîf* half (§ 207).	سدس *súds, súdûs* ¹/₆.
ثلث *súlûs, súls* ¹/₃.	سبع *súb'* ¹/₇.
ربع *roub', ouroub* ¹/₄.	ثمن *súmn, súmûn* ¹/₈.
خمس *khoums* ¹/₅.	تسع *tûs'* ¹/₉.

عشر *úshr, úshûr* ¹/₁₀; *éôshûr* tithe (pl. اعشار *ashar*).

§ 691. In forming compound numeral adjectives in Arabic, the smaller number always precedes the larger, while و *vé* is put between every number and that which follows it: that is to say, in reading they begin from the right, as they write and read from the right (§ 13).

مثاللر *Misal'lér* Examples.

تسعة و ثلاثون *tisét vé sélasoun* (or *sélaseen* [§ 573]) thirty-nine.

تحريراً فى أَلْيومِ الْخَامس وَ الْعشرين ٬ مِن شهرِ ذى أَلْقعدةِ أَلشَّريفه ؛

لسنة سبعةَ عَشَرَ وَ ثلثُمائة وَ الف *Tahreerén fil yévmil khamis vél îshreen,*
min shéhri zilqadétish shérifé, lisénétin sébét-ashér vé sélésoumiyétin
vé élf. (This Firman) was written on the 25th of the sacred month
Zilqadé, in the year 1317 (of the Hejira).

شهور ثلثه امتحانلرى ختام بولدى *shouhourou sélésé imtihanlarî*
khitam bouldou. The term examinations were finished.

اوقات مباركهٔ خمسه *évqatî mûbarékéyi khamsé* the five blissful
times (of daily prayers). الفُ ليله و ليلة *élfû léylé vé léylét* the
1001 nights, *i. e.* the Arabian Nights, Turk. *Biñ bir géjé.*

The Diminutive Noun.

§ 692. The Diminutive noun is made by the
measure فُعَيْل *fouqéyl* (§§ 156, 167, 544):

عبد *abd* a servant: عبيد *oubéyd* a little servant.

حسن *hasan* beautiful: حسين *houséyn* darling, prettiest.

سلمان *sélman* prop. name: سليمان *souléyman* Solomon.

تعليم ١٤٨   Exercise 148.

١ آحاد ؛ عَشَرات ؛ مآت ؛ الوف ؛ آلاف [1] ؛ ٢ أَحَدِيَّت ٬ ثلثان ٬ سُدسان [2] ؛
٣ كتابِ رابع ٬ فُصولِ [3] اربعه ؛ ٤ فصلِ [3] تاسع عشر ؛ ٥ جزائر [4] سبعه ٬
عمليات [5] اربعه ؛ ٦ اوچ ربع ٬ آلتى تسع ٬ يدى عُشر ؛ ٧ مادةٔ [6] رابعه ؛
سنهٔ ثامن وَ عشرين ؛ ٨ دفعهٔ اولى ٬ شهورِ [7] سِتّهٔ عشر محصول [8] ؛ ٩ رسومِ
سِتّه ٬ شهورِ ثلثه ؛ ١٠ حواسِّ [9] خمسه ؛ ١١ خمسين [10] ٬ اربعين [11] ٬
كسرِ اعشارى [12] ؛ ١٢ عيدُ أَخْمسين [13] ؛ اوامرِ عشره ؛ احادِ ناس [14] ·

Words. 1. *ahad, ashérat, miyat, oulouf* or *alaf*; the units, tens,
hundreds and thousands. 2. ²/₃, ²/₆ (duals [§ 568]). 3. *fousoul* seasons, pl. of *fasl* a season; a section, subdivision of a book. 4. *jézayir*
islands, pl. of *jéziré* (§ 646). 5. *améliyat* processes (Arith). 6. *mad'dé*
article (§ 644 b). 7. *shouhour* months (pl. of *shéhr*). 8. product
(méf. of *housoul* [§ 604]). 9. *havass'* sense, faculty. 10. *khamseen*
a period of 50 days, following the Erbayeen, ending at the Vernal
Equinox. 11. *érbayeen* the forty days of midwinter, beginning
with the winter solstice, 21st December, and ending 30th January,
when the severest cold is experienced. 12. *késri asharee* the
decimal fractions. 13. *eed* festival (Pentecost). 14. individuals.

Exercise 149. تعليم ١٤٩

١ مسكرات[1]، دخان[2]، طوز، تمغا[3]، حرير[4]، صيد ماهى[5] رسومنه رسومِ ستّه[6] تعبير اولونور؛ بونلر دخاندن ماعدا ديون عموميه عثمانيه ادارهسنه ترك و احاله اولونمشلر در . ٢ كچن سنه اربعين خفيف كچدى ايسهده، بوسنه خمسين اولقدر خفيف كچمهدى ٣ . دولتِ عليه عثمانيهنك ملكيه[7] درجاتِ رتبهسى[8] آشاغيدن يوقارى چيقهرق شونلر در: رتبهٔ خامسه، رتبهٔ رابعه، رتبهٔ ثالثه، رتبهٔ ثانيه صنفِ[9] ثانيسى، رتبهٔ ثانيه صنفِ ممتايزى[10]، رتبهٔ اولى صنفِ ثانى، رتبهٔ اولى صنفِ اول، رتبهٔ بالا[11]، وَ رتبهٔ وزارت[12] . ٤ عَمَلياتِ اربعه شو آتيده كيلر در: جمع، طرح[13]، ضَرب[14]، تقسيم . ٥ فصولِ اربعه دخى بونلر در: صيف[15]، خزان[16]، شتاء[17]، وَ بهار[18] . ٦ مصادر[19] عربيه اساساً[20] ايكى قسمدر: اوّلا مجرّد[21]، ثانياً مزيدٌ فيه[22] . ٧ مصدرِ مجرد دخى ايكى قسمدر: برى مصدرِ ثلاثئ مجرد و ديكرى مصدرِ رباعئ مجرد . ٨ مصدرِ مزيدٌ فيه دخى ايكى نوعدر: مصدرِ ثلاثئ مزيدٌ فيه وَ مصدرِ رباعئ مزيدٌ فيه . ٩ عيد ألخمسين كوننده باركاه أحديته عرضِ تحميدات ايلهديار .

Words and Notes. 1. *mûskirat* intoxicating liquids. 2. *doukhan* tobacco. 3. *damgha* stamp. 4. *hareer* silk. 5. *sayd* fishing, hunting *mahi* fish; *rousoum* taxes. 6. *tabeer ol."* to be called; *Douyounou Oumoumiyéyi Osmaneeyé Idarési* the Administration of Ottoman Public Debts; *térk* to leave; *ihalé* to refer (IV. of *havalé* [§ 620]). 7. *milkiyé* civil; *askériyé* military (§ 581). 8. *déréjat* degrees (pl. of *déréjé* [§ 576]); *rûtbé* a rank, grade in the Ottoman nobility. 9. *sînîf* class. 10. *mûtémayiz* privileged, superior (fayil of *téma-yûz* [§ 624]). 11. *rûtbéyi bala* the supreme civil grade in the Ottoman nobility. 12. *vézarét* the rank of a vézir. 13. *tarh'* subtraction. 14. *zarb* multiplication (if pron. *darb* it is 'a blow'). 15. *sayf* summer. 16. *khazan* autumn. 17. *shita* winter (§ 591). 18. spring. 19. *mésadir* infinitives (pl. of *masdar* [§ 648]). 20. *ésasén* fundamentally (§ 681). 21. *mûjér'réd* simple, primitive (méfoul of *téjreed*). 22. *mézeedoun fiyhi* augmentative: *mézeed* (§§ 605, 670); *fityhi: fiy* preposition, *hi* pronoun ([§ 671 i] = augmented in itself).

مكالمه **Conversation.**

Congratulations and Felicitations.

تبریکات و تهنیات

I have heard with great pleasure that H. I. M. the Sultan has appreciated your services and conferred on you a decoration of the third class of the Osmaniyé.

خِدَمات علیه‌لرینه مكافات اولمق اوزره عواطفِ علیهٔ حضرتِ شهریاریدن عهدهٔ عالیلرینه اوچنجی رتبه‌دن برقطعه نشان عالئ عثمانی توجیه و احسان یورلدیغی كمالِ محظوظیتله مسموعم اولمشدر.

I have heard with the greatest joy that H. I. M. the Sultan has appointed you Minister Pleni-potentiary to London.

ذاتِ حضرتِ شهریاری ذاتِ والالرینی لوندرا سفارتنه تعیین یوردقلری كمال مسرتله مَسموعِ عاجزانهم اولدی.

I read in the newspapers with extreme joy of your promotion to the degree of Mûtémayiz.

عهدهٔ عالیلرینه رتبهٔ متمایزینك توجیه یورلدیغی تعریفی ناقابل بر مسرتله اوراقِ حوادثده مطالعه ایله‌دم.

[**To a Lady.**] My joy was very great on hearing that H. I. M. the Sultan had been pleased to confer on you the Insignia of the third class of the Shéfaqat.

عواطف سنیهٔ حضرتِ تاجداریدن عهدهٔ عالیلرینه ایكینجی رتبه‌دن شفقت نشانِ ذیشانی احسان یورلدیغی معلوم عاجزانهم اولدقده فوق الحدّ مسرور و ممنون اولدم.

Please accept my congratulations on this honorific distinction.

اشبو توجیهِ وجیهِ حضرتِ پادشاهیدن طولایی ذاتِ عالیكزی تبریك ایدرم.

Please accept my sincere con-gratulations.

بوندن طولایی تبریكاتِ خالصانه‌مك قبول یورلمه‌سی مسترجادر افندم.

I cannot express my gratitude for the interest you feel in me.

حقِ بندكانه‌مده ابذال یوردقلری حسنِ توجهاتِ علیه‌لرندن طولایی نه درجه

I am ever so much obliged
for it.

مُتأثّر اولديغمى تعريف ايدهم . بناءً
عليه تشكراتِ نامتناهيهمى قبول
يورمهلرينى رجا ايدرم افندم .

I perceive from this high token
of the Imperial favour that your
excellent qualities are appreciated everywhere.

حقكزده وقوعبولان اشبو توجّهات
والتفاتِ پادشاهيدن طولايى مُتّصف
اولديغكز صفاتِ جليلهلريكزك هر
يرده تقدير وتحسين اولونفقده اولديغنى
آكلاشيلير .

I hasten to congratulate you on
the new dignity of which Your
Honour is the recipient.

رتبهٔ جديدهٔ عليهلرينك تبريك و تهنيتنه
مسارعت ايدرم .

[**To an Ambassador.**] Sir, Our
August Sovereign, H. I. M. the
Sultan, desirous of affording you
some token of his appreciation
and his regard has been pleased
to confer on you the grand
cordon of His Imperial Order
of the Méjidiyé.

متبوعِ مفخّم ومعظّمز ذاتِ شَوْ-
كتسماتِ حضرتِ پادشاهى ! حق سفير-
انهلرنده دركار اولان حرمت و تَوَجُّهِ
ملوكانهلرينه بر دليلِ جلىّ اولمق اوزره ،
بو كره ذاتِ اصيلانهلرينه برنجى
رتبهدن برقطعه مجيدى نشان ذيشانى
اعطا و احسان يورمشدر:

Will your Excellency therefore
please to accept my very sincere
congratulations on this token of
the Imperial favour of which
you are the recipient?

شو نائل اولديغكز اثرِ جليلِ لطف
و عاطفتِ سنيهدن طولايى تبريكاتِ
خالصهملك قبولنى رجا ايدرم .

I ask you, Sir, to be kind enough
to present to H. I. M. my very
respectful homage and to convey
to him the assurance of my

ثناورلرنجه بَغايت قيمتدار اولان اشبو
نشانهٔ لطف و عاطفتِ سنيهدن طولايى
تشكرات وُ تعظيماتِ فائقهٔ عاجزانهمى
سريرِ شوكتمصيرِ حضرتِ پادشاهىيه

profound gratitude, and to represent to him how greatly I feel
honoured by such a high distinction and how much I am
sensible of his high munificence
and bounty.

عرض و ابلاغ بویورمەلرینی رجا ایدرم

افندم ۰

تَعليم قرائت   Reading Exercise.

وطن Home (Fatherland).

عقل¹ «مربَّع² باشقه ، مثلَّث³ باشقه» قضیەسنك⁴ حقیقتنه نه

قوتده حکم⁵ ایلەیورسه ، وجدان⁶ ده «وطن⁷ باشقه ، خارج⁸ وطن باشقه»

سوزِنك صحتنه⁹ او قوتده اعتماد ایدییور¹⁰ ۰

شـیرخوارلر¹¹ بشیکنی ، چوجوقلر اکلنـدیکی یری ، کنجلر

معیشتـکاهنی¹² ، اختیارلر کوشهٔ فراغنی¹³ ، اولاد والدهسنی ، پدر عائلهسنی

نه درلو حسیات¹⁴ ایله سورسه انسان ده وطننی او درلو حسِّیات ایله سَوَر ۰

بو حسِّیات ایسه سببسز بر میلِ¹⁵ طبیعتدن عبارت دکلدر ۰ انسان وطننی

سور ، چونکه مواهبِ¹⁶ قدرتِك¹⁷ اك عزیزی اولان حیات هوای وطنی

تنفُّسله¹⁸ باشلار ۰

انسان وطننی سور ، چونکه عطایای¹⁹ طبیعتِك اِك رونقلیسی²⁰

اولان نَظَرِ²¹ لحهٔ افتتاحنده خاكِ²² وطنه تعلُّق ایدر²³ ۰

Words and Notes. 1. sense, mind. 2. *mûréb'ba* square
(méf. of *tér-bi'* [§ 615]). 3. *mûsél'lés* triangle (méfoul of *téslees*
[§ 615]). 4. *qaziyé* decision, truth. 5. to judge. 6. *vijdan* conscience. 7. *vatan* home, fatherland. 8. outside, other, non- (*fayil*
of *khourouj*). 9. *sîh'hat* truth. 10. *itimad* to believe (VIII. of
amd). 11. *sheer-khor* that sucks milk, suckling (§ 535). 12. *mayishét*
(n. w. mim of *aysh* + *giâh*) a place where to gain his subsistence
(§ 541). 13. *kéôshé* a nook, retreat; *féragh* leisure. 14. *his'siyat*
feelings (pl. of *hiss*). 15. *méyl* affection. 16. *mévahib* gifts (pl. of
mévhibé). 17. *qoudrét* power; Providence. 18. *ténéf'fûs* to breathe
(V. of *néfés*). 19. *ataya* gifts, bounties (pl. of *atiyé* [§ 646]).
20. p. t. *révnaqlî* splendid, brilliant. 21. looking, glance; *lémhayi*
iftitahda at the first glance. 22. *khak* soil; ground. 23. *té-al'louq*
ét.'' to fasten, to attach (V. of *alaqa* § 622).

انسان وطننى سور ، چونكه مادهٔ[24] وجودى وطنڭ بر جزئیدر[25] .

انسان وطننى سور ، چونكه اطرافنه باقدقجه هر كوشه‌سنده عمر كذشته‌سنڭ[26] بر یاد حزینى[27] تحجّر ایتمش[28] كبى كورور .

انسان وطننى سور ، چونكه حرّیتى[29] ، راحتى[30] ، حقّى[31] وطن سایه‌سنده قائمدر[32] . انسان وطننى سور ، چونكه سببِ وجودى[33] اولان اجدادینڭ[34] مقبرهٔ[35] سكونى[36] وَ نتیجهٔ[37] حیاتى اوله‌جق اولادینڭ جلوه‌كاه[38] ظهورى وطندر .

انسان وطننى سور ، چونكه ابنای وطن آره‌سنده اشتراكِ[39] لسان واتّحادِ[40] منفعت[41] وَ كثرت[42] موانسه[43] جهتیله[44] بر قرابتِ[45] قلب و بر اُخوّت[46] افكار حاصل اولمشدر . او سایه ده بر آدمه دنیایه نسبت[47] وطن ، اوطوردیغى شهره نسبت كندى خانه‌سى حكمنده كورونور .

انسان وطننى سور ، چونكه وطننده موجود اولان حاكیتِڭ[48] بر جزئنه تصرّفِ[49] حقیقى[50] ایله متصرّفدر .

انسان وطننى سور ، چونكه وطن اویله بر غالبڭ[51] شمشیرى[52] وَ یا برکاتبڭ قلمیله چیزیلان مرهوم[53] خطلردن[54] عبارت دكل ؛ ملّیت ،[55]

24. *mad'dé* material (§ 582, 644). 25. *jûz* a part, fragment. 26. p. *gûzéshté* past (§ 555). 27. p. *yad* recollection; *hazeen* sad (adj. qual. *hûzn* [§ 606]). 28. *téhaj'jûr* petrification, embodiment (V. of *hajér* [§ 622]). 29. *hûr'riyét* liberty (§ 581). 30. comfort, rest. 31. *haqq* right. 32. *qayim* existent (fayil of *qîyam*). 33. existence. 34. *éjdad* ancestors (pl. of *jédd* [§ 639]). 35. *maqbéré* a burial place (N. of Loc. *qabr* [§ 598]). 36. *sûkûn* rest, calmness. 37. *nétijé* result, effect (§ 582). 38. *jilvégîah* a place or seat of beauty, life. 39. *ishtirak* participation (VIII. of *shirkét*). 40. *it'tihad* union (§ 628). 41. *ménfa-at* interest (n. w. mim of *naf'* [§ 597]). 42. *késrét* abundance. 43. *mûvanésé* familiarity, friendship (III. of *ûnsiyét*). 44. *jihétiyilé* by means. 45. *qarabét* near relationship. 46. *oukhouv'vét* fraternity. 47. *nisbét* proportion. 48. *hakimiyét* sovereignity (§ 582). 49. *tasar'rouf* disposal, possession (V. of *sarf*). 50. *haqiqi* real (§ 581). 51. *ghalib* conqueror (fayil of *ghalébé*). 52. *shémsheer* sword. 53. *mévhoum* imaginary (méfoul of *véhm*). 54. *khatt* line. 55. *mil'liyét* nationality (§ 581).

حرّیت ، منفعت ، اخوّت ، تصرّف ، حاکمیت ، اجداده حرمت ، عائله‌یه

محبت ، یادِ شباب ⁵⁶ کبی بر چوق حسّیاتِ علویه‌نك ⁵⁷ اجتماعندن ⁵⁸ حاصل

اولمش بر فکرِ مقدّسدر.   ﴿کمال بك﴾

56. *shébab* youth. 57. *oulvi, -viyé* noble (§ 579 of علو *'oulouv*).
58. *ijtima* union (VIII. of *jém* [§ 627]).

درس ٥٧   Lesson 57.

Arabic Compound Words.

§ 693. There are many compound words in use
in Ottoman, composed of two Arabic words. They are
connected together either according to the Arabic or
the Persian systems of Izafét (§§ 515, 668). The
majority of such words are composed according to the
Persian system.

But there are some Arabic words which are in
frequent use in Ottoman in composition with other
words of Arabic origin. Their use will be best understood from the following examples:

§ 694.   **I. Arabic System.** اصول عربی

1. ذی *zi* (sing. genitive), ذو *zou* (nomin.); ذوی *zévi*
(pl.) owner, possessor:

ذیروح *zirouh* animated.   ذیقیمت *ziqîymét* precious.

ذیشان *zishan* glorious.   ذوآلید *zoulyéd* possessed of a
                                           hand, handed.

ذُو ٱلْجَلَل *zoul jélal* possessed of glory, Lord of Glory (God).

ذوی ٱلْاَرْحَام *zévil érham* possessors of relation, relatives

2. صاحب *sahib* possessor; pl. اصحاب *as-hab:* -

صَاحِبُ ٱلْاَمْضَا *sahibúl imza* who signs, the undersigned.

صَاحِبُ ٱلْخَيْرَات وَٱلْحَسَنَات *sahibúl khayrat vél hasanat.* The
possessor (or the author) of this good and charitable work.

3. لا *la* not, without:

لا يُحْصَا *la youh'sa* innumerable.   لايَمُوت *la yémout* immortal.

لا يُخْطَى *la youkh'ti* infallible.   لا بُدّ *la bûdd'* inevitable.

لاشى *la shéy'* nothing.   لا أُبَالى *la ûbali* careless.

§ 695. II. Persian System. اصول فارسى

1. ولىّٰ *vélee, véli* owner; patron. pl. اوليا *évliya.*

ولئ عهد *véliyi ahd* the heir apparent, crown prince.

ولى النعم ' *véli niymét, véliyûn' niyam* benefactor.

ولى نعمت يمنت *véli niyméti bimin'nét* a benefactor who upraids not.

2. ارباب *érbab* (pl. of ربّ *rébb*) owner of, endowed with, master:

ارباب حكمت *érba'bî hikmét* men of wisdom, philosophers.

ارباب هنر *érba'bî hunér* endowed with skill, artisans.

ارباب مراق *érba'bî méraq* men of curiosity, of hobbies.

بو ايشك اربابى در *bou ishiñ érba'bîdîr* he is skilful in this. t.

3. صاحب *sahib*, pl. اصحاب *as-hab* possessor, owner:

صاحب ثروت *sahi'bi sérvét* a man of wealth, rich.

اصحاب ثروت *as-ha'bî sérvét* the rich class.

اصحاب نجابت *as-ha'bî néjabét* the noble class, nobilities.

صاحب فراش *sahi'bi firash* ill in bed, sick.

4. انواع *énva*, pl. of نوع *név*; kinds, varieties:

انواع مشقت *énva'yi méshaq'qat* all kinds of troubles.

5. اهل *éhl* man, person, pl. اهالى *éhali*:

اهل اسلام *éh'li islam* a Moslem.   اهل عرض *éh'li îrz* honorable.

اهل بيت *éh'li béyt* family.   اهل خبره *éh'li khîbré* expert.

اهل هيئت *éh'li hiyét* astronomer.   اهل منطق *éh'li mantîq* logician.

اهليت *éh'liyét* capacity, capability, ability (§ 581).

اهليتلى *éh'liyétli* able, capable. t.   اهليتسز *éh'liyétsiz* incapable.

6. حسن *hûsn* goodness, good: pl. محاسن *méhasin*.

حسن خدمت *hûs'nû khîdmét* good, valuable service.

حسن حال *hûs'nû hal* good condition; character.

حسن خط *hûs'nû khatt'* fine penmanship.

7. سوء *sou* evil, bad (pl. مساوى *mésavi* [§ 649]):

سوء حال *sou'yî hal* bad behaviour, bad condition.

سوء ظن *sou'yi zann* a bad opinion, suspicion.

سوء قصد *sou'yi qasd* attempt to murder.

سوء استعمال *sou'yi istimal* bad usage, abuse.

8. عدم *adém* non-existence, absence (used with nouns):

عدم اطاعت *adé'mi ita-at* disobedience.

عدم رعايت *adé'mi ri-a-yét* dishonour.

عدم قدرت *adé'mi qoudrét* weakness.   عدم وجود *adé'mi vûjoud* non-existence.

ديار عدم *diya'rî adém* abode of annihilation, death.

9. بلا *bi'la* without (used with nouns [§ 530]):

بلا قصور *bi'la qousour* blameless; spotless; perfect.

بلا غرض *bi'la gharaz* without any intention, aimless; sincere.

10. غير *ghay'rî* non-, in-, un- (with adjectives):

غير ممكن *ghay'rî mûmkin* impossible.

غير معلوم *ghay'rî malûm* unknown.

غير لايق *ghay'rî layîq* unworthy.

غير كافى *ghay'rî kiafi* unsufficient.

مسلم وَ غيرِ مسلم *mûslim vé ghay'ri mûslim* Moslem and non-Moslem.

11. كمال *kémal* perfection; perfect:

كمال دقت *kéma'li dîq'qat* perfect attention.

كمال تشكّر *kéma'li téshék'kûr* perfect gratitude.

12. نفس *néfs* person, self:

بِاَلْنَفْس ، بِنَفْسِهِ *bin'néfs, binéf'sihi* personally.

نفس شهرده .t *néfsi shéhirdé* in the very city.

كندى نفسم اوزه‌رينه .t *kéndi néfsim ûzériné* on my person.

13. عين ، عينى *ay'ni* the very same:

بعَيْنِهِ ، عينيله .t *ayniy'lé, biay'nihi* exactly the same.

عين صورت *ay'ni sourét* the exact copy; the very same way.

عينى زمانده .t *ay'ni zémanda* at the same time.

تعليم قرائت Reading Exercise.

نكبت و ذات اهل ظلمت

بر عبدِ حبش¹ دهره² اولور بخت ايله٣ سلطان،

ضحاكلِكُ⁴ ايدر ملكنى⁵ بركاوه⁶ پريشان⁷.

اقبالنه ادبارينه⁸ بل باغلامه⁹ دهرك،

بر دائره‌ده¹⁰ دور ايده‌مز چنبرِ دوران¹¹.

ظالم¹² ينه بر ظلمه كرفتار اولور¹³ آخر¹⁴،

البته اولور او يبقانك خانه‌سى ويران.

Words and Notes. Nékbét ou zil'léti éhli zoulmét the overthrow and abasement of tyrants. 1. *abd* slave; *habésh* Abyssinian; a negro. 2. *déhr* world. 3. p. *bakht* fortune, destiny. (Allusion is made to Nadir Shah, the conqueror of Tartary, Afghanistan and India 1735—45.) 4. *Dah'hak* name of a celebrated Arabian tyrant, who conquered Persia and slew king Jémshid. He is said to have had two snakes living between his shoulders, which were fed daily with the brains of two little children, Zohak (Astyages? Deioces?). 5. *milk* kingdom. 6. *Kîâvé* name of the blacksmith of Ispahan, Kava (Cepheus), who killed Zohak's tax-gatherer who came to seize his children, hoisted his own leather apron as a standard of revolt and made Feridoun (Phraortes), a descendant of Jemshid, king, and delivered Persia. 7. *périshan ét.''* to scatter or ruin. 8. *iqbal, idbar* prosperity, misfortune. 9. *bél baghlamaq* to trust. 10. *dayiré* circle (§ 582). 11. *dévr ét.''* to turn, revolve; *chénbéri dévran* fortune's wheel. 12. *zûlm* wrong; the fayil of which is *zalim* tyrant. 13. *giriftar ol.''* to be subjected to. 14. *akhîr* at last (fayil of *akhér*).

اكثر¹⁵ كورولور چونكه جزا جنسِ عملدن¹⁶ ،

انجامده¹⁴ آهندن¹⁷ اولور رخنهٔ سوهان¹⁸ .

تذكير اولونور¹⁹ لعن²⁰ ايله حجّاج²¹ ايله³⁴ جنكيز²² ،

تبجيل ايديلير²³ نوشيروان ايله³⁴ سليمان²⁴ .

قابلميدر²⁵ الفاظ ايله²⁶ تغيير²⁷ حقيقت ؟

ممكنمى²⁵ كه تفريق اولونه²⁸ كفر²⁹ ايله ايمان ؟

برخاكدن انشا اولونور³⁰ دير ايله مسجد³¹ ،

بر در نظرِ حقده³² مجوس³³ ايله³⁴ مسلمان .

هر دردك اولور چارهسى ، هر ايكلهين³⁵ اولمز ؛

هر محنته³⁶ بر آخرِ¹⁴ اولور هر غمّه پايان³⁷ .

صبر ايت سِتَمه ! ايستر ايسهلك حسنِ مكافات³⁸ ؛

فِكر أيله³⁹ ! نه ظلم ايلهديلر يوسفه اخوان⁴⁰ .

ظالمِلره¹² بركون ديديرير قدرتِ مَوْلَى :

"تَاللّٰهِ لَقَدْ آثَرَكَ اللّٰهُ عَلَيْنَا"⁴¹ .   ⟨تركيب بند : ضيا پاشا⟩

15. *éksér* for *éksériya* frequently (§ 683); *jéza* punishment.
16. *jins* kind, sort; *amél* crime, sin, guilt (= tooth for tooth and
eye for eye). 17. *ahén* iron. 18. *rakhné* ruin, death; *souhan* a file,
rasp. 19. *tézkeer ét.''* to remember, remind. 20. *lan* cursing.
21. *Haj'jaj* a celebrated tyrant, governor of Iraq. 22. *Jéngiz* the
great cruel and conqueror of the 13th century. 23. *tébjeel* treating
with great honour. 24. *Nousheervan* name of the greatest king of
the Sassani line of Persian sovereigns; *Souléyman* Solomon. 25. *qabil,*
mûmkin (fayil of *imkīan*) possible. 26. *élfaz* words, terms. 27. *tagh-*
yeer to change, verify (§ 615). 28. *téfreeq* to distinguish (§ 615).
29. كفر if pron. *kûfr* means blasphemy; if *kéfr* covering, atonement;
belief. 30. *insha ét.''* to build. 31. *deer* a monastery; *mésjid*
a mosque. 32. *nazari Haqq* in God's sight (comp. Matt. VI., 45).
33. *méjous* fire-worshipper. 34. *ilé* for *vé.* 35. *iñlémék* to moan,
to suffer. 36. *mih'nét* affliction; *ghamm* sorrow. 37. p. *payan*, a. *akhîr*
end, limit; *sitém* injury. 38. *muktafat* reward (III. of *kéyf* [§ 706 b]);
hûsnû— (§ 695 ⁶). 39. think about; *Yousouf* Joseph. 40. *ikhvan*
brothers. 41. *Tal'lahi léqad asérékél lahou aléyna* Truly (By God!),
God has appointed you ruler over us (these are the words which
the brothers of Joseph spoke — according to the Qoran — when
he made himself known to them).

مكالمه Conversation.

بر زيارت A visit.

ايشته افندم! خانهنك افنديس وَ خانمى
بزه طوغرى كلييورلر.

اخشام شريفلر خير اولسون، افندم!
صفا كلديكز! خوش كلديكز!

احباى كرامهمدن عزيز افندىيى ذات
عاليكزه تقديم ايتمكله افتخار
ايدهرم.

تشكر ايدهرم افندم! وَ ذات عاليكزى
طانيمق شرفنه نائل اولديغمدن طولايى
درجهٔ نهايهده ممنونم.

بندهكز ده اويله افندم! بو جهتله
كنديمى غايت مفتخر عَدّ ايدهرم.

صيره بندهكزه كلينجه اقربامدن بولونان
رامز اوحانس افندينك مخدومى آرام
افندىيى ذات عاليلرينه تقديم ايدهرم،
تقديراتكزدن طولايى فوق العاده
تشكرلر ايدهرم. ذات عاليكزى
كورديكمه پك ممنون اولدم افندم.

قولكزى بوشرفله مشرف يوردينغكزه
تشكر ايدهرم. رامز اوحانس افندى
حضرتلرينك نام عاليلرينى چوق دفعه
مدح وُ ستايشله ايشيتمش ايدم.

خانم افندى! ذات عصمتانهكزى
كورديكمزه نهايت درجهده ممنون
و مسرور اولدق.

بكم! بنده خانهيى تشريفكزله مشرَف
بويورديغكزه پك بويوك افندللك
ايتديكز.

درس ٥٨ Lesson 58.

كلمات مترادفه Synonymous Words.

§ 696. In the Arabic and Persian languages it is customary to use two and even three words of the same meaning (*Kélimatî Mûtéradîfé*) in the same sentence to express one idea. This is considered one of the beauties of the language. That was the case with the old Ottoman literature too, in which the Turks imitated this characteristic of the said languages.

But through contact with European languages and their literature, the new generation of writers has begun gradually to forsake the old wearisome system and to

adapt the use of simple and single words. Yet there remain some instances of the old system, which by the sanction of centuries have been stereotyped and consolidated even in the common speech.

§ 697. The synonymous words are united together by a وَ, which is generally pronounced *ou*, *vû*, not *vé*. The shorter of the two comes first.

For instance, the Turkish word چاليشهلم *chalîshalîm* is expressed by سعى وُ اقدام ايدهلم *say ou iqdam édélim*, or سعى وُ غيرت ايدهلم *say ou ghayrét édélim*: the words سعى ، اقدام ، غيرت all meaning 'effort'; and the meaning of the sentences is 'let us try'.

جناب اللهﯔ كرم وُ عنايتى دوكنمز *jénabi Al'lahiñ kérémou inayét dûkénméz* the mercy of God does not come to an end.

لطفكزى تمنّى وُ ترجّى ايدهرم *loutfounouzou témén'ni vû téréj'ji édérim* I ask for your kindness.

دينمى ادا وُ ايفا ايلهدم *déynimi éda vû iy-fa éylédim* I paid my debts (وَ is pronounced *vû*, after vowels).

The words ترجّى ا۔ ؛ تمنّى ا۔ both mean 'to ask' and ادا اۛ ؛ ايفا اۛ mean 'to pay'.

Note. **ou** is appended to the last syllable of the previous word.

مثاللر Examples.

مدح و ثنا اۛ	*méd'hou séna ét."*	to praise.
تقدير و تحسين اۛ	*taqdir ou tah'seen ét."*	to praise and appreciate
قتل و اعدام اۛ	*qatlou idam ét."*	to kill.
اخذ و كرفت اۛ	*akhzou girift ét."*	to arrest and seize.
حاضر و آماده	*hazir ou amadé*	ready.
علوم و فنون	*ouloum ou fûnoun*	arts and sciences.
علم و عرفان	*ilmou îrfan*	science and art.
عرض و تقديم اۛ	*arzou taqdîm ét."*	to present, to offer.
دولت و اقبال	*dévlét ou iqbal*	prosperity and good fortune.

II. كلمات مُسَجَّعَه Symphonious Terminations.

§ 698. It was a great task in the ancient Ottoman literature, in imitation of Arabic and Persian to accumulate in a sentence words of the same termination; as:

هنكام طعام رسيدهٔ انجام اولونجه *héngîamî ta-am résidéyi énjam oloun'ja* when dinner(-time) was over.

ولادت باهرالسعادت حضرت پادشاهى *véladéti bahirûs'-sa-a-déti hazréti padishahi* the prosperous birth-day of H. I. M. the Sultan.

جلوس ميمنت مأنوس حضرت ظل اللهى *jûlousou méyménét-mé-é-nousou hazréti zil'loul-lahi* the auspicious accession of H. I. M.

نشان ذيشان عثمانى *nishanî zishanî Osmani* the glorious Ottoman order (of knighthood).

III. كلماتِ مُتَضادَّه Antonyms.

§ 699. There is another class of words which, though they are not synonymous and have contrary meanings, are yet connected together by و *ou, vû:*

اخذ و اعطا *akhzou ita* a taking and giving, buying and selling, trade, business. Turkish *alish vérish.*

بو يولك ابتدا و انتهاسى يوقدر *bou yoloûñ iptida ou intihasî yoq dour* this road has no beginning and no end.

اقبال و ادبار اثناسنده *iqbal ou idbar ésnasînda* in the time of prosperity and misfortune.

چوجوقلره جزء و كلّى بر شى وير *chojouqlara jûz ou kûl'li bir shéy vér* give the children something more or less.

استانبوله عزيمت و عودت ايلهدم *Istambola azeemét ou avdét éylédim* I went to Constantinople and came back.

مثاللر *Misal'lér* Examples.

خير و شرّ	*khay'rou shérr'*	good and evil.
حيات و ممات	*hayatou mémat*	life and death.
سوال و جواب	*souval vé jévab*	question and answer.
كار و ضرر	*kîar vé zarar*	gain and loss.
صفا و جفا	*séfa vû jéfa*	pleasure and pain.
مكافات و مجازات	*mûkîafatou mûjazat*	reward and punishment.

ايفاء وُ استيفاء	iyfa vû istiyfa	payment and receipt of a debt.
ايجار وُ استيجار	ijar ou istijar	leasing and hiring.
تسليم وَ تسلّم	téslim vé tésél'lûm	delivery and receipt.
اقراض وُ استقراض	iqraz ou istiqraz	lending and borrowing.
تعليم وُ تعلّم	ta-lim ou té-al'-lûm	teaching and learning.

تعليم ١٥٠ Exercise 150.

I. ١ ١ انسان حيواناتدن معدود١ در : فقط ذوالروح ، ذوالّيد وَ صاحبِ
عقل وُ فكر در . مخلوقاتك حكمدار ذيشانى اولوب لايموت بر روحه
مالكدر٢ . ٢ بو چشمه صاحبُ الخيرات وَ الحسنات مرحوم٣ وَ مغفور
متوفا٣ كتهجيان حاجى٣ بوغوث افندينكدر٣ . ٣ پاپا٤ لايحتى يم ديو
ادّعا٥ ايدرسه‌ده ، اربابِ حكمت وُ كمالتدن هيچ بريسى بوكا ايمان
واعتقاد٦ ايتمزلر . ٤ لسان فارسيده ذيروح اولان اسملر "ان" ايله وَ غير
ذيروح اولانلر ايسه "ها" ايله جمعله‌نيرلر . ٥

*ذيقيمت مالگى١ * صات٧ * حالك٧ عرض ايتمه٨ * زامرده٩ ؛*
همان كه١٠ كلّه١١ صاغ اولسون * كلاه١٢ آكسيك دكلدر مَرده . . * (ضيا پاشا)

II. ٦ عَينى زمانده نفسِ شهرده دخى برحريقِ مُهيل١٣ ظهور ايله‌دى .
اطفاسى١٤ غيرِ ممكن اولديغندن اهاليدن چوقلرى اهلِ بيتلريله ديا . عدمه
هجرت ايله‌ديلر١٥ . پك چوقلرى اقبال وسعادتك اوج بالاسنده ايكن ،
برقاچ ساعت ظرفنده فقر وضرورتك درجهُ سُفلاسنه١٦ اينديلر . بعضيلرى

Words and Notes. 1. *ma'doud* regarded. 2. *malik dir* he has,
owns. 3. *mérhoum* deceased and admitted to God's mercy (méfoul
of *rahmét*); 3. *mûtéréf'fa* dead, asleep (méfoul of *téréf'fi* [§ 623]);
3. *haji* Jerusalem pilgrim (fayil of *hajj'* is *hajij* = *haji*); *Kétéjîan
Haji Boghos Efféndi*. 4. *papa* the pope of Rome. 5. *id-diya,
id-da-a* to claim. 6. *itiqad* conviction (VIII. of *aqd* [§ 627]), *eeman*
belief. 7. *haliñ'* for *haliñi* your situation, distress. 8. *arz étmék*
to state politely. 9. *namérd* coward (§ 530), cruel. 10. *héman ki* since.
11. *kél'lé* skull, head. 12. *kûlah'* cap; *mérd* a manly man. 13. *mûheel*
dreadful (fayil of *ihalé*, IV. of هول). 14. *itfa* to extinguish (§ 619).
15. *hijrét ét."* to pass. 16. *sûfla* lower, lowest (fem. of *ésfél* [§ 610].

مجروح اولوب صاحب فراش اولدیلر • ٧ انکلایز حکومتی ولئ عهدی فخامتلو

پرنس دی غال حضرتلاری ۱۷ هندستانه مُتَوَجّهاً سَیر و سیاحته ۱۷ چیقمشلر •

٨ معلمكز السید ۱۸ حاجی ۱۸ کریم افندینك حقّكیزده حسن ظنّی میوار ؟

یوخسه سؤ ظَنّی می ؟ ٩ افندم ! معلّم مومی الیهك حقّ عاجزانهمده

حسنِ توجُّهلری باقی و دائمدر ۱۹ • ١٠ حاضر و آماده امریکزده منتظرم •

17. *séyr ou séyahat* journey; 17. *préns dî Gal* the Prince of Wales. 18. *és-séy'yid* a descendant from Mûhamméd, Lord; 18. *haji* pilgrim to Mecca. 19. *baqî* everlasting (*fayil* of *baqa*), *dayim* permanent (*fayil* of *dévam*).

ترجمه ۱۵۱ Translation 151.

I. 1. The speaker[1] began[2] his speech, by saying, 'Honourable hearers.'[3] 2. Where is the residence of the undersigned? 3. The word 'who' is used for those who have sense[4], and 'which' for things which have no sense. 4. My uncle is wealthy: his property is immense (innumerable). 5. Kojaman oghlou is a skilful (capable) artisan, he is a thorough master of his business: but Bîchaqjî oghlou is an incapable man, his family is always in poverty[5]. 6. Scientists and artists have done great services to humanity[6].

II. 7. The teacher of penmanship in the College is Haji Nahid Effendi. 8. The pupils who have been disobedient[7], the teacher disgraces[8] them. 9. There was a great multitude[9]: the Moslem and the non-Moslem inhabitants of the city, with their families, were all present there. 10. I have not the habit of lending and borrowing. 11. The leasing and the hiring of this house are finished[10]. 12. The question[11] of education[12] is a question of life and death for a nation. 13. The payment and the receipt of your debt are impossible now. 14. Ali-Mouzafför Effendi was appointed guardian (patron) to this orphan.

Words and Notes. 1. *natîq* (*fayil* of *noutq* speech). 2. *ibtidar ét.''* 3. *houz'zarî zévil vaqar hazaratî*: *huz'zar* pl. of *hazîr*, *zévil vaqar* (§ 694[1]); *hazarat* pl. of *hazrét*. 4. *zévil ouqoul*: *ouqoul*, pl. of *aql* sense (§ 694[1]). 5. *faqr ou zarourét*. 6. *insaniyét* (§ 581). 7. *adémi ita-atda boulounan*. 8. *adémi ri-ayétdé boulounour*. 9. *iz-diham* (§ 620). 10. *khitam boulmaq*. 11. *mésélé* (n. w. *mim* of *souval*). 12. *talimou térbiyé*.

تعليم قرائت **Reading Exercise.**

ترکیب بند

اللهه توکّل ¹ ایدهنك یاوری حقّدر ،

ناشاد ² کوکل برکون اولور شاد ² اولهجقدر .

پك رنكنه آلدانه ! فلك ³ اسكی فلكدر ،

زیرا فلككك مشرِب ناسازی ⁴ دونك ⁵ در .

اللّٰهه صیغین ⁶ شخص حلیمك ⁷ غضبندن ⁸ ،

زیرا یومشاق ⁹ خویلو آتك چیفتهسی ⁹ پك ¹⁰ در .

یاقدی نیجه جانلر او تزاکتله تبسّم ¹¹ ،

شیرك ¹² دخی قصد ایتمهسی ¹² جانه ، کوله رکدر .

بداصله ¹³ نجابت می ¹⁴ ویریر اونوفورمه ¹⁵ ؟

زردوز ¹⁶ پالان وورسهاك ¹⁷ ، اَشك ینه اشكدر .

بدمایه ¹⁸ اولان آكلاشیلیر مجلس مَیده ¹⁹ ،

عشرت ²⁰ گرِر ²¹ آدمی تمیزه ²² محك ²³ در .

Words and Notes. Térkibi-bénd a poem in stanzas of similar metre but of different rhyme; the distiches of each stanza rhyme, excepting the last distich (pp. 302, 396). 1. *tévék'kûl* to trust (in God) [V. of *vékîl*]; *yavér* helper; *Haqq* The True One, God. 2. *shad* happy; *nashad* unhappy (§ 530). 3. *félék* a revolving sphere of the heavens; fortune, destiny. 4. *méshréb* natural disposition; *nasaz* discordant, incorrect. 5. *déônék* inconsistent, changeable (§ 439). 6. Take refuge! Trust to God! (= May God keep you). 7. *halim* mild, gentle (adj. q. of *hilm* [§ 606]). 8. *ghazab* anger. 9. *youmshaq khouylou* mild-natured; *chifté* a kick with both hind feet at once. 10. *pék, pérk* violent, severe. 11. graceful smile: *nézakét* (pseudo-Arabic from p. *nazik*) grace; *tébés'sum* smile (§ 622). 12. p. *sheer* a lion; *qasd ét''* to intend to kill. 13. *béd-asil* whose family or origin is vile, bad; mean, nasty. 14. *néjabét* nobility. 15. *ûniforma* uniform [It.]. 16. *zérdouz* gold-laced (§ 535). 17. to saddle: *palan* a pad substituted for a saddle in the East; it resembles a large cushion. 18. *béd-mayé* vile-natured (§ 536). 19. pleasure party, society: *méy*, wine. 20. *ishrét* drinking, wine. 21. *gihér* disposition. 22. *tém'yeez ét.''* to distinguish. 23. *méhékk'*, vulg. *méhéng* a touchstone, test (n. i. of *hékk* [§ 599]).

نصح ⁲⁴ ايله يوله كلمه‌يه‌نى ايتمه‌لى تكدير ⁲⁵ ،

تكدير ايله اوصلانغايانك حتّى ²⁶ كوتك ²⁷ در .

ايمان ايله دين ²⁸ : آقچه در ارباب غناده ²⁹ ،

ناموس و حميت ³⁰ سوزى قالدى فقراده .

بر يرده كه يوق نغمه‌گى ³¹ تقدير ايده‌جك ³² كوش ³³ ،

تضييعِ نَفَس ايلمه‌مه ³⁴ ! تبديل مقام ³⁵ ايت !

عورت ³⁶ كبى مغلوبِ هوا ³⁷ اوله ! ارِ ³⁸ اول ار !

نَفسك ³⁹ سنى رام ايتمه‌سين ⁴⁰ ، سن نَفسكى رام ايت .

مانندِ شجر ⁴¹ نابت اولور ⁴² ثابت اولانلر ⁴³ ،

هرهانكى ايشك اهلى ⁴⁴ ايسه‌ك ؛ اونده دوام ايت !

نقصانكى ⁴⁵ بيل ! بر ايشه يا باشلامه اوّل !

يا باشلاديغك كارى ⁴⁶ پذيراى ختام ⁴⁷ ايت . ﴿ضيا پاشا﴾

24. *nous-h', nousouh'* advice; *yola gélmék* to come right.
25. to punish (§ 615). 26. *haqq'* right, claim. 27. *kéôték* beating,
cudgelling. 28. belief and religion. 29. *érbabî ghina* the rich people
(§ 695 ²). 30. *namous* a sense of honour, decorum; *hameeyét* honesty.
31. *naghmé* song, a melody sung. 32. *taqdeer et.''* to appreciate.
33. p. *gûsh* ear. 34. *tazyee* to waste [II. of *zay'*]; *néfés* the breath.
35. *tébdeel ét.''* to change; *maqam* a tune. 36. *avrét, avrat* woman.
37. *maghloub ol.''* to be defeated; *héva* any unreasonable bias. 38. *ér*
brave man (Armenian). 39. *néfs* the carnal man, the spirit of
conscupiscence. 40. *ram ét.''* to submit. 41. *manén'di shéjér* like
a tree. 42. *nabit ol.''* to grow, to vegetate. 43. *sabit ol.''* to be
firm. 44. *éhl* a capable man (§ 695 ⁵). 45. *noqsan* deficiency.
46. work. 47. *pézira'yî khitam ét.''* to bring to an end.

مكالمه Conversation.

A Visit on Ship-board.

صباح شريفلريكز خير اولسون !	صباحلر خير اولسون ! بويورك !
نره‌دن كليورسكز ؟	ازميردن كلييورز افندم !
سواريكزك اسمى نه‌در ؟	قپودان جون سيمور در افندم !
سفينه‌كزك اسمى نه‌در ؟	سفينه‌مزك اسمى 'اسقوچيا' در افندم !

بر شیئه احتیاجکز وار می؟

تشکر اولونور شمدیلك هیچ برشیئه
احتیاجمز یوقدر.

دیشاریده هوا نصل ایدی؟

هوالر پك مساعد ایدی.

بوراده نه‌قدر بولونه‌جقسکز؟

بر هفته قدر.

مُدّت سیاحتکز نقدر امتداد ایله‌دی؟

صوك اسکله‌ن اولان ازمیردن بوصالی
کونی حرکت ایتدك.

اوحالده ایکی کوندنبری دکیزده
بولونویوررسکز؟

اوت افندم!

نه‌ره یه کیتمکی تصمیم ایدییورسکز؟

پك اصابت ایدرسکز؟ ماکنه‌کزده
وقوع‌بولان سَقَطلنی بلا معاونت تسویه
ایده‌بیلیرمیسکز؟

اکر مُخْتَلِف هوایه تصادف ایتمز
ایسه‌ك بیروته قدر کیده‌جکز.

بورایه نصل کلدیکز؟

معاونتکزه تشکرلر اولونور ، لکن ایکی
ساعته‌قدر بزجه تعمیری ممکندر.

الله ایصمارلادق! آلمش اولدیغم معلوماتی
قرودانفه اخبار ایده‌جکم.

یلکن ایله کلدك.

لطفیکزك منتداری‌یم ، لکن شمدی طورمغه
وقتمك عدم مساعده‌سندن طولایی
انشاالله معامله‌ً مهمان‌نوازانه‌کیزدن وقت
آخرده مستفید اولورم.

بر فینجان قهوه ایچرمیسیکیز.

شیمدیلك الله ایصمارلادك!

نه وقت آرزو ایدرسه‌کیز ، تشریف
ایدیکز. تشریفکزله مشرف اوله‌جنم.
احترامات فائقه‌می قودانیکیزه
تقدیمله کسب فخر و شرف ایده‌رم.

خوش کلدیکز! صفا کلدیکز!

---

۵۹ درس   Lesson 59.

Euphonic Changes of the Letters.

A. Assimilation or ادغام Idgham.

§ 700. Idgham is (the imposition of one letter
on another, or) the assimilation of one letter to another.
This occurs when two letters of the same kind have
come together. The imposition (or assimilation) always
takes place on the second letter, provided that the first

is quiescent (§ 42). The assimilation is denoted by a *shéddé* (ّ) over the second letter; the quiescent letter is marked by a *jézma* (ْ) [§ 45].

§ 701. There are four cases in which *Idgham* occurs:

a. **If the First of the double Homogeneous Letters is quiescent,** it is removed or imposed upon the second, and the latter is doubled or marked with a *shéddé*; as:

مِلْلَتْ *mil'lét:* the first *lam* is quiescent: therefore it is omitted and imposed on the second *lam:* and this imposition is indicated by a *shéddé*, which shows that the second *lam* is doubled thus: مِلَّتْ *mil'lét.*

حِدْدَتْ *hid'dét* ʿanger': is written as حِدَّتْ *hid'dét.*

دعوت٬ عفو *davét, afv:* the Obj. Part. of the measure مفقول is مَعْفُوْوْ٬ مَدْعُوْوْ *médouv, mafouv;* the first letter و is quiescent, therefore imposed on the second و; as: مَعْفُوّ٬ مَدْعُوّ *médouv, mafouv.*

There is no change in the pronunciation in either instances.

b. **If the First of the double Homogeneous Letters is punctuated by a vowel,** the vowel is cast back upon the preceding letter and the letter itself imposed upon the second:

إِخْلَال *ikhlal* to spoil: the remainder is خلل (§ 634 a): the Subjective Participle is مُخْلِل: the first of the double letters has a vowel, the vowel is cast back upon the preceding letter: hence مُخْلِلْ *moukh'-lil* becomes مُخِلّْ *moukhill;* after the assimilation مُخِلّ *mou-khill'.*

شديد *shédid* severe: √شَدَدَ: the Noun of Superiority according to the measure أَفْقَل (§ 609) is أَشْدَدْ *ésh'-déd:* Remove the vowel to the preceding: it is أَشَدْدْ *éshédd*, after the assimilation أَشَدّ *é-shédd* ʿseverest'.

c. **If the Preceding Letter already has a vowel,** or **if it is an *élif*,** the vowel of the first letter cannot be carried back to the preceding; therefore the vowel of the first letter is omitted: and the letter itself is placed over the second of the double homogeneous letters:

ارتداد *irtidad* apostasy (VIII of رَدَدَ√ [§ 627]): the remainder is رتدد (§ 634 a): the Subj. Part. is مُرْتَدِدْ *murté'-did:* the first of the double letters دِ has a vowel: that vowel cannot be brought back to the preceding تَ; because it already has a vowel: therefore the vowel of the first دِ is omitted: as مُرْتَدْدْ *murtédd*, and the letter itself imposed upon or assimilated with the second دْ: as مُرْتَدّْ *mûr-tédd'* (vulg. *mourtad, mîrtad*) apostate.

Note. In such cases the Objective Participle is the same with Subj. Part. as: مُرْتَدَدْ *murtédéd* = مُرْتَدْ = مُرْتَدّْ *murtédd;* but the Obj. Part. of the measures *Infiqal* and *Iftiqal* is not used.

مرور *mûrour* to pass: مَرَرَ√: according to the measure فَاقِلْ the Subj. Part. is مَارِرْ *ma'-rir:* the first of the double homogeneous letters (رِ) has a vowel; but that vowel cannot be transported to the preceding letter, because it is *élif:* therefore the vowel of the first *ré* is omitted as مَارْرْ *marr:* and the letter itself assimilated with the second *ré* رْ: as مَارّْ *marr'.*

d. If two *élifs* have come together, the first *élif* is assimilated with the second: but the second *élif*, instead of taking a *shéddé*, has a *médda* placed over it (§§ 29 d, 39, 47, 603):

امر *émr* order: the Subj. Part. of the measure فَاقِلْ is اَامِرْ *é-amir:* the first *élif* is omitted and the second has *médda;* thus آمِرْ *a-mir* commander. اتيان *ityan* to follow: اَتَيَ√:فَاقِلْ: اَاتِ *é-a-ti* = آتِ *a-ti* following.

Note. 1. All double homogeneous letters are not subject to assimilation, there are exceptions; as: مدد *médéd* help, خلل *khalél* injury, ضرر *zarar* loss, سبب *sébéb* reason, اكتتاب *iktitab* copying.

2. The Subj. Part. of حج *hajj* 'pilgrimage' is حَاجِجْ = حَاجّْ *hajj* = حَاجْ *hajj* or حَاجِى *haji* pilgrim [to Mecca (Sûnni Moslems), Jerusalem (Christians), Kérbéla (Persians) and Haji Béktash near Kîr-shéhir (Qizîlbashes)].

تَعْلِيم ١٥٢   Exercise 152.

Change the following words into the prescribed forms, first without *idgham* and afterwards with *idgham:*

Into the Subjective Participle (Fayil §§ 601—3, 634 d):

، اَخْذٌ⁶ ، اِنْضِمَامٌ⁵ ، خُصُوصٌ⁴ ، اَكْلٌ³ ، اِسْتِمْدَادٌ² ، اِخْتِلَالٌ¹

. اِستقلال ، عُمُومٌ¹⁰ ، اِحْمِرَارٌ⁹ ، تَمَامٌ⁸ ، اِضْرَارٌ⁷، اسوداد

Into the Noun of Location (مَفْقَلٌ):

. حَكّ¹³ ، مُرُورٌ¹² ، حُلُولٌ¹¹ ، قوارٌ¹¹

Into the Noun of Superiority (اَفْقَلٌ § 609):

. جلال ، لَذِيذٌ¹⁷ ، عَزِيزٌ¹⁶ ، قَلِيلٌ¹⁵ ، صَحِيحٌ¹⁴ ، تَامٌ¹⁴ ، خِفَّت

Into the Noun with *Mim* (مَفْقَلَتٌ):

. حُلُولٌ ، ذِلَّت ، سُرُورٌ²⁰ ، ضَرَرٌ¹⁹ ، حُبٌّ¹⁸ ، وداد¹⁸

Words. 1. confusion (spoilt). 2. to implore help (who asks help). 3. to eat. 4. case, especiality (especial). 5. addition (added). 6. to take. 7. persistence (persistent). 8. completeness. 9. a becoming red (intensely red). 10. common (general, public). 11. to abide, stay (an abode, place). 12. to pass (a passage, path). 13. to scratch (a touch stone). 14. complete; true. 15. few. 16. beloved. 17. delicious. 18. love (love). 19. loss (loss). 20. joy (joy).

B. Modification of Letters. اعلال *Eelal.*

§ 702. The letters ا و ى are called 'weak' or 'feeble' letters (*houroufou illét*), and all the others are called 'sound' letters (*houroufou sahihé*) by the Arabs. The weak letters cannot bear any burden or 'motion' (vowel), as the sound letters can; they cannot have any vowel, they must be quiescent (§ 42). If in the formation of words they should be in a position in which a vowel would naturally be placed on them, were they 'sound' letters, this vowel is removed or modified.

§ 703. The general principal of modification or permutation of the weak letters is as follows:

When a vowel (ـَ) and a weak letter (ا و ى) which is not analogous to it come together in a word, the ordinary laws of euphony require that one should yield; and in Arabic the vowel prevails.

Note. Élif is analogous to *ûstûn*, *yé* to *ésré* and *vav* to *eôtré* (§ 27).

§ 704. The weak letters و and ى require especial consideration: the changes of ا are not important.

§ 705. Modification of *vav* اعلال واو

a. If *vav* has a vowel and the preceding letter is quiescent, its vowel is transported to the preceding letter; as:

the خَوْفَ ، قَوَلَ ، صَوَنَ ، صَوْن ، قَوْل ، خَوْف *savn, qavl, khavf* √ Obj. Part. by the measure مَفْعُول (§ 604): مَصْوُون ، مَقْوُول ، مَخْوُوف *mas-voun, maq-voul, makh-vouf:* modified مَصْوون *ma-sou-oun* etc. after the assimilation مَخْوُف ، مَقْوُل ، مَصْون *ma-soun, maqoul, makhouf* 'kept, spoken, terrible'.

b. If the letter preceding *vav* has *ésré* as its vowel (ـِو) *vav* is changed into ى (*-i-*); as:

The word.	Root.	Measure.	Natural form[1].	Modified form.
دُعَاء *dou'a*	دَعَوَ	فَاعِل	دَاعِو *da-yiv*	دَاعِى *da-yi*
وَزْن *vézn*	وَزَنَ	مِفْقَال	مِوْزَان *miv-zan*	مِيزَان *miy-zan*
وُجُود *vûjoud*	وَجَدَ	اِفْقَال	اِوْجَاد *iv-jad*	إِيجَاد *iy-jad*
إِدَارَة (§ 620)	دَوَرَ	Subj. Part.	مُدْوِر *mûd-vir*	مُدِير *mû-dir.*

c. If the letter preceding *vav* have *ústún* as its vowel, (ـَو) the *vav* is changed into *élif* (*-a-*):

صَفْوَت *saf'vét*	صَفَوَ	مُفَاقَلَه	مُصَافَوَت *mûsa-fé-vét*	مُصَافَات *mûsafat*
عَدَاوَت *adavét*	عَدَوَ	»	مُعَادَوَت *mou-a-dévét*	مُعَادَات *mou-a-dat*

---

[1] The forms in this column do not actually occur, but are given to show how the rule works.

The word.	Root.	Measure.	Natural form.	Modified form.
رِضَاء riza	رَضَوَ	مَفْقَلَتْ	مَرْضَوَتْ mér-zé-vét	مَرْضَاة mérzat
قَوْلْ qavl	قَوَلَ	مَفْقَلْ	مَقْوَلْ maq-vél	مَقَال ma-qal
دَوْر dévr	دَوَرَ	»	مَدْوَرْ médvér	مَدَار médar.

d. *Vav* after servile *élif* is changed into *hémzé* (§§ 591, 602 a):

The word.	Root.	Measure.	Natural form.	Modified form.
دَوْر dévr	دَوَرَ	فَاقِلْ	دَاوِرْ da-vir	دَائِر da-yir
لَغْوْ laghv	لَغَوَ	اِفْقَال	اِلْغَاو il-ghav	اِلْغَاء il-gha
دَعْوَتْ davét	دَعَوَ	فُقَال	دُعَاو dou-av	دُعَاء dou-a
رِضْوَان rîdvan	رَضَوَ	فِقَال	رِضَاو ri-zav	رِضَاء riza
عُلُوّ ou-louv	عَلَوَ	استفقال	استعلاو is-ti-lav	استعلاء is-ti-la.

تَعْلِيم ١٥٣ Exercise 153.

Change the following nouns into the forms mentioned below: first into the natural and afterwards into the modified forms:

Subjective Participle (§§ 602—603):

اَصْطِفاء ، رِضَاء٧ ، نَوْمْ٦ ، سَمُوْ٥ ، صُومْ٤ ، خُلُوْ٣ ، قَوْل٢ ، دَوَام١ .

Noun with *Mim* (مَفْقَلْ):

مَوْت١١ ، جَوَاز١٠ ، كَوْن ، نَوْم ، ذَوْق٩ ، خَوْف٨ .

Words. 1. to continue. 2. word, agreement (consenting). 3. emptiness. 4. fasting. 5. eminence. 6. sleep. 7. consent. 8. fear. 9. taste (taste). 10. permission (figurative language). 11. death (death).

Derivative Infinitive (اِفْقَال [§ 621]).

وُجوب ، وُقوع ، وُضُوح [15] ، وُجود [14] ، وُصول [13] ، وُرُود [12]·

Deriv. Inf. (اِسْتِفْقَال [§ 631]): وُضُوح [18] ، وَفَاء [17] ، عَفْو [16]·

12. arrival (to bring forward, to cite). 13. arrival (to send). 14. existence (to invent). 15. clearness (to explain). 16. to excuse, pardon (to resign). 17. loyalty (to receive). 18. (to ask an explanation).

§ 706. **Modification of** *yé* يا، اعلال

a. If *yé* would properly and regularly have a vowel and if the preceding letter be quiescent, the vowel is transfered to the preceding letter:

The word.	Root.	Measure.	Natural form.	Modified form.
سَيَلَان *séyélan*	سَيَلَ	مَفْقَلْ	مَسِيِلْ *més-yil*	مَسِيل *mé-sil*
سَيْر *séyr*	سَيَرَ	مَفْقَلَتْ	مَسِيِرَة *més-yi-ré*	مَسِيرَة *mé-si-ré.*

b. If the letter preceding *yé* have *ústún* for its vowel, the *yé* is changed into *élif*:

نَفِي *néfi*	نَوَى	مُفَاقَلَه	مُنَافَيَتْ *mû-na-fé-yét*	مُنَافَات *mû-na-fat*
رِعَايَتْ *ri-ayét*	رَعَى	مُفَاقَلَه	مُرَاعَيَتْ *mûra-'é-yét*	مُرَاعَات *mû-ra-at*
زِيَارَتْ *ziyarét*	زَيَرَ	مَفْقَل	مَزْيَرْ *méz-yér*	مَزَار *mé-zar*
عَيْش *aysh*	عَيَشَ	مَفْقَل	مَعْيَشْ *ma-yésh*	مَعَاش *ma-ash*
هَيْبَتْ *héybét*	هَيَبَ	مَفْقَلَتْ	مَهْيَبَتْ *méh-yé-bét*	مَهَابَتْ *mé-ha-bét.*

c. If *yé* is quiescent and the preceding letter has *êôtré* as its vowel, the *yé* is changed into *vav*:

إِيَجاد *ijad*	(وَجَدَ) يجد	Subj. Part.	مُيِجِد *mouy-jid*	مُوجِد *mou-jid*
إِيَجاب *ijab*	(وَجَبَ) يجب	(§ 621)	مُيِجِب *mouy-jib*	مُوجِب *mou-jib.*

d. After the servile *élif*, *yé* is usually changed into *hémzé* (§§ 591, 602 a):

The word.	Root.	Measure.	Natural form.	Modified form.
نِيَابَتْ *niyabét*	نَيَبَ	فَاعِلْ	نَايِب *na-yib*	نَائِب *na-ib*
هَدِيَه *hédiyé*	هَدَىَ	اِفْقَال	اِهْدَاى *ihday*	اِهْدَاء *ihda*.

تعليم ١٥٤   Exercise 154.

Change the following words into the measures mentioned below: first into their natural and afterwards into their modified forms:

Subjective Participle [§§ 602—603]:

اِيرَاث ‛⁵ سَيَرَان ‛⁴ نَيْلَان ‛³ زِيَادَه ‛² زِيَارَتْ ‛¹ اِيمان ·

اِيجَار ‛ اِزدِياد ‛ انقِياد ‛ احتِياج ·

شِكَايَتْ ‛⁹ كِفَايَت ‛⁸ نَهَايَتْ ‛⁷ كِسْوَتْ ‛⁶ (افتِقال): Deriv. Inf.

Derivative Infinitive (افِقَال):

كِسْوَت ‛¹³ جَرَيَان ‛¹² سَقى ‛¹¹ رَخَاوَتْ ‛¹⁰ بقا ‛ خِفى ‛ نهى ·

Noun with *mim* (مفقِل):

(مفقَقَلَه) نور ‛¹⁷ رِضوَان ‛ حِيلَه ‛¹⁶ زِياده ‛¹⁵ فَيضْ ‛¹⁴ ·

Derivative Infinitive (§ 618): مُفَاقَلَتْ = مُفَاقَلَه

جَزا ‛ كَيْف ‛ نَفى ‛²⁵ بَها ‛²⁴ ‛²³ دَواء ‛²² نَجْو ‛²¹ صَفوَت ‛²⁰ لِقاء ‛¹⁹ رِعايَتْ ‛¹⁸

Words. 1. visit (visitor). 2. much (redundant, superfluous). 3. to obtain (worthy). 4. to leave a remnant, to look (other, remainder). 5. to cause: to leave a legacy (who leaves property to one as heir; that causes). 6. dress, costume (to wear a garment). 7. end (to come to an end). 8. to be enough (to suffice). 9. complaint (to complain). 10. softness (to loosen). 11. drinking (to drink). 12. to act, happen (to perform) 13. (to wear). 14. abundance. 15. much (auction). 16. horror. 17. light (light-house). 18. respect, esteem. 19. meeting, encounter. 20. delight (amity). 21. whispering (supplication). 22. medicine (treatment). 23. pleasure (to vaunt). 24. discord. 25. pleasure (reward).

تعليم قرائت Reading Exercise.

The Ceremony of the Coronation of the King of England.	انكلتره قرالى حضرتلرينك رسم تتوّجلرى

London: Aug. 9., 1902. — The ceremony of the Coronation took place at 12.40 in Westminster Abbey, the interior of which was splendidly decorated.

لوندره : ۹ آغستوس — (وستمينستر) كليساسنده ساعت اون ايكى بى قرق كچه، تتوج مراسمى[1] اجرا اولنمشدر . كليسانك درونى، فوق العاده[2] وَ پك مُشعشع[3] صورتده تزيين ايدلمش ايدى .

A crowd of incalculable numbers was gathered all along the route of the Royal Couple [the King and the Queen] from Buckingham Palace to the Cathedral, making enthusiastic ovations. The King appeared to be in excellent health.

قرال وقراليچه حضراتى[4] (بوكينغام) سرايندن كليسايه قدر كچهجكلرى يوللرده طوپلانمش اولان برجمّ غفير[5] طرفندن آلقيشلانغشلردر . قرال حضرتلرينك احوال صحّيهلرى[6] پك ايى كورونيوردى .

At 2. p.m. their Majesties (after having received the homage of the Archbischop of Canterbury, the Prince of Wales, the Duke of Norfolk, and the representatives of the Nobility) returned

قرال و قراليچه حَضْراتِ[4] ، ساعت ايكيده : اهالينك آلقيشلرى آره سنده ؛ (قانتربورى) باش پسقپوسى[7] ايله[8] پرنس (دوغال)[9] وَدوق (دونورفولق) وَ زادكان صنفِ[10] هيئت مبعوثهسى[11] طرفندن عرض اولونان تبريكات

Words and Notes. Ingiltérra Qralî hazrétlériniñ résmi tétév'-vûjléri.—1. *résm* pl. *mérasim* (§ 649) ceremony. 2. *févqél-'adé* extra-ordinarily (§ 671 h). 3. *mûsha'sha' sourétdé* splendidly (§ 458): *mû-shasha* méf. of *sha-sha-a* (§ 635). 4. *hazarat* pl. of *hazrét* (§§ 497, 576). 5. *jém'mi ghafeer* a great multitude. 6. *ahvali sih'hiyé*: *ahval* pl. of *hal*, *sih-hi-yé* sanitary: ménsoub of *sih-hat* (§ 579). 7. *bash pisqopos*. 8. *ilé* for *vé* (§ 470). 9. *Préns dî Gal. Dûk dî Norfolk*. 10. *zadégîan* (pl. of *zadé*) nobles (§ 510); *sînîf* the class. 11. *hiyét* assembly, *mébous* (méf. of *ba's*) delegate (§ 604).

to Buckingham Palace, where they appeared on the balcony and were loudly cheered by the throng outside.	وُ احترامانى قبول ايتدكدن صكره ؛ (بوكينغام) سرايينه عودتله ، بالقونه چيقميشلر وَ اهالى طرفندن تكرار آلقيشلانغشلردر .
We are assured that the King experienced no fatigue from (during) the ceremony and looked well throughout it.	قِرال حضرتلرينك مراسم تتوّجيه اثناسنده هيچ بر راحتسزلق وَ يورغونلق حس ايتمەدكارە ، تأمين اولونيور¹² . احوالِ صحيەلرينك بَركمال¹³ اولديغى ناصيەلرندن¹⁴ غايان اولويوردى .
The illuminations in the evening were magnificent; a vast crowd thronged the streets and filled the air with their shouts of joy.	آقشام اوزەرى مشعشع³ شنلكلر اجرا اولونغشدر . بر چوق اهالى آواز بُلَندله مسرّت عظيمە اِظهار ايدەرك سوقاقلرده طولاشمقدەدر .
(The Constantinople Agency.)	(قسطنطينوپل)

London: the same (day) — Coronation day was favoured with splendid weather; the city was richly beflagged and a vast crowd filled the streets.	لوندره : كذا — رسم تتوّجك اجراسى كوننده هوا پك لطيف ايدى . شهرپك پارلاق بر صورتده دونادلمش ايدى . بر ازدحام فوق العـاده سوقاقلرى دولدورمشدر .
The ceremony in the Abbey, of which the duration was an hour and a quarter, was magnificent. The King showed no signs of fatigue.	كليساده آيين پك مطنطن¹⁵ اولمشلردر . قِرال حضرتلرى تَعَبْ وَ مَشَقَّتْ¹⁶ حس ايتمەمشلردر . آيين¹⁷ يتمش بش دقيقه امتداد ايتمشدر .

12. *té-é-min ét.''*: to assure (2 of *émn* [§ 615]). 13. *bér kémal* perfect (§ 557 e). 14. *nasiyé* looking, face (§ 582). 15. *moutantan* magnificent (méf. of *tantana* [§ 458]). 16. *té-'ab ou méshaqqat* fatigue and suffering; *hiss ét.''*: to feel. 17. *ayin* ceremony.

The procession (of the Coronation) was gorgeous. All the Peers and Peeresses were in State attire and produced a grand effect. (and among them were) Lord Kitchener, General Sir A. Gaselee, and Admiral Seymour. The hotels were decorated, and the ordinary prices were maintained. The terms for places on the platforms were very moderate. The enthusiasm was great. King Edward, although very thin, looks very well. No accident occurred. (The National Agency.)

رسمِ تتوج آلايى پك مطنطن ايدى .
لوردلر ايله⁸ زوجهلرينك لابس اولدقلرى
البسه رسميهلر آلايه¹⁸ برشعشعه³
ويرييوردى . لورد كيچنر ايله جنرال
(غزالى) وَ آميرال (سهيور) هركسك
نظرِ دقتنى جلب ايدييورلردى . اوتللر
تزيين و اسكى فيأتلر ابقا ايدلمشدر .
اهالىيه مخصوص انشا اولنان صرهلرك¹⁹
فيأتى پك دوندر²⁰ . مَسَرَّت عظيمدر .
قرال حضرتلرى هرنه قدر ضعيف
ايسهلرده احوالِ صحيهلرى ايبدر . هيچ
برحادثه²¹ وقوع بولمامشدر .
(آژانسُ ناسيونال)

18. *alay* procession. 19. *sira* bench, platform. 20. *doun* low, moderate. 21. *hadisé* (fayil of *houdous* [§ 582]).

The Coronation in Westminster Abbey and the procession lasted an hour. The weather is magnificent. After the ceremony the King and Queen returned to Buckingham Palace.

The King, who looks thinner, declares that the ceremony caused him no fatigue.

(Fournier.)

لوندره : كذا — (وستمينستر) ده
تتوج آيينى وَ آلايك مرورى برساعت
دوام ايتمشدر . هوا غايت لطيفدر .
قرال و قراليچه حضرتلرى تتوجدن
صوكره (بوكينغام) سراينه عودت
ايتمشلردر .

خستهلق مناسبتيله دوچارِضَعف اولمش
بولنان قرال حضرتلرى هيچ بريورغو-
نلق حس ايتمدكلرينى بيان ايتمشلردر .
(فورنيه)

---

٦٠ درس Lesson 60.

Miscellaneous Idiomatic Phrases.

Eldén géléni yap. — Do as much as you can.

Shimdi gélir. — He will be here presently.

Iki gûndé bir. — Once in two days.

Bén olmasam boghoulajaq idi. — But for my help he would have been drowned.

Az qaldi béni bir géôzdén édi-yoroudou. — He came very near causing me the loss of an eye.

O qadari él vérir. — That was sufficient.

Baña él vérméz. — I cannot afford it.

Baña él étdi. — He beckoned me.

Oña géôz étdi. — He winked at him.

Aqli bashina géldi. — He came to his senses.

Bashi dara géldiyi gibi. ⎫
Bashi tasha gélir gélméz. ⎭ — When he got into trouble.

Onou bir shéy yériné qomaz. — He regards that as of no account.

Pék chapouq aliniyor. — He is easily touched.

Yûzûnû asmish. — He is out of humour.

Aqlima géldi. — It occurred to me.

Aqlina braq. — Remind him of it.

Dédiklérimi fikriñdé tout. — Remember what I say.

Dépétaqla gétdi. — It went down head foremost.

Eodûm patladi. — It alarms me excessively.

Ustûñû bashiñi déyishdir. — Change your clothes.

Séôzûnû achmaq. — To commence conversation.

Né qadar vaqit sûrér? — How long will it take?

Bou hich bir shéyé yaramaz. — This is good for nothing.

Géôzdén géchir. — Cast your eye over it.

Elimé béôylé bir kitab géch-diyi yoghoudou. — Such a book I had never seen.

Yéméyé gélir amma saqla-maya gélméz. — It is good to eat, but will not do to keep.

Dérisi qirmîziya chalar. — Its skin is reddish.

Sijimi iki qatla. — Double the string.

Evléri iki qat dir. — Their house is two stories high.

Bir dil baghi vérmishlér. — They had given a token.

Kitaba bir qab géchir.	Put a cover on the book.
Ordan oraya, ordan oraya né olajaq béôylé?	Why move it about from place to place?
Qoulaq asma.	Don't care.
Tashî yériné qodou.	He has hit the nail on the head.
Top atdî.	He has become bankrupt.
Séôyléméyé aghzîm varmayor. ⎫ *Dilim ûsté varmayor.* ⎭	I cannot bear to speak (on so painful a subject).
Eli ouzoun (éyri) dour.	He is thievish.
Sén né iséñ, béndé o youm.	I have equal claims with you.
Adam var adam da var.	There are more sorts of men than one.
Bizi alt ûst étdi.	He has put us all to confusion.
Baña yazîq dîr?	I am to be pitied.
Baña yazîq déyil mi?	Am I not to be pitied?
Sésiñi kés!	Be quiet!
Eli achîq bir adém dir.	He is a liberal man.
Béni dé'mi bashdan chîqarajaqsîn?	Will you lead me also astray?
Evimi barqimî bashîma yiqdî.	He has lost me all my property.
Géôzé géldi. Nazara géldi. ⎫ *Géôz déydi. Nazar déydi.* ⎭	He has been affected by an evil eye. He is bewitched.
Dagh dash adam késilmish.	The hill is full of people.
Bashînî yédi.	He was the cause of his death.
Ishimdén gûjûmdén oldoum.	I was hindered in my work.
Aqlîñî bashîña topla.	Come to your senses.
Janiñ' mî chîqîyoroudou?	Were you dying, that you were in such a hurry?
Dili ouzoun dour.	He talks much.
Né oldou isé oldou.	Forget the past.
Hich sorma!	I cannot tell (how badly matters are going).

Appendices.

The Ottoman Literature.

In all literary matters the Ottoman Turks have shown themselves a singularly uninventive people: the two great schools, the old and the new, into which we may divide their literature, being closely modelled, the one upon the classics of Persia, the other on those of Modern Europe, and more especially of France. The old or Persian school flourished from the foundation of the Empire down to about 1830, and still continues to drag on a feeble existence, though it is now out of fashion and cultivated by none of the leading men of letters. These belong to the new or European school, which sprang up some fifty or sixty years ago, and which, in spite of the bitter opposition of the partisans of the old Oriental system, has succeeded, partly through its own inherent superiority and partly through the talents and courage of its supporters, in expelling its rival from the position of undisputed authority which it had occupied for upwards of five hundred years. For the present purpose it will be convenient to divide the old school into three periods, which may be termed respectively the pre-classical, the classical, and the post-classical. Of these the first extends from the early days of the empire to the accession of Suleyman I., 1301—1520 (A. H. 700—926); the second from that event to the accession of Mahmoud I., 1520—1730 (926—1143); and the third from that date to the accession of Abd-ul-Aziz, 1730—1861 (1143—1277).

The works of the old school in all its periods are entirely Persian in tone, sentiment, and form. We find in them the same beauties and the same defects that we observe in the productions of the Iranian authors. The formal elegance and conventional grace, alike of thought and of expression, so characteristic of Persian classical literature, pervade the works of the best Ottoman

writers, and they are likewise imbued, though in a less
degree, with that spirit of mysticism which runs through
so much of the poetry of Iran.   But the Ottomans
did not stop here.   In their romantic poems they chose
as subjects the favorite themes of their Persian masters,
such as Léyla and Méjnoun, Férhad and Shirin,
Youssouf and Zûléykha, and so on.   They constantly
alluded to Persian heroes whose stories occur in the
Shah-Namé and other storehouses of Iranian legendary
lore; and they wrote their poems in Persian metres and
in Persian forms.[1]   The mésnévi, the qasidé, and
the ghazél, — all of them, so far at least as the
Ottomans are concerned, Persian, — were the favorite
verse-forms of the old poets.   A mésnévi is a poem
written in rhyming couplets, and is usually narrative
in subject.   The qasidé and the ghazél are both
monorhythmic; the first as a rule celebrates the praises
of some great man, while the second discourses of the
joys and woes of love.   Why Persian rather than Arabian
or any other literature became the model of Ottoman
writers, is explained by the early history of the race.
Some two centuries before the arrival of the Turks in
Asia Minor, the Seljouks, then a mere horde of savages,
had overrun Persia, where they settled and adopted the
civilization of the people they had subdued.   Thus
Persian became the language of their court and Government, and when by and by they pushed their conquests
into Asia Minor, and founded there the Seljouk empire
of Roum, they carried with them their Persian culture,
and diffused it among the peoples newly brought under
their sway.   It was the descendants of those Persianized
Seljouks whom the early Ottomans found ruling in Asia
Minor on their arrival there.   What had happened to
the Seljouks two centuries before, happened to the
Ottomans then: the less civilized race adopted the
culture of the more civilized.   As the Seljouk empire
fell to pieces and the Ottoman came gradually to occupy
its place, the sons of men who had called themselves
Seljouks began thenceforth to look upon themselves as
Ottomans.   Hence the vast majority of the people whom

---

[1] See the Reading Exercises in pages 259, 306—307.

we are accustomed to think of as Ottomans are so only by adoption, being really the descendants of Seljouks or Seljoukian subjects, who had derived from Persia whatever they possessed of civilization or of literary taste. An extraordinary love of precedent, the result apparently of conscious want of original power, was sufficient to keep their writers loyal to their early guide for centuries, till at length the allegiance, though not the fashion of it, has been changed in our own days, and Paris has replaced Shiraz as the shrine towards which the Ottoman scholar turns. While conspicuously lacking in creative genius, the Ottomans have always shown themselves possessed of receptive and assimilative powers to a remarkable degree, the result being that the number of their writers both in prose and verse is enormous. It ought to be premised that the poetry of the old school is greatly superior to the prose.

When we reach the reign of Mahmoud II., the great transition period of Ottoman history, during which the civilization of the West began to struggle in earnest with that of the East, we find the change which was coming over all things Turkish affecting literature along with the rest, and preparing the way for the appearance of the new school. The chief poets of the transition are Fazîl Béy, Vasîf, notable for his not altogether unhappy attempt to write verses in the spoken language of the capital, Izzét Molla, Pértév Pasha, Akif Pasha, and the poetesses Fîtnét and Léyla. In the works of all of these, although we occasionally discern a hint of the new style, the old Persian manner is still supreme.

More intimate relations with Western Europe and a pretty general study of the French language and literature, together with the steady progress of the reforming tendency fairly started under Mahmoud II., have resulted in the birth of the New or Modern school, whose objects are truth and simplicity. In the political writings of Réshid and Akif Pashas we have the first clear note of change; but the man to whom more than to any other the new departure owes its success is Shinasi Efféndi, who employed it for poetry as well as for prose. The European style, on its introduction,

encountered the most violent opposition, but now it alone is used by living authors of repute. If any of these does write a pamphlet in the old manner, it is merely as a tour de force, or to prove to some faithful but clamorous partisan of the Persian style that it is not, as he supposes, lack of ability which causes the modern author to adopt the simpler and more natural fashion of the West. The whole tone, sentiment and form of Ottoman literature have been revolutionized by the new school: varieties of poetry hitherto unknown have been adopted from Europe; an altogether new branch of literature, the drama, has arisen; while the sciences are now treated and seriously studied after the system of the West.

Among writers of this school who have won distinction are Ziya Pasha, Jévdét Pasha: the statesmen and historians. Ahméd Midhat Efféndi, Sami Béy: the lexicographer and encyclopedist, Ebûz-Ziya Tévfiq Béy, Mouallim Naji Efféndi, Hamid Béy: who holds the first place among Ottoman dramatists, Mihran Efféndi: the grammarian, and Kémal Béy: the leader of the modern school and one of the most illustrious men of letters whom his country has produced. He has written with conspicuous success in almost every branch of literature, — history, romance, ethics, poetry, and the drama.   G.

Sultans of the House of Osman.

The dates are those of the Sultan's accession, according to the Moslem and Christian eras.

				A. H.	A. D.
1.	Osman I.	Son of	Er-Toghroul	700	1301
2.	Orkhan	» »	Osman I.	726	1326
3.	Mourad I.	» »	Orkhan	761	1359
4.	Bayazid (Bajazet) I.	» »	Mourad I.	791	1389
	Interregnum			804	1402
5.	Méhémméd I.	» »	Bayazid I.	816	1413
6.	Mourad II.	» »	Méhémméd I.	824	1421
7.	Méhémmed II.	» »	Mourad II.	855	1451
8.	Bayazid II.	» »	Méhémméd II.	886	1481
9.	Sélim I.	» »	Bayazid II.	918	1512

					A. H.	A. D.
10.	Souléyman I.	Son of	Sélim I.		926	1520
11.	Sélim II.	»	»	Souléyman I.	974	1566
12.	Mourad III.	»	»	Sélim II.	982	1574
13.	Méhémméd III.	»	»	Mourad III.	1003	1595
14.	Ahméd I.	»	»	Méhémméd III.	1012	1603
15.	Moustafa I.	»	»	»	1026	1617
16.	Osman II.	»	»	Ahméd I.	1027	1618
	Moustafa I.			(restored)	1031	1622
17.	Mourad IV.	»	»	Ahméd I.	1032	1623
18.	Ibrahim	»	»	»	1049	1640
19.	Méhémméd IV.	»	»	Ibrahim	1058	1648
20.	Souléyman II.	»	»	»	1099	1687
21.	Ahméd II.	»	»	»	1102	1691
22.	Moustafa II.	»	»	Méhémméd IV.	1106	1695
23.	Ahméd III.	»	»	»	1115	1703
24.	Mahmoud I.	»	»	Moustafa II.	1143	1730
25.	Osman III.	»	»	»	1168	1754
26.	Moustafa III.	»	»	Ahméd III.	1171	1757
27.	Abd-ûl-Hamid I.	»	»	»	1187	1773
28.	Sélim III.	»	»	Moustafa III.	1203	1789
29.	Moustafa IV.	»	»	Abd-ûl-Hamid I.	1222	1807
30.	Mahmoud II.	»	»	»	1223	1808
31.	Abd-ûl-Méjid	»	»	Mahmoud II.	1255	1839
32.	Abd-ûl-Aziz	»	»	»	1277	1861
33.	— —			— —	—	—
34.	Abd-ûl-Hamid II.	»	»	Abd-ûl-Méjid	1293	1876

تاريخ هجرت Arabic Calendar (pp. 96—98).

The Arabic, *i. e.* Lunar, Year being 10 days, 21 hours and $14^2/5$ seconds shorter than the Christian *i. e.* solar year, does not correspond exactly with it. Its reckoning begins from the Hijrét or departure of Muhammed from Mecca to reside in Medina, A. D. 622 July 15/19 (Mouharrém 1).

In order approximately to convert a year of our Era into one of the Moslem Era: subtract 622, divide the remainder by 33 and add the quotient to the dividend.

Conversely, a year of the Moslem Era is converted into one of the Christian Era by dividing it by 33, subtracting the quotient from it, and adding 622 to the remainder; as:

$$1902 - 622 = 1280 \div 33 = 40; \ 1280 + 40 = ١٣٢٠$$
$$1904 - 622 = 1282 \div 33 = 40; \ 1282 + 40 = ١٣٢٢$$
$$1328 - 622 = \ 706 \div 33 = 23; \ \ 706 + 23 = ٧٢٩$$

Conversely

$$١٣٢٠ \div 33 = 40; \ ١٣٢٠ - 40 = 1280 + 622 = 1902$$
$$١٣٢٢ \div 33 = 40; \ ١٣٢٢ - 40 = 1282 + 622 = 1904$$
$$٧٢٩ \div 33 = 23; \ ٧٢٩ - ٢٣ = \ 706 + 622 = 1328.$$

سنه ماليه The Ottoman Financial Calendar.

In the 1205th year of the Héjira ($^1/_{12}$ March 1789), Sultan Sélim III. issued an Iradé to use this calendar in financial and commercial transactions. It corresponds exactly to the Old Style, only the new year begins in March instead of in January. The following table shows the years of the Financial Calendar corresponding to those of ours, till 1909.

F.	C.	F.	C.	F.	C.	F.	C.	F.	C.
1205	1789	1225	1809	1245	1829	1265	1849	1285	1869
6	1790	6	1810	6	1830	6	1850	6	1870
7	1	7	1	7	1	7	1	7	1
8	2	8	2	8	2	8	2	8	2
9	3	9	3	9	3	9	3	9	3
1210	4	1230	4	1250	4	1270	4	1290	4
1	5	1	5	1	5	1	5	1	5
2	6	2	6	2	6	2	6	2	6
3	7	3	7	3	7	3	7	3	7
4	8	4	8	4	8	4	8	4	8
5	9	5	9	5	9	5	9	5	9
6	1800	6	1820	6	1840	6	1860	6	1880
7	1	7	1	7	1	7	1	7	1
8	2	8	2	8	2	8	2	8	2
9	3	9	3	9	3	9	3	9	3
1220	4	1240	4	1260	4	1280	4	1300	4
1	5	1	5	1	5	1	5	1	5
2	6	2	6	2	6	2	6	2	6
3	7	3	7	3	7	3	7	3	7
4	8	4	8	4	8	4	8	4	8

F.	C.	F.	C.	F.	C.	F.	C.	F.	C.
1305	1889	1309	1893	1313	1897	1317	1902	1321	1906
6	1890	1310	4	4	8	8	3	2	7
7	1	1	5	5	1900	9	4	3	8
8	2	2	6	6	1	1320	5	4	9

Parsing. تَحْليل *Tahleel.*

The method of parsing in Arabic includes Grammatical and Logical Analysis. But in Ottoman-Turkish all that is really necessary is to give such particulars as are given in the subjoined parsing of a piece. The genders, numbers, moods, tenses and all particulars about the words must be mentioned, and the parts of Regular and Irregular Verbs must be given. Read first with expression the following Exercise, and analyse it afterwards. Turn up all references to the Grammar.

The Prophet's Speech. خطبهٔ پیغمبری

رسولِ اکرم بر جمعه کوني کندی دوهسنه بیندی وَ یوز نفر اهلِ اسلام ایله قُبادن قالقدی ، وَ نفسِ مدینهیه عازم اولدی . اثنای راهده صول طرفنه مَیل ایله بنی سالم بن عوف یوردنده رانونا دینیلن وادینکٔ اوست طرفنه ایندی وَ اوراده غایت بلیغانه بر خطبه اوقویوب جمعه غازی قیلدی .

خاتِمُ الْاَنْبیا حضرتلرینک اكٔ ابتدا قیلدیغی جمعه غازی بو در . وَ ابتداكٔ خطبهسی او در که خلاصه وجه ایله ترجمهسی بوراده ایراد اولونور .

رسول اکرم قالقوب حق تعالی حضرتلرینه لایق اولدیغی وجه ایله حمد و ثنا ایلهدکدنصوگٔره بویله بویورمش ایدی :

ای ناس ! صاغلیغٔکزده آخرتٔکز ایچون تدارك کوروگٔز . مُحَقَّق بیلیكٔز که ، یوم قیامتده هر فردك باشنه ووروله‌جق وَ چوبانسز براقدیغی قویونندن صوریله‌جق . صوگٔره جناب حق اوگٔا دییه‌جك ؟ اما ناصل دییه‌جك ؟ ترجمانی یوق ، پرده‌داری یوق ؛ بآلْذّات دییه‌جك که : 'ای قولم سكٔا بنم رسول کاوب ده تبلیغ ایتمه‌دی می ، بن سكٔا مال ویردم ، لطف و احسان ایتدم ؛ سن کندك ایچین نه تدارك ایتدك ؟

«اوکیمسه دخی صاغنه صولنه باقه‌جق بر شی کورمه‌یه‌جك . اوگٔونه

باقه‌جق ، جهنّمدن باشقه بر شى كورمه‌يه‌جك . اويله ايسه هر كيم كه كنديسنى
وَلَوْ كه بر يارِم خُرما ايله اولسون ، آتشدن قورتاره‌يله‌جك ايسه ، همان اول
خبرى ايشله‌سين . اونى ده بولاماز ايسه ، بارى كلمهٔ طَيِّبَه ايله كنديسنى
قورتارسين . زيرا اونگله بر خيره اون مثلندن يدييوز مثلينه قدر ثواب
ويريلـير » .

وَ ٱلْسَّلَامُ عَلَى رَسُولُ ٱللهِ وَ رَحْمَةُ ٱللهِ وَ بَرَكَاتِهِ . ﴿جودت پاشا﴾

خطبهٔ پيغمبرى *Khoutbé'yi Péyghambéri* 'the prophetic
sermon, or the sermon of the prophet'. Pers. Izafét: if the
first noun ends in vowel *hé,* a hémzé is placed over it (§ 519):
خطبه is an Ar. noun, measure فُعْلَت (§ 592): 'a special homily
and prayer, in which they praise God, bless Mouhammed and
pray for the reigning Caliph, delivered by an official preacher
(خطيب *khatib*) before the midday service of worship in Friday
(*Jouma'a namazi*).' p. پيغمبر is composed of پَيْغَام ، پَيْغَم *péygham*
'message, revelation' élif is omitted (§ 560) + بر *bér* 'carry'
(§§ 535, 554); by the addition of ى *-i* it is changed into Noun
of Rel. (§ 527).

رسول اكرم *Résou'lou Ekrém.* 'The most venerable
Prophet': Pers. Izafét composed of two Ar. words (§ 517). رسول
'prophet, apostle' Adj. Qual. of رَسَالت of the meas. فَعُول (§ 607).
أَكْرَمْ is a كَرَامَت ، أَفْعَل N. of Superiority of كرامت, masc. meas.
miracle wrought through the agency of a saint, but معجزه *mûjizé*
is a miracle wrought by Divine power.

بر جمعه كونى *bir Jouma'a gûnû* 'on a Friday': بر Turk.
Ind. Article (§ 60), جمعه كونى Turk. Izafét (§ 181). جمعه Ar. noun,
meas. فُعْلَة (§ 592), the fayil being جامع 'collector, mosque', other
derivatives: كون = كونى ؛ تَجَمّع ، مجموعه ، مجموع Turk. noun
with pron. affix third person (§ 105 [3]).

كندى دوه‌سنه *Kéndi dévésiné* 'on his camel': Turk.
Izafét with pron. كندى pers. pron. (§ 147), دوه‌سنه = دوه ، دوه‌سى
Turk. noun with pron. affix third person sing. dative case.

بیندی *bindi* 'he mounted': Turk. intran. verb, Ind. Past sing. third person of the masdar بینمك. Der. بیندیرمك، بینیلمك.

وَ يوز نفر اهل اسلام ايله *vé yûz néfér éhli islam'ilé* 'and with believers two hundred in number': وَ Arab. Pers. conjunctive (§ 470), يوز Turk. Card. number (§ 192), نَفَر Ar. noun meas. فَعَل 'individual' used for men (§ 203): Reg. Fem. pl. نفرات (§ 576); اهلِ اسلام Pers. Izafét 'Moslem'. Comp. noun (§ 695⁵). a. اهل meas. فَعَل, Irregular pl. آهالى (§ 650). تَأَهَّلَ = تَفَعَّلْ *té-éh'hûl* to marry; اسلام submitting himself to the divine disposal, IV. of سلام, fayil مسلم *mûslim* 'one who submissively obeys God, Moslem' (§§ 512, 634 d); ايله Turk. post position, sign of Instrumental case (§ 232).

قبادن قالقدى *Qoubadan qalqdi* 'he started from Qouba': a. قبادن prop. noun, sing. abl.; nom. *Qouba* 'a place near Medina'; قالقدى Ind. Past, sing. third person the primitive masdar قالقمق, deriv.: قالدىريق، قالقيشمق (§§ 263, 268).

وَ نفس مدینه‌يه *vé néfsi Médinéyé* 'to the [main] city of Medina' (as distinguished from its outlying regions): Pers. Izafét: a. نفس 'the very substance, main' meas. فَعْل; a. مدینه prop. noun, sing. dative of the measure فقيله, Abstract noun by the addition of *hé* (ه = *é* [§ 582]).

عازم اولدى *'azim oldou* 'he departed toward': comp. Intrans. verb., Ind. Past sing. third person, formed by using noun with aux. verb اولمق, Masdar عازم اولمق (§ 272): a. عازم fayil of اغرام = اِفقال IV. deriv. عزیمت.

اثناى راهده *ésnayi rahdé, -rahda* 'in the course of the road, or journey, i. e. on the way': Pers. Izafét (§ 518): a. اثناء Irreg. plural of ثنى *sénee* (§ 639 b) 'twisting, winding', used in Turkish as a sing., in the sense of 'the course of a journey,

the time of a stay, a period of time': اثنای اقامته 'in the course of the stay', اول ثناده راهده 'at that time, in that interval'; sing. loc. case.

صول طرفنه *sol tarafina* 'to his left side': Turk. adj. and noun: t. صول adj., a. طرفنه = طرف ، طرفی meas. فَقَل with pron. affix third person singular dative (§§ 99, 105 [3]).

ميل ايدهرك *méyl ilé* 'swerving, turning' for ميل ايله: the Turk. conj. ايله is used to express the meaning of ايدهرك (§ 430). a. ميل meas. فَقْل.

بنی سالم بن عوف يوردونده *Bénee Salim bén Of yourdounda* 'in the settlement of the children of Salim bén Of': Pers. and Turk. Izaféts. سالم (§ 575); بنی masc. pl. of بَن ، بَنُو ؛ يوردنده = يورد ، يوردی stands for patronym (§ 669 [3]); بن : عوف bén عوف 'tent, home' second member of Turk. Izafét, with pron. affix third person sing. locative.

رانونا دينيلن وادينك اوست طرفنه *Ranona dénilén vadiniñ ûst tarafina* 'in the upper part of the valley called Ranona': رانونا Ar. prop. noun; دينيلن méfoul of دينيلمك (§ 402); وادينك first member of the Turkish Izafét, Ar. noun meas. فاعل sing. genitive; اوست Turk. postposition used as an adj. (§ 452); طرفنه = طرف ، طرفی noun, pl. اطراف (§ 639 b); it indicates a. motion (§ 237).

ايندی *éndi* 'he halted': Ind. Past singular third person Primitive masdar اينمك, deriv. ايندرمك (§ 263).

اوراده *orada* 'there': adverbial demonstrative (§ 144), sing. locative case, it indicates location (§ 237).

غايت بليغانه بر خطبه اوقويوب *ghayét bélighané bir khoutbé oqouyoup* 'he recited a very eloquent speech': غايت superl. degree of Turk. adj. (§ 226). a. p. بليغانه pers. adj. or adv. (§§ 528, 684): a. بليغ adj. Qual. of بَلاغَت 'eloquence'; اوقويوب

Turk. Gerund 'having recited' or 'he recited and afterwards ...'
(اوقودی وَ ... قیلدی for).

جمعه غازی قیلدی *Jouma'a namazî qîldî* 'he performed
his Friday prayer': جمعه غازی Turk. Izafét (§ 109): a. جمعه =
فُقْلَةْ first member. غازی second member, third person of p. غاز
'the Divine worship of Islam, consisting of fixed recitals of praise
with prostration of the body, five times a day', غاز قیلمق 'to make
his prayers', comp. trans. verb (§ 272); قیلدی Ind. Past. singular
third person.

خاتم الانبیا حضرتلرینك الثّ ابتدا قیلدیغی جمعه غازی بو در
*Khatim'ul énbiya hazrétlériniñ éñ iptida qîldîghi Jouma'a
namazî bou dour* 'This is the first Friday prayer which
the seal *i. e.* the last, of the prophets (Mouhammed) has
performed': خاتم الانبیاء Arabic Izafét (§ 668 [2]), a. خاتم fayil of
فقال' انبیاء pl. of نبی *nébee* (§ 645 c), which is Adj. Qual. of
نبوت ; حضرتلرینك = حضرت 'حضرتی' حضرتلری *nûbouvvét* 'prophecy';
Ar. noun meas. فَقْلَتْ with pron. affix third person pl. Genitive,
used after the name of God, saints and great personalities (§§ 497,
500). الثّ ابتدا Turk. Superl. adj. (§ 224): ابتداء Ar. deriv. masdar
meas. افتعال (§ 627) of بداء' بدایت ; قیلدیغی Obj. participle of قیلمق
(§ 413); بو Demonstrative (Pron.) Adj.; در copula (§ 67).

ابتداکی خطبهسی او در که خلاصه وجه ایله ترجمهسی بوراده ایراد
اولونور *iptidaki khoutbési o dour ki khûlasa véjh' ilé tér-
jémési bourada iyrad olounour* 'This is his first speech
(or oration), the translation of which is given below in
brief': ابتداکی Turk. pron. adj. (§ 138). که Pers. Relative pron.
(§ 317); تَرْجَمَه Ar. Quadriliteral Masdar meas. فَقْلَلَه (§ 595); ایراد
(§ 274) Turk. comp. passive verb ایراد اولونق اولونور Masdar, Ind.
Aorist, sing. third person.

تصريف افعال Conjugation of Turkish Verbs.

Infinitive of Verbs مصدر *Masdar.*

Masdar: the Root $\sqrt{+mék}$, $\sqrt{+maq}$; *Sérmek'*, *Yazmaq'*.

Negative: *Sév'mémék*, *Yaz'mamaq*.

Verbal Substantives: 1. *Sérméklik'*, 2. *Sérmé'*, 3. *Sérish'* (§ 288).

Derivative Forms (§§ 261—268):
   Otourtmaq', Basdîrmaq', Yatîrmaq', Taranmaq', Yazîlmaq', Chékishmék'.

Potential verbs: *Sérébilmék'*, neg. *Sévé'mémék* (§ 283).

Accelerative verb: *Sévi'vérmék* (§ 286).

Verbs derived from nouns and adjectives:
   Hazirlamaq', Hazirlanmaq', Hazîrlatmaq' (§ 277).

Compound Verbs (Nouns with Auxiliaries) (§ 272):
   Sival' étmék, — éylémék, — qîlmaq, — bouyourmaq.

Participles فرع فعل

Subjective Mood (§ 399).		Objective Mood (§ 411).	
Active *Fayil* *yazan' yazar' yazdiq' yazmish' yazajaq' — olan*	**Passive *Méfoul*** *yazîlan' yazilîr' yazîldîq' yazîlmish' yazîlajaq' — olan*	**Past** *yazdîghîm' yazdîghîn' yazdîghî' yazdîghîmîz' yazdîghîñîz' yazdîqlarî'*	**Future** *yazajaghîm' yazajaghîn' yazajaghî' yazajaghîmîz' yazajaghîñîz' yazajaqlarî'.*

Gerunds رابطه ضيغه لر (pp. 206—207).

1. *yazar'jasîna*
2. *yaz'madan*
3. *yazîn'ja*
   yazar' yazmaz
4. *yazdîq'da*
5. *yazdîq'ja*
6. *yazali'*
7. *yaza' yaza*
8. *yaza'raq*
9. *yazasî'*
10. *yazajaghîña'*
11. *yazîn'ja*
12. *yazdighîmda' yazajaghîndan'*
13. *yazib', yazip'*
14. *yazar'ken.*

Verbal Adjectives صفت مشبهه (§ 436).

1. *Yazîjî'*, 2. *achîq'*, 3. *sûrgûn'*, 4. *côlû'*, 5. *sévinj'.*

Noun of Excess: *Chalîshqan', sûzgéj', dalgîj'.*
Noun of Location: *Yataq', otlaq'.*
Instrumental noun: *Elék', daraq'.*

فعل ، افعال ذاتیه Finite Verb.

Indicative Mood	Assertive Mood	Relative Mood	Conditional Mood

Imperative امرحاضر (§ 316).

yaz'			
yazsîn'			
yazalîm'			
ya'zînîz			
yazsînlar'			

Present حال (§ 318).

sévi'yoroum	*sévi'yor idim*	*sévi'yor imishim*	*sévi'yor isém*
sévi'yorsoun	„ *idiñ*	„ *imishsiñ*	„ *iséñ*
sévi'yor	„ *idi*	„ *imish*	„ *isé*
sévi'yorouz	„ *idik*	„ *imishiz*	„ *isék*
sévi'yorsouñouz	„ *idiñiz*	„ *imishiñiz*	„ *iséñiz*
sévi'yorlar	„ *idilér*	„ *imishlér*	„ *isélér.*

Aorist مضارع (§ 326).

sévé'rim	*sévér' idim*	*sévér imishim*	*sévér isém*
sévér'siñ	„ *idiñ*	„ *imishsiñ*	„ *iséñ*
sévér'	„ *idi*	„ *imish*	„ *isé*
sévé'riz	„ *idik*	„ *imishiz*	„ *isék*
sévér'siñiz	„ *idiñiz*	„ *imishsiñiz*	„ *iséñiz*
sévérlér'	„ *idilér*	„ *imishlér*	„ *isélér.*

Past ماضئ شهودی (§ 344).

sévdim'	*sévdi' idim*		*sévdi' isém*
sévdiñ'	„ *idiñ*		„ *iséñ*
sévdi'	„ *idi*		„ *isé*
sévdik'	„ *idik*		„ *isék*
sévdiñiz'	„ *idiñiz*		„ *iséñiz*
sévdilér'	„ *idilér*		„ *isélér.*

Dubitative ماضئ نقلی (§ 351).

sévmi'shim	*sévmish' idim*	*sévmish' imishim*	*sévmish' isém*
sévmish'sin	„ *idiñ*	„ *imishsin*	„ *iséñ*
sévmish'	„ *idi*	„ *imish*	„ *isé*
sévmish'iz	„ *idik*	„ *imishiz*	„ *isék*
sévmish'siñiz	„ *idiñiz*	„ *imishsiñiz*	„ *iséñiz*
sévmishlér'	„ *idélér*	„ *imishlér*	„ *isélér.*

Future مستقبل (§ 357).

sévéjé'yim	*sévéjék' idim*	*sévéjék' imishim*	*sévéjék' isém*
sévéjék'sin'	„ *idiñ*	„ *imishsin*	„ *iséñ*

Indicative Mood	Assertive Mood	Relative Mood	Conditional Mood
sévéjék'	*sévéjék' idi*	*sévéjék' imish*	*sévéjék' isé*
sévéjé'yiz	„ *idik*	„ *imishiz*	„ *isék*
sévéjék'siñiz	„ *idiñiz*	„ *imishsiñiz*	„ *iséñiz*
sévéjéklér'	„ *idilér*	„ *imishlér*	„ *isélér.*

Optative التزامى (§ 365).

sévéyim'	*sévé' idim*
sévésiñ'	„ *idiñ*
sévé'	„ *idi*
sérélim'	„ *idik*
sévé'siñiz	„ *idiñiz*
sévélér'	„ *idilér*

Suppositive إنشائيه ياخود فرضيه (§ 377).

sév'sém	*sév'sé idim*	*sév'sé imishim*
sév'sén	„ *idiñ*	„ *imishsiñ*
sév'sé	„ *idi*	„ *imish*
sév'sék	„ *idik*	„ *imishiz*
sév'séñiz	„ *idiñiz*	„ *imishsiñiz*
sév'sélér	„ *idilér*	„ *imishlér*

Necessitative وجوبى (§ 384).

sévméli'yim	*sévméli' idim*	*sévméli' imishim*	*sévméli' isém*
sévméli'siñ	„ *idiñ*	„ *imishsiñ*	„ *isén*
sévméli'	„ *idi*	„ *imish*	„ *isé*
sévméli'yiz	„ *idik*	„ *imishiz*	„ *isék*
sévméli'siñiz	„ *idiñiz*	„ *imishsiñiz*	„ *iséñiz*
sévméli' dirlér	„ *idilér*	„ *imishlér*	„ *isélér.*

The Verb To Have.

Bénim var, séniñ var, onouñ var ...	} I have **a** (book).
Béndé var, séndé var, onda var ...	
Béndé dir, séndé dir, onda dir ...	I have **the** (book).
Bénim var îdî, séniñ var îdî, onouñ var îdî	} I had **a** —
Béndé var îdî, séndé var îdî, onda var îdî	
Bénim var îmîsh, séniñ var îmîsh ...	(They say that) I have.
Bénim var îsa; Béndé var îsa	If I had **a** —
Bénim oldou, sénin oldou ...	I got **a** —
Bénim olajaq, séniñ olajaq ...	I shall have **a** —
Bénim olsa; séniñ olsa idi.	If it were mine.

قسم رسمى

The Official Part.

The Imperial Palace مابين همايون حضرت ملوكانه

His Imperial Majesty the Sultan ذات حضرت پادشاهى

تشریفاتِ عمومیه ناظری *Téshrifatî oumoumiyé Nazîrî*, The Grand Master of Ceremony.

دارالسعادت الشریفه اغاسی، قیزلراغاسی *Dar-ûs-sa'adét ûsh-shérifé aghasî, Qîzlar aghasî*, The Chief of the Eunuchs of the Imp. Palace.

سرقرناى حضرت شهریارى ٬ باش ماینجی *Sér qourénayi Hazréti Shéh'riyari, Bash Mabéynji*, The Chief (Lord High-) Chamberlain.

مابین همایون باش کتابتی *Mabéyni Hûmayoun Bash Kitabéti*, The Imperial Chancellary.

مابین همایون باش کاتبی *Mabéyni Humayoun Bash Kŷatibi*, The First Secretary of the Imp. Palace.

کاتب خصوصیٔ حضرت شهریارى *Kŷatibi Khousousiyi Hazréti Shéh-riyari*, The Private Secretary of H. I. M.

دیوان همایون باش ترجمانی *Divanî Hûmayoun Bash Térjémanî*, The Premier Dragoman of the Imp. Divan.

دیوان همایون باش مترجمی *Divanî Hûmayoun Bash Mûtérjimi*, The Premier Translator of the Imp. Divan.

مابین همایون امامی *Mabéyni Hûmayoun Imamî*, The Chief Almoner (Imam) of the Imp. Palace.

یاور اکرم حضرت پادشاهى *Yavéri Ekrémi Hazréti Padishahi*, The Aide-de-Camp of H. I. M.

فخری یاوران ٬ یاور فخری *Fakhri Yavéran*, The Honorary aides-de-camp.

یاور٬ یاوران *Yavér*, pl. *yavéran*, Aide-de-camp, Aides de camp.

باش مصاحب *Bash Mousahib,* The Premier Courtier (French Courtisan).

جيب همايون *Jébi Hûmayoun,* The Privy Purse.

خزينه خاصه شاهانه *Khazinéyi Khassayi Shahané,* The Civil List.

معيت شاهانه اركان حربيه مشيرى *Mayéti Shaha'né Erkiani Harbiyé Mûsheeri,* The Chief of the Military Household.

مابين همايون مديرى *Mabéyni Hûmayoun Mûdiri,* The Director of the Imp. Palace.

اصطبل عامره مديرى *Îstabli Amiré Mûdiri,* The Grand Equerry of H. I. M.

باب السعادت العاليه اغاسى *Babûs Sa'adétûl aliyé Aghasi,* The Director of the Porte of the Palace.

قاپوجيلر كتخداسى *Qapoujoular Két'khûdasi,* The Chief of the Porters.

حطب آنبارى مديرى *Hatab anbari Mûdiri,* The Director of the Dépôt of Combustibles.

مابين همايون سر معمارى *Mabéyni Hûmayoun Sér Mîymari,* The Premier Architect of the Imp. Palace.

مابين همايون سر اطباسى *Mabéyni Hûmayoun Sér atibbasi,* The Premier Physician of the Imp. Palace.

مطبخ وفرونلر مديرى *Matbakh vé Fourounlar Mûdiri,* The Director of the Imp. Kitchens and Ovens.

ارزاق آنبارى مديرى *Erzaq anbari Mûdiri,* The Director of the Provisions.

حبوبات آنبارى مديرى *Houboubat anbari mûdiri,* The Director of the Granaries.

حديقه شاهانه مديرى *Hadiqayi Shahané Mûdiri,* The Director of the Imp. Gardens.

چيفتلكات همايون مديرى *Chiftlikiati Hûmayoun Mûdiri,* The Director of the Imp. Farms.

The Sublime Porte باب عالى

The Council of Ministers مجلس خاص وكلا

صدر اعظم *Sadri A'zam,* The Grand Vizier.

شيخ الاسلام *Shéykh-ûl Islam.* The Minister of the Canon Law of Islam.

داخليه ناظرى *Dakhiliyé Naziri,* The Minister of the Interior.

خارجيه ناظرى *Kharijiyé Naziri,* The Minister for Foreign Affairs.

سرعسكر، حربيه ناظرى *Séraskér, (Harbiyé Naziri)* The Minister for War.

28*

شورای دوات رئیسی *Shourayî Dévlét Réyisi*, The President of the Council of State.

عدلیه و مذاهب ناظری *Adliyé vé Mézahib Nazîrî*, The Minister of Justice and Public worship.

مالیه ناظری . *Maliyé Nazîrî*, The Minister of Finance.

معارف عمومیه ناظری *Méarifi oumoumiyé Nazîrî*, The Minister of Public Instruction.

بحریه ناظری *Bahriye Nazîrî*, The Minister for Naval Affairs (Navy).

طوپخانهٔ عامره مشیری *Top-hanéyi Amiré mûsheeri*, The Grand Master of Ordnance.

اوقاف ناظری *Evqaf Nazîrî*, The Minister of Religious Funds.

تجارت و نافعه ناظری *Tijarét vé Nafiya Nazîrî*, The Minister of Commerce and Public Works.

شهر امینی *Shéhir Emeeni*, The Prefect of the City.

ضبطیه ناظری *Zaptiyé Nazîrî*, The Prefect of the Police.

لیمان رئیس *Liman Réyisi*, The Prefect of the Port.

رسومات امینی *Rousoumat Emini*, Director General of Customs.

دفتر خاقانی ناظری *Déftéri Khaqani Nazîrî*, Director General of the Imperial Archives.

پوسته و تلغراف ناظری *Posta vé Télégraf Nazîrî*, Director-General of Post and Telegraphs.

اورمان و معادن و زراعت ناظری *Orman ré Méadin vé zira'at Nazîrî*, The Minister of Mines, Forests and Agriculture.

اطفائیه آلایی قوماندانی *Itfayiyé alayî Komandanî*, The Commander of the Fire-Brigade.

صدارت عظما The Grand Vizieriate

آمدیٔ دیوان همایون ، آمدجی بك *Amédiyi Divanî Hûmayoun*, Referendary of the Imp. Divan.

مکتوبی اوطهسی *Méktoubi Odasî*, The Bureau of Correspondence.

تشریفات قلمی *Téshrifat Qalémi*, The Bureau of the Master of Ceremonies.

ولایات ممتازه قلمی *Vilayatî Mûmtazé Qalémi*, The Bureau of the privileged Provinces.

سفرا تشریفاتجیسی *Sûféra Téshrifatjîsî*, Introducer of the Ambassadors.

The Council of State شوراى دولت

ملكيه دائرهسى   *Milkiyé Dayirési*, The Civil Department.

تنظيمات دائرهسى   *Tanzimat Dayirési*, The Legislative Department.

محاكمات دائرهسى   *Mouhakémat Dayirési*, The Judiciary Department.

شوراى دولت كتابتى   *Shourayi Déclét Kitabéti*, The Bureau of the Council of State.

امور نافعه قوميسيونى   *Oumourou Nafiya Qomisionou*, The High Commission of public Constructions (Improvements).

شوراى دولت ملازمى   *Shourayi Déclét mûlazimi*, The Auditor of the Council of State.

The Foreign Office خارجيه نظارت جليلهسى

خارجيه مستشارى   *Kharijiyé Mûstéshari*, The Under-Secretary of State for For. Affairs.

ترجمه قلمى   *Térjémé qalémi*, The Bureau of Translation.

مكتوبىٔ خارجيه قلمى   *Méktoubiyi Kharijiyé qalémi*, The Bureau of Correspondence.

تحريرات اجنبيه قلمى   *Tahrirati Ejnébiyé Qalémi*, The Bureau of Foreign Correspondence.

اوراق اوطهسى   *Ecraq Odasî*, The Bureau of Archives.

محاسبه قلمى   *Mouhasébe Qalémi*, Board of Audit.

امور حقوقيةٔ مختلطه قلمى   *Oumourou Houqouqiyéyi Mûkhtélité Qalémi*, The Bureau of Disputed Claims.

حقوق مشاورلرى اوطهسى   *Houqouq mûshavirléri Odasî*, The Bureau of Legists.

تابعيت قلمى   *Tabiyiyét Qalémi*, The Bureau of Nationality (naturalization).

مطبوعات اجنبيه اوطهسى   *Matbou'atî Ejnébiyé Odasî*, The Bureau of the Foreign Press.

سجل احوال قلمى   *Sijli ahval Qalémi*, The Bureau of personnel.

The Ministry of Internal Affairs داخليه نظارت جليلهسى

مطبوعات قلمى   *Matbou'at Qalémi*, The Bureau of the Press.

انتخاب مأمورين قوميسيونى   *Intikhabî Mémoureen Qomisiyonou*, The Commission for the Selection of functionaries.

تقاعد صندیغی نظارتی *Téqayûd sandîghî Nazaréti,* The Direction of the Pension Funds.

باب مشیخت پناهی The Sheikh-ûl Islamate

صدر روم ایلی ، رومایلی قاضیعسکری *Sadrî Rouméli, Rouméli Qazaskéri,* The Vice-Chancellor of Turkey.

صدر آناطولی ، آناطولی قاضیعسکری *Sadrî Anadolou, Anadolou Qazas-kéri,* The Second Vice-Chancellor of Turkey (p. 458).

فتوا امینی ، امین فتوا (فتوی) *Fétva Emini,* The Superintendent of Canonical Decisions.

مفتی (the Fayil of افتاء = فتوی) *Mufti,* a judge of the Canon Law of Islam.

مالیه نظارت جلیله‌سی The Ministry of Finance

واردات اداره عمومیه‌سی *Varidat Idaréyi Oumoumiyési,* The General Directorate of revenues.

مصارفات اداره عمومیه‌سی *Mésarifat Idaréyi Oumoumiyési,* The General Directorate of Expenses.

دیون اداره عمومیه‌سی *Douyoun Idaréyi Oumoumiyési,* The General Directorate of Public Debts.

محاسبات عتیقه دائره‌سی *Mouhasébatî atiqa dayirési,* The Bureau of regulation of ancient accounts.

اعشار و اغنام امانتی *Ashar ou aghnam Emanéti,* The administration of the tithes and taxes on sheep.

وزنه ، مالیه وزنه‌سی *Vézné,* Directorate of Weights and Test.

مع ترجمه تحریرات اجنبیه قلمی *Ma térjémé Tahriratî Ejnébiyé Qalémi,* The office of Translation and correspondence in foreign languages.

دیوان محاسبات *Divanî Mouhasébat,* The Court of Accounts.

مؤسسات مالیه *Mûés'sésatî maliyé,* Financial Establishments.

ضربخانه ، عامره مدیریتی The Imperial Mint

سکه‌زن دائره‌سی *Sikkézén Dayirési,* The department of Minting.

چاشنی دائره‌سی *Chashni Dayirési,* The department of assays.

ماکینه دائره‌سی *Makina Dayirési,* The department of Machines.

قلع دائره‌سی *Qal Dayirési,* The department of Refining.

The Customs Administration رسومات امانت علیه‌سی

رسوم سته اداره‌سی *Rousoumou Sitté Idarési,* The Administration of the six indirect taxes (p. 390).

مع مسكرات ذخیره كومروكی نظارتی *Ma mûskirat zakhiré geômrûyû nézaréti,* The Directorate of the customs on cereals and liquors.

كراسته كومروكی نظارتی *Kérésté geômrûyû Nézaréti,* The Directorate of the Customs on wood.

میوه و سبزه كومروكی نظارتی *Méyvé vé Sébzé geômrûyû Nézaréti,* The Directorate of the customs on fruits and vegetables.

بالقخانه نظارتی *Balîqhané Nézaréti,* The Directorate of the Fishery.

مشترك المنفعه انحصار دخان دولت علیه عثانیه، رژی *Mûshtérékûl Ménfa'a inhisarî dou-khanî Dévléti Aliyéyi Osmaniyé,* The Regie co-interessé of tobaccos of the Ottoman-Empire.

دیون عمومیه اداره‌سی *Douyounou Oumoumiyé Idarési,* The Administration of Public Debts.

دیون عمومیه باش قومیسری *Douyounou Oumoumiyé bash qo-misiri,* Imperial Commissary of the Ottoman Public Debts.

معارف عمومیه نظارت جلیله‌سی
The Ministry of Public Instruction

انجمن تفتیش و معاینه *Enjûméni Téftish ou Mouayéné,* The Council of Inspection and Censure (Supervision).

مطبوعات اجنبیه قلمی *Matbou'atî Ejnébiyé Qalémi,* The Bureau of the Domestic Press.

مطبوعات داخلیه قلمی *Matbou'atî Dakhiliyé Qalémi,* The Bureau of the Domestic Press.

مطبوعات داخلیه مدیری *Matbou'atî Dakhiliyé Mûdiri,* The Director of the Domestic Press Bureau.

مكاتب عالیه مدیربتی *Méktatibi Aliyé Mûdiriyéti,* The Directorate of the Higher Schools.

مكتب ملكیه شاهانه *Méktébi Milkiyéyi Shahané,* The Imperial Civil College.

مكتب ساطانی *Méktébi Soultani,* The Imp. Lyceum of Galata-Séray.

مكتب حقوق شاهانه *Méktébi Houqouqou Shahané,* The Imp. Lyceum of Law.

لسان مکتبی *Lisan Méktébi*, The Imp. Lyceum of Languages.

مکتب صنایع *Méktébi Sanayi*, The School of Arts and Industry.

مکتب ابتدائیه (مکاتب ابتدائیه) *Méktébi Iptidayiyé*, A Primary School.

مکتب رشدیه (مکاتب رشدیه) *Méktébi Rûshdiyé*, A Grammar School.

مکتب اعدادیه (مکاتب اعدادیه) *Méktébi Idadiyé*, An Academy or Preparatory School (which prepares for a College).

مکتب عالی (مکاتب عالیه) *Méktébi Ali*, A Superior (High-) School or College.

دار المعلمین *Dar-ûl Mouallimeen*, A Normal School for teachers.

دار المعلمات *Dar-ûl Mouallimat*, A Normal School for lady teachers.

مکتب طبیهٔ ملکیه *Méktébi Tibbiyéyi Milkiyé*, The Civil Medical School.

عشیرت مکتبی *Ashirét Méktébi*, A School for Nomadic Tribes.

رصدخانهٔ عامره *Rasadkhanéyi Amiré*, The Imp. Meteorological Observatory.

موزهخانهٔ همایون *Mûzékhanéyi Hûmayoun*, The Imperial Museum.

مطبعهٔ عامره *Matba'ayi Amiré*, The Imperial Printing-House.

عدلیه و مذاهب نظارتِ جلیلهسی
The Ministry of Justice and Public Worship

مذاهب مدیری *Mézahib Mûdiri*, Director of Public Worship (Religions).

انجمنِ عدلیه هیئتی *Enjûméni adliyé Hiyéti*, The Board of the Justice.

محکمهٔ تمییز *Méhkéméyi Témyeez*, The Court of Cassation.

باش مدعی عمومی *Bash Mûddayi oumoumi*, The Procuror General of the Court of Cassation.

محکمهٔ استیناف *Méhkéméyi Istinaf*, The Court of appeals.

استدعا دائرهسی *Istida dayirési*, The Section of Requests (in the C. of Cassation).

جنایت دائرهسی *Jinayét Dayirési*, The Criminal Section.

جنحه دائرهسی *Jûnha Dayirési*, The Correctional Section.

حقوق دائرهسی *Houqouq Dayirési*, The Civil Section.

جزا دائرهسی *Jéza Dayirési*, The Court of Criminal jurisdiction.

هیئت اتهامیه دائرهسی *Hiyéti It-hamiyé Dayirési*, The Court of accusation.

محكمهٔ بدایت ، بدایت محكمهسی *Méhkéméyi Bidayét*, The Court of first instance.

محكمهٔ تجارت *Méhkéméyi Tijarét*, The tribunal of Commerce.

برنجی تجارت مجلسی (محكمهسی) *Birinji Tijarét Méjlisi*, The First Commercial Court (where the cases between foreigners and Ottoman subjects are dealt with).

محكمهٔ تجارت بحریه *Méhkéméyi Tijaréti Bahriyé*, The Maritime Com. Court.

حاكم ، حكام *Hakim*, pl. *houk'kiam*, Judge.

رئیس *Réyis*, President. (The presiding Judge.)

محكمه اعضاسی ، اعضا *Méhkémé Azasî, aza*, Member of council.

مدعی عمومی *Müddayi Oumoumi*, Procuror General. (Public prosecutor.)

مدعی عمومی معاونی *Müddayi Oumoumi mou'avini*, The assistant Proc. Gen.

ضبط كاتبی *Zabt Kiatibi*, The Clerk.

معاون *Mouavin*, Assistant.

مستنطق *Moustantîq*, The trial justice.

مقاولات محرری *Mouqavélat Mouharriri*, The Notary Public.

مدعی ، دعواجی ، خاصم *Müddayi, davajî, khasim*, The plaintiff.

مدعی علیه *Müddayi aléyh'*, The defendant.

شاهد *Shahid*, vulg. *shahad* Witness.

دعوا وكیلی ، آووقات *Dava vékili, avoqat*, Lawyer, attorney.

وكالتنامه *Vékialétname*, A power of attorney.

The Prefecture of Police ضبطیه نظارت عالیهسی

پولیس مجلسی *Polis méjlisi*, The council of police.

ژاندارمه مجلسی *Jandarma méjlisi*, The council of gendarmery.

پولیس قومیسری *Polis Qomiséri*, The commissary of police.

پاسپورت اوطهسی *Pasaport odasî* (vulg. *pashaport*), The bureau of passports.

پولیس مدیرلیکی *Polis mûdirliyi*, The prefects of police.

صو نظارتی *Sou nézaréti*, The directorate of waters.

حبسخانهٔ عمومی *Habskhanéyi oumoumi*, The central prison.

شهر امانت بهیهسی *Shéhir émanéti béhiyési*, The Prefecture of the City (of Const.).

برنجی دائرهٔ بلدیه *Birinji dayireyi bélédiyé*, The first municipality circle.

بلدیه دائرهسی *Bélédiyé dayirési*, The municipality.

بلدیه رئیسی *Bélédiyé réyisi*, The mayor (of a city).

بلدیه مجلسی *Bélédiyé méjlisi*, The municipal council.

تیمارخانه *Timarkhané*, Asylum of the insane.

غربا خستهخانهسی *Gouréba Khastahanési*, The hospital for strangers.

تجارت و نافعه نظارت جلیلهسی
The Ministry of Commerce and Public Works

تیمور یوللر ادارهٔ عمومیهسی *Démir yollar idaréyi oumoumiyési*, The general directorate of railroads.

مدیر عمومی *Mûdiri oumoumi*, General manager.

طرق و معابر ادارهسی *Tourouq ou méabir idarési*, The general directorate of roads and bridges.

مهندسخانهٔ همایون *Mûhéndiskhanéyi Hûmayoun*, The School of Engineers.

امور صحیه نظارت بهیهسی
The Council of International Sanitation

ادارهٔ امور صحیه *Idaréyi oumourou sihhiyé*, The sanitary administration.

دائرهٔ صحیه *Dayiréyi Sihhiyé*, The Bureau of Sanitation.

تحفظخانه، قرانتنه، قارانتینه *Téhaffouzkhané*, *Qarantina*, The Lazaretto, Quarantine Station.

اوقاف همایون نظارت جلیلهسی
The Ministry of Religious Funds

فراغ *Féragh*, Alienation, Quitclaim.

انتقال *Intiqal*, Transmission by inheritance.

پوسته وتلغراف نظارت بهیهسی
The Administration of Posts and Telegraphs

دولت عالیۀ عثانیه اتحاد پوستەلری *Dévléti Aliyéyi Osmaniyé Ittihad Postalari*, The International Ottoman Posts.

دفترخانۀ خاقانی نظارتی *Déftérkhanéyi Khaqani Nézaréti*, The Ministry of Archives.

زراعت بانقەسی *Zira'at banqasi*, The Agricultural Bank.

عثانلی بانقەسی *Osmanli banqasi*, The Ottoman Bank.

بانق عثانی مدیری *Banqi Osmani Mûdiri*, The manager of the Imp. Ottoman Bank.

The Ministry of War حربیه نظارت جلیلهسی

باب والای سرعسکری *Babî Valayi Séraskéri*, The Seraskeriat (The War Office).

ارکان حرب *Erkiânî Harb*, The General Staff.

عموم ارکان حرب دائرەسی *Oumoum Erkiânî Harb Dayirési*, The Department of the General Staff.

پیاده دائرەسی *Piyadé Dayirési*, The Infantry Department.

سواری دائرەسی *Suvarî Dayirési*, The Cavalry Department.

طوپجی دائرەسی *Topjou Dayirési*, The Artillery Department.

استحکامات و انشاآت دائرەسی *Istihkiâmat vé Insha'at Dayirési*, The Department of Military fortification and buildings.

محاکمات عسکریه دائرەسی *Mouhakémati askériyé Dayirési*, The Department of Military Justice.

صحیۀ عسکریه دائرەسی *Sihhiyéyi askériyé Dayirési*, The Department of Military Sanitation.

امور صحیۀ انسانیه شعبەسی *Oumourou Sihhiyéyi Insaniyé shûbési*, The Department of Military medical Inspection.

امور صحیۀ حیوانیه شعبەسی *Oumourou Sihhiyéyi Hayvaniyé Shûbési*, The Department of equestrian hygiene.

تفتیش عسکریه قومیسیون عالیسی *Téftishi askériyé Qomisiyonou alisi*, High Military Commission.

لوازمات عمومیه دائرەسی *Lévazimatî oumoumiyé Dayirési*, The Commissary-General's Dep.

محاسبات عمومیه دائرەسی *Mouhasébatî oumoumiyé Dayirési*, The Department of General accounts.

ژاندارمه دائرهسی *Jandarma dayirési*, The Department of Gendarmery.

اطفائیه آلایی · طلومبهجی آلایی *Itfayiyé alayî, Touloumbajî alayî*, The Brigade of Firemen.

مکتب حربیه *Méktébi Harbiyé*, The Military School.

مکتب طبیه عسکریه *Méktébi Tibbiyéyi Askériyé*, The Medical Military School.

عموم مکاتب عسکریه مدیری *Oumoum Mékẗatibi Askériyé Mûdiri*, Director General of the Military Schools.

مأمورین عسکریه Military Grades

سردار *Sérdar*, General (cf. p. 458).

سردار اکرم *Sérdarî Ékrém*, Grand Marshal.

مشیر *Mûsheer*, Marshal.

فریق *Fériq*, General of division.

میرلوا *Miriliva*, General of brigade.

Erkan اركان
Highest officers

میر آلای *Miralay*, Colonel.

قائمقام *Qaymaqam*, Lieutenant colonel.

Uméra امرا
Higher officers

بیك باشی *Biñ bashî*, Major.

قول اغاسی *Qol aghasî*, Adjutant major.

یوز باشی *Yûz bashî*, Captain.

ملازم اول *Mûlazimi évvél*, Lieutenant.

ملازم ثانی *Mûlazimi sani*, Sub-lieutenant.

آلای امینی *Alay Émini*, Intendant of a regiment.

آلای کاتبی *Alay Kẗatibi*, Sec. of a regiment.

Zabit pl. zabita ضابط، ضابطه
Officer

آلای امامی *Alay Imami*, Chaplain of a regiment.

طابور امامی *Tabour Imamî*, Chaplain of a battalion.

باش چاوش *Bash chavoush*, Sergeant major.

صیره چاوشی *Sira chavoushou*, Sergeant.

Efrad افراد
Lower officers

اون باشی *On bashî*, Corporal.

نفر · عسکر نفری *Néfér, askér néféri*, Soldier, Private.

قرعه عسکری · عجمی *Qour'a askéri, Ajémi*, Conscript.

احتیاط عسکری *Ihtiyat askéri*, The army reserve.

Reg. Army

اردو *Ordou*, Army.   فرقه *Fîrqa*, Division.

لواء *Liva*, Brigade.   آلاى *Alay*, Regiment.

طوپجى ياخود سوارى بولوكى *Topjou yakhod souvari bêôlûyû*, Squadron.

طابور، پياده طابورى *Tabour, piyadé tabourou*, Battalion.

بولوك، پياده بولوكى *Bêôlûk, piyadé bêôlûyû*, Company.

پياده عساكرى، نفرى *Piyadé asakiri; -néféri*, Infantry; Footsoldier.

طوپجى عساكرى، نفرى *Topjou asakiri; -néféri*, Artillery; -man.

سوارى عساكرى، نفرى *Souvari asakiri*, Cavalry.

بحريه عساكرى، نفرى *Bahriyé asakiri*, Marines.

عساكر نظاميه (مُوَظَّف) *Asakiri nizamiyé, -Mouvazzaf*, Regulars.

عساكر رديفه *Asakiri rédifé*, Militia.

عساكر مستحفظه *Asakiri moustahfiza*, The last Reserves.

خاصه عساكرى *Khassa asakiri*, The corps of the Imp. Guards.

دردنجى اردوى همايون *Deôrdûnjû Ordouyi Hûmayoun*, The 4th Army Corps.

Note. 1. The centre of the Imp. Guards is Constantinople, 2nd Edirné, 3rd Monastîr, 4th Erzinjan, 5th Damascus, 6th Bagdad, 7th Sana.

Note. 2. All the Moslems in Turkey are called to enter the Army at the age of 20, which is called the age of Maturity *(ésnan)*. The term is 9 years in the Regular Army *(Asakiri Nizamiyé)*: 3 years under arms and 6 years in the army reserve *(Ihtiyat)*; 6 in the territorial army (Militia *Rédif)* and 3 in the territorial reserve *(Moustahfîz)*.

اسلحه Arms

اسلحهٔ ناريه *Éslihayi nariyé*, Fire arms.

اسلحهٔ جارحه *Éslihayi jariha*, Pointed arms.

توفنك *Tuféng*, Gun.   فيشنك *Fishéng*, Rocket.

روولور *Révolvér*, Revolver.   طابانچه *Tabanja*, Pistol.

طوپ *Top*, Canon.   سونكى *Sûngû*, Bayonet.

قےاطوره *Qatsatoura*, Strap.   قيليج *Qilij*, Sword.

قبضه، قين *Qabzé, qin*, Sheath.   بالطه *Balta*, Axe.

مزراق *Mizraq*, Lancet.   خانچر *Khanchér*, Sabre.

قامه *Qama*, Dagger.   ياتاغان *Yatagan*, Yatagan.

بحريه نظارت جليلهسى The Admiralty

شوراى بحريه   *Shourayi bahriyé*, Board of admiralty.

اركان حرب دائرهسى   *Érkiâni harb dayirési*, Staff-office.

بحريه ناظرى   *Bahriyé nazîrî*, Minister of marine.

بحريه مشيرى ، آميرال .(a.امير   *Bahriyé mûshiri, amiral*, Admiral.

دونانغه قوماندانى (الماء)   *Donanma qomandanî*, Admiral of the fleet.

فريق   *Fériq*, Vice-admiral (of the 1st class).

ميرلوا (رياله پاشا)   *Mirilica, riyalé pasha*, Rear-admiral.

قومودور   *Comodor*, Commodore.

ميرآلاى   *Miralay*, Captain.

بيك باشى . كمى سواريسى ، اسوارى   *Bin bashî, gémi souvarisi, souvari*, Commander.

قول اغاسى   *Qol aghasî*, Lieutenant-commander.

قدملى يوز باشى   *Qîdémli yûzbashî*, First Lieutenant.

يوز باشى   *Yûz bashî*, Lieutenant.

ملازم اول   *Mûlazimi évvél*, Sub-Lieutenant.

ملازم ثانى   *Mûlazimi sani*, Midshipman.

تعليم سفينهسنده بولونان مهندس   — — — *mûhéndis*, Naval cadet.

تعليم سفينهسنده بولونان مُعَلِّم   — — — *mouallim*, Naval instructor.

تفنك انداز ضابطى   *Tûféng éndaz zabiti*, Marine officer.

حرب ضابطى   *Harb zabiti*, Executive officer.

اركان حرب ضابطى   *Érkiânî harb zabiti*, Staff officer.

كوكرته ضابطى   *Geôyérté zabiti*, Deck officer.

طورپيدو ضابطى   *Torpido zabiti*, Torpedo officer.

طوپجى ضابطى   *Topjou zabiti*, Gunnery officer.

قدملى ضابط   *Qîdémli zabit*, Senior officer.

قدمسز ضابط   *Qîdémsiz zabit*, Junior officer.

نوبتجى ضابطى   *Névbétji zabiti*, { Officer of the day. » on duty.

واردا ضابطى   *Varda zabiti*, Officer of the watch.

سير سفائن ماموری   *Séyri séfayin mémourou*, Navigating officer.

چرخجی ضابطی، انشائیه ضابطی   *Charkhji zabiti, inshayiyé zabiti*, Civil officer.

چرخجی باشی   *Charkhji bashî*, Chief engineer.

چرخجی باشی معاونی   *Charkhjî bashî mouavini*, Assistant engineer.

قالیون کاتبی   *Qalyon kîatibi*, Fleet paymaster.

سفینه کاتبی   *Séfiné kîatibi*, Paymaster.

بریق کاتبی   *Briq kîatibi*, Clerk.

قلاغوز   *Qlavouz*, Pilot.   دومنجی   *Dûménji*, Steersman.

پورصون   *Porsoun*, Boatswain.   طوبجی   *Topjou*, Gunner.

مارانقوز   *Maranqoz*, Carpenter.   یالکنجی   *Yélkénji*, Sailmaker.

قالافات   *Qalafat*, Caulker.   غایبار   *Gaybar*, Topman.

واردا باندهرا   *Varda bandéra*, Signalman.

سفینه امینی   *Séfiné émini*, Master at arms.

مستعد کمیجی، اونباشی   *Mûstayid gémiji, onbashi*, Seaman.

نفر، طائفه   *Néfér, tayifé*, vulg. *tayʾfa*, Blue jacket.

سلاح انداز نفری   *Silahéndaz néféri*, Marine.

عجمی نفر   *Ajémi néfér*, Dock hand.

موسیقهجی   *Mousiqaji*, Bandsman.   بوروجی   *Boroujou*, Bugler.

ترامپت   *Trampét*, Drummer.   دمیرجی   *Démirji*, Blacksmith.

آتشجی   *Atéshji*, Stoker.   کومورجی   *Kêômûrjû*, Trimmer.

سفینه امامی، سفینه پاپاسی   *Séfiné papasî, séfiné imamî*, Chaplain.

قارانتینه ادارهسی   *Qarantina idarési*, Quarantine administration.

قارانتینه مجلسی   *Qarantina méjlisi*, Board of health.

تمیز پراتیقه   *Témiz pratiqa*, Clean bill of health.

بولاشیق پراتیقه   *Boulashîq pratiqa*, Foul bill of health.

The Imperial Arsenal ترسانهٔ عامره

ترسانه (دارالصناعه .a)   *Térsané, (darûsʾsanaʾa)*, Dockyard, arsenal.

رسمخانه   *Résimkhané*, Drawing office.

انشائیه دایرهسی   *Inshayiyé dayirési*, Constructor's office.

طورپیدو دایرهسی   *Torpido dayirési*, Torpedo department.

دمیرخانه *Démir khané,* Blacksmith's shop.

دوكمه خانه *Deôkmé khané,* Foundery, forge.

بیچقی خانه *Bichqî khané,* Sawmill.

قازانخانه، قزغانخانه *Qazankhané,* Boilermaker's shop.

ماكینه اعمالاتخانهسی *Makina imalatkhanési,* Engine shop.

تسویه فابریقهسی *Tésviyé fabriqasî,* Fitting shop.

تیر كوكرته *Teer géôyérté,* Rigging loft.

چلیك فابریقهسی *Chélik fabriqasî,* Steel factory.

یلكنجی مغازهسی *Yélkénji maghazasî,* Sail loft.

حاوض، حوض *Havouz,* Dock.

سابح حاوض *Sabih havouz,* Floating dock.

صولو حاوض *Soulou havouz,* Basin or wet dock.

قورو حاوض *Qourou havouz,* Dry or graving dock.

آنبار، دهپو *Anbar, ambar,* Stores.

كرسته محلی *Kérésté mahélli-mahali,* Timber yard.

Different Kinds of Ships سفینهنك انواعی

سفینه، سفائن؛ كمی *Séfiné, séfayin; gémi,* Ship.

زرهلی سفینه، سفن *Zîrhli séfiné,* pl. *sûfén,* Armour-plated ship.

باربه تالی زرهلی *Barbétalî zîrh'lî,* Armour-plated barbette ship.

قولهلی زرهلی *Qouléli zîrh'lî,* Armour-plated turret ship.

قالیون *Qalyon,* Line-of-battle ship.

فرقتین، فرقاتین *Firqatin,* Frigate.

قوروت *Qorvét,* Corvette.	بریق *Briq,* Brig.
غولت *Golét,* Brigantine.	غانبوط *Ganbot,* Gunboat.
قروآزور *Qrouazor,* Cruiser.	ایسقونه *Isqouna,* Schooner.

تجار ناویسی، تجار ناولیسی *Tûjjar navisi, tûjjar navlîsî,* Barque.

داولومبازلی واپور *Davloumbazlî vapor,* Paddle boat.

ایسقرو واپور *Îsqrou vapor,* Screw steamer.

تنزه واپوری، یوط *Ténézzûh vaporou, Yot,* Yacht.

قباسورطه سفینه   *Qabasourta séfiné,* Full-rigged ship.

قراغول سفینه   *Qaraghol séfiné,* Guard ship.

زرهلی سفینه   *Zîrhli séfiné,* An Iron-clad.

ساج کمی   *Saj gémi,* Iron ship.

تعلیم سفینهسی   *Talim séfinési,* Training ship.

نقلیه سفینهسی   *Naqliyé séfinési,* Transport ship.

مساحه کمیسی   *Mésahé gémisi,* Surveying ship.

یولجی طاشیان سفینه   *Yoljou tashiyan séfiné,* Passenger ship.

طورپیدو ایستیمبوطی   *Torpido îstimbotou,* Torpedo boat.

تحت‌البحر طورپیدو ایستیمبوطی   *Tahtélbahr torpido* ⎰Submarine torpedo
îstimbotou, ⎱ boat.

طورپیدو که‌جری   *Torpido Kéchîri,* Torpedo catcher.

The Provinces (p. 126, 441) ولایات شاهانه

ولایت ، والی   *Vilayét, vali,* Province, Governor-General.

والئ جدید   *Valiyi jédid,* The newly-appointed Vali.

والی وکیلی   *Vali vékili,* The acting Governor-General.

والی معاونی   *Vali mouavini,* The assistant governor.

لوا ، سانجاق ؛ متصرف   *Liva, sanjaq; mûtésarrîf,* County; governor.

قضا ، قائمقام   *Qaza, qaymaqam,* District, sub-governor.

ناحیه ، مدیر   *Nahiyé, mûdir,* Parish, Mûdir.

ولایت قاپو کتخداسی   *Vilayét qapou Kétkhoudasi,* vulg. *-kéh'yasî,* The
agent of the Governor-General.

دفتردار ، محاسبهجی ، مال مدیری   *Déftérdar, mouhasébéji, mal mûdiri,*
The comptrollers of revenue and expenditure in Vilayét,
Sanjaq and Qaza (p. 352).

مکتوبجی ، تحریرات مدیری ، تحریرات کاتبی   *Méktoubjou, tahrirat mûdiri,*
tahrirat kîatibi, The chief secretaries in Vilayét, Sanjaq
and Qaza.

دفتر خاقانی مأموری ، طاپو مأموری ، طاپو کاتبی   *Déftéri khaqani mémourou,*
tapou mémourou, tapou kîatibi, Registrar of Real-Estate
or Title-deeds (in Vilayét, Liva and Qaza).

نفوس ناظری ، نفوس مأموری ، نفوس کاتبی   *Noufous nazîrî, noufous mé-*
mourou, noufous kîatibi, Census-taker (in Vilayét, Liva
and Qaza. (Who issue the *Tézkérés* and passports also.)

فراغ قومیسیونی *Féragh qomisiyonou*, The quit claim commission.

تحصیلات قومیسیونی *Tahsilat qomisiyonou*, Commission of taxes.

تحصیلدار *Tahsildar*, Tax-collector.

مهاجرین قومیسیونی *Mouhajireen qomisiyonou*, Commission of immigrants.

صندیق امینی *Sandiq émini*, Treasurer.

مع تحریر ویرکو قلمی *Ma tahrir vérgi qalémi*, The bureau of cadasters.

زراعت بانقهسی شبعهسی *Zira'at banqasî shûbési*, A branch of the Agricultural bank.

پولیس سر قومیسری *Polis sér qomiséri*, First commissioner of Police.

قومیسر *Qomisér*, Commissioner.

پولیس *Polis*, Police, policeman.

مفتش *Mûféttish*, Inspector.

محکمهٔ شرعیه *Méhkémeyi shériyé*, The court of Canon-Law.

مفتی (فتوی = افتاء) *Mûfti*, A judge of Canon-Law. (the *Fayil* of

محکمهٔ نظامیه ٬ محکمهٔ عدلیه *Méhkéméyi nizamiyé, méhkémeyi adliyé*, The Judicial Court (pl. *Méhakim*).

نائب ؛ مرکز نائبی *Nayib, mérkéz nayibi*, Deputy judge.

قاضی ٬ حاکم (قضیاء ٬ حکم) *Qadî, hakim*, A judge, magistrate. (from

ممیز ٬ باش کاتب *Mûméyyiz*, Chief secretary.

مسود ٬ خلفا ٬ میبض ٬ مقید *Mûsévvid, khouléfa, mûbéyyiz, mouqayyid*, Clerk.

بلدیه مجلسی *Bélédiyé méjlisi*, Municipality.

بلدیه رئیسی *Bélédiyé réyisi*, Mayor.

بلدیه طبیبی ٬ ــ حکیمی *Bélédiyé tabibi*, Municipality doctor.

آشیجی ٬ آشی مأموری *Ashîji, ashî mémourou*, Vaccinator.

پوسته مدیری *Posta mûdiri*, Post-master.

دیپاوماسی تعبیراتی Diplomatic Terms

سفیر ٬ ایلچی ٬ اورته ایلچی *Séfir, élchi, Orta élchi*, Minister.

سفیر کبیر ٬ بویوک ایلچی *Séfiri kébir, béôyûk élchi*, Ambassador.

سفارت مستشاری *Séfarét mûstésharî*, The counsellor of legation.

مصلحتگذار *Maslahatgûzar*, Chargé d'affaires.

هيئت سفارت   *Hiyéti séfarét,* The personnel of the Embassy.

سفارتخانه   *Séfarétkhané,* Embassy, legation.

باش كاتب   *Bash kīatib,* The chief secretary.

قونسولوسلر هيئتی   *Qonsoloslar hiyéti,* The consular corps.

قونسولوس ، شهبندر   *Qonsolos, shéhbéndér,* The consul.

باش قونسولوس ، باش شهبندر   *Bash qonsolos,* The consul-general.

قونسولوس وكيلی ، شهبندر وكيلی   *Qonsolos rékili,* The vice-consul.

قونسولوسخانه ، قونسولاتو   *Qonsoloskhané, qonsolato,* General-consulate.

قنچلاريا ، قانچه لاريا   *Qanchélarya,* The chancellary.

تعاطئ تحريرات   *Ta'atiyi tahrirat,* Exchange of correspondence.

تحريرات رسميه   *Tahriratî résmiyé,* Official correspondence.

تحريرات غير رسميه   *Tahriratî ghayrî résmiyé,* Unofficial correspondence.

صورت رسميهده ، رسماً   *Souréti résmiyédé, résmén,* Officially.

صورت غير رسميهده   *Souréti ghay'rî résmiyédé.* Unofficially.

مبادلهٔ افكار   *Mûbadéléyi éfkīar,* Exchange of opinions (views).

مباينت افكار   *Mûbayénéti éfkīar,* Divergency of opinions.

مذكرهٔ عموميه   *Mûzékkéréyi oumoumiyé,* Consular dispatch.

مشترك نوطه   *Mûshtérék nota,* Collective note.

تقرير شفاهی ، مذكرهٔ شفاهيه   *Taqriri shifahi, Mûzékkéréyi shifahiyé,* } Verbal note.

صوك و قطعی تكليف ، اولتيماتوم   *Son ré qati téklif, ûltimatoum,* Ultimatum.

صلح ، مصالحه   *Soulh, mûsaléha,* Peace.

قونفرانس ، قونغره   *Qonférans, qongré,* Conference, congres.

مرخص   *Mourakh'khas,* Plenipotentiary.

معاهده ، عهدنامه   *Mouahédé, ahd'namé,* Treaty.

صلح معاهدهسی   *Soulh mouahédési,* Treaty of peace.

تجارت معاهدهسی   *Tijarét mouahédési,* Treaty of commerce.

تضمينات   *Tazminat,* Indemnity.

تضمينات حربيه   *Tazminatî harbiyé,* War Indemnity.

تسليم اراضی   *Téslimi arazi,* Cession of territory.

اشغال ، استیلا *Ishghal, istiyla,* Occupation.

تخلیه *Takhliyé,* Evacuation.

مأذوناً *Méézounén,* On furlough.

حکومت مشروطه *Hûkûméti méshrouté,* Constitutional government.

حکومت مطلقه *Hûkûméti moutlaqa,* Absolute government.

جمهوریت *Júmhouriyét,* Republic.

قانون اساسی *Qanounou ésasi,* The constitution.

مجلس مبعوثان ، پارلامنتو *Méjlisi mébousan, parlaménto,* The Commons.

مبعوث *Mébous,* Deputy, delegate. M. P.

مجلس اعیان *Méjlisi ayan,* Senate.

مجلس اعیان اعضاسی *Méjlisi ayan azasî,* Senator.

نامزد ، قاندیدا *Namzéd. Qandida,* Candidate.

منتخب *Múntakhib,* Elector.

رأی ، رأیلر ، آرا *Rey,* pl. *ara, reylér,* Vote, votes.

اکثریت آرا *Éksériyéti ara,* The majority of votes.

قلیت آرا *Aqalliyéti ara,* Minority of votes.

تکلیف ، تکلیف ایتمك *Téklif, —ét",* Motion, to move.

اکثریت *Éksériyét,* Quorum.

پولیتیقه فرقهلری *Politiqa fîrqalarî,* Political parties.

محافظه کاران فرقهسی *Mouhafazakîaran fîrqasî,* Conservative party.

ترقی پروران فرقهسی *Téraqqî pérvéran fîrqasî,* Progressive party.

حریت پروران فرقهسی *Hourriyét pérvéran fîrqasî,* Liberal party.

حکومت طرفدارانی *Hûkûmét tarafdaranî,* The supporters of the government.

حکومت خلافكیرانی *Hûkûmét khilafgiranî,* The Opposition.

فرقهٔ عوامّ *Fîrqayî avamm,* The Democratic party.

فرقهٔ جمهوریه *Fîrqayî júmhouriyé,* The republican party.

فرقهٔ مخالفه رئیسی *Fîrqayî moukhaléfé réyisi,* The leader of the Opposition.

بحران وكلا   *Bouhranî vûkéla,* A ministerial crisis.

تبدل وكلا   *Tébéddûlû vûkéla,* Change of ministry.

استعفا ' — ايتمك   *Istifa, —étmék,* Resignation, to resign.

عزل ' عزل ايتمك   *Azl, azl étmék,* Removal, to remove.

نصب و تعيين   *Nasbou tayin,* Nomination.

ترفيع رتبه   *Térfiyi rûtbé,* Promotion.

توجيه نشان   *Tévjihi nishan,* Decoration.

رتبه ' صنف   *Rûtbé, sînîf,* Class, order.

آچيق *Achîq,* Deficit.   بودجه *Bûdgé,* Budget.

حاصلات ' واردات   *Hasîlat, varidat,* Income.

مصارفات ' مدفوعات   *Mésarifat, médfouat,* Expenditure.

فضله حاصلات   *Fazlayî hasîlat,* Surplus.

محاربه ' حرب   *Mouharébé, harb,* The war.

محاربه بحريه   *Mouharébéyi bahriyé,* Naval battle.

محاربه بريه   »   *berriyé,* Land battle.

محاربه داخليه   »   *dakhiliyé,* Civil war.

اعلان حرب   *Ilanî harb,* A declaration of war.

اداره عرفيه   *Idaréyi êôrfiyé,* A state of siege.

اتفاق مثلث   *Ittifaqî mûséllés,* The Triple alliance.

اتفاق تدافعى و تجاوزى   *Ittifaqî tédafiyi vé téjavouzi,* An offensive and defensive alliance.

محارب دولتلر   *Mouharib dévlétlér,* The Belligerent Powers.

دولت معاونه   *Dévléti mouaviné,* Allied Power.

بىطرف دولت   *Bitaraf devlét,* Neutral Power.

آبلوقه *Abloqa,* Blokade.   مضاربه *Mûdarébé,* Battle.

محاسره *Mouhaséré,* Siege.   هجوم *Hûjûm,* Attack.

استحكام ' قلعه   *Istihkiām, qala, qalé,* Fortress.

تسليم مقاولهسى   *Téslim mouqavélési,* Capitulation.

غلبه *Ghalébé,* Victory.   فتح *Féth,* Conquest.

متاركه *Mûtaréké,* Armistice.

بين الملل *Béynél milél,* International.

بایراملر وَ یورطولر Festivals

بایراملر وَ یورطولر — *Allah Taɛala Hazrétléri, Jé-nabî Allah, Jénabî Haqq,* God, the Most High.

الله تعالى حضرتلرى ٬ جناب الله ٬ جناب حق — ${Salousou Shérif \atop Éqanimi Sélésé}$ The Holy Trinity.

ثالوث شریف ٬ اقانم ثلثه — *Eesa-él-Mésih,* Jesus Christ.

عیسى المسیح — *Rouhoul Qoudous,* The Holy Spirit.

روح القدس — *Kilisé, Kiliséyi Mésihiyé,* Church, Christian Church.

کلیسه ٬ کلیسه مسیحیه — *Yévmi makhsous,* Anniversary.

یوم مخصوص — *Sélamliq résmi alisi,* The ceremony of Sélamliq (a public procession of the Sultan to mosque at noon on Friday).

سلاملق رسم عالیسى — *Eed,* pl. *ayad* festival. بایرام ٬ *Bayram,* Moslem or Jewish festival.

اعیاد ٬ عید — بیرام *— Yévmi véladét,* The birthday.

یوم ولادت — *Isim gûnû,* The name-day.

اسم کونى — *Séné bashî, yil bashî,* The New Year's Day.

سنه باشى ٬ ییل باشى — *Véladéti Hûmayoun,* The Birthday of Sultan.

ولادت همایون — *Julousou Hûmayoun,* The accession of H. I. S.

جلوس همایون — *Zatî Shahanéniñ qilij qoushanmasî,* The investiture of H. M. with the sword of the Prophet.

ذات شاهانهنك قیلیج قوشانمسى — *Qilij alayî,* The ceremony of investiture.

قیلیج آلاى — *Shahzadégdäniñ sûnnét dûyûnû,* The circumcision feast of the Imp. princes.

شهزادکانك سنت دوکونى — *Khitan jémiyyéti, sûnnét dûyûnû,* A circumcision feast.

ختان جمعیتى ٬ سنت دوکونى — *Véleemé jémiyyéti, dûyûn,* The wedding.

ولیمه جمعیتى ٬ دوکون — *Léyléyi mûbaréké,* pl. *léyaliyi mûbaréké,* The Holy night, — nights.

لیلهٌ مبارکه ٬ لیالئ مبارکه — *Mévloudoun nébi, mévloud,* The birth-day of the Prophet.

مولود النبى ٬ مولود — *Léylétûl miraj, miraj géjési,* The Night of the Ascent of the Prophet (26th Réjéb).

لیلة المعراج ٬ معراج کیجهسى — *Léylétûl Ragayib, léyléyi Ragayib,* The Night of the first Friday of Réjéb, regarded as the anniversary of the conception of the Prophet.

لیلة الرغائب ٬ لیلهٌ رغائت

برات كيجهسى ، برائت كيجهسى *Bérat géjési*, The Night of Absolution, the Night of the 5th of Shaban, in which the re-velation was communicated to Muhammed by the angel Gabriel.

قنديل كيجهسى *Qandil géjési*, Any Night of general illumination for a Moslem festival, of which there are four: Muhammed's Birthday, Conception, Night-ascent and Absolution.

ليلة القدر ، ليلهٔ قدر ، قدر كيجهسى *Léylét'ûl qadîr, léylé'yi qadir, qadîr' géjési, Qadr géjési*, The Night of Power, name given to the 27th night of Ramazan.

ليلة العيد *Léylét'ûl eed*, The night preceding either of the two days of Bayram.

عرفه *Aréfé*, The day preceding the two following Bayrams.

عيد فطر ، رمضان بيرامى ، شكر بيرامى *Eedi fitîr, Ramazan bayramî, Shékér bayramî*, The festival at the end of the fast of Ramazan. (The first three days of Shaban.)

عيد اضحى ، قربان بيرامى ، حاجيلر بيرامى *Eedi adha, Qourban bayramî, Hajîlar bayramî*, The Moslem festival of sacrifice, the Great Bayram falling on 10—13 of Zilhijjé.

خرقهٔ شريف ، خرقهٔ سعادت *Khîrqayî Shérif, Khîrqayî Sa-adét*, The mantle of Muhammed, given to the poet Kiā'b.

صرهٔ همايون *Sourréyi Hùmayoun*, The Sultan's yearly gifts for Mecca and Medina.

موكب حج شريف *Mévkibi Hajji Shérif*, The Sacred Caravan for the Holy Lands of Islam.

Christian Festivals اعياد عيسويه (يورطولر)

ميلاد عيسى ، كوچوك پاسقاليه *Meeladî Eesa, Kûchûk Pasqalya*, Christmas.

ميلاد عيسى عرفهسى ، ختوم *Meeladî Eesa aréfési, Khîtom*, The Christmas Eve.

قارناوال ، ات كسيمى ، بارقاندان *Qarnaval, Ét késimi, Barqandan*, The carnival.

بويوك پرهيز *Béôyûk Pérhiz*, The Lent.

پاسقاليه ، بويوك پاسقاليه ، زاديك *Pasqalya, Zadig*, Easter.

عروج حضرت عيسا (عسى) *Ouroujou Hazréti Eesa*, The Ascension.

عيد الخمسين ، خمسين بيرامى *Eedûl Khamseen, Khamseen bayramî*, The feast of Pentecost.

قداس ، قداس شريف *Qouddas, Qoudda'si Shérif*, The Eucharist.

عشاى ربانى *Asha'yî Rabbani*, The Lord's Supper.

اعیاد یهودیه (بایراملر) Jewish Festivals

خامورسز بیرامی ، فصح *Khamoursouz bayramî, Fisîh',* The Jewish Passover. *(15 Nissan.)*

چوراب بیرامی ، کیپور *Chorab bayrami, Kipour,* The feast of Atonement. *(10 Tishri.)*

قامش بیرامی ، سوککوت *Qamish bayrami, Soukkot,* The feast of Tabernacles. *(15 Tishri.)*

قاره بیرام *Qara bayram,* The Jewish fast for the destruction of Jerusalem. *(9 Ab.)*

کل بیرامی ، صاووت *Gûl bayramî,* The Jewish Pentecost. *(6 Sivan.)*

شکر بیرامی ، پوریم *Shékér bayrami, Pourim,* The festival of Purim. *(14 Adar.)*

Orders of the Ottoman Empire

سلطنت سنیهٔ عثمانیهنك نشان ذیشانلری

1. خاندان آل عثمان *Khanédanî Ali Osman:* Star in brilliants (*Mourassa* مرصع), established by Sultan Hamid.

2. ارطغرل نشانی *Értogroul nishanî:* Gold, established by Sultan Hamid.

3. نشان افتخار *Nishanî Iftikhar:* Star in brilliants, established by Sultan Mahmoud.

4. نشان امتیاز *Nishanî Imtiyaz:* Star in brilliants, established by Sultan Hamid.

5. نشان عثمانی *Nishanî Osmanee:* Star in brilliants, 1, 2, 3, 4, established by Sultan Abdûl Aziz.

6. نشان مجیدی *Nishanî Méjidee:* Star in brilliants, 1, 2, 3, 4, 5, established by Sultan Méjid.

7. نشان شفقت *Nishanî Shéfaqat:* The only order conferred on ladies 1, 2, 3, established by Sultan Hamid.

مدالیهلر Medals

لیاقت مدالیهسی 1. Gold medal of *Liyaqat.*

امتیاز مدالیهسی 2. Gold and silver medals of *Imtiyaz.*

صنایع مدالیهسی 3. » » » » » *Industry.*

جان قورتاران مدالیهسی 4. Silver medal for saving life.

افتخار مدالیهسی 5. » ‘ » » *Iftikhar.*

The Different Ranks in the Ottoman Empire رتب مختلفۀ دولت عاليۀ عثمانيۀ رتب

رتب ملكيه Civil Grades	رتب عسكريه Military Grades	رتب علميه Religious Grades
۱ p وزارت، وزير	۱ p مشيرلك، مشير	۱ صدر روم or صدر ايلي é
۲ é, b رتبۀ بالا	۲ p فريق اول	۲ صدر روم ايلي é پايه‌سي كازعسكرلگي or كازعسكرلك
۳ é, b رتبۀ اولى صنف اول بكلربكي پايه‌سي or رتبۀ اولى é	۳ p فريق ثانى	۳ كازعسكرلك آناطولى پايه‌سي or آناطولى é
۴ é رتبۀ اولى صنف ثانى é or بگ‌مجردان پايه‌سي	۴ پاشا or لوا or بگ‌لربگي b الالای	۴ استانبول كازعسكرلگي پايه‌سي é
۵ é, b رتبۀ ثانيه صنف اول خانزى پايه‌سي	۵ b قائمقام	۵ حرمين شريفين موليتى é
۶ b رتبۀ ثانيه صنف ثانى مير آخر or مير الاحرا پايه‌سي é	۶ é, b قول آغاسى	۶ بلاد خمسه موليتى é
۷ é رتبۀ ثالثه or اصطبل عامره مديرلگى پايه‌سي	۷ é, b بوزباشى	۷ مخرج موليتى é كبار مدرسين
۸ é رتبۀ رابعه or كتب هماين پايه‌سي é	۸ é, a, p بولك أميني	۸ سليمانيه مادوننده مدرسين é
۹ é رتبۀ خامسه خواجۀ قاپوچى باشنلرى é	۱۰ a ملازم	۹ خواجه‌لر é

Note. 1. The title-holders are called p = pasha, $é$ = éfféndi, b = béy, a = agha.
       2. *Rûtéb* is the plural of *rûtbé* 'grade, degree'. *Rûtébi Milkiyé* = *Milkiyé Rûtbéléri*.

Civil Grades *Milkiyé Rûtbéléri*

1. *Vézarét, Vézir,* The Rank of Vezir (the highest civil grade).
2. *Rûtbéyi Bala,* The Rank of Bala (*béy, éfféndi*).
3. *Rûtbéyi Oula sinîfî évvél* (*béy, éfféndi*) yakhod *Rouméli Béylér béyi payési* (*béy, éfféndi*), The Rank of 1st grade, 1st class.
4. *Rûtbéyi Oula sinîfî sani* (*éfféndi*) yakhod *Mirimiran Payési* (*pasha*), 1st grade 2nd class or the rank of Mirimiran.
5. *Rûtbéyi Saniyé sinîfî évvél Mûtémayizi* (*éfféndi*) yakhod *Miyrûl ûméra payési,* 2nd class Mûtémayiz or the Rank of Miyrûl ûméra.
6. *Rûtbéyi Saniyé sinîfî sani* (*éfféndi*) yakhod *Stablî Amiré Mûdirliyi payési,* 2nd class 2nd grade.
7. *Rûtbéyi Salisé* (*éfféndi*) yakhod *Rikīabî Hûmayoun Qapoujou bashîlighî payési* (*éfféndi*), 3rd class.
8. *Rûtbéyi Rabiya* (*éfféndi*), 4th class.
9. *Rûtbéyi Khamisé* (*éfféndi*), 5th class.

Military and Naval Grades *Askériyé Rûtbéléri*

1. *Mûshirlik, Mûshir* (*pasha*), Marshal = Admiral (p. 444).
2. *Fériq, Fériqi évvél* (*pasha*), General of Division I. rank.
3. *Fériqi sani* (*pasha*), Gen. of Division II. rank = Vice Admiral.
4. *Miriliva, Liva pasha,* General of Brigade = Rear Admiral.
5. *Miralay* (*béy*), Colonel = Captain.
6. *Qaymaqam* (*éfféndi, béy*), Lieutenant Colonel = Captain of frigate.
7. *Biñbashî* (*éfféndi, béy*), Major = Commander.
8. *Qol aghasî* (*éfféndi*), Adj. Major = Lieutenant Major.
9. *Yûzbashî* (*éfféndi, agha*), Captain = Lieutenant.
10. *Mûlazim* (*agha*), Sublieutenant = Sublieutenant.

Grades of Religious Hierarchy *Ilmiyé Rûtbéléri*

1. *Sadrî Rouméli* yakhod *Rouméli Qazaskérliyi Payési* (*éfféndi*), The Rank of the Chancellor of Rouméli (corresp. to Archbishop): The Vice-Chancellor of Turkey (p. 438).
2. *Sadrî Anadolou* yakhod *Anadolou Qazaskérliyi payési* (*éfféndi*), The rank of the chancellor of Anadolou (corresp. to Bishop).
3. *Istanbol Qadîlighî payési* (*éfféndi*).
4. *Haréméyni Shériféyn payési* (*éfféndi*).
5. *Biladi Khamsé mévléviyéti payési* (*éfféndi*).
6. *Makhréj mévléviyéti payési* (*éfféndi*).
7. *Kibarî Mûdérriseen payési* (*éfféndi*).
8. *Sûléymaniyé Madounounda mûdérriseen payési* (*éfféndi*).
9. *Hoja, Khoja payési* (*éfféndi*).

Official Titles القاب رسميه

There are numerous expressions to denote 'His Imp. Majesty the Sultan', the followings are much in use:

ذات حضرت پادشاهى ، ذات حضرت جهاندارى ، ذات حضرت شهنشاهى ،
ولى‌نعمتمز ، ولى‌نعمتمز پادشاهمز افندیمز ، شوکتمآت افندیمز ، شوکتلو پادشاهمز
افندیمز ، ذات شوکتسمات حضرت کیتی ستانى .

Zatî hazréti Padishahi, Zatî hazréti jihandari, Zatî hazréti shéhinshahi, Vélinimétimiz, Vélinimétimiz Padishahîmîz éfféndimiz, Shévkétméab éfféndimiz, Shévkétlou Padishahîmîz éfféndimiz, Zatî Shévkétsîmatî hazréti giyti sitani.

Imperial:

، جهانبانى ، جهاندارى ، سنیه ، خسروانه ، همایون ، ملوکانه ، شاهانه ، پادشاهى
etc. شهریاریلری ، ملوکانه‌لری ، شاهانه‌لری ، پادشاهیلری or تاجدارى ، شهنشاهى

Padishahi, Shahané, Mûlûkîané, Húmayoun, Khûsrévané, Séniyé, Jihandari, Jihanbani, Shéhinshahi, Tajdari or *Padishahiléri, Shahanéléri, Mûlûkîanéléri, Shéhriyariléri* etc.

Especial titles of the Mother-Sultana (*Validé sûltan aliyétûsh'shan hazrétléri*):

دولتلو عصمتلو عظمتلو عنایتلو مرحمتلو افندم حضرتلری

Of Foreign Emperors and Kings:

هندستان اینپراطورى و انکلتره قرالى حشمتلو آلبرت ادوارد حضرتلری

Hindistan Impératorou vé Ingiltérra Qiralî Hashmétlou Albert Edward hazrétléri. (H. M.)

حشمتپناها! *Hashmétpénaha'!* Sire!

Of the Shah of Persia:

(H. M.) ایران شاهى شهامتلو مظفر الدین خان حضرتلری

Of the Imperial Princes:

(H. I. H.) دولتلو نجابتلو افندى حضرتلری

Of the Khedive of Egypt, the Presidents of Republics and the Grand vizier:

فخامتلو دولتلو افندم حضرتلری *Fékhamétlou dévlétlou Efféndim hazrétléri.* (H. H.)

ذات فخامتسمات حضرت صدر اعظم *Zatî fékhamétsîmati hazréti Sadrî Azami.*

Of the Ex-Grand viziers:

ابتلو دولتلو پاشا حضرتلری *Ûbhétlou dévlétlou Pasha hazrétléri.*

Of Foreign Ambassadors:

اصالتلو سير (نيقولاس اوقونور) جنابلرى

Of the Shérif (governor) of Mécca and Medina:

(H. H.) دولتلو سَيادتلو افندم حضرتلرى

Of the Chief Eunuch of the Imperial Palace:

(H. H.) دولتلو عنايتلو افندم حضرتلرى

Of the Minister of War and the Husbands of Imperial Princesses:

(H. H.) دولتلو عطوفتلو افندم حضرتلرى

Of the Grand Marshal (*Sérdarî Ékrém*):

(Excellency) دولتلو رأفتلو افندم حضرتلرى

Of Functionaries of Civil and Military Grades.

١ Of Marshals and Viziers:

(Excellency) دولتلو افندم حضرتلرى

Of the Governors General (*Valis*):

(Excellency) دولتلو عطوفتلو افندم حضرتلرى

٢ Of functionaries of *Bala*, of the Imperial Chamberlains, of the Premier Secretary of H. I. M. and of the President of the Council of State:

(Excellency) عطوفتلو افندم حضرتلرى

٣ Of Generals of Division (*Fériq*), Vice-Admirals, and of the functionaries of the First grade of the *Rût-béyi Oula*, and of *Rouméli Béylér Béyiliyi*:

(Excellency) سعادتلو افندم حضرتلرى

٤ Of Brigadier-Generals (*Miriliva*), Rear-Admirals and the functionaries of the 2nd grade *Rûtbéyi Oula* and the *Mûtésarrifs*:

سعادتلو افندم

٥ Of Colonels, Captains of ships (*Miralay*), functionaries of *Mûtémayiz* and *Qaymaqams*:

عزتلو افندم حضرتلرى

٦ Of functionaries of *Rûtbéyi Saniyé*, of Lieutenant-Colonels, Captains of Frigates and the Director of the Imperial Stables:

عزتلو افندی or بك or اغا

٧ Of Majors (*Binbashî*), Commanders (Captains of Corvettes), *Mûdirs* and Intendants of Regiments (*Alay Emini*):   رفعتلو بك or افندی or اغا

٨ Of Adjutant-Majors, functionaries of *Rabiya*, Lieutenant-Commanders and Captains:

فتوتلو بك or افندی or اغا

٩ To those who are below the above functionaries:

حمیتلو بك or افندی or اغا

Of Moslem Clergy.

Of the Sheiykh-ûl Islam:

دولتلو سماحتلو افندم حضرتلری

Given by Clergy:

معروض داعئ دیرینهلری درکه

Given by laymen:

معروض بندهٔ دیرینهلری درکه

Of each Ex-Shéykh-ûl Islam:

دولتلو فضیلتلو افندی حضرتلری

١ ‘ ٢ Of the Judges of Rouméli and Anatolia:

سماحتلو افندم حضرتلری

٣ Of the Istanbol Qadîsî and the Judges of Canon Law: فضیلتلو افندم حضرتلری

٤, ٥, ٦ Of the functionaries of Harémeyn etc.:

فضیلتلو افندی

٧ Of the functionaries of Mûdérriseen (Doctors of Theological Seminaries): مَکرَمتلو افندی

٨ ‘ ٩ Of the functionaries of the 8th and 9th grade:

مَوَدَّتلو افندی

Of Chélébi Effendi (the Shéykh occupying the post
of Mévlana Jélaléddini Roumi at Iconium):

رَشادتلو افندی

Non-Moslem Clergy.

Of the Catholicos, Patriarchs, Bulgarian Exarch
and Grand-Rabbi:

رتبتپناها ! رتبتلو افندی حضرتلری *Rûtbétpénaha!*

Of the Chancellor of Protestants (*Millét Vékili*):

سعادتلو افندم حضرتلری

Of Archbishops and Bishops:

سماحتلو افندم

Of Pastors, Missionaries, Chief Priests and Priests:

حرمتلو افندی given by Moslems ; فضیلتلو افندی

Commercial Terms اصطلاحات تجاریه

Accept (to) *qaboul ét.''*
accepter *qaboul édén;* — ted *maq-
    bouloum dour.*
account *hisab, mouhasébé;* -cur-
    rent *hisabî jari;* on- *alél hisab.*
acquittal *ibranamé, ibra sénédi.*
action *hissé sénédi.*
address *adrés, khitab.*
advance *péshin, téslimat.*
advise *ikhbar ét.'';* letter of ad-
    vice *ikhbarnamé, ikhtarnamé.*
agent *agénta, vékil.*
agio *aqjé farqî, bash.*
agreement *ouzlashma.*
allowance *ikram.*
amount *meblagh, para.*
assets *mévjoud, -at; matloubat.*
assurance *sigourta, tééminat.*
average *avarya, -malî.*
Bail, to be — *kéfalét, -ét.''*
balance *mûvazéné, -diftéri, bi-
    lancho; baqiyéyi hisab, borj.*
bank *banqa;* -shares *ésham;*
    -note *qayimé, banqnot.*
banker *bankér, sarraf.*
bankrupt, -cy *mûflis, iflas.*

bargain *pazarlîq.*
barrel *varél, fichî.*
bearer *hamil.*
bill of exchange *qambiyal, policha;*
    — of lading *irsaliyé qaymésé.*
blank indorsement *béyaz jiro.*
bonds *tahvil, séhim; éshamî ou-
    moumiyé, qonsolid.*
bottomry *géminiñ térhini.*
brévété, chartered *bératlî.*
broker *déllal, sîmsar.*
brokerage *déllaliyé, sîmsariyé.*
budget *irad masraf deftéri, bûdjé.*
bulletin *jédvél, pousoula.*
bureau *qalém, idarékhané.*
business *oumour, ish.*
buy *satîn almaq, ishtira.*
buyer *mûshtéri, alîji.*
Capital *sérmayé, résûlmal.*
cargo *hamoulé, yûk.*
cash *para;* in — *péshin, naqdén.*
certificate *ilmoukhabér, shéhadet-
    namé.*
change *tébdil, bozma.*
charter *bérat, imtiyaz.*
chattel *émvalî ménqoulé.*

check *chék;* coin *sikké, para.*
commerce *tijarét, akhzouita.*
commercial *tûjjari; –* law *canonou tijarét.*
commission *qomisiyon;* -er *qomisiyonjou, -tûjjar.*
company *qoumpanya, shirkét.*
consols *qonsolid, ésham.*
contract *mouqavélé, qontourato.*
copy *qopya, nûskhé.*
correspondence *moukhabéré;* -dant *moukhabir, adém.*
course of exchange *piatsa.*
credit *qrédito, itibar; matloub;* on – *vérésiyé.*
creditor *alajaqlî, dayin.*
currency *rayij aqjé, para.*
custom *géômrûk, rousoum;* – house *géômrûk, rousoumat dayirési.*
customer *mûshtéri, bayi.*
Damage *zarar, ziyan, khasar.*
days of grace *mûsaadé, mûhlét.*
dear *bahalî, fiyatlî.*
debt *déyn, borj.*
debit *zimmét, dûyounat;* (to) *zimmét qayd ét."*
debtor *médyoun, borjlou.*
deduction *ténzil, tarh'.*
deficiency *achîq.*
delay *téékhir;* without – *bila téékhir, sériyan.*
demurrage *îstalya.*
deposit *émanét, déposito.*
destination *mahallî maqsoud.*
discount *îsqonto, ténzil.*
dissatisfaction *khoshnoudsouzlouq.*
dissolution *féskh, laghv.*
dividend *hisséyi téméttû, kiârdan dûshén hissé.*
double *chifté;* -entry *mûzaaf.*
draft *qambiyal, politsa.*
draw a bill (to) *politsa chékmék,* – back *géômrûk résminiñ iyadési.*
drawer *késhidéji.*
due *téédiyési lazîm gélén.*
duplicate *nûskhéyi saniyé.*
Endorsement *jiro, havalé.*
error *séhv', khata, yaneish.*
exchange *éjnébi piatsasî, – politsasî; mûbadélé, trampa.*

exports *ikhrajat.*
Factor *qomisiyonjou.*
fair *panayir.*
final *qati, soñ.*
firm *tijarétkhané.*
foreign *éjnébi.*
forestaller *madrabaz, mûhtékir.*
freight *hamoulé, yûk;* (to) *gémi yûklétmék, tahmil ét."*
fund *méblagh, aqjé; sérmayé, résûlmal.*
Gain *kiâr, qazanj, téméttû;* netsafi *téméttû, safi kiâr.*
goods *ésh-ya, mal.*
guaranty *kéfalét, kéfil.*
Honour *(politsayî) qaboul ét."*
Import(ation) *idkhalat.*
imputable *ténzili lazîm gelén.*
indemnity *tazminat.*
indorsement *jiro, havalé.*
indorser *jiranta, jiro édén.*
insurance *sigourta, tééminat.*
insured *sigourtali.*
interest *fayiz, gûzéshté.*
inventory *mûfrédat déftéri.*
invoice *fatoura, qayimé.*
Letter *tahrirat, méktoub.*
liability *zimmét, borj.*
licence *roukhsat, béhiyé.*
loss *zarar, ziyan.*
Maker *médyoun, késhidéji.*
mark *marqa, alamét.*
market *charshî, piyatsa.*
maturity *vadéniñ ikmalî.*
memorandum *hisab pousoulasî.*
merchandise *mal, émta'a.*
merchant *tûjjar, tajir.*
money *aqjé, naqîd.*
monopoly *inhisar.*
mortgage *réhin, véfa.*
Negotiable *géchér, rayij.*
net *safi; îsqontosouz.*
Offer *satlîgha chiqarilan mal.*
office *idarékhané, oda.*
order *émr, sîparîsh.*
Package *pakét.*
partner *shérik, ortaq;* -ship *shirkét, ortaqlîq.*
patent *bérat, imtiyaz.*
pattern *mostra, éôrnék.*
pawn, pledge *réhin.*
payable *téédiyési méshrout olan.*

payee *aliji, hamil.*

payment *téédiyé, éda.*   [*qoulé.*

personal property *emvali mén-*

post *posta, – vaporou; –* office *postahané; –* order *manda.*

power of attorney *rékiālétnamé.*

price *fiyat, qiymét, baha; -*current *fiyatî jari, rayij.*

principal *sérmayé.*

protest *protésto.*

Quality *nér, jins.*

Real estate *emvali gayrî ménqoulé, mal mûlk.*

ratification *tasdiq.*

receipt *ilmouhabér, maqbouz; on-ba ilmouhabér.*

reference *bir tijarétkhané haq-qînda vérilén malûmat, shéha-dét.*

reimbursement *téslim, téédiyé.*

rent *ijar, kira.*

responsible *mésoul.*

responsibility *mésouliyét.*

retail *pérakéndé satîsh.*

return *avdét, iyadé.*

Sale *satîsh, sarfiyat, sûrûm.*

sell *satmaq, firoukht étmék.*

seller *bayi, satîji.*

satisfaction *mémnouniyét.*

security *kéfil, kefalét.*

S. G. D. G. (sans garanti du gouvernment) *hûkûmétiñ té-éminatî olmaqsîzîn.*

ship *gémi, séfiné; -*ment *tahmil, yûklémé;* (to) *tahmil ét." yûk-létmék.*

simple *safi; adi.*

sign *imzalamaq.*

signature *imza.*

smuggled *qachaq (mal, tûtûn).*

solid *mûtébér, qavee.*

stamp: postage- *posta poulou;* revenue- *damga poulou, sénéd poulou.*

stock *hissé, hissé sénédi.*

superior *ala, aghîr (mal).*

Titledeed *tapou sénédi.*

trade mark *alaméti fariqa.*

trustee *vasi, mûtévélli.*

Ultimo *mahî sabîq, géchén ay.*

usury *téféjilik.*

Warehouse *maghaza.*

warranty *kéfalét.*

weigh *tartmaq, vézn ét."*

weight *aghîrlîq, sîqlét.*

wholesale *topdan satîsh.*

لغتچه

Vocabulary.

Abandon (to) *braqmaq*, a.*térk ét.''*
abate (to) *ashaghi varmaq, chîqarmaq,* a.*ténzil ét.''*
ability a. *qabiliyét, iqtidar; qoudrét.*
able a. *qadir, múqtédir.*
ablution p. *abdést.*
abode *év,* p. *khané,* a. *méskén.*
abolish (to) a. *laghv, mahv, im-
ha ét.''*
abominable p. *napak, mourdar.*
about a. *dayir; taqribén.*
above *yoqarî, yoqarda; ústûn.*
absence a. *ghayboubét; fîqdan,
yoqlouq.*
absent a. *ghayib, namévjoud.*
absolute a. *moutlaq, mústaqil.*
absolutely a. *qatiyan, kúlliyén,
as'la.*
abstain (to) a. *ijtinab ét.'',* p. *pérhiz ét.'', pérhiz toutmaq.*
abstinence a. *ijtinab,* p. *pérhiz
kîârlîq;* a. *imsak, orouj.*
abundant *bol, choq,* a. *késir.*
abuse (to) a. *ifsad ét.'', bozmaq.*
abyss a. *varta, lûjjé, q'ar.*
academy p. *énjûméni danish,
f. aqadémiya;* a. *méktébi ali.*
accept a. *qaboul, akhz ét.'', almaq,* a. *razee olmaq.*
access a. *téqarroub,* a. *doukhoul.*
accident a. *qaza, vouqouat, hadisé.*
acclivity *yoqoush, bayir.*
accompany a. *rifaqat, arqadash-
lîq ét.''*
accord (to) a. *ittifaq ét.''; vérmék.*
according (to) . . . a *geôré, binaén,
nazarén.*
account a. *hisab, mou'amélé.*
accumulate (to) *birikdirmék,* a.*jém
. ét.''; yîghmaq, toplamaq.*

accurate *doghrou,* p. *dúrúst,*
a. *sahih'.*
accusation a. *shikîâyét, ittiham.*
ache *aghrî,* a. *véj'a.*
acid *ékshi;* a. *hamiz.*
acknowledge a. *iqrar, i'tiraf;
tanîmaq;* a. *tasdiq étmék.*
acorn *palamout.*
acquire (to) *tahsil ét.''; eôyrénmék.*
across *tarafîndan; arqîrî.*
act (to) a. *harékét ét.''; étmék, yapmaq.*
act, action *ish,* a. *fi'il;* p. *jéng.*
active *ishgûzar;* (verb) a. *fi'ili
mútéaddi.*
actually a. *filhaqîqa, sahihén;
(now) shimdi.*
acute *sivri, késkin;* a.*fétin,* (angle)
a. *zaviyéyi haddé.*
adamant *polad.*
adapt (to) *ouydourmaq,* a.*mouva-
fiq qîl maq.*
add (to) *qatmaq,* a. *zamm, ilavé ét.''*
adder *éngérék yîlani.*
addition *'ilavé;* (arith.) *jém'.*
adieu! a. *éyvallah, Allaha îsmar-
ladîq,* f. *adiyo.*
adjective a. *sîfét, vasf.*
administer a. *idaré étmék; vérmék.*
admiral *amiral, bahriyé múshiri.*
admire (to) *béyénmék,* a.*tahsin ét.''*
admit (to) a. *qaboul ét.''*
adore (to) *tapînmaq,* p. *pérés-
tish ét.''*
adult *béôyúk, aqla baligh.*
adultery a. *zina, fah'shiyat.*
advantage a. *fayidé, kîâr, istifadé.*
adversary a. *khasim, 'adou,*
p. *dúshmén.*

advice a. *nasihat; khabér.*
advocate, *f. avoqat, dava vékili.*
– (to) a. *iltizam, istis-hab, tércijét.''*
affair *ish,* a. *maslahat;* p. *jéng.*
affection a. *mouhabbet, houbb; illét.*
affiance (to) a. *aqdi nikiah ét.''*
affray *ghavgha,* a. *niz'a.*
affront a. *tahqir, haqarét ét.''*,
  t. *gujendirmék.*
aforesaid a. *salif iz zikr, mézkûr.*
afraid (to be) *qorqmaq,* a. *khafv
  ét.''*
after *soñra,* a. *badéhou, badéma.*
afternoon *ikindi,* a. *badéz zéval.*
again *bir daha,* a. *tékrar, tékrarén.*
age *yash,* a. *sinn;* a. *asr, dévr,
  éyam.*
agent a. *vékil, adém, f. agénta.*
agitator a. *mouharrik, mûfsid.*
agony a. *iztirab; halétûn néz'.*
agree a. *qavl, ittifaq ét.'', razi ol.''*
agriculture a. *zira'at, rénjbérlik.*
ague *sitma.*
ah! *akh!, aman! vakh.*
aid *yardim,* a. *mouavénét, imdad.*
aim (to take) p. *nishan almaq.*
air a. *hava, havayi nésimi.*
alarm *qorqou,* a. *iztirab, héyéjan.*
alas! *éyvah! yaziq!*
alderman a. *ayan, sahibi noufous.*
algebra a. *ilmi jébr, jébr.*
alien a. *éjnébi,* t. *yadîrghi.*
alike a. *mûshabih, béñzér.*
alive *diri, sagh,* a. *hayy'.*
all *hép,* a. *jûmlé, jémi, kûlli.*
alleviate (to) a. *takhfif ét.''*
alley *dar soqaq, chiqmaz.*
alliance a. *ittifaq, ittihad.*
allow a. *izin, roukhsat vérmék.*
allowance a. *tayin, tayinat.*
almanac a. *taqvim,* p. *salnamé.*
almond *badém.*
almost *héman, az qaldi.*
alms a. *sadaqa, eeyané, zékiat.*
alone p. *ténha; yaliñiz.*
aloud *pék,* p. *avazi bûlénd ilé.*
alphabet *élifbé,* a. *houroufou héja.*
already a. *zatén;* p. *hénouz.*
also *da, dakhi,* a. *kézalik.*
altar a. *mézbah.*
alter (to) a. *taghyir, tébdil ét.'''*
  t. *déyishdirmék.*

although *hér néqadar,* p. *éyérchi.*
altitude *yûkséklik,* a. *irtifa.*
altogether a. *jûmlétén, témamén.*
alum *shab, shéb.*
always a. *dayima,* p. *hémishé.*
ambassador p. *élchi,* a. *séfir.*
amber p. *kéhrûba, kéhribar.*
ambergris a. *'anbér, ambér.*
ambition a. *hirsi shan, iqbal pé-
  réstlik.*
amble (to) *rahvan, éshkin, yorgha
  gitmék.* [giah.
ambuscade t. *pousou,* p. *kémin-*
amiable a. *latif,* p. *khosh,* t. *tatli.*
ammunition p. *jébhané.*
amount á. *yékûn; méblagh.*
ample *bol, joshgoun,* a. *késir.*
amulet a. *nouskha, tilisim, hama-*
amuse (to) *éyléndirmék.* [yil.
ancestor a. *jédd;* (pl.) *aba ou éjdad.*
anchor *démir, léngér.*
anchovy *sardéla, sardalya.*
ancient a. *qadim,* t. *éski.*
ankle *topouq,* a. *kiab.*
anecdote a. *hikiayé, latifé, qissé.*
angel a. *mélék, mélayiké.*
anger a. *hiddét, khirs,* t. *eôfké.*
angle a. *zaviyé,* p. *keôshé.*
angry *darghin,* p. *ghazabnak.*
animal a. *hayvan.*
annals a. *tarikh,* (pl.) *tévarikh.*
annoy (to) a. *tajiz ét.'', osandir-*
annual *yilliq,* a. *sénévi.* [maq.
answer a. *jévab,* p. *pasoukh.*
ant *qarînja,* p. *mourché.*
antagonist a. *moukhasim, raqib.*
antelope *jéyran, jéylan,* p. *ahou.*
antichrist a. *déjjal.*
anvil *eôrs, sal.*
anxiety p. *éndishé,* a. *vésvésé.*
ape *maymoun,* p. *kébi.*
apology *eôzûr;* a. *tarziyé; mûda-*
apoplexy *damla,* a. *nûzûl.* [fa'a.
apostate a. *mûrtédd* vulg. *mourtad.*
apostle a. *résoul, havari* (of
  Christ). [méydanda.
apparent a. *zahir,* p. *ashikiar,*
appeal a. *khitab; mûnajat.*
appear (to) *geôrûnmék;* a. *zahir,*
  p. *nûmayan ol.''*
appearance *geôrûnûsh,* a. *sourét,
  shékl; zouhour.*

appendix a. 'ilavé, zamimé.
appetite a. ishtiha, vulg. ishtah.
apple élma, (of eye) geôz bébéyi.
appoint (to) a. nasb. tayin ét."
apprentice oushaq. p. shayird.
apricot (dry) zérdali, (fresh) qa-
yîsi.
apron p. péshtimal, fota.
Arabian, -bic arabi, arabja.
arch kémér, p. taq.
archbishop mitropolit, arachnort.
archer p. kémankésh, tiréndaz.
architect a. mimar, qalfa, p. ousta.
aright doghrou, a. salim. sahih.
arithmetic a. ilmi hisab.
arm qol, p. bazou; a. silah.
army ordou, p. léshkér.
arrange a. tértib ét., t. dizmék.
arrival gélish, a. vûrûd, vûsûl.
arsenal f. térsané.
art a. fénn, pl. fûnûn, sana'at.
artery shah damar, a. shéryan.
artichoke énginar, gangar.
artificer a. ésnaf, éhli sana'at.
artificial yapma, a. soun'i; taqlid.
artillery toplar, topjou éslihasî.
ascend a. sou'oud ét.", chîqmaq.
ascertain a. tahqîq ét."; yoqlamaq.
ashamed (to be) outanmaq, a. hijab ét."
ashes kûl, p. rémad.
ask sormaq, a. istifsar, sival ét."
ass éshék, p. khar, a. mérkéb.
assassin qanlî, a. qatil, p. khounriz.
assist yardim, a. mou'avénét, iané.
assuredly a. filhaqiqa, haqiqatén.
astray yoldan sapmîsh, gûmrah.
astrologer a. mûnéjjim, t. baqîji.
astronomy ilmi hiyét.
atom a. zérré, jévhér; jûz.
atone a. kéfarét ét."
atrocity a. zûlm, mézalim.
attack a. hûjûm, hamlé.   [ét."
attempt (to) chalîshmaq, a. téjribé
attend, (upon) a. khîzmét ét."; (to)
a. hazir ol."
attention a. diqqat; khass dour!
attract a. jézb ét.", chékmék.
auction a. mézad, mûzayédé.
augment artirmaq, a. téksir ét."
August (month) avosdos, okosdos.

aunt (paternal) a. émé; (maternal)
téyzé, a. hala.
Austrian némché, némtsé.
author mûéllif, mûharrir.
auxiliary yardimji; (verb) a. fiyli
iyané, fiyli 'amm (§ 272, 309).
avenge a. t. intiqam almaq.
avenue a. jaddé.
await béklémék, a. mountazir ol."
awake ouyanmaq.
awe qorqou. a. déhshét, héybét.
axe balta, girébi.
axis a. mihvér.
axle dingil.
azure lajivérd, achîq mavi, geôv.
Baby bébék, chojouq, chagha.
bachelor érgén, a. azab, békiûr.
back arqa, sirt. a. véra.
backgammon tavlou.
bacon doñouz pasdirmasi.
bad a. féna, p. béd, t. keôtû.
bag a. késé, chouval; khourj, héybé.
baggage piri pirti. pîrti. a. éshya.
bail a. kéfil. bait yém.
bake pishirmék, a. tabkh ét."
baker ékmékji, fourounjou.
balance a. térazi, p. mizan.
balcony f. balcon, p. shahnishin.
bald daz bashli, daz, p. kél.
ball top, gûllé; qourshoun; f. balo.
balloon f. balon.
ballot a. qour'a.
band bagh, p. bénd; taqim;
bandage sarghi.   [f. banda.
bank sou kénari, qiyi; a. sédd;
f. banka.
banker a. sarraf, f. bankér.
bankrupt a. mûflis, meôhlûz.
banner bayraq, a. além.
banquet a. ziyafét.
baptism f. vaftiz, a. ta'mid.
bar choubouq. siriq.
barbarian a. vah'shi, yabani.
barber bérbér.
bare chiblaq, a. ûryan, t. achîq.
barefooted yalin ayaq. p. bérhéné
bargain pazarliq.   [pay.
barge mavouna; mayét vaporou.
bark aghaj qaboughou; (of dog)
ûrûmék, havlamaq.
barley arpa. a. shayir.
barn a. p. anbar, ambar.

barometer a. *mizan úl hava*,
f. *barométro.*
barracks *qishla.*
barrel *fichi*, f. *varél, varil.*
barrow *él arabasi.*
barter *trampa, déyish toqoush.*
base *alchaq*, a. *édna, déni*, p. *khor;*
(foundation) *daban*, a. *ésas;*
f. *baso (sés).*
bashful *outanjaq*, a. *mahjoub.*
basin p. *léyén;* a. *kiâsé, chanaq.*
basket *sépéd*, a. *zénbil.*
bastinado *dayaq*, a. *falaqa.*
bastion a. *ta'biyé, tabya.*
bat *chomaq; yarasé, géjé qoushou.*
bath a. *ham'mam, sijaq.*
battalion *tabour.*   [*ghavgha.*
battle a. *mouharébé*, p. *jéng,*
bay (gulf) *kéôrféz*, (colour) *dorou.*
bayonet *súngú*, p. *nizé.*
beacon a. *minaré*, p. *nishan.*
beam *kirish;* (of sun) p. *pértév.*
bean a. *baqla;* f. *fasoulya.*
bear *ayi;* (to) *dayanmaq, géôtúr-
mék*, a. *tehammúl ét."*
beard *saqal*, p. *rish.*
bearer a. *hamil.*
beast a. *hayvan;* p. *janvér.*
beat *déôymék; bozmaq.*
beautiful *gúzél*, p. *dilbér.*
beaver *qoundouz.*
bed *yataq, déôshég.*
bee *ari*, a. *zénbour.*
beef *sighir éti.*
beet root *panjar, chúkúndúr.*
beggar *dilénji*, a. *sayil.*
begin *bashlamaq*, a. *iptidar ét."*
behead *bashíni késmék*, a. *qatl.*
behold! *ishté, nah!, na!*
believe (to) *inanmaq, iman ét."*
bell (small) *chíngîrdaq;* (large)
chañ, qampana; (of a time-
bellows *kéôrúk.*   [piece) *zil.*
belly *qarin*, a. *batn, batin.*
beloved a. *mahboub, mashouq;*
(fem.) a. *mashouqa, mahboubé.*
belt *kémér, qayish.*
bend *éymék, éyilmék.*
benediction *bérékét dou'asi.*
benefactor *éfféndi*, a. *véli niymét.*
bereave (to) a. *mahroum ét."*
berry p. *dané*, a. *habbé.*

beseech *yalvarmaq;* a. *istid'a, réja
ét."*
besides, *-dan ma'da, -dan bashqa.*
besiege a. *mouhaséré ét."*
better *éyi, daha éyi*, p. *bih'tér.*
bible a. *kitabi mouqaddés.*
big *béôyúk, iri, qojaman.*
bile *safra, éôd;* a. *ghazab.*
bill a. *hisab*, f. *pousoula;* a. *sénéd.*
billet f. *pousoula, bilét.*
bind *baghlamaq*, p. *bénd ét."*
bird *qoush*, p. *múrgh.*
biscuit f. *béksimét, galéta, gévrék.*
bishop f. *épiscopos, mérkhasa.*
bit a. *júz*, p. *parcha;* a. *loqma.*
bite (to) *isîrmaq, dishlémék.*
bitter *aji.* —ness *ajiliq.*
black *qara*, p. *siyah*, a. *ésvéd.*
blacksmith *démirji*, p. *ahéngér.*
bladder a. *mésané.*
bleed (to) *qanamaq; qan almaq.*
bless (to) *múbaréklémék*, a.t. *bérékét oqoumaq.*
blessing a. *khayr dou'a, bérékét.*
blind p. *kéôr*, a. *a'ma.*
blood *qan*, p. *dém.* —money
a. *diyét.* —thirsty p. *khounriz.*
blossom *chichék*, p. *ghonché.*
blow (to) (wind) *ésmék;* (mouth)
úflémék.
blow a. *darbé, vouroush.*
blue (light) *mavi, géôv;* (deep)
lajivérd.
blunt *kéôr, késméz.*
board *tahta;* a. *méjlisi idaré.*
boat *qayîq*, f. *filiqa, sandal.*
body *géôvdé*, a. *vújúd, bédén*, p. *tén.*
boil (to) *qaynamaq, qaynatmaq;
pishirmék, hashlamaq.*
boiled *souda pishmish, hashlan-
mîsh; qaynar (sou).*
bold a. *jésour*, p. *dilavér.*
bolster *yasdîq, yúz yasdighî.*
bolt *súrmé, súrgú.*
bombshell f. *qoumbara.*
bone *kémik.* book a. *kitab.*
boot *chizmé.* border p. *kénar.*
bore (of a gun) *chap;* (to) *délmék.*
borrow (to) *éôdúnj almaq*, a. *isti-
qraz ét."*
bosom *géôkús*, p. *siné; qoyoun.*
bottle *shishé;* bottom *dib.*

bountiful *bol,* a. t. *bérékétli.*
bow (to) *bash éymék,* a. *inqiyad ét."*
bow *yay;* a. *téménna, sélam.*
bowels *baghirsaq.*
bowl a. *tas, kïasé; lûlé;* f. *qavata.*
bowstring *kirish,* p. *zih.*
box (chest) *sandiq;* (desk) *chék-méjé,* (small) *qoutou;* (on the ear) *sillé, toqat:* (tree) *shimshir.*
boy *oghlan, chojouq.*
brace (pair) *chift;* (braces) *asghi.*
brain *béyin, béyn.*
bran *képék.* branch *dal.*
brandy *raqi.* brass *pirinj.*
brave *yigit,* a. *jésour,* f. *péhlivan.*
bread *ékmék,* f. *pidé.*
breakfast *qahvaltî.* [*maq.*
break *qîrmaq,* a. *késr ét.";* *qirîl-*
breast *géôküs: mémé.*
breath *néfés, solouq;* a. *ténéffüs ét."*
bribe a. *rishvét;* (to) *rishvét vér-*
brick *toughla, kirémid.* [*mék.*
bride *gélin,* a. *arous.*
bridegroom *gûréyi. damad.*
bridge *keoprû.* bridle *bashliq.*
brigade *liva.* brigadier *miri liva.*
bright *parlaq,* p. *roushén.*
brilliant *pîrlantî; parlaq.*
brimstone p. *kûkûrt.*
bring (to) *gétirmék.*
broad *énli; génish.*
brook *chay, šou.* broth *ét souyou.*
brother *qardash,* p. *biradér.*
bronze *touj.* brush *fîrcha.*
buck *géyik.* bucket *qova.*
buffalo a. *jamous. manda.*
bug *tahta biti; béôjék.*
build (to) a. *bina ét.", yapmaq.*
building a. *bina;* a. *tamir.*
bull *bougha.* bullock *tosoun.*
bullet *qourshoun.*
bunch *salqim; démét,* p. *désté.*
burden *yûk,* p. *bar,* a. *hamoulé.*
burial a. *jénazé alayi. défn.*
buried *défn olounmoush,* a. *méd-foun.*
burn (to) *yaqmaq,* a. *ihraq ét.";* t. *yanmaq.*
burning-glass p. *pértévsouz, khour-débeen.*
burst (to) *patlamaq; patlatmaq.*
bury a. *défn ét." géômmék.*

bush *chali. chaliliq.* [*sab.*
busy a. *méshghoul.* butcher a. *qas-*
butter *téré yaghi, kéré yaghi,* p. *kéré;* (clarified) *saghi yaghi* vulg. *say yaghi.*
button *dûymé,* f. *qobja.*
buy (to) *satîn almaq,* a. *ishtira ét."*
buyer a. *mûshtéri,* a. *bayi.*
buzz *vizlamaq. viz-vîz étmék.*
Cabbage *lahana, kélém.*
cabin (in ship) f. *qamara.*
cage *cafés.* cake *qourabiyé.*
calamity a. *afét, mousibét; béla,*
calculate a. *hisab ét."* [*qaza.*
calendar a. *taqvim,* p. *salnamé.*
calf *dana.* calico *chit. basma.*
call *chaghîrmaq;* a. *tésmiyé ét."*
calm a. *asoudé;* (weather) a. *mûla-*
calumny *iftira, bûhtan.* [*yim.*
camel *dévé,* a. *jémél,* p. *ûshtûr.*
camp *ordou.* candle *moum.*
cane *qamish; déynék.*
cannon *top.* canvass *yélkén bézi.*
cap *fés,* p. *kûlah,* f. *kép.*
capital p. *paytakht;* (money) *sér-mayé.*
captain (army) a. *zabit;* (navy) p. *sûvari,* f. *qaptan.*
captive a. *ésir* vulg. *yés'sir.*
caravan p. *kérvan,* a. *qafilé.*
carcass *lésh,* p. *lashé.*
card a. *mouqava;* f. *kart.*
carder (of cotton) a. *hallaj.*
caress *oqshamaq, taltif ét."*
cargo *yûk,* a. *hamoulé.*
carnal a. *jismani, néfsani.*
carpenter (house) *dûrgér;* (joiner) *doghramaji;* (ship's) *maranqoz.*
carpet *hali, khali, kilim;* a. *séjjadé* (prayer-carpet).
carriage *araba.*
carrier *éshékji, qatîrji;* a. *hammal.*
carrot *havouj,* a. *késhour.*
carry *tashîmaq, géôtûrmék.*
cart *araba, qañli, qañni.*
cascade *chaghlayan,* a. *shélalé.*
case *sandiq.* cash a. *naqd.*
cask *fîchi.* cast (to) *atmaq.*
castle a. *qala'.* cat *kédi.*
catch (to) *toutmaq.* catgut *kirish.*
catholicos *qatoghigos.*
cattle a. *hayvanat. davar, sîghîr.*

cauliflower *qarnabit.* [*yiri.*
causal (verb) a. *mûtéaddiyi* tas-
cause a. *sébéb, moujib, bayis, badi.*
cavalry *atlî,* p. *sûvari.*
cavern *maghara, in,* a. *ghar.*
ceiling *tavan;* celery *kéréviz.*
cell a. *hûjré.* centre a. *mérkéz, orta.*
cement *toutqal, zamq; alchi.*
certain a. *mouhaqqaq,* a. t. *shûbhé-*
chaff *saman.* chain *zénjir.* [*siz.*
chair *sandalya.* chalk *tébéshir.*
challenge *méydan oqoumaq.*
chamber *oda;* (of mine) a. *khaziné.*
change *déyishmék; déyishdirmék.*
channel *sou yolou,* a. *méjra.*
chapel a. p. *ibadétkhané,* a. *mabéd.*
character a. *siyrét* (moral); (written) *yazi,* a. *khatt;* (quality)
a. *kéyfiyét.*
charcoal *kéômûr.* [*gûzar.*
chargé d'affaires a. p. *maslahat-*
charity a. *khayrat, sadaqa.*
charming a. *latif,* p. *dilbér,*
t. *gûzél.*
cheap *oujouz.* cheek *yanaq.*
cheat *aldatmaq, dolandirmaq.*
cheerful p. *shén, shénshoukh, kéyfli.*
cheese *péynir.* chess p. *satranj.*
chemise *qadîn géomléyi,* a. *qamis.*
cherry *kiraz;* (morella) *vishné.*
chestnut *késtané.* chew *chiynémék.*
chicken *pilij.* child *chojouq.*
chief *bash, sérgérdé, shéykh.*
chimney *ojaq, baja; lamba jami.*
chin *chéné.* chip *yonya.*
chisel *qalém.* cholera *qoléra.*
choice a. *ikhtiyar, yédi ikhtiyar.*
chop (cut) *késmék;* (mince) *qiymaq.*
Christ *Hazréti Isa, Kristos.*
Christian *khristiyan; isavee, mé-*
sihi; mûmin, dindar.
church f. *kilisé.*
cigar *sigara;* (-case) *tabaqa.*
cinnamon *tarchin.* circle a. *dayiré.*
circular *youvarlaq,* a. *mûdévvér.*
circulate *déônmék,* a. *déveran ét."*
circumcise (to) *sûnnét, khatn et."*
circumstance a. *hal, kéyfiyét.*
city p. *shéhir, shéhr.*
civil a. *nazik, zarif, térbiyéli.*
civilisation a. *médéniyét, téméd-*
dûn.

class a. *sinîf.* clean a. t. *témiz.*
clear *témiz;* a. *bérraq;* t. *achîq.*
clergyman a. *rouhani, rouhban*
girouhou. (Moslem) *ouléma.*
clerk a. *kiâtib,* t. *yaziji,* p. *mirza.*
climate p. *ab ou hava,* a. *iqlim.*
cloak *qapoud, aba;* clock a. *sa'at.*
close *qapali; yaqin.*
cloth *béz; chouha.* cloud *boulout.*
clover *yonja.* coal *kéômûr.*
coarse *qaba, qalin, bayaghi.*
coast *qiyi, yali,* p. *kénar,* a. *sahil.*
coat f. *sétri, sûrtouqo.*
cobbler *éskiji, paboujjou.*
cobweb *éôrûmjék aghi.*
cock *khoroz; mouslouq.*
coffee f. *qahvé.* coffin a. *tabout.*
coin a. *sikké;* (pl.) *méskûkât.*
cold *sovouq;* a. *névazil.*
colic *sanji;* collar *yaqa.*
collect (to) *toplamaq, jém étmék.*
collection a. *méjmou'a.*
college a. *médrésé, méktébi ali.*
colonel a. t. *miralay.*
colour p. *réng.* colt *tay, sipa.*
comb *taraq,* p. *shané.* [p. *jéng.*
combat a. *mouharébé, ghargha.*
come *gélmék,* a. *vasîl olmaq.*
comet *qouyrouqlou-yildiz.*
commend a. *émr, émir;* f. *qomanda.*
commence *bashlamaq,* a. *ibtidar*
commentary a. *téfsir, shérh'.* [*ét."*
commerce a. *tijarét, akhzou ita.*
common *'oumoumi, amm;* (-people)
avamm, avam'mi nas, éhali.
communion a. *ûnsiyét;* (Holy-)
Ashayi-rabbani.
community a. *jéma'at; millét.*
companion *arqadash,* a. *shérik.*
company a. *rûféqa, arqadashlar.*
compare a. *mouqabélé, tatbiq ét."*
compass f. *pousoula;* (pl.) *pérgél.*
compatriot p. *hémshéhri.*
complain a. *shikiâyét, ishtikiâ ét."*
complete a. *tékmil, tamm, kiâmil.*
compose a. *tértib, tasnif ét."*
composition a. *meqalé.*
comrade *arqadash,* a. *réfiq.*
condition a. *hal; shart, shourout,*
shérayit.
conduct a. *harékét; tavrou haré-*
confidence a. *itimad, émniyét.* [*két.*

congratulate a. *tébrik ét."*
conquer (to) *zabt, fét-h ét."*
consent a. *razi olmaq, qaboul ét."*
consider *dûshûnmék,* a. *mûtala'a*
consist (to) a. *ibarét olmaq.* [*ét."*
console (to) a. *tésélli ét."*
consul f. *qonsolos,* p. *shéhbéndér.*
consulate f. p. *consoloskhané,*
  p. *shéhbéndérkhané.*
contain *almaq,* a. *mûhtévi ol."*
content a. *razi,* p. *hoshnoud.*
contraband *qachaq, yasaq.*
contrary a. *khilaf, zidd.*
controversy a. *mûbahasé, bahs.*
convenient a. *mûnasib.*
convent f. *manastîr.*
convert a. *mûhtédi.*
cook *ashji;* (to) *pishirmék.*
cool *sérin.* cooper *fichiji.*
copper *baqîr; qazan.*
copy a. *sourét, ayn.*
coral *mérjan.* cord *ip.*
cork *mantar.* corn a. *zakhiré.*
corner p. *kéôshé,* t. *boujaq.*
corporal *onbashi.* [*ét."*
correct *doghroultmaq,* a. *tas-hih*
correspondence *méktoublashma,*
  a. *moukhabéré.*
correspondent a. *moukhabir.*
corrupt *bozouq, chûrûk.*
corsair *qoursan. — gémisi.*
cottage f. a. *qoulibé, tounjik.*
cotton *pamouq.*
cough *éôksûrûk; éôksûrmék.*
council a. *méjlis, shoura.*
counsel a. *nasihat; — vérmék.*
count *saymaq, ta'dad étmék.*
counter p. *péshtahta.*
counterfeit p. *sakhté,* a. *qalb.*
country a. *mémlékét,* p. *éôlké; kéôy.*
couple *chift.*
courage *yigitlik,* a. *jésarét.*
courier *tatar.* p. *chapar.*
courtyard *havli, havlou.*
cover *éôrtû; éôrtmék.*
coverlet *yorghan.*
cow *inék.* coward *qorqaq.*
cream *qaymaq, sûd yûzû.*
creation *khîlqatî 'ålém.*
credit a. *itibar; alajaq.*
creditor *alajaqli,* a. *dayîn.*
crescent *yarîm ay,* a. *hilal.*

crime a. *jinayét.* crier a. *déllal.*
criminal a. *jani.* cripple *cholaq.*
crooked *éyri. qambour.*
cross p. *hach, khach,* a. *salib.*
crowd *qalabaliq.*
crown a. *taj;* (of head) *dépé.*
cruel a. *zalim, mérhamétsiz.*
crumb *ékmék ichi, ékmék oufan-*
  tisî.
crust *qabouq.*
cry (to) *baghirmaq, aghlamaq.*
crystal a. *billor, billour.*
cucumber *khiyar.* cudgel *sopa.*
cup *finjan; —* board *dolab.*
cure *shifa vérmék, éyilétmék.*
curiosity a. *méraq;* a. *tohafiyé.*
currants *fréng ûzûmû.*
curse a. *lanét,* vulg. *nallét.*
curtain p. *pérdé.* cushion *yasdiq.*
custom a. *adét;* (tax) *résmi géôm-*
  rûk, résm (pl. *rousoum*).
customer *mûshteri.*
customhouse *géômrûk dayirési.*
cut *késmék,* a. *qat étmék.*
cypress p. *sérv, sélvi.*
Dagger a. *khanchér, qama.*
daily *gûnlûk,* a. *yévmi.*
damage *saqatliq,* a. *zarar, ziyan.*
damp p. *ném, némnak.*
dance a. *raqs ét.",* t. *hora tépmék.*
danger a. *téhliké, moukhatara.*
dark *qaranliq,* a. *zoulmét.*
darling a. *mahboubé, mahboub.*
date a. *tarikh;* (fruit) *khourma.*
dated a. *tarikhli, mûvérrakh'.*
daughter *qîz,* p. *dûkhtér,* a. *bint.*
dawn *chinsabah,* a. *shafaq, féjr.*
day a. *yévm,* t. *gûn,* p. *rouz.*
deacon a. *shémmas,* f. *saryavak,*
  diaconos.
dead *éôlû,* p. *mûrdé, jansiz.*
deaf *saghir, ishitméz.*
dear *bahali.* p. *giranbaha;* a. *aziz*
  (loved). My-. *azizim.*
death *éôlûm,* a. *mévt, mémat.*
debt *borj.* a. *déyn* (pl. *dûyoun, -at*).
debtor *borjlou,* a. *médyoun.*
deceitful *aldadiji,* p. *hiylékiar.*
deceive (to) *aldatmaq.*
decide (to) *qarar vérmék, qarar-*
  lashdirmaq.
deck f. *géôvérté.* (It. *cuverta.*)

declare a. *i'lan ét.*, *néshr ét.*
decline a. *zéval.*
decree p. *férman;* a. *fétva.*
dedicate (to) *taqdis.* a. *takhsis ét.*
deep *dérin; qoyou* (colour).
deer *géyik, qaraja.* [*mék.*
defeat (to) *yénmék,* a. *ghalib gél-*
defence a. *mouhafaza, múdafa'a.*
defendant a. *múd'dayi aléyhi.*
deficient *éksik,* a. *noqsan.*
deformed *bichimsiz, bodour.*
degree a. *déréjé.*
deign a. *kérém, loutf ét.*
delay (to) a. *tévaqqouf, téékhir ét.*
delicate a. *nazik,* t. *injé.*
delicious a. *léziz, lézzétli.*
delight *sévinj,* a. *súrour.*
deliver (to) *qourtarmaq,* a. *khélas*
deluge a. *toufan.* [*ét.*
demand a. *istid'a, dava.*
demolish *yénmék, bozmaq.*
den *in,* a. *maghara.*
deny a. *inkiar ét.*
depart (to) *ayrilmaq,* p. *révan ol.*
depend a. *tabi ol.*, *baqmaq.*
deprive a. *mahroum étmék.*
depth *derinlik,* a. *oumq.*
deputy a. *vékil, nayib.*
derision a. *istihza, zévqlénmé.*
derogatory *yaqishmaz.*
descend *énmék,* a. *nazil ol.*
describe a. *tarif étmék.*
desert *chéôl, béyaban;* (to) *qach-*
   maq, a. *firar ét.*, *térk ét.*
design a. *niyét, méram.*
despair *úmidsizlik,* a. *yés, fútúr.*
destiny a. *qadér, qismét.*
detach *ayîrmaq.*
devil a. *shéytan, iblis.*
devote (to) *takhsis ét.*
dew *chih',* p. *shébném.*
diamond *élmas.*
diarrhæa a. *is-hal.*
diary a. t. *múkhtiré déftéri.*
dice *tavlou zari, zar.*
dictionary *loughét kitabî.*
die (to) *éôlmék, véfat ét.*
difference a. *farq, ikhtilaf.*
different *farqli, bashqa.*
difficult *gúj,* a. *múshkil.*
dig (to) *qazmaq,* a. *hafr ét.*
digest (to) a. *hazm ét.*, *siñdirmék.*

dignity p. *shan,* a. *mansîb, izzét.*
dike *sédd, séd, khéndék.*
diligent *chalishqan,* a. *ghayour.*
dine (to) *yémék yémék,* a. *ta'am ét.*
dinner *yémék,* a. *ta-am.*
dirt *kir, mourdarlîq.*
disabled a. *saqat.* [*khosh.*
disagreeable p. *namaqboul, na-*
disappear (to) *géôrúnméz ol.*
disappoint (to) *aldatmaq.*
discharge (to) *boshaltmaq.*
discipline a. *téédib, inzibat.*
disease *hastaliq,* p. *dérd,* a. *illét.*
disgrace a. *rézalét.*
disgust (to) a. *néfrét étmék.*
dish *tabaq; qab; yémék.*
dishonest a. *múrtékib,* t. *khîrsiz.*
disorder *qarîshiqlîq.*
disperse (to) *daghitmaq.*
distance *ouzaqliq,* a. *mésafé.*
distant *ouzaq, iraq.*
distinguish a. *téfriq ét.*
ditch p. *héndék, khandék.*
divide (to) *béôlmék, taqsim ét.*
divine a. *ilahi, réb'bani.*
do (to) *étmék,* a. *ijra ét.* (p. 128).
doctor a. *hékim, tabib.*
dogma a. *aqidé.* p. *aqayid.*
doll *bébék, qouqla.*
door *qapou, qapî,* a. *bab.*
dormitory *qovoush,* f. *ninjaran.*
double *iki qat; chifté.*
doubt a. *shúb'hé; shúbhé ét.*
doubtful *shubhéli;* -less *shúb-*
   hésiz.
dough a. *hamour, hamîr.*
downy *túylú, havli.*
dragon *azhdérha; atli.*
drain *laghîm, gériz.*
draughts (game) *dama.*
drawers *ich donou; chékméjé.*
draw (to) *chékmék;* a. *résm ét.*
drawing-room, *músafir odasî.*
dream a. *rouya,* t. *dúsh.*
dress f. *rouba,* t. *ústbash.*
drink *ichmék.*
drop *damla; damlamaq.*
dropsy a. *istisqa,* vulg. *sîsqa.*
drown (to) *boghmaq; boghoulmaq.*
drum *davoul.*
drunk p. *sérhosh, sérkhosh.*
dry *qourou,* a. *yabis.*

duck *êôrdék.* dumb *dilsiz.*
dung *gûbré, fishqi.*
dungeon p. *zindan.*
dust *toz.*
Dutch *filéménk.*
duty *vazifé, khizmét.*
dwarf *jûjé; bodour.*
dye *boya; boyamaq.*
dynasty a. *sûlalé,* p. *khanédan.*
dysentery *qanli is-hal.*
Each *hér bir,* p. *béhér.*
ear *qoulaq,* a. *ûzn.*
earn *qazanmaq,* a. *késb ét."*
earth *topraq;* a. *dûnya.*
earthquake a. *zélzélé,* vulg. *zérzélé.*
ease a. *rahat; qolayliq.*
east *gûndoghou,* a. *sharq.*
Easter f. *pasqalya.*
easy a. *rahat; qolay, souhoulétli.*
eat *yémék,* a. *ékl ét."*
echo *yanqo,* a. *aksi séda.*
eclipse (*gûnésh, ay*) *toutoulma.*
economic a. t. *idaréli.*
edge p. *kénar, ouj; aghîz.*
education a. *talim ou térbiyé.*
effect a. *nétijé, séméré, téésir.*
effort a. *say, ghayrét, jéhd.*
egg *youmourta,* a. *béyza.*
either *ikisindén biri.*
elbow *dirsék.*
electricity f. a. *éléktriq, -iyét.*
element a. *ûnsûr,* pl. *anasîr.*
elephant *fil.*
embark *gémiyé binmék, -bindir-
mék.* a. *tahmil étmék.*
embassy a. *séfarét, — khané.*
embrace *sarîlmaq,* p. *dér aghoush
ét." qoujaqlamaq.*
emerald a. *zûmûrrûd, zûmrût.*
eminent a. *mésh-hour, shêôhrétli.*
emperor f. *impérator.*
empire a. *dévlét, saltanat.*
employ (to) *qoullanmaq.*
empty *bosh,* a. *khali.*
enamel *miné;* -ed *minéli.*
enclose *chévirmék;* a. *dakhil, léff
et."*
end *soñ, ouj;* (to) *bitmék.*
endure *dayanmaq;* a. *téhammûl*
enemy a. *dûshmén,* p. *khasim.* [*ét."*
energy a. *qouvvét, ghayrét.*
engaged a. *méshghoul.*

engagement a. *méshghouliyét.*
engine f. *makina;* (fire) *touloumba.*
engineer a. *mûhéndis;* f. *makinist.*
English *ingiliz; ingilizjé.*
engrave *qazmaq.* a. *hékk ét."*
engraver a. *hak'kûk,* p. *kalémkûar.*
enigma a. *mou-amma,* t. *bilméjé.*
enlarge a. *tévsee ét.", génishlétmék.*
enmity a. *adarét,* p. t. *dûshménlik.*
enough *elvérir,* a. *kûafi.*
ensign (flag) *sanjaq; bayraqdar.*
enter *girmék,* a. *dakhil ol."*
entire *hép, bûtûn,* a. *jûmlé.*
envelope a. *zarf.*
envy a. *haséd,* t. *qisqanjliq.*
equal p. *bérabér,* a. *mûsavi; aqran.*
equator a. *khatti istiva.*
equip *donatmaq.*
error *yanlish,* a. *khata,* a. *séhv.*
escape *qachmaq, qourtoulmaq.*
especially a. *khousousa.*
eunuch *khadim; harém aghasî.*
Europe *Avropa.*
European *Avropali.*
evacuate a. *takhliyé ét."*
evangelist a. *mûbésh'shir.*
even *bilé,* a. *hatta.*
even (adj.) *chift; dûz: doghrou.*
evening *akhsham, aqsham.*
evil *féna, kéôtû; fénaliq.*
ewer *ibriq;* (— bason) — *léyén.*
exact a. *tamm, témam, doghrou.*
examine a. *téftish, imtihan ét."*
examination a. *imtihan.*
excellent a. *ala, aliyûl ala.*
except — *dan ma'da, bashqa.*
exchange *trampa,*
excuse (to) a. *mazour toutmaq,
roukhsat vérmék.*
execute (to) a. *ijra ét."; qatl ét."*
expect a. *mémoul ét.", béklémék.*
explain a. *iyzah ét."; añlatmaq.*
extensive a. *vasi, génish.*
exterminate *bitirmék,* a. *mahv ét."*
extol a. *médh ét.",* t. *êôymék.*
extraordinary a. *févq-él-adé.*
extravagant a. *mûsrif.*
extremely a. *ghayét,* t. *pék.*
eye *gêôz.* eyebrow *qash.*
eyelash *kiprik,* p. *mûzhgûan.*
Fable a. *hikûayé, masal.*
face p. *chéhré,* t. *yûz,* a. *souret.*

facilitate a. *tés-hil ét.,qolaylatmaq.*
fact a. *haqiqat;* (in-) a. *fil haqîqa.*
factory f. *fabriqa, kîarkhané.*
faint (to) *bayîlmaq.*
fair f. *panayir;* t. *gûzél.*
fairy p. *péri,* a. *jinn.*
faithful a. *sadiq, émin.*
falcon *doghan,* a. *shahin.*
fall (to) *dûshmék,* a. *souqout ét.''*
false *yalan;* -*ji,* a. *kîazib.*
fame a. *shéôhrét,* p. *shan.*
family f. *familya,* p. *khanédan.*
famine *qitliq,* a. *qaht.*
fan *yélpazé.*
far *ouzaq,* p. *dour.* a. *bayid.*
farewell a. *véda; él véda!*
farm *chiftlik.*
farmer *chiftji,* p. *rénjbér.*
ferrier a. p. *nalband.*
fast *chapouq,* p. *téz;* a *orouj.*
fat *sémiz, yaghli; yagh.*
fate a. *qadér, qaza, qîsmét.*
fathom *qoulaj.*
fatigue *yorghounlouq.*
fault *qousour,* a. *qabahat.*
fear *qorqou,* a. *khavf.* p. *déhshét.*
feast a. *ziyafét,* p. *bézm.*
February *shoubat, pédirvar.*
feeble a. *zayif,* t. *zaboun.*
feed (to) *béslémék, yédirmék.*
feel (to) a. *hiss ét.'', douymaq.*
felt *kéché, kébé.*
female *dishi,* p. *madé.*
fever a. *hûmma; hararét.*
few *az,* a. *qalil.*
fidelity *sadaqat, véfa.*
field a. *sahra;* t. *tarla.*
fierce *azghîn, sért.*
fife *dûdûk, qaval.*
fig *injir, aydin yémishi.*
fight *ghavgha (qavqa);* p. *jéng.*
figurative a. *méjazi.*
figure a.*raqam, adéd; shékl, résim.*
filbert *findiq.*
file *yéyé; sira,* a. *saff.*
fill (to) *doldourmaq; dolmaq.*
filth *mourdarliq, pislik.*
filthy *mourdar, pis,* p. *napak.*
final *soñ.* -ly a. *én nihayé.*
find *boulmaq.*
fine *injé, nazik;* a. *khalis, khass..*
finger *parmaq,* p. *éngûsht.*

finish (to) *bitirmék,* a. *khitam vér.''*
fire p. *atésh.* fish *baliq.*
flag *bayraq.* flame *aléf.*
flat *dûz, yassi.*
flea *piré.* fleet *donanma.*
flesh *ét.* flood a. *sél,* a. *toufan.*
flint *chaqmaq tashî.*
floor *déôshémé.* flour *oun.*
flower *chichék,* p. *shûkûfé.*
fluxion (cold) a. *nevazil, zûkkîam.*
fly *sinék;* (to) *ouchmaq.* [*lumaq.*
foal *tay, qouloun;* (to) *qouloun-*
fodder *ot, arpa-saman, alaf.*
foe p. *dûshmén,* a. *khasim.*
fog *douman,* p. *mih, migh.*
fond *méraqli,* a. *haris.*
food *yémék, yéyéjék.*
foot *ayaq,* p. *pa,* a. *qadém.*
forage *ot, arpa-saman.*
force p. *zor,* a. *jébr; qouvvét.*
ford *géchid, sigh.*
forehead *alin, ann.*
foreigner a. *éjnébi.*
forerunner p. *péshrév,* t. *qilavouz.*
foresight a. *basirét, firasét.*
forest *orman;* a. *méshjéré.* [*ét.''*
forget *ounoutmaq,* p. *firamoush*
forgive a.*afvét.'',* t. *baghîshlamaq.*
fork *chatal.*
form *bichim,* a. *sourét;* (to) *yap-*
fortifications a.*istihkîamat.* [*maq.*
fortnight *iki hafta.*
fortress a. *qala, qalé.*
forward *iléri; iléridé.*
foundation f. *témél,* a. *ésas.*
fountain *pouñar;* (jet) *fisqiyyé.*
foul *tavouq.* fox *tilki.*
fraud a.*hiylé.* free p.*azad,sérbést.*
freedom *azadliq,* a. *hûrriyét.*
freemason *farmason.*
freeze (to) *doñmaq; doñdourmaq.*
freight a. *naqliyé,* p. *navloun.*
frequent *siq, choq,* a. *késir.*
fresh p. *tazé.* friend p. *dost.*
Friday a. *jouma'a, jouma'.*
frigate f. *firqateen.*
fringe *sachaq.* froth *kéôpûk.*
frog *qourbagha.*
frontier p. *serhadd,* a. *houdoud.*
frozen *doñmoush.*
fruit p. *méyvé,* t. *yémish.*
fry (to) *tavada pishirmék.*

frying-pan *tava.*
fugitive *qachaq,* a. *firari.*
full *dolou,* a. *mémlou.*
funeral a. *jénazé alayî, jénazé.*
fur *kürk.*
furious *azghîn.* furnace *ojaq.*
furlough a. *izin, mézouniyét.*
furniture a. *éshya,* f. *mobilia.*
fury a. *hiddét, ghazab.*
fuse *tapa;* (to) *éritmék.*
future *géléjék,* a. *mûstagbél.*
Gain p. *kīar,* t. *qazanj; qazanmaq.*
gallant a. *zarif, nazik, kibar.*
gallows *dar aghají.*
game *oyoun;* (prey) *av,* p. *shikīar.*
garden p. *bahjé, baghché.*
garlic *sarmisaq.*
garnet a. *lal.* gate *qapou.*
gather (to) *toplamaq.*
general a. *oumoumi;* f. *général.*
generous *jéômérd,* a. *ali jénab.*
genius a. *firasét, zékīavét.*
gentiles a. *tayifé.* p. *poutpérést.*
gentle a. *mûlayim, halim,* t. *tatli.*
genus a. *jins,* pl. *éjnas.*
geography *joghrafiya.*
geometry *ilmi héndésé.*
get *almaq;* b. *hasil ét.''*
ghost a. *khayal; rouh,* p. *jan.*
 (the Holy ghost) *Rouhoul qouds.*
gift (divine) a. *mévhibé, dadî haqq;*
 (superior to inferior) p. *bakh-*
 shish, a. *ihsan, atiyé;* (inf. to
 sup.) a. *hédiyé,* p. *péshkésh;*
 (brought back from a journey)
 armaghan.
gipsy *chingīané, posha.*
girl *qîz.* girth *qolan.*
give (to) *vérmék,* a. *ita ét.''*
glad a. *mémnoun,* p. *shadman.*
glass p. *jam;* a. *qadéh.*
globe a. *kûré.*
gloom *qaranliq;* a. *gham, kédér.*
glory *shan ou shéréf,* p. *jélal.*
glove *éldivan.* glue *toutqal.*
go *gitmék.* good *eôyéndéré.*
goat *kéchi.* gold *altoun.*
God a. *Allah, Allah Ta'ala, Jenabi-*
Godhead a. *oulouhiyét.* [*Haqq.*
good *éyi,* a. *ala.* goose *qaz.*
gospel a. *injil,* pl. *énajil, bésharét.*
gourd *qabaq, qantar qabaghí.*

gout a. *niqris.*
grace a. *létafét; inayét, loutf.*
grape *ûzûm.* grass *ot.*
grateful a. *mûtéshékkir.*
gratis a. *méjjanén; mouft.*
grave a. *mézar, qabr.*
grease *yagh, ich yaghi.*
great *béôyûk,* a. *azim, jésim.*
greedy a. *oubour, shish boghaz.*
green *yéshil.*
greyhound *tazi.*
gridiron *ísqara.*
grief a. *kédér, élém, gham.*
grocer a. *baqqal.*
groom *séyis.* ground *yér; 'arsa.*
growl *khirlamaq.*
guard *neôbétji;* a. *khassa askéri;*
 (to) *béklémék.*
guardhouse *qoullouq.*
guess (to) a. *zann, qîyas ét.''*
guest a. *mûsafir.*
guilt a. *qousour, qabahat.*
gulf *keôrféz.* gum *zamq.*
gums *dish éti.*
gunpowder *barout.*
gutter *héndék, olouq.*
gymnastic f. *jimnastiq.*
Habit a. *adét,* p. *khouy;* a. *résm;*
hail *dolou, ghîrji.* [*tabiyat.*
hair *sach; qil, tûy.*
half *yarim. nim,* a. *nisif* (§ 207).
halt *dourmaq, éylénmék.*
hammer *chékij;* (sledge) *varya.*
hamper *sépéd.*
hand *él;* (hour-) a. *aqréb;* (minute-)
 yélqovan.
handkerchief *méndil.*
handle *sap,* a. *qabzé.*
handsome *gûzél, yaqîshiqli.*
hang *asmaq;* (-down) *sarqmaq.*
happy a. t. *sa'adétli.*
harbour f. *liman.*
hard *sért, pérk; gûj.*
hare *tavshan.*
harem a. *harém, zénané.*
harm a. *zarar, ziyan.*
harness *araba taqimî, qoshoum.*
harvest *bichin;* (-time) *hasad,*
 hasad vaqti, oraq vaqtî.
hasten a. *ajélé ét.''* hat f. *shapqa.*
hatchet *balta, girébi.*
hate (to) a. *ikrah ét.''*

haughty a. *maghrour, kibir.*
have (to) a. *malik olmaq* (§§ 119 to
hawk *atmaja (qoushou).* [122].
hay *qourou ot.*
hazard p. *bakht,* a. *qaza, qadér.*
haze *sis, douman.*
head *bash;* p. *sér;* a. *rés* (§ 203).
headlong *bash ashaghi, sérnigûn.*
heal (to) *éyilétmék,* a. *shifa vérmék.*
health a. *kéyf, mizaj, sih'hét.*
heap *yighin;* (to) *yighmaq.*
hear (to) *diñlémék, ishitmék.*
heart *yûrék,* a. *qalb,* p. *dil.*
heat *sijaqliq,* a. *hararét.*
heaven *geök,* a. *séma,* (pl.) *sémavat.*
  (paradise) a. *jénnét,* p. *firdévs.*
heavy *aghir,* a. *saqil.*
Hebrew *Ibrani, Yéhoudi.*
hedge-hog *kipri,* p. *khar-púsht.*
heel *eôkjé,* a. *aqab.*
height *yûkséklik,* a. *irtifa'.*
hell a. *jéhénném.*
help *yardim,* a. *imdad, mou'avénét,*
  iyane; (to) *yardim, mou'avénét*
  ét.''
hemorrhoids *mayasil,* a. *basour.*
hen *tavouq.* herb *ot.*
herd *sûrû.* hero a. *qahriman.*
hesitate (to) a. *téréd'dûd étmék.*
hide *déri;* (to) *saqlamaq.*
high *yûksék,* a. *mûrtéfi.*
highway a. *jaddé,* p. *shah'rah.*
hill *dépé.* hip *qalcha.*
hinge *rézé, méntéshé.*
hire *kira;* (to) *kiralamaq.*
history a. *tarikh,* pl. *tévarikh.*
hit (to) *vourmaq.* hoarse *boghouq.*
hold (to) *toutmaq;* (ship's) *ambar.*
hole *délik.* holiday a. *tatil.*
hollow a. *khali, téhi, ichi bosh.*
holy a. *aziz, mouqaddés;* (of God)
  a. *qouddous;* (-Spirit) *Rouhoul*
  Qouds.
home *év,* a. *ayilé; vatan, mémlékét;*
  (to go —) a. *sila étmék, silaya*
  gitmék.
honest a. *émin, sadiq,* t. *doghrou.*
honey *bal,* a. *asal,* p. *mikh.*
honour a. *izzét, itibar, shéréf,*
  namous; (to) *izzétlémék, ihtiram*
hoof *tîrnaq.* hope p. *ûm'mid.* [*ét.''*
hook *chéngél; qanja, ilik.*

horizon a. *oufouq,* (pl.) *afaq.*
horrible a. *makhouf, déhshétli.*
horse *at,* p. *ésb; béygir;* (-man)
  atli, p. *sûvaree.*
hospital p. *khasta-khané.*
hostile p. *dûshmén.* hot *sijaq.*
hound *keôpék, zaghar, tazi.*
hour a. *sa'at.*
house *év,* p. *khané,* a. *béyt; qonaq.*
humanity a. *insaniyét, mûrûv'vét.*
humble a. *mûtévazi, halim; khim-*
hunger *ajliq.* hungry *aj.* [*bil.*
hurry (to) a. *ajélé ét.''*
hurt (to) *injitmék, ajitmaq.*
husband *qoja,* a. *zévj.*
hymn a. *ilahi.*
hypocrisy a. *riya, mûrayilik.*
hypocrite a. *mûrayi, mûnafiq.*
Ice *bouz.* icy *bouzlou.*
idea a. *fikir, tasavvour.*
idiom a. *istilah,* p. *shiyvé.*
idle *ishsiz, témbél, bosh gézén.*
idol p. *pout,* a. *saném,* (pl.) *asnam.*
ignorance a. *jéhalét, jéhl.*
ignorant a. *jahil,* p. *nadan.*
ill *kéyfsiz,* p. *hasta,* a. *mériz.*
illness *hastaliq,* a. *maraz.*
imagine (to) a. *tasav'vour ét.''*
imitate (to) a. *taqleed, iqtida ét.''*
impartial p. a. *bitaraf, insafli.*
impatient a. t. *sabirsiz.*
implore (to) *yalvarmaq;* a. *rija,*
  niyaz ét.''
important a. *mouhimm, mûtébér.*
impression a. *tééssir; éfkiar.*
imprison a. *habs, mahbous ét.''*
inch *parmaq.* incline (to) a. *méyl*
incognito a. *tébdil, — qiyafét.* [*ét.''*
income a. *irad.* increase *artmaq.*
indebted *borjlou,* a. *médyoun.*
indeed a. *haqiqatén; eôylé mi!*
industry a. *hirfét, sana'at.*
inform (to) a. *khabér vérmék, ikh-*
  bar ét.''
ingratitude p. t. *nankeôrlûk.*
inhabit (to) *otourmaq,* a. *sakin ol.''*
injury a. *zarar; saqatliq.*
ink a. *mûrékkéb.* (-stand) *divit.*
inn *khan.* inquire (to) *sormaq.*
insane p. *divané,* t. *chîlghin.*
insect *beôjék.* insert a. *dakhil ét.''*
inspect (to) *yoqlamaq.*

instruct(to) *eôyrétmék,* a. *talim ét.''*
integrity a. *témamiyét;* t. *doghroulouq,* a. *istiqamét.*
intercede a. *rija, shéfa'at ét.''*
intercession a. *shefa'at.*
interest a. *ménfa'at,* f. *éntéréso;* a. *fayiz.*
interesting *mérak jélb édiji, jalib.*
internal a. *dakhili.*
intimate *sîqi,* a. *mahrém.*
intolerable a. *téhammûlû naqabil.*
invitation a. *davét.*
iron *démir.*
irregular a. *nizamsîz;* (soldier) *bashi bozouq.*
irrigate *yiyqamaq.*
island *ada,* a. *jéziré.*
itch (to) *gijishmék.*
ivory *fil dishi.*
ivy *sarmashiq.*
Jackal *chaqal, ghiyab.*
jacket f. *chakét; mintan.* [*var.*
January *kĩanounou sani, Hounjar qavanos, désti, kûp.*
jaw *chéné.*
jealous *kisqanj,* a. *hasoud.*
jealousy a. *haséd,* t. *kisqanj.*
Jehovah *Yéhova.*
Jesus *Isa-él-Mésih, Isa.*
Jew *yéhoudi, chifit.*
jewel a. *jévahir, mújévhér.*
join (to) *bitishmék, bitishdirmék.*
joke a. *shaqa, lateefé.*
journal p. *rouznamé.* f. *journal.*
journey *yol; séyahat, yoljoulouq.*
joy *sévinj,* a. *sourour, shazliq.*
judge a. *hakim, qadî.*
jug *désti,* p. *gûzé.*
juice *sou;* (grape-) p. *shira.*
jump (to) *sîchramaq.*
Jupiter *mûshtéri yildîzi.*
just a. *adil, mounsif.*
justice a. *adalét, haqqaniyét.*
justify a. t. *haqqlî chîqarmaq.*
Keep (to) *saqlamaq,* a. *mouhafaza ét.''*
kettle *gûgûm;* f. *chaydan.*
key f. *anakhtar,* a. *miftah.*
kick (to) *tépmék, chifté atmaq.*
kid *oghlaq.* kidney *beôbrék.*
kill *eôldûrmék,* a. *idam ét.''*
kind a. *jins,* t. *soy, dûrlû; tatli.*

king *qral,* p. *padishah, hûkûmdar.*
kiss p. *bousé, eôpûsh;* (to) *eôpmék.*
kitchen p. *ashkhané,* a. *matbakh.*
kitten *kédi yavrousou, pisik.*
knee *diz,* p. *zanou.*
kneel (to) *diz cheôkmék.*
knife *bîchaq;* (pen-) *qalémtrash.*
knit (to) *eôrmék.*
knock (to) *(qapou) chalmaq.*
knot *dûymé; dûyûm.*
know (to) *bilmék.*
kuran *qouran, kélami qadim.*
Label *yafta.*
labour a. *amél,* t. *ish,* p. *kãr.*
labourer a. *amélé,* t. *ishji.*
lace (gold-) *sîrma;* (false-) *qîlabdan* :(thread-) f. *dantéla ;* (tape-) *shérid.*
lad *oghlan, chojouq, déliqanli.*
ladder *mérdivén,* p. *nérdûban.*
lady *hanim.* lake *geôl.*
lamb *qouzou.* lamp *lamba.*
lance a. *mîzraq,* p. *nizé.*
land *qara;* (to) *qaraya chîqmaq.*
language a. *lisan,* p. *zéban,* t. *dil.*
lantern f. *fénér, fanos.*
lap *qoyoun, qoujaq.*
large *beôyûk, iri.*
last *soñ;* (— night) *duñ géjé,* (to) *dayanmaq, sûrmék.*
late *géj; sabîq; mérhoum.*
lattice *qafés.* laugh *gûlmék.*
laundry *chamashîrkhané.*
laundress *chamashirji qari.*
law a. *qanoun; shériyat, shér'.*
lawyer f. *avoqat,* a. *dava vékili.*
lay (to) *yatmaq; yatirmaq.*
lazy *témbél, ténbél, ayar.*
lead *qourshoun;* (to) *geôtûrmék.*
leaf *yapraq,* a. *varaq.*
lean *zaboun;* (to) *dayanmaq.*
leap (to) *sîchramag, hoplamaq.*
learn (to) *eôyrénmék,* a. *tahsil ét.''*
leather *méshin, sakhtiyan.*
leave (to) *braqmaq; chîqmaq.*
led (horse) *yédék.*
leech *sûlûk;* leek *prasa.*
left *sol.* leg *bajaq.*
legation a. *séfarét,* — *khané.*
legend a. *hikãyé, masal.*
legislator a. *vaziyi qanoun.*

leisure *bosh vaqit,* a. *foursat.*
lemon *limon.* length *boy.*
lend (to) *eôdûnj vérmék, vérmék.*
leopard *qaplan.* lesson a. *dérs.*
letter *yazi,* a. *harf; méktoub.*
lettuce *maroul.* level *dûz.*
lever *manavéla.*
liberal *jeômérd, jivanmérd.*
liberate (to) *qourtarmaq,* a. *khélas. ét."*
liberty a. *hourriyét,* p. t. *azadliq.*
library p. a. *kitabkhané.*
lick (to) *yalamaq.* lid *qapaq.*
lie *yalan,* a. *kizb;* — *seôylémék.* (— down) *yatmaq, ouzanmaq.*
life p. *jan,* a. *rouh;* (-time) a. *eômûr.*
lift (to) *qaldirmaq,* a. *réf ét."*
light a. *nour,* t. *îshîq;* a. *khafif.*
lightning *shimshék,* a. *barq.*
like *bénzér, yibi;* (to) a. *hazz ét."*
lime *kiréj.* limited a. *mahdoud.*
line *chîzgi,* a. *khatt; satir.*
linen *kétén bézi;* lining *astar.*
linseed *kétén tohoumou, zéyérék.*
lip *léb, doudaq.*
listen (to) *diñlémék, qoulaq vér- mek.*
litter (for the sick) *téjgéré.*
little *oufaq, kûchûk,* a. *saghir.*
live (to) *yashamaq.*
lively *janlî; qani sîjaq.*
liver *jiyér, qara jiyér.*
living *géchim,* a. *téay'yûsh.*
load *yûk;* (to) *yûklémék.*
loaf *somoun; kéllé shékér.*
lock f. *kilid;* (to) *kitlémék.*
locksmith *chilingir.*
log *kûtûk.* long *ouzoun, boylou.*
longitude a. *toul.*
look (to) *baqmaq; bakish.*
loom *dézgûâh.* loose *gévshék.*
lose (to) *yitirmék,* a. *ghayb ét."*
lord *éfféndi;* a. *Rabb.*
love a. *ashq, mouhabbét; sévmék.*
lover a. *ashîq.* low *alchaq.*
luck p. *bakht,* a. *tali, taléh.*
luggage a. *éshya, pîri pîrtî.*
lump *parcha.* lunch *qahvaltî.*
lute a. *'oud, 'oud chalghî.*
luxury f. *fantazi.*
lynx *vashaq, eôshék.*
Macaroni f. *maqarna,* p. *érishté.*

mace *topouz, gûrz, chomaq.* [a. *alét.*
machine f. *makina,* p. *charkh;*
mad *déli, divané;* (-dog) *qoudouz.*
madam f. *madama, hanîm, qoqona.*
magazine f. *maghaza,* p. *ambar;* (powder-) p. *jébhané;* (periodical) a. *résaléyi mévqouta.*
magician a. *sihirbaz,* a. *sahhar.*
magic lantern a. *sihiri siraji.*
magistrate a. *zabit, hakim.*
mahomedan a. *mûsliman, mou- hammédee.*
maiden a. *bakiré,* t. *qîz.*
mail f. *posta;* p. *zirkh,* a. *silah.*
maintain (to) *béslémék.*
major *biñ bashî.*
make (to) *yapmaq,* a. *imal ét."*
mallet *toqmaq.* mamma *anné.*
man a. *adam, adém, insan.*
manage (to) a. *idaré, zabt ét."*
mane *yélé.* manger *yémlik.*
mankind a. *béni adém, névi insan.*
mantle f. *qapot,* a. *férajé.*
manufacture (place of-) f. *fabriqa;* (article) a. *mal;* (to) *yapmaq.*
manure *gûbré,* a. *zibil,* t. *térs.*
manuscript *él-yazîsî.*
many *choq.* map f. *kharta.*
marble *mérmér.*
march (musical) f. *marsh;* (soldiers) *yeôrûmék;* (command) f. *arsh!*
mare *qîsraq.*
marine a. *bahri, bahriyé.*
mark a. *isharét,* p. *nishan.*
market p. *pazar; charshî.*
marriage a. *nikûâh, izdivaj.*
marry (to) *évlénmék, évléndirmék.*
martyr a. *shéhid.*
masculine *érkék;* a. *mûzékkér.*
master *éfféndi, agha; ousta.*
mat *hasîr.* maxim a. *qayidé.*
matches a. *kibrit.* [*ziyé.*
mathematics a. *ouloumou riya-*
meadow *chayîr,* p. *chimén, -zar.*
meaning a. *ma'na.*
measure *eôlchû,* a. *mîqyas.*
measles *qîzamouq.* meat *ét."*
medicine a. *ilaj, déva.*
meet (to) a. *tésadûfét." rastgélmék.*
melon (musk) *qavoun;* (water) *qarpouz.*

melt (to) *érimék.*
member *aza* (pl. *azavat*).
memory a. *qouvvéyi hafîza, fikir.*
mend (to) a. *tamir, térmim ét.''*
merchant a. *tajir, tûjjar.*
mercy a. *mérhamét, rahmét.*
merely *dûzjé,* a. *adéta.*
merit a. *istihqaq, liyaqat.*
merry a. t. *kéyfli,* p. *shén.* [*dén.*
message a. *khabér.* metal a. *ma-*
method a. *ousoul, qayidé,* t. *yol.*
microscope p. *khourdébeen.*
middle *orta,* a. *vasat.*
middling *orta,* a. *évsat.*
midsummer *yaz ortasî.*
might *qoudrét, iqtidar.*
mighty a. *qadir, mûqtédir.*
mild a. *mûlayim, hafîf.*
milk *sûd.* mill *déyirmén.*
mind a. *aqîl, fikir, zihin.*
mine a. *ma'dén,* (pl.) *mé-a-din.*
minute a. *daqîqa; mazbata.*
mischief a. *zarar, ziyan.*
miser a. *khasis,* a. p. *tamakiâr.*
mist *sis, douman.*
mistake a. *khata,* t. *yañlish.*
mix (to) *qarîshdirmaq,* a. *mézj ét.''*
mob *qalabalîq, ayaq taqîmi.*
mock (to) *zévqlénmék,* a. *istihza ét.''*
model p. *nûmouné,* f. *eôrnék.*
modern *yéni,* a. *jédid.*
modest a. *mahjoub, térbiyéli.*
moist p. *ném,* t. *yash.*
momentous a. *mouhimm, éhémm.*
monarch p. *hûkûmdar padishah.*
Monday *pazar értési.*
money *para, aqjé,* a. *naqd.*
monkey *maymoun.*
month *ay,* p. *mah,* a. *shéhr.*
moon *ay,* p. *mah,* a. *qamér.*
moral a. *akhlaqî; hissé* (p. 119).
more *daha,* a. *ziyadé* (p. 101).
morning a. *sabah.*
morrow *érté,* a. *sabah.*
mosque a. *jami, mésjid.*
most *éñ,* a. *ziyade* (p. 101).
moth (flying) *pérvané; gûvé.*
mother *ana,* p. *madér* (p. 58).
motion *harékét.*
mould *topraq;* a. *qalib.*
mound *dépé, tépé.*
mount *dagh;* (to) *chîqmaq, binmék.*

mountain *dagh,* a. *jébél.*
mourn p. *fighan ét.''; yas toutmaq.*
mournful p. *ghamkin,* a. *mahzoun.*
mouse *sîchan,* a. *faré.*
mouth *aghîz,* p. *dihan.*
move (to) *qîmildanmaq,* a. *harékét ét.''*
mow (to) *bichmék.* mud *chamour.*
mug a. *mashrapa.* mule *qatîr.*
multitude *qalabalîq.* [*ét.''*
multiply (to) *choghaltmaq;* a. *zarb*
murder (to) *eôldûrmék.* a. *qatl et.''*
murderer *qanli,* a. *qatil.*
museum f. *mûzékhané.*
music a. *naghmé,* f. *mousiqa.*
musician f. p. *mousiqi shinas,
mousiqaji.*
musquito *sivri, sivri sinék.*
mustache *bîyîq.*
mustard *hardal.*
mutton *qoyoun éti.*
mystery a. *sirr, ésrar.*
Nail (finger) *tîrnaq;* (iron) *éksér,
chivi, mikh;* (to) *mikhlamaq.*
naked *chîplaq,* a. *ûryan.*
name *ad,* a. *isim,* p. *nam.*
named a. *mûsémma,* p. t. *naminda.*
namely a. *yani;* naphtha *néft.*
narrow *dar, énsiz.*
nasty *pis,* a. *mékrouh, mourdar.*
nation a. *millét, qavm, ûmmét.*
native *yérli.* natural a. *tabiyi.*
naughty *yaramaz.* navel *geôbék.*
naval a. *bahri, bahriyé.*
navigation a. *séyri séfayin, gézmé.*
navy *donanma.* near *yaqin.*
necessary a. *lazîm, mouqtazi.*
necessity a. *hajét, zarourét.*
neck *boyoun.* need a. *ihtiyaj.*
needle *iyné.* negro a. *zénji, arab.*
neighbour *qonshou.*
nest *youva.* net *agh.*
never p. *hich,* a. *asla,* a. *qat'an.*
new *yéni,* p. *név,* a. *jédid.*
news a. *khabér, havadis.*
next *yandaki,* a. *atidéki; soñra.*
nice *gûzél,* a. *ala.* night *géjé.*
no *khayr; hich, hich bir.*
noble a. *néjib; jins.*
noise *sés, shamata, gûrûltû.*
nonsense *sachma, bosh laf.*
noon *eôylén vaqtî, eôylén.*

noose *ilmék*.
north a. *shimal*, f. *poryas*: (due-)
   yîldîz; (-west) *qara yél*.
nose *bouroun*. not *déyil*.
nourish (to) *béslémék*, p. *pérverdé
   ét.*"
now *shimdi*, a. *hala*, *élan*.
number *sayî*, a. *adéd*, *miqdar*.
nurse (wet-) *sud-ana*; (dry-)
   dada; (sick-) *hastaji*.
nut *fîndiq*.
nutmeg *hindistan jévizi*.
Oak *méshé*, *pélit*.
oar *kûrék*. oath a. *yémin*.
obedience a. *ita-at*.   [*ét.*"
oblige (to) a. *kérém ét.*"; *méjbour*
obscure *qaranliq*; a. *moughlaq*.
observe(to)a.*diqqat ét.*"; *baqmaq*.
obstinate a. *inadji*, *mouannid*.
obtain *élé gétirmék*, a. *istihsal ét.*"
occupy (to) a. *zabt ét.*", t. *toutmaq*.
ocean *bahrî mouhit*, *oqianos*.
odd *ték*; a. *touhaf*.
ode a. *ghazél*, *qasidé*.
offence a. *qabahat*, *qousour*, *souch*.
offer (to) a. *taqdim ét.*"; *sounmaq*.
oft, often a. *éksériya*, *choq défa*.
oil *yagh*, p. *roughén*.
old *ésgi*; (-man) *ikhtiyar*, *qoja*.
olive *zéytoun*, *zéytin*.
omelet *qayghana*.
omen *fal*. on (p. 105).
once *bir kérré*; (at-) *birdén*.
onion *soghan*. only *salt*.
open *achîq*; (to) *achmaq*.
opinion a. *réy*, *éfkîar*, *zann*.
opium p. *afiyon*, *tiryaq*.
opportunity a. *foursat*.
opposition a. *moukhaléfét*.
oppose (to) *qarshî qomaq*, a. *mani
   ol.*"   [*ét.*"
oppress (to) *zoulm ét.*", p. *jéfa*
orange *portouqal*, p. *narénj*.
oration a. *khitab*, *noutq*.
order a.*émr*,*iradé*;*nizam*,*intizam*.
ordinary *bayaghi*, a. *adi*.
organize (to) a. *téshkil ét.*"
original a. *asîl*, *aslee*.
ornament *sûs*, a. *ziynét*, *haliyé*.
orphan *éôksûz*, a. *yétim*.
outrage a. *haqarét*.
oven *fouroun*.

overtake *yétishmék*, *toutmaq*.
ox *éôkûz*. oyster f. *istridya*.
Pace *adim*, a. *qadém*; *yéôrûyûsh*.
pack p. *désté*, f. *basta*; *déng*;
   (-horse) *yûk hayvanî*, *béygir*;
   (-saddle) *palan*.
padlock *kilid*, *asma kilid*.
page a. *sahifé*. pain *aghrî*, *sîzî*.
paint *boya*; (to) *boyamaq*.
painter a. *naqqash*, *réssam*(§ 610).
pair *chift*. palace p. *saray*.
palate *dimagh*, *damaq*.
pale *réngsiz*, *dounouq*, *solghoun*.
palm (tree) *khourma aghajî*; (—of
   the hand) *él ayasî*, *avouj*.
pan *tava*, *saplî*.
pantry *kilér*, f. *maghaza*.
paper *kîûghid*, vulg. *kéhad*.
parasol a. *shémsiyé*.
parcel (bundle) *boghcha*, *bohjé*.
pardon a. *afv*; (to) — *ét.*"; *baghish-
   lamaq*.
parsley f. *maghadanos*,*maydanos*.
part p. *parcha*, a. *qîsîm*; *taraf*.
partake p. *hissédar olmaq*.
partial a. *khousousi*; *tarafgir*.
partner *ortaq*, a. *shérik*.
partridge *kéklik*, p. *kébk*.
party *taqîm*; a. *taraf*.
pass *géchid*; (to) *géchmék*.   [*ré.*
passage *yol*; *géchid*; p.*bénd*, a.*iba-
passion a. *ghazab*; *mouhabbét*.
passport *yol tézkérési*, f.*pasaport*.
past *géchmish*, *gechén*, a. *mazi*.
pastry *hamour ishi*; f. *pasta*.
patch *yama*; (to) *yamalamaq*.
path *yol*, a. *jaddé*, *tariq*.
patience a. *sabr*, *tehammûl*.
patient *sabirlî*; p. *hasta*.
patriarch f. *patriq*; a. *ébûl aba*.
patriot p. *vatan pérvér*.
patriotism — *lik*, a.*houbbou vatan*.
pattern a. *nûmûné*, *éôrnék*, *qalib*.
pavement *tash déôshémé*, *sal*.
pavillion *kéôshk* a. *qasr*.
paw (fore-) *pénché*; (hind-) *ayaq*.
pay a. *ûjrét*; t. *gûndélik*; *ayliq*;
   yilliq; (to) *éôdémék*, a. *éda ét.*"
peace *barishîq*, a. *mûsaléha*.
peach *shéftali*.
peacock *tavous qoushou*.
pear *armoud*.

pearl *inji.* peasant *këöylû.*
pebble *chaqîl tashî, chaqîl.*
peculiar a. *makhsous; touhaf.*
pedlar *qoltouqjou, chértji.*
peel *qabouq;* (to) *soymaq.*
pen a. *qalém;* (-knife) *qalémtrash.*
pension a. t. *téqa'ûd ma'ashî.*
people a. *éhali; millét, qavm.*
pepper *qarabibér, bibér.*
perceive (to) *gëörmék,* a. *féhm ét."*
perfect a. *kïamil, tamm; témam.*
perform (to) a. *ijra ét." étmék.*
perfume *hosh qoqou,* a. *rayiha.*
period a. *mûddét, vaqît, zéman.*
perish (to) *hélak ol."; bitmék.*
permanant a. *dayimi, qadim.*
permission a. *roukhsat, izin.* [*ét."*
permit (to) — *vérmék, mûsa'adé*
perpetual a. *dayim, démirbash.*
persecute (to) *qovalamaq.*
Persia *Ajémistan, Iran.*
Persian *ajém, irani;* (lang.) *Farisi.*
person a. *shakhs, zat; adém.*
persuade (to) *qandîrmaq,* a. *iskïat*
perverse *térs,* a. *mou'annid.* [*ét."*
pest a. *véba,* t. *baba, youmourjaq.*
petition a. *arzouhal, istid'a.*
petticoat f. *miso fistan, miso.*
pharmacy a. p. *éjza-hané.*
pheasant *sûylûn qoushou.*
philosopher a. *féylésof, hakeem*
  (pl. *hûkéma).*
philosophy a. *ilmi hikmét, hikmét.*
photograph *fotograf;* -er -*jî.*
physician *hékim, tabib* (pl. *atîbba).*
pick *qazma;* (to) *qoparmaq.*
picture a. *résim, tasvir.*
piece *parcha.* pierce (to) *délmék.*
pig *doñouz.* pigeon *gëöyérjin.*
pile *yîghîn; hav, khav.*
piles *basour, mayasîl.*
pilgrim (to Mecca) *haji* (§ 409).
pillow *yûz yasdîghî.*
pin *toplou, toplou iyné.*
pinch (to) *chimdiklémék.*
pious a. *dindar, mûtédéyin.*
pipe (smoking) *chibouq, choubouq;*
  (water) *borya.*
pistachio f. *fîstîq.*
pistol *tabanja.*
pit *qouyou, chouqour.*
pitcher p. *désti.* place *yér.*

pity a. *mérhamét;* (to) — *ét."*
plague *véba,* (vulg.) *baba.*
plain *dûz ova;* a. *sadé, safi.*
planet a. *séyyaré.* plant f. *fidan.*
plaster *souva, sîva; yaqî.* [*maq.*
play *oyoun;* (to) *oynamaq; chal-*
pledge a. *réhin;* (to) — *qomaq.*
plot a. *fitné, fésad.* plough *saban.*
plum *érik.* plump *dolgoun, sémiz.*
plunder *yaghma.* pocket *jéb.*
poem a. *sheer; ghazél, qasidé.*
poet a. *shayir.* poetry *shir.*
point *ouj; bouroun; gëöstérmék.*
poison a. *zéhir:* poke (in) *sokmaq.*
pole (of heavens) a. *qoutb; sîrîq.*
policy f. *politiqa;* a. *ousoul.*
polish *perdah,* a. *jila;* (to) — *vér-*
  mék.
polite a. t. *nézakétli, térbiyéli.*
pomegranate *nar.*
pond *gëöl, havouz.*
pony *midilli.* poor a. *faqir.*
porcelain f. *chini, farfouri.*
pork *doñouz éti.*
porte *qapou; Babî Ali.*
portion a. *hissé,* p. *pay.*
portrait a. *résim.*
possess (to) a. t. *malik olmaq.*
possible *olour,* a. *mûmkin.*
post *dirék; posta;* a. *mémouriyét,*
  p. *post.* pot *qab, chanaq.*
potato *patatés.* potter *chëömlékji.*
pound *libra; lira £;* (to) *dëöymék.*
pour (to) *dëökmék.*
poverty a. *fouqaralîq, zarourét.*
powder (dust) *toz;* (gun-) *barout.*
power a. *qouvvét; dévlét, hûkûmét.*
practice p. *méshq,* f. *pratica.*
praise a. *médh, séna, hamd.*
prayer a. *niyaz, rija; dou'a.*
preach a. *vaz ét.*
preacher a. *vayiz, vazjî.*
precedent a. *émsal.*
prepare a. t. *hazîrlamaq, hazîr ét."*
present (time) *shimdi, shimdiki;*
  (gift) p. *bakhshish;* (to) a. *taqdim*
  ét."
preserve (to) a. *hîfz ét."; saqlamaq.*
president a. *réyis,* t. *bash.*
pretence p. *béhané, mahana.*
pretty *gûzél,* p. *dilbér.*
pride a. *kibr, ghourour.*

Turkish Conv.-Grammar.   31

priest f. *papas, késhish.*
prince *béy;* p. *shahzadé;* f. *préns.*
princess a. *soultan;* f. *prénsés.*
principle a. *ésas, ousoul, qayidé.*
print *basmaq,* a. *tab ét."*
printed *basma,* a. *matbou.*
prison a. *habs, mahbés.*
privilege a. *imtiyaz.*
probably a. *ihtimalén,* p. *belki.*
professor a. *mouallim, mûdérris.*
profit p. *kâr,* a. *fayidé.*
progress *ilérlémé,* a. *téqaddûm.*
promise *vad, séōz.*
proof a. *isbat, délil, bûrhan.*
proper a. *mûnasib,* p. *shayésté.*
prophet p. *péyghambér,* a. *nébi.*
proposal a. *téklif.*
prose a. *nésir, shir olmayan.*
proselyte *déōnmé,* a. *mûhtédi.*
protect (to) a. *himayé, siyanét ét."*
proud a. *maghrour, kibirli.*
proverb a. *darbî mésél* (p. 208).
province a. *vilayét* (pl. *vilayat*).
provisions a. *zakhiré, zahra.*
pull (to) *chékmék.*
pulley *maqara.* pulse *nabz, navz.*
pump *touloumba.*
punish (to) a. *tékdir, mûjazat ét."*
purchase (to) *satîn almaq.*
pure a. *saf, safi, khalis, témiz.*
purple *mor.*
purpose a. *niyit, méram, maqséd.*
purse a. *késé.* pursue *kovalamaq.*
push *yitmék, sûrmék, qaqmaq.*
put (to) *qomaq,* a. *vaz' ét."*
puzzle a. *mouam'ma; loughéz,*
  (to) *shashîrtmaq.*
Quadruped *déōrt ayaqli,* p. *charpa.*
quail *bîldîrjin.*
quality a. *khassiyét, kéyfiyét; jins.*
quantity a. *miqdar.*
quarantine f. *qarantina.*
quarrel *qavga,* a. *niza, mûnaza'a.*
quarry *tash-ojaghî, tashlîq.*
quarter *roub, déōrtdé bir* (§ 208).
quarters *yér,* a. *sémt, nahiyé.*
queen f. *qralicha,* a. *méliké.*
quench (to) *séōndûrmék.*
question *sival;* (to) — *ét."* *sormaq.*
quick *chapouq, téz.* (-silver) *jiva.*
quicken (to) *chapouq ét."* a. *istijal*
  ét."

quiet p. *asoudé,* a. *rahat, ouslou.*
quince *ayva,* vulg. *hayva.*
quinine f. *qina qina; solfato.*
quire p. *désté; éōzbé.*
quite *bûsbûtûn,* a. *kûlliyén.*
quiver p. *tirkésh,* t. p. *oqdan.*
Rabbit *ada tavshani.*
race (running) *yarîsh;* a. *mûsaba-*
  qat.
radish *tourp.*
rag *pachavra, chapout.*
railroad, -way *démir-yol.*
raiment f. *rouba,* a. *élbisé, ésvab.*
rain *yaghmour,* a. *rahmét;* (to) —
  yaghmaq; (-bow) *éléyim-saghma.*
raise (to) *qaldîrmaq,* a. *térfi ét."*
raisins *qourou ûzûm,* f. *chamich.*
rake *daraq, dîrmîq.*
ram *qoch;* (to) *sîqî doldourmaq.*
ramble (to) *gézinmék, sûrtûnmék.*
random (at-) *tésadûfén.*
ransom a. *fidiyé.*
rapid p. *chapouq,* a. *séri,* t. *hîzlî.*
rare a. *nadir.* rascal *chapqîn.*
raspberry *aghaj chiléyi, îzma-*
  voula.
rat *iri sîchan, gévél, pospol.*
rather (somewhat) *bir az;* (in
  preference) *daha éyi.*
ravage a. *khasarat;* (to) *talan ét."*
raw *chiy, pishmémish.*
razor *oustoura.* reach *yétishmék.*
read (to) *oqoumaq,* a. *mûtala'a ét."*
ready a. *hazîr, mûhéy'ya.*
real *gérchék,* a. *haqiqi.*
reality a. *haqiqat.*
really *gérchékdén,* a. *filhaqîqa, fil-*
  vaqî.
reap (to) *bichmék.* rear *géri.*
reason a. *aql, sébéb, hikmét; rajon.*
rebel *asî, zorba;* (to) *isyan ét."*
rebellion a. *isyan, toughyan.*
receipt a. *maqbouz sénédi, ilmou*
  habér.
receive (to) *almaq,* a. *akhz ét."*
reckon (to) *saymaq, hisab ét."*
recognize (to) *tanîmaq.*
recommend (to) a. *tavsiyé ét."*
reconcile (to) *barîshdîrmaq.*
record (to) a. *qayd ét.* red *qîrmîzî.*
redeem (to) *qourtarmaq,* a. *khélas*
  ét."

redeemer *qourtarîjî, khélaskïār.*
reed *qamîsh.* (-pen) — *qalem.*
refuge *sighínajaq yér,* a. *mélja.*
regard *nazar; itibar;* (to) — *ét."*
regeneration *yéni doghoush.*
register *déftér.* regular *mûntazam.*
regularity *nizam, intizam, ittirad.*
reign (to) *saltanat ét."*, *húkûmét*
reins *dizgin, térbiyé.* [*sûrmék.*
rejoice (to) *sévinmék,* p. *shaz ol."*
relative a. *khîsîm, aqrîba.*
reliance a. *itimad, émniyét.*
religion a. *din, mézhéb.*
remainder a. *baqîyyé, mabaqî.*
remarkable a. *mésh'hour.*
remember (to) *dér khatîr ét."*
remove (to) *qaldirmaq.*
renegade *déônmé, mûrtéd.*
renewal a. *téjdid, yénilémé.*
rent (to) *ijara vérmék,* — *toutmaq, istijar étmék.*
repair (to) a. *tamir ét."* [*lamaq.*
repeat (to) a.*tékérrûr ét." tekrar-*
repent (to) *tévbé ét." pûshman ol."*
reply (to) a.*jévab vérmék.*
report *raporto;* (to) — *vérmék.*
republic a. *júmhouriyét.*
reputation a.*izzét, itibar, shéôhrét.*
resemblance a. *mûshabéhét.*
resemble (to) *bénzémék.*
residence *qonaq,* a. *mékïān, év.*
resist (to) a. *mougavémét ét."*
resolve (to) a. *qarar vérmék,
   tasmim ét."*
respect a. *hûrmét, riayét.*
rest *qalan,* a. *baqî; rahat.*
retire, retreat (to) *géri chékilmék.*
return (to) *déônmék,* a. *avdét ét."*
revenge a. *intiqam,* t. *éôj.*
review a. *tékérrûr; résmi géchid.*
reward a. *mûktāfat, ûjrét.*
rheumatism *yél,* f. *rûmatizm.*
rhyme a. *qafiyyé.*
ribbon f. *qordéla, shérid.*
rich *zéngin; yaghli, sémiz.*
ride (to) (*hayvana*) *binmék.*
right *doghrou, haqq; sagh taraf.*
ring *yûzûk;* (to) *chalmaq.*
ripe *olmoush, yétgin.* [*chîqmaq.*
rise (to) *qalqmaq, yûksélmék;*
rival *éngél,* a. *raqib.*
river *îrmaq,* a. *néhr; sou, chay.*

road *yol;* a.*jaddé.*
roast (to) *qavourmaq, kébab ét."*
   (-meat) *qîzartma, rosto.*
robber *khîrsîz, haydoud, harami.*
roll (to) *youvarlamaq.*
roof *dam.* room *oda.*
root *kéôk.* rope *ip, halat.*
rose p. *gûl.* rotten *chûrûk.*
rough *qaba, pûrûzlû.*
round *youvarlaq, top;* a. *mûdévvér.*
royal a. p. *mûlûkïāné, shahané.*
rub (to) *ovalamaq, sûrmék.*
rude a. t. *térbiyésiz, édébsiz.*
rug *kéché, kilim, séjjadé.*
ruin a. *kharabé, kharabiyét.*
rule *qayidé, qanoun.*
run (to) *qoshmaq; aqmaq.*
rust *pas.* rye *chavdar.*
Sabbath a. *sébt,* f. *shapat; giragi.*
sabre *qîlîj.* sad *kédérli.*
sacred a. *mouqaddés, aziz.*
sacrifice a. *qourban, fidiyé.*
saddle *éyér.* saddler a. *sarraj.*
safe a. *émin; sagh, saghlam,*
   a. *salim.*
sage *aqîllî, ouslou; ada chayî.*
sail *yélkén; yola chîqmaq.*
salt *touz.* salutation a. *sélam.*
salute (to) *sélam vérmék,* – *almaq.*
sand *qoum.* satellite p. *péyk.*
sausage (dry) *soujouq;* (fresh)
   boumbar.
savage p. *yabani,* a. *vahshi.*
save (to) a.*khélas ét."*, *qourtarmaq.*
saw p. *déstéré.* say (to) *démék.*
scarce *nadir.* school a. *méktéb.*
science a. *ilm.* scissors a. *maqas.*
scold (to) *azarlamaq,* a.*tévbikh ét."*
scoundrel *oughoursouz, chapqîn.*
scourge *qamchî, qîrbaj.*
screw *vida.* scythe *tîrpan.*
sea *déñiz.* seal p. *méôhûr.* [*sim.*
seam *dikish yéri.* season a. *mév-*
second a. *saniyé.*
secret a. *sîrr; gizli.*
see (to) *géôrmék.* seed *tohoum.*
seek (to) *aramaq.*
seem (to) *géôrûnmék; bénzémék.*
seize (to) *yaqalamaq; qapmaq.*
select (to) *séchmék; séchmé.*
sell (to) *satmaq; vérmék.*
send (to) *géôndermék,* a. *irsal ét."*

separate *ayri;* (to) *ayîrmaq.*
series *sîra.* serious *aghîr.*
sermon a. *v'az.* serpent *yîlan.*
servant *oushaq, khîzmétji.*
serve (to) p. t. *khîzmét ét."*
set *taqîm;* (to) *qomaq; dikmék.*
settle (to) *hisablashmaq; yérlésh-mék; isklân étdirmék.*
sew (to) *dikmék.* shade *gêôlgé.*
shake (to) *sallanmaq.*
shallow *sigh; sachma, dibsiz.*
shame a. *hijab.* shame! *ayîb!*
shape *bichim.* share *hissé.*
sharp *késkin.* shave p. *trash ét."*
sheath *qîn.* sheep *qoyoun.*
shell *qabouq.* shepherd *choban.*
shield *qalqan.* shine *parlamaq.*
ship *gémi.* shirt *gêômlék.*
shoe f. *qoundoura;* p. *pabouj.*
shoot (to) *atmaq, vourmaq.*
shop a. *dûkklân,* f. *maghaza.*
shore a. *kénar, sahîl,* t. *yali, qîyî.*
short *qisa.* shoulder *oumouz.*
shut (to) *qapamaq; qapali.*
sick *hasta, kéyfsiz,* p. *namizaj.*
side *yan,* a. *taraf, janib.*
siege a. *mouhaséré,* f. *abloca.*
sieve *qalbour, élék.*
sight a. *nazar, baqîsh; témasha.*
signal a. *isharét.* signify (to) *démék;* a. *délalét étmék.*
silence a. *sûkût.* silk *ipék.*
silver *gûmûsh.* sincere a. *samimi.*
sing (to) *térén'nûm ét.";* (bird) *êôtmék.*
single *yalîn qat; ték,* p. *yégîâné.*
sink (to) *batmak; batîrmaq.*
sit (to) *otourmaq;* a. *jûlûs ét."*
situated a. *vaqî.* size *boy,* a. *qîta.*
skill p. *hûnér,* a. *marifét.*
skin *déri.* sky *gêôk yûzû.*
slave *yésir; kêôlé;* a. *jariyé.*
sleep *ouyqou;* (to) *ouyoumaq.*
sling *sapan.* slip (to) *qaymaq.*
slow *aghîr, yavash,* a. *bati.*
small *kûchûk, oufaq,* a. *saghir.*
small-pox *chichék.*
smell *qoqou;* (to) *qoqmaq; qoqla-*
smile (to) a. *tébéssûm ét."* [*maq.*
smith *démirji.* smooth *dûz.*
smoke *dûman, tûtûn;* (to) *tût-mék,* (tobacco) *tûtûn ichmék.*

snake *yîlan; nargilé marpoujou.*
sneeze (to) *aqsîrmaq.*
snow a. *qar;* (to) *qar yaghmaq.*
snuff *énfiyé;* (-box) — *qoutousou.*
soap *saboun.*
society *dayiré, souhbét;* (company) *shirkét; ortaqliq.*
soft *youmshaq.*
soil (to) *kirlétmék.*
solder *léhim;* (to) *léhimlémék.*
soldier a. *askér,* (private-) a. *néfér.*
song *tûrkû,* a. *sharqi, mani.*
sorrow a. *kédér,* p. *dérd,* a. *qasavét.*
sort *soy, dûrlû, chéshid.*
soul p. *jan,* a. *rouh.* soup *chorba.*
sound *sés; saghlam;* (to) *sés-lémék; yoqlamaq.*
south *qîblé,* a. *jénoub;* (-east) *késh-ishlémé;* (-west) f. *lodos.*
sow (to) *ékmék.*
space *yér, méydan; araliq.*
spade *bél.* span *qarish.*
spark *qîghîljîm,* p. *shéraré.*
spectacles *gêôzlûk.*
speech a. *noutq, kélam; khitab.*
spell (to) *héjélémék.* (-ing) a. *imla.*
spend (to) *kharjamaq; sarf, téléf*
spice *bahar* (Ar. pl. *baharat).* [*ét."*
spider *êôrûmjék.*
spinage *ispanaq.*
spirit a. *rouh;* (liquor) f. *ispirto;* (courage) a. *jésarét;* (Holy —) a. *Rouhoul Qouds.*
spiritual a. *rouhani.* (-ity) -*yét.*
spittle *tûkûrûk.* spleen *dalaq.*
spoil (to) *bozmaq, bozoulmaq.*
sponge *sûngér.* spoon *qashîq.*
spot *léké;* (place) a. *mévqi, yér.*
spread (to) *yaymaq, sérmék.*
spring *bahar, îlk bahar; yay.* (-wagon) *yayli araba.*
spur *mahmouz.* spy a. *jasous.*
squadron f. *filo,* t. *donanma.*
square *dêôrt kêôshé,* a. *mûrébba.*
stable *akhîr; tavla.*
stain *léké.* stag *géyik.*
stair *basamaq;* (pl.) *mérdivén.*
stale *bayat.* stalk *sap.*
stammerer *pélték, kéké.*
stamp *damgha, poul;* (revenue-) *sénéd poulou;* (postage-) *posta poulou, méktoub poulou.*

stanza a. *béyit, béyt.*
stand (to) *dourmaq, ayaqda dour-maq; a. t. qayim olmaq.*
standard (flag) *sanjaq, bayraq.*
star *yildîz,* a. *kérkéb,* p. *sitaré.*
starch *qola.* start (to) *yola chîq-maq; mûtévéjjihén harékét ét.''*
state a. *hal; dévlét; béylik, miri.*
stay (to) *qalmaq, otourmaq; éylén-mék.*
steady *mûhkém.* steal (to) *chal-maq; sîrqat étmék.*
steam a. *boukhar,* vulg. *boughou, islim.*
steamer f. *vapor.* steel *chélik.*
step *adîm.* steward *rékilkharj.*
stick *déynék;* (to) *saplamaq.*
stir (to) *qimildanmaq,* a. *harékét ét.; qarîshdîrmaq, altûst étmék.*
stirrup *ûzéngi.* stockings *chorab.*
stomach a. *mi'dé,* t. *qarîn.*
stone *tash;* (of fruit) *chéyirdék.*
stool *iskémlé; chouqali, havroz.*
stoop (to) *éyilmék; méyillénmék.*
stop (to) [intr.] *dourmaq, éylénmék;* [trans.] *alîqomaq, dourdourmaq.*
storage *maghaza kirasî; ardiyé.*
store a. *dûk'kian,* f. *maghaza;* (pl.) a. *zakhiré;* (-room) *kilar,* a. *makhzén,* a. *ambar.*
stork *léylék, haji léylék.*
storm f. *fourtouna.* storey *qat.*
story a. *naqliyét, hikiayé; masal.*
stove f. *soba.* strange a. *gharib.*
stranger a. *gharib; éjnébi; yabanji.*
strangle (to) *boghmaq.*
straw *sap; saman.* (-berry) *chi-stray yoldan sapmaq.* [lék.
stream *chay, sou, aqîndî.*
street a. *soqaq, mahallé.*
strength a. *qouvvét.*
strengthen (to) *qouvvétléndirmék, taqviyé ét.''*
stretch (to) *gérmék; gérilmék.*
stretcher *téjgéré (déstkéré).*
strike (to) *vourmaq; chalmaq.*
string *ip, sijim.*
strip (to) *soymaq; soyoulmaq.*
strong a. *qouvvétli,* t. *sért.*
stupid *sûrtûk, boudala; shashqîn.*
submission a. *ita'at, inqiyad.*
substance a. *jism; jévhér.*

substantive a. *ism, ismi moutlaq.*
suburb f. *varosh, kéôy,* a. *jivar.*
succeed (to) a. *mouvaffaq ol.''; yé-riné géchmék.* a. *khaléf olmaq.*
suck (to) *émmék.* suet *ich yaghî.*
suddenly *nagéhan, birdén biré.*
suffer (to) *chékmék, zahmét chék-mék;* (trans.) *qomaq, braqmaq.*
suffocate (to) *boghmaq; boghoul-*
suffix a. *édat.* [maq.
sugar *shékér.*
suit (of clothes) *qat.*
summer *yaz.* sun *gûnésh.*
superior *fayiq, ala, éfzal; béôyûk.*
supper *akhsham ta'amî.*
(Lord's -) *Ashayi Rabbani.*
support (to) *dayanmaq; arqa ol-maq,* a. *iltimas, iltizam étmék.*
suppose (to) a. *zann, farz étmék.*
sure (to be) *éyi bilmék, émin ol-maq.* surety a. *kéfil.*
surely a. *élbétté, moutlaqa.*
surface a. *sath (sat-h), yûz.*
surgeon a. *jér'rah.*
surgery *jér'rahliq.*
surname a. *laqab, kûnyé (§ 669).*
surprise a. *té-ajjûb;* (to) *basqîn vérmék; shashîrtmaq.*
surrender (to) a. *téslim ét.'' – ol.''*
suspect (to) *shûbhélénmék.*
suspicious *shûbhéli,* a. *méjhoul.*
swallow *qîrlangîj;* (to) *youtmaq.*
swear (to) *yémin ét.''* sweat *tér.*
sweep (to) *sûpûrmék,* sweet *tatlî.*
swell (to) *shishmék, qabarmaq.*
swelling *shish.* swift *téz.*
swim (to) *yûzmék.*
sword *qîlîj.* syllable a. *héjé.*
sympathy a. *riqqat, tévéjjûh.*
symptom a. *alamét, ésér.*
syntax a. *nahv.* system a. *ousoul.*
Table *sofra,* f. *masa;* a. *jédvél.*
table cloth *sofra bézi.*
tail *qouyrouq.* tailor p. *térzi.*
take (to) *almaq;* (– by force) *zabt ét.''; jébrén almaq.*
tale a. *hikiayé, masal, fiqra.*
talk *laqîrdî;* (to) – ét.'', *laflashmaq.*
tall *ouzoun boylou.*
tallow *don yaghî.*
tame *alîshîq, alîshqan, mazloum.*
tar *qatran.* target p. *nishangiah.*

tariff a. *narkh.* Tartar *Tatar.*

taste a. *lézzét,* t. *tad;* (to) *tatmaq.*

tavern p. *méyhané. qoltouq.*

tea f. *chay.* (- pot) *chaydan.*

teach (to) *éöyrétmék, talim étmék.*

teacher p. *hoja,* a. *mouallim.*

tear (to) *yîrtmaq; géöz yashî.*

telegram *télégraf.*

telegraph *télégraf;* (to) – *vour-maq, télegraf chékmék.*

telescope p. *dourbin* vulg. *dûldûl.*

tell (to) *séöylémék, démék.*

temper a. *mizaj, méshréb, tabiyat.*

tempest f. *fourtouna, bora.*

temple a. *héykél, ma'béd;* (of the face) *shaqaq yéri.*

tender a. *nazik,* t. *youmshaq,* a. *mûlayim.*

tent *chadîr.* tepid *ilijaq.*

terrace f. *taratsa; dam, baja.*

terrible *qorqounj,* a. t. *déhshétli.*

terrify (to) *qorqoutmaq.*

thank (to) a. *téshékkûr ét.''* (- you) *téshékkûr édérim, mémnounoum* (493, 498).

thanks, thanksgiving a. *shû-kraniyét, téshékkûr.*

thick *qalîn.* thief *khîrsîz.*

thimble *yûksûk.* thin *injé.*

thing a. *shéy,* pl. *ésh'ya.*

think (to) *dûshûnmék; zann ét-mék; téfékkûr étmék.*

thirst (to) *sousamaq; sousouzlouq,* a. *hararét.*

thirsty *sousouz.*

thorn *dikén.* thorny *dikénli.*

thorough a. *kiamil, tamm.*

thought a. *fikir, téfékkûr, mûta-la'a.*

thread *tél, iplik, tiré, ébrûshûm.*

threshold *qapou éshiyi,* p. *asitané.*

throat *boghaz.* throne *takht.*

throw (to) *atmaq, éndakht ét.''*

thumb *bash-parmaq.*

thunder *yîldirim.*

thus *béöylé.* tie (to) *baghlamaq.*

tiger *péléng.* tile *kirémid.*

timber *kérésté.* till (to) *hérg ét.''*

time a. *vaqît, zéman; déf'a, kérré.*

timid *qorqaq.* timidity – *liq.*

tin *qalay; ténéké.*

tinder *qav.* tithe *éöshûr, ondaliq.*

title a. *laqab,* pl. *élqab, ûnvan.*

toast (to) *ékmék qîzartmaq; qa-déh toqoushdourmaq.*

tobacco *tûtûn,* p. *doukhan.*

toe *ayaq parmaghî.*

together *bérabér.* token p. *nishan.*

tomb a. *mézar; tûrbé, marqad.*

tongs *masha.* tongue *dil.*

tooth *dish.* top *dépé.*

torrent a. *sél.* torch a. *méshala.*

torment a. *azab.* tortoise *tosbaghî.*

torture p. *iskénjé,* a. *éziyyét.*

total a. *yékûn.* -ly a. *kûlliyén.*

touch (to) *doqounmaq, déymék.*

touchstone a. *méhékk, méhéng tashî.*

towel *havli.* tower a. *koulé; bourj.*

town a. *qaryé; shéhir.*

toy *ojounjaq.*

trade a. *tijarét, alîsh vérish.*

trademark *alaméti fariqa, marqa.*

trader a. *tajir, tûjjar* (512).

tradition *hadis,* pl. *ahadis; riva-* [yét.

train *démir yol qatarî.*

traitor a. *khayin, yéhouda.*

trample (to) *chighnamaq, dépé-lémék.*

translate (to) a. *térjémé ét.''*

translator a. *mûtérjim.* tray *tépsi.*

transmigration a. *ténasûkh.*

trap *douzaq, faq; sîchan faqî.*

travel (to) a. *séyahat ét.'', gézmék.*

treacherous a. *khayin, chiftéli.*

treacle *pékméz.*

tread (to) *basmaq.*

treacherous *khayin.* -chery *khî-yanét, khayinlik.*

treasure a. *khaziné, mal.*

treaty a. *mou'ahédé, ahdnamé.*

tree *aghaj.* tremble *titrémék.*

trench *météris, héndék.*

triple *ûch qat.* tribute *vérgi.*

trinity *salousou shérif.*

troop *sûrû, kéömé;* pl. *béölûk.*

trouble *sîqîntî,* a. *zahmét.*

trousers *don;* p. *shalvar.*

truce a. *mûtaréké.* true *doghrou.*

truly a. *filhaqiqa, haqiqatén.*

trumpet p. *borou; borouzén.*

trunk *géövdé; sandîq.*

truth a. *haqîqat.*

try (to) *ghayrét ét.'', chalîshmaq.*

tube *borou;* *peôhréng.*

tumble (to) *youvarlanmaq.*

turban *sariq.* tune a. *maqam.*

Turk *türk.* Turkish *türkjé.*

Turkey *mémaliki mahrousé, Túr-kiya* (p. 126); *hind tavoughou, teôkteôk, choullouq.*

turn a. *névbét, neôbét, sira;* (to) *deônmék; chévirmék.*

turnip *shalgam.*

turpentine *neft yaghi.*

turtle *tosbaghi.* twilight a. *shafaq.*

twin *ékiz.* twine *sijim.*

tyranny a. *zoulm, ghaddarliq.*

tyrant a. *zalim, jébbar, dérébéyi.*

Ugly *chirkin.* ugliness – *lik.*

ultimate *soñ,* a. *akhir.*

umbrella a. *shémsiyé.*

unanimous a. *müttéfiq, müttéhid.*

unbeliever a. t. *dinsiz, imansiz.*

uncircumcised a. t. *sünnétsiz.*

unclean p. *napak, mourdar.*

understand (to) *añlamaq, féhm [étmék.*

uniform f. *úniforma.*

union a. *ittifaq, ittihad.*

universal a. *oumoumi.*

universe a. *além, jihan, kîayinat.*

university a. *darúl fúnun.*

unless p. *mégér, égérchi* (478).

unofficial a. *ghayri résmi.*

unspeakable a. *malakélam, seô-züm ona!*

unusual a. *nadir´úl vouqou.*

unwell *namizaj, hasta, kéyfsiz.*

unworthy p. a. *nalayiq.* up p. *bala.*

usage a. *adét.*

use a. *faydé;* (to) *qoullanmaq.*

useful a. *faydéli.* usual a. *adi.*

utter (to) a. *téléffúz ét.; seôylémék.*

urgent a. *ajélé, músta'jél, béjid.*

Vacant *bosh;* a. *mahlúl.*

vaccinate (to) *ash étmék, ash-lamaq.*

vaccination *ashi, chichék ashisi.*

valet *oda oushaghi, oushaq.*

valley *déré.* valour a. *shéja'at.*

vanish (to) a. *ghayib ol. nihan ol.*

variety *chéshidlénné, ténév´rü.*

various *dúrlú dúrlú,* a. *múténévvi.*

varnish (to) a. *jila súrmék, jila-lamaq.*

vault p. *kémér.* veal *dana-éti.*

vegetables p. *sébzévat,* vulg. *zar-zavat.*

veil *yashmaq; eôrtü,* f. *vélo.*

vein *damar.* velvet *qadifé.*

venerable a. *múhtérém, múkérrém.*

vengence a. *intiqam.*

Venus a. *outarid.*

veranda *tahtaposh,* f. *taratsa.*

verbal *aghizdan,* a. *shifahi.*

verge *kénar.* vermicelli *shéhriyé.*

verse (of Bible) a. *ayét;* (poetry) a. *béyt,* pl. *ébyat.*

version a. *térjémé.* vest *qaftan.*

veterinary surgeon a. *baytar.*

vex (to) *gújéndirmék, éziyét vér-mék.*

vial *shishé.* victim a. *qourban.*

victor a. *ghalib.*

victuals *yéyéjék.*

view a. *ménzaré;* (opinion) *réy.*

vigour *qouvvét.* village *keôy.*

vine *asma.* vinegar *sirké.*

vineyard *bagh.*

violate (to) *bozmaq.*

violent *shiddétli, sért.*

violet a. *bénéfshé;* (colour) *mor.*

violin *kéman.* viper *éngérék.*

virgin a. *bakiré, qiz.*

virtue a. *fazilét.*

visible *geôrünúr.* vision a. *rouya.*

visit f. *vizita,* a. *ziyarét;* (to) – *ét-mék, vizitaya, ziyarété gitmék.*

visitor a. *músafir, ziyarétji.*

vocabulary a. p. *loughétché* (544).

voice *sés,* a. *séda.*

volcano *atéshfishan.*

volley *yaylim atésh.* volume

volunteer *geônúllú.* [a. *jild.*

vomit (to) *qousmaq.*

vow a. *ahd, nézr;* (to) – *ét.*

vowel a. *harfi imla; haréké.*

voyage *déniz yoljouloughou, séfér.*

vulgar a. *adi, qaba.*

vulture *aqbaba.*

Wag (to) *sallamaq; sallanmaq.*

wager (to) *bahs toutmaq, bés tout-maq.*

wages a. *újrét,* t. *gúndélik, ayliq.*

waggon *araba.* waist *bél.*

waistcoat *yélék.*

wait (to) *béklémék.* [*maq.*

wake (to) *ouyanmaq, ouyandir-*

walk (to) *yeôrûmék.* wall p. *divar.*
walnut a. *jéviz.* want (to) *istemék.*
war *qavga,* a. *harb, mouharébé.*
warehouse f. *maghaza,* a. *dûkkïan.*
warm *sîjaq.* warmth *-lïq.*
wash (to) *yîyqamaq.* waste a. *téléf.*
watch *sa'at; néôbét;* (to) *béklémék.*
water *sou.* wave *dalga.*
wax *bal moumou.* way *yol.*
weak a. *zayif; hafif.* -ness *-lik.*
wealth *zénginlik, sérvét.*
wealthy *zéngin.* weapon a. *silah.*
wear (to) *géymék; ashînmaq.*
  (-out) *esgimék, ipranmaq.*
weary *yorgoun.* weather a. *hava.*
week *hafta.* weep (to) *aghlamaq.*
weigh (to) *tartmaq.* weight *tartî.*
welcome! *boyour, bouyourouñ!*
well *qouyou; éyi; pék éyi!*
west *gûnbatî, batî,* a. *gharb.*
wet *îslaq, yash.* wharf f. *isgélé.*
wheat *boughday,* a. *hînta.*
wheel *tékérlék;* (machine) *charkh.*
whip *qamchî;* (to) *qamchîlamaq.*
whisper (to) *fisildémék.*
whistle (to) *îslîq chalmaq.*
white *aq,* a. *beyaz.* whole *bûtûn.*
wick *fitil.* wicked *kéôtû.*
wickedness *-lûk,* a. *fésad, shérr.*
wide *énli, génish.*
widow *doul qarî.*
will *géônûl,* a. *mûrad; vasiyét.*
wind p. *rûzgïar,* t. *yél.*
window *pénjéré.*
wine *sharab.* winter *qîsh.*
wing *qanad; qol.*
wipe (to) *silmék.*
wire *tél.* wisdom *aql.*
wise a. *aqîllî, aqil.*
wish a. *arzou, khahish; istemék.*
without *- sîz.* - home *évsiz.*
witness a. *shahid; shéhadét.*
witty a. *zarif.* wolf *qourt.*
womb a. *rahim,* t. *qarîn.* [*ét.''*
wonder a. *hayrét, té'ajjûb;* (to)
wood *aghaj; odoun; orman.*
wool *youn, yapaghî.*

word *séôz,* a. *kélam; lafz, kélimé.*
work a. *amél,* t. *ish;* (to) *ishlémék.*
workman a. *amélé,* t. *ishji.*
world *dûnya, kûréyi arz.*
worm *soghouljau.* worn out *ésgi.*
worse *dah'a kéôtû,* p. *bétér.*
worship a. *ibadét.* (to) *– ét.''*
worst *éñ kéôtû.* worth a. *qîymét.*
worthy a. *layîq.* wound *yara.*
wounded *yaralî,* a. *méjrouh.*
wrap (to) *sarmaq.* wrath a. *hiddét.*
wrestle (to) *gûlésh toutmaq.*
wretched p. *perishan,* a. *zevalli.*
wrist *bilék;* p. *bazou.*
write (to) *yazmaq,* a. *tahrir étmék.*
writer *yazîjî,* a. *mouharrir.*
writing *yazî,* a. *khatt.*
written *yazîlmish,* a. *mouharrér.*
wrong *yañlîsh,* a. *khata.*
Yard *arshin,* f. *yarda; havlî.*
yawn (to) *ésnémék.*
year *yîl,* a. *séné,* p. *sal.*
yearly a. *sénévi, yîllîq.*
yeast *maya.*
yell (to) *baghîrmaq,* a. *féryad ét.'';*
  av'avé.
yellow *sarî.* (– berries) *jéhri.*
yes! *évvét, évét,* p. *béli.*
yet a. *émma, vélakin, faqat.*
yoke *boyoundourouq; chift.*
yolk *youmourta sarîsî.*
young *génj, déliqanli,* a. *jahil.*
youth *génjlik,* a. *shébabét.*
Zeai *ghayrét; hamiyét, té'assûb.*
zealous a. *ghayyour, mûté'assib.*
zenith *sémtûrrés.*
zephyr p. a. *badî saba, nésim.*
zero *sîfir.* zinc *chinqo.*
zigzag *éyribûyrû, dolambaj, yî-*
  lanqavi.
Zion *Siyon, Sih'youn.*
zodiac a. *mintaqat ûl bourouj.*
zone a. *mintaqa.* torrid, tempe-
  rate, glacial —. a. *mintaqayi*
  harré, mintaqayi mûtédilé,
  mintaqayi mûnjémidé.
zoology a. *ilmi hayvanat.*

فهرست عمومی

General-Index.

(The figures refer to the sections.)

دارمستادده ق . . ف . . وینطایر مطبعه‌سنده طبع اولوغشدر .

Printed by C. F. Winter, Darmstadt.

بدرقهٔ لسان عثمانی

یعنی

لسان عثمانیك تحصیلنه تسهیلك مخصوص و سهولتمنه براصول

محرّرتن

واخیا اوحنا ایّوبیا

هر درسڭ صوڭنده واقع املاطوله قوله جنبه ادبیات عثمانیه

معلمی

طابع و ناشری،

اسلامبولك بابعالی برغ شهنده مقیم

جولیوس غروس

۱۳۱۹ سنه

مدخل

حروف هجاء عثمانيه

١	١ ١ ١	ب	غ	غعغع
ب	بببب	ن نرن	ف	ففف
ت	بببب	ز زرز	ق	ققق
ث	ننن	مم سسس	ك	ككك
ت	ننن	مم ششش	كك	ككك
ج	ججج	ص صصص	ل	للل
چ	چچچ	صه صصص	م	مسم
ح	ححح	ط ططط	ن	ننن
د	ددد	ظ ظظظ	و	ووو
ذ	ذذذ	ع عظع	ه	ههه

لا لا لا ل

بيم

١ ٢ ٢ ٤ ٤ ٥ ٦ ٧ ٨ ٩ ١٠

تَعْلِيم . ١ .

ا بْ بَ تْ تَ ثْ جَ جْ دّ ا

هْ ةِ وْ زْ رُ ا عِ طْ ى

كَ كْ لْ مْ نْ ا سْ سَ عْ فْ

مى ؛ ڢ رسه ن ؛ تَ دْ جْ

صه طَ عْ ا

ابجدهوز حطى كلمه سعفصه قرشت

تخذ ضظع

تَعْلِيم . ب .

عَ عْ عُ هَ هِ هُ صَ صِ صْ

شَ يْ شَ قَ قَ يَ بْ كَ كِ كْ

ثَ نْ نْ لَ طِ طَ طْ بْ بِ بَ .

ءَ ءَ ءِ جِ جَ جُ دُ دَ رَ رُ عِ نَ

عُ وَ ىَ

تَعْلِيم . جِ .

دَك دُم رَسِي رَن نَل وَ وجِ

دِك ذُم رِسِي رَن نِل وِد وجِ

دُك ذُم رِسِي رَن نُل وُر وجِ

رَف رَف رُف

تَعْلِيم . هـ .

بِ سِهِ . بِسِهِ . جِ . بِبِ . نَ لَ ئَل

ءُم . ئُم . جِ م . جِم . جِ ك . جَك .

سِهِ سِي . شِسِهِ . سِي سِي . سِي كُم

كُم . وَ لَ . قِل . فَ سِ . فِس . جِ جِ

تَعْلِيم . وَ .

بایه بی بو ، ماه می سو ، ناء فی نو ، ساسی
سو، دابه دی دو ، ناقه فی قره ، غا
غه می غر ، لا له لی لو ،

ـ

قل ، قال ، قل ، قبل ، قول ،قُل ، قسه
قاسه ، قسه ، قبسه ، قسه ، قرسه ، لاف
لیف ، لوف ، بال ، بیل ، بول ، غام ، غیم
غوم ، عام ، میم ، میرم ،

ـ

صُوُل قول ، جوُر،چوُب ، بوُل مال ، یول
واز ، قوب ، کیت ، موُم صانت ، دانِ
یوُل ، جوُق ، طلوُز

ـ

جاف یاف یائا یائا یالی یاناه بودی
قوداه قوناه مالی صاری جیران یاف
صودی صوغاه بای دولا جیر،با وغلا

نوتون اوقو قوقو اوقور اوموز اوقوز
اوغوز قورو اوددوت جوروك بوغو
چولاق سولوك لوقوك

P15

صحيفه ١٥ — و ١٨

آت ايت اوت . بال ، بايس ، اوروپا مولا
مولى ، عيسا ، عيسى ، پاشا . آمپه ، آباد
او . وقت . آلو . بول . لونده ، دوست
منصوره . خواجه خزانه

P16   § 31

بل سرمى : قسه . دبلسه . يه . والب
هنز . قهوه . أصه . بنه . كله چلم ، أصه

P17   § 34   حكايه ، حكايه ، حكايت .

قوماه . قامه . قابسه . كبه جك . كتاب كده
كول : كو . كول . كل . طاغد . كامل . آطا ه .
دكز ، دكز . بالكز ، بالكز . سك . دكل
دكبل . اكرى . بك

تعليم "ـر"

ئاو . طاو . آقمى . الملك . الملك . آلمى . قول .
كول . قار . كار . اك . اك . الك . قيو قويلك
بته . بنه كنز . بانه دس . بانه ديكنز . كول . قول
كاتب . اوكود . اوكون . دكرمسه . بكمز . دكلك
بكه . بكيت . كونسه . طوكون . طقون . كوكرته
 كوكرجيه . صوكره .

§ 35

مَعْلُومُ . عَالِمَه . آغا . اوغلان بلغ . اوغلُوق
قوغه . صُغوق . صوغوق . قوغمق . اُوغَلامَق
هوغمر . غلادبستويه . غا دياسه . غزة غاز

§ 38

ـــ

اول . اثر . اَثَر . ال . اُل . آبت . اُبت .
آلمه . آلمه . الت . آت . تأير . مأمور .
قائل . دائر

§ 42

جزم

بشلك . بربر . مكتب . بالوى . بالق .

٨

تعليم . ح

P.20

ساعت . لازم . طاورن . جوجون . جوجه .
صاحب . قاسه . جالس . راحت . صيوك وبلك
جبلك . ونسه كلدن . كيدن . كندن . شفقته
كتاب II احشام . اسلام . اقرا . اقبال . ايآ
اسراف . اتساله . تبديل . تشريف . تعريف نسيم
تقسيم . مخصوص . مظلوم . مشهور . مكتوب . محبوب

P.21   —   III

كتاب . كتاب . كتابه . فو . فيروب . فيربه
بالى . بالى . بالىه . باره . باروب . باوة
بابا . باباب . بابابه . آنا . آنابى . آنابه
قار . قارى . قاره

P.21   —   IV

شربجى . كتابنك . كتابيده . كيابى . هارو چى مجلسة
مكتبده . سرمايه . حبردار . دولتلى . هوسلى . مظلفا
باعده ده يجمه ده

P.21 صحيفه ١١ تشديد

صالاس . جدّدت . مدّت . مللت . ملت .

P.22 صحيفه ۱۱ تعليم ط

جرّاح . حمّال . فزّان . صرّاف . جلّاد . مدّاح .
بقّال . ثقّا . شمّاس . دلّوك . هرّت . جنّت .
هنّا . محرّك . نكرّم

§ 47 صحيفه ۱۱ . مت

انّ . آنّ . انت . آت . اميه . آيبه . اه . آه .
او . آو . ال . آل . اى . آى . اسه . آسح .
اك . آك . آنسه . آلت . آباء . آدم . آلدمآج

صحيفه ۱۱ تنوين

ت . تًّ . ةً . ةً . ؤً . ؤً . فً . نلبًا .
نظامًا . قرضًا . صانت . حقًا . عبد لطفًا . يومًا

§ 49 صحيفه ۱۱ اكست Accent

او . كوبك . آغلاس . صالاس . صرّاف بصر .
نقدم . مهّل كريم . آتس . خصوص آلبه آلله . قدوه

P23

صحیفه ٤٤ بوشنى آهلك

اولدى . آلنى . آله حبنمزك . سوزنى . كوردك
كوستروحكمز اللر

طعام . طعامى طعام . ال الى . الله قول دولاقولا
كرلى . كوردم . جردم . قولد . كورده . كولسه .
آنا . آناىه . آرا . آياسن . قنره . سلادوكيبيوده لمبروت

صحیفه ٥٥ اوريوغرافى املا

P25

بتره . بولتوه . قبلندى . قبلندى . قلبذك . قلزك
ایسته مك . سیه كلدك . كطیم . باشلر . اولجك . آلمى .
اوده . شكم . كونز . جردل . قول . كوزك بكل اولمر .

قسم اول صرف ترکى

صحیفه . تعلیم ء ١

P29

١ بر جومعه . جو جود ۰ بر قوسه . قوسه ٣ اوكوز
بر اوكوز ٤ شوردم . بورده . بر باقیه كوتى
باقیه بر كوتى ٦ بوركسك بر طاغ (داغ) بر بوركسا
داغ ٧ اوز نله شهر . شهر اوزاقده . اوشهد اوزاقده

٨ بوبوك طاغ . داغ. بو طاغ بوبوك مید. . بر
بروك طاغ . ٩ ابو چوچو . ابی چوچو ك چو
چوده ابو در . او ابو چوچوده . او چوچوده ابو
بر چوچوقده . ١٠ بو آت . بر آت . ابی آت . ات . ابی آت
بو بر ابی آتده . بر ابی آت . ات ابی در . ١١ اوزاره
بر شهر . بر یاقیده شهر . شهر یاقیده مید. . شهر
اوزاقده . ١٢ هوا ابی در . هوا اصجانه مید. هوا
صغوقده . صوغوقده در . ١٣ قرداسه قاره داسه
قاره داسه وقیز قاره داسه نی کیمه درلر . قاره وسه قیز
قاره داسه . بابا . وآنا . ابی درلر ١٤ سه بوبروك
میسه؟ كو مروك بیسه ١٥ قره . قاره . قاره قوسه
قره طاغ . قره دكیز ،، دكیز ،، دوكیز آده
دكیز . آده بابا . آده طاغ .

ترجمه ٢

١ . آت . بر آت . ابی بر آت . ابی آت . بر آت
و بر اوكوز . ٢ براو . بو بروك براو . بوبروك

او . اوبویوکدر . ۲ برآدم . آدم . آله برآدم
آله آدم ٤ قاره دکیز . قاره طاغ . آله دکیز .
آله طاغ . ٥ برآله کل . آله کول . قیرمیزی کل .
٦ کوتو بر چوجوق . بو برکوتو چوجوقدر .
کوتو چوجوق بودر . ۷ اربافیسه در . اوباغینه
شهر اوزاقدر . شهر اوباقده . ۸ برآت . برقوسه
و براوکوز . اللی آت و بوربوک اوکوز ۹ بوقوسه
آله در . بوقوسه آقده . بوقوسه آله میدر؟
قاره در . ۱۰ قاره داسه کبح در . کبحدر . اوللی
برآومدر . آدم در . ۱۱ قاره قوسه بوبوک
برقوسه در . قوشدر . اوقوسه کوزل برقاره
قوشدر . ۱۲ آله دکیز . بوبوک بر دکیز در .

—

ابه کومیوک ایم . ۲ سه کمجه به . ۳ اوطلر زنگینه دیر
٤ بابا ایی در . ٥ آن کوتو در . ٦ اوشهر اوراقده .
۷ شهر اوزاقده . ۸ هوا میبان میدر . ۹ اوتی میبان در .

١٠. قورسه بربوكده...

معمّا

P.30

جواب	سؤال
اوت زنگینم .	سه‌نڭ ایكڭه میسڭ؟
اوت فقیردر ..	قار داسڭ فقیر میدر؟
اوت اوغلڭ ایجیدر	او غلده ایجی میدر؟
به ایی بم .	سه ایوه سیوه كردركمیسڭ؟
اوت قبزقار داسلری فیزدر	اوت قار داسڭ ایچمیدر؟
اوت بویكسك..	بو داغ بویكسك می.؟
اوسه اكیح دیلر	اوكلر كیجه میدر؟
بز زنگینسه اینه .	بیز فقیر میسكز؟
قاره دكڭز كومورك در	آنه دكڭز بریوك می؟
اوت بربوك برقورشدر	آنا بابا بریوك برقورسه میدر؟

—

سند ایلان اونواعی س؛

عادی دین سنده

عمزوشمده

کارمجمده اعبا اً طغانه برکوده ویهدلبره شهری بکرمحلمیه
باسه فاسطله تجاسره معتبر اذنده ازمیر لباده اوهانس افندی
سنده بروجه بالو بالکذ دست بلک عنزوسه اخذ واسئکذا

الملدم ٦٤ اسویسالح   المدیوده
                                    نقیب

یولیجه سنذنف

سید عثمان غنی

a Draft

قیصریه ده مدیر غلمنده بالیفجیان اسبه افندیه ماینجئلته اوریه
کوده مسوکده همبه یولیجه ملك ماسلی برلئه کبا یاده کیدکوه اغایه

وبا امرنه بر وجه بالا بالبکذ المنصه عحد و لیرای عثمانی نأدیه بوڭزه

حسابك کمده سکز بیك نقداً اخذ والمندس ح مربرشیه

نورییس

Jndorsement   جیرو

لسان عثمان معلی مهری افندیه نأدیه ایده سکز بدل حسابا

مأخوذ در   » ح مربرشیه   کیاه بایدکرکور

امرسندی قبوذده بولنز

مدرای عثمانی

a Note

وظیفه ناجری هرمتلد کریم افندیده سابیه بلمدیکم مال بیك

اولدسه بر وجه بالا بالبکذ قرده بسه عحده لیرای عثمانی دیم

اولوب ناجنده اوقته برکوده صورنده کندی امرنه ادا

ایده جکم ح لحصی شلیه   مراه یانس

a Receipt   مقبوصه سندی

مکبنز طلبظاننه نصرب لی طاجاطور افندیك اشوبیاطغنی

يوز اوچ شس المعلی انداسنده شباطی نیابته دك الفوالمعه

مكتب اجرتی اولّ سكز عدد لیرای عثمانی مقبوضدر ٦ الجلدلیلیه

من شعرمنه واقع الحوله

قوله جی عزیزه داروب

جمیع هوایتس

اشبر بلك اوجیون اوده لحضرن شس ثمنه معاتم اوللّ ورثه

یوز غروسه معاده وننه سنده مقدمهم الحعد اجرسنده قلیخ

بیح بورشیح بعد قلد ایبنی بکبوغ

ساكنك معلمی بیدغا

چك نموزیسی

a Check

دمعاده نه قرو دك لیوه باننه سنه

اشبر سنك ابرازنده بابا بیامه به دوس افغتیخ یوزعده

عثمانی بیراس نأره اید مكد تاریخ للطلاع الجمدس

ابرا انامه

an acquittal

تاریخ ابرا نامه دكیمه بابا ارجی اوحاصی انماردنه اورون

مقصر قلك قاوضنی امذه واستیفا الجمه والسیاسه كندبنه كبرا

صو و مطلعوبم خالادینی بایه اولنوس ۹۶ لایولیمیه
الیکتابان

كفالتنامه

شنافع دولت ز مملكة مصر اولیباده هرنوع كتب و رسائلم
طبع و تمثیل ایتمك اوزره به مطبعه كتابیه طالب ولاتبعه
دولت علیه دره سعادطوراغمب ماطبوعباده افندینك طبقاً
نظامنامه سی احكامه توفیقاً هركتابه دیكه شتكفل اولدیمریه
اشبو كفالتنامهم جانب حكومت سنیه ه تقدیم قلصم جریه
استنابتا بل دیكباله

قونطوراطو

مر ز بقوزنك بانباد وهسی سوقعنده واقع معلوم الحدد و
جماعاتی دوبم نردامی ودونشه هفرة ابسترالیه زیع ایتمك ن
موجود ت اتجاره سیره لری رضی كدبسة عائد اولنی اوزره
سنة عالبه قاسی ابتداسنده كله جلت سه درتة حجریه قنده
به سنه مدك دیبنا ناوریه اولفس اوزره هودبسه لبایبل باب
باتجنواده علی ایباد ایجابایلیم ح بربلقتبی سیلسلباه

وكالتنامه

بادئ نظره وكالتنامه للملك

درسعادتده نور عثمانیه ده رمرك افندنك خانئسنده مقیم اوطوبانی
رئائك اغانذستده اوللا بنمه عده دلیرای عثمانك مطلوبك
استخلاصیله طرفه تسلیمرضنده هرنا ایجاب ایده سه کندی نامه و
طرفمدن اولمده اجرا ایتمك اوزره ارغاوه خانئسده
٦ نومروولی اوطه ده مقیم برنجی صنف دعوا وکیللرندن یه غطور
ماه غایوس افندی یا وکیل مطلوبه نصب وتعییله ایلدیكمی سبب
اشبو وکالتنامه بالامضا افندی موماالیه اعطا قلنمشدر

درسعادتده كلیسه خانئده مقیم   نه تموزت۱۳۰
دبغراده اغزبیه

بالاده موضوع امضانك دیغراده آغرابابه افندبك كندی
امضاسی اولدیغی تصدیقه اولنور   منهر

درسعادتنده معارفة محلکتی

علوم وخبرلر

مملكتمز شهكلنك نده ساه دیدوسی ولد سركبی اغا جیرلك قاعنه

ذكرا بها يوسف اغانك بتصرف اولديغى ٤٦ نومروله بللو
اغانك شذلش مع باغجه تكرى درت بيك غروسه بدلله اشتراو
مبايعه ايده بلك اولمعله شتذئ مرقومك تبعذ ودلتعلقه
ايدوكنى شهد اشبو علم وخبر اعط قلنمشدر   محمد   نخأ

      فى ١٨ مورللع   قريه يوسف نجمدون

مقدما اينجى اردو دحملايرنده بياده برنجى آلاينك برنجى بلوكلك
بورت ينباشيسى متوفا صالح اغانك بيوله اولادردن ترك ايلديكى
خديجه و موسى و تامارا ايتامك محلمزده شكمه اولوبدأله
بر حيات اولدوقلديئى و مرقوماننده خديجه نك هنوز اره داريبنى
ميبه اشبو علم وخبر بالتمهير اعط قلنمشدر   جزره بلدشيجى

     ممتار محلة حاجى بالى

شهاده تنامه لر

دارنده وثيقة واكاده كغام افندى مكتبرك علوم والسنه
مقرره نى ترتيب مخصوصى وجهله تدريس وتحصيل ايتمه محلال
والخلاد حميده بلد هيئت معلمونك توجيه نظاراولابعنه

فنون داربیات اجازتنامه‌سنه معادل اولوب علوم علیه
شهادتنامه‌سنی حسب المدیریه طرفندمد بالامضا افندی مومی الیه
بنیه اعطا قلندی ۸ تموز ۱۳۳۵؟

انقطرولیه قولاجی هیئت میدلری
طرفندن اودارد ریکسی

انقطرولیه قولاجی هیئت معلموفی طرفندن
ریسی چارلیز ترانسی

حامل دثیقه زبور بها حصر افندینك مدت سنه مكتبمزه
مداومتله علوم والسنه شد بیسكد دوبی منظماً تدیسی وتحصل
ایتمیه وبو مدت طرفنده سوالبا ابراز شعاحسه سیزلطراتیا
نائل بالمسه اولدیغنی بیه اشبو شها دتنامه افندی مومی الیه
بنیه اعطا قلندی ۸ لیلول ۱۳۳۵   برهان ذرقی مكتبی میدیری

مكتوبات تنوعه

سال جدیده تبریکنامه‌سی

سوکیلی بیدرم !

نجیبه سال مناسبیله حیات شكراده و صداقتمی تكرار ایلیكب

فخر شرف ایلدم .

سزلر نجده انیدکه عبودیتم تزاید ایتمکده ! افندیمزده اولان
طور مع محبوب اولدیغمی دوشوندکچه کریم نشده ایله صکمده تۀ
سزک کمال خلوصله سوند روجوم ؛ دعای تمادئ عمر وقبال
عالیکزه ابد شغولدر . هر حالده توجهات سامیۀ ولانعمیزیۀ
بقاسی استرحامایله خنم کلام ایمرم افندم ح

محب ومکرمز : صلیفنم

ان دواج تبریکنامه سی

کریمه کزک تزوجنده دولابه تبریکمی عصه ایه اخلایدیم
قیزمزک اوبه شرفلی ناموسلی بر فامیلیابه دخولی حیتم مرتبه
کوردیوجك احوالددندر . دوکرنشنده برلامدیفیمۀ دولابی
مناسعنم جناب رحمان طرفنی مسعود ایدهسیه افنم ح

محبکزز : بابا .

تعریفنامه

قادائم افنم !

عمره نمای فضل و عفت اولان خانمله عالیلرینك دنبیله

املده دوجار اولدیغی صباع عظیمه دولوب عالمجه صدمه
افزوده مكدر و دلخوذه اوله سنه بو مقوله احوال طائفكنداره
مرهم تعدیل اولا صبرجیل بانیك برآنده آقدم قلوب تمالرته
دوومله سكو تتبنسهالم اولمسنی جناب حملاومونده بالضرع
نبان: الملكه بزافنم ٦٢ شعباان

هدره ديكنى : يىقومى

الايشى هديه سنده دولوب بردوستة شكرنامه

محب وفا شعاریم افنم

هدره: كرمطابريبنى كمال مهونتڭد الدم. سری تأميه يوم
بهیج برشی بنده كزی بوقده سرورايتمه شده . هدركزی
هركسی بكندی . نظر عاجزانه سده بوئدر بك قيمتداردر
هزكم محصول دست ماهراه كزدر . بولطفكر بنده كزی
شكره مجبوره ايدى . شوصورتله باوعدهال ابتمه بى . بقای
توجهاكز استدعاسنه بروسيلة مهنده عداه درم افنم

١٧٢ احمد رعو

معذرت نامه

قارہ داتم افندم

مكتوبكزه جراب ويره مديكمده طولابي نه درجه آغراساغه
كوسترديكمى بنده كزده بليرم . فقط مشاغلك كثرتى بلكز
بنى تعذير ايتمز . حتى حالها امريكنز . بو دنياده برشيئ مخامم
اوده مجتمكز ده دست مجتمكزى بنده جكمك دأئماً ووجار دوليرم
آلوسى تشديد ايتمك ديمكدر . مكتوبكزه جابجمده منتظم .

برادرم افندم ع ح

توصيه نامه

محب و قائمقامم افندم

اعزا امباى عاجزى سليم افندى يه توصيه دمك كب شرف
ايده رم . مومى اليه حقنده لازم كلان معاونت و رعايتك
دريغ بيورلمامه جعنى اوته دنبرى سلم كذرانم اولا شيئ
مروت سازفا ساميدرنيده اميد ايده رم . بير مومى اليه
ايده جلكز ايكلكك حمدسنى عاجزلريه راجع بلديكمده
بر لطفكز ايله ايكى كيشى يه منتاد ايتمسه اوله جقكز افندم

تذكره لر

دلیم جمعیته دعوت تذکره سی

افندیم : بلطف تعالی اوكدره كليجك كون ساعت بشه
قراردنده بنه خانه ده دلیم جمعیتزك اجراسی حكم اولديغنده
ذات عالی برادرانه لرينك دخی جمعیت تذکرهسی تشریفی ایله
بنه لرینی احیا بیورمه لری خصوصه نیازه مخلصيدرم

٧ اکتوبر سنه

عائله جه برجمعیته دعوتنامه

ماه حالده دینك بشنجی جمعه ايرتسی اخشامی ساعت بشده
بنه خانه کرده عائله جه برجمعیتك انعقادی حكم اولديغنده
ذاتعالیلرینك دخی عائله جه نشریفلری بالخاصه رجا اولنور افندیم

جواب موافقت

تذکرۀ علیه کزی کمال متنونیتله اوقودم ، دعوتنه بربه کزه
اجابت ایده جکسی عهد اجه درم افندیم ،

دعوت تذکره سی

معار پرور افندیم ،

مكتبنه تشكر دانلك سوى استمالى بو دفعه ختام برلوب ماه
حالك اون... نجى صالى كوتى قبل الزوال ساعت برجوب یادلرنهٔ
نر ربع مكافات یمی اجرا ایدیه جکندره جمعیت عاجزانز
حضور ... عالى شریفنله هلدیه ... انتخاب اولی اوننه بوم
مذكوره ده لطفاً و تنزله تشریف بلا داعیلرنك ده دعا
مفخرت و مسار بویورلسی ... جامعله عصها حدامات سائمهٔ
اولنغو ... انتم ٢ حزیران سنه ٩

عرضحال لر

معارف عمومیه نظارة جلیله سنه

دولتلو افندم حضرتلری

سوده سی اشبو استدعامان جاكریدیه معا تقدیم قلمناده ،
انكلیزجه ده ایتجیه لغت نام اثر عاجزانهٔ مك
طبع و نشرینه دائر بر قطعه ... مضمونهٔ مك محاسن یاینهٔ
امیدوار ماله حضرت مه الامركده ... ... خانوملنی

اوحانس

مرزيفون ده بلديه محكمه‌سى حقوقده وارهسى
رياستى جانب عاليه‌نه

معروضه چاكريمدركه

حاجى بالى مجلسى شمكلكنده سراج طرسوس اغاذمنده بالتحويل
غيرا به تسليم اولونوز التى عدد ليراى عثمانى مطلوب عجزايم
اولوب وعده سنده ايكى مرو ايتمسه ابه وهنوزايفا
ديه ايتمسه اولديغنه مبلغ مزكورك مع فائضه ومصارف محاكه
تحت حكمة النفس صمنه و ايجاب حالك اجرا بيورلمسى استرحام ولنر
اولبابده امرواراده افنم حضرتلرنكدر سنه ٩ مايس ٢٩

لمدياماه مهيوسفك

دفعه خطنده مستعمل بعضه كلماتك
اشكال متنوعه‌سى

طا . ط . كا . طا . ده . ص . نك بل . لى لى . لوج
سى سى . مال حال . بول يول . يوم بوم . افنك افضا
افنم افنم افنم . افندى . افضه اراده . ايا ص .

مبصوصه . چیوجیله . حفتری . مصارفه . اوّلا اولان
اولوب اولوب . اولدیغنده اولهیغندن . بولاآ بوشاه

تعلیمات

اوّلا طلبه هرهانکی بطر بیانده جناولارلامره کلهلرن دیتجه

ثانیاً قرائتی دمغتنی بایملیب ۔ طلبه بیلکه کلنه بغد کلهلری بیلمه

علالعمله بامغه جربه ثمبوکلهنك هر بر بارجوسی بر ۔۔۔ بر یعنی قلمی کزدیج
قاله بنابه بایلی . ثلاد محمر . کلهسنی بردوه مد سلوه منفح
محمرسه دنشابازملی

ثالثاً رقعه بایسنی بك مصلی کوسترده ماللا ده بریحی نوه دیك بابغرا اولرقه
خط مستقیم اردنیه دیزیلکه کی ولملی

ثلاد معلمنر حاجی صدقی افندی محمود باشاده
عجم فانده متکلمر . بردوه بابه بغه
نردوه معلمنر حاجی صدق افندی محمود باشاده عجمحانده ثملکه

ابعا بایه لك لطیف وطریقه داراولو . مناسب دریتریکلهلری بعضا
انشفا اصولیله بایلی ثلاد ذوات عالی صنیاستحو عاجزی
ذوات عالی صنیاستحو عاجزی کمی بابیه بلیو .

رتبهٔ ثانیه

Divanee

باب سرعسکری ترجمه و تحریر بوله سنه لجنهٔ قلمی خلفا

سندن افتخارلله ماجد و لله کارم

مهری افندی غلام مجده شایسته عاطفه

سنیه بولندیغنه بناءً شرف منسوح و صدور

بیورللهٔ لمرو اراده حضرت لام غایهٔ

جناب شهنشاهی موجبنجه رعو لطف علیه

ملوکانه مدد کاموسی البهه فکر لاقافانه

رتبهٔ ثانیه توجیه اولندی

۱۳۴ ربیع الاول سنه ثمان مائه وهـ

اما ما علينك برمُناجاتى

خط اجازت

Ijazét

اى صاحب جود ، حامد كم ، اى كان معبود ،
متعاليسڭ . عباد زكدن ايستيدڭكى مظهر
احسانڭ بايان ايدرسڭ ، ديلمڭكڭ رجا
خسران وحرمانٮ المزسڭ .

خط قلم : التحطكاهم انجق سنسڭ ، عسر حالنڭ كى
يسر حالنه قدر سكا راجعت ايدرم سكا يالوارريم
آلهى : اكرجه كناهيم بيوكدر فقط سنڭ عفول
اوندن دها بيوك دكلميد .

ستایش حضرت پادشاهی

ویرمش بزه رازدان ادوار

بر پادشه ستوده اطوار

هر درلو ستایشه سزاوار

بر حامئ بی بهانه مزوار

بزل ایتدیکی لطفه غایت اولمأ

بوندن ده بیوك سعادت اولمأ

ای عرش سریر سده سایه

سنسن بزی ایلین وقایه

کلمکده در اهل النجایه

سایه کده صفای بی نهایه

فرق صفاده ظل حقتین

سلطانلغه حق بیلیر احقسین

Taliq

Sülüs

Nésikh

خط شمه

Riqa

خط دیوان جلی

۳۲

Jélee Divanee

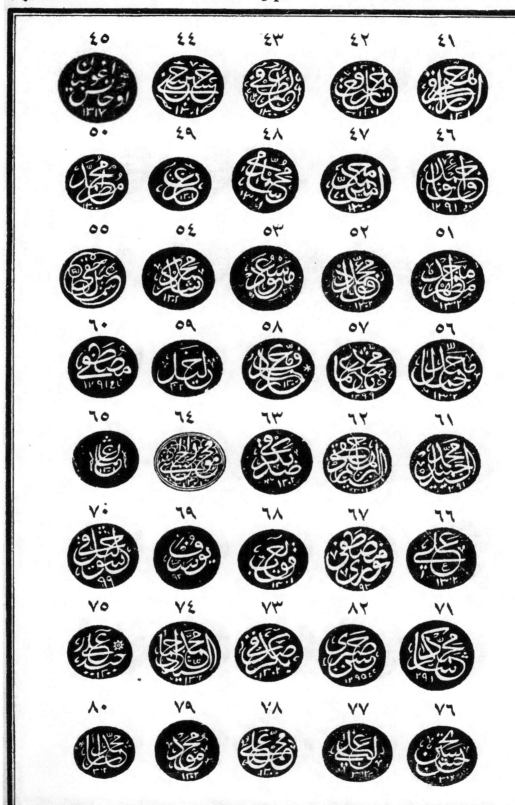

Educational Works and Class-Books

Method Gaspey-Otto-Sauer

FOR THE STUDY OF MODERN LANGUAGES.

PUBLISHED BY JULIUS GROOS, HEIDELBERG.

———

‹With each newly-learnt language one wins a new soul.›   Charles V.

‹At the end of the 19th century the world is ruled by the interest for trade and traffic; it breaks through the barriers which separate the peoples and ties up new relations between the nations.›

William II.

„*Julius Groos, Publisher, has for the last fifty years been devoting his special attention to educational works on modern languages, and has published a large number of class-books for the study of those modern languages most generally spoken. In this particular department he is in our opinion unsurpassed by any other German publisher. The series consists of 200 volumes of different sizes which are all arranged on the same system, as is easily seen by a glance at the grammars which so closely resemble one another, that an acquaintance with one greatly facilitates the study of the others. This is no small advantage in these exacting times when the knowledge of one language alone is hardly deemed sufficient.*

The textbooks of the **Gaspey-Otto-Sauer** *method have, within the last ten years, acquired an* **universal reputation,** *increasing in proportion as a knowledge of living languages has become a necessity of modern life. The chief advantages, by which they compare favorably with thousands of similar books, are lowness of price and good appearance, the happy union of theory and practice, the clear scientific basis of the grammar proper combined with* **practical conversational exercises,** *and the system, here conceived for the first time and consistently carried out, by which the pupil is really taught* **to speak and write the foreign language.**

The grammars are all divided into **two** *parts, commencing with a systematic explanation of the rules for pronunciation, and are again subdivided into a number of* **Lessons.** *Each Part treats of the Parts of Speech in succession, the first giving a rapid sketch of the fundamental rules, which are explained more fully in the second.*

The rules appear to us to be clearly given, they are explained by examples, and the exercises are quite sufficient.

To this **method** *is entirely due the enormous success with which the* **Gaspey-Otto-Sauer** *textbooks have met; most other grammars either content themselves with giving the theoretical exposition of the grammatical forms and trouble the pupil with a confused mass of the most far-fetched* **irregularities and exceptions without ever applying them,** *or go*

Method Gaspey-Otto-Sauer
for the study of modern languages.

to the other extreme, and *simply teach him to repeat in a parrot-like manner a few colloquial phrases* without letting him grasp the real genius of the foreign language.

The system referred to is easily discoverable: 1. in the arrangement of the grammar; 2. in the endeavour to enable the pupil to understand a regular text as soon as possible, and above all to teach him to **speak** *the foreign language; this latter point was considered by the authors so particularly characteristic of their works, that they have styled them — to distinguish them from other works of a similar kind — * **Conversational Grammars.**

The first series comprises manuals for the use of **Englishmen** *and consists of 38 volumes.*

Our admiration for this rich collection of works, for the method displayed and the fertile genius of certain of the authors, is increased when we examine the other **series,** *which are intended for the use of foreigners.*

In these works the chief difficulty under which several of the authors have laboured, has been the necessity of teaching a language in a foreign idiom; not to mention the peculiar difficulties which the German idiom offers in writing school-books for the study of that language.

We must confess that for those persons who, from a **practical** *point of view, wish to learn a foreign language sufficiently well to enable them to* **write** *and* **speak** *it with ease, the authors have set down the grammatical rules in such a way, that it is equally easy to understand and to learn them.*

Moreover, we cannot but commend the elegance and neatness of the **type** *and* **binding** *of the books. It is doubtless on this account too that these volumes have been received with so much favour and that several have reached such a large circulation.*

We willingly testify that the whole collection gives proof of much care and industry, both with regard to the aims it has in view and the way in which these have been carried out, and, moreover, reflects great credit on the editor, this collection being in reality quite an exceptional thing of its kind."

. . . . t.

(Extract from the Literary Review.)

All books bound.

Method Gaspey-Otto-Sauer
for the study of modern languages.

English Editions.

	s.	d
Elementary **Modern Armenian** Grammar by Gulian	3	—
Dutch Conversation-Grammar by Valette. 2. Ed.	5	—
Key to the Dutch Convers.-Grammar by Valette	2	—
Dutch Reader by Valette. 2. Ed.	3	—
French Conversation-Grammar by Otto-Onions. 13. Ed. . . . net	4	—
Key to the French Convers.-Grammar by Otto-Onions. 8. Ed..	2	—
Elementary French Grammar by Wright. 3. Ed.	2	—
French Reader by Onions	3	—
Materials for French Prose Composition by Otto-Onions. 5. Ed. . .	2	(
French Dialogues by Otto-Corkran	2	—
German Conversation-Grammar by Otto. 28. Ed.	5	—
Key to the German Convers.-Grammar by Otto. £0. Ed.	2	—
Elementary German Grammar by Otto. 8. Ed.	2	—
First German Book by Otto. 9. Ed.	1	(
German Reader. I. 8. Ed.; II. 5. Ed.; III. 2. Ed. by Otto . . each	2	(
Materials for translating English into German by Otto-Wright. 7. Ed.	2	(
Key to the Mater. f. tr. Engl. i. Germ. by Otto. 3. Ed.. . . .	2	
German Dialogues by Otto. 5. Ed.	1	
Accidence of the German language by Otto-Wright. 2. Ed. . . .	1	(
Handbook of English and German Idioms by Lange	2	—
German Verbs with their appropriate prepositions etc. by Tebbitt .	1	—
The **Hausa** language (Die Haussasprache; la langue haoussa) by Seidel	4	—
Italian Conversation-Grammar by Sauer. 8. Ed.	5	—
Key to the Italian Convers.-Grammar by Sauer. 7. Ed.	2	—
Elementary Italian Grammar by Motti. 3. Ed.	2	—
Italian Reader by Cattaneo	2	—
Italian Dialogues by Motti	2	—
Japanese Conversation-Grammar by Plaut	6	—
Key to the Japanese Conv.-Grammar by Plaut	2	—
Modern Persian Conversation-Grammar by St. Clair-Tisdall .	10	—
Key to the Mod. Persian Convers.-Grammar by St. Clair-Tisdall . .	2	—
Portuguese Conversation-Grammar by Kordgien and Kunow .	5	—
Key to the Portuguese Convers.-Grammar by Kordgien and Kunow . .	2	—
Russian Conversation-Grammar by Motti. 3. Ed.	6	—
Key to the Russian Convers.-Grammar by Motti. 3. Ed.	2	—
Elementary Russian Grammar by Motti. 2. Ed.	2	—
Key to the Elementary Russian Grammar by Motti. 2. Ed. . . .	1	—
Russian Reader by Werkhaupt and Roller	2	—
Spanish Conversation-Grammar by Sauer-de Arteaga. 7. Ed. net	4	—
Key to the Spanish Convers.-Grammar by Sauer-de Arteaga. 5. Ed. . .	2	—
Elementary Spanish Grammar by Pavia. 2. Ed.	2	—
Spanish Reader by Sauer-Röhrich. 2. Ed.	4	—
Spanish Dialogues by Sauer-Corkran	2	—
Elementary **Swedish** Grammar by Fort	2	—
Turkish Conversation-Grammar by Hagopian	10	—
Key to the Turkish Convers.-Grammar by Hagopian	4	

Arabic Edition.

	s.	d
Kleine **deutsche** Sprachlehre für Araber von Hartmann	3	—

Armenian Edition.

	s.	d
Elementary **English** Grammar for Armenians by Gulian	3	—

Method Gaspey-Otto-Sauer
for the study of modern languages.

	s.	d.
Bulgarian Edition.		
Kleine **deutsche** Sprachlehre für Bulgaren von Gawriysky . .	2	6
German Editions.		
Arabische Konversations-Grammatik v. Harder	10	—
Schlüssel dazu v. Harder	3	—
Chinesische Konversations-Grammatik v. Seidel	8	—
Schlüssel dazu v. Seidel	1	—
Kleine chinesische Sprachlehre v. Seidel	2	—
Schlüssel dazu v. Seidel	1	—
Dänische Konversations-Grammatik v. Wied	5	—
Schlüssel dazu v. Wied	2	—
Duala Sprachlehre und Wörterbuch v. Seidel	2	—
Englische Konversations-Grammatik v. Gaspey-Runge. 24. Aufl.	4	—
Schlüssel dazu v. Runge. (Nur für Lehrer und zum Selbstunterricht.) 4. Aufl.	2	—
Englisches Konversations-Lesebuch v. Gaspey-Runge. 6. Aufl. . .	3	—
Kleine englische Sprachlehre v. Otto-Runge. 6. Aufl.	2	—
Englische Gespräche v. Runge. 2. Aufl.	2	—
Materialien z. Übersetzen ins Englische v. Otto-Runge. 3. Aufl. . .	2	—
Englische Chrestomathie v. Süpfle-Wright. 9. Aufl.	4	—
Handbuch englischer und deutscher Idiome v. Lange	2	—
Ewe Sprachlehre und Wörterbuch v. Seidel	2	—
Kleine **finnische** Sprachlehre v. Neuhaus	2	—
Französische Konversations-Grammatik v. Otto-Runge. 28. Aufl.	4	—
Schlüssel dazu v. Runge. (Nur für Lehrer und zum Selbstunterricht.) 5. Aufl.	2	—
Franz. Konv.-Lesebuch I. 9. Aufl., II. 5. Aufl. v. Otto-Runge. à . .	2	6
Franz. Konv.-Leseb. f. Mädchsch. v. Otto-Runge I. 5. Aufl., II. 3. Aufl. à	2	6
Kleine französische Sprachlehre v. Otto-Runge. 8. Aufl.	2	—
Schlüssel dazu v. Runge.	1	—
Französische Gespräche v. Otto-Runge. 8. Aufl.	2	—
Französisches Lesebuch v. Süpfle. 11. Aufl.	3	—
Italienische Konversations-Grammatik v. Sauer. 12. Aufl. . .	4	—
Schlüssel dazu v. Cattaneo. (Nur für Lehrer und zum Selbstunterricht.) 4. Aufl.	2	—
Italienisches Konversations-Lesebuch v. Sauer. 5. Aufl.	4	—
Italienische Chrestomathie v. Cattaneo. 3. Aufl.	2	6
Kleine italienische Sprachlehre v. Sauer. 9. Aufl.	2	—
Schlüssel dazu v. Cattaneo	1	—
Italienische Gespräche v. Sauer-Motti. 5. Aufl.	2	—
Übungsstücke zum Übers. a. d. Deutschen i. Ital. v. Lardelli. 4. Aufl.	2	—
Japanische Konversations-Grammatik von Plaut	6	—
Schlüssel dazu von Plaut	2	—
Marokkanische Sprachlehre v. Seidel	3	—
Neugriechische Konversations-Grammatik v. Petraris	6	—
Schlüssel dazu v. Petraris	2	—
Lehrbuch der neugriechischen Volkssprache v. Petraris	3	—
Niederländische Konversations-Grammatik v. Valette. 2. Aufl.	5	—
Schlüssel dazu v. Valette	2	—
Niederländisches Konv.-Lesebuch v. Valette. 2. Aufl.	3	—
Kleine niederländische Sprachlehre v. Valette. 3. Aufl.	2	—
Polnische Konversations-Grammatik v. Wicherkiewicz. 2. Aufl. .	5	—
Schlüssel dazu v. Wicherkiewicz. 2. Aufl.	2	—
Portugiesische Konversations-Grammatik v. Kordgien. 2. Aufl.	5	—
Schlüssel dazu v. Kordgien. 2. Aufl.	2	—
Kleine portugiesische Sprachlehre v. Kordgien-Ey. 4. Aufl. . .	2	6
Russische Konversations-Grammatik v. Fuchs-Wyczliński. 4. Aufl.	5	—
Schlüssel dazu v. Fuchs-Wyczliński. 4. Aufl.	2	—
Russisches Konversations-Lesebuch v. Werkhaupt	2	—
Kleine russische Sprachlehre v. Motti. 2. Aufl.	2	—
Schlüssel dazu v. Motti. 2. Aufl.	1	

Method Gaspey-Otto-Sauer
for the study of modern languages.

German Editions.

	s.	d.
Schwedische Konversations-Grammatik v. Walter	5	—
Schlüssel dazu v. Walter	2	—
Kleine schwedische Sprachlehre v. Fort	2	—
Spanische Konversations-Grammatik v. Sauer-Ruppert. 9. Aufl.	4	—
Schlüssel dazu v. Ruppert. 3. Aufl.	2	—
Spanisches Lesebuch v. Sauer-Röhrich. 2. Aufl.	4	—
Kleine spanische Sprachlehre v. Sauer. 6. Aufl.	2	—
Schlüssel dazu von Runge	1	—
Spanische Gespräche v. Sauer. 3. Aufl.	2	—
Spanische Rektionsliste v. Sauer-Kordgien	2	—
Suahili Konversations-Grammatik v. Seidel	5	—
Schlüssel dazu v. Seidel	2	—
Suahili Wörterbuch v. Seidel	2	6
Tschechische Konversations-Grammatik von Maschner	5	—
Schlüssel dazu von Maschner	2	—
Türkische Konversations-Grammatik v. Jehlitschka	8	—
Schlüssel dazu v. Jehlitschka	3	—
Kleine **ungarische** Sprachlehre v. Nagy	2	—

French Editions.

	s.	d.
Grammaire **allemande** par Otto-Nicolas. 17. Éd.	4	—
Corrigé des thèmes de la Grammaire allemande par Otto-Nicolas. 6. Éd.	2	—
Petite grammaire allemande par Otto-Verrier. 9. Éd.	2	—
Lectures allemandes par Otto. I. 7. Éd., II. 5. Éd., III. 2. Éd. à	2	—
Erstes deutsches Lesebuch von Verrier	2	6
Conversations allemandes par Otto-Verrier. 5. Éd.	2	—
Grammaire **anglaise** par Mauron-Verrier. 10. Éd.	4	—
Corrigé des thèmes de la Grammaire anglaise par Mauron-Verrier. 5. Éd.	2	—
Petite grammaire anglaise par Mauron. 6. Éd.	2	—
Lectures anglaises par Mauron. 2. Éd.	3	—
Conversations anglaises par Corkran	2	—
Grammaire **arabe** par Armez	10	—
Corrigé des thèmes de la Grammaire arabe par Armez	3	—
Grammaire **grecque** par Capos	6	—
Corrigé des thèmes de la Grammaire grecque par Capos	2	—
Petite grammaire **hongroise** par Kont	2	—
Grammaire **italienne** par Sauer. 10. Éd.	4	—
Corrigé des thèmes de la Grammaire italienne par Sauer. 6. Éd.	2	—
Petite grammaire italienne par Motti. 4. Éd.	2	—
Chrestomathie italienne par Cattaneo. 2. Éd.	2	—
Conversations italiennes par Motti	2	—
Grammaire **japonaise** par Plaut	6	—
Corrigé des thèmes de la Grammaire japonaise par Plaut	2	—
Grammaire **néerlandaise** par Valette. 2. Éd.	5	—
Corrigé des thèmes de la Grammaire néerlandaise par Valette	2	—
Lectures néerlandaises par Valette. 2. Éd.	3	—
Grammaire **portugaise** par Armez	5	—
Corrigé de la Grammaire portugaise par Armez	2	—
Grammaire **russe** par Fuchs-Nicolas. 4. Éd.	5	—
Corrigé des thèmes de la Grammaire russe par Fuchs-Nicolas. 4. Éd.	2	—
Petite grammaire russe par Motti. 2. Éd.	2	—
Corrigé des thèmes de la petite grammaire russe par Motti. 2. Éd.	1	—
Lectures russes par Werkhaupt et Roller	2	—
Grammaire **espagnole** par Sauer-Serrano. 5. Éd.	4	—
Corrigé des thèmes de la gramm. espagn. par Sauer-Serrano. 4. Éd.	2	—
Petite grammaire espagnole par Tanty. 2. Éd.	2	—
Lectures espagnoles par Sauer-Röhrich. 2. Éd.	4	—
Petite grammaire **suédoise** par Fort	2	—

Method Gaspey-Otto-Sauer
for the study of modern languages.

	s.	d.
Greek Editions.		
Kleine **deutsche** Sprachlehre für Griechen von Maltos	2	6
Deutsche Gespräche für Griechen von Maltos	2	—
Italian Editions.		
Grammatica **tedesca** di Sauer-Ferrari. 7. Ed.	4	—
Chiave della Grammatica tedesca di Sauer-Ferrari. 3. Ed. . .	2	—
Grammatica elementare tedesca di Otto. 5. Ed..	2	—
Letture tedesche di Otto. 5. Ed.	2	—
Antologia tedesca di Verdaro	3	—
Conversazioni tedesche di Motti. 2. Ed.	2	—
Avviamento al trad. dal ted. in ital. di Lardelli. 4. Ed. . .	2	—
Grammatica **inglese** di Pavia. 5. Ed.	4	—
Chiave della grammatica inglese di Pavia. 2. Ed.	2	—
Grammatica elementare inglese di Pavia. 3. Ed.	2	—
Grammatica **francese** di Motti. 3. Ed.	4	—
Chiave della grammatica francese di Motti. 2. Ed.	2	—
Grammatica elementare francese di Sauer-Motti. 3. Ed.	2	—
Letture francesi di Le Boucher	3	—
Grammatica **russa** di Motti	5	—
Chiave della grammatica russa di Motti	2	—
Grammatica **spagnuola** di Pavia. 3. Ed.	5	—
Chiave della Grammatica spagnuola di Pavia. 2. Ed.	2	—
Grammatica elementare spagnuola di Pavia. 3. Ed.	2	—
Grammatica elementare **svedese** di Pereira	2	—
Dutch Editions.		
Kleine **Engelsche** Spraakkunst door Coster	2	—
Kleine **Fransche** Spraakkunst door Welbergen	2	—
Kleine **Hoogduitsche** Grammatica door Schwippert. 2. Dr. . .	2	—
Polish Edition.		
Kleine **deutsche** Sprachlehre für Polen von Paulus	2	—
Portuguese Editions.		
Grammatica **allemã** por Otto-Prévôt. 3. Ed.	4	—
Chave da Grammatica allemã por Otto-Prévôt. 2. Ed.	2	—
Grammatica elementar allemã por Prévôt-Pereira. 3. Ed. . . .	2	—
Grammatica **franceza** por Tanty-Vasconcellos. 2. Ed. . . .	4	—
Chave da Grammatica franceza por Tanty-Vasconcellos. 2. Ed. .	2	—
Livro de leitura franceza por Le Boucher	3	—
Grammatica elementar **sueca** por Pereira	2	—
Rouman Editions.		
Gramatică **germană** de Leist	4	—
Cheea gramaticiĭ germane de Leist	2	—
Elemente de gramatică germană de Leist. 2. Ed.	2	—
Conversațiunĭ germane de Leist. 2. Ed.	2	—
Gramatică **francesă** de Leist.	4	—
Cheea gramaticiĭ francese de Leist	2	—
Elemente de gramatică francesă de Leist. 2. Ed.	2	—
Conversațiunĭ francese de Leist. 3. Ed.	2	—

Method Gaspey-Otto-Sauer
for the study of modern languages.

Russian Editions.

	s.	d.
English Grammar for Russians by Hauff	4	—
Key to the English Grammar for Russians by Hauff	2	—
Deutsche Grammatik für Russen von Hauff	4	—
Schlüssel zur deutschen Grammatik für Russen von Hauff	2	—
Grammaire **française** à l'usage des Russes par Malkiel	4	—
Corrigé de la Grammaire française à l'usage des Russes par Malkiel	2	—

Servian Editions.

Elementary **English** Grammar for Servians by Petrovitch	2	6
Petite grammaire **française** pour Serbes par Petrovitch	2	6

Swedish Edition.

Kleine **deutsche** Sprachlehre für Schweden von Walter	2	—

Spanish Editions.

Gramática **alemana** por Ruppert. 2. Ed.	4	—
Clave de la Gramática alemana por Ruppert. 2. Ed.	2	—
Gramática elemental alemana por Otto-Ruppert. 6. Ed.	2	—
Gramática **inglesa** por Pavia. 2. Ed.	4	—
Clave de la Gramática inglesa por Pavia. 2. Ed.	2	—
Gramática sucinta de la lengua inglesa po Pavia. 4. Ed.	2	—
Gramática **francesa** por Tanty	4	—
Clave de la Gramática francesa por Tanty	2	—
Gramática sucinta de la lengua francesa por Otto. 4. Ed.	2	—
Libro de lectura francesa por Le Boucher	3	—
Gramática sucinta de la lengua **italiana** por Pavia. 3. Ed.	2	—
Gramática sucinta de la lengua **rusa** por d'Arcais	2	—
Clave de la Gramática sucinta rusa por d'Arcais	1	—

Tchech Edition.

Kleine **deutsche** Sprachlehre für Tschechen von Maschner	2	—

Turkish Edition.

Kleine **deutsche** Sprachlehre für Türken von Wely Bey-Bolland	3	—

Conversation-Books by Connor
in two languages:

	s.	d.		s.	d.
English-German	2	—	Deutsch-Dänisch	2	—
English-French	2	—	Deutsch-Französisch	2	—
English-Italian	2	—	Deutsch-Italienisch	2	—
English-Russian	3	—	Deutsch-Niederländisch	2	—
English-Spanish	2	—	Deutsch-Portugiesisch	2	—
English-Swedish	2	—	Deutsch-Rumänisch	2	—
Français-Espagnol	2	—	Deutsch-Russisch	3	—
Français-Italien	2	—	Deutsch-Schwedisch	2	—
Français-Portugais	2	—	Deutsch-Spanisch	2	—
Français-Russe	3	—	Deutsch-Türkisch	4	—

in three languages:
English-German-French. 13. Ed.	2	6

in four languages:
English-German-French-Italian	4	—

Method Gaspey-Otto-Sauer
for the study of modern languages.

«As long as Bellamy's 'state of the future' is no fact yet, as long as there are millionaries and Social Democrats, until every cobbler can step on to the scene of his handicraft, fitted out with an academic education, so long will private tuition be a necessity.

Since no pedagogic considerations fetter the private tutor, one should think that the choice of a classbook could not be a difficult matter for him; for it is understood, and justly so, that any book is useful if only the teacher is of any use. But the number of those who write grammars, from the late respected Dr. Ahn down to those who merely write in order to let their own small light shine is too large. Their aim, after all, is to place the pupil as soon as possible on his own feet i. e. to render a teacher superfluous, and to save time and money.

Then the saying holds good: «They shall be known by their works», and for that reason we say here a few words in favour of the books of the Gaspey-Otto-Sauer Method which have been published by Mr. Julius Groos.

Valuable though these books have proved themselves to be for the use at school, it is for private tuition that they are absolutely indispensable. They just contain what I claim for such books, not too much and not too little. The chapters of the various volumes are easily comprehended and are arranged in such a way that they can well be mastered from one lesson to the other; besides, the subject-matter is worked out so as to lead the pupil from the commencement to converse in the foreign tongue.

What success these books have met with will best be seen from the ever increasing number of their publications which comprise, in different groups relating to Englishmen, Germans, Frenchmen, Italians, Spaniards, Russians etc. etc. not less than 160 works the following volumes of which I have successfully used myself and am still using for the instruction of Germans: — the French grammar (24th. edition), the English grammar (21st. edition), the Spanish, Italian, Dutch, and Russian grammars; for English and French students: — the German grammar, not to mention minor auxiliary works by the same firm.

It is surprising what splendid results one can obtain by means of this method in a period of 6 to 12 months. After such a course the student is enabled to instruct himself in commercial correspondence in a foreign language without a master's helping hand.»   (. . . . .)

	s.	c
German Language by Becker . . . . net	2	-
Spanish Commercial Correspondence by Arteaga y Pereira **net**	3	-
Richtige Aussprache d. Muster**deutschen** v. Dr. E. Dannheisser, br.	—	7
Englische Handelskorrespondenz v. Arendt. 2. Aufl.	2	-
Kurze **französische** Grammatik von H. Runge	2	-
Franz. Sprachl. f. Handelssch. v. Dannheisser, Küffner u. Offenmüller	2	-
Italienische kaufm. Korrespondenz-Gramm. v. Dannheisser u. Sauer	5	-
Anleitung z. **deutschen, franz., engl.** u. **ital.** Geschäfts- briefen von Oberholzer u. Osmond, br.	1	-
Spanische Handelskorrespondenz von Arteaga y Pereira . . .	3	-
Kleines spanisches Lesebuch f. Handelsschulen v. Ferrades-Langeheldt	2	-
Langue **allemande** par Becker	2	-
Correspondance commerciale **espagnole** par Arteaga y Pereira .	3	-
Lengua **alemana** de Becker	2	-

The Publisher is untiringly engaged in extending the range of educational works issuing from his Press. A number of new books are now in course of preparation.

The new editions are constantly improved and kept up to date.